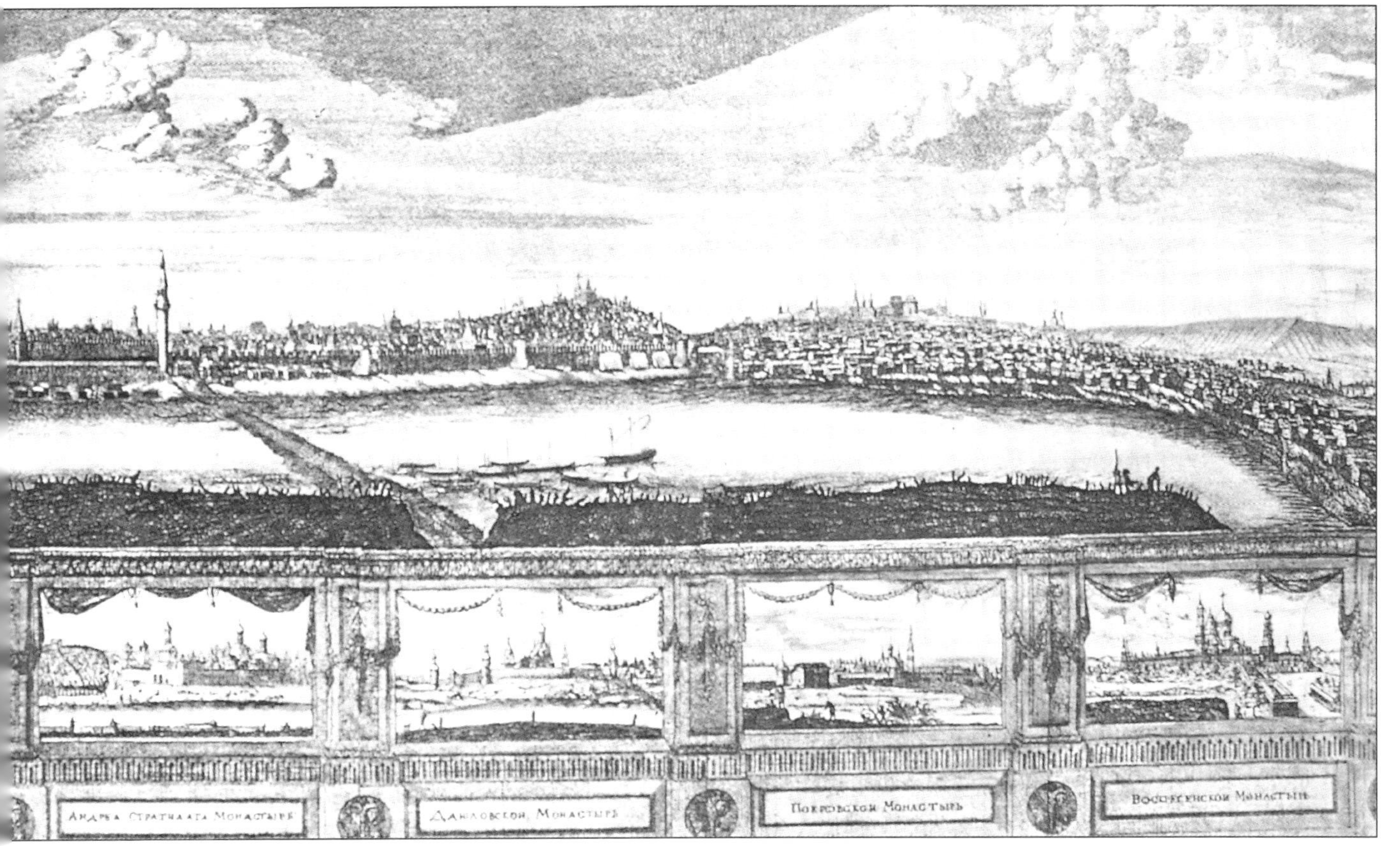
Даниловской Монастырь
Покровской Монастырь
Воскресенской Монастырь

Editorial Board:
Luzhkov Yu.M. – Chairman
Patriarch of Moscow and All Russia **Alexius II**
Belov L.A.
Vinogradov V.A. — Editor-in-chief
Kezina L.P.
Kirichenko E.I.
Moleva N.M.
Muravjov V.B.
Resin V.I. — Deputy Chairman
Trofimov A.S.
Shantsev V.P.

Reviewers:
Bocharov Yu.P.
Potapova N.A.

"Moscow 850th Anniversary" — jubilee edition in two volumes (under the general edition of V.A.Vinogradov). — I volume 368 ps.: ill. 420. Publishing House AO " Moscow Textbooks", Moscow — 1996.

    The edition touches upon the formation of historical Moscow, combination of Eastern and Western traditions in the city's artistic image, succession of symbolics of Jerusalem, Rome, Constantinople, Kiev and Vladimir. The basic principles of town-building art are shown in the planning, composition, building in, landscape, toponymics, connected with the key historical events of Moscow kingdom, imperial Russia, the USSR and the Russian Federation.
    The edition is for the general public.

The edition is dedicated to the 850th anniversary of Moscow with financial support of Moscow Government.

ISBN5-7461-0033-1

МОСКВЕ 850 ЛЕТ

ТОМ I

Yuriy Luzhkov — Moscow Mayor

A Word about Moscow

The **850**th anniversary of Moscow is an especially remarkable date. The majesty of people's glory of many ages and the quite visual and sensible destiny, full of vivid details and peripetia, the destiny of today's generations, of each capital family, each Mu scovite mixed in one whole in these eight centuries.

Thus is the date — thus is Moscow image itself — of the ancient city, which is eternally new, proudly capital-like and native and close in a home-like style, which embodies valour and sufferings, sense and insanity, tragedy and glory, beauty and barbarism of the changing epochs.

The typical picture of today's Moscow, so dear to heart, is similar to this date and this image.

The golden miracle of the cupolas, the famous forty of forties bounded by modest construction scaffoldings. One is unthinkable without the other — for this is the embodiment of the national self-consciousness, succession of traditions, glory, love to the past and the care about the present and the future.

Memorials of town-building, and there are plenty of them in the capital, are the durable guards of spiritual and moral human values, an evident and bright expression of people's attitude to the world, evolution, to God. The level and the way of life of the society are assessed according to their condition. That is why it is necessary to provide high quality of the natural and aesthetic environment of the historical centre of the Russian State — Moscow, because this spiritual centre is the creative source of transformation of the society. Our spiritual influence in the world depended and will depend to a great extent on the fact how we bring the images of our holy things and memorials to the other nations of the world, on our attitude to our historical memory and to the consciousness, and so, to the memory and consciousness of other nations, to their history and culture.

From time immemorial Moscow collected holy things of national and Christian importance together with gathering nations and lands which had been hostile before, turning them into allies, into blood brothers, retaining their national character, giving them the opportunity to develop on the basis of the richness and power of all the state.

Comprehending itself as the "Third Rome", it tried to embody outwardly the ideals of the first Rome and of the "Second Rome", which Constantinople was. The best masters of the East and the West were attracted to this work. In the image of Sacred Moscow Russia accumulated talents and experience of different nations in itself, their striving for the better, spiritual life, formed a united, unrepeatable look of a Eurasian state, full of dignity and power.

Many native philosophers, thinking about the specialities of the Russian spirit, made a resolution, paradoxical at first sight, — resisting the new and alien to it, it was gradually imbued with the essence and inevitability of these influences, being carried away by the logic of the outside world, but not losing its soul.

Walking along the city streets, we see magnificent samples of baroque and classicism. Empire-style and pseudo-Gothic style, rococo and constructionism... But in each of them there are some individual Moscow features, and there are many styles in everything — an original unity of a huge town-building ensemble, which had to be revived not once with new streets, avenues and squares, to restore its holy things. Only during the last five years, a minor period according to historical measures, Moscow brought hundreds of memorials of history and culture back to life and glory. They are the cathedral of the Kazan Icon of the Theotokos in Red Square, the Red Porch in the Kremlin, Voskresenskie gate with the chapel of the Icon of the Theotokos, the cathedral of the Ascension behind Serpukhovskie gate, the church of the Ascension "Maloe" in Big Nikitskaja street, the grandiose complex on the Poklonnaja Hill, and, certainly the national holy thing the unique cathedral of Christ the Saviour.

A simple enumeration of the restored temples, boyars chambers, estates and mansions will occupy impermissibly much place, and the process of reconstruction of Moscow centre is in full swing. Soon Manege Square will be transformed, creation of pedestrian areas is stipulated in Zamoskvorechie and Stoleshnikov lane. A competition for the best building, restoration and reconstruction of the object in the historical centre of the capital is conducted annually.

Moscow independent international political, economic, scientific and cultural connections are getting wider and stronger. New economic relations in Russia allowed to attract Finnish, German, English, Turkish, Polish, Bulgarian, Czech, Yugoslavian and other firms to the construction and restoration works at the objects of the architectural heritage. Foreign businessmen not only carry out construction works, but make investments in them on a mutually beneficial basis.

The mastery of architects and builders shows itself today in the fact that they work carefully, tactfully and skilfully in the preserved corners of the immortal city, reviving our antiquity, retaining the precious plies of architecture of generations and solving simultaneously today's functional problems. Restoration of the look of ancient Moscow is coordinated with the construction of new buildings: the hotel "Balchug-2", the business centres in Osipenko and Tverskaja streets, Novinskiy and Petrovskiy boulevards. For from ancient time it was considered that architecture is based on three whales — strength, usefulness and beauty. Time is necessary to be sure in it, to get used with this or that construction, to test it in operation, in the city everyday life, and the city cannot be treated otherwise than with love and carefully, with this unforgettable Moscow tenderness, which is felt in the names of the streets, lanes and even transportation facilities today too: the tram "Annushka", the trolley-bus "Bukashka"...

Certainly, this should be promoted by big work on comfortable arrangement of the city, overcoming of the consequences from the cheap construction technologies of the 60s, settlement of the dwelling and transportation problems, improvement of ecology. The latter, for instance, will be promoted by the "Complex program of development of planting of trees and shrubs and flower arrangement of Moscow", stipulating restoration of the historical landscape, creation of new gardens and parks.

No doubt that the most important point in implementation of the ecological program is solving of the transportation problem. Laying of the third automobile ring, construction of subways, multi-storey garage-parkings, reconstruction of MRAR (Moscow Ring Automobile Road), use of the inside ring of the railway for transportation of passengers, the program of the metro development till 2010 — these are the main points of development of this important sphere of Moscow infrastructure.

Within the framework of the program "Conversion" and "Science to Moscow" academical institutes and enterprises of VPK develop and introduce the technologies necessary for the city, master the production of equipment and new preparations.

In spite of the complicated financial situation, the wide-scale city program of social support is realised, in accordance with which nearly one third of the capital's inhabitants receive different social help. Big attention is paid at health care, culture, insurance.

But there is another important task directly connected both with town-building and the city economy — a task of social and moral importance — revival of the spiritual climate in Moscow, the atmosphere of community, friendliness, optimism, the feeling that both the home and Moscow are at the two sides of the flat's porch. I see a great potential of spiritualizing of the city space, potential of the real flourishing of our capital in this overcoming of the isolation, estrangement of people, which have recently appeared, in the reviving of the feeling of a creator and a master.

Our dear Moscow has a great and glorious past. I believe that its future is not less glorious. It depends on us, today's citizens, whom I believe and whom I gladly congratulate on the 850th anniversary of Moscow. I wish you success, my dear Muscovites — the continuers of the history of the sacred and immortal capital city of Russia!

Moscow Mayor Yuriy Luzhkov

Building of Moscow Government.

Holiest Patriarch of Moscow and All Russia Alexius II. (Picture of artist V. Shilov)

DEAR BROTHERS AND SISTERS!
DEAR READERS!

Eight hundred fifty years that have passed since the time of Moscow foundation by Suzdal prince Yuriy Dolgorukiy, testify evidently to the ways of the salvatory Divine Providence in the history of Holy Russia and its capital. Ivan Petrovich Zabelin, a famous historian of Moscow, commented: "Such cities of world historical importance like Moscow are born in their places not upon a whim of some kind and wise prince Yuriy Dolgorukiy or by a lucky capricious chance, but by the force of the reasons and circumstances of much higher and much deeper kind..."[1]

Moscow was neither a centre of political life like Vladimir, nor a great trade city like Novgorod or Tverj, nor an owner of vast lands like Rostov, but showed itself in Russian history as the most precise expression of the character of *Russian people*, as *their soul*. Even the first Moscow governor Saint Prince Daniel, the youngest son of St. Alexander Nevskiy, Grand Prince of Vladimir, showed to the world an image of a wise tsar in his small domain and at the same time an image of a man of a holy life. The life history of Moscow, closely connected with the history of Russian holiness, began with his name, the name of the first Moscow Saint.

And only a quarter of a century after decease of Saint Prince Daniel the first confirmation to this effect appeared in our history: St. Peter, metropolitan of Kiev and All Russia, fell in love with the God-loving small town of Moscow, its pious and cordial prince John, St. Daniel' s son, who got the nickname Kalita due to his love to give alms always , and the people of Moscow themselves, young, energetic, willing to live a God-serving and creative life. Foreseeing Moscow future exalted position, St.Peter transferred the department of Saint Hierarchies to Moscow and not long before his decease blessed the Moscow prince to built a temple of the Most Holy Theotokos in Moscow and predicted to prince John Danilovich: "If you do what I say, my son, you will glorify both yourself with your dynasty more than other princes, and your city among other Russian towns, and hierarchs will live in it, and my bones will be buried here"[2]. The pious prince implemented the hierarch's will and in 1326 in the Kremlin the stone cathedral of the Assumption was founded, and when in the same year St.Peter deceased, his holy relic was put into a shrine in the cathedral of the SAssumption, where it rests now in the sacrarium of Sts. Apostles Peter and Paul. As for prince John Danilovich, he continued temple-building in Moscow. Soon the churches of St.John, the author of "The Ladder", and Archangel Michael were raised, the monastery of the Transfiguration (of the Saviour "In Bor") appeared, and in the lands near Moscow, in Khotjkovo, the convent of the Intercession acquired life, which gave shelter to Righteous Cyril and Mary, the old parents of St.Sergius of Radonezh, the future Hegumen of Russian Land.

The second half of the 14th century is often called by historians as the time of Moscow's exalting, but for the history of Russian Church this time is the epoch of three greatest Moscow Saints: St.Sergius of Radonezh, St.Alexius, metropolitan of Moscow and All Russia, and St.Prince Demetrius Donskoy. Due to their praying intercession before God, their labour, monastic feats and feats of arms Russia was brought together, freed from foreign yoke and exalted spiritually and in its statehood. Russia's soul — Moscow became stronger due to their belief and deeds. St.Sergius presented Russia with many Saints — his disciples, who spread the Great Light of his Hod-carrying soul in all Russia. These cloisters became the centres of enlightenment and moral reformation of people.

After the Holy Trinity-St.Sergius Lavra they created new great monasteries: Christ the Saviour — St.Andronicus, the Nativity of the Most Holy Theotokos in Simonovo, the Miracle of Archangel Michael in Colossae (Chonae), founded by St.Alexius, metropolitan of Moscow.

---

[1]. I. Zabelin History of Moscow. M., 1990, p. 6.
[2]. St.Macarius (Bulgakov), metropolitan of Moscow. History of the Russian Church. Book three. M., 1995, p. 25-26.

Prince Demetrius, the victor of Kulikovo battle, grew up and gained strength due to tireless cares of St.Alexius, the tutor and protector of the young Moscow sovereign. And, perhaps, it is especially symbolical, that exactly in 1378, in the year of decease of St.Alexius, the Moscow army, led by prince Demetrius, won the first victory over the Tatars at the river Vozha. Only two years were left before the main battle in Kulikovo field. And the day, when prince Demetrius came to St.Sergius for blessing to the great battle, was close already. And the latter, blessing the prince, sent two monks with him Peresvet and Osljabja, who were men of Herculean build, and he himself with the brethren stood at indefatigable prayer for saving of the Russian land.

In the 15th century Moscow was consolidated as the head of the Russian State, but discords and hostility turned up inside it. And a Moscow hierarch, metropolitan Jonah this time, rose for defence of the real tsar again, grand prince Basil Temny. Well known Russian historian M. V. Tolstoy wrote: "Moscow consolidated and became strong under the protection of the activity and prayers of three marvellous hierarchs. Great in his meekness, metropolitan Peter transferred the throne of metropolis to a small and wretched town of St. Prince Daniel: he announced prophetically Moscow future majesty. Great in his belief, metropolitan Alexius strengthened the grand princely dignity in the dynasty of John Kalita, supporting his little grand-son and rising Moscow above the other cities of independent principalities. Great in the law and truth, metropolitan Jonah returned the throne to the legal grand prince, subdued the internecine war, was a strong support of the wretched blind man in the state affairs and an indefatigable guard of Orthodoxy in the church affairs "[3].

The 16th century gave the capital city of Moscow three Saint Hierarchs: the outstanding orthodox enlightener, creator of the Grand Menology, the protector and initiator of the Russian book-printing metropolitan Macarius, who belongs now to the history under the name "wonderful", St.Hieromartyr metropolitan Philip, who rose his voice fearlessly to defend his flock and convicted the incomparable oprichnina and the tsar, who forgot the God's testimonies, and Job, the first Russian eparchy, who was honoured with the highest worthiness of Patriarch service.

But the Troubled Time was already coming in Russia. And God called His Saints again for defence of Holy Russia. Moscow Patriarch Germanus, taken in Moscow by Poles and by the troops of the False Demetrius the second, called by people as the "thieve of Tushino", rejected all the enemies' promises. 'They tried in vain to force the Patriarch by hunger and humiliation to commit a treachery or at least to keep silent. God gave strength to the hierarch to stand up for the Fatherland, the Patriarch spoke up against the enemies and called his flock: "... keep your soul in purity and live like brothers, 'seek to sacrifice your lives for the House of the Most Holy Theotokos and the Miracle-workers, and for the belief, as you have vowed; write to all towns, so that they will write to regiments to boyars and atamans... We bless all of you and assail you for the present and future life as you stand firmly for the belief; and I must pray to God for you"[4]. Then the enemies decided to starve the Patriarch to death, and on 17 February 1612 the Saint Elder deceased. The voice of the Saint Hieromartyr became silent, but the Holy Trinity-St.Sergius Lavra, which had just stood the unprecedented 16-month Polish siege, spoke up. And from the cloister of St.Sergius charters were sent to Russian towns, calling up for the battle, in Nizhniy Novgorod the elective district council Cosmas Minin had a vision of St.Sergius: "St.Sergius came and ordered to collect money for the military people and go and clean the Moscow State from its enemies". So the church memory holds with veneration together with the names of Cosmas Minin and prince Demetrius Pozharskiy the names of St.Hieromartyr Germanus and Righteous Dionysius, an archimandrite of the cloister of St.Sergius.

After St.Hieromartyr Germanus the Patriarch Department in the Russian Church had no leader for seven years. Then, metropolitan Phylaret, the father of Michael Fedorovich, the first tsar of the Romanovs Dynasty, was elected the pontiff of Moscow and All Russia, after he had returned from the long Polish captivity.

---

[3] M. Tolstoy. History of the Russian Church. M., 1991, p. 265.
[4] The charter of Patriarch Germanus, written in August of 1611 to Nizhniy Novgorod and other Russian towns. — Works of St.Germanus, Patriarch of Moscow and All Russia. M., 1912, p. 101.

Moscow lived through the 17th century, which was so complicated for the Russian Church with its reforms and with the opposition to the Patriarch and tsar's power, in a dignified way: expressing the love for God's churches, typical for Muscovites, they decorated the Kremlin with new great creations — the temples of the Twelve Apostles, of St. Apostle Philip and of the Resurrection "Slovutschee", in Nikitniki the extremely beautiful church of the Holy Trinity appeared, in Red Square the chapel of St. Alexander Nevskiy rose and many other monasteries, temples and chapels. And at the end of the century an event happened, which did not attract much attention at that time, but was remarkable in the history of our spiritual life — the foundation of Moscow Ecclesiastical Academy, which became the source of the church knowledge and enlightenment.

Probably this spiritual knowledge and deep orthodox self-consciousness allowed Moscow to retain its character during new tendencies, in the epoch of Peter the Great and his successors, when the Patriarchate was liquidated in Russia and the leadership of the Church was transferred to the Holy Synod, which realized its activity in Petersburg under tireless control of a secular clerk — Ober-Procurator. At that time Moscow stopped being the official capital of Russia and became the "ancient capital", and the Moscow Department stopped being the supreme in the Russian Church. But in people's hearts and souls Moscow was always the first capital city, and Russian emperors, ruling the state from the new capital, were crowned and anointed in the ancient cathedral of the Assumption in Moscow Kremlin.

By God's mercy the Moscow Department was never left without hierarchs and organisers, in the late 18th century there was metropolitan Platon (Levshin) at the head of Moscow eparchy, who is rightfully considered the founder of the church science of the last century, soon after him Moscow Department got a great hierarch metropolitan Phylaret (Drozdov) for nearly half a century. Moscow metropolitan Phylaret, who has been recently canonised by the Russian Church, became a wise teacher, priest and elder for all Russian and especially Moscow flock. After St.Phylaret there were always great hermits, scientists and enlighteners at Moscow Department too[5]. Thus the cathedral of Christ the Saviour, founded in 1839 upon the blessing of St.Phylaret, was consecrated in 1883 already by Moscow metropolitan Ioannicius, a successor of metropolitan Macarius (Bulgakov).

Orthodox Moscow met the year of 1917 with worry and hope. Hard and fearful time came, but God gave strength to His flock, granting Patriarchate to the Russian Church again. At the All-Russian Landed Council in 1917 Moscow metropolitan Tychon, a meek hierarch, was elected by God's will the new Pontiff of All Russia and took the ancient orders of the Patriarch of Moscow and All Russia. The feat of hierarch Tychon was great, for he preserved the Orthodox Church in the time of most cruel repressions and persecutions, schisms and heresies, and was glorified and canonised by the Russian Church. The destiny of Moscow priests and their flock was full of sufferings too: the city of the forty of forties of temples, the pious city of millions of parishioners was disfigured, robbed and abused. And, probably, the most horrible -event of this epoch is the demolishing of the cathedral of Christ the Saviour, the national holy thing of Russia.

But Russia was not frightened by the persecutions, washed and made stronger by the blood of new Christ's martyrs, showing a great example of patriotic service in the years of the Great Patriotic War, living through the persecutions of the 60s, the Russian Church began to acquire strength again in the years after the celebration of the 1000th Anniversary of Christening of Russia. In the ancient Kremlin the bells rang again, Moscow temples, the quantity of which is growing from year to year, are full of praying singing of thousands of parishioners again. By the efforts of all Russian people the cathedral of Christ the Saviour is revived in its former majesty, prayings are raised already to God and the Most Holy Theotokos in the cathedral of the Kazan Icon of the Theotokos and in the chapel of the Iveron Icon of the Theotokos in Red Square.

There is plenty of work in the future, connected with restoration and construction of temples, with enlightenment of our people, revival of the orthodox spiritualness, which was characteristic for the pious capital city

---

[5] For example, metropolitan Macarius (Bulgakov), the author of the famous books "History of the Russian Church" and "Dogmatic Theology", t.Hieromartyr metropolitan Vladimir (Bogoyavlenskiy), the future hierarch of Kiev, or metropolitan Macarius (Nevskiy), the enlightener of the Altay.

of Moscow from ancient time. Again the prayer about the capital of Moscow, addressed to God by St.Hierarch Phylaret one hundred and fifty years ago, is of vital importance again:

We glorify Your blissful choice and Providence concerning us, for You turned a small settlement into a city, and through Your hermit St.Hierarch Peter You said beforehand, that this city would be glorified, it would conquer its enemies and glorify Your name, then the throne of the Orthodox Church was made strong and the root of the Russian autocracy was implanted by You, You exalted the throne of the kingdom and from here You made the faded light of the tsar's family to shine even brighter; upon Your wish Your saint hermits lived and deceased in fragrance here, by their prayers, like by a diamond wall, You defended this city from troubles and disasters, and in our time You reconstructed it from ashes and ruins, adorned with new splendour and filled in with abundance.

For conclusion I would like to remember great Russian icon-painter Simon Ushakov, who lived in the 17th century and created a wonderful icon: 'Inplantation of the Tree of the Russian State". In the branches of this allegorical tree there is the national holy thing: the Vladimir Icon of the Most Holy Theotokos, around Her image there are those who cherished this precious tree: righteous princes, hierarchs, saints, God's fools. John Kalita and St.Hierarch Peter were depicted at the roots of the Tree on the back ground of the cathedral of the Assumption. Today we can imagine plenty of other saint faces. Probably it contains the essence of the Russian history, the great importance of orthodox Moscow, preserving in its sacred earth the roots of the tree of the Russian State System. Thus we bear responsibility for the moral and spiritual situation in Moscow and its flourishing before God and History!

Alexius II, Patriarch of Moscow and All Russia

Patrimony. Icon. End of 14th century.

Preface

This edition in two volumes consisting of four books is dedicated to the 850th Anniversary of the capital of Russia.

In contrast to the previous anniversary editions and other books, planned by Moscow government, this central edition is dedicated to the capital's town-building image: the main stages of its formation, presentation of the symbolical contents, its historical role in the development of the Russian State, society and personality.

In the new conditions of democratic forming of the Russian State System Moscow image as an image of a capital becomes an extremely .important factor, determining the quality of life, ideals and purposes of the development of the society, family, man.

Moscow Government attributes great importance to the preservation and development of the historical look of the capital, reconstruction of the national, religious and state holy things, ruined during the soviet period, to the town-building settlement of many social problems — ecology of the environment, education and culture, dwelling and communal construction, engineering and transportation provision of the city, creation of new forms of public and private property.... But the main task is to make the people of the capital and Russia understand the importance of those Moscow historical holy things, which have become the basis, the corner stone of the construction of the Russian State, forming of the Russian people. Due to these spiritual holy things Russia in the image of Moscow acquired the status of a great power and, so, in spite of the temporary loss of the international prestige, great Russia will be revived through the revived holy things of Moscow.

The contents of the four books were conditioned by the specific features of the historical forming of the city of Moscow. The first volume, consisting of two books, shows the development of the city from its foundation till the first quarter of the 20th century — the beginning of the radical reconstructive transformation.

The first book "Ancient Moscow" covers all the pre-Petrine period, showing the forming of the historical image of the city in the Christian traditions of the East and the West, embodied in the artistic image of the city through its likening to Jerusalem, Rome, Constantinople and the Divine City (the Archetype).

Historical graphic pictures, made by foreigners and countrymen, scientific and artistic reconstructions of views of ancient Moscow will help to imagine the place and the role of ensembles, monasteries, fortifications of the Kremlin, Kitaygorod, Bely Tsar-gorod, Skorodom, gardens, public and private buildings and the spatial structure of the city and in the social and political life. Description of town-building reforming expressed in the structure, planning, building in, composition, landscape, toponymy, and the key historical events show the essence of the stone chronicles of old Moscow.

The second book — "Images of Historical Moscow of the 18th — early 20th centuries" — touches upon the period of Peter's innovations of the 18th century, classicism in the architecture of Moscow before the fire, the city reconstruction in the Empire style, appearance of the neo-Russian style and modernism of the early 20th century.

The chapters of this book show how together with the change of the way of social, political and cultural life the ancient traditions of town-building and architecture changed. These images of historical Moscow are preserved in archive materials, prints, photographs, creations of painters, sculptors, architects, poets, writers, historians. Many of memorials which kept till our time were restored and acquired their historical look.

The second volume, consisting of two books, is dedicated to Moscow town-building of the 20th century and its anticipation in the 21st century.

The third book — "Revival of Historical Moscow" — tells about the soviet period of the city reconstruction beginning from the 1920s with its achievements and losses, as well as about the reconstruction of the lost cultural values, which took place in the last ten years of the 20th century. The projects of the 20s-30s and 60s-70s in the process of their realisation show the ideas stipulated in the general plans of 1935 and 1971 in regard of historical Moscow. The second half of this book shows the practice of reconstruction and restoration of memorials, illustrated by photos of their condition before the revolution, after the reconstruction, during the restoration and after it. The process of revival of historical self-consciousness is revealed visually.

The last ten years from 1987 to 1997 are dedicated to a new approach to the historical town-building heritage and reconstruction of the lost holy things and memorials with their adaptation to modern life. The qualitatively new policy of making the historical environment humane is of special importance. It is: historical and town-building researches, designing of reconstructed buildings in conformity with the environmental conditions, public discussions of projects of reconstruction and regeneration of historical buildings with scientists and population of the reconstructed territories, return of historical names to the streets and squares, revival of theatres, museums, exhibitions, church life of different confessions and other parts of spiritual and social life.

The fourth book — "Architectural Invitation to the 21st century" — is a point of view of future Moscow image, a search after two thousand years of Christian civilisation on the basis of today's architectural and town-building projects, development of historical traditions taking into account the ecology, new forms of dwelling, development of industry and engineering infrastructure.

Personalities of today's Moscow architects are at the basis of the fourth book, their competition projects create the images of future Moscow already today, form the town-building and social philosophy of the city ensembles.

The Editorial Board thanks the colleagues of the museum of Russian architecture after A.V.Tschusev and the institute "Spetsproektrestavratsiya" for the provided graphic and photo material for publication of the book and is grateful to the reviewers Yu.P.Bocharov, A.S.Trofimov, N.A.Potapov for the additions and comments, which enriched the contents of the first and the second books.

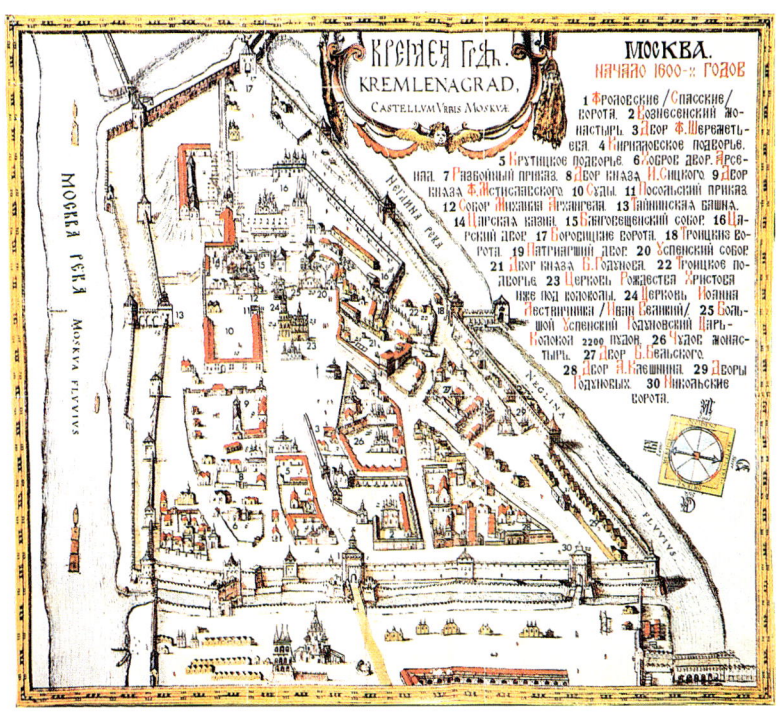

BOOK ONE
Ancient Moscow

Moscow is not an ordinary city, one of thousands. Moscow is not a dumb enormous gathering of cold rocks, composed in symmetrical order... No! It has its own soul, its own life... Each of its stones has an inscription made by the Time and Fate, an inscription, which can not be understood by the crowd, but rich with thoughts, feelings and inspiration for a scientist, patriot and poet! Like the ocean, it has its own language – a strong, sonorous, prayerful language...

*What can be compared with this Kremlin, which, going round with its merlon walls, standing in splendour with the cathedrals' domes, is reclining on a high hill, like the crown of a Great Power on the head of a formidable lord?
It is the Altar of Russia!
On it many sacrifices worthy of the Fatherland, must be committed and were already committed!..*

M. Lermontov

Vladimir Icon Mother God

Spas Icon Novgorod 12 century.

View of the Kremlin from Uspensky Vrazhek in 17th century. Reconstruction of M. Kudriavtsev.

St. Sergius of Radonezh. Pall of 20s of 17th century. Fragment.

Introduction

The word "icon" is of Greek origin and means "image", "portrait". Icon is a church image in general: pictorial, sculptural, architectural, town-building. Through this "portrait", similar to the Prototype, the Lord's Home-building, icon-thrown-church-town-kingdom, on earth is fulfilled. The image of the church – Christ's body – is personified in the image of the Mother of God, Who"Contained the uncontainable Lord". Through this image and its personification in churches, houses, vessels and objects, transfiguration and salvation of degraded Adam's mankind and all creatures is fulfilled by the Holy Spirit.

All man's life from birth to death and Resurrection got in the row of Saints comprehension and sanctified personification. Man's anthropologism in the moral Prototype of God's Son obtained new basis for creation of new life. Upon birth a person was measured and according to it an icon of a Saint of a holiday, connected with the event, was painted. Church's Holy Altar was measured by icon, by church a monastery or kremlin were measured, town was measured by module of monastery or kremlin, thus the town became the measure of space of sacral kingdom.

Theology of Image

"Christianity is the revelation not only of God's Word, but of God's image, revealed by the God's Son." "Nobody and never saw God; He revealed the Only Born Son existing inside the Father, he revealed"[1] the image-icon of God. Through personification God Word – "Being the light of glory and Image of His Entity" (The Father's)[2] – reveals the Father's Image to the world in His Deity. To Philip's request: "God, show us the Father"[3], God answers: "Have I been so long time with you, and yet hast thou not known me, Philip? he that hath seen me hath seen the Father, The Son is one entity with the Father "in the Father's lap", as well as upon personification, being His sacred inscription in Deity.

This truth, revealed in Christianity, is in the basis of its art. So, the category of image, icon-like painting not only does not contradict the essence of Christianity, but, being the basis of its truth, is its integral part. On this the legend was established firmly, showing that exhortation of Christianity to the world is from the beginning carried out by the Church by word and image.

The major principle of Christian art is figurative expression of the Church's doctrine through painting of concrete events of the Holy History and indication of their interior meaning, which shall not reflect problems of life, but give answers to them, from the very beginning it is the conductor of evangelic doctrine.

Christian art from the first centuries was deeply symbolical, and it was not the phenomenon characteristic only of this period of Christianity. It is inseparable from church art, because that spiritual reality, which it expresses, cannot be shown in any other way, but by symbols.

Church gradually creates new art in form and contents, which shows revelations of Divine World in images and forms of material world, makes this world accessible to comprehension and understanding. This art develops together with the church service and, like the service, expresses the Church's doctrine, corresponding to the word of the Holy Writ Scripture. This correspondence of image and word was especially clearly stated by the definition of the Seventh Oecumenical Council, which reestablished iconolatry. On behalf of the fathers of this Council Church, rejecting compromise suggestion to venerate icons equally with sacred vessels, established to venerate them equally with the Cross and Gospel: with the Cross as the differential sign of Christianity, and with the Gospel as full correspondence of word image to visual image[4].

Church sees in image (icon) not only art, serving to illustrate the Holy Writ Scripture, but its full conformity, and thus gives the image (icon) the same dogmatic, liturgic and educational significance as to the Holy Writ Scripture. Like the word of the Holy Writ Scripture is the image, the image is the same word. "What the word communicates through hearing, art shows silently through expression", – St.Basil the Great[5] says, "and by these two ways, conforming to each other, we receive knowledge about the same"[6]. In other words, image (icon) contains and exhorts the same truth as the Gospel, so, like the Gospel, it is based on precise, concrete data, not on fiction in any way, for otherwise it would be able neither to explain the Gospel, nor to conform to it.

Thus image (icon) becomes equal to the Holy Writ Scripture and the Cross as one of forms of revelation and divine knowledge, in which Divine and human wills and actions are combined. Both of them, besides their direct meaning, are reflection of heaven; both sure symbols of the Holy Spirit, that is in them. So, contents of word and image, as well as their meaning and role are the same. Image, like divine service, is a conductor of dogmatic definitions and expressions of bliss of the Holy Writ Scripture in Church. Through divine service and icon revelation becomes the property and life's essence of people. So, from the very beginning church art gets the form conforming to what it expresses. Church creates an absolutely special category of image, corresponding to its nature, the very meaning of which specifies its special character. Church, "Kingdom not of this world"[7], lives in the world and for the world. It has special nature, different from the world, and serves the world exactly because it is different from it. So the Church's expressions through which it serves, word, image, singing etc.,differ from the same world's expressions. All of them have the sign of the above world, which is different in exterior. Architecture, art, poetry stop being the types of art, developing in their own ways, independent from each other, in search of their own characteristic effects, but become parts of one liturgic whole, which not making them less significant in any way, stipulates rejection of all of them of independent role, self-establishment. Out of art with independent purposes all of them become the means of various kind, each expressing the same in its own area: the Church's Entity, i.e. become various means of divine knowledge. Thus, the church art in its essence is the liturgic art. Its liturgic nature is not in the fact that image surrunds divine service or adds to it, but in their perfect conformity. The carried out sacrament and expressed sacrament are a unity, like the interior in its essence, and the exterior in the symbols, which express this essence. So orthordox church image, icon, is defined not as art of this or that historical epoch or as expression of national peculiarities, but exclusively by conformity to its purpose defined by the essence of image and its role in Church. Being the liturgic art in its essence, icon, like word, always was and is now an integral part of religion, one of means to comprehend God, one of means to communicate with Him.Thus, it is clear what significance the Church gives the image. It is of such kind that of all victories over many different heresies the only victory over iconoclasm and reestablishment of iconoltry was announced as the Triumph of Orthodoxy, which is celebrated by the Church on the first Sunday of the Lent.

About the Prototype

So, God Word, the second Entity of the Holy Trinity, undescribable either by word, or by image, accepts human nature, is born by the Virgin, the Mother of God, remaining the perfect Lord, becomes the perfect Man, becomes visual, touchable, thus, describable. So, the mere fact of icon's existence is based on God's personification. Immutability of God's personification is confirmed and proved by icon. So, in Church's opinion rejection of Christ's icon is rejection of the truth and immutability of His personification, and, so, rejection of all God's homebuilding. Defending icon during the period of iconoclasm, the Church defended not only its educational role and even less its esthetic meaning; it taught for the basis of Christianity itself, for the visual evidence of God's personification, as the basis of our salvation. "I have seen the human image of God and my soul is saved", – St.John Damascene says[8]. Such understanding of icons explains why their defenders went to tortures and martyr death without any compromise during the period of iconoclasm.

The fathers of the Seventh Oecumenical Council say: "He (God) recreated him (man) for immortality, giving him this irrevocable gift. This recreation was more godlike and better than the first creation – it is an eternal gift"[9], the gift to communicate with divine beauty, glory. Christ, the new Adam, the origin of new creature, heaven-like, spiritually divine man, takes man to that purpose, for which the first Adam was created and from which he fell; He takes him to implementation of the Holy Trinity's idea of hint: "Let us make man in our image, after our likeness"[10]. According to this idea, man shall be not only the image of God, Who created him, but shall be like Him. However, in the description of already fulfilled creation – "so God created man in his own image, in the image of God created he him"[11] – nothing is said about likeness. It is given to man as the task implemented by action of bliss of the Holy Spirit with free participation of man himself. Man freely and conscientiously, "for the sentence "in the image" indicates mental capability and freedom", enters the Holy Trinity's idea of him, creates, in accordance with his capabilities, his likeness to God, "for the sentence "after our likeness" means like-ness to God in virtues (perfection)"[12], thus remaining a participant in the divine creation.

So, if divine entity of God's Son became Man, a reverse process is happenning to us: man can be god, not in nature, but in bliss. God descends, becomingman, man ascends: becoming similar to God. Becoming like Christ, he becomes "the temple of the Holy Ghost which is in you"[13], reestablishes his likeness to God[14]. Human nature remains what it is, but his personal entity, having obtained the bliss of the Holy Spirit, communicates with divine life, thus changing the life of its created nature. The Holy Spirit's bliss enters nature, combining with it, filling in and transfiguring it. Man as though roots into eternity already here, on earth, obtaining the beginning of eternal life, beginning of godlikeness, which shall appear fully in future life. Revelation of this coming transfiguration was shown to us in on the Tabor. "And was transfigured before them: and his face did shine as the sun, and his raiment was white as the light"[15] i.e. the whole God's body transfigured becoming as though enlighted raiment of Deity.

"As for the nature of the Transfiguration, – the Fathers of the Seventh Oecumenical Council say, referring to St.Athanasius the Great, – it did not happen as though the Word took off human image, but sooner only through the enlightment of the Word with glory"[16]. So, in the Transfiguration "on the Tabor not only deity appears as man, but mankind appears in divine glory"[17]. Man, who has obtained the Holy Spirit's bliss, becomes participant of this divine glory, upon this "uncreated divine enlightment", as St.Gregory Palama calls the light of the Tabor[18].

In human creation, beauty, given by God, conforms to the Prototype like a copy, a replica of the depicted original. Icon's beauty is the beauty of the obtained likeness to God, so its value is not in its own beauty as a beautiful thing, but it is valuable because it depicts Beauty.

Being a divine and human body, just like God and Man Jesus Christ, the Church combines inseparably and integrally two realities: historical, worldly one and the reality of all-sanctifying bliss of the Holy Spirit. Essence of the church art, for instance icon, church, town is in the fact that they tell, or, better, visually testify to these two realities, realities of God and world, bliss and nature. They are realistic in two essences. Like the Holy Writ Script, icon (image of church, town) shows historical fact of an event of the. Holy History or a historical personality, depicted in his own real, physical image and indicates non-temporary revelation, contained in certain historical reality. So, through icon, like through the Holy Writ Scripture, we not only learn about God, but comprehend Him.

If picture is education of man, prayful enlighting of his material contents by uncreated light of divine bliss, appearance to man of live God's icon, icon is an exterior expression of this transfiguration, picture of man full of the Holy Spirit's bliss.

Icon is an exterior expression of transfigured man, of his enlighting by uncreated divine light. Like in the holy paternal written language, in painting of orthodox saints we often encounter this appearance of light, as though internal sunlike radiation of saints' faces at the moments of their highest spiritual raising and glorifying. This appearance of light is shown by nimbi, which is the exact artistic picture of the real phenomenon of spiritual world. Spiritual composition, interior perfection of man, the exterior appearance of which is this light, cannot be expressed .either in icons, or verbally. When Fathers and ascetic writers usually come to description of the very moment of enlighting, they characterize it only as complete silence because it is not possible to be described or expressed.

So, it is exactly in icon where all human feelings, thoughts and actions, like the body itself, are shown to their full value. Icon, church, town is thus the way and means; it is the prayer itself.

Transfiguration of man communicates to all his surroundings, for the quality of holiness is sanctifying everything around, contacting the holy world. Holiness has not only personal significance, but general and cosmic. That is why all visual world in icon changes, becomes the image of coming unity of all creatures, the Kingdom of the Holy Spirit. In accordance with this all expressed in the icon does not reflect disorder of our sinful world, but divine order, peace, where neither worldly logic, nor human morals reign, but divine bliss.

It is a new order among new creatures. So, what we see in icon is not similar to what we see in ordinary life. Divine light penetrates through everything, so there is no source of light falling on the picture from any side; objects do not give shades, for there are no shades in God's Kingdom. All is full of light, and in the technical language of icon the artists icon's background is called the "light". People do not make gestures, their movements are not chaotic, casual; they are committing the religious rite, and their every movement has sacramental, liturgic quality. Starting with clothes of a saint, everything takes off its usual, worldly chaotic look: people, nature, architecture, animals. Together with the saint himself all abides by the same rythmic law, all is concentrated on the spiritual contents and acts in full unity: earth, nature and animals are shown not to make man closer to what we see in our environment, but to make nature a participant of man's transfiguration and, thus, to communicate it to the eternal life. Like through man's fault all creatures fell, they get sanctified by his holiness. So there cannot be any separate creature's icon without man.

Taking into account the essence and contents of icon, the Fathers of the Seventh Oecumenical Council, establishing the possibility to convey through the Mother of God sanctified by the personification, man's blissfull state, ordered to put icons everywhere for veneration, like the Precious and Life-giving Cross "in holy God's churches, on sacred vessels and ephods, on walls and boards, in houses and roads"[19]. This resolution of the Holy Council testifies that the Church understood that the icon's role, told by the Legend, is not limited only to the memory about the holy past. Its role, in Church and in the world, is far from being conservative, but dynamically constructive. Image (icon) is regarded as one of ways by which it is possible and necessary to strive for the given to man task of gaining likeness to the Prototype, to implementation in life of what was revealed by God and Man. In consideration of this images (icons) are put everywhere as Revelation of the future world's holiness, its coming transfiguration, project of its realization and, finally, as sermon of bliss and the presence in the world of Deity sanctifying it. "For the saints during their lives were full of the Holy Spirit, and in the same way after death their bliss of the Holy Spirit is unexpirably stays in the souls and bodies living in coffins, in the features and in their holy pictures."[20].

It is in Russia where it was given to show the perfection of the artistic language of image (icon), which most powerfully opened the depth of contents of the liturgic image, its spirituality.

It is possible to say that if Byzantium gave to the world mostly theology in word, theology in image was given by Russia. It is characteristic that up to the times of Peter the Great there had been a few spiritual writers among Russian saints; but many saints were icon-painters, from usual monks to metropolitanates.

Christianity is a revelation not only of God's Word, but God's Image, in which His likeness was shown. This godlike image is a characteristic feature of the New Testament, being the visual evidence of man's making God-like. The ways of icon-painting here are the same as those of theology, the ways to express what refers to Deity. Both are to express what is not possible to express by human means, because the expression will be always unperfect and insufficient. There are no such words, paints or lines by which we could express God's Kingdom like we express and describe our world. Icon-painting, as well as theology encounter wittingly unsolvable task – to express by means of the created world what is unlimitedly higher the creature. In consideration of this there are no achievements, because the expressed one is incomprehensible, and no matter how high in contents and wonderful, an icon is, it cannot be perfect, like no word image can be perfect. In consideration of this theology and icon-painting are never a success. The value of both of them is exactly in this failure. The value is exactly in the fact that icon-painting and theology reach the highest pick of human' capabilities and turn out to be insufficient. So, those means which are used by icon-painting to indicate God's Kingdom can be only icon-allegorical, symbolical, like the language of the legends in the Holy Writ Script. The contents expressed by this symbolical language, is fixed both in the Scripture and in the liturgical image*.

Figuratively-Symbolical Language of Sacred Town

Soviet historical science, having rejected orthodox religious consciousness as social and state property of people and civilization and making the headstone of life marxist-leninist philosophy, introduced into people's consciousness, artificially made up factual version of history of the Russian State. In this way it deprived all of us of the opportunity to understand and comprehend the previous purposes of social development, coded in cultural monuments.

Radical liquidation of religious people put all the system of up-bringing and education on the unstable and unfruitful soil of limited, plane feeling and vision of the world. The lost figuratively-symbolical language deprived man of the most important quality of being one entity and communicate with his anscestors, people, culture, religion, civilization, finally, to God. We stopped understanding icons, churches, towns as created ark of our salvation. We absolutely stopped understanding the meaning of salvation. That is why people of Russia turned out to be separated into languages, like after the Babel; people stopped understanding each other and, certainly in this situation recreation of Russia is not possible.

One of the main tasks of this book is to help the reader to learn the lost figuratively-symbolical language of our anscestors, incarnated in architecture and town-building like in subject-spacial life's environment, in which the purposes of social development were coded. Today for realization and understandingof the world to full value it is not enough to be able to read, write, retell. and to know the system of signs based on this knowledge, to have so-called higher education. Creative activity requires from modern man free orientation in cultures of civilisation, which are not readable and hidden behind the "seven seals" for majority of people not knowing the specific figuratively-symbolical language.

---
* L.A.Uspensky. Theology of icon of the Orthodox Church. M., 1989.

Together with this, image is a qualitatively new combination of signs, carrying much bigger volume of information and much more densely packed layers of culture. Historical and cultural environment invisibly forms personality of man and people, even when they do not realize conscientiously all its depth. Means of mass media, in spite of the most powerful influence in forming social consciousness, however, do not have a global impact on man's personality through his subconsciousness like the figuratively-symbolical language of holy things and cultural monuments. It is quite natural that the ability "to read" and master by consciousness and feelings the figurative essence (through the divine law of likeness to the Prototype) of the environment with the predecessing aims of social development discloses, the sphere of Logos step by step, connects us by neo-spherical memory consciousness and opens in man himself "sudden spring of great means".

In other words, man becomes the possessor of the opportunity to comprehend oneself as the inheritor of evolution, obtains connection with the Creator due to sudden filling of his memory with the knowledge of the main treasures and holy things, created by man in the name of God.

This method of figuratively symbolical education of man through the images of stone chronicle of Divine testimonies (God's home-building), becomes, to our mind, the main direction of social development – neo-spheric ecology.

850-years of Moscow is a sufficient reason to disclose the figurative symbols of the Sacred Town, reading of which help us to acquire again after the "Bible" the language clear to all Russians, like the Apostles who suddenly started speaking different, but clear to each nation, languages, on the day of the Ascension of the Holy Spirit.

Kluchevsky already noted that our ancient ancestors thought with images, rituals, legends, i.e. mythological consciousness was the vital reality of whole life. Events and facts of life acquired essence and meaning entering this mythological structure of life, or were rejected as carriers of theomachistic consciousness.

These circumstances were the cause for writing the first book, in which ancient Moscow was shown and expressed by the Word and Image for the first time, through likeness to the Prototype, disclosure through Christ's Image of tsar's and patriarch's service to the Sacred Town of God, to clarify through light and colour combination of objective symbolism of the world surrounding us and the Kingdom of Glory.

Secularized temporary consciousness does not ask in vain the sacramental question about peculiar backwardness and even poverty of Russian philosophy and theology, having fundamentally studied and analysing written sources and comparing these historical facts with European enlightenment, brilliant philosophic thoughts and not less bright theology. However, all these researchers passed by the absolutely evident, open and visible phenomenon of Russian orthodoxy – Evangelic

Word, incarnated in the Images of icons, communion tables, churches, towns, kingdom. All the philosophy and theology were expressed not in scribal and phrariscal explanation of Logos – God's Word, but in his incarnation in images through likeness to the Prototype. Home-building and the Acts introduced the everyday life of ancient Russians into the lap of the church divine home-building.

"Man is the first image of God, for he was created "after the image" and "likeness" of God"[21]", – the father Lev Lebedev writes. The fall clouded and distorted this primary likeness. But it was restored and increased in Christ. "*He that hash seen me hath seen the Father*,"[22] – the Saviour says. St. Apostle Paul calls Christ the image of His person[23], stressing at another point that in Christ *all fullness of Deity lives bodily*[24]. God's birth in a creature, God's incarnation, combining integrally, but indivisibly Deity with matter, makes the reflection of Deity in material possible, because it makes peace between creature and its Creator, restores their blissful unity infringed by sin. If Christ is God's incarnated image, in body, then the Christ's Body – the Church – cannot be anything else, but also God's image, "dwelleth all the fullness of the Godhead bodily". That is the great salving significance of God's incarnation both for man and Being. Now it is ascending through man and Church (Christ's body), as God's image, to the Prototype, to a new heaven and *a new earth* (!) *and new Jerusalem*[25]. From here are all the Church's liturgical images: architectural forms of churches, their interior arrangement and decoration, icons and painting of walls, sacred vessels, things and ephods, rank order and rhythms of divine service, sacraments and rituals, church reading and singing and the like; all these images, not loosing their earthly material qualities, are at the same time images of Divine powers and phenomena, Divine World of Angels and Saints. Images inevitably contain sacramental presence of prototypes, have the same energies as the prototypes. Such is the divine-earthly, spiritual-material nature of the Church's liturgical images, including holy icons. In the rank of icons the icons of the Saviour and the Mother of God have the first significance and spiritual value. Through Christ's image communication of people with the Founder of our salvation Who accepted the image of a slave, but did not stop being God, whose name is the "Real" (oωv). Icon of the Mother of God is not only the image of Her blessed Personality, but also a joint image of Church, image of Divine Love and Wisdom, God's kingdom and coming eternal boons, because the Virgin Mary, being Christ's Mother in body, is thus the Mother of His body – the Church. Christ is unthinkable without His Church. On both sides of the Holy Gates of orthodox churches from ancient times Icons of Christ and the Mother of God have been placed. The meaning is clear: God's birth in a salvation of people ("access" into the Divine Kingdom) is implemented through communication with Christ not anywhere and anyhow, but only in His Church which is personified by Virgin Mary.

Holy Eucharistia is the top of blissful life in Christ. It goes far above the limits of any symbols, but partially stays within them. In this Sacrament it is possible to see especially clearly God's Providence about salvation of people. In Eucharistia bread and wine do not lose their material qualities (nature) at the same time becoming "immaterial" Holy Sacraments of the Body and Blood of the Saviour. The most remarkable defender of icon-veneration of the 8th century St.Joahn Damascene says that is someone asks how this combination of material with Deity happens in the Sacrament of Eucharistia "it is enough (to the asking one) to hear that this is carried out by the Holy Spirit, just as God made for Himself and inside Himself body by the Holy Spirit from the Saint Mother of God"[26]. So, in all other exterior material images, icons of the Orthodox Church, unmergeable, but indivisible combination of material and Divine natures, corresponding to the same combination of natures in the Personality of Jesus Christ, is carried out by the Holy Spirit. The main conditions of the combination are similarity to the Prototype (by compliance of images to God-inspired canons of church symbols) and sanctifying of images (symbols) of the Church by "water and Spirit" in rules of sanctifying, similar to rebirth and sanctifying of man by *water and Spirit*[27] in font for Christening.

Thus, icon-veneration, taking into account Christian dogma, comes naturally to preaching blissful, salving, transfigurative action of the Holy Spirit in regard of everything created, being in the lap of the Church, of all *church matter*.

For man earthly Church is a surprizing existence in the world of image, icon, in the world, which is not of this world, but is not the Divine Kingdom yet. Church is not equal either to God, or to creature, but is a personified kernel of God's presence in the world and the world in God! The Divine Kingdom is already present in Church (*is within you*)[28], but has not opened fully yet. It is already sensible reality (the innermost spiritual depths of earthly Church), but at the same time it is the purpose of bellicosity, travelling, sailing and arc-salving. Such movement is nothing, but transformation (Pascha!) of man and creatures in church into being of another reality of the new world – Divine Kingdom. In all this is the basic beginning of the Church.

About the Annivesary Date

The first mention of Moscow in chronicles of 1147 does not mean the city's "birthday", but testifies to the existence, presence at that time of some inhabited place. It was mentioned by chance together with others during telling about events of that time. When it appeared, what it was like – chroniclers wrote nothing about it. But Russian people always wanted to know as much as possible about the "beginning of Moscow". Even without regard to its first mention.

People always said: "**Moscow was not built at once**". This widely known saying is still used figuratively in respect to my affair, which cannot be done at one stroke, one action. The surprising saying came to us from depths of centuries and in its direct meaning contained, supposedly, the initial truth. Anyway, in the 16th century, i.e. very late, chroniclers appeared, who wrote: **the town of Moscow was built at once** in the mouth of the river Neglinnaya by the Prince Yuri Dolgoruky of Suzdal in 1156 (chronicles of Tverj) on the place of a dense forest (added one of chronicle legends of the 17th century). Verbal genuine truth was thus refuted in writing.

Anyway, from this contradiction "rope pulling" began.

In the middle of the last century during earth excavation in different places of the Kremlin remnants of two lines of fortification (artificial moats) of an ancient town-fortress were found. In 1847 under brick wall of the credence of the most ancient church of nativity of St.John the Predecessor on Bor, which was torn down in the year of Moscow's 700th anniversary, some bones were found: a horse head and two shins – one of a bull, the other of a cow. At the same time two big silver neck grivnas (necklaces) and two seven-fanned Vyatich ear-rings were found. Taking into account all this it was supposed: the first line of the fortifications belonged to a pagan fortified settlement (perhaps to a cult centre) of Slavs-Vyatiches of 11th or even 10th centuries, the second one be longed to a fortress of Yuri Dolgoruki. Certainly, they had to write that **Moscow had not been built at once**, but at two stages, that a town of the middle of the 12th century had some earlier town-predecessor (I.E.Zabelin, S.I.Bertenev).

At Moscow 800th anniversary of 1947 the material, that had been collected concerning the problem of two-stage "beginning of Moscow", both historical and archaeological, was reconsidered from a "class point of view". This time not only educated people, but scientists-academicians wrote, that **Moscow neverthless was not built at once** by the prince of Suzdal as a feudal centre, and the early town was, evidently, a fortified mansion-castle of a local boyard Kuchka (M.N.Tikhomirov, then B.A.Rybakov). The new historical decision was fundametally fortified with the bronze-stone monument to the "Founder of Moscow Yuri Dolgoruky" – so that there shall not be any doubts in this question.

But archaeology interfered again. Just when the monument was installed in 1955, in 1965, then in 1975 during earth excavation in Cathedral and John's Squares of the Kremlin they found out: the second exterior line of the fortifications of the ancient town appeared not in the middle of the 12th century, but earlier, at least at the end of the 11th century, testifying, presumably, to the beginning of class distinctions of its inhabitants already before the coming of the prince of Suzdal (N.S.Sheliapina – N.S.Vladimirskaya). The resolution ripened itself: **Moscow nevertheless was not built at once**, but in three stages. To tell the truth there happened to be many stages and Dolgoruky had nothing to do with this: the town with two lines of fortifications appeared long before him. In consideration of the official policy-ideology it not good – there was the monument already! Though they did not take history into account then, but it was necessary to find a way out of the preposterous situation. In 1982 the first book of the fundamental issue "Architectural Monuments of Moscow" appeared under edition of a big collective body. Setting forth the problem the three-stage "beginning of Moscow", the authors of the monograph first quoted as the "support" of their report all previous famous historians of Moscow, paying homage to them. But the they stated absolutely their own, certainly, refined in such a complicated ideological situation option of explanation of town-building implementation of class distinction of Vyatiches in the 11th century. The following scheme was suggested:

Unified town of two parts "fell out" now into two separated fortified settlements, round in configuration and paled (p. 23-25, 259-261). The tandem was a unique one, because nowhere in Russia two independent fortresses were so close to each other (there was only a moat between them).

As in a small cape village during recent excavations a suspended seal of the 11th century was found, supposedly belonging to a metropolitanate of Kiev, it was classified as "some political and administrative centre", and saying even more clearly for the beginning of the 11th century – and also the castle-yard of Stephan Kuchka, titled as the "last owner of the pre-princely Moscow". In a bigger settlement on top of a hill a freedom-loving pagan Vyatiches community, which had already got into slavery to the feudal lord, crowded. Evidently, the two fortresses should have had two different names. And being unnaturally close to each other and certainly being antagonistically at war with each other socially and religiously, servants of a big feudal lord and the free Vyatiches, who had got "in plucking" to him, could, from time to time, shoot each other out of bows right from the fortress walls. Fortunately, already in the middle of the 12th century here a more powerful feudal lord Yuri Dolgoruky appeared. He killed Kuchka, conquering his yard for his administration, then both differently named fortresses united with the help of freed Vyatiches by common round and stronger fortress wall (towns on old-fashioned hook-like substruction). Thus arranged "suburban residence" of the prince of Suzdal, this well-fortified newly born town acquired in 1147 one name – "Moscov". Finally, they got what was to be proved: **Moscov was built at once** by Yuri Dolgoruky before 1152. In this way the authors of the monograph answered the question about the date of appearance of Moscow.

And already now, at the end of the 20th century, after a new research of the completely intricate problem it is found out that at the beginning in 11th-12th centuries on the place of the Kremlin it was **not Moscow which was built**! And certainly **not Moscov**!

Verily "Great are, God, and wonderful are Your deeds!" It was quite clear in totalitarian 1947: it was resolved that "Moscow is 800 years old!", but it turned out again to be unknown from the scientific point of view: "What is the truth?" Willingly or not this "Pilat's question" has to be answered. And certainly in this situation it has to be answered. And certainly in this situation it has to be answered most thoroughly.

---

[1] John, 1, 18.
[2] Hebrews, 1, 3.
[3] John, 14, 8-9.
[4] So it is not possible to understand image of feast or saint, make out the essence and importance of its details, not knowing the service corresponding to it, and for an icon of a saint it is necessary to know his life. Existing explanations of icons usually have this drawback of perfunctory or absolutely no knowledge of image.
[5] Talk 19, on the day of 40 St.Martyrs, P.6.31 Col.509 A.
[6] Acts of the Council, Act 6.
[7] John, 18, 36.
[8] The First Word in Defence of Holy icons, ch. 22.
[9] Acts, as above, p. 437.
[10] Genesis, 1, 26.
[11] Genesis, 1, 24.
[12] St.John Damascene. Account of Orthodox Belief. Book 2, ch. 12, "About Man".
[13] 1 Corinthians, 6, 19.
[14] From here comes the Slavic term "prepodobny" (saint) (literally "very similar"), used to monastic type of holiness. This word, made during the time of St.Cyril and Methodius for translation of a Greek word, indicates acquisition by man of lost similarity to God; it has no corresponding word in other languages, However, the opposite term and idea: "unlike", "improper", "evil" can be traced down to very ancient epoch. Platon uses it in philosophic meaning... or... on the dialogue "Politician" to show uncompliance of the world to his idea. St.Athanasius the Great uses it already in Christian meaning: "The One, Who created the world, seeing it possessed by passions and in danger to be drowned into the "place of indecency", stood at the wheel of his soul and came to its help, mending its transgressions". The Great Augustin says in his "Confession": "I saw myself far from You, in the place of indency."
[15] Mathew, 17, 2.
[16] Acts, as above, p.540.
[17] Works of Phlaret, Metropolitanate of Moscow and Kolomna. M, 1873, p.99.
[18] Quotation acc. to Krivoshein V. Ascetic Theologian Doctrine of St.Gregory Palamas".
[19] Definition of the Seventh Oecumenical Council.
[20] St.John Damascene.
The First Word in Defence of Holy Icons. & 19. P.C.col.1249 C.D.
[21] Genesis, 1, 26.
[22] John, 14, 8-10.
[23] Hebrews, 1, 3.
[24] Colossians, 2, 8-9.
[25] Revelation, 21, 1-2.
[26] III, 6, p. 252.
[27] John, 3, 5.
[28] Luke, 17,и 21.

Vowed crosses. Hieromonk Stephan (Linitskiy).

CHAPTER ONE

Forgotten Moskovj

*There saw the Grand Prince
Daniel Ivanovich
A huge and wonderful beast, with three heads
And very beautiful...
And Basil Grechenin said to him:
"Grand Prince, On this place great town
will be created and triangle kingdom
will extend, and people of different hordes
will increase in it,
id est will transform this beast
with three heads..."*

Tale about creation
of the reigning city of Moscow

**Sts. Equal-to-the Apostles Cyril and Methodius.
Icon of 19th century.**

**St. Apostle Andrew the First Called.
Icon of 19th century.**

**Sts. Equal-to-Apostles princess Olga
and prince Vladimir. Western portal of the
cathedral of St. Vladimir in Kiev.**

The Intercession. Icon of 15th century.

Epyphany. Icon of 15th century. School of Novgorod.

Many most ancient and largest cities in the world do not have data about their conception. They were rising as though mysteriously and unexpectedly foreverybody already large and beautiful from the depth of their unknown "child-hood". Only late legends tried to tell something mythical about this "childhood". Thus, Babylon, Jerusalem, Athens, Rome, Paris raised...

"Beginning of Moscow" is also concealed in depths of centuries. There are also late legends about this "beginning". But here the case turned out to becomplicated: the unknown predecessor – "Moscovj" – which existed before Moscow, was found out.

Data about mysterious Moscovj are absolutely scarce and obscure – because if they were not so, everything was known and clear long ago. Besides many ofthem were distorted by different versions of Moscow historians. So it is difficult to give undoubtful, final answers to all obscure news and explain scarce facts.

Archaeologists cannot help here either. The point is that, Moscow archaeology of the 20th century dragged out a miserable existence. It is common knowledge that instead of scientists the unique historical centre of Moscow (2% of the present city's territory) was dug out by... excavators during more than half a century. Though, sometimes it was allowed to archaeologists to lay two or three prospecting pits in the place of foundation pits of future huge buildings. And that was all. Only in the recent years an archaeological expedition was organized in Moscow, which carries out systematical research and study of the cultural layer.

Anyway, it is possible to make the first step, to try to tell about mysterious Moscovj: with the help of modest archaeological data, attracting the city's toponimy, explaining retrospectively early Moscow historical information, analysing the landscape. In future, with collecting of more concrete, wide archaeological material, still obscure face of Moscow's predecessor will be more clear.

Historycal news

Moscovj was mentioned in the news of the 12th century of the most early and reliable Russian chronicles. In their essence they incidental indications of an address of events which happened at those distant times.

The first mention of 1147 is connected with invitation to the meeting by the Suzdal Prince Yuri Dolgoruky of the Novgorod-Seversky Prince Svjatoslav Olgovich (the father of Prince Igor – the main character of the "Word about Igor's regiment"). In Moscow united chronicles of the end of the 15th century (PSRL., 25) the address of the meeting is indicated as follows: – "said to Yuri: "Come, brother, to me to Moscovj".

In the scripture of Ipatjevskaya chronicle of the end of the 14th – beginning of the 15th centuries (PSRL.,) 2) the address is the same – "to Moscow". But researchers of the scripture already in the 19th century noticed the correction: "y' was written in by the same copier of the chronicle and with the same ink in the place of the rubbed as if "Ъ" (er). In all issues of the chronicle (1843, 1871, 1908) the chronicler was unrightfully "corrected back" and "Moscov" was printed. At the same time the word-name, which never existed, was artificially invented and established in press by mistake, because in scripture "Ъ" was erased (erj) and the address was first read – "Moscovj".

The news of Ipatjevskaya chronicle testifies undoubtedly about corrections of later chroniclers of the most ancient term "Moscovj", beginning at least from the border line of the 14th-15th centuries. At that time Moscow was commonly recognized as the grand princely capital, and its name was well known even abroad. The name was not confused with the name of the river as it could be in ancient times. Naturally encountering the most ancient term~chroniclers changed it into the new one, which was already habitual, which can be found, for instance, in Voskresenskaya chronicle (PSRL., 7). Its main source was the Moscow chronicle summary of the end of the 15th century. But in it the address "to Moscovj" of the news of 1147 was already changed by chronicler of the middle of the 16th century to "to Moscow". So it is possible to consider a good luck the fact that the most ancient term was kept in the early news of the indicated oldest and most reliable chronicles.

It is appropriate to note here that in speech, in the process of furtherchange of the term "Moscovj" to the word "Moscow" the second "o" disappeared as being without stress. So, the stress in the most ancient term fell on thefirst "o" and it was read and pronounced as "Moscovj"!

The last mention of 1177 is connected with the news about the raid of the Riazanj prince and stayed in Lavrentjevskaya, Voskresenskaya, Lvovskaya (PSRL., 1, 7, 20) and other chronicles:

"That autumn Gleb came to Moscovj and burnt the whole town and villages",

"Gleb burnt Moscovj and went to Rjazanj", "burnt all Moscovj: both the town and villages".

First of all it is necessary to indicate that the first mention of 1147 is not the only one and the term "Moscovj" is not a mistake, slip of the pen of chroniclers. We really deal with special term, which can be seen in Russian chronicles of the 12th century. However, after 1177 the term "Moscovj" disappeared from chronicles forever. More than that, this mention is the lastfor the 12th century, too, because the next "Moscow" News is encountered under 1207, 1208, and they tell actually only about the town.

Intermediate mentions, encountered in different chronicles of 1156, 1175, 1176, are chronologically between the first and the last mentions. Their characteristic feature is the use of the term only in declension (to Moscow, of Moscow), which can be formed equally from the term "Moscovj", as well as from the word "Moscva" (later corrections should not be forgotten). However, if to take into consideration the presence in this news of "inflected" terms:

"Moskjvu" of 1156, "Mosjcvi" of 1175, "to Moskve", "moskjvliani" of 1176, but especially the chronicles of 1147-1177, it is possible to make the following three resolutions:

1 – all the terms of intermediate news were made from the term "Moscovj";

2 – this term was mentioned through the whole of the 12th century;

3 – the name of our capital "Moscva" appeared only in the 13th century.

For historical clearness this last resolution is important. So, we should not say "the town of Moscow in the 13th century", – at that time there was also Moscovj, like we cannot state that Petrograd was founded in 1703.

Among historians only S.F.Platonov tried to explain the change of terms, but he presented it as confusion of chroniclers: "In the news of 1176-1177 single name of the town was not defined yet: it is called sometimes "Moscovj", or Kuchkovo, or Moscva; – does it not prove that chroniclers dealt with new settlement, to the name of which they were not used yet?"

Analysis of all the news, and not only those indicated by S.F.Platonov, does not say about confusion of chroniclers, but about variants of the old term before its transformation to the new one. Hesitations, change of terms, as it will be shown later, were the result of a real process of change of one form of settlement into another.

The term "Moscovj" is mentioned in 1147 and 1177 in accusative case. But itsform of nominative case is the same, i.e. "Moscovj", according to the declension rule of Russian words with the end " ", meaning inanimate object of feminine gender. The same form of accusative and nominative cases is also present in toponyms: Tverj, Rjazanj, Kazanj, Sibirj... But the word "tzerkovj" (church) is rather instructive.

The word comes from the Greek "kiriakos" – God's church. From here comes German "kircha" and ancient Russian "tserki". Then the word "tserkovj" appeared and "tserkva", similar to "Moscovj" and "Moscva". Sometimes it is thought that the Moscow words are synonyms, just different readings of the same object (town).

However, "tserkva" is temple, and "tserkovj" is temple and community of believers (each believer is also "vessel" or "God's temple"). And communi-ty of believers can be of state or religious rate: Greek church, Russian church, catholic church... and it is not possible to say Georgian church (tserkva), protestant church (tserkva)... In general, volume and contents of the notes "tserkovj" and "tserkva" are sufficiently different. Similarly the notions "Moscovj" and "Moscva" are not the same: their volume and contents are also different. What did ancient Russian people mean by the word "Moscovj"?

Moscovj-Land

It is possible to find out,even in the latest variant of the notion's contents, upon the news of 1177. Here the oldest term is as though specially mentioned and was explained. According to the Lavrentjevskaya chronicle it is "town and villages", according to the Lvovskaya one it is "all Moscovj", which is "both town and villages".

According to the Tverskaya chronicle, Yuri Dolgoruky founded the town in 1156, and in 1177 this town was mentioned. Then for earlier time, for example, for the 11th for the 11th century, they were to tell only about villages. In any case, the whole Moskovj is nestle of various settlements, some inhabited territory, PORECHIE (on the banks) of the river Moscow.

It is not by chance that in the news of the 12th century "territorial"prepositions "on", "from", "to" (to Moscovj, in Mosjkvi, from Moskve) prevail instead of "city's ones" – "in", "near" (to Kiev, from Novgorod,near Rostov), encountered more and more often in regard of Moscow later, beginning from the 13th century. Certainly this rule is not absolute. Today we also say in regard of territories – in the Crimea, from Belorussia. In the 12th century, though seldom, we can see directions "to Moscovj" (1147), "from Moscovj" (1176), and later – on the contrary: in Moscow, from Moscow. Perhaps in the mentioned "territorial character" there is the secret that "town" is a notion of musculine gender, but inherited a feminine name!

On the other hand, the late news of 1177 – tandem "town and villages" accompanied news about Moscow for a long time. For example, under 1237 it was written that Baty's hordes, having torn Riazanj, Kolomna, "burnt the town and villages" at Moscow again. Only after such "total" disasters of the 13th century villages separated from the town, final "separation of the town from the villages" happened even in people's notions at that time. With this it is necessary to stress specially that exactly by such disasters Moscovj was torn down, and instead of it the town of Moscow remained. In ancient Russia a town's name meant simultaneously the name of surrounding land. With appearance of Russian principalities in the 11th – 12th centuries from the territories of such Eastern Slavic tribal units which had fallen apart, lands, not towns, stood out in some cases. Only later in the centre of such land a town could appear with delay, but it already had the feminine name of land, volost (small rural district). That is how, perhaps, the names: Tverj, Riazanj, Kolomna, Lopasnja, etc., appeared... But Metschera did not acquire a town of the same name. In "Moscow" case there are two names, first "Moscovj" for the land-volost, then slightly corrected – "Moscva" – for the town-volost.

Moscovljane (Moscovites) – inhabitants of Moscovj are mentioned in the 1176 notification of Ipatjevskaja chronicle about movements of the troops of two princes Mikhalko and Vsevolod Yurjevich from Chernigov to Vladimir Zalessky. Moecovljane first accompanied the princes, making their troops stronger. But having learnt somehow that the hostile army of Yaropolk ("passed by in the forest") passed by another road by mistake, retreated:

"Moskovljane, having heard that
Yaropolk did not go against them, retreated,
coming back to their houses."

In the word "Moscovljane" chronicler wrote "j" in the place of erased letter "v". The chronicler seemed to start writing already normal for the 15th century word – "Moskvichi", but then corrected the precious for us word inaccordance with the protograph.

According to this news, Moskovljane are armed warriors who make decisionsindependently from the princes act in conformity with the situation. Later, beginning with the scripture of 1213 in the chronicle of Pereslavl Suzdalsky, "Moscvichi" appear as the town's inhabitants, and this name is finallyestablished till our time. And for the 12th century in full concord "Moscovj" – as some inhabited territory, and its inhabitants "Moskovljane" arementioned. Where did Moscovljans' territory extended?

Archaeologists discovered on the territory of Moscow region long ago manybarrows, barrow groups of Slavs Vyatichi. On Moscow territory and near it pagan cemeteries of the 11th – beginning of the 13th centuries were kept until recent time (and are still kept in some places) on the Yauza, in Ostankino, Tushino, Odintsovo, Matveevskoe, Ochakovo, Cheremushki, Chertanovo, Tsaritsino, Teply Stan, Konjkovo, Birjulevo, Brateevo, Kosino, Ljubertsy and many others. Near the village Rudnevo of Moscow region hundreds of barrows were kept before "kolkhozny" (collective farm) ploughing.

Ancient Russian independent principalities, which appeared in 11th-12th centuries, often inherited the borders of "tribes". Moscow principality appeared at the beginning of the 13th century in the middle flow of the river Moscow with the princes of Vladimir-Suzdal Home, while Mozhaisk had princes from Smolensk at the upper reaches, and Kolomna had ones from Rjazanj at the lower reaches. If Moscow principality was the inheritor of Moscovj-land conquered in the middle of the 12th century by Yuri Dolgoruky (Long Hands), then this land extended from Ruza nearly up to Bronnitsy. Exactly in this place barrows of Moscow Vyatichi are encountered with characteristic funeral ritual and things: burials at the level of horizon (earth surface) or with slightly deeper (up to 0,5 m), seven-fanned temple rings-pendants, lattice rings, lamellar bracelets with turned ends, bipyramidal glass beads...The borders of Moscovj-land were even, perhaps, guarded. It was its "isolated" at a certain time position which was reflected in burial ritual of moscovljane. E.I.Gorjunova indicated plenty of Vyatichis' towns of the 10th-12th centuries on Moscow territory, and T.N.Nikolskaya, who had studied materials about all land of Vyatichis, indicated the chain of 5 towns (town settlements) along the western border of Moscow land from Old Ruza to the North, a chain of seven town settlements along the rivers Pakhra, Moscow in the south; there are town settlements also in the North-East. Chain of town settlements surrounds the territory of Moscovj-land, testifying, perhaps, its earlier autonomy (during the period of existence in town settlements of town-fortresses). Is it possible to indicate this time at least preliminarily, taking into consideration the results of available historical research?

Vjatiches, burning according to the all-slavic ancient tradition their dead people, first installed urns with ashes in special burial houses (pilars) near roads at the suburbs of villages and towns. Christianity, which had started to penetrate to them from the 11th century (with return home of christened Vyatiches warriors from Kiev, Chernigov, Rostov; with move to their land of christened Kriviches, people of the North and Slavs) in a way corrected the old way to bury the dead, which did not leave traces. Vyatiches-pagans started more and more to bury the dead since that time under earth barrows. So early dating of barrows – the 11th century is far from being the time of coming to the Moscovj-land of Vyatiches: they could come earlier (there are barrows with the burnt dead of the 8th-10th centuries).

Where did Vyatiches come from to the upper reaches of the Oka ia still a secret. Some think they came from the Don, Kubanj's land, some think – from Prikarpatje, "from Ljakhs". Anyway it was significant move of many people, besides peasants.

Moscovj was inhabited by Vjatiches from the South of the Oka with two streams. The first one was connected with general colonization of Vjatiches in the 7th-9th centuries of the upper, then the middle reaches of the Oka and with possible enforced ousting of Mordva tribes (erzes, metschers), and in the reaches of the Moscow-river from the end of the beginning of the 9th centuries, perhaps, also Baltic ones (goljads). The stream of kriviches and Slavs from Ilmenj in the 9th-10th centuries already turned round Moscow in the north, moving along Volga and Kljazma. As a result of the above process Arab sources from the middle of the 9th century indicate Slavic some half-state unity here "Vantit". But being weak after fight for land Vyatiches from about the middle of the century, perhaps, were attacked by khazars, and then got into some dependence to Khazar kaganat and had to pay him a donation. The unsubjugated, the most powerful Vyatiches communities, probably, retreated to the North, to the zone of middle flow of the Moscow-river (the second tributary) and joined the Slavs-Kriviches of Zalesskaya land who did not pay the donation. In the North a small country "Moscovj" as if separated from the country "Vantit". At the border line of the 9th-10th centuries Moscovj could have its own administration, army, town-fortresses in the centre and suburbs. In such situation this small free country could exist half a century.

In 964-966 the prince Svjatoslav of Kiev defeated in union with Vyatiches Khazar kaganat. Moscovj, probably did not separate itself from this union with Slavs-Kriviches

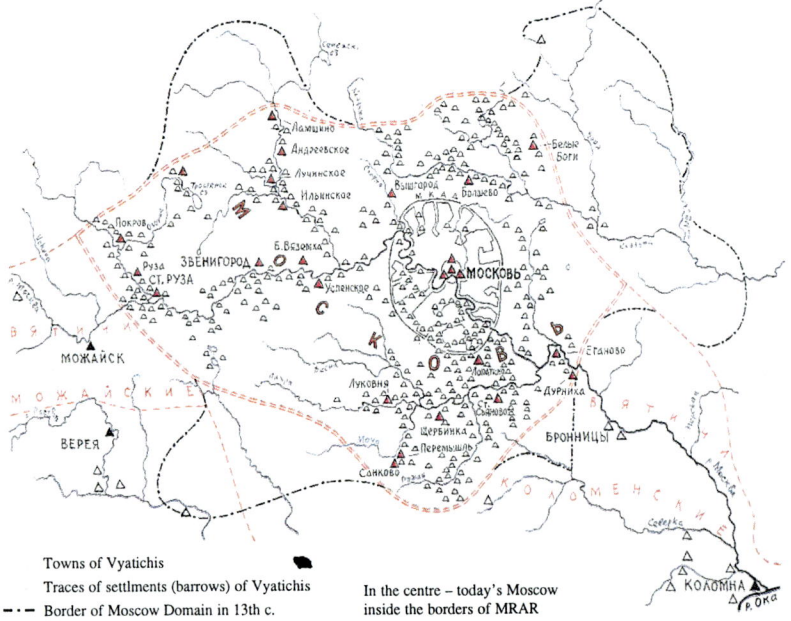

Moskovj-land: fortresses, barrows of Moscow Vjatitcis. 8th – 12th centuries.
Scheme of G. Mokeev according to the information of T. Nikolskaya, E. Goryunova.

Jewelry of Moscow Vyatichis:
necklaces, seven-blade pendants, bipyramidal beads.

of Zalessk, but did not amalgamate as before with general Vyatiches association. In this we can see the reasons of its integrity (its own development), which resulted finally in its submission in the middle of the century to the "Slav-Kriviches" Rostov-Suzdal Principality.

But up to the middle of the 12th century, the princes of Smolensk and Rostov hardly extended here their power. Anyway, Vladimir Monomakh remembered with pride on his death-bed that he had ridden several times "through Vyatiches" (during the period from 1073 to 1117). From Kiev, Pereslavlj, Smolensk to Rostov, Suzdal it was necessary, by the way, to ride "through Moscovj", as it was lying then at the connection of these land route-roads between these important centres at that time.

In the 11th – first half of the 12th centuries Moscovj was one of the strongest volosts of Vyatiches. There were already feudal principalities around it: Novgorodskoe, Smolenskoe, Chernigovskoe, Rjazanskoe, Rostovskoe, Suzdalskoe. And it still kept some customs and regulations of tribal life, pagan rituals. At that time it was one of those territories of Eastern Slavs, on which as if in the last fire primitive communal life was fading away. As a whole existed during 400 years. Its history has to be studied and written.

The Town of Power

Any land of Eastern Slavic tribes had its centre of administration: communal, juridical, religious. For example, in 1146 the town of Dedoslavl was mentioned in regard of Vyatiches, where they called their vetche (meeting). There was a judge-prince in Kordnja. "K n-az" is from "az", which means I, and "kona" is positive, establishing life rules, "zakona" means rejecting rules, and together it is "pravdy" (of truth); "knjaz" (prince) is translated as "I am the law", the judge, "I am the truth". At the end of the 11th century the prince Khodota is mentioned in regard of Vyatiches, with whom Vladimir Monomakh was at war. The third town – Perevitsk – was the religious centre. There, perhaps, was a huge idol (wall-like) of the highest god of Vyatiches Perevit with five heads.

All the three centres were somewhere in Tula's region (though late Perevitsk is mentioned at the Oka, too).

In Nikonovskaya chronicle (PSRL., 9) in 1177 it is said that Gleb of Rjazanj "burnt the whole Moscow, the town of power and villages and captivated all". Topographical sign of "town of power" of Moskovljane were the two lines of fortifications of the central town at the Moscow river at the mouth of Neglinnaya, and the "historical" sign was its capture and reconstruction by Yuri Dolgoruky.

As Moscovj was part of Vyatiches' land, their special power, the centre's square was less and all administrative bodies (vetche, court, religious centre), probably, were placed in one of them. Such centre should have appeared at about the end of the 9th – beginning of the 10th centuries with appearance of Moscow-volost.

As the term "Moscovj" meant nestle of settlements, territory, then the town at the mouth of the Neglinnaya, probably, had its own name. There is nothing new in this statement, because the town was named "Kremnik" later too, and now it is called the "Kremlin". But these names are not the most ancient ones.

Bor-town. ("Bor" means dense forest). In the Western part of the Kremlin there were two most ancient churches of Moscow: one of the Nativity of St.John the Predecessor at Bor and the other of the Transfiguration at Bor. The first church was in the site of cape town and the other – in mainland town. I.E.Zabelin dated the cape town back to the 10th century (near it in Chertolje Arabic coins were found dating to the 9th century); today archaeologists date it back to the 11th century like the mainland town in the Kremlin's Makovitsa. First of all the same name of the churches "at Bor" means that the toan at the Neglinnaya was one unit (exterior fortress was at the suburbs of the town). For explanation of the toponim "at Bor" there are three hypotheses "forest", "view" and "warehouse".

Already in 1461 Moscow chronicler wrote the legend about the time of appearance of the church of St.John the Predecessor: "They say it is the first church in Moscow, – there was dense forest there and the church was built in this forest then." It seems the archaeological dates of the cape town(the end of the 11th century) and the seal of the metropolitanate of Kiev (1093-1096) are close, and the church and the fortress could be really built "then in that forest", which seemed to grow on the Kremlin hill before foundation of the town.

But simple logic contradicts this "forest" hypothesis: if the forest had been felled, buildings cannot be "at Bor" any more" (the toponim will not live). Find of bones of domestic animals under the church's credence means that the town here was more ancient than the church.

The second "view" hypothesis explains better the toponim "at bor". If to draw in a plan the "borovitskie objects", it is possible to see that all of them occupy the end of the Kremlin's hill-cape. So that the churches seemed to be visually "on bor", i.e. standing above the forest, it is enough for the forest to grow not on the top of the hill, but lower, along its slopes, on the bank of the Neglinnaya. Really, the river, which was stormy in high-floods, washed the Kremlin hill. In the North a "pocket" was made in it by the ice. Growing forest, its protection for a long time at the foot of the high bank are not only reasonable, but extremely necessary. The forest could cover for the same reason also the other slope of the hill at the side of the Moscow-river (Naberezhny Sad– Quay Garden). The forest hid the town's fortress wall from sight, but left the churches "on bor" visual. Such forest on the slopes of the hill could appear in the middle of the 12th century for fortification of the slopes of Yuri Dolgoruky, together with installation of "hook-like" substruction under the walls.

M.P.Kudriavtsev suggested the third explanation of the toponim. The word "bor" means not only the "forest", but also taxes, donations – "pobor". A "cherny bor" ("black tax") is known, which was collected in the 14th-15th centuries over schedule by khans of the Golden Horde from captivated Russia. The fortress at the Neglinnaya in the 10th-12th centuries was, most probably, the place where the taxes collected from all Moscovites (pobor, bor) were kept, that is why, perhaps, it had the name "Bor-town". Besides, later churches appeared not only "on bor", but around the town "under Bor" (not necessarily "under the forest"), and in Zanetlimje there was "Borovskaya road".

"Warehouse" hypothesis can be confirmed by another group of toponims. Under 1331 and 1354 in chronicles there is the word "kremnik" as a new name of Moscow fortress. This name preceded the word "kreml", which appeared only from 1365 to define the larger stone town built then by the prince Demetrius (later of the Don). "Kremnik" is a common name as it was also used for definitions of fortresses in Tverj, Torzhok under 1315-1317. If to go further to the North-West, in Sebezh 16th, Velikie Luki 15th, Pskov 14th-15th centuries, it is possible to find the term "krom" or "krem" for their fortresses. In Veliky Novgorod "Nerevsky krom" was mentioned in the scripture of the end of the 11th century, and "Kromny town" – in the 12th. On the map it is possible to follow movement of similar toponims from the North-West to the South-East, besides from century to century they changed along the chain: *krom* (krem) – kremnik – kreml.

The same chain is found in Moscow fortress, but here it meant fortress constructions of different time. In the kremlin cape first krom appeared (without it there would not be further toponims, then with assimilation of town suburbs the fortress became *Kremnik,* and with new assimilation building from stone everything became the *Kremlin.*

Krom in Novgorod, Pskov, Velikie Luki, Sebezh was *town-warehouse* crowded with *closets-bins*. There family valuables were kept, bread, corn, weapons, armour in case of wars, sieges, disasters. During attack of enemies the town's inhabitants locked inside the fortress and fought with siegers, using the stocks.

The notions "bor" and "kremnik" in Moscow, thus, give characteristic of the cape town and the warehouse for keeping public taxes, which was levied from Moscovites, as well as the krom, where in other, family bins, corn, valuables, weapons of the suburban inhabitants were kept. Besides, in some of these bins charter with seal could get, which belonged to metropolitanate of Kiev and which had been brought from the south, and not sent from "one office to another".

The square of vetches (meetings) of Moscovites was in the centre of the suburbs. Not only the traditional presence at this place of the square (Cathedral one) allows to say so. Russian copy of the "Tale about Mamay's Bloody Battle" of the 17th century – a copy of the original of the 15th century (according to attribution of D.S.Likhachev) is kept in the British Museum (London). There are two pictures of the Cathedral of the Repose of the Kremlin dating back to the 14th century in sheets 14 and 15. In one of them Prince Demetrius and his cousin Vladimir pray to an image of the Savior before the fight on field. On the other the brothers pray St.Peter, metropolitanate, near his coffin. In both pictures behind the cathedral of the Repose (in the south) there is a big town bell under wooden shelter, and closer to the cathedral there is a stone round *vetche square*. In form it is the same as the digged out by V.D.Beletsky, an archaeologist, vetche square in Pskov. In ancient Izborsk (the town of Truvorov) archaeologist V.V.Sedov digged out round square which was used both during the pagan period (9th-10th centuries) and the Christian one (11th-13th centuries), probably, for vetche meetings. As for Moscow, the last vetche was called in 1382. All this allows to say that the vetche square was not only in Moscow Kremnik, but traditionally existed here from pagan time.

If the vetche platform was in the eastern end of the vetche square, the opposite western end was occupied by *house for public use or Gridnitsa*. In it elders of Moscovites solved questions of Moscovj's life, judged (big judgments were made by the vetche itself). Both demand in this kind of building with judicial function and analogy with the Canopy in vetche square of Pskov allow to say that Gridnitsa existed.

Later princely Gridnitsa appeared in Moscow in the place of vetche's one, in which the prince made the judgment, and he was the master. Octahedral building, shown in

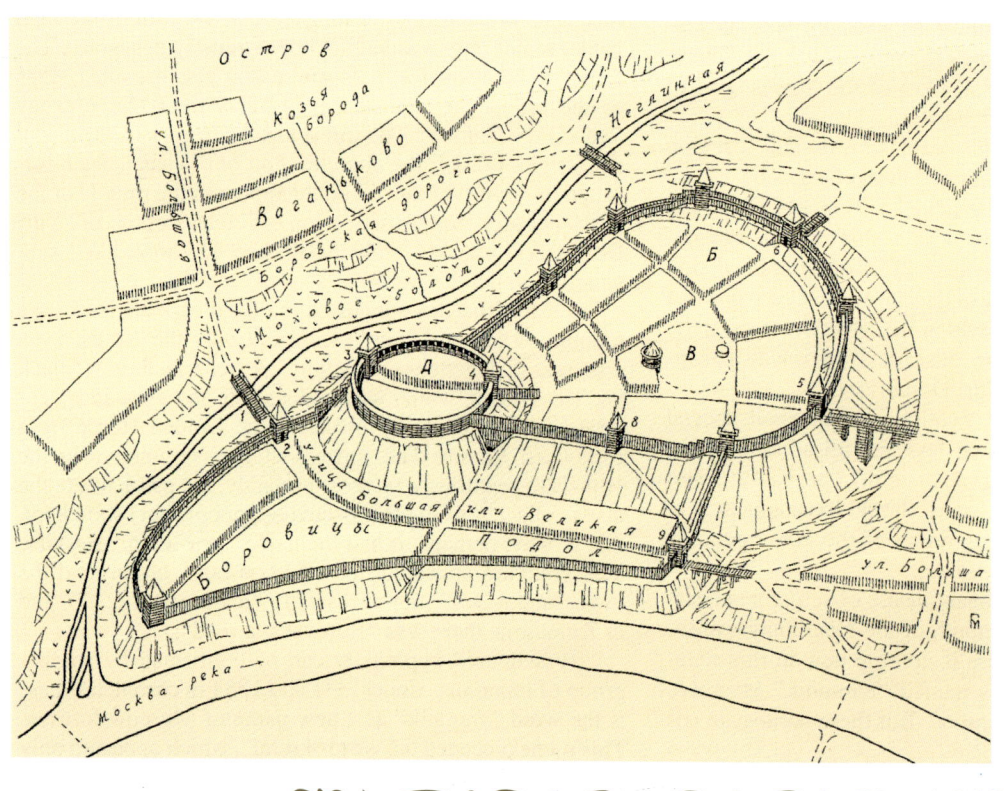

"The town of power"– Bor-town in 7th century:
А – Krom (Krem),
Б – Foothills,
В – vetce square with vetche platform and Gridnitsa (judgement house).
1 – Borovitskiy bridge across the Neglinnaya in Big or Great street of Podol,
2 – Borovitskie gates.
The following gates are conditionally mentioned :
3 – Borovskiye on the hill (now there is Arsenal Tower here, which was on-gate one)
4 – Kremskiye (Krasniye Kolymazhniye),
5 – Great-the upper,
6 – Old,
7 – Neglinenskie, for pedestrians,
8 – Moscow ones, for pedestrians,
9 – Big Podols ones (Taynitskiye Water Gates, turning to the river-Moscow).

Reconstruction of G. Mokeyev.

one chronicle miniatures, depicts the wedding of Symeon the Proud in the 2nd quarter of the 14th century. Later in the place of Gridnitsa the existing Granovitaya Palata (Faceted Palace) with throne was built.

Still nothing can be said about dwelling buildings in the suburbs, whichcrowded right round the vetche part. Even if there were yards, they were small and were used, most probably, as siege yards. Moscovites lived mainly in the villages surrounding Bor-town, where they could keep domestic animals and poultry, and have gardens.

The Bor-town in the 10th-12th centuries stood out among other Moscovj's settlements by its wonderful location. It was on the hill which was 25 metershigh above the river's level. Steep banks together with artificial fortifications made it the strongest fortress of the region. The Bor-town was placed in an original focus of river valleys, small rivers, ravines and, so, was well seen from everywhere and from it the ways to it were well seen, too.

The crossing near the town-fortress of water and land routes made it strategically important point. Public warehouse for taxes (bor) in the cape town, vetche square near it, two fortification lines, finally rich archaeological finds (silver jewellery), found on the territory – all this allows to suppose that Moscovljanes' "power existed" in the Bor-town, that it really was Moscovj's administrative centre.

Presumably, the main Moscow troops lived in it and in surrounding settlements. Entrances into the Bor-town were made, probably, through four gates whichcan be preliminary named: Neglinskie, Starye, Velikie and Moskvoretskie. Therewas also an entrance from the West, through Borovitskie gates (presumably), which were in the place of Armoury Tower of the Kremlin (in the 17th century it was still a gate). People went up through Borovitskie Gates from Borovitsky Bridge along the hill's slope outside the fortress.

Borovitsy was fortified settlement near the Bor-town in Podol. We can say about its existence due to "Borovitsky" bridge across the Neglinka and"Borovitskie" gates, which always were and are now not on the hill, but under it. These gates lead to the fortified Borovitsky settlement. In ancient time the Neglinnaya fell into the Moscow-river nearly at the Lenivka, and the territory in the river's mouth in Podol was significant. It was only during the building of the stone wall of the Kremlin in 1367 when from Borovitskaya Tower to Sviblovskaya Tower the direct moat was digged from the Neglinka to the Moscow-river, cutting out in this way Borovitsky settlement from the Kremlin's Podol. "Bolshaya" (big) or "Velikaya" (great) street Borovits extended at two directions: to the East – by "Bolshaya"

The Kremlin's Arsenal Tower on the place of the first gates of Bor-town. The Kremlin's Borovitskie Gates are near by on the place of the most ancient gates of the forttified Podol settlement of Borovitsy.

street of Porechie (Zarjadje), and to the north-west – also by "Bolshaya" street of Vaganjkovo (Znamenka).

Nestle of the centre's settlements

The Bor-town, Borovitsy were surrounded by other Moscovljanes' settlements.

It is reasonable to consider them in groups in the East, North, West from the "town of power". Not all of them are archaeologically researched and dated. It is difficult to find them, to detect; their names are unknown. It is interesting that nearly in all ancient "villages" there are churches of St.Nicholas Miracle-worker and they can be certain indications of such "villages".

Porechie occupied the territory of Zarjadje (Podol of Kitaj-gorod). It wasmentioned in the 15th century: "Pogore Porechie is all near *Nichola Wet*." The village was the biggest and was separated from the Bor-town by a morass: the churches of the Annunciation and the Saviour of Smolensk were first "on morass". The church of St.Nicholas Wet was famous as one of the most ancient churches of Moscow and was in "Bolshaya" street (Mokrinsky (wet) Lane). During archaeological digging it was detected by A.F.Dubinin that the lower culture layer of the settlement dates back to the end of the 11th century. Porechie stopped being village early and became town handicraft settlement. The change of social structure and quick growth were conditioned by location of the village near the Moscow-river (fish trade point was probably here) and nearness to the Bor-town.

Staroe (old) village extended along Nicholskaya street of the latest Kitay-gorod. Then in the centre of it the church of *St.Nicholas in Stary*, monastery of the Saviour in Stary (Zaikonospassky), as well as Nikolsky Krestets (Cross) in Stary appeared. This village is likely to be also "Kuchkovo", because right near it Kuchkovo field began. Presence of village in the 11th-12th centuries between the Bor-town and Kuchkovo field is quite possible.

Podkopaevo left memory about itself in the name of the church of *St.Nicholas in Podkopaevo,* first mentioned in the 15th century. There are different explanations of the toponim "Podkopaevo" and among them is "goroditschenskoe" (town). In documents of the 17th century a "moat" is mentioned, which divided the site of Ivanovsky Monastery from the Alabovo Hill. If there was at certain time "Kopay-gorod" in the monastery cape, then at its foot, near the river Rachka there could be small village "Podkopaevo". There was no archaeological research of Ivanovsky town and Podkopaevskoe village.

Gostina {guest) Hill and Pristanitsche (refuge) were on the Yauza's right bank: the first one was upper, and the second one was lower and closer to the river's mouth. The church of St.Nicholas in Vorobjino kept the memory about the settlement, which was earlier *"on the Gostinaya Hill"*. Refuge was needed for guests-merchants, sailing along the Moscow-river from the lower land, from the Oka, upper reaches of Yauza, Klyazma. It was at the foot of the hill where the church of *St.Nicholas in Kosheli* was. There was no research of remnants of the settlement.

Yauzskoe town in the place of the church of St.Nicolas the Martyr was mentioned in Gubnaya scripture in 1486. In one of "Tales about the Conception of Moscow" it was said that there was "small town", and the place was called "initial", "exactly moskovskoe" (the 17th century). M.G.Rabinovich who had made excavations here, wrote: "Presence of traces of pre-Mongolian culture layer means that there was in the Yauza's mouth some settlement before the Mongolian attack. This settlement was at least of the same date as Moscow of Yuri Dolgoruky".

Lytschikov town and village were mentioned in Gubnaya scripture of 1486 and chronicle news about Moscow fire in 1547. In the place of the town first,in the 15th century, Pokrovsky Lytschikov monastery appeared, and the churchof the Intercession (Pokrov), which later became a parish one, "which is known in Lytschikovo", is mentioned in the 17th century. There are no archaeological data.

Zolotorozhskoe settlement was found in the place of Andronikov monastery and is dated back to the 10th-11th centuries by archaeologists.

Samoteksky town with the church of the Holy Trinity is on high hill at the fall of the Napridnaya-river into the Samoteka (the Neglinnaya's middle flow was called so). The town of the 11th-12th centuries is under control ofarchaeologists now. There must be a settlement of the same time nearby.

Drachevsky town with the church of *St.Nicholas at Drachi* is known according to the latest document. In the church the chart of 1682 of the Patriarch Joachim was kept, with resolution to build stone church in the place of the wooden one "at Drachi, in the old town". Archaeological research did not giveany results, because the pit happened to by made in the church cemetery. Theremust be settlement along the Neglinnaya banks.

Vysokoe village left the memory about itself in the names of Petrovsky monastery "on Vysoky" (high) (Vysoko-Petrovsky) and Voskresensky one "on Vysoky" (it was in Tverskaya street). The monasteries appeared in the 14th-15th centuries at the outskirts of an ancient village which was between them on the western bank of the Neglinnaya. The village was connected with Kuchkovo field by ancient Kuznetsky bridge. There are archaeological data.

Vaganjkovo village was in the place of Rumjantsevskaya library (Pashkov House) and nearby quarters. The village left memory about itself in the namesof three churches: of the Holy Trinity, the Annunciation (was destroyed) and St.Nicholas – all in "Old Vaganjkovo". "Vaga" means "balance and the village's-name is often connected with the customs, which was here near the prince yard. But according to another version "vaganitj" means "to play", and "vaganjkovo"means "place for games". By the way, "Vaganjkovo field", i.e. "field for games", also existed near Moskvoretsky Studenets (near very ancient villages on Three Hills). And the balance was made in old time like swing, an indispensable attraction of all holidays and games.

Turygino village left memory about itself in the name of the church of *St.Nicholas in Turygino*. Here during earth excavation for the foundation of the cathedral of Christ the Saviour in the middle of the last century Arab coins of the 9th century were found. Even if the coins got here in the 10th-11th centuries, this place is one of the most ancient anyway: according to the "view" hypothesis "borovitskie" names of the Kremlin's objects should have appeared in Turygino. Some historians supposed that here, on the cape at the fall of the Chertoryja-river into the Moscow-river

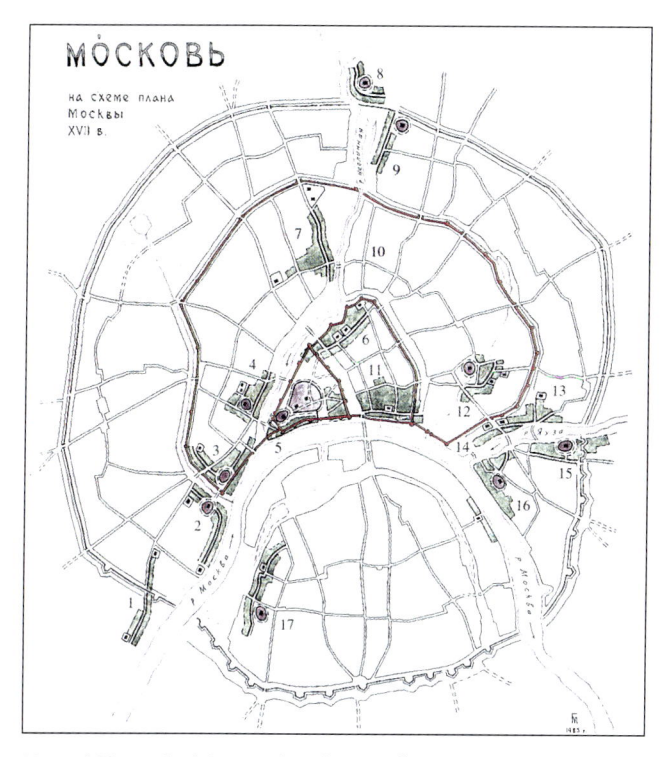

Moskovj. The nestle of the centre's settlements. Gen. plan-scheme of G. Mokeev
1 – Semchinskoe, 2 – Kievets, 3 – Turyguino, 4 – Vaganjkovo, 5 – Bor-gorod and Borovitsy, 6 – Staroe (Old), 7 – Bysokoe, 8 – Troitskoe town, 9 – Drachi, 10 – Kuchkovo field, 11 – Porechie, 12 – Podkopaevo, 13 – Gostina Hill, 14 – Pristanische (Shelter), 15 – Lytschykovo, 16 – Gonchary, 17 – Babiy town in Zamoskvorechie.

there was *Chertoljsky town* in the century, which was liquidated by the construction of the Palace of Soviets.

Kievets village left memory about itself in the church of *St.Nicholas in Kievets,* which was on the bank of the Moscow-river, as well as in the church of Ressurection the New "which was in Kievtsy". The village extended between the churches' yards. But in the middle of this space there was, probably, the town Kievets (Obydensky town of the 11th-12th centuries is under archaeological control according to preliminary list). The village was, probably, famous for its products (lances), but, perhaps, special troops of lance-carriers lived here. There is also suggestion that people who had come from Kiev lived here.

Semchinskoe village was on the territory between the churches of *St.Nicholas* in Khamovniki and the Assumption, "which was Semchinskoe village". The village was mentioned in the earliest Moscow acts, beginning from 1328, and for the last time even at the beginning of the 18th century. There are no archaeological data.

Babiy town in Zamoskvorechie left memory about itself in the name of the church of St.Maron the Miracle-worker, "which was in Baby Gorodok". The village near the town extended up to the church of *St.Nicholas* in Goletvino. Information about the town and village is most doubtful. There was no archaeological excavation.

The nestle of settlements of different kinds, described here, which existed up to the 13th century, is thus found on the territory of ancient Moscow. The nestle existed from towns-fortresses, which crowned the hills, and villages- settlements lying at the foot of the hills. This picture differs so sharply from the one which historians drew not so long ago, indicating that our capital appeared in the middle of the 7th century among forests and morasses in nearly uninhabited place.

Certainly, it is necessary to stress again, that today not all the nestleof Moskovljanes settlements of the 9th-12th centuries was researched by archaeologists and, so, not all the above-mentioned traces may turn out to be the traces of the most ancient and besides Slavic settlements. But if, at the worst, half (!) of the said ten towns and fifteen villages existed till the 13th century (which is absolutely certain in this case the nestle will also be crowded and original enough.

Moscow nestle of towns and villages represented typical form of Slavic settlements in Eastern Europe. For example, the archaeologist P.N.Tretjakov wrote the following about drevljanes (ancient people): "Drevljanskie towns are situated as though they were nestles: towns are built on neighbouring capes... These are towns near the village Gorodki on the bank of the Teterev, nestle of towns at the river Sluchi... But the largest nestle is Iskorostenj: 5-6 towns of the 8th-10th centuries. Besides the numerous towns in the region of drevljanskie lands many unfortified settlements of that time are known. "Nestle-like settlements" of drevljanes towns go back to the primitive-communal time, reflecting family-tribal rules.

Using only one example-analogue from the history of Slavic tribal settlements, we should remember the shrewdness of the remarkable historian I.E.Zabelin, who wrote: "Our ancient towns, like Moscow itself, in the way of their lives were similar most of all to villages and as for their construction they presented simple combination of separate villages, settlements, which were close to each other on one town territory."

Cherished holy places

Vyatichis-Moskovljane venerated pagan idols, celebrated their pagan holidays. *Idols of gods* (cteni) were, probably, both in the *Bor-town* (kapitsche) and around it among settlements of the nestle. There are data about them andthey can be indicated only supposedly. For instance, the *idol of domestic animals* (Volos) could be in the place of the *church of St.Blaise* behind the river Chertory: from here they took herds to the fields Devichje and Luzhniki. The *idol Perun* was, perhaps, on the hill of Obydenskoe town of the 11th-12th centuries in the place of the church of St.Elijah Gromovnik (Thunder-worker) Obydenny. Idol Tur was, perhaps in Chertolje town of the 10th century, on the bank of the river-Moscow near the village Turygino. In the Eastern and Western parts of the Bor-town idols, perhaps, in the places of the church of St.Elijah the Prophet in the field of Gostinaya Hill, *in Bolvanje* behind the Yauza, near the church of St.Nicetas ("who drives devils away") in Nikitskaya street, on Taganskaya Hill, in the place of the church of St.Nicholas "near the Pillar"(Stolp) or "on the Pillars", on Troitskaya Hill above Samoteka in the town of the 11th century. But all this is a supposition based only on "close to pagan" toponimi.

In the centre of Moscow there were several hills where pagan cemeterieswere, and in early soring inhabitants celebrated the sunny holiday *Krasnaya Gorka* or *Radunitsa* (time of weddings and parents commemoration).

The main hill, probably, was the closest to the Bor-town in Zaneglimenje,on which later the church of St.George, "which is famous on Krasnaya Gorka", appeared. The holiday was, perhaps, celebrated also on Ivanovskaya hill, Taganskaya hill, on one of the Three Hills in Presnya...

Ritualjnoe (ritual) field is mentioned in chronicles already as Kuchkovo field. The first news about it is in 1176 in Ipatjevskaya chronicle in connection with the above-said movement of the princes from Chernigov to Vladimir Zalessky and their meeting by vladimirskie envoys:

"Going... to Kuchkovo, say Moscow, and meeting there the Vladimirtsy".

M.N.Tikhomirov, summarizing the scientists' opinion about the news of 1176, wrote that "rekshe to Moscow" (say Moscow) can be translated by today's "id est" and read: "Kuchkovo, id est Moscow" or "Moscow, id est Kuchkovo". Thus, V.P.Neroznak made the following logical resolution: "Moscow's second name, according to historical evidences, was Kuchkovo. The village before the foundation of the town was named so (compare in the chronicle: Moscow, say Kuchkovo)." Not seldom the name "Kuchkovo" was transferred from the unknown village to the town and the Neglinnaya's mouth, seeing here the castle of boyard Kuchka (M.N.Tikhomirov, B.A.Rybakov and others). What does this news about Kuchkovo have to do with the nestle of settlements under the name "Moscovj"?

Regarding the way from Moscow region, for instance, "to Chertanovo, i.e. toMoscow" or from the other side "to Medvedkovo, i.e. to Moscow" nobody will say that Moscow is Chertanovo or Medvedkovo... that Moscow has the second, the third name. We just speak about part and the whole. Here is double address: first smaller one, not much known, then the bigger one, generally known. The same is in the news of 1176. But Kuchkovo of the 12th century is not necessarily village, small town or mansion. In the news of the 14th-15th centuries "Kuchkovo field" is mentioned three times. The most precious is the mention under 1379 connected with the liquidation by the Grand Prince Demetrius (later Donskoy) of tysjatsys (commander of a thousand of warriors) in Moscow. In August that year the son of the last tysjatsky Ivan Vasiljevich, who had come against the Prince, "went with sword to Kuchkovo field near Moscow... And there were plenty of people there, and many cried for him, for his nobility and grandeur". According to the news of 1394 and 1488 Kuchkovo extended from the church of the Holy Trinity "which is near Polj" (field) to Sretensky monastery, occupying the most beautiful Eastern slope of the Neglinnaya bank. Town buildings surrounded the field in the 15th century yet, leaving it free.

From the above news, from the ancient meaning of the word "pole" (field) V.A.Prostov made an interesting and truthful resolution: Kuchkovo field was Ritual field, place of celebrations, fist fights, judgement fights, prosecutions of criminals and, it is possible to add, the place of gatherings and seeing-off of Moscow army during wars, the place of joyful and sorrowful meetings afterwards. Exactly because it was used for so many purposes it could remain for such a long time (till the end of the 15th century) among town buildings during Christian time. It was public one, did not belong to anybody (belonged to the whole town), and it was so from ancient time, from the 10th-11th centuries. In conformity with the above different functions, it was, perhaps, divided into several squares. Probably, because of this the church of the Holy Trinity in the outskirts of the village Staroe, had the address "near the Stary Polj", and in Zaneglimje, before Kuznetsky bridge across Neglinka, the church of St.Hieromartyr Anastasia, Deliverer from Bonds, appeared, "which was near Pole" or "which is near Polj".

In the middle of the 12th century on the Ritual field in the presenceof people, probably Kuchka was executed. He seemed to be the "boyard", who owned beautiful villages here, as late legends say (the 17th century), or even the tysjatsky of Suzdal as V.N.Tatitschev wrote. But the above titles, big private ownership are the notions from vocabulary of feudal time. Among Vyatiches in Moscoviya Kuchka was, most probably, the main volost (rural) elder and judge (judge's function is nearly princely). Kuchka was executed not by Yuri Dolgoruky, who adopted his children, but by Moscovljanes themselves, perhaps by those who were against the prince-conqueror. Moscovljanes executed Kuchka, most probably, for treachery in favour of Dolgoruky. In any case, the fact of Kuchka's death was undoubtedly connected with joining of Moscow to Suzdal Principality and was used for it by the prince of Suzdal. Besides, Kuchka was evidently a Christian already: it was not by chance that Ritual field "carried" his name in Christian Moscow during three hundred years and half – till the end of the 15th century, when it was liquidated by John III during construction of Moscow – the capital.

The place Kulishky is surprising in its beauty and mystery – a big slope tothe Moscow-river of the high Alabovo Hill (inside the borders of the latest Bely town). Here in ancient time nine churches appeared "in Kulishki": those of All Saints, St.Hieromartyr Parasceva of Iconium, Sts.Cyrus and John, Nativity of the Mother of God, St.Nicholas in Podkopaevo, St.Apostles Peter and Paul, St.Andrew of Crete, St.John the Predecessor, of the Three Saints (St.Basil the Great, St.Gregory the Theologian, St.John Chrysostome). According to one of explanations, "kulishki" means "ognitscha" – lands of burned forest for fields or gardens... The forest was certainly burned by the first settlers-Moscovljanes, and Kulishki was likely to appear in Moscovj already in the 9th-10th centuries.

Yuri "Long Hands"

In the middle of the 12th century due to the efforts of the prince of Suzdal Moscovj joined Rostov-Suzdal domain. Yuri Dolgoruky is still considered to be the founder of Moscow. So it is reasonable to mention here the prince's rolein Moscow town-construction.

According to Tverskaya chronicle, the prince appeared here in 1156 and founded the town. The chronicle was published in 1863 according to the only copy of that time, which is kept now in the library named after M.E.Saltykov-Tschedrin in St.Petersburg. The scripture is the following: "The Grand Prince Yuri Volodimerech founded the town Moskjva on ustnizhe of the Neglinnaya upper from the river Yauza."

The indication "ustnizhe" was the talk of the town of all Moscow scientists, because there is no such word in Russian. Really, the confusion has been settled quite recently, when another copy of Tverskaya chronicle was found, which is kept now in the State Historical Museum of Moscow. In the word "ustnizhe" instead of "n" there is the letter "i", and the address if "on ustii zhe of the Neglinnaya". This address, written without mistakes, allows to make the unequivocal conclusion: Yuri Dolgoruky is not the founder of Moscow, because in the news there is the exact indication of repeated action – the town was founded at the same place where it had been before: "on ustii zhe of the Neglinnaya" (at the mouth).

Historians noticed long ago that the date "1156" is also doubtful. In summer that year Yuri Dolgoruky was in Volynj and could not build fortress at the River Moscow. He became the Grand Prince of Kiev in 1154, and at the same time his family left Suzdal for Kiev through Smolensk. In both cases of evidently artificial damage-correction of the text (in the address and date) it is possible to notice the following tendency of chroniclers.

V.N.Tatitschev pointed out, being guided by some chronicles which are notknown now, that Moscow fortress (Moscow) was built in 1146, when Yuri was usual rural prince of Suzdal. The transfer of the date in ten years forward already in protograph of both Tverskie copies of chronicles (Vladimirsky polichrone?) was needed in order that "Moscow was founded" not by usual prince,role but a Grand Prince (just like, for example, Constantinople was as though founded by the emperor Constantine). The chronicler "did not write, only one letter of many years (M – 40, N – 50) to get the desired. Probably, for the same purpose the chronicler of the printed copy of Tverskaya chronicle was damaged the first "i" of the address "on ustii zhe of the Neglinnaya", which disproved by its repetition the act of foundation of the town by the "grand" prince.

Thus, Yuri Dolgoruky really rebuilt the Bor-town at the mouth of the Neglinnaya, but he did it in summer-autumn of 1146, as V.N.Tatitschev wrote about it correctly. In winter the prince went with war to Novgorod land, conquering "the whole Msta" and robbing Torzhok, and in spring 1147 invited "to Moscovj" Novgorod-Seversky prince Svjatoslav Olgovich, who had robbed Smolensk land along the river Protva.

However, a more important event is seen in the chronicles: in 1146 the prince of Suzdal conquered Vyatiches' Northern volost Moscovj, thus separating it from all the other Vyatiches' tribal settlements.

In the rebuilt Bor-town Yuri Dolgoruky accommodated his princely yard, perhaps, instead of the yard of Kuchka executed by Moskovljanes (the prince "adopted" his three children). The settlement turned out not to be in Krom, but in front of it in the outskirts, where later the palace of Moscow princes, then tsars was found. The prince of Suzdal did not conquer, did not rob the town of warehouses of Moscovljanes. And kept it in the newly built fortress not in vain: so, finally, Moscovljanes themselves were to guard the fortress at the Neglinnaya. In general, Yury created what was later named "Kremnik", i.e. the town, in the part of which krom (krem) still functioned.

Christening, the first churches

Mass christening in Russia, as it is known, took place in 988-992 in Pridneprovje, in Volynj, in Zalessk land, Novgorod. After that the process of spreading of Christianity is considered to be gradual. However, there is number of facts, testifying that in Moscovj in the middle of the 12th century Christening of the inhabitants was carried out simultaneously and in mass order, as it had been in Kiev and Novgorod at certain time...

In the 11th-12th centuries Christianity did not enter smoothly East Slavic far lands – and Vyatich Moscovj was just such a far land. Vyatichies did not accept the new world relipion very fast. Their long resistance to its spreading was

The first mention about Moscow in chronicle. The meeting of Suzdal's prince Yuriy Vladimirovich Dolgorukiy with prince Svyatoslav Olgovich on 4th of April, 1147. Chronicle miniature. 16th century.

conditioned by long autonomous existence of the powerful Vyatich tribal union, paying Kiev off by tributes. The chronicler Nestor already at the beginning of 12th century wrote that Vyatichies had been observing their pagan rituals from old time, and "still practice" burial rituals with turning dead. At the beginning of the 12th century Vyatichies killed the missioner Kuksha – a monk of Kiev-Pechersky monastery – for his preaching the Lord's Word. In Moscovj with its pagan barrows, in the middle of the 12th century there was the same situation as in Kiev, Novgorod at the end of the 10th century: presence of pagans as the prevailing majority of inhabitants. So, there was the possibility and "need" in mass, which enforced their Christening.

On the other hand, it is common knowledge, that all the sons, grandsons, great-grandsons of the prince-Christian Vladimir Svjatoslavich considered it to be their duty to spread Christianity. And the first prince in Moscovj turned out to be Yuri Dolgoruky. And here is the new, more contrasting situation: Christian (!) army of the prince during the whole summer and autumn of 1146 were building with help of local pagan (i) people new fortress at the Neglinnaya instead of the old one. More than that, the prince's builders, certainly, in the same 1146 made the first wooden Christian church near the princely yard – the one of the Transfiguration in Bor (by the holiday of 6, August). A bit later, perhaps in 1147, by already Christened Moscovljanes the second wooden church of St.John the Predecessor in Bor was built in Krom (by the holiday on 24, June, to substitute the pagan holiday of Ivan Kupala), and "near Bor" the other two churches of the same name on Ivanovskaya Hill and in Zamoskvorechie.

Finally, from the middle of the 12th century the ritual of barrow burials started to disappear quickly among Moskovljanes, and the last barrows on the territory of ancient Moscow (Yauzskie ones and those in the outskirts) date back to the beginning of the 13th century. Two generations were needed for paganism to disappear, substituted by Christianity.

As christening of Moskovljanes in the above situation could happen only according to Kiev ritual which everybody knows as the initial one, in Moscow places toponims similar to Kiev ones should be left, which reflected the same event. And they are really found not only in "wordy" comparison, but also in topographical one.

Yuri Dolgoruky already in young years was in Kiev several times, especially when his father Vladimir Monomakh was the Grand Prince of Kiev. Surely Yuri learned about and knew well the place of mass christening in 988 by his great-grandfather Vladimir. In Moscovj Yuri could be puzzled by the similarity of the topographical situation, the initial toponymy. And this similarity could also stimulate the prince for the mass Christening of Moscovljanes following the example of the great-grandfather. Opinions about appearance of all "Kiev's" toponims in Moscovj before or after the mass Christening are not very similar. The third opinion is better – the golden mean: part of toponims are previous, part of them are additional, consequent. To date the toponims exactly is, certainly, hopeless affair.

SIMILAR TOPONIMS OF THE PLACES OF MASS CHRISTENING

Kiev Inhabitants in 988	Moscow Inhabitants in 1147
1 – Kiev settlement	1 – Kievets village
2 – Kiev town	2 – Kievets (?) town
3 – Chertory – channel in front of Kiev behind the Dnepr	3 – Chertory – a brook near Kievets
4 – Idol of Tur – supposed place of idol veneration (kapitsche)	4 – Idol of Tur – supposed place of idol veneration (kapitsche)
5 – Tur bozhnitsa, substituted the near and place of Tur kapitsche	5 – the village Turygino upper the Tur kapitsche
6 – Trade place near Tur bozhnitsa place of people gathering for mass Christeningchristening	6 – Lazy Trade Place – place of people gathering for mass Christeningchristening
7 – Borichev Tik – the road from Kiev to the place of christening	7 – Borovskaya road – the road of to the place of christening Moscow people
8 – Borichev town	8 – Bor-town
9 – Borichev settlement	9 – Borovitsy settlement
10 – Podol	10 – Podol
11 – the church of St.Elijah	11 – the church of St.Elijah
12 – the mouth of small river (Pochaina), falling into the big into the big one (Dnepr)	12 – the mouth of small river (Neglinnaya), falling one (Moscow)
13 – "Jordanj" on the Dnepr under Tur bozhnitsa	13 – "Jordanj" on the Moscow-river under the village Turygino

In the above comparison it is possible to see quite clearly the beginningof future Moscow equalling to Kiev, its endeavour to rise up to the all-Russian scale. And it so happens that this tendency was initiated by Yuri Dolgoruky, with his famous strong, fanatical striving to Kiev.

There is some data for the supposition about the exact date of Moscow people christening. Here earlier attention was paid to the fact that nearly inall *ancient villages* of Moscovj there were *churches of St.Nicholas.* They were noted in Porechie, Staroe, Podkopaevo, on Gostinaya Hill, Pristanitsche, in Drachi, Vaganjkovo, Turygino, Kievets, Semchinskoe, Golutvino, there also was such a church in Lenivy Torzhok (Lazy Trade Olace). *All the churches appeared as though at once,* simultaneously, on some holiday of St.Nicholas, archbishop of Myra in Lycia: on 9 May, or 6 December (old style).

Yuri Dolgoruky gave great party for Svjatoslav Olgovich on 4, April, 1147, after which the princes parted. Having had rest after the hard winter war in Torzhok, Yuri, probably, though up good deed, not only induced by the described situation, but by the Seversky prince who had been his guest: Svjatoslav had a rare for princes name "Nicholas" and, so the 9th of May, was name-day. Besides on the day of St.Nicholas Veshny (of spring) people usually start swimming in rivers, lakes. Yuri, supposedly, remembered about all this and his stay near the Moscow-river, building of the fortress in the centre of Moscovj ended in mass, enforced christening of Moscovljanes. Like in summer of 988, the army drove people into the river, and the prince's priests christened them at once. We only can add the chronicler's words here, said about the Kiev event: "If some not with love, but through fear of the ruling one christened: for his belief was combined with power".

Thus, on the day of Christening, on the 9th of May, 1147, in all the oldest Moscow villages the churches of St.Nicholas could appear simultaneously: first, perhaps, chapels, churches-obydenka (built in one day). Later they did not disappear, but on the contrary there became more of them with growth of town settlements. There is also an argument confirming this supposition...

From the beginning of the 14th century the "Eulogy about the move of relics of St.Nicholas from Myra in Lycia to Bor-town" of the presbyter Andrew, who was clergyman of the Cathedral of the Dormition. In this "Eulogy" St.Nicholas is said about as the undefeated armour and establishment of our town.

Symbolically the "town" can be the "church" in general, besides that in Kremnik of the beginning of the 14th century there was no church in the name of St.Nicholas. However, E.V.Barsov, who published the "Eulogy", supposed that as "our town" Andrew could call early Moscow. In this case the presbyter showed the ancient wordy tradition of Moscow people about appearance of divine protector first for the christened nestle of Moscovj's settlements.

By the way, here can be the secret that St.Nicholas the Miracle-worker became, finally, the divine protector not only of ancient Russian towns and villages, but Moscow people, then Moscovites (according to the foreign term). It was was not by chance in the 16th-17th centuries that foreigners and expatriates too on the territory of Russia called the Miracle-worker "St.Nicholas – Russian God", and for Russian trade people St.Nicholas was the first Christian locally venerated saint.

МОСКОВЬ
Крещение московлян в 1147 году

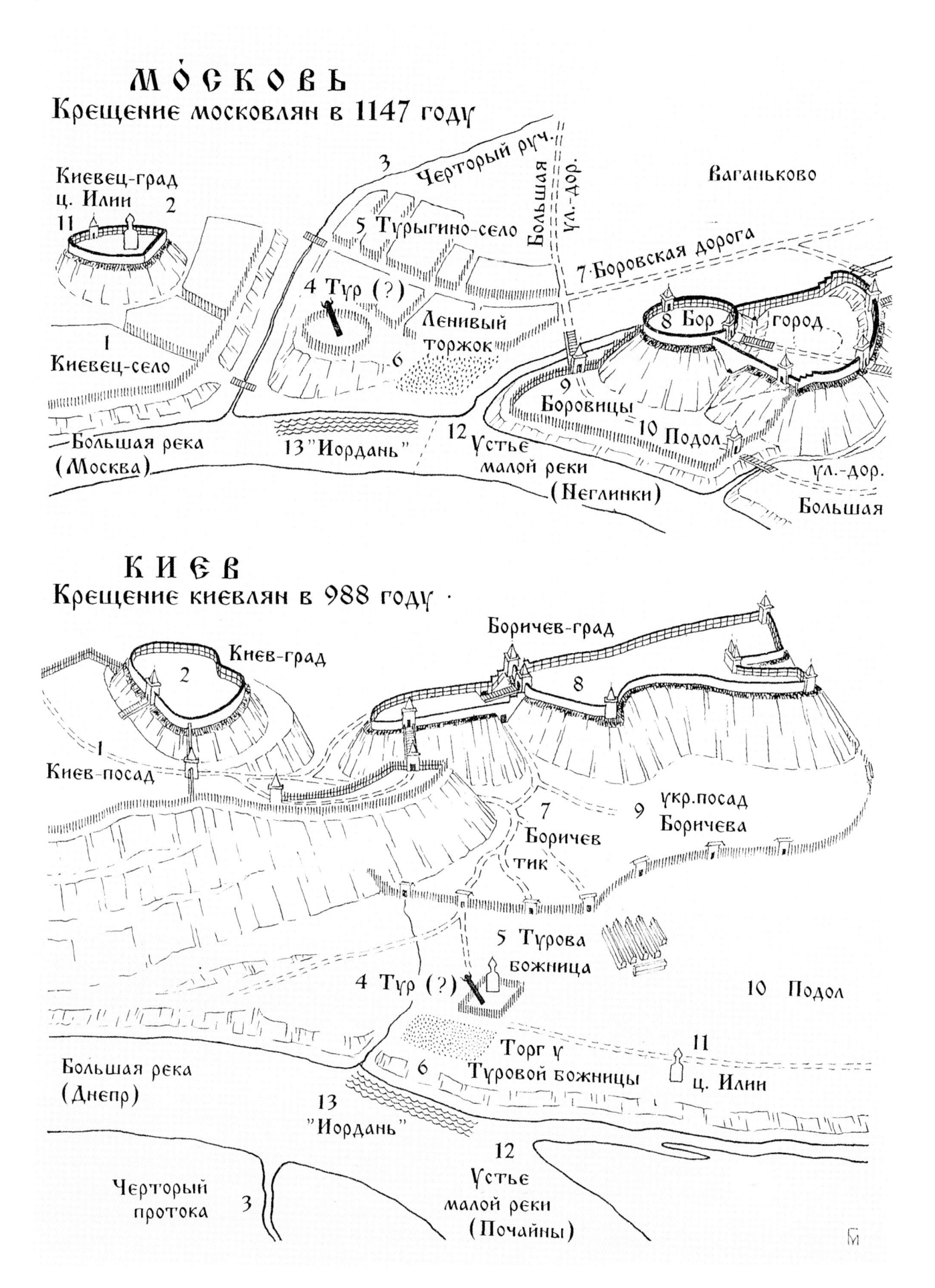

- Киевец-град ц. Илии 2
- 11
- 1 Киевец-село
- 3 Черторый руч.
- 5 Турыгино-село
- Большая ул.-дор.
- Ваганьково
- 7 Боровская дорога
- 4 Тур (?)
- Ленивый торжок
- 6
- 8 Бор — город
- 9 Боровицы
- 10 Подол
- Большая река (Москва)
- 13 "Иордань"
- 12 Устье малой реки (Неглинки)
- ул.-дор.
- Большая

КИЕВ
Крещение киевлян в 988 году

- 2 Кнев-град
- Боричев-град
- 8
- 1 Киев-посад
- 7 Боричев тик
- 9 укр.посад Боричева
- 5 Турова божница
- 4 Тур (?)
- 10 Подол
- Торг у Туровой божницы
- 11 ц. Илии
- Большая река (Днепр)
- 6
- 13 "Иордань"
- 12 Устье малой реки (Почайны)
- 3 Черторый проток

Moskovj and Kiev. Similar toponimy of the places of mass christening. The scheme of G. Mokeev.

All that can be added is that in 1881 in the place of Moscow people christening round stone font was made – "Jordanj" – for the Cathedral of Christ the Saviour!

About Church

The first wooden churches, certainly, gave new "Christian" look to Moscow nestle of settlements. Later the churches became of stone, and Christian Moscow look became more and more complex. Knowing the denomination, symbols of church and its parts, people who believe in God, admired the town's image more deeply and in Christian manner, "reading" it as an original icon, iconostasis.

In order to be the part of such deep understanding of Moscow it is first necessary to have at least general knowledge about our Christian orthodox church.

The word "khram" (church) comes from the Russian word "khorom" used about church building. The church represents God's home, and being sanctified by the Highest Bliss after the service of sanctifying, it is the *Dwelling of the High Entity*. People believing in God, bring their sacrifices to Him here, eulogy and confession. The above-said refers to any church, being town or monastery cathedrals, and independent parish church or interior lateral church.

In order to distinguish them from each other they are consecrated to the names of God's saints or Christian holidays, for example, the Entry of the Lord into Jerusalem, the Descent of the Holy Spirit, etc. These consecrations are an old tradition, which first appeared during the prayers at graves-relics of the first Christians, then got established in connection with the annual cycle of Christian commemorations and celebrations.

Russian orthodox church in its idea was brilliantly explained by Nicholay Troitsky*. So it is reasonable to quote here, though briefly, his explanation.

"The initial word for definition of the main idea of church is its name – "*tserkovj*". Though the notion of church in Christian art had many symbols (ship, sheep yard, refuge, mother, bride), but none of them reveals all the deep idea of church, like architecture of orthodox church and all the iconography decorating it.

Church like Christ's Kingdom, in its denomination, and so, in its historical

development had to include all peoples of the world and envelope all the ends of the universe[1].

If the notions temple and church internally common, which is indicated by calling temple as church, or are united in one idea and are related with each other, like form and its idea, temple's architecture, in its best, fully developed type, as the most perfect work of art, has to correspond to its idea – church of universe, even represent *image of world*. In ancient and the best architectural types of orthodox temple it is so observed. The *building* of temple-church itself is image of Universe, certainly such as it was imagined by ancient Cosmography. So, it is necessary to consider temple to clarify its exterior and interior idea exactly from this point of view at its organization and decoration.

Temple is a majestic and deeply ideological image of Jesus Christ's church, spread all over the world, existing in it from the beginning and seen in perspective of all its centuries.

Making closer the Church of believers, this vivid God's temple with the temple's building itself, St. John Chrysostome teaches that each believer and all together are the temple[2], and all the peoples are the four walls from which Christ made one temple.[3]

In the 12th century Peter Karnatsky wrote: "At the temple's foundation stone is layed with picture of temple and twelve other stones which means that the Church rests on Christ and twelve Apostles. The walls mean peoples; there are *four* of them, because they accept those who are coming from the four parts."[4]

It is rather notable that the temple which from the point of view of St. John Chrysostome and Peter Karnatsky symbolizes Christ's universal church, has four walls, corresponding to the four parts of the world, which means with equal dimensions, in other words temple is *cubic*; and to this corresponds also the ancient architectural type of churches both Byzantine and Byzantine-Russian (those of Kiev, Novgorod, Vladimir, Moscow, etc.).

If, according to the view-point of ancient liturgists, the cubic or quadrangular temple is the world's image; then, certainly, each its wall-part has to correspond to one of the four ends of the world and, according to the corresponding symbolics, has to comply to one or another sphere of church life. And it is really so.

East side of the temple, according to the Bible, to ancient Cosmography and church's opinion, is the area of light, "country of the alive ones" and paradise bliss. Church's idea about the East side was the basis for making the *altar* from ancient time always in direction to the East, in front of which they prayed and carried out the divine service, as Polidor Virgily tells. Christians did so in order to remember what is for them.

This church's opinion so early established has remained till now. And in accordance with this idea church's altar will conform to the paradise area. The same is in liturgy and church memorials.

The name altar means high credence or credence on the *height (alta ara)*. And thus its meaning makes us think about very ancient times.

Noah installed his first credence on top of a hill, where his ark stopped. Abraham makes his sacrifice his son Isaac on the Moria – (one of the Zion tops). The marquee was installed by Jesus Navin on the Garizin, by St. Davis on the Zion. The Cathedral of Solomon, Zorovavel, Herod – on the same hill. Here the faithful venerated: they and those who avoided the true belief made sacrifices with pagans again on tops. So firm was this longing to the top.

Finally, the first Christian Eucharistia is committed in Zion chamber. And even His sacrifice the Saviour made Himself on the Golgotha *Hill*... All such historical testimonies fully explain why Christian credence – communion table is put on top.

The idea of height or ascension is expressed so that either the whole temple is built on high land, or the altar is higher in few steps above the floor, and part of the higher place, which mostly stands forward in the centre of the temple, is called *ambo* (from the Greek ano – veno) – ascend to the top.

But how can an altar, being on the hill together with the temple or on high place in the temple, symbolize at the same time paradise?

---

* N. Troitsky. Christian orthodox temple in its idea. // Eparchial Records of Tula. 1916. No. 3-8.

Christening in the the upper lands of the Dnepr. Painting of V. Vasnetsov in the cathedral of St. Vladimir in Kiev.

It is known that ancient people connected the notion of paradise with the idea about the mountain of the blessed ones: gods lived on tops of mountains, which people could not reach, to them souls of the righteous were striving and ascended.

But does the altar conform to paradise, if the Sacrifice is made in it on the communion table, and the sacrifice was made outside the paradise? It is necessary to take into consideration that, having placed the first people in the paradise, "out of the ground made the Lord God to grow every tree that is pleasant to the sight, and good for food; the tree of life also in the *midst of the garden*"[5]. This "Tree of Life" in Christ's Church if Christ Himself, more precisely – His Holy Flesh and Blood, given in the sacrament of Eucharistia and being the *source of immortal life* to those who receive the Eucharist, according to the Church's word. And rather often the symbol of this "Tree of Life" is placed on the Holy Gates, which is the vine with which Christ compared Himself right after His Euchsristia in the Zion Chamber[6].

This connection between altar-credence and the mountain Zion, as the place of the first Eucharistia, are also symbolical "Zions" or "arks", where the Holy Sacrament – God's Flesh and Blood – is placed. They have the look of a small temple with pictures of Apostles on its sides, are the image of the Zion Chamber, where the Saviour made the Eucharistic Sacrament for the first time. Thus, their name "Zions".

By the same Zions remind of the Old Testament ark of the Marquee and Temple, which were also on the Zion. They are called "*arks*" quite meaningfully. Like in the Old Testament golden shrine manna was kept, this "bread of life", which had ascended from heaven, in "the New Testament" *shrine (ark)* God's Flesh and Blood are kept, this "true bread of life, which ascended from heaven", and of which manna was only the prototype[7].

The image of Zion Chamber is also represented by Kivory sletering the communion table with the Holy Sacrament on it, and surrounded by bishops and presbyters, like at certain time Christ was in Zion Chamber with Apostles.

The idea that altar is and image of heavenly bliss is expressed in the name of the Holy Gates and partially in their iconography. Holy Gates were called *Paradisiacal Gates* in ancient time.

The idea of altar-paradise is illustrated by different images referring to paradise. So, sometimes on altar Northern door the temptation and fall of the foreparents is shown; sometimes "the prudent brigand Rah" with cross in hand; sometimes the First Martyr Stephan the archbishop, for at the moment of his death he saw "the heavens opened, and the Son of man standing on the right hand of God"[8], sometimes Archangel Michael, leader of heavenly powers and divine gate guard of the paradise, etc.

Finally, idea of altar-paradise is approved liturgically. Thus, when "during the evening admittance the tsar's gates are opened, it means that paradise was shuttered by Adam's crime, and nowadays not only paradise will be opened through Christ's arrival but heavens, too"[9].

The tsar's gates are opened on the day of Easter. Idea of symbolic act is presented by a song of the Easter canon devoted to Christ: *Christ has arisen from grave... and opened paradise doors for us.*

***

If East is the area of light, "country of alive", place of paradisiacal bliss; the West is, on the contrary, as the country of the setting, as though dying, sun, is the area of darkness, grief, death, the area of eternal dwelling of the dead expecting the Resurrection and Judgment. That was its idea of ancient people and then of the Christian Church.

In Egypt there was the tradition to place coffins to the West from the town on hill's slope. The same we can see in Minor Asia (Lycia). According to the common Greek belief, the underground *world of Hades (hell)* was in the West.

It is notable that in Jerusalem, to the West from the Holy Zion and the Temple, that narrow vally of "the Sons of Ennom" begins or the famous *Gehenna*, which was the image of perdition place, for Jews – sheol.

The valley of "Ennom's Sons" could be the best visual image of hades according to its location and its religious denomination.

Narrow, deep and gloomy the gehenna began at the North-West from Zion, surrounded all the Western part of the Sacred Town; altogether it was the place of burial or according to Jeremiah, the place of lany coffins: there were many burial caves on its both sides. It was the place of darkness, grief – the kingdom of death... So, on its part, it served the definition of the West as the country of sufferings, death and – Hades. Another circumstance confirmed it – here at certain time at evasion of Jews into paganism there was the sacrificial tomb of Moloh-Baal, on which fire was kept constantly, because here during the gloomy hours of late night human sacrifices were brought with horrible tortures, groans, tears and wild howls. Being thrown into scorching depths of this idol, these victims were as though eaten alive by Satan himself, the personification of which was the disgusting idol of Moloh placed in this hellish valley[11].

That is why Christ the Saviour took this valley of Ennom's sons as a grand homage of valley of darkness, grief, crying and hellish tortures. And after Christ had passed over on the Golgotha Hill, in the West, near the top of this gehenna, where He had gone into hell and freed the souls which had been kept there, the country of the West and its valley of death – gehenna – became for the Christian Church too the country of death and the area of hades.

Thus the opinion of the Fathers of the Church about the Western part as the place of darkness, death and hellish torture, is clear. In accordance with this opinion about the Western country, the same opinion about the hades as the area of the dead, was transferred to the Western part of temple; and it was considered to be more decent to bury the dead at this part.

The Liturgics also adopted the same opinion about the Western temple's side. St.Symeon of Thessalonica says: "Hierarch, who is going to do the religious rite, descends from the communion table to the centre of the temple, which means the God's Son descends to us. Putting on the sacred clothes, he signifies His holy personification; descending from the gates to the West he signifies – His coming to life on earth, death and descend to the hades. For this means to go to the West and descend to the gates". And more: "When the Bishop ascends to the Western gates to put on the sacred clothes, this signifies the embodied Lord, Who descended (from heaven) to earth and even to the deepest end of earth – the *hades*, defeating the prince of darkness and freeing the souls, which had been kept there for ages".

As soon as the temple's idea in its main parts-sides is explained, on the basis of it is easy to understand iconographical scenes of these parts. Usually in ancient temples on the Western part the Final Judgement is shown, sometimes – the vision of St.Prophet Ezekiel of resurrection of bones on the field etc.

***

If the East is the area of light, heaven and paradise, the West is the area of darkness, neither regions and hades; then the centre of temple is all the earthy space, where the Universal Christ's Church exists in its whole. So the Greeks call it *Katholikon*, which is the same as *oecumene*, i.e. the Universe. That is also the Liturgics' opinion of this space. St.Herman says: "Coming with the Gospel (out of the altar) signifies the coming of God's Son into the whole world, as the Apostle says: as when *He leads the First-Born*, i.e. the Lord and Father, into the universe, says: *and all God's Angels shall bow to Him*"[12].

Architectural type of the temple's centre with its four walls, four sails and cupolas covering – so called cubic type– also conforms to this idea of the Universe.

The philosopher Platon taught that earth had the cubic form. Platon's idea was inherited by translators of the Bible into Greek and geographers of Alexandria.

So, if temple is image of the world, and its central part is the image of earth – Universe, then Christ's universal church shall be expressed in it also as whole. If the cubic architectural form shows the scheme of the Universe; then the universal church shall be shown by iconography on all the four walls of this cube – temple.

But how can iconography express on all temple's walls all the universal church? *Not in any* other way, but in the perspective of centuries, all its history, from the first built church to the end of its existence, till the day of the Last Judgment, according to the main epochs. The primitive church – till the end of the Deluge, the *patriarchal* one – before Moses, *under the law* – before the prophets, *prophetical* one – before Christ, the Apostolic one and, finally, the *cathedral* – oecumenical – one till the end of the world, i.e. the Resurrection of all the dead and the Last Judgment (according to the Revelation) shall be shown here iconographically.

The most important events from the Evangelic and Apostolic histories and Oecumenical Councils are placed on temple's walls (Northern and Southern ones). This placement conforms well to the opinion of church fathers about the meaning of 0ecumenical Councils: by the Seven Councils the main structure of the oecumenical church was finalized; they also serve as firm basis of its historical existence, its *protecting walls*.

There are usually four columns in the centre of the temple: on them those representatives of the Oecumenical Church are shown, who spread, enlightened and firmly established it by word, image and heroic deeds of their lives, i.e.: Apostles, Bishops, Martyrs, hermits, etc. They are the church pillars. St.Ignatius the God-bearer, comparing the Apostles with patriarchs, Moses and prophets, says that the *"world's pillars are the Apostles"*[13].

Then the idea of the person-pillars is transferred to the architectural pillars (columns) inside the temple's building. In the Apocalypse God's Spirit says to the Angel of Philadelphia: "him that overcometh will I make a pillar in *the temple of my God*... and I will write upon him the name of my God, and the name of the city of my God, which is new Jerusalem", i.e. Christ's Church.[14]

According to the temple's four corners, above the capitals of its four central pillars, where the arcs are supported, better saying – in the sails, usually images of the four Evangelists are placed. Like the temple's pillars, these images of the Evangelists have special meaning in the general system of its iconography. Such images of the Evangelists and their location here have deep foundation: on the one hand, it is in the ancient Cosmography, on the other hand – in the Gospel and in the Holy Patristic view upon the oecumenical church. According to St.Irenaeus, the Evangelists with their Gospels are the four pillars of the Oecumenical Church, and the Gospels are the four main winds of one God's Spirit, reviving the Church, spread in all the four parts of the Universe.

In St.Irenaeus's opinion, cherubs are compared with the four winds, and with them the four Evangelists. This comparison conforms to the biblical one, to the vision of St.Prophet Ezekiel of "God's glory" as bright and glittering cloud, carried by the wind together with four Cherubs, standing at four sides and serving the Lord. According to church understanding, these four cherubs are pre-images of the four Evangelists. Temple iconography quite conforms to this idea of them in holy patristic scriptures.

As in the Christian church idea the four Gospels conform to the four mainwinds, the four Evangelists with their Gospels are shown in Christian churches in the corners – in the sails, and above the main, central columns, so that according to St.Irenaeus's idea (i.e. the "Church musts have four pillars") to show this way that in the Oecumenical Church from the four sides of the world instead of four columns and natural four winds there is God's Spirit, giving it true life through the four Gospels.

But according to St.Irenaus the Evangelists are compared with the Cherubs, who support the throne in heaven and the Pentacrate sitting on it, – as St.Ezekiel saw in his vision of "God's glory" at the river Habar. that is why in temple's sails there are sometimes only cherubs, like in Tsargradskaya Sophia, sometimes there are old testament cherubs with the Evangelists, as their pre-images or symbols, life in Sophia in Kiev and Novgorod and others. Above the four walls of the main or the "real" part of temple (katholikon) there usually is a vault in the form of a dome-semisphere – like above the four parts of the world heaven spreads: so the dome above this temple's part is like heaven above the earth.

As soon as the idea of heaven was transferred on temple's dome, the idea of God the Pentacrate, which was first of all referred to heaven, was now transferred to temple's dome, like to the image of heaven above the earth. And here it was to get its visual expression iconographically, – in corresponding image.

But what image was to be placed on temple's vault – inside the dome? Old Testament man imagined Iegova to be God the Pentacrate; however, already in the Old Testament God the Pentacrate showed Himself in the form similar to the *Son of man* on the throne of glory, – above the four sides of world, i.e. as the Pentacrate.

The Old Testament Script teaches: by the *word of the Lord* were the heavens made; and all the host of them by the breath of his mouth.[16] So the heavenly stronghold is the creation of the Word and Mind of God or the Personal God's Wisdom, and all the heavenly powers are the creation of God's Spirit. The New Testament defines more clearly that this God's Mind (Logos), like the Creator, is the embodied

God's son, whose image had been already revealed in the Old Testament by the prophets.[17] So, transferring the idea about the Pentacrate from the heaven to temple's dome, Christian icon-painter was to place here not the image of Iegova, but right the image of the embodied Word – God's Mind, i.e. Jesus Christ's Image, as the world's King and Pentacrate.

Thus, evidently, in the place, where exactly *the centre of earth* was presented, Christ's image was placed, as the wise Creator and Pentacrate, according to the St.Isaiah's prophecy.[18] And later, when temple's centre started to symbolize the centre of the earth; then above it, already in temple's dome, as though on heavenly stronghold, Christ's image began to be shown, as the Lord.

But if the temple is the image of the Universe, and also of the Oecumenical Church of Christ, which is His Body, and Christ is its Head; then Christian art – iconography and architecture were to express and expressed this idea each in its own way.

Really, Christian icon-painters already in dome of the most ancient temples, in this symbolic heaven, showed exactly ascended Christ, sitting on the heavenly stronghold, sometimes on the rainbow (according to the vision of St.Prophet Ezekiel), sometimes among stars, etc.

But the fact ascended Christ, showed in temple's dome, not only as the Lord, but also as the Head of Oecumenical church, was especially expressed by painter-architect by the fact that above the temple's body, on its shoulders and neck he placed the head.

Christian orthodox church as a piece of art, represents one majestic image of the Universe and the Oecumenical church existing within its borders, revealing itself multilaterally during all periods of its existence with gradual development in its life of divine Revelation, on the basis of one idea of atonation of the mankind by the personification, teaching, death, resurrection and ascension of Christ, as the Divine Entity of Wisdom.

Thus, are the historical and symbolical circumstances and archaeological data of appearance and establishment of our state's capital.

---

[1] St. Mathew, ch.28, v. 18-19. Acts, ch. 1, v. 18.
[2] Chrysostome, X, 50.
[3] Chrysostome, VI, 167.
[4] Quotation according to: Tarasov N., Romansky Style, p. 884
[5] Genesis, ch. 2, p. 3.
[6] St.John, ch. 15, v. 1 and the next.
[7] St.John, ch. 27, 31-33, 45-58.
[8] Acts, ch. 7, v. 56.
[9] Archbishop Benjamin. The New Testimonies. Spb., 1884, p. 87.
[10] St. Jeremiah, 6, 1st.
[11] St. Jeremiah, ch. 2, p. 23-24, 33-34.
[12] Mansvetov U.K. Icons of God's Feasts... Spb. 1855, p. 343-344.
[13] 1 Thessalonians, ch. 9.
[14] Revelation, ch. 3, v. 12.
[15] Ezekiel, ch. 1-2, 1.
[16] Psalms, 32, v. 6.
[17] St.Isaiah, ch. 6; Ezekiel, ch. 1-2; John, ch. 1.
[18] Isaiah, ch. 40, v. 5, 12-23.

Moscow. Construction of the fortress walls on the Borovitskiy Hill at the time of Yuri Dolgorukiy. Watercolor of G. Borisevich.

CHAPTER TWO

Domain Capital Town

St. Daniel, prince of Moscow.
Fresco of the
Archangels Cathedral
in the Kremlin.
The 17th century.

The Nativity of Christ. About 1660. School of Yaroslavl.

МОСКВА

850 ЛЕТ

The Theotokos the Great Panhagia. About 1224.

The Land of Holy Russia. Hieromonk Stephan (Linitskiy)

In the history of Ancient Moscow there were three political ranks. Town's status raised at intervals: first - the capital town of rural principality, then – capital town of grand domain, finally – the state capital. The stages of growth were connected with growth of titles of social and church hierarchies: prince, Grand Prince, 'tsar, metropolitanate, patriarch. Principality territory and population grew too, and the state extended on the lands of other tribes and nations. As soon as Moscow rose to another rank, monarchs did everything to raise it to the next rank. So, for example, at the rank of grand domain objects of already tsar's Moscow (the Kremlin, Kitai-gorod...) were constructed. In the same way the scale of town-building symbolics raised equalling at Vladimir, Kiev, Constantinople, Rome, Jerusalem, finally, the Heavenly Town. So the process of Moscow growth from a small town to a large medieval town-symbol of Russian people and state should be considered not gradually with time periods, but taking into account the abruptness of town-building process, marking the contribution of outstanding Russian political and religious man in it. Also remembering that the process of the town's stable raise was accompanied from time to time by its nearly complete liquidation: in 1238 Baty ransacked it, in 1383 – Toktamysh, in 1571 Devlet-Guirey burnt it, in 1612 the Poles, Lithuanians, Germans burnt it... It burnt itself with "great blazes" in 1343, 1390, 1395, 1445, 1470, 1474, 15... There was an uncountable number of disasters.

Moscow was not built at once

The time from the middle of the 12th till the beginning of the 13th centuries was not a long, but very important crucial period. Yuri Dolgoruky made in Moscovj a sharp change from "the primitive communal epoch to the feudal one" by conquering it, separating from the Vyatiches, liquidation of communal-tribal power, change of paganism... But this was a social change. Town-building situation did not change so quickly. Half a century was needed (1146–1212) to change the old system of settlements in accordance with the new feudal regulations, private ownership. At this crucial moment the pagan Moscovj "agonized", because in the centre of the nestle of its settlements the feudal town was developing "internally". By the end of this development, at the beginning of the of the 13th century the first Moscow prince appeared, and the town became the capital one. Right at this time it inherited the name of some pagan nestle-land, a little changing its ancient name to the "new one" – "Moscva".

In the second half of the 12th – beginning of the 13th centuries Moscovj was included into active life of Zalesskaya land. Among many events of that time those are interesting which clarify Moscow town-building situation.

In 1175 Moscow "kuchkovichi", who had been cherished in 1146 by Yuri Dolgoruky, hatched a plot and killed his son, the Grand Prince of Vladimir St.Andrew Bogoljubsky. The second young Andrew's wife from Bulgary Ulita (perhaps a thought up name) joined the plot, probably taking revenge for the recent massacre by the Prince of Bulgarian towns. After killing the Prince the conspirators with everything that they had robbed, left for Moscovj, where, perhaps lived in Bor-town, in the settlement of Yuri Dolgoruky (the former Kuchka's yard). In autumn the new Grand Prince Michalko Yurievich (brother of Bogoljubsky) called them to Vladimir to snem (boyard council) and after consideration of the case executed kuchkovichis and Ulita. The robbed princely property was confiscated in Moscovj and distributed to people in Vladimir. But Michalko Yurievich could not continue to be the prince of Vladimir and had to leave for the south.

In 1176 he was called again by people of Vladimir. In Moscow Kuchkovo field a delegation of them met the prince, at the head of which was the prince George Andreevich (the son of Bogoljubsky, the tsar of Georgia in the nearest future, married to the legendary tsarina Tamara). The joyful Moscow banquet after the meeting was suddenly interrupted by the news that hostile troops of Rostov were coming and Michalko had to fight his way to Vladimir. However, after that he did not reign in Vladimir for a long time either: the same year he was probably poisoned by Rostov boyards, and the Grand Prince of Vladimir became his younger brother Vsevolod Yurievich, who later got the nickname Big Nestle.

In 1177 a coalition of princes at the head of which was the prince Gleb of Rjazan, opposed the new prince of Vladimir. In autumn Gleb with the troops of the coalition attacked the borders of Moscovj unexpectedly: burnt Dolgorukov's fortress, surrounding villages and, supposedly, old dilapidated pagan, small towns, and captured the inhabitants. The robbery was a horrible one because Mounted Polovetskaya Horde, which had been invited by the prince of Rjazan, took part in it. At that time the old family-tribal nestle of settlements of Moscovj's centre died in blazes.

After Vsevolod's victory over Gleb on the Pruskovo Hill not far from Vladimir and return of Moscow captured people, it seems that only the Christian town with villages was restored in the 70–80s. Pagan Moscovj could exist yet as land, but in its centre the feudal town developed already. And here the construction of the new wooden church of St.Hieromartyr Demetrius of Thessalonica in the northern part of vetche square in the restored fortress can be noted.

Moscow Cathedral of Dormition from ancient time had the lateral church of St.Demetrius. For the first time the chronicles mention it in 1326: "bringing from the Horde (the body) of the Grand Prince Yuri Danilovich" and "putting it in the church of Theotocos of Her Holy Dormition in the lateral altar of St.Demetrius". However, the Stepennaya (rank) Book says that Yuri Danilovich was buried in the church of St.Demetrius, "which is now the big lateral altar of the cathedral church".

Really, the body of the prince Yuri was brought in February of 1326 (according to the March calendar it was 1325 yet), and the Cathedral of Dormition was founded by the metropolitanate Peter in August 1326, i.e. more than half a year after. To this effect in 1873 I.M.Snegirev commented: "The lateral altar could appear... only after abolishment of the separate church of St.Demetrius". In other words, the church of St.Demetrius preceded the Cathedral of Dormition of the metropolitanate Peter, besides, as the scientist thought then, it was a wooden church.

In 1963—1965 during excavations in the square near the Cathedral of Dormition of the Kremlin a Christian cemetery was found, which functioned till 1325 – the time when the yard of the metropolitanate Peter appeared here. N.S.Sheljapina, who had published the information about the excavations, made the conclusion that the appearance of the cemetery was connected with the building of the church here. The ancient burials dated back to the second half of the 12th century.

Thus, the wooden church of St.Demetrius of Thessalonica, most probably, appeared at the end of the 70s of the 12th century. And it was raised as the memorial church for the killed Moscow people in 1177. The Grand Prince Vsevolod of Vladimir built the temple "in his name", he had the Christian name Demetrius.

In 1207 during Vsevolod's march against the princes of Chernigov his sons came to Moscow: Constantine from Rostov, as well as Yuri, Yaroslav, Vladimir. A big army gathered, in which not only people of Suzdal, Rostov, Perejaslavl, but also from Novgorod, Pskov, Ladoga, Novy Torjok... "Moscow is shown in this news as an important strategic base. Here it is possible to get food and have rest for a big army before a new march... Moscow of the beginning of the 13th century is not just a border point, but a convenient place for gathering and rest of troops, base for actions against the princes of Chernigov," – M.N.Tikhomirov wrote in 1947.

Now knowing about the existence in Moscow already from pagan time of the majestic nestle of settlements, it is not surprising that it could be turned into a "military base" in such cases.

The First Prince – Vladimir Vsevolodovich

"Stol" (table) in Russia was first of all called the throne of tsar-prince. A town became "stoljny" with building in it a princely yard, princely table. Speaking about the beginning of stoljnaya Moscow, about the first important stage of its development, it is necessary to tell about the appearance in it of the first Moscow prince. As the prince had come from table Vladimir Zalessky and his gaining of power was complicated by circumstances of that time, it is reasonable to tell about everything in detail. Besides, historians did not write anything about the first Moscow prince.

On 13, April, 1212, in Vladimir Zalessky the Grand Prince Vsevolod the Big Nestle died. He seemed to get this characteristic nickname, because he grew up six sons (other two twins died in childhood). Before death he had an argument with his son Constantine. So, he left the grand princely table to his second son, Yuri (George, Geurgi). Yuri now owned the main town Vladimir and Suzdal, and Constantin had got earlier Rostov and Yaroslavl. The son Yaroslav got Pereyaslavlj and Tverj, Svyatoslav got Yuriev Polsky and a small town Radilov, Vladimir got Moscow and Dmitrov, and the little one, John, got Starodub Ryapolovsky.

Having got from his father the grand princely table and making sure of support of his brother Yaroslav, Yuri, being of stern tempo, soon distributed again the towns increasing his ownership. In addition to table Vladimir and Suzdal he joined to his ownership Kostroma and Solj Velikaya from his elder brother Constantine and in the West – Moscow from his brother Vladimir. The Grand Prince added to Yaroslav Dmitrov, taking it from Vladimir, and the outskirts Nerehta, taking it away from Constantine. Instead Yuri gave to Vladimir the town of Yuriev Polky, taking it from Svyatoslav, and Starodub Ryapolovsky, taking it from John.

Redistribution of property raised natural discontent of the elder and the youngest brothers. Peaceful talks did not give any results, and armed conflict started. Young Vladimir was quick. According to the chronicles, "Vladimir Vsevolodovich" not wishing to reign in Gyurgev (Yuriev Polsky) and running to Volok... and (upon advice of Constantine) from Volok to Moscow and stayed there, in his brother's town... and locked in it". It is unknown why Moscovites accepted Vladimir. Probably, because it was for the first time when they had their own prince, and Moscow from outskirts was raising to the rank of a table town; probably, their decision was influenced by Vsevolod's advice. It is significant that moscovites, being on Vladimir's side, went against even the Grand Prince Yuri without any fear.

Timid Svyatoslav acted in another way: "Went from Constantine to Yury and gave him... (the Grand Prince) Yury Polsky". In this way Yury punished Vladimir, leaving him only Starodub taken away from John. But the main opponent of the redistribution was still Constantine, who, being the elder one, had the right to the grand princely table and the main town Vladimir. Yury and Yaroslav decided to impose their will on him, with troops they went to Rostov in 1213.

Having learnt about the march, Vladimir "went with Moscovites and his troops to Dmitrov, to Yaroslavlj, the town of his brother... People of Dmitrov heard about it and burnt all beyond the town's walls and locked inside". Defending themselves they nearly shot the "self-styled" Moscow prince. The latter had to retreat, besides he got the news about reconciliation of princes-brothers near Rostov. During Vladimir's retreat, Dmitrovtsy unexpectedly "went out of town, bit the behind flanks of his troops. And followed Vladimir up to Moscow".

Having returned from Rostov, Yury with brothers "came and surrounded Moscow, his town" and made Vladimir to leave it. More than that, he had to go to the south, to reign in Russian Pereyaslavlj near Kiev. In this way Moscow went down back to the rank of outskirts, and its prince turned out to be sent away from Zalesskaya land.

At this Vladimir's misfortunes were not over. In 1215, in Pereyaslavlj he got married "to Gleb's daughter, the prince of Chernigov". "But having heard that Polovtsy were going against Pereyaslavlj, he went to meet them, and after that there was a great battle. The Polovtsy won the battle and captured the prince Vladimir". In this battle the prince was, probably, injured, because later he did not take part in any battles, did not live long and had no children.

In 1216 the famous Lipitsk battle near Yuriev Polsky happened. Constantine in union with Novgorod and Smolensk defeated utterly the troops of Yuri, Yaroslav Svyatoslav... Becoming the Grand Prince of Vladimir he sent Yuri to the small town of Radilov, and the other brothers he simply sent to their domains. After contacting the Polovtsy, Constantine, probably, ransomed his brother. In 1217 Vladimir "went from Polovtsy to the brother and gave him Starodub and another volost". So it was written, intentionally not indicating this "another volost", later in the chronicle Simon, bishop of Vladimir, – Yuri's servile chronicler.

V.N.Tatitschev informed, on the basis of some unknown now chronicle source, that Vladimir died in 1227 being the *prince of Moscow*. Precision of the scripture of the great Russian historian is undoubtful, because he called Vladimir when he returned from the captivity "the prince of Pereyaslavlj" and it was true at that time. So, becoming the great prince of Vladimir, fulfilling the precept of his father prince Vladimir, in 1217 Constantine returned Moscow to Vladimir, taking away this "another volost" from Yuri. In February 1219 (in 1218 according to the March calendar) Constantine suddenly fell ill and died. However, after returning to the grand princely table, Yuri, probably, did not begin taking Moscow away from Vladimir, otherwise he would have infringed two wills: those of the deceased father and brother. There is no reason to think that Vladimir could get Moscow from Yuri's hands.

So, Vladimir Vsevolodovich reigned in Moscow nearly wilfully in 1212–1213 and by the princes-brothers' consent in 1217–1228. Except his fight for Moscow table, short-term reign in Novgorod (people of Novgorod did not like him), alter the unfortunate battle with Polovtsy near Pereyaslavlj Zalessky, his activity was not marked with anything else. The prince was born on 26, October, 1194, died on 6, January, 1228 (1227 according to the March calendar), and before death he traditionally, "took monastic vows and schema, he was put in Vladimir in the church of Theotocos Zlatoverhaya". The first Moscow prince lived "thirty three years" (the age of Jesus Christ), reigned in Moscow for 12 years totally. There is his portrait at the age of four.

N.N.Voronin, after studying historical material about the fretted white stone cathedral of St.Demetrius of 1198 in Vladimir Zalessky, wrote: "The composition in the Eastern part of the Northern wall is of special interest... There is an enthroned man's figure with a child on his knees here; at its sides there are symmetrically situated half-kneeling (two figures at each side) four figures in short clothes with hands outstretched to the sitting man in prayer. It is undoubtedly the image of Vsevolod III... the five masculine figures conform to the quantity of his sons (till 1198 – the end of the cathedral's construction – his last son John was not born yet (G.M.). Then, whom is Vsevolod holding on his knees?

We think it is Vladimir born in 1194. According to the chronicle he was horn on the eve of the day of St.Demetrius (Vsevolod's patron). Vsevolod "ordered to give his son the name Demetrius, which was his own name after christening, and Vladimir was given as the princely name – after his grandfather – Vladimir Monomakh"... The central position in this sculptural "family portrait" on the cathedral's wall exactly of Vladimir was determined by the tact that both father and son had the Christian name Demetrius".

The relief of north-east chamber of the Cathedral of St.Demetrius is special. Here portrait similarity was required from the artist. And this complicated task was quite different from the task of other masters who cut abstract symbols from stone: mythical Heracles, biblical David or unknown by the face Alexander of Macedonia. The portraitist's task was complicated by strict judgement. The

Big Nestle – the Grand Prince of Vladimir Vsevolod III with his sons. Relief in the North-Eastern chamber of the cathedral of St. Demetrius. 1198.

Grand Prince was alive and evaluated the work together with his family, there were 30–40 other professional engravers-judges. And as Vsevolod's portrait with sons was finally installed on the cathedral's wall for the descendants to see, it can be said that the artist had managed his task successfully: his work was approved. All this proves that the appearance of the people of the "Big Nestle" is real. The portrait of the father with his sons is very realistic and decorative, monumental "for the cathedral", symbolic. Here ancient Russia left not only the single in its way "family

Grand Prince of Vladimir Vsevolod Big Nestle with his four-year son Vladimir – the future first Moscow prince. Fragment of the relief of the cathedral of St. Demetrius. 1198. The fretman is unknown.

portrait", but a portrait of "father with a little son". The same was only on the icons of the Mother of God.

Vladimir on the portrait is about four years old. His little long nose and full lips are seen in profile. He sits not just on the father's knee, but as though on the throne together with his father. As if according to God's Words: "The winning... I shall let to sit with Me on My throne." To this effect N.N.Voronin was right when he wrote: "As this heir was so meaningfully called after his famous great-grandfather, probably, Vsevolod had some special dynastic considerations connected with him." It seems that finally Vsevolod was mistaken in his hopes: Vladimir of Moscow did not become a new Monomakh. But the symbolics, the little miracle, is still here.

All that happened in that ancient time, seems now "from the height of the passed centuries" to be some Divine Omen, the sacred meaning of which, certainly, nobody knew, including the Grand Prince of Vladimir himself. Could Vsevolod suppose in 1198 that taking on his knees little Vladimir (to pose for the portraitist), he took out of his "Nestle" and in this way singled out of the four future grand princes, as though showed to the whole world the future first Moscow prince? Could he then know before his death in spring 1212 that after making Vladimir the first Moscow prince and Moscow itself the table town, he committed a symbolic act: "Vladimir-Suzdal land gave birth to and raised Moscow" – the future capital of all Russian land, the huge Russian state. The described symbolic miracle, which cannot be called otherwise, is now on the Northern wall of the famous fretted cathedral of St.Demetrius in Vladimir.

The cathedral is knitted from paradisaical plants;
The Big Nestle is seen above,
But time stands still... the high chorus is silent...
The nestlings hardened into stone long ago...

Moscow Domain

After death of the first Moscow prince Vladimir Vsevolodovich in 1228 Moscow goes again to Yuri Vsevolodovich, besides the prince of Vladimir gave it at once to his son who was also *Vladimir*, but *Yurievich*. The little prince was 12 and juridically he became quite rich and relatively independent. Though at difference to the first Vladimir, he lived mostly with his father, and came to Moscow only from time to time. In 1236 the father married him off together with the younger brother Mstislav.

In winter of 1237–1238 Baty's Horde attacked Russia. Separate Russian principalities could not join together before the terrible danger and were defeated utterly one after another. After Ryazanj's fall the Grand Prince of Vladimir tried to make a covering detachment near Kolomna, for which he attracted Moscovites. However, nearly all the detachment was killed: the prince Roman Ingvarovich of Kolomna, the commander Eremey Glebovich of Vladimir were killed, and the prince Vsevolod Yurievich, who had been sent here, ran away: "As for Moscovites, they ran away not seeing anything".

Moscow fortress was defended by Vladimir Yurievich himself with his commander Philip Nyanok. The Nyankovs boyard family comes from a noble Kiev family: already in the 12th century near the banner of Yaropolk of Kiev Damian Nyanok is mentioned. However, "taking Moscow, tatars killed the commander... captured the prince Vladimir with their hands... Massacred people from the old to infants. The burnt town and the Holy churches, all the monasteries and villages. They robbed a lot and went away".

There was a sad scene near table Vladimir, which was written by chroniclers. When tatars came close to the fortress walls, they shouted: "Do not shoot!" – and pushed forward the captured Moscow prince. He had a pitiful look to such an extent that Vsevolod and Mstislav who were standing on the town gates "with their boyards and citizens cried seeing Vladimir". As M.N.Tikhomirov noted: "tried to make effect and were proud of conquering strong Moscow". Moscow prince was killed here during the attack at the town of Vladimir together with his brothers. And their father, the Grand Prince Yuri Vsevolodovich was killed in a sword fight at the river Citj. Vladimir Yurievich reigned in Moscow for about 10 years.

After Baty had gone from the robbed Zalesskaya land Vladimir's table in 1238 was taken by Yaroslav Vsevolodovich, Moscow's table – by his son, the prince *Michael Yaroslavich*. The prince got the nickname Horobrit for his fearless but uncontrolled tempo, which finally ruined him. After Yaroslav's death, who was poisoned in Horde in 1246, Vladimir's table was taken by timid Svyatoslav Vsevolodovich being the elder. But in 1247 Michael Horobrit sent his uncle away and enthroned himself on the grand princely table. In 1246 he was killed in collision with Lithuanians at the Moscow border near the river Protva. Michael Yaroslavich reigned in Moscow for about 10 years.

Vladimir's throne was taken by Svyatoslav again, but in a year he was sent away again by another violent yaroslavich – Andrew, who had got from the Horde khan a tag for the reign. Kiev's throne was given to his elder brother *Alexander Nevsky*. From 1252 Alexander Nevsky became the Grand Prince of Vladimir and held to himself his native Pereyaslavlj and Moscow.

Before death in 1263 (probably, he was also poisoned by tatars) he had left Pereyaslavlj to his elder son Demetrius, and Moscow – to his youngest son Daniel, who was born in 1261.

Little Daniel first lived with his uncle in Tverj, the Grand Prince Yaroslav Yaroslavich. In 1272 Yaroslav died, but Daniel was 12 and he took the Moscow throne, being probably under protection of his elder brother the Grand Prince Demetrius Alexandrovich of Pereyaslavlj. Daniel reigned 31 years totally and died on 5, April, 1303. As Moscow throne was inherited by children and grandchildren of Daniel, he became the forefather of future Moscow princes. As his elder sons Yuri and John later became the Grand Princes of Vladimir, Daniel as though finished by himself modest existence of Moscow domain.

But Daniel is remarkable not only as the forefather of Moscow princes. He made the first important steps for the rise of Moscow in the 14th century to the next grand princely stage. In 1302 childless prince John Dmitrievich of Pereyaslavlj left the town before his death to the Moscow prince whom he loved "more than others". The situation changed: Alexander Nevsky was the prince of Pereyaslavlj, but held Moscow to himself; Daniel was Moscow prince, but held also Pereyaslavlj. At the same time together with

Pereyaslavlj he got Dmitrov. At the beginning of the 14th century he conquered Kolomna, capturing with some ruse prince Alexander of Ryazanj. Thus, Daniel at the end of his princehood reigned besides Moscow in other three towns and their lands around Moscow. Practically he started gathering the lands of the divided north-east Russia. His elder children – Yuri and especially John continued his business with great energy.

The First Stone Church

To speak about the change of the face of the town on the Neglinnaya in the dlirection of the "capital one" it is necessary to understand first how table town was different in Russia from a usual one. In the 10th – 15th centuries the "signs" of such difference were stone churches, because ancient Russian towns were wooden. As E.E.Golubinsky noted, stone churches "were firstly considered the necessary adornment and appurtenance of grand princely capitals, secondly, they prevailed in the towns which had exclusive social status... The comparatively big quantity of stone churches was built in the capitals of grand principalities – Kiev, Vladimir Klyazemsky... Holm... Moscow, Novgorod and Pskov".

Appearance among wooden town houses and even wooden churches of a stone church with white and painted walls, semi-circular sides, leaden-coloured or golden cupolas, crowned with golden cross – all this was the appurtenance of a table, i.e. princely town. It can be compared with the look of the prince himself who always stood out from the warrior of his troops. "Oh, Vsevolod, man of courage!.. As he rode, sparkling with his golden helmet, there the vile polovetskie heads lie". Or in the chronicles of 1201: "Then Vladimir Monomakh drank the river Don with a golden helmet..."

As soon as in some towns of Zalesskaya land an independent prince appeared, he tried to build a stone town cathedral at least. If the first prince failed to do it, the church was built by his son and grandson... It was so in Rostov, Suzdal, Vladimir, Pereyaslavlj, Yaroslavlj, Nizhny Novgorod, Uglich, Yuriev Polsky... Moscow was not an exception.

In 1966–1969 during restoration and fortification work inside the Cathedral of Dormition in the Moscow Kremlin the floor was partially uncovered and the foundation was found. By several pits the culture layer was researched down the death of 4 m. The layer consisted mainly of remnants (stones, broken brick, lime) of preceding stone churches. But there were also found some undamaged lower parts of columns, foundations, floor of the cathedral of 1472–1474 of the masters Krivtsov and Myshkin, floor of the cathedral of 1326–1329 of the metropolitanate Peter, as well as, unexpectedly for everybody, the floor of even earlier white stone church!

From this unknown church the following was found: lower part of south-east column of size 1,36 x 1,36 m), to the east from it – remnants of half-ruined altar, in the south– remnant of east wall frame ledge. Near the column and the wall fragments of lime-sand preparation for floor plates were found. N.S.Sheljapina, who had carried out the excavation, made the conclusion that it is possible to identify the found church with the church of St.Demetrius of Thessalonica. In her opinion, the church substituted the wooden one at the end of the 13th century.

The first reconstruction of the plan of newly found church was taken up by V.I.Federov, who made architectural observation of the excavations. The remnants of the southern frame ledge allowed him to take as analogues the churches of Archangel Michael 1227–1230 of Nizhny Novgorod, St.Hieromartyr George 1230–1234 of Yuriev Polsky and to reconstruct graphically the plan of the Moscow church similar to the plans of these churches (with three frame ledges, open inside the quadruple). G.K.Vagner tried to reproduce some elements of decoration according to fragments of ferreted sculptures found nearby. Style of the decoration was characterized as of Vladimir-Suzdal one.

The excavations allowed to make a wonderful discovery: to find a stone church on wooden square of Moscow. But very scarce volume – the church's remnants were found only in two pits – did not allow to date it according to direct archaeological data. The dating was made according to the historical situation, in essence, according to indirect historical considerations. And here not everything was impeccable and acceptable.

First of all, the stone church did not exist long and already in 1326 was dismantled. It is difficult to believe that a functioning church during some 30–40 years became so hopelessly ramshackle. N.S.Sheljapina's idea about a storm which ruined it or about its possible burning by Djudenj's Horde in 1293 is not sufficient (St.Daniel of Moscow just let the horde inside the fortress and it turned out to be only robbed). Finally, intentionally or not they impute to the metropolitanate Peter a rather absurd wish for the situation of that time (Mongolian yoke, stone churches are rare) to substitute the churn which was not old yet by another: the old one could be repaired, the new one could be built nearby. All becomes clear, if to suppose that the church of St.Demetrius did not appear at the end of the 13th century, but earlier, and at the beginning of the 14th century it really became ramshackle because of many fires and disasters and was to be changed. It is common knowledge that princes from the time of christening tried to build churches "with their names" in the names of their Saints-guards: Vsevolod-Demetrius not only followed this tradition but bequeathed to his son Vladimir who was also Demetrius, his towns Dmitrov and Moscow with their wooden churches of St.Demetrius of Thessalonica. It is quite possible that he precepted to his son to build in Moscow a stone church instead of the wooden one, like in Vladimir: it was not by chance that Moscovites accepted Vladimir in 1212 in spite of the actions of prince Yuri. Could not they build a stone church in Moscow at that time, i.e. in the first half of the 13th century?

After digging of the cemetery outside the Cathedral of Dormition N.S.Sheljapina wrote: "At the depth 3,30-3,80 m several white stone smooth and ornamented plates probably moved from the burials and broken, were found... 'The most ancient burial under smooth burial white stone plate was found at the depth of 5,92 m. It dates back to the first half of the 13th century."

Moscovites in the first half of the 13th century brought stone plates for themselves, worked on the white stone and could, one should think, not only grave plates. Outside the

Cathedral of Dormition during excavations majolica floor plates were found. "Moscow plates like the plates of the church of St.Joachim and Anna in Vladimir (1196) were made from red roughly treated clay and have almost the same thickness. Plates with prominent frame on the back side and square deepening are most close to the plates of the Cathedral of the Nativity in Suzdal of 1222-1225", N.S.Sheljapina wrote. Materials of the excavations are modest, but make the dating of the white stone church of St.Demetrius in Moscow possible by the first half of the 13th century too, and not only by the end of the 13th century. In this case it is possible to date it even more precisely.

After Vsevolod's death construction of stone churches in table towns of Zalesskaya land was carried out by deeply believing Constantine, who gathered for this purpose his father's masters. Right after Vsevolod's death in 1213 he founded the huge cathedral of Dormition in Rostov, which was finished in 1231. In 1214-1218 in Rostov's princely yard the church of Sts.Boris and Gleb; in 1215-1219 the cathedral of Dormition is built in Yaroslavlj; in 1216 the cathedral of Transfiguration was founded in Yaroslavlj and finished in 1224. Finally, in Vladimir during one summer of 1218 in trade square the church of Adoration of the Holy Cross. According to the dates it is clear that by 1219 the works were over in three churches: Sts.Boris and Gleb, Dormition and Adoration of the Holy Cross. Line of the three artels of bricklayers was sent already in 1218 by Constantine for construction of the cathedral of Sts.Constantine and Helen in the monastery near Vladimir.

The plan of the church of St. Demetrius of Thessalonika – the first Moscow stone church. Reconstruction of V. Fedorov.

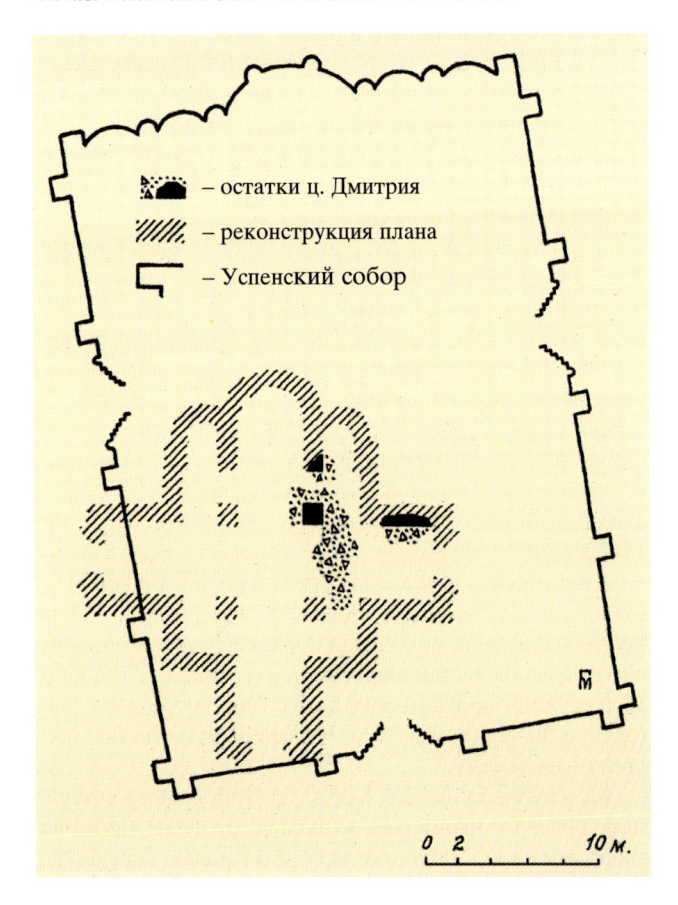

- остатки ц. Дмитрия
- реконструкция плана
- Успенский собор

And before his death Constantine, probably, gave to his brother Vladimir the third of the artels which became tree after construction of the church of Adoration of the Holy Cross – to construction of a white stone church in Moscow. It was in 1219-1221 in the flow of stone construction when a "window" is found in the dates, and besides after the construction of stone churches by Constantine who loved and protected Vladimir.

The Grand Prince Yuri sends then part of bricklayers to his towns: for construction of a cathedral in Suzdal in 1222-1225, then the church of Transfiguration in 1225-1227, the church of Archangel Michael in 1227-1229 in Nizhny Novgorod. After that he gave the bricklayers to Svyatoslav for construction in Yuriev Polsky of the cathedral of St.George in 1230-1234. From 1225 and 1231 bricklayers and fretters became free after construction of the cathedrals in Yaroslavlj and Rostov. Part of them could be sent to improve artels in Uglich, Vladimir, and part – in Nizhny Novgorod, Yuriev Polsky. Increase of quantity of bricklayers and trotters, probably, made the look of the church richer: their facades were decorated more and more, they were covered with white stone fretwork.

Moscow church was not mentioned in chronicles, it was discovered archaeologically. It has to be dated according to the complex of sources: indirect (not local) archaeological data (stratigraphia), traditions of consacration of churches (St.Demetrius), historical situation (pre-Mongolian period), the gap in chronicles of construction of stone churches in table towns of Zalesskaya land. The sample for the Moscow church was, probably, the church of St.George in Yuriev Polsky, built already in 1152 by Yuri Dolgoruky and dismantled in 1230.

Moscow church of St.Demetrius of Thessalonica of 1215-1221 took chronologically medium position in post-Vsevolod pre-Mongolian stone construction in Zalesskaya land. That is why, perhaps, it was decorated richer than the churches of Rostov and Yaroslavlj, but poorer than the churches of Nizhny Novgorod and Yuriev Polsky. Stone for the church and for the grave plates near it was taken from the quarry in Dorogomilovo – the oldest and the nearest to Moscow. It was floated on ferries down the Moscow-river to the mouth of Neglinnaya at a comparatively short distance. From the same Dorogomilovsky white stone later the churches were built at the time of Daniel, Kalita, finally, the white stone walls and towers of the Kremlin of Demetrius Donskoy.

Built by the first Moscow prince Vladimir Demetrius in the centre of Moscow fortress on Makovitsa the "glittering in all directions" white stone church of St.Demetrius first singled out Moscow as one of the most perspective table towns of Great Russia.

Reconstruction of Moscow at the time of Michael Horobit, then active growth of the town in the second part of the 13th century at the time of Alexander Nevsky, his sons Demetrius and especially Daniel were stimulated by the inflow of people from southern Russian lands. From tatars' attacks people went away to the North-East "behind the forest" and settled here in Moscow land. It was not very cosy for the southern people to move further to the snowy North. It is known that at that time and later many families from Kiev, Chernigov, even from Volynj land moved to Moscow.

Though in Moscow the great handicraft-merchant settlement was developing in the east part from Kremnik, in the general town structure the *nestle of villages* still dominated, which gave Moscow majestic look. And the built monasteries, mentioned in 1237 as though substituted the former pagan towns on tops of the hills. According to I.E.Zabelin's supposition these monasteries could be in Zaneglimenie the nearest to Kremnik monasteries of Adoration of the Holy Cross, St.Nicetas and Resurrection. So, they appeared at the time of the first princes Vladimirs. At the Great Settlement in 1296 at the time of Daniel the monastery of Epiphany, and behind the Moscow-river near the prince yard the monastery of St.Daniel with the stone church of Transfiguration appeared.

Besides the monasteries on the town's territory several more churches appeared. At the end of the first quarter of the 13th century Vladimir Vsevolodovich could build in the country prince yard a domestic church of St.Vladimir in Old Gardens, because already in the pre-Mongolian period the prince Vladimir Svyatoslavovich, who had baptized Russia, was canonized (the holiday is on 15, July). Michael Horobit till 1248, probably, built "in his name" the wooden church of Archangel Michael in the southern part of the vetche square in Kremnik. At the end of the 13th century during Daniel's time this church became a stone one. It is unknown by whom of the princes the wooden domestic church of Annunciation was founded, which became a stone one in 1293.

In one of Pskov chronicles kept in Pskov museum, there is the scripture: "In the summer of 6799 (1291) on 21, July,... , the town of Moscow was established near the Moscow-river." It is quite possible that in that year Daniel *extended* the Moscow fortress and this *Kremnik* existed till 1365, the time of the Kremlin's construction during Demetrius' time (Donskoy). The data about existence on this joined territory of khan yard, which in 1365 was bought out by the metropolitanate Alexius who founded here Chudov monastery, allows to speak about extension of the ancient Bor-town to the East to the wall line of the present Red Square.

About Town

In ancient Russia a fortified settlement was called "gorod" (town) sometimes, its fortress, defence structures: walls, gates, towers. Defence is the main town's function. Other settlement functions: dwelling, hunting, trade, administrative, religious were under the town's cover, it provided stability of their existence. It is not possible to raise one of the functions, for instance, handicraft or trading, to the criteria of existence or non-existence of a town. But the presence of a fortress – "grad" – is such criteria.

In different time there were totally more than three thousand towns in Russia, and more than 150 of them were table towns. Almost all of them were wooden, small and only a few dozens of towns were relatively large.

The structure of the ancient Russian town was made of three parts. Usually, there was a fortress on the hill near a river, lake, called grad, gorod, krom, kremnik, detinets, ostrog. Outside near the main fortress gates, using the space for shooting in front of the wall, there was a trade place with stores and trade rows. Further, behind the trade place there was a settlement with yard buildings and gardens. During extension the town did not change its structure, it was just gradually corrected, became more complex: extending fortress pushed the trade place, which also became a big one, and growing settlement surrounded the trade place at all sides, stretching its streets to it. Settlements of big towns got the barriers: ostrog, middle town, outskirts town... Correction of growth was usually made after town fires. The above three-parts structure could be found both in hundreds of small towns, such as Ryazhsk, Shuya, Rzhev, Torzhok, Mozhaysk, Volokolamsk, Izborsk..., and in big ones: Pskov, Tverj, Rostov Veliky, Suzdal, Murom, Yaroslavlj... even in huge, according to medieval standards, Moscow.

Beginning from the 10th century there was another one and the main town structural element. If the town's basic part was a central wooden church, its main holy thing was the *cathedral* inside the fortress. The look of wooden town cathedrals of the 16th century is almost unknown. But from the 11th century till our time there are stone churches in many cities and towns. There are still moats and banks in some places, their descriptions and pictures are in historical documents of the centuries. There is the same data for trade places and settlements. Consideration of temple, fortress, trade place, settlement as a whole allows to understand the *contents and form* of a usual small ancient (Russian town as a creation of town-building art. Consideration should be, certainly, started from the town holy thing.

The "true marquee" of God and men is the *new Heavenly Town of Jerusalem*, descending from heaven... Now the *church is its image*", – St.Andrew of Caesarea wrote about the Christian temple in the Commentary on the Hevelation of St.John the Theologian. It seems to be difficult to see in the image of a small church building the image of a whole town. However, if to compare the ancient pictures of the Divine Town, some Jerusalems-Zions (shrines) of our temples, as well as stone temples of our ancient towns, the result is amazing.

The Divine Town, according to the description of St.John the Theologian, has four corners on its plan, equal in width, length, height (cube), has 12 gates: three ones in the direction of each part of the world. "Christ is called the great church wall, high and protecting everybody living in the Sacred Town; its twelve gates are the Apostles, by whom we are *led to the Father*," – St.Andrew explained. There is Cod's Table in the centre of the Town, made by divine powers. Cod film- sell is sitting "on cherubs".

Showing the Divine Town, ancient artists often used short forms of its image, limiting themselves only to its characteristic elements-signs. Thus, the walls often were not shown, and the gates were moved. In this case the town consisted only of the gates indicating the Apostles. Above the town (or in its centre) sometimes the Table was shown, crowned with cross, – Christ's symbol. Exactly in these forms, for example, the two Jerusalems of the 15th century of Moscow Cathedral of Dormition, are made. The forms of the Small Jerusalem are most clear: it is a cube with walls made from gates in which there is Christ, Theotocos, St.John the Predecessor, Apostles, signifying the christened peoples of the four parts of the world; Angels serve at Table; above all is the church dome finished with the cross,– Christ's symbol. There are only the Apostles at the bottom in the Big Jerusalem.

After these descriptions and comparisons it is not difficult to read now also the heavenly symbolics of forms of our stone churches which fully conform to our town-like forms of shrines – Jerusalems. The forms of the churches of the 12th century are especially similar to this effect: the churches of Intercession near Nerli, of Transfiguration in Pereyaslavlj, of Nativity in Bogolyubov, of St.Demetrius of Thessalonica in Vladimir... Many similar, canonically pure in their town-like symbolics one-cupola churches were hunt in the 11th – 13th and other centuries.

If *cathedral meant the Divine Jerusalem*, which as though descended to Russian town from God's heaven, fortress signified earthly Jerusalem. Appearance of Golden Gates like those in Jerusalem (then in Constantinople) in the time of Christ, in Kiev, Vladimir allow to say so. There were also Iron Gates in Vladimir and Jerusalem. Besides inside an ancient Russian town there was a krom – warehouses, used in siege. And one passage from Synodal Bible a Russian bibliophile of the 15th century translated: "and David existed in krom"– it is about Jerusalem of the time of King David. It should be recognized, however, that the symbolics of the earthly Jerusalem was shown slightly and from time to time in ancient towns-fortresses of Russia, sometimes its traces can be met only in large table towns.

Trade place and settlement were evaluated "closer to earth". Trade people were as though sent away out of temple and fortress. The principle "commodity- money-commodity" flourished outside Russian town and had nothing to do with it, though some towns got "trade" names (Torzhok, Menjsk, Laljsky torg...). Certainly merchants-guests built churches at trade places, especially in the names of their guards – St.Nicholas the Miracle-worker, St.Parasceva the Iconium, Sts. Cosmas and Damian, and settlement people united into church-street communities built churches in settlements. Nevertheless, the ancient Russian town as a whole was not just "the product of separation of agricultural economy from handicraft", as it used to be thought of. Almost all Russian people in ancient towns (even artisans) were occupied in agricultural work, did not with mother-earth. It was not by chance that 90% of Russian population was agricultural.

Iconic, architectural and town-building images come from sacral sources of culture. Understanding of these images is not possible without personal comprehension of the essence of Christian outlook. All European and Eastern Christian art can be understood only under one condition – necessary realization of each onlooker of sacramental world of Christian mythology, running through the entire history of our civilization. Church has the gift to communicate each person to the most High, to the universe, including nature, culture, civilization. Through the Church's Images and Word we are capable of penetrating into sacramental secrets of being and to build God's house inside ourselves, Man's purpose and denomination in the world and the world's structure as the image of God's Town – Divine Kingdom and Paradise – become clear. Explaining church's object symbolics, father Leo Lebedev describes in his works canonical understanding of this phenomenon.

Church's Object Symbolics

Dogma states the presence of certain blissful connection between icon (image) and the prototype (archetype), that is why it becomes possible, venerating icon, venerate what is shown in it, and icon itself becomes a holy thing, requiring "respectful veneration". Dogma also mentions in general context Cross, Gospel and "other holy things", which means that not only icons as images of Christ, Theotocos, Angels and Saints, but all other church liturgical symbols have the same connection with the prototypes, i.e. with what they depict or symbolize. This is quite in conformity with the theory of image which was developed in Eastern Church for ages. Byzantine theory of image always had as the starting point the truth of the "real not imaginable" God's embodiment. As a result of Cod's embodiment all heavenly and spiritual in Christ and his Body – Church – is inevitably striving to its expression in the earthly material. So, icon and other Church symbols become such expression. Icon's doctrine significance is evident. So let's pay more attention to the principle of similarity to the Prototype. This principle concerns not only icons of Jesus Chris, but all icons and all images and sign of the Church's liturgical life as a whole.

These principle roots are in the furthest ancient time. For ages various symbols-images and symbols-signs are used in religion and magics of all peoples and always serve one purpose – to establish contact between image and original, and the more likeness to the original the more successful is the contact.

Heavenly Jerusalem in symbolic forms of canonical Russian ortodox temples of 10th-12th centuries. Scheme of G. Mokeev.

Combined experience of the mankind since the most ancient time kept identical knowledge about mysterious real contact of image with the original and that this contact is reached by likeness, that all these roots in the ontological nature of existence.

If pagan religions and magics by their images and signs reached contact either with earthly creatures or with demonic powers of the hegenna, images and signs of Christ's Church are to provide vivid blissful contact with true God, divine world of God's angels and Heaven of the Victorious Church of Saints. Principle of likeness is kept here too, but it is significantly changed and implemented by other new conditions.

The most important thing in contact between image and original in church symbolics through likeness is that such contact is implemented in Christ, through Christ and by the Holy Spirit. ...According to St.Theodore of the Studion, "original and image in some way exist in each other". "The mores the image is similar to the original, – this teacher of the Church writes, – the more it incorporates adoration in general without adoration of the matter on which it is based. The nature of the image is that it is identical to the original in likeness and is different in essence. (nature – L.L.).

...Hallowing of church symbols and Images "from water and the Holy Spirit" in the font of Christening to such extent as man is "from ashes and earth (mother) is different from man's Christening to the extent as mar is different from an other visual creation. But hallowing by water and the Holy Spirit of church things is nothing but their mysterious change into objects of new matter, spiritual one, ascending by such hallowing to the existence "of new sky and new earth", "new Jerusalem". Thus, the purpose of all sacraments, prayers, rites of the Church with all their material subjects and symbols the top and focus of which is the Holy Eucharistia, is the "pass over (Jewish – "pascha") of man and creature from this world to the other... new reality, realization of new creation in Christ and the Holy Spirit".

Overwhelming figurativeness of church existence also includes all object symbolics of the Church. Spiritual and material, eternal and temporary, divine and earthly nature of images stipulates, as it can be seen easily, that image, not loosing its earthly material qualities natural to this temporary existence, at the same time belongs to the other reality of the Divine Kingdom. Image is a special reality. It is equal neither to earthly, nor to the divine being, but is, like the whole Church, according to the brilliant sentence of A.Riu, the personal kernel of God's presence in the world and the world – in God. According to St.Maximus the Confessor, image "returns to the prototype".

After all the above-said we can understand how it happens. Hallowing of Images by the Church, including sanctifying of object symbols by water and the Holy Spirit, makes the direct blissful penetration by energy of the pure divine reality of the Heavenly Kingdom into material forms of the

EXTERIOR SYMBOLICS OF RUSSIAN ORTODOX TEMPLES OF 10th – 13th CENTURIES.
Scheme of G. Mokeev.

Form	Contents
THE TOP, WITCH IS HIGHER THAN HEAVEN – THE HEAVEN OF HEAVEN	
Dove	– Symbol of the Holy Spirit
Cross	– Symbol of Christ
Tsata (⤻ – up/down)	– Symbol of the highest worthiness, here of the King of Kings (Heavenly/Earthly)
Orb-mirror (later)	– Autocraty over the Heavenly and Earthly kingdoms (handed to Archangel Michael)
Lob, "lemekh" (later)	– the Frontal place from Adam's forehead), great quantity of the Heavenly Powers
Rings, triangles...	– Ranges of the Heavenly Powers
"Drum"	– Throne from the Heavenly Powers (cyboria-carrying ranges)
Windows	– Heavenly light: of Christ, also through the Theotokos, Apostles
"Tribun", later Increased by arches	– "Podprestolie" - Heavenly Powers (cherubs, rings)
Temple's wall as a whole	– Christ's body
UPPER PART OF THE WALLS – HEAVEN HEAVENLY CHURCH, HEAVENLY TOWN	
Arches-chambers	– Gates of the Heavenly Town
Images of the walls	– Pictures of the seen Paradise
Images of David, Soloman, Heracles...	– Souls of the righteous in the Heavenly Kingdom
Flora, birds, animals	– Paradisical gardens
Windows	– Christ's light, through the Apostles
LOWER PART OF THE WALLS - THE EARTH, EARTHLY CHURCH	
Archature with Saints	– "Earthly angels" near the Paradise
Walls, the lower part	– Christian peoples, coming from the four parts of the world and making the temple
The Holy Gates	– the Advent of Christ into this world, Christ's via dolorosa

The structure of a usual ancient Russian town: temple – town – trade place – settlement. Temple symbolized Heavenly Jerusalem...
Trade place was "sent away" from the temple and even from the town nearer to the trade-handicraft settlement. Scheme of G. Mokeev.

present temporary existence. Unity of the image and the prototype in the face (look) of the expressed becomes possible, so the Church's symbol is not a conventional sign of the expressed. Through the likeness to the prototype and sanctifying it gets united with it not in nature, but in the entity of the expressed one and in those energies, which act in both of them in the same way. ...As we have partially seen already, there is the tightest bilateral connection between the Church's object images and man, people, included into it through belief and Christening. In the basis of it is the fact that people carry God's image and that they are "small churches", even their bodies are "God's temples", for man was created "to the image and likeness" of God. So, the main principles of his unity with God also are the likeness and sanctifying by "water and the Holy Spirit". But unlike material images of the Church Man in his earthly spoilt state is called to strive to God-likeness by conscious, "often very difficult!" spiritual heroic deed. This spiritual-praying heroic deed is also committed not casually, not at one's own sweet will, but according to the canons and rules of the church's Acts and rules of orthodox asceticism, which have been developed for centuries by hermits of piety and compose a whole science of true ascend to God, unity with Christ. One of the most important elements of this science are the rules of mutual relations of a believer with the Church, including with the temple and all that is carried out and is in it, i.e. with object symbolics too.

Salvation of creature in Christ begins from man. But for his salvation, in its turn, the sanctified basis of all the world – "water" ("world's matter") is used. Then man creates material images and symbols of the Church with this most important purpose, so that they served for the salvation of man, but in this way he also implements salvation of all the sanctified matter... All world's elements are sanctified in the Church: earth, water, fire, air, as well as various metals, substances, minerals, paints, forms, images, sounds, melodies, rhythms, wordings, etc., thoroughly chosen by the Church. All this, not loosing its earthly qualities, communicates the Divine World, together with man commits its pass over ("pascha") from the earthly reality to the reality of the other existence of the Divine Kingdom). This is in the literal meaning the construction of that "new Jerusalem", about which the Revelation of St.John the Theologian tells us.

...Till now we talked about subject symbolics only in iconography, icons in their narrow special meaning. What about the other symbols-images and symbols-signs in the object symbolics of the Church? For many of them are used by the Church historically by chance... For example, structure of orthodox temple and its altar seem, at first sight, to be fortuitous. Catacombs chapels were the prototype here. Thus, the starting point was the coffin of the venerated martyr, around which and in front of which all the rest was arranged in accordance with concrete conditions of underground premises, where the ceilings are supported by the necessary in such case pillars. But already in the Roman catacombs it is possible to see the purposeful, symbolical separation of the altar from the main space of the temple by making it higher and by altar barrier (railing). Figuratively speaking, this form of temple in the most general principal features was as though cast in the earth of catacombs, so that later, after persecutions of the Church stop, being taken out to the surface of earth, to serve as sample (type) for the majestic cross-cupolas churches of Byzantine style. In them the clear features of catacombs are kept. Narrow windows, through which the day light hardly penetrates, it has more symbolical than practical meaning: the quantity of windows– two or three – indicates Christ's light, cognised in two entities and that of the Holy Trinity – "light" which "shines in the darkness, and the darkness did not envelope him". Arched ceilings and especially the space under the cupola in the central part of Temple conforms to what was in catacombs. But there it was necessary to take out as much of rock as possible to be closer to the surface of the earth and make a well of light (luminair) for the practical purpose to light the premise during the day time. In cross-cupola Byzantine churches the under-cupola space of the central part is mad high purposefully, and in the centre of it there is already not the luminair, but the image of "The true Light

That came into the world" – God Jesus Christ, blessing the faithful... The pillars, supporting the arched church's roof and implementing its symbolical division into three parts: altar, the church itself, the frame ledge (space for the proclaimed in ancient time). The Church sees in such temple's structure a great dogmatic meaning. Division of the temple into three parts is understood as conformity to the Holy Trinity, as well as to the division of the world into three parts: Divine being, angelic world, earthly human being. Or to the three-parts composition of man: spirit, soul, body. In three-parts division of the temple altar signifies the "heavenly" area of being, the other space signifies the "earthly one"; or soul and body of man (in dichotomic terminology). There can be other conformities.

Numerous images of the heavenly dwellers in icons and wall paintings, splendid, and in some cases just luxurious decoration of temple inside and outside, and especially inside make the whole temple the image of the Universe. But transfigured Universe, i.e. the image of "the new heaven and new earth", as well as the image of the Church and besides the Triumphant Church (both meanings of the "new earth" and the Divine Church of Saints become so close that are often synonyms). Here we find – again the double character of symbolism: the temple is the cave, underground and at the same time it is the Divine World shining in the glory of the Divine Kingdom.

Attention must be paid to the fact that such symbolism of the temple providentially coincides with the symbolics of the Holy Sepulchre. The latter is historically also the underground, a cave where in the main part of the burial chamber there is the stone bed on which the Saviour's Body rested till His Resurrection. However, spiritually, it is the paradise and even more than that. "As the Life-giver, as the most Splendid in the Paradise He truly appeared to be the lightest in the Kingdom, oh, Christ, Your Sepulchre, the source of our Resurrection," – they sing in canticles of the Orthodox Church...

In any case, taking into account any comments, the meaning of the "Divine dwelling", "the Highest Heaven", some "divine" holy place, is firmly attributed to the altar. About it much is said in all the liturgical comments, various "Testimonies", in many words of saint fathers, in all the Helms books, in separate works like the "Book about Temple" of St.Symeon of Thessalonica (15th c.), in the modern text-books about liturgies.

How true is all this? How is the orthodox temple, especially its altar, similar to the "divine" prototype. Is there such prototype at all? Let us dare check this circumstance.

For this it is enough to take the Revelation of St.John the Theologian and read it attentively, as though to have a look at the other reality of the mysterious Divine World.

Through "a door was open in heaven" a marvellous view is seen: "a throne was set in heaven and one sat on the throne". Around this throne there were other seats for 24 elders-priests. There were "seven lamps of fire" burning before the throne (table) of God Almighty; before the throne there was the golden credence, under which there were "the souls of those killed for God's Word". Angels tightened with golden belts come to the throne and credence and commit the divine service. They have golden censers, cups, books, "the eternal Gospel". Angels, elders-priests and the righteous bring to God eulogy, prayers, requests, sing: "Holy, holy, holy, Lord God Almighty", "Halleluia", etc. This Temple is sometimes "open in heaven"...It is easy to see how all this conforms to everything which goes on and is in the altar of the orthodox church (especially a big one, for instance, a cathedral), when the Divine Liturgy is implemented by a bishop with priests and clergymen. Here also sometimes the Holy Gate opens in the iconostasis, through which it is possible to see the bishop occasionally, sitting in the "Heavenly Place" (the inside eastern part in the centre of altar). There are smaller seats for the clergymen around the bishop's seat. There are "seven lights of fire" in front of the "Heavenly Place", as well as the credence or "meal" (now – "table"), under it or more often in today's practice on it, in the corporal there are relicts of martyrs (or other saints). Deacons girt on breasts and waists, enter and exit, doing various rites, sometimes they hold censers, cups, books, the Gospel... They read and sing glorifications, prayers, requests, including "Holy, holy, holy, Lord God Almighty", "Halleluia", etc.

As it was already said above, in all works and comments on organization of Temple altar is made like the Divine World, "heaven", etc., but no work says; that in the Church's history altar was made or shall be made in accordance with the facts from the Revelation of St.John the Theologian! Altar of the orthodox Church was arranged historically by chance and not at once. Some important things (for example, the seven lights of fire) appeared in it in the Russian Church only in the 18th century.

Thus, we see a surprising example of providential and not occasional church symbolics, when God's Providence, the mysterious governing of the Holy Spirit, not infringing human free will and not supressing human creativeness, nevertheless lead it so that church symbols made by people come to full compliance with divine architypes.

If to remember that according to the common opinion of many saint fathers, people who are honoured to be in the Divine Kingdom, will see there nothing else, but the developing and disclosing Divine Liturgy, and take part in it, then the Liturgy carried out now during the earthly being, is the image of this Divine Liturgy, as it is especially well shown in "Mystagogia" of St.Maximus the Confessor.

It gives us full basis to come to the conclusion that not only the altar and its main holy things, but all the liturgical symbols of the orthodox church, introduced into the service conscientiously or by chance, but accepted by the Church's common intellect, comply to certain divine prototypes, are like them, have their energy, mysteriously contain their presence. So that means the canons in the church symbolics are originally not only human invention: they are God-aspired. It cannot be otherwise in the true Christ's Body – the Church! Here "there is nothing in exterior which was not the phenomenon of the interior world", for the "Word became body to unite all the divine and earthly under one Head – Christ".

The Flourishing Cross. Hieromonk Stephan (V.D. Linitskiy).

CHAPTER THREE

The Table Russian Land

The Grand Prince, John I (Kalita).
Painting. Faceted Palace.

The Grand Prince, St. Demetrius Donskoy.
Painting. Faceted Palace.

The meeting of the Vladimir Icon of the Theotokos. Moscow icon from the temple of St.Alexius the Metropolitanate of Moscow in Glinitschi. 1640s.

The Holy Trinity. Icon of A. Rublev.

St. Peter the Metropolitanate of Moscow with Life-description. Studio of Dionysius. 80s of 15th century.

St. Alexijis the Metropolitanate of Moscow with Life-description. Studio of Dionysius. Studio of Dionisius. 80s of 15th century.

Metropolitanate Hilarion, addressing in 1049 – the Grand Prince of Kiev Yaroslav the Wise, said about his father, prince the baptiser, the great Vladimir Svyatoslavich and about Kiev: "See the one who make the *table of your land beautiful...*" Better understanding of the table town of the Russian land was given by the chroniclers in the 14th century already not in respect of Kiev, but Vladimir Zalessky: "Glorious Vladimir is the table of the Russian land... In it Russian grand princes reign and have the table of the Russian land, where the grand prince of all Russia is nominated, they are first honoured. There is the marvellous grand *cathedral of the Host Holy Theotocos*, which is the Eulogy and Glory to all Christians of the world, the Source and Root of our piety..."

Here we see again the same signs of a table town, which were indicated for Moscow of the beginning of the 14th century. However, a much bigger scale is shown here: the prince is grand and of all Russia; the cathedral is the one of all orthodox Christians of Russia.

The princes of the small rural Moscow domain put the highest goal at the beginning of the 14th century – to make Moscow the Table of the Russian Land. At that time it was not easy to reach the highest grand princely power in the fight with many almost equal princes, and besides in the conditions of the Mongolian-Tatar yoke which robbed Russia. But in Moscow a bellicose prince was found for the first fight.

We shall tell in more details about the first grand prince Yuri Danilovich here only because his short reign in Vladimir was connected with the second grand princely raise of Moscow. As for Yuri, he did not do anything for Moscow town-building. But in contrast to his "power fight", the "spiritual and town- building" line of Moscow development, offered by metropolitanate Peter of Kiev and Vladimir, looks absolutely different. And if young Yuri could reach his goal only for a short period of time, finally, but quietly and for a long time it was done by the very old elder, who arranged his grave himself in the centre of Moscow Kremnik, for the second prince John Danilovich.

The First Grand Prince

Actions of Daniel Alexandrovich in connection of joining the nearest domains to Moscow were not firmly strengthened. In Pereyaslavlj – though the childless prince John Dmitrievich left it by his will to Daniel – in 1302 tributaries of the grand prince Andrew of Vladimir (Daniel's brother) enthroned

themselves. Moscow prince had to send them away by force and to leave them to reign in the town of his elder son Yuri. But Daniel died in the spring of 1303. "People of Pereyaslavlj came to his son, prince Yuri, and did not let him go to the funeral of his father", being afraid that the grand prince could take their towns by his power. Andrew Alexandrovich went to the Horde to look for his own truth. At that time Yuri with brothers unexpectedly conquered Mozhaysk and captured there prince Svyatoslav Glebovich, the younger brother of prince Alexander Glebovich of Smolensk. In 1304 Andrew Gorodetsky (the prince of Vladimir) died. Michael Yaroslavich of Tverj and Yuri Danilovich of Moscow went to the Horde now for the grand princely tag. Elder Michael got the tag, so for Yuri the perspective of promotion closed for many years.

While the princes argued in the Horde, sure of Michael's victory people of Tverj tried to conquer *Pereyaslavlj*. However, there was foreseeingly Ivan Danilovich already. Meeting the people of Tverj half-way, Moscovites and Pereyaslavtsy defeated their army utterly, killing the commander in this fight, boyard Akintha of gorodets. Returning from the Horde in 1306 Michael, being annnoyed, "went to Moscow, against the princes Yuri and John... and made peace with them". In winter Yuri ordered to kill prince Constantine Romanovich, who had been captured by his father, and finally made Kolomna his town. All the flow of the Moscow-river became the possession of the Moscow prince.

Somebody could hardly approve of such predatory extension of Moscow domain. Probably, in connection with this in 1308 Michael Yaroslavovich went from Vladimir with war against Yuri and "there war a fight near Moscow... and not conquering the town, he went back". Moscow appeared to be in a long and hard confrontation with Tverj and coalition of allies of the grand prince. Nevertheless, when in 1314 Yuri was called to the North-West, to the table of Novgorod, he left John in Moscow, and defended Novgorod and Pskov against agressive actions of German knights of Livonsky order.

Time went by and the Moscow prince had only one opportunity to get the grand princely table, which he used. In 1316 Yuri went to the Horde and lived there for two years. During this time he gained trust of khan Uzbek and even became his relative. Having got married to his sister Konchaka (after christening she became Agape), he got the tag for the grand princehood! With tatars army under the commandment of prince Kavdygay Yuri went against Michael. But the latter meeting him half-way near Kostroma... refused the grand princehood himself in favour of Yuri. It turned out that in Tverj the Kremnik burnt down and Michael returned there to build a wider fortress.

However, the tatars did not want to come back to the Horde empty-handed and were going to cross the Volga for robbery. Then the people of Kashin joined Tverichies and at the distance of 40 versts from Tverj near the village of Bertenevo Yuri was utterly defeated. During the battle Kavdygay treacherously went aside, and Michael captured Konchaka during the battle, as well as Yuri's brother Boris. Yuri himself escaped to Novgorod.

In Tverj Konchaka died unexpectedly: the news that she was poisoned spread out. And when Michael and Yuri came to the Horde again, Michael was killed atrociously. His body was brought to Moscow, from Moscow – to Tverj to the funeral; Konchaka's body was brought from Tverj to Rostov for the funeral. Yuri occupied triumphantly the grand princely table in Vladimir in 1319.

In 1322 Yuri was called again to the North-West and he led the war there of the people of Novgorod and the Swedish knights of king Magnus. At that time in the Horde Dmitry Mikhailovich of Tverj obtained the tag for the grand princehood. In 1325, whrjnYuri with dangerto his life got through Russia to the Morris, Dmitry killed him there "without the tsar's word", for which he was slaughtered himself already "upon the tsar's word". Alexander Mikhailovich got the tag for grand princehood. All returned to what it was before.

Yuri Danilovich was the grand prince not longer than three years. He got what he wanted. But by what efforts and means? M.N.Tikhomirov gave the following characteristic to the violent and self-willed Moscovite: "Behind the short and reserved chronicles we can see the image of a brave and rapacious prince, who could use the situation and not very scrupulous in means. The following short chronicle tells about the gloomy tragedy: "In that same winter prince Yuri killed prince Constantine of Ryazanj..." Yuri showed unusual activity and was not afraid of hardships and dangers. Enemies made a trap for the Moscow prince in Suzdal, but in vain. Perfidity, treachery, traps, sudden stacks are the features of knight- bandits modes of fight, so characteristic for medieval West-European barons, attract our attention when we read the chronicles about the reign of Yuri Danilovich. Anyway, his enemies were the same, the princes of Tverj who poisoned the captured Yuri's wife".

Historians made the shades a little darker. Konchaka could be secretly poisoned by some of Moscovites (if she was poisoned at all), and not Tverichies, who realized very well that it would lead to a very dangerous conflict with the Horde. Certainly, everybody condemned Yuri, who had got the khan's tag by slyness and marriage. Hut Yuri, for example, like a knight, did not leave the people of Novgorod in their battle with the Swedish. He continued to fight: sieged Vyborg, even founded the fortress Oreshek in 1323 at the mouth of the Neva, while the Tverichies took his grand princehood behind his back, for which he had been fighting desperately for nearly 20 years.

Evidently, many liked Yuri, even the people of Novgorod famous for their obstinacy and the people of Pskov, even his enemies – tatars. His honour and haughtiness were not less than those of the three grand princes, with whom he had to fight. But it was the fight for power and... that speaks for itself.

Sage And Cunning One

Russian metropolitanate Peter conferred in Constantinople, appeared in Vladimir Zalessky in 1309. At once he was on very bad terms with grand prince Michael, and especially with bishop Andrew of Tverj. Living in Vladimir he started visiting more often Yuri and John in Moscow. Hospitable Danilovichies gave him a yard in Kremnik (more exactly, in the Krom liquidated for this purpose) near the church of St.John the Predecessor on Bor. However, churches in Moscow were not big, they were crowded and not quite suitable for the Head of the Russian Church. Besides, the metropolitanate had a numerous retinue: body-guards, vicegerent, foreman, many other boyards and servants. The priestly yard was the focus of spiritual power, embracing all parts of the Russian land. M.N.Tikhomirov wrote about it: "The old tradition connected for Russian people the idea about the "reigning town" with the place where the tsar and metropolitanate lived. Magnificent divine services for the occasion of confirmation for bishop, when in the capital the highest hierarchies gathered from other towns, constant contacts with Constantinople and princely capitals in Russia , meetings and seeing-off of metropolitanates and bishops, splendid religious rites, which medieval people liked so much, – became the property of Moscow".

Metropolitanate Peter said to John Danilovich: "If you, my son, listen to me and build the *church of the Host Holy Theotocos* in your town... *you will be more famous than other princes*, and your sons and grandsons from generation to generation will be famous as well; and *the town will be glorified* among all Russian towns; and *priests will live* in it. Its hands will be on the shoulders of its enemies, and God will be glorified in it; and my bones will be buried in it, too." In the words of metropolitanate Peter, told by writers of his life, the way, which Ivan Danilovich was to follow, was indicated. First of all it was necessary to build a church in the name of the Theotocos. Then the three wills were implemented by themselves: to obtain the grand princely table, to make Moscow the table town of Russia, to transfer the centre of the Russian Church to it.

However, seeing that neither Yuri, nor John does or is able to do anything about it, Peter decided to move this hard business himself from the dead point – he began to realize his own advice. First, he arranged a new permanent metropolitan yard to the North from the square. Then on 4, August, 1326, he himself with his own hands founded on the place of the ramshackle church of St.Demetrius of Thessalonica the new white stone cathedral of Dormition. Founding the cathedral during the time inconvenient for construction. Peter hurried, because he felt the death coming: he even established a coffin for himself in the cathedral's altar. Really, in December Peter died and was buried in the started cathedral. Moscow princes later acquired from the Constantinople's Patriarch canonization of Peter, who became the first "Moscow and all Russia miracle-worker".

St. Peter, metropolitanate, at the foundation of the cathedral of the Assumption of Moscow Kremlin. Icon feast "St.Peter, metrqpolitanate". 15th century.

After Peter's death all his prophecies became true. The new metropolitanate Greek Theognostus gradually began to live in Moscow more in the new metropolitan yard. Besides that in 1328 the new stone cathedral was built, and prince John Danilovich got the khan's tag for grand princehood. It so happened that at that time Tverichies did not stand tatars' violences and rose against the tributaries. Prince Alexander Mikhailovich had to support them. Tatars were defeated in Tverj, and the grand prince ran away first to Pskov, then abroad.

The cathedral of Dormition in Moscow was made at once the real symbol of the new "raising" grand princely capital of Russia. Near the northern inside lateral altar of Veneration of St. Apostle Peter's Chains metropolitanate Peter – the recent head of the Russian Orthodox Church – was buried, who got the title of "the first Moscow metropolitanate" after his death. In the southern inside lateral altar of St.Demetrius of Thessalonica the first grand prince Yuri Danilovich was buried.

Thus, Moscow announced its pretensions seriously and irrevocably in 1329. Time of reign of John Danilovich was remarkable in many respects. After the killing of tatars' tributaries in Tverj, he made the unrealized "brother-in-law" khan Uzbek give him the right to collect the Horde's taxes from Russian domains. Collecting it, Moscow prince got a big "economic" and very "visual" advantage in regard of rural princes in addition to the political one. Chronicler of Tverj gave Kalita the following characteristics: "Great constraint began, because grand princehood was given to great John Danilovich of Moscow". Not robbing rural princes, he did not forget to fill in his bottomless kalita (wallet). And being a cunning politician, he managed to become famous among people as a generous tsar: "They called him Kalita because he was very generous and always had a kalita on himself full of silver coins which he gave away as much as he took out wherever he went..."

In connection with this John Kalita's reign was noted in Russian chronicles. "Sat Grand Prince John Danilovich in grand princehood of all Russia and since then there was great silence for 40 years and the vile people stopped attacking the Russian land and killing Christians. And Christians had a rest and restored after the great hardships and violences of tatars, and there was great silence since then all over the earth".

The First Builder Of Table Moscow

After foundation of the cathedral of Dormition metropolitanate Peter called "somebody by the name Protase to make him the town's elder: because there was no prince then in the town. As for Protase, he was an honest man and famous for good deeds. And said to him: "Child, I am leaving this life." After these words the metropolitanate gave all his savings, "bequeathing to spend them on finishing the cathedral. In two years after his righteous death, the cathedral was finished and hallowed by Prochorus, the bishop of Rostov". In 1329 the cathedral was finished with building of the inside lateral altar in the northern part of Veneration of St. Apostle Peter's Chains. In the same 1329 to the South from the cathedral the high octahedral white stone church of St.John, author of "The Ladder" was built "under the bells". If the cathedral was built for the account of the metropolitanate this one was Kalita's promised church, built in the name of the saint prince's son Ivan Ivanovich Krasny (handsome).

In 1330 at Kalita's wish (in his yard) the stone cathedral of Transfiguration on Bor was built instead of a wooden one. Near it a monastery was arranged under the government of an archimandrite and here the monks from the robbed country monastery of the Saviour were transferred. But the latter was not liquidated. As the chronicler noted: "Together the both monasteries underdone governing and by one flock are well arranged."

In 1331 "there was a blaze in Moscow and the town of Kremnik burnt (in the analogous news of 1354 Moscow fortress was also called "Kremnik").

In 1333 after liquidation of consequences of the blaze, the white stone church of Archangel Michael is built, which soon became the place of repose of John Kalita and his descendants. The dimensions of the church were not less than that of the cathedral of Dormition and it was built during three years.

In this year prince Symeon Ivanovich got married, the elder Kalita's son. In one of miniatures, as mentioned above, the wedding was shown in the octahedral chamber Gridnitsa – throne hall of grand princes, covered by helmet-like coating. The stone Gridnitsa was, perhaps, also built instead of the wooden one after the fire in 1331. Two octahedral buildings: the church under the bells of St.John, the author of "the Ladder" in the East and Gridnitsa in the West occupied the places on both parts of the vetche's square, being at the flanks of the southern facade of the cathedral of Dormition. The square, surrounded by white stone buildings from all sides got, perhaps, from that time the name "Krasnaya (beautiful) Cathedral Square".

I.K.Kondratiev wrote at the end of the last century, according to some detected data, that the cathedral of Dormition, founded in 1326, fell down (perhapns during the fire of 1331) and was rebuilt in 1336. The wide temple columns, which were found recently during archaelogic excavations (2 x 2 m) testify about the possibility of possible reconstruction and fortification of the columns during the restoration works after possible fall of the tower-like cathedral's, too.

In 1337 "there was a fire in Moscow again, 18 churches burnt down", and in 1343 during another fire the chronicler noted that during 15 years there were four great fires (probably, Moscow was burnt intentionally by Tverj's supporters). Besides reconstruction of wooden churches and repair of stone ones they had to build again and this time oak Kremnik in 1338-1339.

Finally, before the decease (March of 1340), John Kalita "founded the church of Epiphany, and after his passing away up to God and upon his order, this marvellous church was finished in this sacred monastery by his boyard called Protase".

The church was built in Kremnik in the yard of the settlement monastery of Epiphany, founded at the time of Daniel in 1296, but, probably, destroyed several times by fires and Tverichies. Like in case with the monastery of the

Kremnik of table Moscow in the middle of 14th century.

Protase's complex of buildings.
1 – white stone cathedral of the Assumption, founded by St. Peter, metropolitanate, in 1326 and finished by Protase by 1329,
2 – white stone church of St.John the author of "The Ladder" under the bells of 1329,
3 – white stone cathedral of the Saviour of 1330,
4 – white stone cathedral of Archangel Michael of 1333,
5 – white stone cathedral of Epyphany of 1340-1342,
Oak town Kremnik restoreff by Protase in 1338-1340 after the fire of 1337:
6 – Great gates (the second upper ones),
7 – Dmitrievskie,
8 – Nikolskie,
9 – Neglinenskie gates and bridge (the names of the gates are supposed).
The following is also shown:
10 – Vetche Platform,
11 – Town's bell,
12 – princely Gridnitsa,
13 – grand princely temple of the Annunciation of 1293

Reconstruction of G. Mokeev

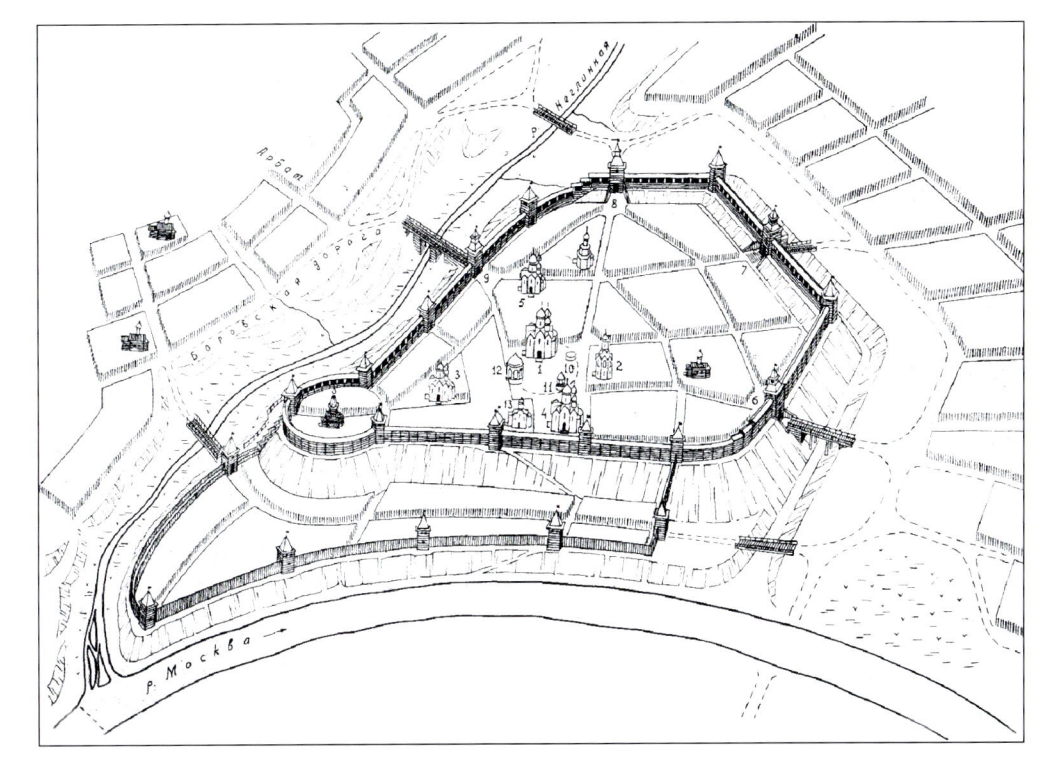

Saviour, here the monasteries of Epyphania "became double" and "both started to he well arranged". The town cathedral, in spite of its foundation by the grand prince, shall be also excluded from the definition "Kalita's temples". It became the burial-vault of Moscow boyards and, so, was built at their combined money. In it the builder of the cathedral Protase was buried himself, then his family.

Protase's house was near the cathedral of Epiphany, to the East from it. It is quite possible that the boyard gave himself part of his yard for construction of the town's monastery of Epiphany when it was necessary to transfer it from the settlement to Kremnik. It was very important for that time, because the monastery became the source of enlightenment. Two of its monks soon became outstanding ones:

Alexius (future metropolitanate) and Stephan, the brother of St.Sergius of Radonezh, who became the Hegumen of the monastery (as well as the spiritual father of the grand prince Symeon the Proud and Moscow nobility.

As soon as the first cathedral of Dormition and the last cathedral of Epiphany were "finished" by Protase, it is logical to to think that the other stone buildings were built not without his participation during that period of time. Besides that his administrative role in creation of the main Moscow cathedral is undoubtful.

If earlier, in the 12th-13th centuries, inside the Moscow fortress wooden and stone churches appeared one after another in different time, in 1326-1342 due to continuous construction a *single ensemble* of white stone temples of Moscow central square was created. Besides, oak Kremnik was built anew. There were several customers of the construction: the metropolitanate, the grand prince, boyards, and the constructor was one!

The whole complex of all Kremnik's buildings was constructed by Protase. At that time it was of state importance.

"A man honest and faithful", of noble origin and "responsible" was to be the head of it participate directly in it. That is why this affair was trusted to a boyard, though he had been a commander in his youth, prince's vicegerent. He could be and was the chief of the contract, even a work superintendent and architect. In any case Protase could be called the creator of the single town's complex of the new all-Russian capital, the first builder of table Moscow.

Protase came from Vladimir together with prince Daniel Alexandrovich and already during his time he was the commander of a thousand warriors. During Yuri's time he was, probably, a commander and at the time of Kalita he took part in expulsion "of the best people" from Rostov the Great, besides he built Radonezh for the refugees. Daniel died in 1303; Protase was to be 30 (as the commander) in case he came late, at the border of the 13th-14th centuries. During construction of the cathedral of Dormition he was over 55, and during the construction of the cathedral of Epiphany – over 70. The temples, Gridnitsa, oak Kremnik, were thus, built by an old experienced man who could not hold the sword.

The Preceptor And Warrior

Getting up to the grand princely table, in the first half of the 14th century Moscow princes undertook during that difficult time the hard responsibility for thr destiny of Russian people, for whom everything was destroying, slaughtering, fatal then.

First there was the *civil fight* for the supreme power of Moscow, Tverj and other princes. Tverichies came to Moscow several times, burnt its settlements,robbed, captured people; Moscovites answered in the same way. When Moscow princes won the fight for power inside the Russian land, battles with outside enemies began.

John Kalita and Protase – the first builders of table Moscow. Icon feast "St. Peter, metropolitanate". 15th century.

Upon instigation of princes Lithuanian troops came to Moscow several times with Olgerd at the head, capturing people, burning villages on their way, destroying town settlements of Mozhaysk, Volokolamsk, Moscow. At that time Lithuania conquered one after another the Southern Russian domains ravaged by Mongols, and began to seek power over the Russian land. "Litovtschina" made the process of "Moscow rise" hard.

In spite of it Moscow princes after the middle of the 14th century were already ready morally for the battle with "*tatartschina*". First Symeon the Proud and John Krasny (Kalita's children) defended actively Russian border towns and lands from tatars' attacks, kept the "Horde's exit". Finally Demetrius Donskoy started active war with the Horde.

The start of war with tatars was connected, strange as it might seem, with the activity of metropolitanate Alexius. It is directly said to the effect in a chart of Constantinople's Patriarch: "After some time, the grand prince of Moscow and all Russin died, who did not only leave before his death his son the present grand prince Demetrius for the care of that metropolitanate, but also *trusted the administration and defence of all the domain*, not trusting anybody else because there were many exterior enemies, ready to attack from all sides, and interior ones, who envied his power and looked for a convenient moment to grab it."

The monastic name Alexius got at 20, entering the community of the monastery of Epiphany in 131&. Unusual sharp mind, big talents, virtuos life, self-perfection made him famous already during the time of Symeon the Proud, – when he was close to another monk, Stephan, the brother of St.Sergius of Radonezh: becoming the Hegumen of the monastery, Stephan became the spiritual father of the grand prince and many Moscow boyards. During the time of Symeon Alexius became the bishop of Vladimir.

Soon the old metropolitanate Greek Theognostus made him close to himself, making him his vicegerent for the time of his absence in Moscow. And when Theognostus died in 1353 from the "black death" – plague (from it Symeon the

Moscow plan of the 1st half of 14th century. Appearance of "three merlons" of the main streets in the Great settlement in Zagorodie (Zaneglimenie) and Zarechie (Zamoskvorechie). Reconstruction of G. Mokeev.

Gridnitsa in Moscow Kremnik of 1st half of 14th century. According to the miniature of 15th century, depicting the wedding of prince Symeon the Proud.

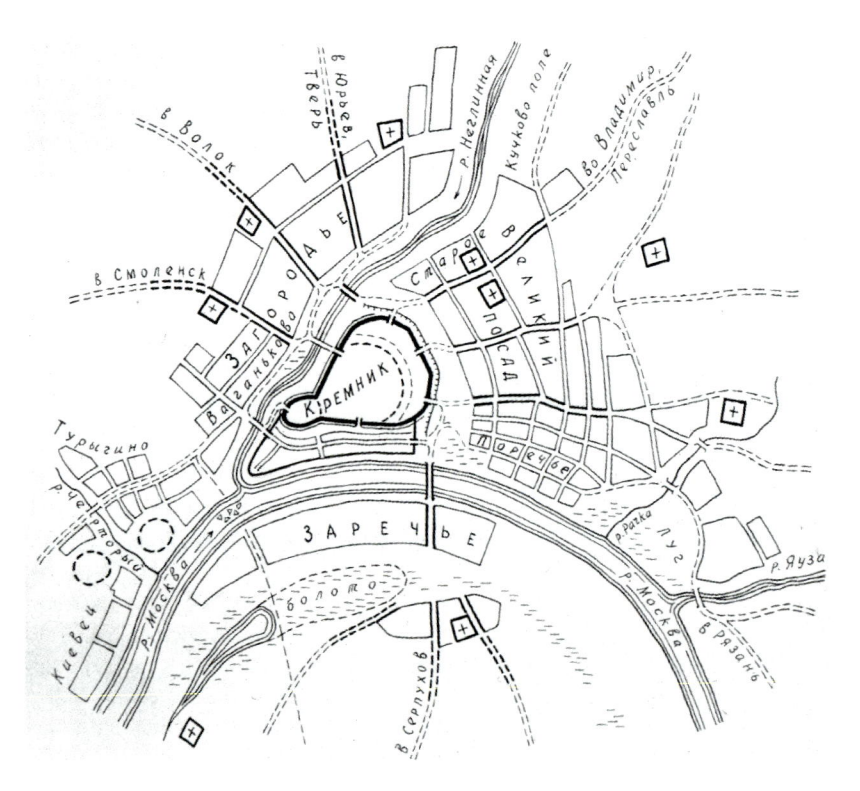

Prod with all his big family dies too), Alexius was sent to Constantinople. Living there for a year he came back to Moscow as the metropolitanate during the time of prince John Ivanovich Krasny.

After decease of John Krasny in 1359 the role of metropolitanate Alexius was especially remarkable. His son Demetrius was 9 then and the tag for grand princehood was given to prince Demetrius Konstantinovich of Suzdal. At that time the metropolitanate became Moscow's governor: "Called to teach peace and consent, he was carried away by wars, battles and arguments." In 1363 Demetrius became 12.

At that time there was "confusion" in the Horde and two khans appeared instead of one. Demetrius with the help of boyards got another tag for grand princehood. Putting Demetrius on a horse, Moscow boyards went in troops against the prince of Suzdal and sent him away from the grand princely table to Vladimir. Behind all the actions of Demetrius and Moscovites the firm handling of an experienced preceptor was felt. Even in the following episode: in 1366 Demetrius married Eudocia, the daughter of Demetrius Konstantinovich; the enemies were thus reconciled. Life of Demetrius Donskoy was full of military battles. From 1363 to 1380 there nearly was not one year when the Moscow prince did not go somewhere with Moscow troops. In 1365 his mother, grand princess Alexanra died, and after Moscow fire he had to be busy with construction of the new Kremlin in 1367. In 1368 he defends Moscow together with metropolitanate Alexius from prince Olgerd's army. In 1370 Demetrius made his own battle in Tverj, then defended Moscow again from Olgerd. In 1371 the Moscow prince defeated utterly the people of Ryazanj near Skornitschev, in 1372 he was with his army near the Oka-river against Olgerd, in 1373 he was with his army near the Oka-river again in expectation of tatars' attack, who ravaged Ryazanskaya land, in 1375 he sieged Tverj, in 1376 he defended the Oka's banks again from Mamay's tatars. During all this time Demetrius Ivanovich "guarded and defended the Russian land by his courage". But since that year the character of the guard changed, because two contrasting events happened.

In 1377 the army of Moscow and Suzdal (without participation of Demetrius) sieged the Great Bulgary, and then was fully crushed in the battle near the river Pianj. However, in 1378 in the battle near the river Vozh Uemetrius crushed Begich's army in open battle. The significance of the Vozh battLe was that Demetrius had to change abruptly from the tactics of defence to offensive one through the force of circumstances and events. And it led directly to the collision of all Russian forces with the Golden Horde in 1380.

The victorious Kulikovskaya battle is widely known. It glorified the name of Demetrius Donskoy, and his brothers-in-arms Vladimir Andreevich of Serpukhov, Demetrius of Bobrok-Volynsky and others. And though Russia had to pay the tributary to the Golden Horde, all Russians knew that being united they will be free. But these hundred years were spent on the union of Russian lands.

The image of prince Demetrius Donskoy, whom not everybody knows well enough till now, is interesting. Already at 30 the prince "was very strong and courageous, tall and stout, with wide shoulders and very heavy; with

Round stone vetche Tomb and Town's bell in Moscow Kremnik of 2nd half of 14th century. According to the miniature of 15th century, depicting praying to the Vernicle of princes Demetrius and Vladimir before Kulikovo battle.

Vetche Tomb and Town's bell in Kremnik of 2nd half of 14th century. According to the miniature of 15th century, depicting princes Demetrius and Vladimir praying at the coffin of St.Peter, metropolitanate of Moscow, before Kulikovo Battle.

black beard and hair and marvellous look". The prince's horse was not, evidently, a slim and viperous one, but sooner it was a heavy draught-horse. After such description of Donskoy one can remember the mighty Elijah Muromets in the famous V.M.Vasnetsov's picture "The Three Heroes".

During the Kulikovskaya battle Demetrius was 30. He was in the first row of guards, who were on foot, which was cut out by tatars entirely. And the chronicler writes about Demetrius: "First of all he started fighting with the tatars, who were to the right and left from him like water and they bit, cut and thrust his head, shoulders and belly, but the Lord God saved him from death by His mercy, the prayers of His Mother, the great saint miracle-worker Peter and all saints' prayers; he was tired and exhausted from the terrible tatars' violence so as though close to death." That is why, perhaps, the grand prince lived only 39 years.

Stone Wooden Kremlin

In 1365 Moscow was ruined by the horrible All-Saints fire. Hut since that time the word "Kremlj" appeared in chronicles and it turned out to be connected not only with reconstruction, but also with renovation of the Moscow fortress. In 1365 "grand prince Demetrius Ivanovich decided to build the stone town Moscow, and he implemented what he decided to do. That very winter they started carrying stones to Moscow". By the summer of 1368 it was just ready and was regarded with curiosity by Olgerd with troops being here just in time, and in 1382 Moscovites got ready to defend from the huge army of khan Tokhtamysh, hoping for "the stone walls and iron gates".

All this data together with other mentions about the stone walls and loop- holes of Moscow Kremlin in the chronicles of the end of the 14th – beginning of the 15th century allowed the historians to think that in 1367 it was all built from stone. The news of 1451 about the assault of it by tsarevich Mazovsha's tatars, "there was no stone fortress anywhere", or the news of an Italian A.Contarini of 1474 about "the wooden Kremlin" in Moscow were explained by the scientists that the walls after many firm, even after one earthquake in 1445, fell down in many places" and repaired with wood, looked like wooden ones.

However, it is doubtful that the Kremlin of Demetrius Donskoy could be all built from stone during only one summer season. During a short period such work was done, the volume of which is unbelievable for Russia of that time. There seemed to be raised a dozen of three or four-tire towers and about two kilometers of stone walls up to ten meters high (N.M.Voronin). And nearly the same parameter of walls, hut twice as many towers, were built a hundred years later during 15 years.

It is also difficult to believe that the Kremlin of the crowded grand princely capital presented itself as ruins patched with wood for several dozens years. As though after 1367 there were no bricklayers in Russia anymore and nobody could mend, repair the fortress walls when necessary (for example, the name of the master – Demetrius Ermolin – who repaired the Kremlin wall near Borovitskie Gates a hundred years later in 1460s, is known).

Taking into account the news of 1451 about absence in some Kremlin's places of "stone fortresses", the news of A.Contarini about the presence of wooden walls in 1474 it is more logical to consider the Kremlin of Demetrius Donskoy *combined*. From stone were the walls in the Eastern part from the Moscow-river to the Neglinnaya and in the West, from Borovitskie Gates to Sviblova Loop-Hole. The walls were on the banks and were low "and the town was low then". From stone were the Gates Bolshie (Timofeevskie), Frolovskie (later Spasskie), Nikolskie, Rizopolozhenskie (later Troitskie), Borovitskie and Taynitskie. From stone were the corner towers of Sviblova, Beklemishevskaya, Neglinskaya (Malaya Arsenalnaya) and, probably, two-three small towers at the front. The walls and towers along the rivers Moscow and Neglinnaya were from *wood*.

It is confirmed by archaeologic observations over excavation works inside the Kremlin near Troitskie (the Holy Trinity) Gates. The existing now Western brick wall of the Kremlin, extended earlier along the river Neglinnaya (now there is the Alexander Garden instead of the river taken into the pipe), was built in 1495 "adding to the town not on the old foundation". Cut on the way of this "old foundation" inside the Kremlin the fortification line with wooden-earth construction was found twice.

First it was found in the last century three sazhenjs away from the Kremlin stone wall. These were low timber sets of a wooden wall, which was on the earth bank. As it was known according to the chronicles; that the oak Kremnnik was built by Kalita, the wall was dated back to 1333. The logs were taken out, from the underground and for some time were demonstrated openly till they fell apart.

For the second time the fortification line war; found during excavation of the foundation area for the Palace of Congresses. The basis of the earth bank was open, it was fortified from the outside with logs kept from rolling outside by transversal with hooks. The fortification line was dated dy the middle of the 12th century and referred to as the fortress of Yuri Dolgoruky. From this way, from the "old foundation", the wall was moved in the direction of the Neglinnaya-river only in 1495. So, here, from the 11th till the 15th century, along the shore-line of the Neglinnaya-river there was the fortification line with timber-earth construction (similar to the hook-like construction of Novgorod of the 11th century).

The Kremlin's wall of 1367 extended along the same way and was wooden. If it was at that time in good condition since Kalita's time, it was not touched at all during the time of Demetrius Donskoy (it could be repaired, closets could be substituted at some places). By the way, here in 1365 for the first time in Moscow a stone bridge was built across the Neglinnaya-river, which allowed, together with construction of stone Kuryatnye Gates, to "move" the Kremlin further to the East, closer to the present Red Square.

There is no definite data about the character of the fortification line along the Moscow-river. They suppose, that some white stone ruins in earth near the brick walls and towers can belong to the Kremlin of 1367. Rut it is very doubtful for two reasons. Firstly, the wall and towers were

Stone-wooden Kremlin in 1367. Reconstruction of G. Mokeev.

dismantled here at the end of the 18th century for construction of Bazhenov's Big Kremlin Palace. Here big quantity of white stone was brought, even some work was started. As it is known, the construction was rejected, and the Kremlin's walls and towers were reconstructed again. Secondly, chroniclers say definitely that the walls of 1367 were on the banks, not on earth. But even if there were some white stone ruins of the 14th century in earth, then, taking into account spring floods, it is possibie to support that in 1367 on the shore of the Moscow-river only stone foundations-socles were installed under some shore wooden loopholes. And the bank under the walls could be also fortified with stone along the bottom from floods.

It can be also noted that construction of the Kremlin at the end of the 15th century at the time of John III was started not from the fortified parts, but from Moskvoretskaya, perhaps, less fortified, thus, more dangerous part. In 1485 the stone Taynitskaya Tower was founded first along the centre of the defense line, in 1487 the corner Beklemeshevskaya Tower was built in 1488 – the corner Sviblova Tower, which centered fire on the whole line along the Moscow-river.

Moscow Kremlin of Demetrius Donskoy was, thus, stone-wooden and so existed from 1367 till 1485, i.e. nearly for a century and a quarter. The Kremlin looked originally and was beautiful in its style. There was the complex of white stone temples of Protase in its centre. Demetrius wooden palace on the shore included tower chamber with golden roof and vitreous windows. From three sides to the central complex there were three monasteries very close to it also with white stone cathedrals: to the West – that of the Sviour on Bor of the princes, to the North – the boyards' one of Epiphany, to the East – Chudov monastery of metrorolitanates. On the Eastern part of the Kremlin there was the "stone town's breast" with three gates' loop-holes. On the opposite part the Kremlin was also covered with a stone wall. The panorama of Moscow central complex opened spectacularly to the Moscow- river in Zamoskvorechie at that time already. There was no similar complex neither in Kiev, not in Novgorod, Vladimir, Pskov, though there were more stone buildings. In Moscow everything looked well thought of, estimated, for the ensemble of the Red Cathedral Square was built by Protase all together 15 years.

In 1382 Moscovites trusted the perfidious khan Tokhtamysh and opened the Kremlin's gates. Tatars slashed 24 thousand Moscovites who had gathered here: men, women, old people, children, and burnt the Kremlin. At the end of the 19th century during construction of a statue of Alexander II a gigantic common grave of slashed skeletons was found on the hill, historians supposed it was connected with the horrible tragedy of 1362.

About The Holy Russia

Depressed with cross burden,
The King of Heaven, looking like a slave,
Walked all over you, my motherland,
Blessing you.

F.Tjutchev

At the end of the 19h century the historian V.S.Soloviev wrote in the article "What is Russia?": "Usually people, wishing to praise their nationality, express their national ideal in this praise, what is best of all for him, what he wants most of all. Thus, a French man speaks about beautiful France and French glory (la belle France, la gloire du nom francais); and English man says with love: old England (old England); a German man rises higher and, giving ethic character to his national ideal, says with pride: die deutsche Treue ("German loyalty").

What do Russian people say in that case, how do they praise Russia? Do they call it beautiful or old, do they speak about Russian glory or Russian honesty and loyalty? You know that they do not say anything like that, and wishing to express their best feelings towards the Motherland only say "the Holy Russia".

That is the ideal: neither liberal, nor political, nor aesthetic, but moral and religious!"

"Motherland" and "Holy Russia" are surprising terms. What is even more surprising that you cannot see them in our chronicles nearly at all (not in the acts either), which have been written during eight hundred years, mostly by monks or clergymen. Though it seems that it was the church which was on guard of morals and religiousness. So, the conclusion comes itself: both notions were from common people, and noisily ostentatious, but concealed, intimate. They belonged to deeply intimate parts of soul of a Russian person, and showed themselves only in exclusive cases. So, Holy Russia does not belong to Russian history, but to Russian Spirit. That is why we find it not in historical documents, but in folk poetry, legends, bylinas (bylina about Elijah Muromets and Solovey the Highwayman, Jerusalem conversation, etc.).

The word "Rusj" from ancient time had a double meaning, which was people and land. The notion "Holy Russia" also acquired double meaning. This was reflected, for example, in the terms "Holy Russian heroes" and "Holy Russian land". But the notion "Holy Russia", which referred to our country till the 18th century, did not appear at once, but during some period of time, was formed due to certain circumstances.

The first written testimonies about Holy Russia, more exactly about Holy Russian land are encountered in the works of prince A.M.Kurbsky of the third quarter of the 16th century. but they clearly showed the notions which had been already established firmly among people. The scale of land, people speaks about the long and complicated process of conception and establishment of these notions. Not pretending to full treatment of the question, some its important moments can be discussed.

Not all *people of Russia* became "holy" in Christian meaning. Partially, because the church excluding for many centuries step by step their originally pagan nature, could not substitute it fully. Partially because Christianity was not strong in all layers of society. But developing struggle with paganism, the church constantly educated people in the area of Christian moral and religious "holiness". The "Shepherded flock" was brought up first of all by the secular clergy. And the regular clergy – monkhood – was in the forefront. So, the chronicler Nestor wrote about Kiev in a hundred years after christening of Russia: "Where the pagans served demons on the hills, there are holy churches now, with golden cupolas, stone-built, and the monasteries are full of regular clergy, constantly glorifying God in prayers, vigils and fastings, in crying: and due to their prayers the World exists!"

After the monkhood "new lights of fire" appeared soon in Russian land – Holy Equal-to-the-Apostles Great Prince Vladimir and Blessed Equal-to-the-Apostles Olga, princess of Russia, the first Russian Saints Boris and Gleb, the princes,then saint pastors, elders, finally fools for Christ. The pantheon of national saints increases from century to century. And people had contacts not only with the secular clergy, but more with the regular one. Pilgrimage increased to many monasteries: Kiev Caves (Kievo-Pecherskaya Lavra), monasteries of Novgorod, Chernigov, Smolensk, Rostov, Suzdal, Vladimir, Pskov, Moscow, Tverj, Ryazanj... Russian pilgrims visited Constantinople, the Holy Land of Palestine, the Holy Town of Jerusalem.

During the tatar-mongolian yoke many town monasteries were defeated utterly. And only in the middle of the 14th century in wild places, "deserts" sketes, small and secluded monasteries began to appear. The new form of ascetism was connected with the name of *St.Sergius of Radonezh*.

"Ancient Russia fires its light of culture directly from the holy light of Byzantine, taking from hand to hand, as its precious property, the Promethean fire of Hellas," – Paul Florensky wrote. "Sergius of Radonezh touched the most fiery top of the Greek Middle Ages, in which all its fiery lives were collected, and from it he fired his spirit." In the depressing 14th century an idea was necessary, which was absolutely clear to thousands, millions of ordinary Russian people, and at the same time the highest, unlimitedly deep, light and mostly required. St.Sergius finds such idea. He builds a temple in the name of the Holy and Life-Giving Trinity, "to gain victory by constantly looking at it over the fear of the hated partitiveness of the world". Among the chaotic circumstances of time, conflicts, civil discords, general wildness, tatars' massacres and murders, which corrupted Russia, the undestroyable Divine "Most High World", unlimited and unperturbed opened to spiritual sight. Mutual, unlimited Love, streaming in eternal consent, spiritual parcification, in eternal silent talk was opposed to enmity and hatred reigning? in the Earthly world...

"Comparatively late statement of the symmetrical Trinity formula, – P.Florensky continued, – makes the idea of Trinity the subject of special attention and thus leads to construction of Trinity temples, development of Trinity iconography, creation of the cycle of Trinity holidays and new liturgy poetry."

Byzantine did not know the holiday of the Holy Trinity. Appearing as a local church holiday of the cathedral of the Holy Trinity, it became all-Russian holiday, spread according to the

Blissful Russia. Hieromonk Stephan (Linitskiy).

Acts as a sample. The day of the Holy Trinity inspires creation of folk songs, domestic popular beliefs...

The idea of the Holy Trinity for St.Sergius was also the testimony of monastic life. It was established in his monastery and from here widely spread: after the middle of the 15th-16th centuries in Russia more than 150 communal monasteries appeared. In the Life Description of St.Sergius of Radonezh Pachomius the Serb in about 1440 wrote that the saint "shined not from Jerusalem and Sion, but in Great Russian land brought up his peity". St.Sergius' travellings, and then those of his spiritual children, grandchildren, great-grandchildren, generations of Russian Saints spread this piety all over the Russian land. St.Sergius' House of the Holy Trinity became the centre of the idea of spiritual, territorial, economic, artistic, educational, finally moral unity. Here Russian people began to seek moral support and the high approval of their activity. The Grand Moscow Prince Demetrius Ivanovich gave a special example of it, asking for the saint's blessing for Kulikovskaya battle with the unfaithful. So, it is not by chance that the field church of grand princess, and from the time of John the Terrible of tsars too, was consacrated to St-Serrius of Radonezh.

In the 15th century too, exterior events were tightly connected with the interior ones into one flow: 1439 – condemnation by Russians of the Florentine union of the Latin and Greek Churches, 1448 – annunciation of autonomy of Moscow metropolis, 1453 – the Turkish conquer Constantinople by storm, 1470– Constantinople's Patriarch confirms a Lithuanian priest as "the metropolitanate of all Russia", 1471 – refusal of John III from the Horde's tributary, then his marriage to Sophia Paleologus, 1479– construction of Moscow cathedral of Assumption, 1480 – liberation from Tatar-Mongolian yoke.

Russia became "autocratic" – the only free orthodox state. According to the words of John III, "Greek orthodoxy destroyed itself". In literature, in the point of view of all Russian of the end of the 15th century the idea of special significance of Russian ortnodoxy is established, about the special, *different from Greek piety of Russia.* Already in the 60s, after the fall of Constantinople Russian publicist-monk, the author of "the Word about the Latinism" said: "Now and forever, blissfully educated Russian land, by saint government of God's Church is to rejoice in the Universe and under the sunshine with people of the true in belief orthodoxy, being enveloped in the *light of piety,* ...by the autocracy of the Grand Prince Basil Vasilievich."

The idea of Russia as the only custodian of orthodoxy spreads widely from the end of the 15th century. Hermits of national consciousness in the direction of "saint-Russian kingdom", even "saint Russian empire" appeared three times: at the border of the 15th-16th centuries, when John III "tried on" his grandson Demetrius the tsar's throne (the grandson died); at the beginning of the 16th century, when the monk-elder Philotheus of Pakov announced the idea "Moscow is the third Rome"; finally in 1547, when metropolitanate Macarius raised John IV Vasilievich (the Terrible) to the tsar's throne. As a result of such activity in the middle of the 16th century the notion "Holy Russia" established firmly among people. Here is an effective example of it. In the "Legend about Azov's Siege Expectation", written after the middle of the 17th century by some Cossack scribe, it is told about that contingent of Russian people, which made it Holy. Before the last deathly attack out of the fortress to the huge Turkish army the Cossacks said farewell to each other, and then began to pray and ask Holy Russia for forgiveness of sins.

"By origin we are servants of the tsar of the Christian Moscow kingdom, our calling is forever being the Cossacks of the Don-river, who are free and fearless for we are God's people... And we stayed in Azov with small people... just for the experience: we will see the Turkish ideas and plans! And all of us are striving for *Jerusalem and Tsartown:* we would like also to conquer Tsartown, – for it was a Christian state...

And Moscow state is crowded, great and large, is shining brightly in the middle, more than other states and hordes of unfaithful, Persian and Hellenic, like the sun in the sky!

And in Russia we are regarded as stinking dogs. We are running away from this Moscow state, from constant work, from forced slavery, from boyards and nobility of the tsar. And here we came and inhabited wild desert, looking at Christ, Heavenly God...

We shall not return to *Holy Russia!* Our death is in the deserts for our miracle-working icons, for Christian belief, in the name of the tsar and all Moscow state!

Forgive us, your sinful slaves, the tsar and grand prince Mikhailo Fedorovich of all Russia the autocrat. Order, our star to commemorate our sinful souls. Forgive us, our lords, all oecumenical patriarchs. Forgive us, all saint metropolitanates. Forgive us, all archbishops and bishops. Forgive us, Archimandrites and Hegumens. Forgive us, hieropriests and priests, deacons and all clergymen. Forgive us, all monks and recluses. Forgive us, all fathers. Forgive us, *all orthodox Christians,* commemorate our sinful souls with your righteous parents. What we committed was for the shame of the Moscow state".

Holy Russian land was also mentioned by the Cossacks in their farewell prayer, though they were speaking only about Don's land. "Forgive us, dark forests and green woods. Forgive us, clean fields and quiet creeks. Forgive us, blue sea (perhaps, Azov – G.M.) and quick rivers. Forgive us, Black sea. Forgive us, the quiet lord, Don Ivanovich: neither our ataman with formidable troops, nor we are to ride here and hunt for wild animals in fields, nor to fish in the quiet lord Don Ivanovich." And what was Holy Russian land like?

Priest-historian G.P.Fedorov wrote: "All Russian life begins with that magnificent image of Russian land: "Oh, most light Russian land, beautified with many rivers and various birds, animals and creatures of all kind: God rejoicing man, created all for his sake; and then God rejoyced with orthodox belief, christening, filling it with large towns and churches, and with God-loving books, showing by them the way to salvation and the joy of all saints."

The unknown reteller of life gives the key to religious meaning of national life. There are three areas indicated clearly in his words. At the bottom there is the natural created life, wonderful and blessed by God, physical substratum of people's life. On top there is the "light and joy of all saints", the Heavenly Kingdom, adjacent to all boundaries. In the middle there is the way of salvation – not personal, but national way. Showing the way to salvation, "God filled in Russian land with *large towns and churches*", as well as with "sowed" God-loving books all over the land.

Byzantium, West Europe built Christian temples, first using basilica and rotundas. Then in the West they started to build basilics in the shape of Latin cross on plan, and in the Kast – temples of cross-cupola type. "I excelled you, Solomon!" – Byzantine Emperor Justine exclaimed, looking at the gigantic cathedral of St.Sophia built by him in Constantinople. The sample for construction of temples was also the temple-rotunda of the Holy Sepulchre (of Christ's Resurrection) in Jerusalem. As a whole the temples of Byzantium and its provinces were oriented, at the temples of the sacred earthly towns of Jerusalem and Constantinople.

But Greek architects invited by Vladimir to Kiev after christening of Russia in 988 and who built in 996 the Dessiatinas stone church with 25 cupolas (symbol of 75 thrones of the Heavenly Town), showed to the Russian the sample which should be followed in ideal during construction of Christian temples, – the *Heavenly Town*. The Greeks built in Kiev the cathedral of St.Sophia with twelve pillars inside and thirteen cupolas, the consacration, as though following the example of Constantinople, but actually – the ideal again – the Heavenly Town (Christ's and Apostolic church, 12 Apostles – 12 pillars on the wall of the Heavenly Town).

In Byzantium itself there were no temples with clearly expressed forms and symbolics of the Heavenly Town. Russians turned out to be understanding; and accurate pupils of the architects invited at the end of the 10th century from Greece, because stone temples in all Russian towns became the symbols of the Holy Trinity Home, Heavenly Paradise, Divine Jerusalem. In the highest Christian ideal of God's Dwelling, embodied for instance, in our temples of the 11th-15th centuries, Holy Russian land. Holy Russia was born.

Besides, Russia became full of its own new holy places, about which John

the Terrible and other tsars told, who often went there as piligrims, to pray to the sainth. Religious processions around the temples, inside them, on the walls, around towns, between the holy paces: monasteries, sacred towns, were of special significance. Such "processions" around towns and all over the Russian land with prayers, holy icons hallowed the land itself. Visual images were added by the sonic ones: each day chime of church's good annunciation (the Gospel) sounded over the towns, villages, monasteries.

The sacred image of Russian towns, villages, monasteries, lying in the fields, forests, valleys, on the hills, gave a special, national, Russian image to the landscape. From here also comes the notion of Holy Russian land! Such landscapes can be seen on pictures of artists: M.Nesterov "Vision of the lad Bartholomew" (future Saint Sergius of Radonezh), I.Levitan's "Over the Eternal Quietude", "Vesper Chime", V.Linitsky's pictures and many, many others.

"We made to live and pray around us nearly all objects", Sergey Esenin wrote in the article "Mary's Keys", showing further the every day life and work of Russian peasant, symbolics of things surrounding him, buildings, natural environment. Our Motherland was called Holy Russia before appearance in the 18th century of multilingual, multinational, multireligious Russian Empire. But it was not forgotten since that time and still finds its place in the heart of a true Russian person as priceless patrimony. So, in the beginning of the 20th century the vow of Azov's hero-Cossacks of Holy Russia was as though reborn:

We shall fight bravely the battle for Holy Russia
And we shall all give away our young lives!

The famous theologian Kartashev noted that from the time of christening of Russia till the fall of Byzantine orthodox empire with its capital Constantinople – the Second Rome before the Turks the image of Holy Russia in orthodox consciousness revealed itself only in folklore. Rejecting the union with the catholic church, blessed prince Basil Vasilievich entrusted Moscow state with the oecumenical responsibility for the purity of orthodoxy in the whole world. Thus, he raised people to the level of the world's nation, and the princely domain – to the level of state, which since that time became the guard of the true Christ's Kingdom. Both the state and the church called Moscow the Third Rome. Thus, the great autocratic consciousness of Russian people appeared and his last and important mission was determined – to keep the Truth of Christ's Church till the Second Advent. This sacred mission enlightened with the Holy Spirit many orthodox hermits of Russia. By the time of metropolitanate Macarius canonization of Russian saints changed the image of ancient Russia, transferred Russian Spirit, into the kingdom of Holy Russia. Synaxis of All Russian Saints is the sacrificial Christ's Body, making around Christ the lightest kernel of the church, ark of salvation, visual image of God's town. Since then the Byzantine tradition of symphony of the church and the foundation of people's, state and church life. Holy Russia in the person of people, state and church directed their service to transfiguration into the image of Christ, the priest forever after the order of Melchizedek and King of kings.

The unexpectedly important indication of what was behind the people's beloved definition "Holy Russia" is the church rule of prayers for health, by which drinking, of spirits was ennobled.*

In Moscow before the time of Peter I each celebration of a tsar or Patriarch included short divine service and for reading the prayer over the toast cup a corresponding rule was made. The rite began with singing for health of feast prayers by tsar's, metropolitanate, patriarch's or monastic chorus depending on who had lunch and why.

After singing feast prayers they came down to action. The nominated drink was poured into a big cup, over which a prayer was read and a specially prepared text, which got the name of "cup for health". Sometimes already full cup was sprinkled with holy water. In ancient time the cup was sent from hand to hand, which was a far image of communion rite. But in the 16th-17th centuries specially nominated boyards poured from the bowl and delivered wine in goblets, vodka – in cups, honey and beer – in ladles. In case of tsar'e celebration the ritual became complicated. Bowlers poured the bowl, cup-pourers poured out of it and gave the cups to table servants selected from the boyards close to the tsar, and only they could bring the goblet to the tsar. At each

---

* G.A.Romanov's text is to the end of the passage.

stage each of them was to pour a little for himself and drink in front of everybody, thus ensuring the tsar's safety from danger of poisoning. As for the tsar, he had the right to send his goblet to someone with a table servant as an award.

The first bowl was always consecrated to the Host Holy 'Theotokos, the intercessor and protector of Russian land. Then bowls with prayers to saint Russian miracle-workers could follow. The prayer over the first toast bowl was followed by the speech for the health of the tsar, protector of orthodox Christians. At this the chorus sang "long ages", next bowls were for the health of the royal family and the metropolitanate (when the Russian church became patriarchate, for the patriarch's health). In order to assess what "long ages" was let's have a look at the observation of Paul Alepsky. Usually "long ages" was repeated to the tsar Alexius Mikhailovich 12 times, and to the patriarch and members of the royal family – three times each.

The toast cup for the health of the metropolitanate Macarius had the text with a deeply symbolic meaning: "The cup of our lord Right Reverend Macarius the Metromolitanate of all Russia. So that our lord is in good health and prayed to the Lord God and the Host Holy Theotokos and the great miracle-workers and all saints about the tsar, grand prince John Vasilievich, autocrat of all Russia, for good health for long ages and salvation... and about all orthodox Christendom, for he occupies tine same table and is the vicegerent of the great saints and miracle-workers Peter, Alexius and Jonah, and is in their place, and is always looking at the miracle-working image of the Most Holy Theotokos and always venerates the health-giving coffins of the great miracle-workers. So that by his lordship prayers the Lord God will give all blessings to the tsar grand prince John and all orthodox Christendom; and to him, our lord, to shepherd the wordly flock entrusted to him by God and give it back to Him chaste.

Blissful is the *Holy Russian Kingdom*, which was honoured to receive from God such a good fruitful royal ripe garden, multiplied by piety and virtuous management, due to which we flourish like a tree with rich leaves, change for the better spiritually and physically from any wrong deed, from which we take the sweetest wisdom and rejoice".

The document shows us the veneration of the Russian Church as the cause and basis of Holy Russia. Upon prayers of Theotokos God granted Russian Kingdom with many Saints "shining in Russian land", and saint priests with the one sharing the table and the vicegerent of "the miracle-workers Peter, Alexius and Jonah" at the head. All together they make the united earthly and Heavenly, Holy Russian Orthodox Church. So, our land is the temple, "garden' of this Church – Russia of Saints, Holy Russia.

Sanctifying of Russian land. Hieromonk Stephan (Linitskiy).

Theology Of Russian Land

The idea of Russian land as the image of the "promised land" of the Heavenly Kingdom, "New Jerusalem"[1], *development* and implementation of this idea in visual architectural images and names of different places – is the most amazing and carrying away speciality of church-theologian and people's consciousness of Russia of the 10th-17th centuries.

In the famous "Word about the Testament and Bliss" of Hilarion, the metropolitanate of Kiev (the first metropolitanate Russian by nationality), written in 1037-1050[2], Constantinople was directly and without any stipulations called "New Jerusalem"[3], from which, according to Hilarion, prince Vladimir with his grandmother Olga brought the precious cross like Constantine the Great with his mother Helen brought the cross from Jerusalem. The fact that Constantinople was called "New Jerusalem" without any ground, is the evidence that the idea of Tsargrad in Ancient Russia was widely spread and generally accepted. In the same work metropolitanate Hilarion compares Yaroslav the Wise with Solomon. The Comparison is not occasional, if to note that Yaroslav did the same as Solomon in Jerusalem, – built new fortress walls with four gates and in the centre – the magnificent temple (cathedral of St.Sophia).

Thus, the Golden Gates in Kiev in Russian mind had the prototype not only Constantinople, but also Jerusalem. Now it is clear why they were not only just the main, but sacred (sometimes were called so). They as though invited the Lord Jesus Christ to enter Kiev, like He entered Jerusalem, and to bless the table town and Russian land. There was the church of Annunciation on the Colden Gates. And the event of the Blissful Annunciation to the Virgin Mary about the birth of the Saviour from Her is the beginning of the Gospel, it is "the entrance" of

God's Son into human world. The Golden Gates lead directly to the main holy thing of Kiev – the cathedral of St. Sophia.

Novgorod (with its St.Sophia), the second capital of Russia – Vladimir (with many "Kiev's" names, with the cathedral of Assumption of "Sophia's" type with Golden Gates), other princely centres, finally, Moscow began to follow Kiev's examnie in this or another way or scale.

We shall note another detail which made ancient Russian Christian town similar to the historic Palestinian Jerusalem. It is the "veneration" hills. They were in Kiev, Vladimir, Novgorod, Moscow and nearly all large Russian towns and monasteries. It is the clear parallel to the "veneration" hill near Jerusalem. It was described in one of our most ancient written sources of the beginning of the 12th century as follows: "...There is a sloping hill near the road, at the distance of nearly a versta from Jerusalem, – on that hill all people get off their horses, make there cross bows, and venerate the Holy Resurrection in view of Jerusalem. And there is a great joy to every Christian when he sees the sacred town of Jerusalem, and believers cry here. For nobody is able to hold tears seeing this desired land and the holy places where Christ our God suffered for us, sinful. And all go on foot with great joy to the town of Jerusalem."[4] "Veneration" hills near Russian towns are also high places from which travellers first saw the panorama of the town, and where they got off their horses and carriages too and prayed and bowed to the town.

So, the ancient Russian town was understood by people not just as a dwelling centre, centre of trade and handicraft, where people seemed to go with usual everyday needs, hut as a *sacred thing, sacred town, object of praying veneration, like Jerusalem...*

The Russian's interest in historic Palestinian Jerusalem appeared simultaneously with christening. It is quite natural for believers in Christ.

It is one of spiritual and historical lines, which connected from ancient time christened Russian land with Sacred Land of Palestine, Russian table towns – with the town of Jerusalem.

As it was mentioned above, this connection began through *Constantinople*, because it imitated Jerusalem in certain features. But Constantinople was built not only "in the image" of Jerusalem, but first of all, – "in the image" of Rome as a traditional capital of empire. Thus, Constantinople is "new" or "the second Home". Thus, comes the idea about Moscow as the "third Rome".

Due to imitation of Constantinople, Russian capitals from old time got double significance – as church (so, sacred) centres and as political, autocratic centres. And in them two images were created – those of Jerusalem and Rome, which quite complied to the double unity of spiritual and physical nature in man, double unity of church and state power in Christian human society.

Golden-*sacred gates* became the prototype of all "sacred gates" of monasteries. It is not just the main *entrance* into the monastery; it is right the sacred entrance of God, symbolizing spiritual-mysterious entrance of God Jesus Christ into the monastic town, like western (in old time called "tsar's") doors – leading into the temple, as well as "tsar's" gates of the temple's altar are the symbols of entrance of the "Heavenly King" – Christ and together with Him of all his Saints.

The main, *sacred* town's gates (whatever can be their name – Golden or anything else) are situated in the fortress wall. The halls of an ancient Russian town after Russia's christening are not only defence constructions. Walls of large towns got sacral meaning. Spiritual-symbolic meaning could be given to configuration of the walls, fluantity of towers. Quantity of gates in them, consecration of the churches on the gates or towers. As a rule, the quantity of gates was determined by the sacred number: one, two, four, eight, twelve. Gates (sometimes towers, too) had holy icons outside and insicie, in front of which icon-lamps were often burning. So, town's wall (and that of monastery) was understood as the image of divine power, protecting the faithful from enemies, testified that orthodox town's people

hoped not so for the strength of material town's walls, but for God's power and prayers of saints, invisibly protecting the town.

If a separate orthodox temple (with its altar and holy table) was venerated by people who were coming closer to it, an ancient Russian town with its many temples and monasteries was to be comprehended as a holy thing, as the place of special presence and stay of the Heavenly King of Glory (God Jesus Christ, His Most Holy Mother, regiments of angels and triumphant Church of Saints, in other words – as the *image of the Heavenly Town.*

But in this case the space of Russian land between its towns and villages (with churches in them) could not be left without efforts to give them sacral (sacred) character. Really, as today's research shows, in ancient Russian toponymy we can see here and there Jordans, Tabors, Zions, Gethsemanes, Bethanies, Jerusalem valleys... Confirmation of this very ancient Russian tradition can be the area around the Holy Trinity – St.Sergius Lavra, some other monasteries, as well as spiritual-praying practise of some Russian hermits-monks. An example to it is St.Seraphim of Sarov, who gave the names of the Sacred Land to certain places in the forest where he led the life of a hermit.

So, from ancient time, from christening *Russian land was consciously arranged (tried to be arranged) simultaneously as the image of the historic Sacred Land of Palestine and as the image of "the promised land" of the coming Heavenly Kingdom.*

Town's geometrical centre was often marked by some open (frontal) place which was often arranged in a certain way. It was the place from which sanctifying of the town was begun, where holiday divine services were carried out, where in such cases a lectern for reading the Gospel was installed. From the frontal place they addressed people with sermons, princely messages and decrees. In such case it corresponded to *ambo* of an orthodox church.

In Kiev, for instance, the frontal place was in the square near the cathedral of St.Sophia. In this case, for people's meeting under the open sky in the square the cathrfiral wns to be the object of praying, i.e. as though God's altar. In the 11th century five altar apses of the cathedral stood out in the square in front of the frontal place – the symbolics of Christ and the Four Evangelists, the cathedral's roof was crowned with thirteen domes in the image of Christ and twelve Apostles.

In connection with this it should be remembered that the Desyatinnaya church of the Assumption was crowned at that time by 25 domes. The first possible explanation of it can be the quantity of eulogy prayers of the only Akathist existing at that time "Laudation of the Most Holy Theotokos"", but it also complied to the throne of God Almighty and 24 seats for the elders near Him from the Revelation of St.John the Theologian[5]. ...Later, in the 16th century, in front of the frontal place in Moscow in Red Square the cathedral of Intercession (St.Basil's cathedral) will be built with 25 domes already.

...If to remember the simplest temple composition of town – cross sign, then with further development of town to its temple-building such images could be added as "Christ and the Four Evangelists", "Christ and 12 Apostles", "The throne of God Almighty and seven lights of fire in front of it", the same throne and seats of 24 elders[6]. In this case only symbolics of numbers was implemented: 5, 13, 7, 24. As for the consecration of temples and their inside lateral altars, we dare add to the observations of our historian the following:

...Names (consecrations) of town's temples were not accidental. They were governed naturally by two main ideas: *holidays* of Gods, Theotokos and most venerated saints in this place, as well as to the sequence of saints' rank (angels, prophets, apostles, saint priests, martyrs, saints, unvercenaries...). It is easy to

Golden gates in Jerusalem, closed acceding to the legend till the Second Advent of Jesus Christ.

Plan of Jerusalem. Historical periods of development: the wans which belong to the time of earthly life of Jesus Christ till destroyntent of the town by Romans are marked with blue and black; the walls built by emperor Adrian at the begijnning of 2nd century are marked with red.

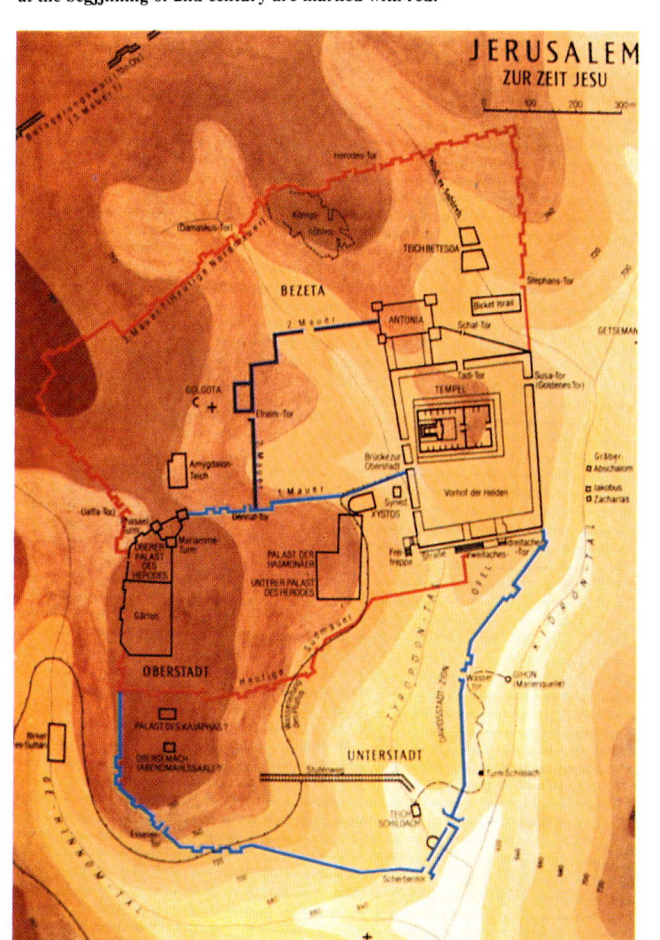

see that in the basis of all this there is the same idea or logic, which is in the church paintings, especially in iconostasis with its tires: local, festal, apostolic, prophetic, – and with composition of intercession of Theotokos and St.John the Predecessor to God Almighty (Deisis) in the centre. But all these are the images of heaven dwellers, combined image of the triumphant Heavenly Church of Saints! Deisis can be encountered not only in iconostasis, but always in icons or frescos of the Last Judgement on the Western temple's wall! It is the image of end of the present earthly life and beginning of the eternal life of the Heavenly Kingdom!

Thus, any more or less developed ancient Russian town with its temples consecrated to Christ, the Mother of God and many saints is to contain the *architectural image of the Heavenly Church, Heavenly Town.* This way the old Russian town was understood, especially at far distance, from the "veneration" hill, when its wonderful panorama opened to the traveller, where domes and bell towers of temple, monasteries, fortress walls with churches and towers above gates dominated.

Still a town is a town and there is not only the image of the Heavenly town, but also that of the earthly one, the image of "this world" with all its passions; there are prisons, trade places, stores, pubs, etc.

...In all mentioned above there are two conformities with regularity. On the one hand, since christening of Russia the town is arranged, independently from people's will and consciousness, subdueing to some natural order, as the image of circle – the symbol of eternity, includes in itself the cross and images of the divine world only due to the existence in it of God's temples with their divine symbolics. On the other hand, in town-building and temple-building ensembles of ancient Russian towns they try already consciously to create some images (symbols) of the divine world, "New Jerusalem".

Moscow collects consciously the number of features and images of all capitals of former princely domains, thus underlining its significance as the uniting centre of all Russian land. So the most important tendencies of ancient town- and temple-building are rightfully developed in Moscow. At the same time Moscow is trying consciously to arrange itself as the spiritual centre, sacred capital of Russia, so the efforts to create certain images of the sacred town, New Jerusalem get in Moscow a brighter, more definite, distinct expression.

It is possible to speak about the number of "New Jerusalem" images in Moscow, as it was built in the middle of the 17th century, quite definitely that they were created intentionally and consciously. First of all it concerns the cathedral of Intercession, known as the cathedral of St.Basil in Red Square. It was noticed long ago that its numerous inside lateral churches are so small and crowded, that they could take only small quantity of parishioners, so the cathedral was constructed not so as the place of prayer, but the object of prayer. In the latter meaning it was made multi-cupola, picturesque, elaborate "paradise garden", as image of Paradise or "the House of the Heavenly Father", where there are "many mansions" for saints[7]. According to A.V.Bunin, "being situated like that Red Square provided a huge useful territory", while the cathedral itself became its original altar. Really, after construction of the cathedral of St.Basil the tradition of wide people's prayings and processions in Red Square established". The religious procession in the 17th century on Palm Sunday was especially portentous from the Kremlin to the cathedral of Intercession, in which there was an inside lateral church of the holiday of God's entrance into Jerusalem. The religious procession signified also the historic entrance of Jesus Christ into Jerusalem on the eve of cross passions and symbolic entrance of the righteous into the Heavenly Kingdom. Patriarch, symbolizing Christ, rode on horse from the Kremlin, the tsar led it by the bridle, willow was carried on a carriage, decorated with various

Jerusalem. The town of David with the Temple.

Constantinople. Panorama.

sweets as a symbol of tree of life. Eparchs, many clergy men went in the procession, strelitz troops were standing. All this was going on when a very big crowd gathercd in Red Square. First the Patriarch, tsar and some holy orders rose onto the white stone Frontal place, where the portentous service beran, then they entered the cathedral of St.Basil and in the inside lateral church of the Entrance of Christ into Jerusalem they read the prescribed Gospel, then returned to the Frontal Place, finishing the service and blessing Moscow people with cross. Because of this procession they started to call the cathedral of Intercession (St.Basil) as Jerusalem. M.P.Kudriavtsev quotes the following I.E.Zabelin's evidence: "Foreign travellers of old time, for example of the 17th century, were amazed by Moscow phenomenon. They called it mostly Jerusalem, saying that it was called so among people at that time"[8].

The Frontal Place in Red Square attracts everybody's attention. M.P.Kudriavtsev compares it with a lectern in front of God's throne (the cathedral of St.Basil). But it will be more exact, as we have already seen, to define it as *ambo in front of altar*. When necessary lectern is installed on ambo, which was done on Moscow Frontal place during portentous public prayers. But from the same ambo (without a lectern) patriarchs and stars addressed people in many other cases. In this respect Red Square with the Frontal Place and cathedral in front of it does not seem to be very different from the squares known to us already in front of the cathedrals of ancient Kiev, Novgorod, Pskov, other big cities and big monasteries. But Moscow Red Square is not just continuation of ancient tradition, it is a full disclosure of interior kernel of the tradition.

Above the main central altar of the Intercession the main central marquee of the temple of St.Basil is raised. It is octahedral, crowned by a golden dome. If the golden dome is, according to our Helms Book, "God's head, for the church's head is held by Christ"[9]. (He, being the "Sun of Truth", is symbolized by temple's golden dome), the octahedral marquee, which is already proved[10], symbolizes Theotokos as the Sovereign and Mother of the Church, protecting it with Her holy omophorion (omophorion of the Virgin Mary in orthodox icons has octahedral stars on the main part and shoulder parts). But the number eight also means the eighth age – eternal life in the Heavenly Kingdom, where the mysterious wedding between the Lamb and His bride – Church – is committed. "And I John saw the holy city, new Jerusalem, coming down from God out of heaven, prepared as a bride adorned for her husband." "And there came unto me one of the seven angels... and talked with me, saying, Come hither, I will shew thee the bride, the Lamb's wife... and shewed me that great city, the holy Jerusalem, descending out of heaven from God"[11]. Here the notion about *New Jerusalem*, as the Heavenly Kingdom, and the notion about Christ's Church, the personification and Mother of which is the *Virgin Mary*, for from Her Christ got His Body (and the Church – "Christ's Body", according to the Apostle) become identical. Thus, in the orthodox consciousness the *Holy Theotokos is simultaneously the sign of the Church and the sign of the "New Jerusalem"*. Such identity was reflected in Russian temple architecture. Cross-cupola temple of Russian-Byzantine type (it was the main in Russia from the 10th till the 17th centuries; there was also a circular temple and temples of complex composition, there were no baziliks at all) contained simultaneously new ideas – about the church as the place where believers gather and about the Heavenly Kingdom as the result of belief in Christ. It is not by chance that in the Russian language the word "tserkovj" means assembly of believers, the temple's building, the forms and icons of which are to testify to the eternal, enveloping "new sky" and "new earth" Heavenly Kingdom.

The symbolics of eight, octahendral, from the sign of the Mother of God transfers to the symbol of the Heavenly Kingdom ("the eighth" century). This symbolics of eight repeats itself in the cathedral of Intercession many times: in the main eight

Constantinople. Plan of 15th century.

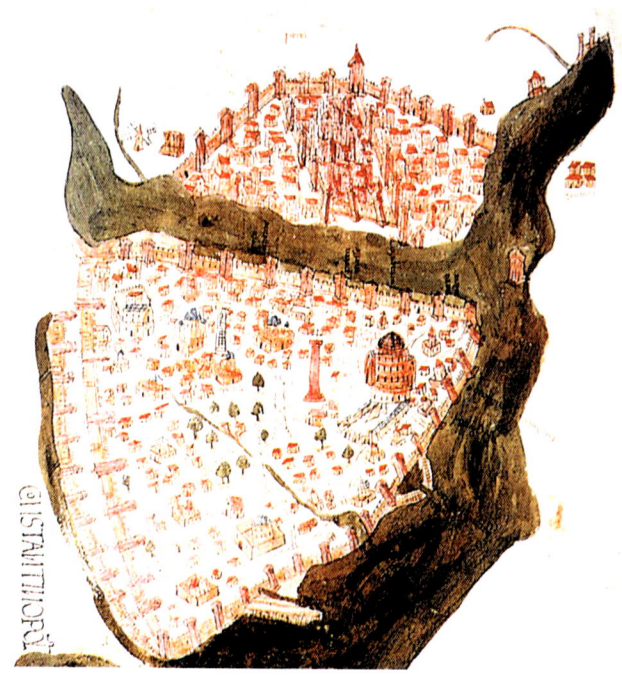

The Calvary intrant of the cathedral of St. Sophia in Kiev. 18th century.

Heavenly Town. Miniature from the Apocalipse.
17th – beginning of 18th century.

domes, surrounding the ninth (marquee-like), and in smaller eight cupolas, which were on the kokoshniks of the central marquee in the 16th-17th centuries, in the octahedral planning of all the cathedral, all the four inside lateral churches were made right in the direction of the four parts of the world, and the other four – between these parts, so that there was a figure of two squares, combined under the angle of 45 degrees, i.e. *octagonal star*. All together with the eight edges of the central marquee are the evidence of intentional presentation of the temple as the symbol of Theotokos and tale symbol of New Jerusalem, the life of the "eighth", "future age". If to add to this that in the 16th-17th centuries the total quantity of all cupolas of the cathedral of St.Basil was 25 (several more small cupolas were on the Western dome of the cathedral, it is better evidence of the initial "New Jerusalem" symbolics of the cathedral: 25 – means God Almighty and 24 elders near His throne in the Revelation of St.John the Theologian, and at the same time – 13 condaks and 12 icoses (short and long eulogy prayers) of the "Laudation" of Theotokos – the only Akathist of that time existing by rule, which was read during the Lent to glorify the Virgin Mary (at that time icons of the "Laudation" were widely spread, which presented 24 scenes, complying to the contents of the Akathist). In future small cupolas on the marquee and the Western dome were removed, so that the cathedral of Intercession in Red Square represented mostly symbolics of eight. Theotokos symbolics, complying to symbolics of the Heavenly Kingdom, is not accidental in the centre of Moscow: Moscow and all Russia were understood long ago as the "house of the Most Holy Theotokos". Russian spiritualness has Theotokos character, which is noticed by all. Special care of the Virgin Mary for the (destiny of Russian land showed itself from ancient time in all parts of Russian land, including in Her spiritual-mysterious guidance in creation of Russian towns, temples, monasteries.

In the Revelation of St.John the Theologian we see evidences, which may seem contrasting; at first sight, about the temple in Divine Jerusalem. In one place St.John says: "And I saw no temple therein: for the Lord God Almighty and the Lamb are the temple of it"[12]. But in the number of other places of the Revelation it is clearly said about some mysterious "temple of God", which "is open in the heaven"[13] and in which there is the "throne of God and Lamb", "and one sat on the throne" – God, and near His throne there were 24 small seats for the elders – priests, and in front of the throne of God Almighty "there were seven lamps of fire burning", then there is the "golden-credence"[14], and around all this certain divine service is carried out[15]. So, in the Divine Jerusalem there is no temple in the earthly meaning, as a special building for public prayers, but still there ir some mysterious "temple of God"!

As the cathedral of Intercession (St.Basil's) was made intentionally not like a cathedral populous meeting of the praying, but as an object of prayer for people standing in Red Square, like an altar, then, certainly, M.P.Kudriavtsev is correct defining Red Square as a temple under the *open sky*, in which, according to his words, "the most complicated for symbolic implementation phrase of the Revelation" was realized: "And I saw no temple therein"[16]"[17]. We would like to add this comment that here another fact of the Revelation was reflected, concerning the mysterious heavenly "temple of God", which is just symbolized by the cathedral of Intercession (St.Basil's).

Then we have to point out that in Moscow, in Red Square, the idea of other Russian towns and monasteries, beginning from ancient Kiev, where there were squares in front of the cathedrals and frontal places for prayers under the open sky, finds its brightest and absolutely final expression.

The cathedral of St.Basil was arranged as the symbol of "New Jerusalem" gradually. In the 16th century its cupolas were usual, smooth, and the walls did not have picturesque paintings on the white background. In 1594 the cupolas become figured, but not coloured, they had golden coating. In the 17th century rich wall paintings appear with a floral ornament, the cupolas become of different colours. If to take into account that the temple is at the edge of the Moscow-river, then in its finished variant it is to be associated with another fact from the Revelation: "And he showed me a pure river of water of life, clear as crystal, proceeding out of the throne of God and of the Lamb. In the midst of the street of it, and on either side of the river, was there the tree of life, which bear twelve manner of fruits, and yielded her fruit every month: and the leaves of the tree were for the healing of the nations[18]".

On the one hand, Moscow is the main church centre of Russia, on the other hand, it is the political, worldly centre. Sacred town arki the town of worldly vanity (Babylon). Patriarch's town – and tsar's town. The town of God's temples and monasteries – a town of tsar's prisons and pubs. God's town and a town "of this world". Unity of the head of the state and of the head of the church, unity of Russian people in orthodox belief since the time of prince Vladimir provided quite a peaceful alliance also of two main ideas: "capital of Russia – new Jerusalem" and "capital of Russia – the third Rome". As "the second Rome" – Constantinople was considered and called "New Jerusalem" too, both above-said ideas were almost synonymous. It is natural, however, that church's thinking was more inclined to the idea of "New Jerusalem", state, political thinking was more attracted by the idea of "the third Rome". And in case of some discord in relations between the tsar and patriarch, i.e. between the state and the church, there appeared a gap between the ideas of "New Jerusalem" and "the third Rome".

In the 17th century, continuing and developing traditions, tendencies and theological ideas of Russian domain towns, Moscow is arranged providentially and intentionally as the image of "New Jerusalem" (as the heavenly town), "the second Jerusalem" (as successor of the glory of the historical, Palestinian one), "the third Rome" (similar to Constantinople, "the second Rome") and as the image of Rome as autocratic capital of the world (with pagan, cultural and political meanings). All these tendencies come from ancient Kiev of the epoch of the princes Vladimir and Yaroslav the Wise. If the idea of "the third Rome" was double, the idea of "New Jerusalem" turned out to be double, too. In spiritual depths many symbols get connected; but in the exterior, emperic reality the creation of architectural images of historic Jerusalem and Divine (New) One was going on in two *parallel lines* till a certain time.

Nicon was the Patriarch of All Russia – the only powerful orthodox country in the world, who thought much about the world historical and spiritual significance of the Russian Orthodox Church, which was not comprehended only by him as Holy Russia – image of Heavenly Jerusalem and Divine Zion. Nicon was inclined to these Divine images for a long time. It becomes clear that for Patriarch Nicon his ecclesiastical point of view and two tendencies in the symbolics of Russian town- and temple-building, which developed in two independent, but parallel ways, – personification of images of historical Palestine (historic Jerusalem) and personification of images of the divine world ("New Jerusalem"), as it was described in the Revelation of St.John the Theologian, did not combine in any way with each other in the theological synthesis of his ecclesiastical view point. The latter tendency as though found already its expression in Moscow, about which Nicon knew well. But he also knew very well the fact that Moscow is first of all "the third Rome" and not only in spiritual meaning, as the successor of the church capital of orthodoxy – Constantinople, but it is also the worldly capital, autocratic centre, in a way even imitating pagan Rome and other capitals of world's empires. Besides, Moscow is still the town of worldly vanity, "the sea of every-day life, raised by storms of sorrows"... A man of deep spiritual-ascetic life and experience, who had escaped at a certain time to an island in the White Sea, Nicon felt by the subtle hermetic sense, that the mixture of different worlds and ways of life did not allow Moscow to be the image of Divine Jerusalem to a full extent. Here this image is dissolved with the images of quite another character and spirit. Besides, if to speak about the cathedral of Intercession in Red Square, it could be "New Jerusalem" only in the meaning of a sign, but not the image, because except for some features "New Jerusalem" as Heavenly Kingdom was not shown even in the Revelation in a descriptive enough way. So, it followed that, firstly, to create a relatively clear image of the Heavenly Kingdom it is possible only outside worldly, town's vanity. Secondly, how should it be created? Here the theologian question of theory of image got the most important meaning.

Does the architectural image have the right (and to what extent) to be for believers the same that an icon image? With icons everything was more or less clear long ago. According to the orthodox doctrine, image through its symbolical similarity to the prototype, reached by observation of ancient God-inspired canons of icon-painting and sanctifying by water and the Holy Spirit according to a special church rule, become the possessor of the same blissful energies as the prototype, mysteriously, but really contains the *presence* of the prototype. But does the same happen to the architectural image? Can the energies of the prototype act in it, too? Will it be the mysterious *presence* of what it expresses?

...But does it mean that patriarch Nicon found the necessary link, that now he understands the connection between the historic Sacred land of Palestine and the promised land of the Heavenly Kingdom? Yes, what happened cannot be called otherwise than a great insight granted by God to the searching mind of a great saint priest! How did it happen?

In 1653, at the beginning of construction of Iversky monastery in Valday, patriarch Nicon got from the patriarch of Jerusalem the second gift which as if settled problems, which raised because of the first gift (cypress model of the Holy Sepulchre) – the book "Testimony". It was composed by a Greek monk John Nathaniel and presented explanations, taken from many fathers and teachers of the Church, of symbolic meaning of temple and its most important parts, spiritual- mysterious symbolic explanation of Divine liturgy, church vessels and ephods, other images and symbols of the church.

...What did "surprise" the fathers of the Synaxis so much, and so, Patriarch Nicon himself in this book? First of all this spiritual-mysterious, symbolic comment on temple and Divine liturgy, which sums up the devedopment of the Byzantine theory of image.

Much of what in Russia was considered just a sacred tradition given together with belief from the ancient Greek Church, as if became alive due to "Testimony", was lit up from inside and filled up with the deepest spiritual meaning. For example, it turned out that the altar is the image of the heavenly altar, the heaven and even the throne of the Holy Trinity and at the same time it symbolizes some events of life and passions of the Saviour. So, the throne (in today's understanding) means Jerusalem, Calvary and the Holy Sepulchre; the credence means Bethlehem and the mountain Olivet; the eparch, and if he is absent, the priest committing the divine service, mainly symbolizes Christ (that is why he wears chesubles similar to Christ's clothes in his earthly life and at the same time symbolizing

His glory as the King of the world), that in the better world all granted the Heavenly Kingdom will see nothing else, but Divine Liturgy as it is the image of all God's home-building for salvation of man, image of all God's Providence about the world created by Him. As the altar first of all symbolizes the divine world, mysterious heaven and kingdom of first-born, the rest of the temple means the earth, world (the temple is divided into three parts, but its symbolics does not change). According to the saint patristic doctrine, its spiritual logic, as it was shown in " Testimony", not only painted images (icons), but all images and symbols in general, which we see in Church, its religious rites, divine services, sacred objects and ephods, including the temple's buildings themselves, their interior arrangement and decoration, just like icons, if they are made canonically correctly (and sanctified with water and the Holy Spirit) possess the same energies as the prototypes, contain the mysterious, but real presence of the expressed one.

Near Myasnitskie gates of Bely town. Artist A.H.Vasnetsov. 1926.

All this conforms absolutely to the ancient general Church's belief, is an integral part of the Holy Legend. For example, in the "History of the Church" of Eusebius Pamphilius there is a speech of some man made for the occasion of sanctifying a temple in Tyr at the beginning of the 4th century, that "the temple envelopes all the universe" and is created not only by people, but by "the great Builder – the Word" and "exists on earth as mental likeness of what is above the firmament", that in the temple we see the "examples" (i.e. images) of "Jerusalem, called the Divine, the heavenly mount Zion and the existing above all this (earthly) world town of Living God, in which there are reignments of angels and the Church of the first-born, written in the heaven"[19].

All this is not just a free human allegory, some meaningless comparisons. Church symbolics is a *"real symbolism"*, as V.M.Zhivov says. In "Mystagogia" of St.Maximus the Confessor it is said that "the Holy Church bears the type and image of God, because it possesses typically and imitatively the same energy (action)", and further, that "God's Holy Church posses in respect of us the same actions as God, like the image and archetype posses them" (prototype)[20]. All this is directly rooted in christological dogma, in doctrine about Christ, as incarnated God, combining in His personality the divine and human, heavenly and earthly, and about the Church as Christ's Body. Thus, the prototypes of the other heavenly life can be reflected under certain conditions in earthly images. This theory of image, according to St.Maximus, gives answers to the questions put by him: "How does the created according to the image rise, to the image, how is the Prototype adored, where is the power of our salvation and for whose sake did Christ die?"[21]

The iconographic doctrine of the Orthodox Church in Russia was known long ago, understood and honoured, that is why the book "Testimony" was aknowledged "impeccable". But it "was worthy of surprise" of the Local Synaxis of the Russian Church in 1656 because for the Russians for the first time, on the basis of the primordial iconographic doctrine, the *spiritual-mysterious*, real-symbolic essence of well-known rules of the divine service, separate objects of the divine service, ephods and parts of temple were explained in detail.

Patriarch Nicon was to pay special attention to the fact that the altar of the orthodox temple was connected with the Divine "New" Jerusalem by the relation of image and prototype. According to the law of orthodox iconography, image shall posses *likeness* to the prototype, and this is possible only if the prototype appeared in quite a *describable look*.

Besides the walls, in "New Jerusalem", according to the Revelation of St.John the Theologian, only the mysterious divine temple is describable enough. So, St.John the Theologian was granted to see in such images this temple, and what is going on in it.

Though in different liturgical works and the "Testimonies" the altar was constantly mentioned as the image of the divine world, but nowhere in any work it was said that the altar was arranged or should be arranged purposefully in conformity with the facts of the Revelation of St.John the Theologian! The altar was arranged historically – by chance. The best example of it is the "seven ligts of fire", which were not found in our temples in ancient time. It appeared here only in the 18th century from the West, but entered organically the symbolics of the altar, adding to it image of those "seven lights of fire", which St.John the Theologian sees right in the same place – between Enthroned

God and the credence. So, the fact that the altar of the orthodox temple conforms nearly precisely to the one in the heaven and to what is going on in it, during the liturgy, is God's Providence, inspirations of the Holy Spirit, which led mysteriously the Church's mentality and taught how the altar was to be arranged. Something of the kind we already saw in conformity between the cross structure of the ancient Russian town and the altar's arrangement.

Now it is important to note that conformity of the orthodox temple's *altar* to the Heavenly Altar testifies to the fact that the "temple in heaven" is strictly speaking the *altar*, not the *temple*, because in reality there is no temple in the Divine Jerusalem, "for the Lord God Almighty and the Lamb are the temple of it"![22] On the other hand, in this heavenly altar we see full assembly of all the Divine Church of Saints – angels and the righteous. But at the same time God's town "New Jerusalem" is not the same as the heavenly altar. And "the new heaven and the new earth"[23] are not the same as the descending from the heaven from God "New Jerusalem". Still, according to the essence of the Revelation, "New Jerusalem" is nothing, but all the area of eternal life of the righteous, the Heavenly Kingdom, and so it envelopes all "the new earth and the new heaven". In this case the heavenly altar spiritually-mysteriously is also the altar of the heavenly city and all the Heavenly Kingdom, new earth as a whole. Altar, town, new earth are only different types or phenomena of the whole Heavenly Kingdom.

How all this complies to our earthly images, altar – church – frame ledge; cathedral – square in front of it – town; cathedral – square – monastery!

So the most remarkable thing for Patriarch Nicon was the following. The altar of the earthly temple repeats almost exactly the arrangement of the altar of "the heavenly temple". And it can be regarded as the image of the latter. However, in the earthly altar some most important sacred places of historical Palestine: the Holy Sepulchre, Bethlehem, the mountain Olivet are symbolized (mainly by the communion table and credence of the present). There are no such signs in the heavenly temple, their prototypes are in historical Palestine. In the earthly altar they are symbolized so laconically that they cannot be the icon, image of the Holy Land. But, on the other hand, it is not by chance that all the Heavenly Kingdom (and so its mysterious altar) is called "Jerusalem", though the "New" one. It is enough to state that it has heavenly archetypes (prototypes). It cannot be otherwise! For "the promised land" of Palestine always was the prototype of "the new earth" of the Heavenly Kingdom "promised" by Christ to the faithful! So, it is due to God's Providence that earthly Palestine, location of all its holy places, especially those of life and passions of the Saviour, is the aspect *reflection* (in accordance with early life in space and time) of *the Heavenly Kingdom on earth*. And it "comes back to the prototype" according to the same laws as any correct icon. Icons can be copied many times; it was general practise since ancient time! So, in order to create in Russian land an icon of "the new earth", Heavenly Kingdom, it was necessary as though "to take" out of the altar, to refill and locate on earth images of holy places of historical Holy Land of Palestine. Then together with the altar, where these places are repeated laconically, the required completeness of image appears, by which it gets the necessary blissful connection with the prototype!

Patriarch Nicon not only expressed the most interesting speciality of the church's mentality of Ancient Russia in the brilliantly and creatively implemented constructional-architectural ensemble of New Jerusalem, but developed, on the basis of saint patristic doctrine, orthodox theory of image which was a serious step forward. For the first time Nicon proved theoretically, that architectural ensemble can be the same icon, coming back to the prototype, as the icons themselves, as all other images and symbols, belonging to the Church and its divine service.

Town-building in Moscow at the end of 14th century. Miniature of chronicle summary. 16th century.

[1] Revelation, 21, 1-2.
[2] A.M.Moldovan. "Word about the Testament and Bliss" of Hilarion. Kiev, 1984, p. 5.
[3] As above. p. 97.
[4] Life and Actions of St.Daniel, the Hegumen of Russian Land// Memorials of literature of Ancient Russia. 12th century. M., 1980, p. 32-33.
[5] Revelation, 4, 2-4.
[6] Revelation, 4, 2-5.
[7] St.John, 14, 2.
[8] M.P.Kudriavtsev. Moscow at the End of 17th Century (analysis of town-building composition): Dessertation for candidacy of architecture. By khe right of manuscript. M., 1981 (typewriting). P. 144.
[9] Russian Orthodox Church. M.: p.h. of Moscow Patriarchate, 1980, p. 190.
[10] As above, p. 203-207.
[11] Revelation, 21; 2, 9-10.
[12] Revelation, 21, 22.
[13] Revelation, 11; 1.19; 15. 5-8.
[14] Revelation, 4, 2-5; 8, 3.
[15] Revelation, 15, 6,; 4. 8; 19, 1.
[16] Revelation, 21, 22.
[17] M.P.Kudriavtsev. The above work, p. 144.
[18] Revelation, 22, 1-2.
[19] Eusebius Pamphilius. The History of the Church. Book 10. Ch. 4. Theologic works.1985. Issue 26, p. 76.
[20] M.V.Zhivov. "Mystagogia" of St.Maximus the Confessor and develonment of Byzantine theory of image// Belles-Lettres Language of Middle Ages. M., 1982, p. 119.
[21] As above, p. 120.
[22] Revelation, 21, 22.
[23] Revelation, 21, 1.

Big Zion. 1486, Moscow.

CHAPTER FOUR

The Capital of Great Russia

Who could ever hope for or heard of that the town of Moscow would be a Kingdom and reign in many kingdoms and many countries?

   Legend "About the Concept of the Reigning Town of Moscow"

The cathedral of the Holy Trinity on the Ditch. 1561. Architect Postnik (Faster) Yakoviev with the nickname Barma.

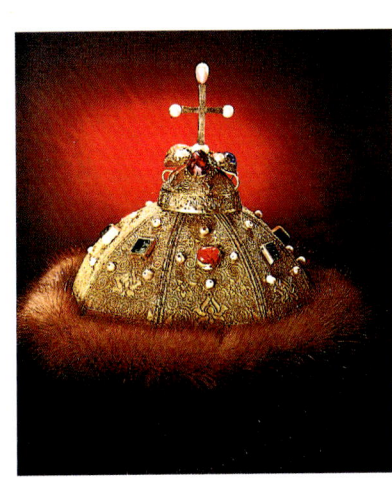

Monomakh's fur-cap. End of 13th - beginning of 14th century.

"Petrov drawing" of Moscow. About 1597-1599.

The Kazan icon of the Theotokos. 1649. T.Rostovets (monk Timothy).

The Transfiguration. 70-80s of 15th century.

Seal of tsar John III.

Grand prince John III.

St. Macatius, metropolitanate of Moscow.

Tsar John IV and metropolitanate Philip.

St.Job, patriarch. Portrait from the Titular Book of 17th century.

Tsar Theodore Ioannovich (1584-1598).
Portrait from the Titular Book of 17th century.

St.Germanus, patriarch.

Tsar Boris Godunov (1598-1605). Miniature from the Titular Book of 1672.

For two and a half centuries outstanding princes of North-East Russia were confirmed for the Grand princely table in the cathedral of Assumption in Vladimir Zalessky. In 1432 this tradition was interrupted. The grandson of Demetrius Donskoy Moscow prince Basil Vasilievich won in the Horde his suit for grand princehood against his uncle prince Yuri Dmitrievich Galitsky and first took the grand princely table near the Golden Gates in Moscow cathedral of Assumption. By this significant act rural princes lost the opportunity to get grand princehood forever. "The Table of Russian Land" moved finally to Moscow since that time.

Probably by the end of the 15th century, after liberation from the Tatar-Mongolian yoke and acquisition of independence, in Russia the word "stol" (table) was gradually changed by the word "stolitsa" (capital), which is of feminine gender according to the name of the town. Perhaps, by the middle of the 16th century the new and better wording appeared «the capital of Holy Russia».

At the beginning of the 18th century the word "stolitsa" stopped being "personal" and, first used in regard of Petersburg and then the main cities of other countries, became widely spread.

It is not easy to tell about the creation of the capital of Holy Russia, besides that, this process has not been considered for obvious reasons: before the revolution there was no science of ancient Russian town-building, and after the revolution there is nothing sacred for scientists-materialists. It seems to be necessary to state as usual in chronological order the facts of construction of well-known objects of the Kremlin, Kitay-gorod, Bely gorod, Skorodom, about the system of monasteries around Moscow. However, impassive wide historical statistics is not the most important thing for such presenting, but the factology, first opening the form, and then the contents of the created by Russian people unique piece of town-building art. It is also important to remember the architects themselves, not to forget the historic background of this creative process.

Liberation From The Yoke

In 1480 North-East Russia liberated from the Horde power, and Moscow state became "autocratic", i.e. independent. The liberation, like the beginning of new construction in Moscow, is connected with the name of the great politician and strategist grand prince John III (Vasilievich). Besides, the liberation from the yoke happened without "great massacre" in a very complicated situation.

The khan of the Big Horde Akhmat (Akhmed), threatening with merciless war, demanded from John III payment of tribute, which the tatars had not received from Russia for nine years already. After refusal Akhmat made an agreement with Polish-Lithuanian king Kazimir IV about utter defeat of Russia by simultaneous attacks from East and West, and in the summer of 1480 he moved a huge army to the Oka-river. Learning that the Russians occupied the crossings, the khan went to the West along the Oka-river, and along the Ugra-river to join Kazimir. Russian troops also moved to the Ugra. Coming to the Lithuanian border, Akhmat started to wait for the troops of allies, trying to cross the river several times. From endless encounters at the crossings the famous long "stay at the Ugra" began.

At the end of October, when the river was frozen, John III unexpectedly moved the Russian troops from the Ugra, intending to retreat even to Borovsk and to occupy a flank position in regard of the tatars and Lithuanians.

Not finding the Russians in front of him, Akhmat was at a loss because of the unclear manoeuvre. He did not venture to cross the river, find the Russians and fight with them with his rather weakened army and retreated to Dikoe field. Both armies after many months of "making no headway" ran away from each other in opposite directions. Thus the liberation of Russia from the Tatar-Mongolian yoke happened.

In fact everything was not so easy. This great event happened also due to a number of political actions of the most careful of all grand Moscow tsars.

Several years before "the stay at the Ugra" John III concluded an agreement with the Crimean khan Devlet-Guirey about joint defence actions against the Big Horde, Poland and Lithuania. Already at that time, the grand prince, stopping to pay the tributary to the Horde, estimated the possible positive result of the coming encounter with the Big Horde (with actions of Devlet-Guirey from the rear).

But in the situation of 1480 upon request of John III the Crimean khan attacked Polish Podolia, thus distracting the forces of king Kazimir: the Polish and Lithuanians did not come to the Ugra, and Akhmat went to join them and waited at the border in vain.

By the autumn after the long stay at the Ugra the huge tatar army "ate up" quickly all the surrounding area, besides after snow began to fall and because of lack of forage the army started losing the horses.

By the same autumn John III organised the march of Russian detachment with the Kazan tatar allies to the rears of Akhmat's uluses in the low reaches of the Volga. People of the Horde at the Ugra were worried about the security of their families.

Returning with shame after that situation Akhmat was soon killed by tatars in khan's conflicts.

There was another important result of the unsuccessful Akhmat's march against Russia. Retreating to the south from the Ugra, the tatars robbed the lands and towns of Russian princely domains in the upper lands (Serensk, Mtsensk, Belev, Vorotynsk...), which were the part of the great Lithuanian domain. After that at the end of the 15th century these domains joined Moscow of their own free will.

The strengthening of the grand Moscow domain in divided Russia in the second part of the 15th century, the result of which was the liberation from the Tatar–Mongolian yoke, was pre-determined by many objective reasons too. In Russian land it was first of all the general growth of uniting efforts of thousands and thousands of ordinary Russian people who were in different domains, jeopardised by powerful foreign enslavers, centralising policy of the Russian orthodox Church, finally, successive, persistent and efficient actions in "gathering" of Russia of Moscow grand princes. Moscow rapidly strengthened at the time of John III after joining the principalities of Yaroslavl in 1463, Rostov in 1474, but especially of Novgorod the Great in 1478 with its huge territories as far as the Arctic Ocean and the Urals.

On the other hand, the Golden Horde fell in decay – the most Western state of Tatar-Mongolian conquerors. By the middle of the 15th century it divided into smaller feudal-formations, which were at the state of war with each other. After establishment of the balance of forces the liquidation of dependence on the central Big Horde became possible, and in 1471 John III rejected the subordination, stopping to pay the tributary to the tatars.

In 1453 Turks took by storm Constantinople, the largest centre of civilisation of that time, "the second Rome", the last pillar of the eastern orthodox church. All orthodox countries became enslaved by muslems. Only Russia had the opportunity in the situation of that time to get free from the yoke. And it managed to do it in 1480. Russian people had the right to consider Russia as the inheritor of the Byzantine empire, continuer of its traditions in ideology, politics, culture, religion. Growth of self-consciousness immediately showed in the first real deeds. In 1473 John III married the nephew of the last Byzantine emperor Sophia Paleologus and received the Byzantine emblem – a double-headed eagle. After that connections with the countries of Europe and Asia quickly extended and became more active. Understanding the great importance of the events which happened at the end of the 15th century, Russian people began assessing the importance of Moscow in a special way. The elder Philotheus of Eleazarov monastery in Pskov in his messages to Moscow grand prince Basil III called Moscow "the third Rome", clearly formulating the idea of the new cultural and historical importance of Russian capital for the world, perspective of its development.

Liberation from the Tatar-Mongolian yoke did not decrease, but increased the danger of military conflicts. In the capital of the centralised Russian state construction of fortifications and temples was to develop on a large scale. And it really began at once. But it continued on the new ideological basis, and as for the sphere of architecture the most up-to-date town-building ideas of that time were used in it.

The Kremlin

Like at the time of metropolitanate Peter renovation of Moscow began from the reconstruction of the main temple of the capital and the state. In 1472 the contractor John Golova, architects Krivtsov and Myshkin founded at the place of the ramshackle one the cathedral of the Assumption, larger and more majestic.

But in 1474 the unfinished cathedral fell down unexpectedly. Masters of Pskov called to investigate the accident, indicated its reasons, but refused to continue the construction of the cathedral. The situation was even worse because other stone temples and fortifications of the Kremlin were in a very ramshackle condition. John III tried to preserve them in normal condition by repairs, but the look of the Kremlin as a whole did not conform to the new denomination of Moscow.

Then John III authorised his ambassador in Italy Semen Tolbuzin to invite a good architect for the construction. In 1475 the architect and engineer from Bologna Aristotle Fioravanti with his son and master Peter came to Moscow to build the main temple of the capital, as well as to cast cannons, bells, coins... The Italian architect was shown the sample for construction of the temple – the cathedral of the Assumption in Vladimir. By 1480 the Moscow cathedral of the Assumption was built, and Russian people celebrated their liberation in it. Thus the cathedral became the symbol of uniting Russia after subduing Novgorod and at the same time the symbol of *autocracy*, freedom of orthodox Russia.

Much was said about the similarity of the cathedrals in Moscow and Vladimir.

Really, their sizes are close, both have six pillars, monumental proportions and five domes. The domes of both cathedrals were close in form to a helm, and the architectural coulisses were finished with small triangular frontons. The great Italian managed to catch the originality of Russian architecture and to under stand its essence.

What about the features of Italian architecture? Perhaps the precise geometry, spaciousness, "chamber-like" interior? But it was just the creative understanding of the task. Perhaps, the "Byzantine" caps of pylons and columns, which disappeared after the 17th century, can

Synaxis Russia. Suthern portal and fragment of the archature range of the cathedral of the Assumption. Of the middle of 17th century.

Russian embassy of Z.I.Sugorskiy to emperor Maximilian II.

be noted, and Latin kryzh in the altar laid out by Fioravanti, which was immediately cut off. The most "Italian" in the cathedral's appearance seems to be the fact which makes Italian and Russian architecture so close: the unity of volume, wholeness, its indivisibility. This quality was well expressed by a Russian chronicler – "Like one stone".

The cathedral of the Assumption, like at the beginning of the 14th century, opened the succession of reconstructions of the Kremlin's buildings. In 1484-1489 the cathedral of the Annunciation – domestic temple of grand Moscow tsars – was profoundly reconstructed including the wooden parts. The masters of Pskov, who built the temple, not only constructed an amazingly beautiful, cosy temple, but also found the general style of the objects of the ensemble of the Cathedral Square – *archature belt*. The three-dome and smaller in volume cathedral was subordinated in composition to the main cathedral of the Assumption. On the edge of the Kremlin hill the Pskov masters built a two-tire building more exquisite and the roof was made in the shape of sharp-edged, keel-shaped coulisses, the necklace of which was also made around the central dome. Like the cathedral of the Assumption, the cathedral of the Annunciation got the archature belt, and at the same height and with windows in it. However, the belt was made in the Eastern part of the temple, as it looked out at Cathedral Square. The latter makes the two cathedrals different: there is no archature on the apses of the cathedral of the Assumption.

The mode of equal height of placing archatures and other details immediately led to unification of the square's ensemble and was used during the construction of other buildings. So, in the small church of the Chasuble-laying, built by the Pskov masters in 1484-1486, the figured terracotta cornice begins at the level of the bottom of the archature of the cathedral of the Assumption. At the height of this archature and at its level the windows of the Faceted Palace were placed, which was built in 1487-1491 by other Italian masters: first it was built by Marco Ruffo, then it was finished by Pietro Solari (later in 1684 the Palace's windows were made wider and decorated with fretwork by Osip Startsev). At the same height were the windows of the Golden Tsaritsa's Chamber, intermediate cornice of the cathedral of Archangel, as well as archature belt of the Patriarch's Palace and the cathedral of Twelve Apostles, which appeared in 1642-1655. But the Patriarch's domestic temple has the second archature belt higher at the whole tire. And it stretches at one level with the archature of the bell tower of John the Great and the former cathedral of the Miracle of Archangel Michael of 1502 in the Chudov monastery which was near by.

Saints were depicted at full length in the architectures, so the saints surrounded all Cathedral Square. If to imagine archatures on painted buildings, temples, including the painted cathedral of the Assumption, the ensemble of Cathedral Square will look differently and like a really unique one.

Construction of the Kremlin objects was not over after John III, but increased already at the time of his son Basil III, then at the time of John IV the Terrible. In 1505-1508 architect Bon Fryazin builds instead of the church of St.John the author of "The Ladder", a new bell-tower with the church of the same consecration, but higher. In 1504 Aleviz the New, another outstanding architect, arrives in Moscow, who is to reconstruct the cathedral of the Archangel Michael. Raised four years after at the time of Basil III the cathedral had helm-like domes covered with small scaly tiles from black slate. The cathedral was red and white with golden crosses. For the ensemble of Cathedral Square the two-tire division of temple was

Coloured print of 16th century.

quite correct from architectural point of view, because it was in unity with other temples.

In 1532 construction of a bell-tower for the cathedral of the Assumption began under the management of the Italian Petrok the Small. The same architect built in 1535-1538 the defence walls of Kitay-gorod, then he returned to Italy. After that the bell-tower was built by Russian architects, which was over only in 1543 at the time of John the Terrible.

At the time of Basil III the construction of the palace complex in the Kremlin was over, which had been started by John III after the destroying fire in 1499 and finished in 1508. The architect of the palace was Aleviz Fryazin from Milan. The Golden and Faceted Palaces are the centre of the composition. The golden roof of the first palace looked very exquisite in combination with the golden domes of the nearby cathedrals and patterned tops of other chambers.

John the Terrible inherited a wonderfully built town and a palace. But neither he, nor moscovites were to live there. Three cruel fires in 1547 burnt Moscow down to ashes. So, from the beginning of his reign he had to start a wide construction activity. However, in 1571 Moscow was burnt by the Crimean tatars headad by Devlet-Guirey. The famous tsar's Oprichny Palace was burnt down, the Kremlin's Palace had to be rebuilt, in Kitay-gorod the Gostinny (Guest) Yard was rebuilt. By the end of the 16th century the Kremlin's temples were restored, the palaces were built again. In the cathedral of the Annunciation inside lateral altars were built in the corners. The Golden Palace was restored. A new golden roof with a weather-vane in the form of golden horses beautified it. The roof's edge was covered with metallic gold-coated decorations and inscriptions made from golden letters. The Palace's facade was decorated with fretwork and sculptures, partially by those left from the Palace of John III. Paintings of the Palace and the Kremlin's temples were meaningful. In them the idea of Moscow's succession after the large capitals of Christendom, Rome and Constantinople, was embodied.

Construction of the Kremlin's *walls* and *towers* at the time of John III was also carried out with the participation of Italian architects. In 1485 the master Anthony founded the first Taynitskaya (Storage) Tower on the shore of the Moscow-river; Marco Ruffo founded Beklemishevskaya Tower in 1487; in 1489 Antony founded Sviblova Tower and, perhaps, the Annunciation Tower in i486. In 1491 Pietro Antonio Solari together with Marco Ruffo founded and built Frolovskaya (the Saviour, Spasskaya) gate tower, Nikolskaya and Borovitskaya gate towers, as well as the wall from Borovitskaya to Sviblova Towers and all the Eastern Kremlin's wall.

Sobakina (Arsenal) Tower, founded by Pietro Solari in 1492, is the most remarkable architecture from among those which have remained till our time. Its forceful high building with small loop-holes strictly situated for curved

Heralds in the Kremlin esutly in the morning. Artist A.M.Vasnetsov.

fire amazes with simplicity and majesty of form. Sixteenhedron of the tower is a bright example of polyhedron not used before in such buildings. Mastery of brick-laying really creates a jewellery beauty. Construction of the tower was the swan-song of Pietro: he died when it was finished in 1493.

In 1494 Aleviz from Milan starts building the most complicated in regard of engineering Northwest Kremlin's wall along the Neglinnaya's shore and the towers: Rizpolozhenskaya (The Chasuble-laying) (Troitskaya (The Holy Trinity)), Srednyaya Arsenalnaya (Middle Arsenal), Oruzheinaya (Armoury), Kutafia, and on the East wall – Nabatnaya (Alarm) and Senatskaya (Senate) (later names). Aleviz builds (jams on the Neglinnaya and makes ponds, builds a new bridge from the Tower of the Chasuble-laying to Kutafia Tower, lays a ditch in front of the Kremlin wall at the side of the Great Settlement, to which in 1506 he starts water from Neglimensky pond. The works were over only in 1516.

Built by the Italian architects, Kremlin was different in its architecture from the earlier one. During its long existence its walls and towers were rebuilt, repaired, raised many times, which almost fully changed their look by the present. The walls were covered by wooden roofs, the towers did not have patterned stone superstructures, but were covered with wooden marquees with tops or without them. Construction of protuberance for the curved fire on the towers was a significant innovation. All the rest was known to Russian fortification art, which flourished in Novgorod and Pskov lands and which was reflected already in the Kremlin of Demetrius Donskoy.

As for the "swallow's tails", which are on top of the Kremlin's walls now, during restoration works near Borovitskaya Tower on an evidently "Italian" wall, below the existing ones, the previous "Italian" merlons appeared and they were rectangular! Besides, we do not know any "swallow's tails" on other Russian fortresses till the second half of the 16th century, i.e. the time of work of the great Russian architect Theodore Savelievich the Steed, he built in Moscow, for instance, the huge wall of Bely (White) town, which had double merlons. It is quite possible that the tsar's town master Theodore the Steed decorated the Kremlin with such merlons during its overhaul at the time of the tsar Theodore Ioannovich at the end of the 16th century. The merlons of Milan's Palace in Italy (the only comparison with the Kremlin) can be dated not earlier than the end of the 16th century.

Aristotle Fioravanti complained in his letters to Italy that he could not make a step without informing Moscow authorities. It is undoubtful that the activity of other architects and masters was also strictly controlled. It is known that earlier boyards were occupied as architects (Protase, Ermolin, Khovrin) or were responsible for construction of separate Kremlin's architectures, evidence of which are "boyards" names of the Kremlin's shooting-ranges of the time of Demetrius Donskoy: Tomofeevskaya, Beklemishevskaya, Sviblova, Chishkovskaya.

Certainly, the construction of all objects at the time of John III was also under close boyards' control, and it is possible that the construction of the main Frolovskie Gates was supervised by John III himself.

Later in 1599-1600 the facing supporting walls of the ditches at the side of the Great Settlement were repaired and the second row of lower walls was built along the Moscow-river. Besides the engineering purpose – defence of the main Kremlin walls from floods, the low walls became an original "pedestal" for all the complicated complex of town-fortress, which the Kremlin was at that time. All the town-fortresses looked as though they grew from the earth first by one-two low walls with patterned double merlons, and already above them the whole Kremlin raised with high walls and many other architectures.

At that time the architectonic look of the highest building of ancient Moscow – the bell tower of John the Great was finalised. The third tire was raised and the bell-tower's height became eighty-one metres. The building is interesting because it is an absolutely one unity in its forms and does not produce the impression of a building which was reconstructed and added for almost a century – and not just by different architects, but by representatives of different national cultures. The bell-towers' tires, growing from each other, are the continuation of the same architectural theme, which can be figuratively called "ascension of chime". Arcades of the chime are on the tops of the first two tires. Above the second tire another more narrow arcade raises, where the chime is increased by the golden flame of high three-tops kokoshniks with golden stars. Location of windows conforms to the chime location and is an original finish of the main theme, which is crowned by the ranges of the golden inscription on the blue background and a dome with a cross.

Already in 1532-1543 near the Ivanovsky Pillar Petrok the Small builds a belfry for big bells of the cathedral of the Assumption, into which first the consecration of the church of the Resurrection, then in 1555 the consecration of the church of the Nativity of Christ were transferred.

Near the strict bell-tower's pillar the patterned volume of the belfry with its fretted ranges, rich top, complicated dome's drum, is very beautiful. Thin rich decoration preserved during the reconstructions of the belfry in 1685 and 1781, can he seen on the water-colour by G.Quarenghi and on ancient (drawings from the collection of Bergolts in Sweden (18th century). According to these documents, using axonometric plans of Moscow and the Kremlin, it is possible to recreate quite precisely the former look of the belfry.

In 1624 upon the task of Patriarch Phylaret an architect's apprentice Bazhen Ogurtsov added to the previous ones another bell-tower, known under the name of "Phylaret's out-house". Strict and exquisite, with a light top, it completed the ensemble of the main Kremlin's belfries. This ensemble became an original symbol of united Russia, architectonic and "sonic". Here the bells of the former capitals of Russian lands and domains were collected.

During the 16th-17th centuries the ensemble of Cathedral Square acquires a finished appearance. The

Moscow Kremlin at the time of John III. Artist A.M.Vasnetsov.

porches of the Faceted Palace, the Golden Porch, galleries and parvises of the cathedrals of Archangel Michael and the Annunciation were remade and extended. During these two hundred years the colour composition of the ensemble changed several times: from red-white painting with tiles, coloured fretwork and scenery frescos to unusual richness of geometrical and floral paintings. But in spite of the changes in form and colour, the general character of the ensemble of Cathedral Square was preserved very strictly. All was subordinated to the cathedral of the Assumption and the bell-tower of John the Great. Coloured and fretted, rich in ornaments of various types churches, cathedrals, palaces of the square as though surrounded the white stone, nearly without small details and "excess" decorations the cathedral of the Assumption. Even when all the archature belt of the cathedral had the figures of saints, it only stood out with its asceticism.

From the middle of the 16th century the Kremlin's buildings became more diverse. The ensemble of Ivanovskaya Square developed and improved. In 1565 to the East from the cathedral of Archangel Michael Ambassadorial Chamber was built. In 1675 the construction of Departments buildings was begun – which were certain ministries of that time, which were finished in 1680. Having the length of 142 and the width of 27 metres, the range of the buildings contained seven departments: Ambassadorial, Categorising, of the Big Fisc, Novgorodian, Estate Kazansky and Streletsky. Each department had its own porch. According to the kept drawing, till the end of the 18th century each department had its own, special in configuration and colour roof. In the same drawing there is the temple of St. Michael and Theodore of Chernigov in the middle part, as well as the temple of St. Alexander Nevsky. These churches were fetched here from the bell-tower of John the Great in 1681-1683.

By the end of the 16th century Ivanovskaya Square presented an extremely interesting ensemble. Streets stretched from the Saviour, the Holy Trinity and St.Nicholas Gates of the Kremlin to the square, it was possible to come to it from Taynitskie Gates. By two passages Ivanovskaya Square was connected with Cathedral one. The highest dominating group of buildings of the square is the ensemble of belfries with the bell-tower of John the Great and the cathedral of St.Nicholas Gostunsky in front of it made its transversal axis. Longitudinal axis was made by the double church at the Departments in the Southern part and the church of

St. Andrew the First Called of the Chudov monastery in the Northern part. Both under the churches at the Departments and under the churches of the Chudov monastery there were gates, which even more underlined the unity of the architectures along the longitudinal axis. Crossing of the square's axises divided the longitudinal axis nearly into two halves, the transversal axis was divided in proportion to the difference between the height of the ensemble of the belfries and the church of St. Nicholas Gostunsky from which the point of crossing is further.

The complex of the tsar's palaces was a tire-like, very extended ensemble. History kept the names of main Russian architects, who took part in its creation. At the border of the 16th-17th centuries Theodore the Steed could take part in the construction, and in the 17th century – Bazhen Ogurtsov, Stepan Karaulov, Gregory Zagryazhsky, Antip Konstantinov, Trefil and Nicetas Shaturin, Larya Ushakov, (Osip Startsev, David Okhlebin, Lyubim Grigoriev, Safon Sysoev, Jacob Sharygin), the elder Hippolytus.

The Kremlin decorated by the last quarter of the 17th century with high marquees, steeples on Three corners and two gate towers, included large, wonderfully elaborate, rich in colour and fretwork cathedrals, monasteries, palaces, state offices, churches and palaces of high officials. Combining in the purely Russian ensemble creative work of many nations of Europe and Asia, it became the monument of world's importance – conscious town-building symbol of ecclesiastic unity of mankind not by usurpation and military force, but through the disclosing of the highest achievements of cultures of different nations.

Hierarch and the First Tsar

Flourishing of Russian national architecture, beginning of change of Moscow's appearance as the capital of Holy Russia are connected with the activity of a man of genius – extremely active hierarch metropolitanate Macarius. The hierarch raised Moscow to the next "royal" stage, provided, blessed the construction of religious buildings special in appearance, which later served to rapid development of individuality of Russian architecture, unique look of all Moscow.

Macarius was born in Moscow at the beginning of 1482, at the end of the 15th century he took the monastic vows in Paphnutievsky monastery in Borovsk, since 1523 he was the Father Superior of Luzhetsky monastery in Mozhaysk, and since 1526 he was the archbishop of Great Novgorod and Pskov. In March 1542 at the age of 60 the hierarch becomes the Head of the Russian Church. Already in 1547 and 1549 he prepared and held two councils on "glorifying and canonisation of Russian Saints. Among the new miracle-workers there were the Saints of Kievskaya Rus, Great Novgorod, Pskov, Rostov, Suzdal, Smolensk, Tver, Great Ustyug, Moscow, Murom, Perm and other places. A contemporary notes gladly to this effect: "Since that time God's Churches are not like widows without memory about Saints of all Russian land. As though some luminary is shining on the candle-stand of Russian land, with Orthodoxy and true belief and doctrines of the Divine Apostolic Epistle in all the Universe".

The above councils resulted in great spiritual inspiration in Russian society. This was the epoch of new miracle-workers, new page of canonisation of Russian Saints. The third Stoglavy Council is associated with the name of Macarius, which in 1551 put an end to discords in the Russian Church that had accumulated for the long period of scattered existence of Russia.

The name of Macarius is connected with composition of the Great Menology (Chetji Minei). The work of partial writing, collection, systematising of all "read books" in Russia was begun by him in Novgorod in 1529 and continued in Moscow.

The Menology of St. Macarius included the memorials of ecclesiastic literature, which appeared at the sunrise of Slavic writing language, the first Russian works and further memorials, here is the "Word about the Testament and Bliss" of the first Russian metropolitanate Hilarion (the middle of the 11th century), the works of St. Cyril, bishop of Turov (12th century), "Pilgrim" of Hegumen Daniel (12th century), the works of Pachomius the Serb (15th century), Epistles of Metropolitanates of all Russia, etc. The Menology included the memorials of ecclesiastic literature, lives of saints, also newly canonised, doctrine material, memorials of struggle with schisms, with the Tatar yoke, cosmology. "The Menology is the act of church-state importance. Motives of its appearance are the same as those of Stoglavy Council and the Councils of canonisation – to renew and extol the Russian Church", – the academician A.S. Orlov wrote.

The influence of metropolitanate Macarius on Russian art was immense, including icon-painting. "Art loses local specialities, and the style of the whole Moscow state is created. It was because of the metropolitanate move to Moscow and icon-painting masters of Novgorod and Pskov with him, who assimilated with Moscow masters making "Makarievskaya studio". One of the most important memorials of the studio is the icon "Blessed Is the Regiment of The Heavenly King", – the famous memorial of the victory in Kazan.

One of the most important events in history of Rus was the church wedding of the first tsar, 17-year old grand prince John IV Vasilievich, in future the Terrible. Rise to the tsar's Throne was prepared and blessed by metropolitanate Macarius and all the Saint Synaxis of Russian Metropoly..." After the wedding, liturgy, congratulation of the new tsar metropolitanate Macarius made a proper speech wishing the new tsar to love the Church and observe God's testaments, take care of his citizens. In 1551 in the cathedral of the Assumption a praying place was arranged for the tsar. And in 1561 the blessing chart with the signatures of 37 hierarchs of the East Orthodox Church was received from Patriarch Ioasaph, which confirmed the tsar's rank of John IV Vasilievich.

But it was stipulated in the chart that "what was done by metropolitanate Macarius cannot be final and binding and that only the chiefs of priests of Rome and

Constantinople are entitled to marry tsars in church". This note insulted the Russians deeply, the Patriarch who needs himself the confirmation of his order from the Turks, takes the right to grant or not the tsar's title to the Tsar of the free orthodox Russian Kingdom, direct heir of the fallen Byzantine Empire. It insulted John IV too, who started to criticise the Greeks after that as the Latins. Still the chart made the Russians to understand that they lack one important person for the complete inheritance of the Greek Empire – Patriarch.

Metropolitanate Macarius knew all that very well, but he had made such a step, using the situation, to extol the title of the Russian Tsar, and his estimation was absolutely correct.

The young tsar got a hard political inheritance. Five tatar Muslim khanates surrounded Russia in the East and South: the khanates of Kazan, Astrakhan and the Crimea, Nogayskaya Big and Small hordes. Russian people had to make enormous efforts to defend their East and South borders. It was very difficult to fight with the heirs of the Golden Horde. Historian S.F.Platonov wrote about the specialities of the war at the steppe borders: "The enemy's qualities, with whom they had to fight and about whom they had to be very careful, were original: it was a steppe wild animal, movable and fearless, but at the same time inconsistent and difficult to catch. He "stole" Russian "outskirts", did not fight in an open war, he captured and robbed the country, but did not conquer it, he kept Moscow people in constant fear of his invasion, but at the same time he did not try to take away forever or even for some time to appropriate the lands which he attacked like a sudden, but short thunder".

The main purpose of tatars' invasions was the capture of "polonjanniks", who after that were sold at East markets. This capturing began in the 15th century and continued till the 18th century. And during the Troubled Times at the beginning of the 17th century East bazaars were so overcrowded with "polonjanniks" (captured people), that the Persian shah Abbas, receiving Russian ambassadors expressed his surprise that there were still some people in the Russian state...

In 1552 young John the Terrible and the Russian army took Kazan by storm and liquidated Kazanskoe khanate. In 1556 Astrakhanskoe khanate was also liquidated.

The death-bearing circle of tatar hordes was destroyed Russian orthodox state was saved, the main merit in which is given to John the Terrible.

After that Rus could not turn its face to catholic Lithuania and Poland, which oppressed Russian population in Malorossiya and Belorussia and often attacked Russians from the rear and flank when they defended from tatars their centralised Moscow state. Wars and robberies on the part of Lithuanians and Polish were often done in union with tatar hordes and khanates, besides, hetman Radsivil, for example, said cynically in one of such cases: "I do not argue if it is good to let the vile loose upon Christians from the point of view of theology, but according to earthly politics, it turned out to be very good".

So, in those conditions the Russian capital was built in the 16th century at the time of John the Terrible, then at the time or his son Theodore Ivanovich.

Kitay-Gorod

The stirring up of construction at the turn of 15th-16th centuries resulted in the fact that the Kremlin and, certainly, Moscow changed beyond recognition. Out of the grand princely town Moscow became the capital of the united Russian state. But the construction did not stop. Fortifying the Kremlin, reconstructing its buildings by increasing the cathedrals, palaces, Moscow authorities started to make the whole city more beautiful. In the area of 109 sazhens cleaned around the Kremlin gardens and convenient trade squares were made, a new stone bridge was built across the Neglinnaya. At the beginning of the century architecton Aleviz raised more than ten stone temples on the territory of the city. Soon the first stone fortification was built in the Great Settlement of Moscow.

The word "kita" means wattled grass or tree branches. In 1534 "in Moscow a town was made from earth... The cunning people made it very wisely, it was begun from the big wall (of the Kremlin), they wattled thin branches near big wood and poured earth inside and pressed very hard, conducted it along the Moscow-river and led to the same stone wall (of the Kremlin) and at versta made a traditional wooden town... and gave it the name "Kitay".

But next year grand princess Helen – the mother of the five-year old John (in future the Terrible), around the town Kitay "ordered to build a stone town near the earth one". At the same time "the foundation of the town was made by the master Peter the Small Fryazin". By 1538 the walls of Kitay-gorod were built. Today it is possible to see what remained of them in two places: near the hotel Rossiya" and in the square in front of the Bolshoy theatre. The walls have loop-holes, which first were similar to the Kremlin's loop-holes. The difference between the walls of Kitay-gorod and the Kremlin was in the presence of curved fire, and the walls themselves were lower. All the towers of Kitay-gorod had curved fire (mashikuli), the towers were first covered with wooden marquees. At the field side of Kitay-gorod a deep ditch was made, faced with stone and filled with water from springs.

Entrances of the new Moscow fortress were protected by images of saints, which were in icon-cases above the gates. It is known that after the fire of 1547 masters from Novgorod and Pskov were called to paint the repaired stone plates and "the images of saints above the town's gates".

In 1668 a wooden chapel for the Iveron icon of the Most Holy Theotokos appeared outside between the double Neglinenskie gates. In 1680 the gates were dismantled and the new ones were built instead with two towers and emblems at the top of the marquees, which were called Voskresenskie (Resurrection), because above the gates there was the icon of the Resurrection. The Iveron chapel was raised again and the gates were sometimes called Iverskie. There was also a wooden chapel of Solovetsky monastery outside near the double Moskvoretskie gates.

The Frontal place and St. Basil's cathedral in 17th century. Patriarch Ioasaph blesses tsar Michael Federovich in 1636. Print from A. Clearly's album.

Kitay-gorod gradually built in with unique architecture, got several original ensembles too.

The frontal (Lobnoe) place was first mentioned in 1549, when after the fire and riot in Moscow the religious procession first came out of the Kremlin and the young tsar John Vasilievich (the Terrible) in the presence of metropolitanate Macarius was at the divine service and then told the moscovites about the reasons of disasters in the state. A round stone tomb was brought here from Cathedral Square and put on the new place in front of Frolovskie (the Saviour) gates. Frontal Square became the place of public prayer under the open sky, and the Frontal place became like an ambo for the holy orders. From here the tsars addressed to people, tsars' decrees were announced from the Frontal place; here various celebrations were organised, the troops were met and seen off. In 1606, for example, here the relicts of the killed tsarevich Demetrius – the last of the Ryurikovichis – were places for public valedictory.

Moscow Frontal place became the geometrical place of the capital. From it distances to all towns of the huge Russian state were measured and indicated.

The importance of the Frontal place will he mentioned later during the description of the capital's symbolic structures.

The cathedral of St.Basil is a "national miracle" (according to Zabelin), an "ultranational work" (according to German scientist Kugler), which appeared after the Frontal place. In 1552 tsar John Vasilievich gave the vow: to build a temple in Moscow if Kazan was taken. In 1553 the stone vowed temple of the Holy Trinity was built at the ditch, near Frolovskie (the Saviour) gates outside the Kremlin. In 1555-1560 the temple was rebuilt eight more inside lateral altars were added. According to the names of some of them the temple was called at different times as the temple of the Holy Trinity at the Ditch, then the one of the Intercession at the Ditch, of the Entrance into Jerusalem at the Ditch, finally, since the 18th century – the temple of St.Basil – according to the inside lateral altar of 1588 -in the name of the glorious fool-for-Christ.

The world's famous memorial of subjugation of the khanates of Kazan and Astrakhan, final liberation of Russia from Tatar-Mongolian yoke, from real threat of moslem enslavery of Russian orthodox people, the cathedral of St.Basil has such unusual forms that it is still commented on and interpreted differently. It is really rich in its forms and especially in meaningful symbolic contents.

In accordance with the consecration of the main East altar of the Holy Trinity the cathedral represents the symbol of the "House of the Holy Trinity" – Divine Jerusalem, Heavenly Town. With this consecration the vowed stone church was built in 1533 right after taking of Kazan. In this way the stone cathedral of 1561 is indicated on all axonometric plans of Moscow of the 17th century. In capital forms of the cathedral four purely Russian temple types: multi-cupola, marquee-like, tire-like and fiery were used together ("combination of types", as I.E.Zabelin said).

The *multi-cupola* type was first represented by 25 cupolas: 9 were on the main inside altars, 8 small cupolas were installed at the bottom of the marquee of the central altar of the Intercession, 4 – on the West altar of the Entrance into Jerusalem, 4 – on the inside altars "under the chime". The cathedral became, on the one hand, the symbol of rebirth of multi-cupola style of Kievskaya Rus of the 10th-12th century, on the other hand, the main sample of the new, Moscow stage of construction of multi-cupola temples of different forms.

It is known that the construction in Russia of multi-cupola temples ("multi" is understood as "more than five"). There were no such temples in Byzantium, from where Christianity came to Russia, not in any other christian countries of East and West. It was a purely Russian novelty. It started from the wooden cathedral of St.Sophia in Kiev in 952 built by St.Olga, princess of Russia. According to the legend, the cathedral had seventy cupolas. The construction of stone churches at the time of prince Vladimir began from the stone Desyatinnaya church with 25 cupolas – the symbol of the Heavenly Town in the centre of Kiev. Then the stone cathedral of St.Sophia in Kiev with 13 cupolas, the cathedral of St.Sophia in Novgorod with 6 cupolas, the cathedral of St.Sophia in Polotsk with 7 cupolas, the church of Archangel Michael in Kiev with 15 golden cupolas were built.

Construction of multi-cupola temples in Moscow Rus, as is known, began from the church of St.John the Predecessor in Diakov with 15 cupolas, then the 15-cupola church of the Transfiguration in Ostrov, finally, the cathedral of the Holy Trinity on the Ditch with 25 cupolas – the symbol of the Heavenly Town in the centre of Moscow. Like in Kievskaya Rus, in Moscow Rus multi-cupola temples are the token of unity of Russian people, rebirth of the huge and united Russian state after the period of scattering of the 12th century and Tatar-Mongolian yoke of the 13th-15th century. The perpetual value, uniqueness of Russian multi-cupola cathedrals is in this religious, civil, warriors symbolics. The Moscow cathedral of the Holy Trinity on the Ditch can he compared in this symbolics only with the Desyatinnaya church in Kiev.

The marquee-like temple – the altar of the Intercession in the centre of the cathedral – makes the temple of St.Basil also one of marquee-like temples of Moscow and Russia. Marquee as a form of a church roof first appeared above wooden churches, probably, already at the time of christening of Russia and spreading of Christianity over the Russian land in the 11th-12th century. And when near Moscow in tsar's residence near the village of Kolomenskoe in 1532 the first stone church of the Ascension with high stone marquee was built, the chroniclers wrote that its top was like that of the wooden one. So, wooden marquee-like temples, that had beautified villages and towns since ancient time, were not unusual in Russia. Marquee underlines strongly "centricity" and this quality was used for the creation in the centre of Moscow, near the Frontal place, of a centric cathedral. Besides, only a marquee could hold 25 cupolas.

Tire-like (pillar) temples are situated inside the cathedral of St.Basil along the cross at the four sides of the central marquee-like inside the lateral altar. Each temple reminds of the bell-tower of John the Great and has a special pattern decoration. All the four pillars first looked high, because there was no gallery above the porches. Tire-like temples in Russia, like marquee-like ones, appeared long before St.Basil and after it many different temples of the kind were built. The favourite ones were not only the temples of the type "octahedron on octahedron", but "octahedron on tetrahedron" and other numerous variants (up to 4-5 tires), especially in temples with chime.

Fiery temples (altars) of the cathedral of St.Basil are situated along the diagonal cross in relation to the central marquee-like temple and pillar-like altars. These are four churches with tires of semi-circular kokoshniks at the bottoms of the cupolas. Fiery temples were built in Moscow later, at the end of the 16th-17th century, as though spread from St.Basil's (cathedral.

The "national miracle" was built by the great Russian architect *Postnik Yakovlev* with an associate, who had the nickname of *Barma*. It is quite clear that a young man, a novice in creation, theology, doctrine in Christian symbolics, could not build the tsar's vowed temple in the centre of Moscow and to create one of the greatest pieces of architecture. Certainly he was an acknowledged master, who had already built stone temples, chambers, fortress walls and towers. It was not by chance that he got the nickname Barma – tsar's oplechie (precious jewellery) before the construction of the cathedral of the Holy Trinity on Ditch. And if contemporaries acknowledged his architectural talent, we can say that he also built such original architecture like the church of St.John the Predecessor in Diakov in 1547 in honour of the tsar's church wedding of John IV Vasilievich, the amazing marquee-like churches of St.Sergius in Troitskoe settlement in the Kremlin, and even the tsar's residences in the villages Ostrov and Kolomenskoe. Only such tsar's temples could be the reason of the nickname "Barma".

In some of the above-said temples, besides many original architectural forms, scientists also find some of Italian style and concluded that Italian architects could participate in the construction. As Italians built in Moscow at the end of the 15th and beginning of the 16th century, it is certainly possible. But this logic is not unquestionable. And the copyright of Postnik-Barma's Moscow national "miracle" is out of the question.

We must comment too that only due to the strong will power of grand Moscow princes and utter responsibility before God of metropolitanates, especially of the metropolitanate Macarius and the tsar John the Terrible, such individual Russian orthodox temples could appear in Moscow in the 16th century, which were drastically different from the canonical cross-cupola Greek temples. Besides, no new type deviated from the symbolics of the Heavenly Town. The best example of ultranational creation was the cathedral of the Holy Trinity on the Ditch – St.Basil's cathedral.

At the end of the 16th century the "miracle" is rebuilt, becomes even more miraculous. Instead of the cupolas from plain white iron (tinned) it gets the new famous cupolas, which are even coated with gold. The cupolas shone in the sun in the centre of Moscow. During the 17th century the temple is decorated even more: a gallery with a roof is built, the porches are carved; at the end of the century instead of the three-marquee church under the chime the bell-tower appears which exists till now. The temple is painted with floral ornament outside, as a symbol of the Paradise. Frontal square began to be called as "Troitskaya".

By 1637 near Neglimenskie (gates of Kitay-gorod the cathedral of the "Kazan" *Icon of the Most Holy Theotokos*. With this miracle-working and victorious icon people's volunteer corps of Cosmas Minin and prince Demetrius Pozharsky liberated Moscow in 1612 from Polish-Lithuanian invaders. The memorial of the saving of Russian orthodox people from catholic expansion raised on the shore of the Neglinnaya near the Kremlin's Nicholskie Gates, like the cathedral of St.Basil - on the shore of the Moscow-river near Frolovskie (the Saviour) gates. In front of Kazansky cathedral Zemsky Department was built, and around the cathedral a smooth wooden floor was laid – that is why the square of the cathedral was called "Red" "Krasnaya". Wide smooth flooring – "Krasny bridge" – was also made for religious processions of the tsar and church hierarchs from the Frontal place to Kazansky cathedral. Thus, these two squares: Troitskaya at the cathedral of the Holy Trinity and Krasnaya at Kazansky cathedral are connected and get the single name of Krasnaya Square (first mentioned in

Ancient Moscow buildings. Stone building of the Printing Yard. End of 17th century. Reconstruction of M. Kudriavtsev.

1662). But, finally, the ensemble of *Red Square* was composed by 1700, when the altars of 15 temples on the Ditch were carried into St.Basil's cathedral, and the temples with their yards were liquidated.

Town-building measures in the 16th-17th centuries took place also on the territory of Kitay-gorod. The second after the Kremlin centre of the capital's departments forms here. First, at the end of the 16th century, the future Red Square is bordered in the East by the line of the Verkhnie (Upper) trade rows. Monetny (Coin) Yard is arranged in the North end, behind the Upper rows and Kazansky cathedral. In the South sine of Kitay-gorod, from the Lower trade rows to Moskvoretskie gates customs Mytny Yard is built. Behind the Middle rows Guest Yard appears. The monastery of Epiphany and the monastery of Our Lady of the Sign gradually become splendid behind the yards. Dense net of yards – representations of Russian towns and big monasteries – forms gradually behind this huge town-building complex of the Upper, Middle and Lower trade rows, tsar's yards and monasteries; it forms inside the walls of Kitay-gorod. By the end of the 17th century the representations occupy a big part of the territory. Here also a number of embassies were situated : English, Polish, Roman, the monastery of St.Nicholas Stary becomes St. Nicholas Greek (representation), Tatar representation was at the corner of Kitay-gorod.

Since 1551 after Stoglavy Council near the cathedral of the Holy Trinity on the Ditch the Priest House appeared for management of seven Moscow Synaxis (later it became the Department of Church Affairs, Tiunskaya Chamber). Since the time of John the Terrible the Printing Yard appeared in Nicholskaya street. Its organisation is connected with metropolitanate Macarius and the first Russian publisher John Fiodorov, a deacon of the Kremlin's church of St.Nicholas Gostunsky. In the 17th century the Printing Yard was rebuilt by the architects Sharutin and Neverov and like other yards got portentous entrance in the form of a high picturesque gate tower. There were solar clocks on the tower.

Kitay-gorod was united in strict and well functioning structure, exquisite town-building composition. At the same time it was a sample of ideal subordination of the complex second architecture to the first one – the Kremlin. In spite of the fact that its main ensembles and buildings are well known, it still must be studied in the general history, archaeology and most of all in town-building. Being in the past the second Moscow centre of state government, international trade and political connections, science, education, Kitay-gorod is a unique monument of ancient Russian architecture.

The Tsar and the First Patriarch

John the Terrible took great care of consolidation of the tsar's power. So his son, a meek and pious tsar Theodore Ioannovich had just used the results of the well regulated system of monarchist state structure, though, as it often happens, near the flabby heir the decisive, intelligent and smart "manager", as the boyard Boris Godunov was, acted. This stable power and appeasement of the autocrat could result in the period of the quiet reign of Theodore Ioannovich both in the sphere of politics, ideology (enslavery of peasants, establishment of patriarchate etc.) and especially in the capital's town-building. The most important event was, certainly, the establishment of patriarchate.

"Latins" and orthodox Greeks did not recognise John the Terrible as "strong tsar" because of the above-sale minor formality: he was raised to the tsar's throne not by the patriarch, but metropolitanate Macarius. Because of his cruelty, repressions of orthodox boyards tsar John the Terrible gave the reason to Russian people to see in him the false tsar and even antichrist of the last times (Hegumen Cornelius of Pskovo-Pechersky monastery). So after the death of tsar John the Terrible in 1584 Moscow authorities started to make efforts in order that there was the Patriarch in Russia: a free orthodox tsar cannot be crowned in unfaithful Turkey or catholic Rome. With appearance of high church hierarch the tsar's power will he generally acknowledged. The Greeks understood it too, so the efforts of Russians were successful in five years already.

In 1589 patriarch Jeremiah came to Moscow from Constantinople with suite and with participation of All-the-Right Reverend Synaxis of bishops of the Russian

Church raised metropolitanate Job to the throne of the patriarch of all Russia.

And "the Right Reverend Jeremiah, by God's mercy archbishop of Constantinople, *New Rome's* oecumenical patriarch... said with all his heart:

"Oh, faithful and Christ-loving and crowned by God... great lord Tsar and Grand Prince Theodore Ioannovich..." (and further – there were nearly exactly the words of Pskov's elder Philotheus of the beginning of the 16th century): "As ramshackle Rome fall down through Apollinaris' schism; the second Rome, which is Constantinople, is under the power of unfaithful Turks; your, pious Tsar, great Russian Kingdom, the *third Rome* is higher in piety than the others, and all pious tsars gathered into yours, and All-the-Right Reverend Synaxis of the great Russian and Greek kingdoms, elected and established as the patriarch to the great throne...of the reigning town of Moscow Job, the Right Reverend Metropolitanate of all Russia". By the same Establishment Charter all church hierarchy raised to the new stage: four metropolitanate were established in it, six archbishops, eight bishops.

The news about establishment of patriarchate in Russia was written in all Russian chronicles. But in the chronicle of Pskov it had an unusual commentary: "Patriarch Jeremiah...upon the Tsar's will and order (?).. blessed and established in Moscow metropolitanate Job to the Russian patriarchate instead of the fallen away Roman Pope". The commentary reminded in its own way the dissidence of the christian church in 1055 and confirmed the theory of the elder Philotheus: «upon the insistence of Russians in the Patriarch's Establishment Charter their claim of the estimation of Moscow as «the Third Rome» was written in». The fact that in 1593 upon establishment by Eastern patriarchs of the rank implemented in Moscow this claim was not stipulated, speaks to this effect.

However, the Russian public opinion was sure that it was right. Though the Moscow Patriarch was established by the Greeks as the fifth after that of Jerusalem, he was understood as the first because of his status in the only free powerful orthodox state and because he substituted also free hierarch of the catholic church (at Florentiysky Council in 1439 the priority in the Christian church was given by the Greeks to the Roman Pope). In this public opinion there is the reason of firm existence in Russia of the theory "Moscow – the Third Rome" up to the end of the 17th century, while the Russian government and Tsar of Moscow did not presume this theory in any official international document (the theory was not official in the state). Here again, like with Holy Russia, all was understood and established at the level of people's consciousness.

The life of the first Russian patriarch Job was full of troubles. At his time The murder of tsarevich Demetrius happened (1591). In 1598 he took the side of Boris Godunov, the elected tsar, – the first tsar crowned by the Russian Patriarch, – though many did not recognise him as the tsar. After several years of bad harvests there was famine in Russia, of which millions of people became the victims and the country gradually fell into the chaos of the Troubled Time. With appearance of the self-called tsar Lzhedmitry I (False Demetrius) patriarch Job in sermons and epistles exposed and ordered to anathematise Lzhedmitry. After the death of tsar Boris Godunov in 1605 there was a riot in Moscow. The rebellious assaulted the old patriarch in the cathedral of Assumption and outraging his order, fetched him to the Frontal place. But he stayed alive and was sent to Staritsky monastery under supervision.

In 1606 at the time of tsar Basil Shuisky patriarch Job renounced his order and blessed Germanus to be the patriarch. At the time of Job many new saints were canonised: St.Basil, St.Joseph, abbot of Volokolarnsk (or Volotsk) etc.

Bely – Tsar's Town

The third range of Moscow fortifications is usually called "Bely (White) town". But it was forgotten that initially the fortification line was called by the name of "Bely" tsar" – tsar of the free state, as Theodore Ioannovich was.

Resides in the area of Bely town, mainly, tsar's and church's officers lived who were freed from taxes.

At the beginning of the 16th century the big territory of Moscow along the line of Boulevard Ring was surrounded along the old bank of the second half of the 14th century with new wooden walls of Okolnichy town (their remnants were found during the construction of the first metro stations). At the time of John the Terrible, and especially of Theodore Ioanovich the construction on the territory of Okolnichy town included reconstruction and extension of yards, growth of dwelling houses. At the end of the 16th century stone walls of Moscow monasteries were built.

In 1586 according to the tsar's decree outside the walls of Okolnichy town Bely town was built from stone and brick, which was finished in 1593. The architect of the new fortification line was famous *Theodore Savelievich* the Steed, who was from the nobility of Zvenigorod's prince. The stone wall was at that time one

The church of the Ascension "Maloe" and Patriarch's court in 17th century in Big Nikitskaya street. Reconstruction of M.P.Kudriavtsev.

Ancient Moscow buildings. Stone chambers of boyard V.V.Golitsyn in Okhotny Row. Drawing of D.P.Sukhov.

of the biggest – the length was about 10 km with 27 towers, 10 of which were gate ones.

Bely – Tsar's town was dismantled at the time of Catherine II, and unfortunately, neither drawings, nor detailed descriptions were left. Till now there were no special excavations and research of its remnants. Though the remnants were encountered a few times during earth works near the Palace of Councils, during dismantling of Sukharevskaya Tower, near the former Educational house... But today still there are houses near Petrovskie, Sretenskie, Pokrovskie gates, into which parts of the ancient fortress wall are bricked up. The bottom part of the wall higher than the socle also remains in different places of the Boulevard Ring under the ground.

It is known that the wall was a little inclined inside, the loop-holes for a curved fire had the merlons in the form of a «swallow tail». In the majority of ancient plans of Moscow and pictures wall gates have three marquees, and the towers have one marquee, the south-west tower near Chertolskie gates on the shore of the Moscow-river has the design of seven marquees.

Surrounding the Kremlin and Kitay-gorod, Bely-Tsar's town was in the 17th century the proper frame for two central fortresses. In the northern part its wall conformed to the north line of four monasteries-guards, which controlled the North roads: Tverskaya, Dmitrovskaya, Yurievskaya, Yaroslavskaya. These were the monasteries Strastnoy (of the Passions), Vysoko-Petrovsky, Rozhdestvensky (of the Nativity of the Theotokos), Sretensky (of the Presentation of Christ in the Temple). From them only the latest monastery of the Passions was outside the wall behind the ditch. In the west the wall went above the brook Chertory, in the East – near the shore of the Yauza-river, including into its ditch the small river Rachka which dried out. At the flanks of the Kremlin and Kitay-gorod there were the walls and towers of Bely-Tsar's town in the panorama of Moscow's centre in the south, from Zamoskvorechie.

Many temples in the settlement and yards of Bely-Tsar's town were the monuments of war history, adjoining of Russian principalities to Moscow. The church of the Ascension Maloe in Nikitskaya street and the church of the Resurrection in Uspensky Vrazhek are the monuments of liberation of Moscow from Polish-Lithuanian intervention during the Troubled Time; the churches of the Holy Trinity in Khokhlovka, St.Nicholas in Kleniki are connected with the reunion of Russia and Ukraine; the church of All Saints in Kulishki is the monument of the victory in Kulikovo field, the church of the Presentation of the Virgin in the Temple in Lubyanka is the monument to joining Pskov; the church of the Grebnevskaya Icon of the Most Holy Theotokos and the church of St.Sophia in Lubyanka are the monuments to the joining of Novgorod, etc.

Buildings of Bely-Tsar's town in the 16th-17th centuries are mostly from stone - the temples and the lower storeys of dwelling chambers. But household buildings, gardens and upper storeys of dwelling houses and chambers were all from wood cut, fretted, painted. Russian people, peasants, handicraftsmen, streltsy, boyards preferred to live in wooden houses believing that stone houses are hazardous for health. That is why stone buildings which stayed till our time are household lower premises, and rooms for official receptions are on the second floor. Certainly, the chambers of princes, boyards were the richest, their yards surrounded the Kremlin and Kitay-gorod. The most outstanding were the yards of the princes Khovanskys, Golitsyns, Sheremetevs, Troekurovs, prince Pozharsky and others. Some buildings still remain, we know about many of them from the chronicles and other documents.

Skorodom

In 1591 during a very short period of one summer another fortification line was built – the wall of Skorodom or Derevyanny (Wooden) town, which went along the highway of today's Garden Ring. Austrian ambassador Nicholas Varkoch described Moscow with this fortification in 1593: "The whole town is surrounded by a wooden wall of three sazhen of width and fortified with many wooden towers which makes it look beautiful and majestic at the distance: all its gates are absolutely similar, big and beautiful, all have three-top towers". At different times the look of Skorodom changed because of many rebuildings, during some time the gates even were one-marquee. But the appearance which Varkoch describes, is very remarkable. The length of Skorodom's walls was 15 km, there were 58 towers on the walls, from which three-marquee 12 towers were on the gates and each three of them looked at the four parts of the world.

Skorodom's walls were badly destroyed during the Troubled Time. After the liberation of the capital by the people's volunteer corps under the commandment of prince Pozharsky the town was restored quickly. But the fortifications were from earth now (partially of bastion type), so 12 main gates became more contrasting, part of them were from stone now.

What was left of Skorodom's town – Earth town stayed for a long time and was mentioned in descriptions of the 80s of century. Inside this huge fortress there were handicraft and military settlements, the yards of nobility and boyards took less place, as well as those of the clergy men. Military settlements were in the four main areas at four sides of the world.

Skorodom's architecture was rather rich. Wooden and stone houses covered with fretwork and painted went along the streets or inside the yards surrounded by palings or cut fences with fretted gates. There was its own social centre in each Skorodom's settlement, which consisted of a temple with a cemetery and brethren yard with a meeting house or chamber, which were close to each other. Now there are only three such centres left: the settlements Ovchinnikovskaya and Kadashevskaya in Zamoskvorechie, and Bronnaya settlement, where the church of St.John the Theologian was separated from the brethren yard by a later dwelling house. Only the main temples were left from the centres of other settlements.

Most of settlements' centres were of fiery type. Nowadays these are the churches of St.Nicholas in Pyzhi, the Theotokos in Sadovniki (it is know according to the inside lateral altar of St.George in Endov), St.Sophia in Tsaritsin meadow (Sophiyskaya quay), the Holy Trinity in Bersenevo (It is known as the church of St.Nicholas according to the inside lateral altar), of the Saviour in Pesky, of St.Symeon Stylites in Povarskaya, of Our Lady of the Sign near Petrovskie gates, etc. There were also other types of temples. For example, tire-like were the churches of the Assumption in the (Cossacks' settlement, of St.Elijah the Prophet (Obydennaya (built in one day). The temples of marquee-cupola type were special, their marquees had neck-drums at the bottom, which were on the temple's vault: on the closed one or, if there were three cupolas – on the parted one. Now there is only one such church of the Nativity of the Theotokos in Putinki (near Pushkin Square, which was earlier Strastnaya). Certainly, in Skorodom's settlements there were temples of the older traditional cross-cupola type: four-pillar ones (like the restored church of the Holy Trinity in Listy), marquee-like ones (like the church of St.Hieromartyr George the Victory-bearer in Ordynka, rebuilt in the 19th century). There were also many wooden churches.

The church of St.Hieromartyr George the Victory-bearer in Vspolie in 17th century in Bolshaya Ordynka. Reconstruction of M.P.Kudriavtsev.

The houses of the settlements' people had two storeys and more, but they were always lower than the nearby churches. They usually consisted of three parts: there was the passage in the middle, on the one side there was the warm part of the house, on the other – the cold one to live during hot summer. There were many gardens, kitchen-gardens, sometimes pastures. Streets, lanes and blind alleys were locked by railings for the night time, near which there were guards.

From other buildings: representations, business yards, mills, production buildings, Kadashevsky textile yard was a unique one in Skorodom. Now there are only two fragments left from it, but the drawings of the 18th century and pictures allow to reconstruct the outside look of the building.

The yard was built in the middle-third quarter of the 17th century under the order of the tsar Alexius Michailovich as a production building for textile workers of Kadashevskaya settlement. Before its construction the requirements of the masters for its dimensions, situation, technological connections and outside look of all the needed premises, were written down carefully. As a result of co-operation between textile workers and architects a

Kadashevskiy Textile Yard in 17th century in Bolshaya Polyanka. Reconstruction of M.P.Kudriavtsev.

Voskresenskaya street of Kadashevskaya settlement in 17th century. Reconstruction of M.P.Kudriavtsev.

house was built which excelled many boyards' yards in its functional reasonability and exterior beauty. It was built from white stone, covered with tiles and non-ferrous metal, painted, decorated with painted and golden patterns and symbolics. The building's forms of tile Textile yard were still reserved and laconic, a little reminding of a fortress, only with a very rich top. Inside it was an elaborate palace with fretted porches and galleries, towers and cosy terraces, there were flower-beds in the middle of the yard.

Another yard – Krymsky, which is still in Zamoskvorechie, is of great interest, in its structure it reminds of Asian caravanserais. It is a monument of trade relations between Russia and East. The third yard, small and reserved in its architecture, is in the north-west part of Skorodom (Spiridonovskaya street). Only one of its two buildings connected by a passage with a tower is left. This yard was the centre of Russian military engineering, established by John the Terrible, it acted even during the time of Peter I, i.e. nearly two centuries and a half.

Military elite, cannon people, streltsy and Cossacks, were also located inside Skorodom, Bely-Tsar's town, Kitay-gorod and even the Kremlin, besides the holy orders, merchants, handicraftsmen. Their total quantity

Pokrovskie gates of Skorodom. Reconstruction of M.P.Kudriavtsev.

was about forty thousand (according to historian S.K.Bogoyavlensky). It was the quarter or the third part of the Russian army of that time. Most of the military men lived inside the town, near its sacred gates. So, Moscow is the largest "military base" of Russian land, which was created because of Russia's hostile strong environment.

System of Planning

After the construction of Bely-Tsar's town at the end of the 16th century, as well as of Skorodom, part of their dwelling buildings was burnt by the Polish-Lithuanian invaders in 20 years, then it was restored by moscovites, taking into account the above-said fortification lines in the second quarter of the 17th century. At that time Moscow's planning formed finally. Written sources of the 16th-17th centuries, and especially the first geodesic plan of medieval Moscow, made under the leadership of architect Ivan Michurin in 1739, allowed to make analysis of this planning.

Like in a living human body there were separate life systems of bones, muscles, blood, nerves, so in a huge body of an ancient town there are separate systems of settlements, defence constructions, trade places, streets. Considered in their development and formation, they allow to clarify the essence of the general, complicated system of Moscow planning.

The system of *fortresses and three open settlements*: Veliky, Zagorodje and Zarechie, existed in the 13th-15th centuries after the transformation of the nestle of settlements of pagan Muskovy. Appearance of three separately located settlements near the Kremlin happened because of appearance and development of the feudal town on the cape at the fall of two rivers Moscow and Neglinnaya, dividing the territory into three parts. Besides three settlements did not appear at once, but one after another. It so happened because of different dimensions of the rivers, i.e. different sizes of crossings over the rivers.

First there was a settlement between the rivers directly under the Kremlin: here it was called Big or Great already in early documents (the first stage of the town's growth). After it Zagorodje began to develop – the settlement behind the small river Neglinnaya (the second stage). With bigger growth of population Zarechie appeared (settlement behind the bigger river Moscow (the third stage). Different sizes of the rivers influenced the sizes of the growing settlements: Great settlement – about 59%, Zagorodje – 30%, Zarechie – 20%. The ancient system of the Kremlin and three settlements composed the first stage of "fortress" development of the town.

The system of *four fortresses*: the Kremlin, Kitay-gorod, Bely-Tsar's town, Skorodom (wooden town) appeared in the same order. The stone wall of Kitay-gorod separated and defended between the rivers the nearest to the Kremlin part of the Great settlement (the second "fortress" stage of the town's development). After that the stone wall of Bely-Tsar's town "crossed" the Neglinnaya and surrounded the large part of Zagorodje (the third stage of the town's development). The ring wall of Skorodom surrounded Moscow's outskirts and protected Zarechie (the fourth stage).

The system of *four fortresses* has not survived by our time as a whole. All know only the Kremlin, some moscovites know about the fragments of the wall of Kitay-gorod. In the place of dismantled Bely-Tsar's town (the end of the 18th century), the boulevards appeared, and in the place of Zemlyanoy (Earth) town (Skorodom) the Garden Ring appeared.

The system of *four towns*: the Kremlin, Kitay-gorod, Zaneglimenie, Zamoskvorechie appeared after the construction of settlement fortifications. Besides, the fortification lines separated from three settlements the parts of land, which comprised approximately the following ratio: Kitay-gorod – 20%, Zaneglimenie – 30%, Zamoskvorechie – 50%. Sequential appearance of the fortifications not only influenced the change of the settlements' names (instead of Zagorodie – Zaneglimenie, instead of Zarechie – Zamoskvorechie), but finalised the sizes of the towns and influenced the planning of all dwellings inside the fortification lines.

The system of *town-building* remained till our time, though the liquidation in the last century of the river Neglinnaya (it was taken into the pipe) resulted in disappearance of the name "Zaneglimenie", and dismantling of the walls of Kitay-gorod in the 30s of our time led to disappearance of the name Kitay-gorod. Now only the Kremlin and Zamoskvorechie are known.

The system of the trade places was very well developed in Moscow. Three settlements created three trade places near the Kremlin. The largest one was Kitaygorodskoe trade place, the Upper, Middle, Lower Rows with a second-hand goods market in front of them in the square (the future Red). The smallest was Zaneglimenskoe trade place: Okhotny, Kuryatny, Obzorny and other rows, connected with Kitaygorodskoe trade place by Neglimensky bridge (Voskresensky) from stone. Zamoskvoretskoe trade place was small – Nogaysky trade place (later with relocation it became Bolotny market), connected by Moskvoretsky wooden floating bridge with Kitay-gorod.

During floods the trade places were separated, and in winter they joined together, on the frozen rivers there was (Gribnoy (Mushroom) market near the bridges.

Besides the main trade places there was a whole system of small trade lands, as a rule, outside the fortress gates. There was Konevoy (horse) market near Kitaygorodskoe Varvarskie gates, Sennoy market near Iljinskie gates, Lubyanoy market – near Nikolskie gates.

Planning of ancient Moscow. System elements are singled out on the town's plan of 1739. Scheme of G. Mokeev.

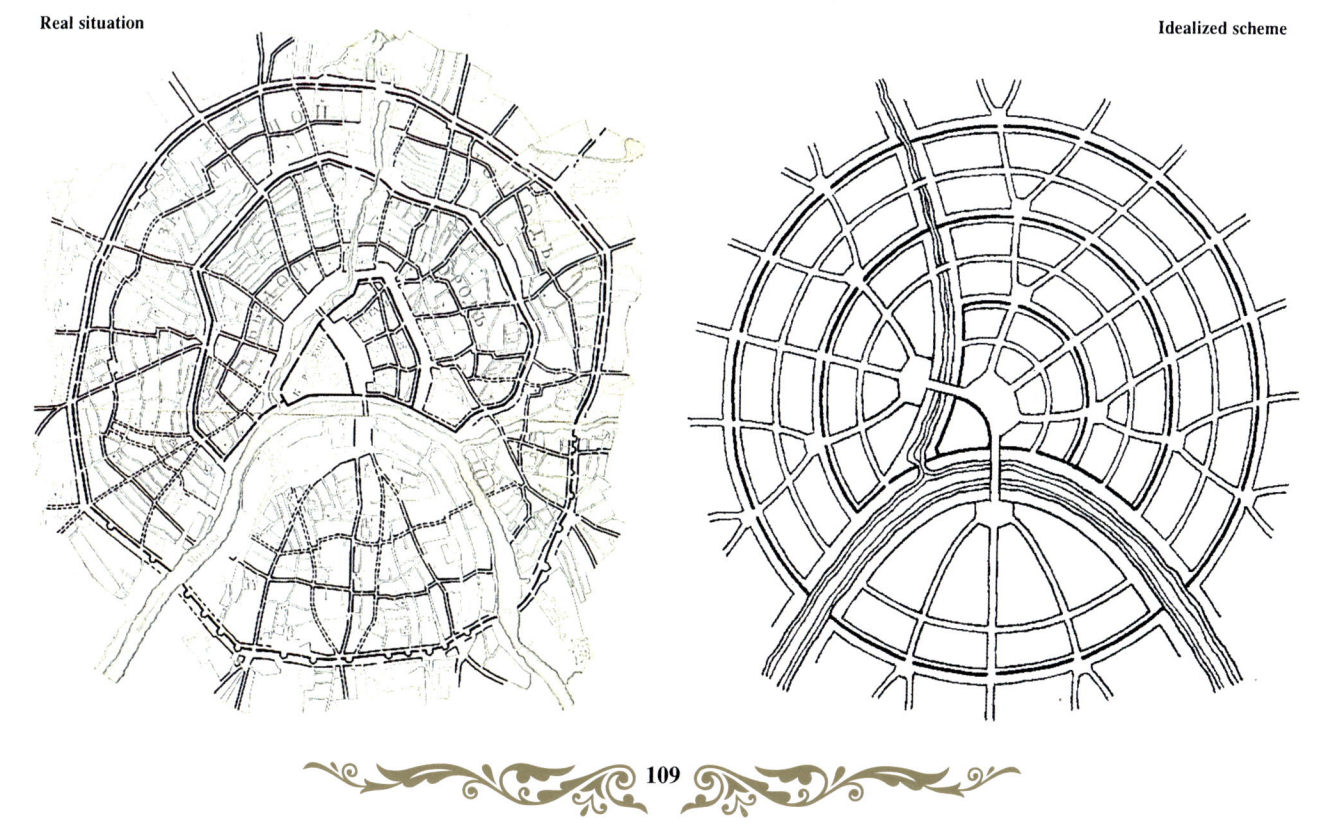

Real situation   Idealized scheme

There were trade lands outside Chertorylskie, Arbatskie, Tverskie, Petrovskie, Sretenskie, Pokrovskie, Yauzskie gates of Bely-tsar's town; Prechistenskie, Smolenskie, Tverskie, Dmitrovskie, Yaroslavskie, Myasnitskie, Pokrovskie, Taganskie, Serpukhovskie, Kaluzhskie gates of the Wooden (Earth) town. This network of trade places was the result of the need of a huge medieval town.

The system of *fan-like* ramified streets was also very well developed. First the fan-like character of planning of three settlements should be noted: Kitay-gorod ramification went from the Kremlin, and the fan-like ramification of the streets of Zaneglimenie and Zamoskvorechie went from the bridges across the rivers. The bridges led to the main trade place of the town. In each ramification there were three main streets. The middle street was the axis in each settlement (I1jinka, Nikitskaya, Ordynka), and side streets ramified later during the growth of settlements from the centre to the outskirts. The branches and fans of the streets allowed, using the shortest ways, to walk to the centre of the town to the main trade places.

The roads to other towns went only along some ways of the fan-like ramification system of the streets, and sometimes along secondary branches (the roads to Tver, Vladimir). It is clear: the roads can radiate from the town in open places (fields), but the dwelling town's architecture could not grow all the time and expand along one road, without making street branches, homogeneously enveloping all the built-in territory.

The fortification lines especially influenced the order of the ramification system of ancient Moscow. From each outside settlement two-three streets stretched to the fortress gates. Such street bunches, which appeared with the growth of the town from the centre to the outskirts, appeared usually in the far areas near the rivers. Thus, with appearance of three settlement walls, three ramifications of the side streets formed between the rivers. In Zaneglimenie *two ramifications* corresponded to two walls, in Zamoskvorechie, protected by one wall, there was *one ramification*.

Taking into account the three-branch system of the main streets of three town settlements, as well as the

Planning of ancient Moscow. System elements are singled out on the town's plan of 1739. Scheme of G. Mokeev.

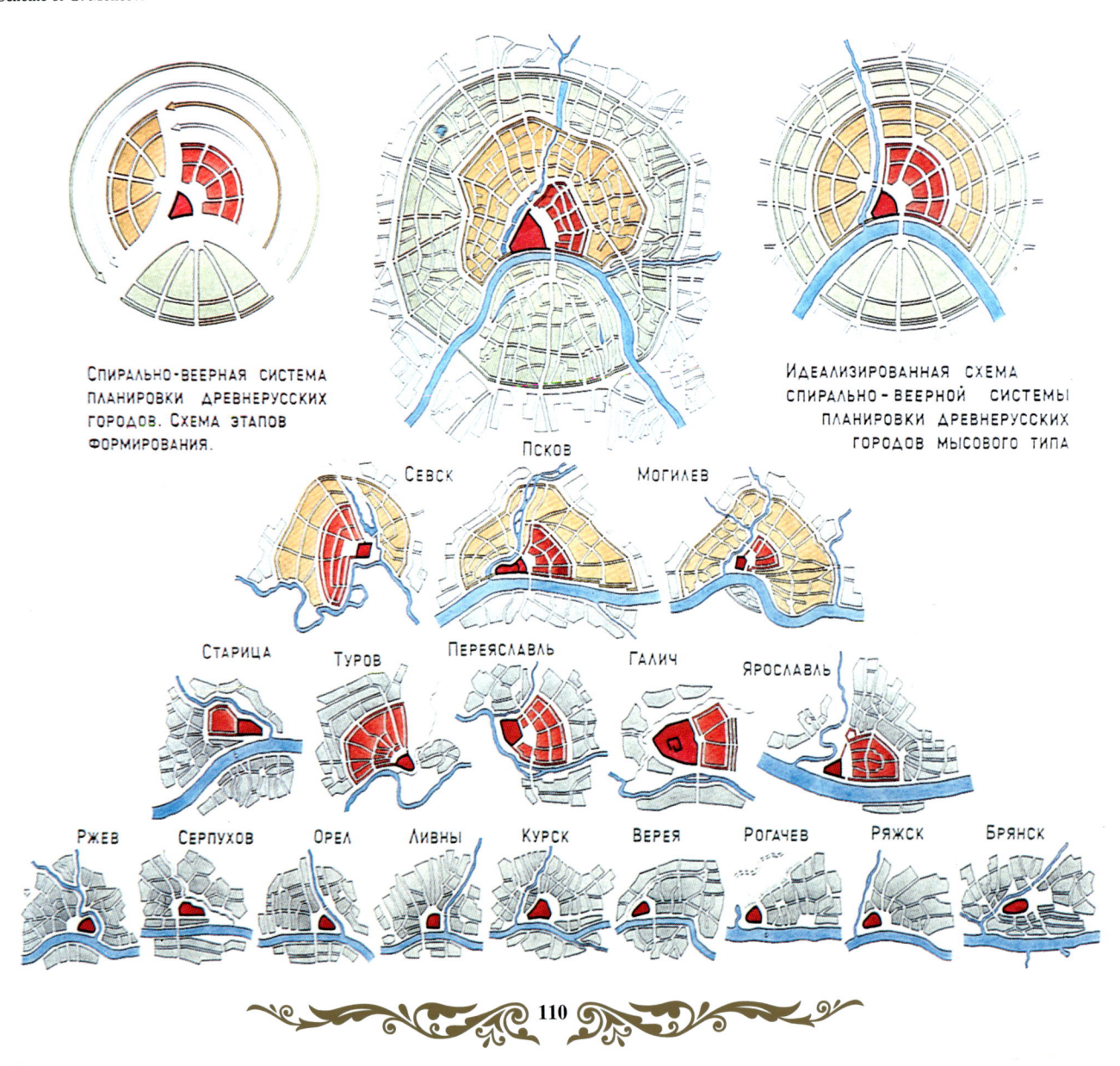

above order of ramification of their side ways after the lines of town fortification, it is easy to specify the main ways, which define the system of *fan-like ramification* of the streets of all ancient Moscow. The system is nearly the same today (all the streets have names).

The system of *streets-connections*: sectorial, semi-circular, ring-shaped appeared due to the system of fortresses, the necessity to move along the walls and ditches, as well as among the buildings which were between the walls.

The fortification line in front of Kitay-gorod made it necessary to lay out an interior street along the fortress wall and exterior street near the ditch. A chain of streets, which allowed to walk from one river to another, appeared in Kitaygorodsky dwelling quarter. These three "sectorial" streets corresponded to the sector form of town settlement. In the same way in semi-circular Bely-Tsar's town two fortress streets were laid at both sides of the fortification line and the third "intermediate" semi-circular street for connection on the territory of the dwellings, which was between the walls lines (this chain of streets and lanes went across the Neglinnaya by Kuznetsky bridge). In circular wooden town (Skorodom) three similar circular streets appeared, among which the intermediate street-connection is a unique one, which stretches like a serpentine along all the ring territory of the dwelling buildings.

During pulling down of settlement fortifications in the 18th-20th centuries "fortress" streets-connections (interior and exterior) joined together, and squares were made in their places, as well as boulevards and a transportation ring (Garden Ring). This system of streets-connections of ancient Moscow exists today.

The system of *planning* of ancient Moscow is an organic combination of all its separate systems .The national principle of bringing the form and function closer can be fully seen here. From all that people built they left only what was reasonable and necessary.

The system of planning of Moscow can be approximately called as "spiral-fan-like", if to take into account the general dynamics of development of the town and to specify in this development the most original feature: three fan-like town settlements appeared and were situated as though along a spiral in relation to the central town settlement – the Kremlin (they were surrounded one by one by fortification lines).

This system of planning does not look as one created by human hands as a result of a way of life of a huge town situated on a certain land (at the fall of two rivers big and small). Anyway, if the architects, who do not know the above-described system, are requested to make a project of the most reasonable town on the place of ancient Moscow, it is possible to be a hundred percent sure, that no project will be similar to the existing plan of Moscow! People's thinking does not embrace all the necessary, ideally functional body of a huge town, which was already created by collective thinking of people during several centuries. The town's structure did not just reflect the structure of an ancient town settlement, it reflected the life and the system of connections of this community during the time of its growth.

Moscow was not single in its planning. The same system of planning was characteristic for all towns of sector-cape type (which appeared on capes at the fall of two rivers), which made nearly half of all ancient Russian towns. If to look at their plans, it is possible to see that hundreds of towns at the end of the feudal period, in the middle of the 18th century stopped in their development at the first "fortress" stage (a fortress and open settlements), dozens of towns reached the second stage of development (they had outskirts and settlements between rivers), and only Moscow developed to the fourth stage, getting four fortification lines (with defence of the settlement behind the big river). Among hundreds of ancient Russian towns of original planning Moscow was a unique sample, which crowned all the "pyramid" of evolution of towns of sector-cape type.

The planning system of ancient Moscow as a whole: in completeness of its form, the beauty of outlines close to ideal, is a unique sample and undeniably a unique memorial of Russian medieval town-building art of large scale. It can be valued even more if to remember about the re-planning of nearly all ancient towns, that Moscow almost did not undergo this re-planning.

Delivery of the Big Vetche Novgorod Bell in 1478.

Monuments of Syntaxis Russia

Already at the beginning of the 14th century under the Tatar-Mongolian yoke the grand prince John Kalita with the first steps of "gathering Russia" developed the way of firm joining of principalities to Moscow domain. This way was so effective that, it was used by his heirs till the 16th century.

The "best people" were repatriated by force from the joined principalities to Moscow: boyards, merchants and handicraftsmen who made in the capital special dwelling settlements and communities. Thus, new regions appeared, Dmitrovskaya, Rostovskaya, Ustyuzhskaya, Khlynovskaya, Rzhevskaya, Novgorodskaya, Tverskaya or just communities from Pereyaslasl Zalessky, Staritsa, Yaroslavl, Pskov, Novgorod, Smolensk...

Becoming, voluntarily or not, the officers of Moscow tsar rural princes became gradually Moscow citizens: boyards in the government, commanders in the Moscow army... The yards of the officers were mainly in Bely-Tsar's town and Kitay-gorod, even in the Kremlin. Palaces, domestic temples of princes were included into the town's composition.

With such expatriates specially venerated, holy things were brought in so that here together they symbolise the unity of Russian land and people. Thus, in the iconostasis of the Kremlin's cathedral of the Assumption the holy icons of the Saviour from Novgorod, of the Intercession from Pskov, of the Annunciation from Ustyug, Hodegetria from Smolensk appeared. In the bell-tower of John the Great to the bells of Moscow Kremlin's cathedrals the bells from the cathedrals of Tver, Smolensk, Novgorod, Pskov were joined. But holy things were brought not only into the Kremlin.

Beginning from the 14th century in Moscow yards-representations of towns and the biggest monasteries of Russian land began to appear. They were often located in the communities of fellow townsmen. In the 17th century there were more than a hundred of such representations in the capital, including the Kremlin. There was at least one small temple, more often from stone, in each representation. Together with other temples of expatriates they filled in the Moscow panorama with plenty of church cupolas, copper and golden crosses.

This surprising architectural symbol of Synaxis Russia was as though scattered. Thus, it was included into the architecture of the town, its social and functional structures, making the capital of ancient Russia outstanding. It was included even into the synaxis chime of the town, into the "multivocal chorus" of Moscow. The contemporaries noted that it was (grandiose and was not similar to any chime of other towns. Here is, for instance, A.Olearia's evidence: "With great surprise and special attention we were listening to the foreigners being in Moscow for the first time, highly diverse speech of several thousand bells, the chime of which made a special and unknown, till that time, impression on us". The powerful voice of thousands of Moscow bells was the voice of Holy Russia in its capital.

Russian chroniclers noted in the 15th century not just the "fall of Constantinople": in 1453 "Tsargrad was taken by the Turkish sultan; but the Russian (i.e. Greek) belief was not changed, and the Patriarch was not dismissed, but just took *away the chime*; in the cathedral of St.Sophia God's Wisdom they serve the Divine liturgy, matins and vespers they sing *without chime*..."

In the 17th century the Kremlin guards had the rule of the call-over on the walls, which began with glorification of God and was over with the mention of the largest Russian towns:

Glorious is the town of Moscow!
Glorious is the town of Kiev!
Glorious is the town of Vladimir!
Glorious is the town of Novgorod!
Glorious is the town of Smolensk!
Glorious is the town of Pskov!

Town-building memorial of Synaxis Russia. Scheme of M.P.Kudriavtsev.
Conventional signs:
Settlements of expatriots near Moscow:

- – according to S.K.Bogoyavlenskiy;
- – according to P. and B.Goldenberg;
- – Red and Cathedral Squares are the main centres of the memorials of Military Glory and Synaxis Russia;
- – temples built in the memory of adjoinment to Moscow of Russian lands;
- – representations of monasteries and adjoined lands in Moscow.

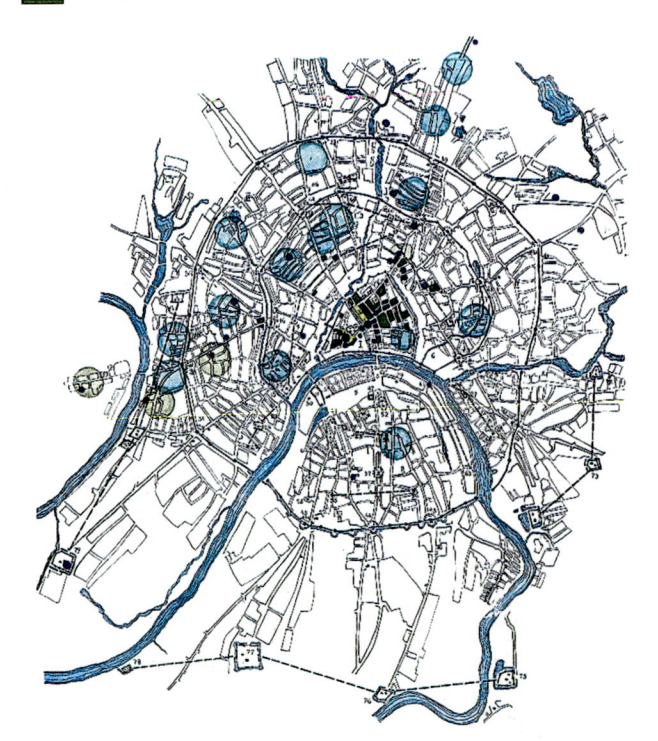

CHAPTER FIVE
Regal Moscow

There, behind the blue mountain chain,
Behind the wide fields,
Where the tired glance sees
Only the earth and the sky, -
There the town-giant sleeps,
Leaning on the hills,
Bowing to the low valleys,
Muffling itself in the fog.
Being all cupolas; it is shining
With a golden crown on the head;
The wind is playing with its belt,
The blue belt – the river.
It is the majesty's holy daughter,
It is – the head of RussiaOur dear mother
Moscow the Golden Head!

L. May

Helm of Michael Romanov. 1621.

The Gates of the Resurrection with the chapel of the Iveron Icon of the Theotokos. Rebuilt by Moscow government in 1995. Architect O.I. Zhurin.

Sceptre and orb of Alexius Mikhailovich. 6Os of the 17th century.

Iveron icon of the Theotokos. The icon was painted by hieromonk Luke of Athos. 1995.

King of Kings. Icon of 1616. N.Istomin.

Jerusalem icon of the Theotokos.

Thou art a Priest. Icon of 17th century. Northern school.

Црь и Великїй Кнзь
Михаилъ Ѳеодшровичь
всеѧ Великїѧ Рѡссїи
Самѡдержецъ.

Tsar Michael Fedorovich (1613-1645). From the book "Russian Regal House of the Romanovs"

Tsar Alexius Mikhailovich. Portrait from the Titular Book. 17th century.

St. Philatet, patriarch.

St. Nicon, patriarch.

Riverain Ensembles and the Natural «Bowl»

*I am not full of water, and I do not stretch on the map
as a long line, as you do, the rivers of my Fatherland;
But on my shores the Capital is standing proudly in its splendour,
The Kremlin's golden cupolas are looking into my waters.*

F. Miller "About the Moscow-river"

Sometimes construction in ancient Moscow started far from the town. Those were *the riverain ensembles* of the Moscow-river, Yauza, Setun, They consisted from riverain country palaces and villages of tsars and Moscow aristocracy. The ensembles' characteristic feature was a visual chain of stakes (usually, temples), which as though straightened endless windings of rivers. Each riverain ensemble was inclined to the town. In other words the chain of each ensemble began or finished with the town. There were four chains situated like a cross in relation to the capital. By the riverain ensembles Moscow was rooted in Moscow region.

The upper riverain ensemble of the Moscow-river started at the river Skhodnya from the marquee-like church of the Transfiguration in the monastery near Tushino and went down the river flow to the town. The villages and their churches followed one after another: the churches of the Holy Trinity in Troitsko-Lykovo and Khoroshovo, the temples of the villages Krylatskoe, Kuntsevo, Pokrovskoe Phili, finally, Dorogomilovo near the town. Moscow was seen already from the country palace ensembles in Khoroshovo and Phili.

The lower riverain ensemble of the Moscow-river began from the town with the palace of Krutitsky and Kolomensky metropolitanates and went down the river first with the group of the temples of Simonov, Nikola-Perervinsky monasteries, Kolomenskoe palace complex, then with the chain of the temples of the villages Bratsevo, Kapotnya, Besedy, of Nikolo-Ugreshsky monastery, and was over with the tsar's palace in the village Ostrov again with the high marquee-like stone church of the Transfiguration.

Riverain ensemble of Setun began from the upper lands of the river with the church of St. Nicholas the Miracle-Worker in Troekurovo and stretched to the town with the

Moscow surrounded by 12 veneration hills, situated on the roads to the capital. Scheme of M.P.Kudriavtsev.

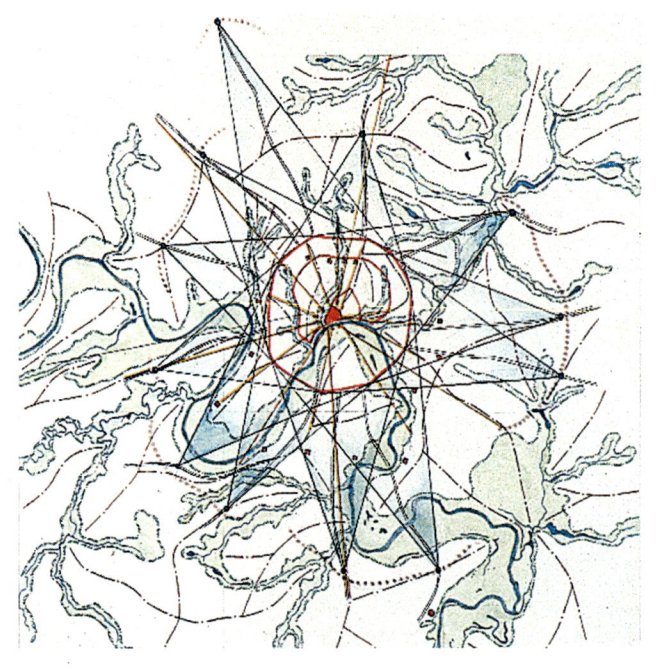

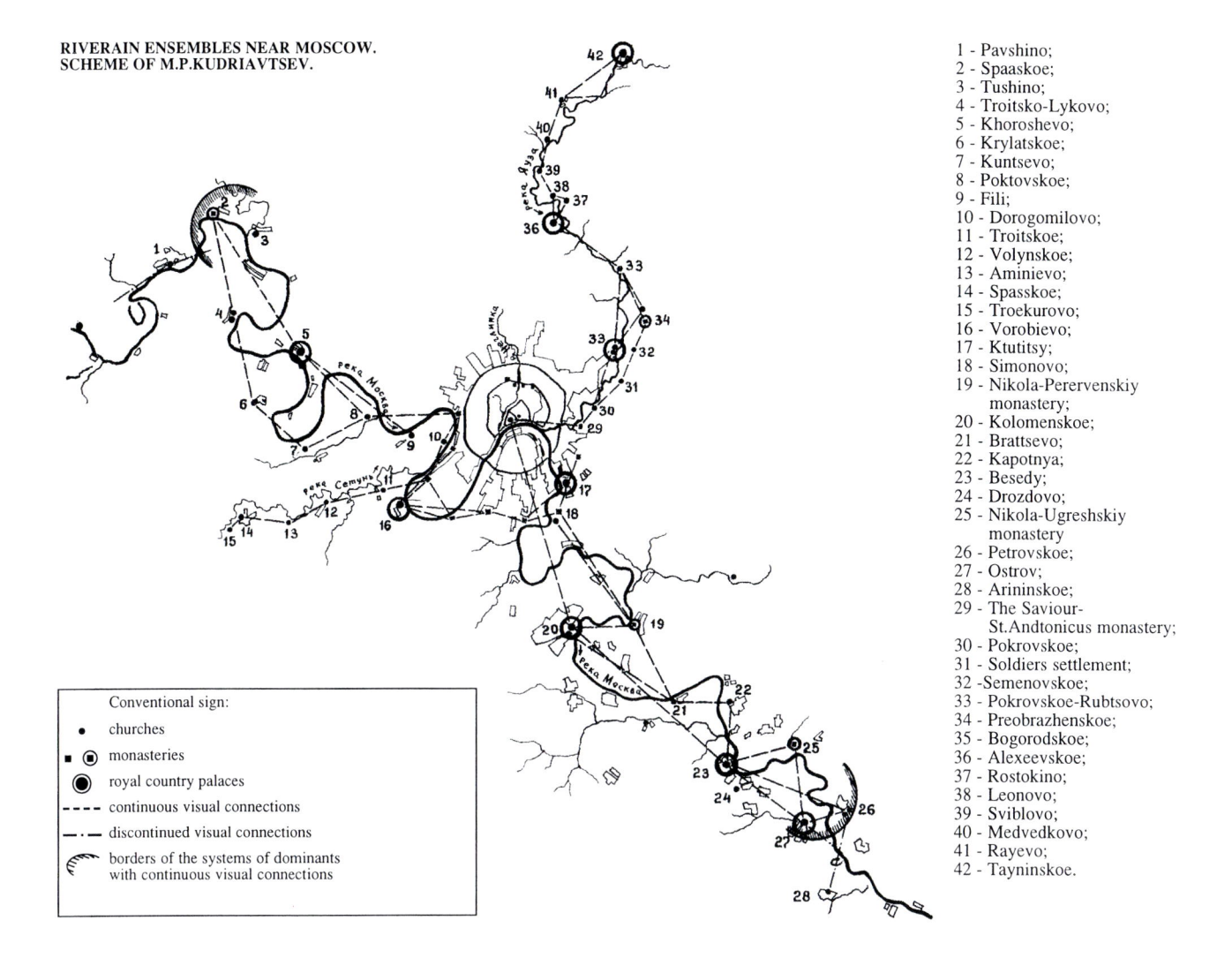

RIVERAIN ENSEMBLES NEAR MOSCOW.
SCHEME OF M.P.KUDRIAVTSEV.

1 - Pavshino;
2 - Spaaskoe;
3 - Tushino;
4 - Troitsko-Lykovo;
5 - Khoroshevo;
6 - Krylatskoe;
7 - Kuntsevo;
8 - Poktovskoe;
9 - Fili;
10 - Dorogomilovo;
11 - Troitskoe;
12 - Volynskoe;
13 - Aminievo;
14 - Spasskoe;
15 - Troekurovo;
16 - Vorobievo;
17 - Ktutitsy;
18 - Simonovo;
19 - Nikola-Perervenskiy monastery;
20 - Kolomenskoe;
21 - Brattsevo;
22 - Kapotnya;
23 - Besedy;
24 - Drozdovo;
25 - Nikola-Ugreshskiy monastery
26 - Petrovskoe;
27 - Ostrov;
28 - Arininskoe;
29 - The Saviour-St.Andtonicus monastery;
30 - Pokrovskoe;
31 - Soldiers settlement;
32 - Semenovskoe;
33 - Pokrovskoe-Rubtsovo;
34 - Preobrazhenskoe;
35 - Bogorodskoe;
36 - Alexeevskoe;
37 - Rostokino;
38 - Leonovo;
39 - Sviblovo;
40 - Medvedkovo;
41 - Rayevo;
42 - Tayninskoe.

Conventional sign:
• churches
■ ⊙ monasteries
⊙ royal country palaces
---- continuous visual connections
—·— discontinued visual connections
⌒ borders of the systems of dominants with continuous visual connections

chain of temples of the villages Spasskoe, Aminievo, Volynskoe, having at the end three-marquee church of the Holy Trinity of the patriarch's yard in the village Troitskoe-Golenitschevo and tsar's Vorobievsky palace on the Vorobievy hills near by. The Setun at the fall into the Moscow-river has steep banks and from it the amassing view of Novodevichy monastery opens near the town. The river was not a water route, so its ensemble was the most modest one.

On the contrary, the rich riverain ensemble of the Yauza formed on the lively ancient water route from the Moscow-river to the river Klyazma, here also aroad was to Zalesskaya land: to Vladimir, Suzdal, The Holy Trinity-St.Sergiusmonastery. So, a whole system of regal, boyard and aristocratic palaces developed along the rather long and deep Yauza.

On the upper territory the ensemble was started with the royal palace in thevillage of Tayninskoe with a wonderful church of the Annunciation, then afterthe village Raevo it included the palace of Pozharsky with a marquee-like church in Medvedkovo, and after the villages Sviblovo, Leonovo, Rostokino – the royal Alexeevsky palace with the church of the Tikhvin Icon of the Most Holy Theotokos, the palace in Bogorodskoe, fretted wooden Preobrazhensky palace with the monastery, the palace in the village of Pokrovskoe-Rubtsovo with a splendid one-cupola church. Down the river there was Semenovskoe village, Soldatskaya settlement, Pokrovskoe, finally, Spaso-Andronikov monastery on the Yauza's steep bank, from which even the Kremlin was seen.

Diversity of the valleys of the Moscow-river, Yauza, Setun with a curved relief, elaborate rivers windings, contrasts between high and low banks gave wonderful opportunities for such location of monasteries, palaces, separate churches,when they were visualised as an absolutely different natural background. The view from any point at the golden cupolas town was very important, besides it opened most impressively from the Yauza, the lower flow of which turned round the capital as a semi-circle, nearing to it. The town was seen already from the village of Alexsevskoe, but it was especially impressive from Preobrazhensky palace and soldiers' settlements near it, besides, the view of the town did not disappear at each river's winding.

The system of any riverain ensemble was seen differently (from water and the shores, the upper shore views took a big territory. Though at various distances the town was already seen, objects of the ensembles were seen separately, especially in far away places. It showed the hierarchy of the ensembles, their objects, and so, the visual connections between them.

Kolomenakiy Palace. The artist is unknown. 1832.

It is not possible to describe in words all the beauty of Moscow's riverain ensembles. Near the rivers and dams there were fairy-tale palaces, monasteries, tsar's villages, ordinary villages. Not only had they the buildings of capital's style and quality, but also real masterpieces of Russian architecture. And all this was in the countryside, among the fields, near the forests, near water reservoirs. National architectural style transferred the unique Russian character to the landscapes.

The most interesting thing in the riverain ensembles, and near the town too, was the country palaces: regal, patriarchate, boyards. Information about them is very scarce, because they were wooden and at the beginning of the 18th century nearly all of them disappeared. There is historical data only about the main regal palaces: Kolomenskoe (there is even the model), Izmailovskoe, Vorobievskoe.

The palace in the village of Kolomenskoe is considered the largest and the most interesting. Complicated in its painting, composed from many buildings of different height, covered with different roofs of elaborate forms Kolomensky palace was a whole encyclopaedia of architectural forms and modes of Russian building of the 17th century. The palace had a stone domestic temple of the Kazan Icon of the Theotokos in honour of one hundredth anniversary of adjoinment of Kazan and Astrakhan. Its architect was Ambrose Maximov, who had built the cathedral of the Kazan Icon of the Theotokos in Red Square twenty years before.

Being the largest regal country residence Kolomensky palace implemented the same functions as the Kremlin one, including receptions of foreign ambassadors. For this the palace had the Throne Chamber with a spacious hall and front porch. The ambassadors waiting to be received were accommodated in splendid marquees and tents on the other side of the Moscow-river, in the low Kurianovskaya floodlands. On the day of reception the ambassadorial procession crossed the river by boats to the palace, walked up the steep bank of the river passing by the church of the Ascension and entered the territory of the palace by Spasskie (the Saviour) gates. In this way the symbolical community between Kolomensky palace and the Kremlin was underlined, for the Kremlin's main entrance was also through Spasskie gates near the cathedral of the Ascension of the monastery of the Ascension.

Izmailovsky country palace of the tsar was a little away from the Yauza and its tributary Khapilovka. It was like a huge tsar's academy. There were gardens, kitchen gardens, fields, mills, ponds, woods, forests, where many animals and birds lived. It was a paradise on earth, to which all regal court liked to come. In Izmailovo different acclimatised exotic plants grew, there was a zoo, and the conditions in it were the closest to the natural ones, a large space of forests

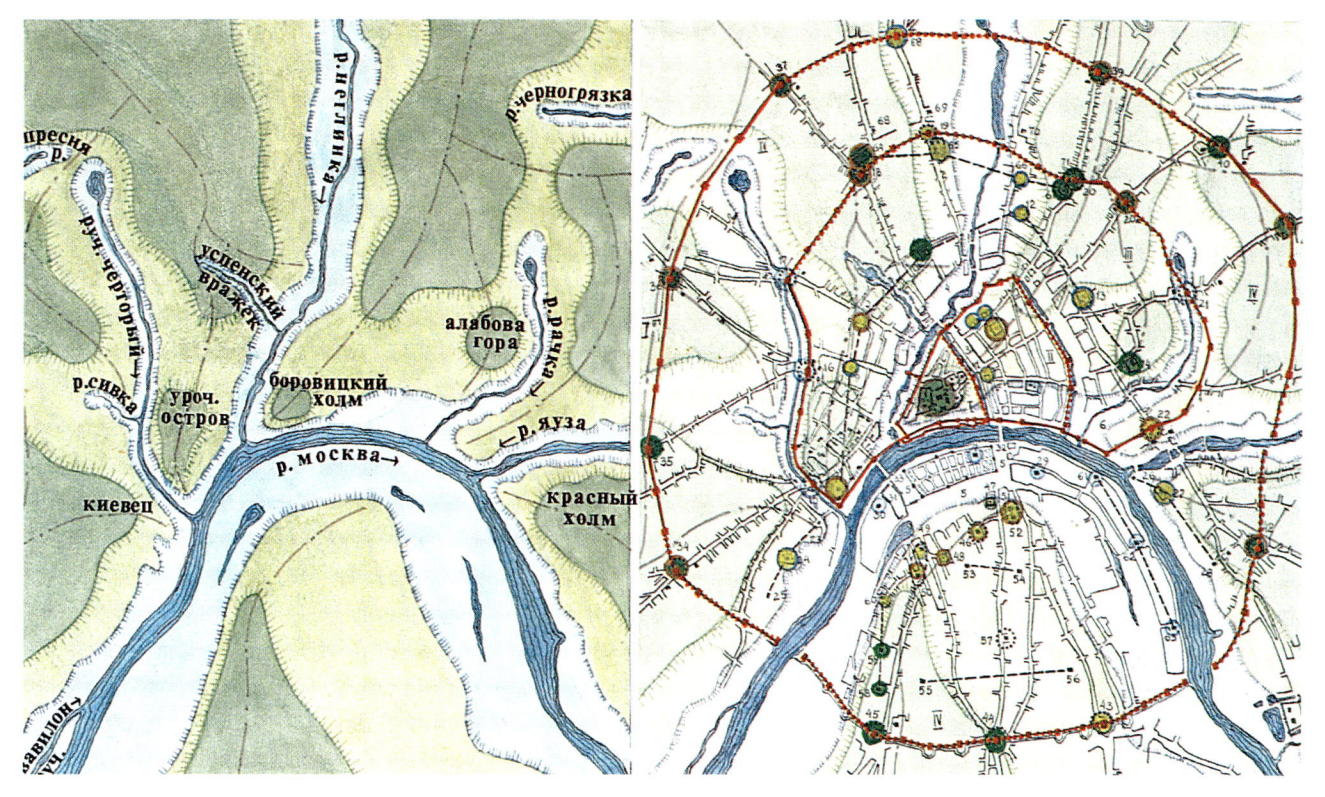

Interconnection between the town and nature. Location of buildings of the ancient town on the relief's elements. Scheme of M. Kudriavtsev.

- ▭ – 1st and 2nd shore terraces – rivers' valleys;
- ▭ – valleys' edges;
- ▭ – slopes covered with forest;
- ▭ – borders of table-lands;
- ▭ – territory of upper forests;
- ▭ – lines of watersheds

Ensembles and buildings located on:
- ○ – shore terraces;
- ○ – valleys' edges;
- ● – near the borders of the table-land;
- ○ ● – near the lines of watersheds;
- ━━ – walls, following the relief's structure;
- ••••• – walls, crossing the natural relief's structure

and meadows, surrounded by deep ditches, which were the borders "dividingdifferent" animals.

Vorobievsky regal palace on Vorobievskie hills was a reserve one: the royalfamily lived there and was occupied with state affairs only during repairs andreconstruction of the Kremlin palace and during the Kremlin fires. It was awhole building, not a connection of different ones, and only the roofs of separate rooms were various.

The mansion of prince Pozharsky – Medvedkovo can be noted as one of those which villages near Moscow had in the 17th century. Here in the place of his prayer before the battle for Moscow with Polish-Lithuanian invaders, the prince built a memorial marquee-like church of the Intercession, which still exists.

Not only the riverain ensembles and country palaces connected Moscow and its regions. The town is situated on the low land, as though on the bottom of a huge *natural "bowl"*. The edges of the "bowl" are 12 veneration hills on 12 roads leading to the capital from the towns near Moscow. Those were such points on the land, from which the capital was fully seen. There were lower edges of the "bowl": seven table-lands included inside Skorodom. The bottom, the lowestplace, – Tsaritsin meadow in Zamoskvorechie (Tsar's garden), in the middle ofwhich there was the church of St. Sophia. These are the main three levels ofthe natural "bowl" of Moscow. How were its possibilities used for constructionof the city?

The main regularity of the combination of the structure of the ancient town with the landscape was *the likeness of location of the architecture*, as well as compositional units, system of the streets to *the location of the types of flora* at the levels of the relief. Along the river, on the places covered with floods, the zone of less valuable flora is (mainly bushes), here, besides piers, there were, as a rule, a lot of saunas. Big leaf-bearing forests grew on the flood-land terrace, – here above the flood level dwelling buildings were, which protected them from the moisture of river fogs and winter snow-drifts. The dense coniferous forest, "bor", grew on the high table-land, on top of the hills, – here at watersheds, on steep banks, as a rule, the biggest constructions were built which were the basis of the towns' composition. So, Moscow was situated on the landscape relief *also at different levels like the types of the flora.*

Taking into account the above regularity, it is possible to indicate three rules in location of town's buildings. The first one is the rule of compositional choice of relief levels: like the forest shows the relief, rising up the hill so the buildings which were the most expressive compositionally, single out the highest bank edges of the valleys and watersheds. The second rule is the compositional apportionment (fixation) of crossings of the natural relief of the landscape with artificial systems, town's fortifications, streets, roads. The third rule is the compositional outline of directions of the relief structures and water systems: it showed itself

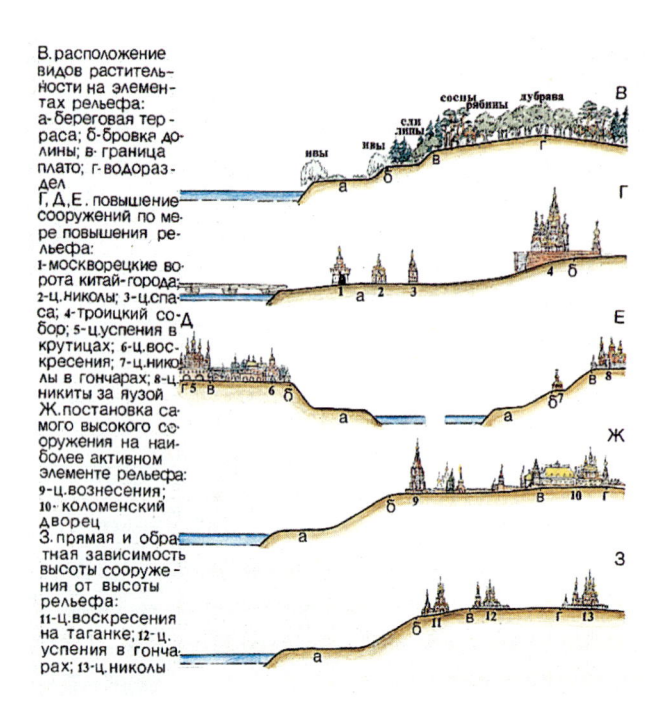

Interconnection between the town and nature. Location of the buildings of the ancient town on the relief's elements. Scheme of M.P.Kudriavtsev.

mostly in location of the chains of the churches along the axises of the watersheds and river valleys.

The favourite places for construction of ensembles and buildings were at the watersheds and edges of the river valleys. On the watershed line in the Kremlin there is the ensemble of Cathedral Square and regal palaces: Faceted Palace, Terem Palace, Reserve Palace, Golden Palace, the cathedral of the Saviour on Bor, Guerbovaya Tower. In the middle of Kitay-gorod there was the monastery of Epiphany, near Spasskie Gates of the Kremlin and the cathedral of the Kazan Icon of the Thetokos in front of Nikolskie Gates. In Bely-Tsar's town and Skorodom a lot of objects with such location can be noted. For example almost all the city and even near the city monasteries, as well as the city churches in the streets Iljinka, Pokrovka, Maroseyka, Nikitskaya, Arbatskaya, Tverskaya, Ordynka, Polyanka, Yakimanka...

There were also riverain ensembles inside the city very rich in their appearance, those of Neglinnaya, Chertory, Rachka, even Uspensky Vrazhek. Their landscape offered an amazing view of the city buildings, fortress walls and towers, and the Kremlin with golden cupolas. The ponds in Neglinnaya were especially beautiful, coming down like a cascade along Kitay-gorod and the Kremlin into the Moscow-river. M.P.Kudryavtsev presented the fairy-tale view of Uspensky Vrazhek in his reconstruction.

Moscow Temples

Cathedrals, churches, particularly their cupolas, which rose above the dwelling buildings, prevailed in appearance of Moscow, like in the appearance of any other ancient Russian town. In spite of many fortress walls, towers with their hip roofs and armorial bearings, Moscow became golden-cupola, certainly, because of an even bigger quantity of golden cupolas. Gilding of cupolas was the last stage in the construction of a church, after the gilding of crosses. If one is to remember that yellow (gold) colour is the symbol of God, each church community tried to gild at least the central cupola of its temple, symbolising Christ. Sometimes communities appealed to the tsar for help in that sacred affair and got it.

In the 16th-17th centuries Moscow "was full" of very original temples, which had not been seen nearly at all in Russia before. So, these churches were typically Moscow ones. It happened during the time of John the Terrible (1530-1584) and during the service of metropolitanate Macarius (1542-1563). First hip roof and multi-cupola stone churches, then hip roof and cupola ones and the fiery churches appeared, and later, at the end of the 17th century, the tradition of construction of tire temples was continued. Here, the diversity of temples was mentioned during the explanation of St.Basil's cathedral. Now it can be explained in detail.

Hip roof stone temples, in contrast to wooden hip roof temples, appeared, firstly with the hip roofs open inside the church, secondly, with additional small symbolical cupolas. For example, as M.P.Kudryavtsev supposed, the first temple of the Ascension in Kolomenskoe had four small cupo-

Hip roof temple of the Ascension in Kolomensloe. 1532. Reconstruction of M. Kudriavtsev.

las at the bottom of the hip roof, together with the central cupola, which were the symbols of Christ and Evangelists (in the 18th century the cupolas and corner kokoshniks under them were removed). 12 symbolic small cupolas at the bottom of the hip roof were installed on the church of the Transfiguration in Ostrov together with the central cupola symbolising Christ and 12 Apostles. Today the cupolas are covered with iron and are almost unnoticeable. Initially they were gilded and shone together with the gilded cupolas of the main temple and two inside lateral altars (the temple had 15 cupolas).

The central altar of the Intercession in St.Basil's cathedral with 8 small cupolas at the bottom of stone patterned hip roof was mentioned already. It is also interesting to note other two hip roof stone temples with 8 cupolas at the hip roof. The first one is the temple of St.John the Predecessor in the village Dyakovo, the octahedron of which is formed of 8 necks of small cupolas, the top of the temple was hip roof (reconstruction of M.P.Kudryavtsev). The second was the highest hip roof stone temple of Sts.Boris and Gleb in Borisovsk, a town near Mozhaysk. It was built by the tsar Boris Godunov in the name of his Saint at the end of the 16th century and sanctified the presence of the tsar in 1602. 8 small gilded cupolas were installed right on the hip roof under the central ninth one. Stone hip roof temple of the Intercession in Medvedkovo built by Pozharsky soon had many cupolas.

So the first stone hip roof temples in Moscow and in the palaces of Moscow region were built multi-cupola, and the small cupolas were everywhere just symbolical. The novelty was not only in stone hip roof temples, but in appearance of symbolic many cupolas.

There were several more hip roof temples in Moscow: the temple of St.Sergius and the temple of St.Hieromartyr Theodore Stratelates in Troitskoe settlement in the Kremlin, the temple of the Transfiguration in Kopie, the temple of St.John the Predecessor near Novodevichy monastery, the cathedral of Alexeevsky monastery, probably, the church of the Ascension (Maloe) in Nikitskaya street, the church of St.Hieromartyr George in Ordynka, the church of St.Prophet Elisha in Uspensky Vrazhek, even the cathedral of Ivanovsky monastery. There were also hiproof temples in the villages of Moscow region apart from those in palaces and monasteries.

Stone octahedral hip roof open inside the temple, has its own symbolic explanation. The basis of the symbol is the cross of the Theotokos made from two Greek equal crosses with one centre: one is straight, the other diagonal. The cross of the Theotokos is seen from inside the temple if to look up inside the hiproof. On the planes of the straight cross there are usually four windows in the hip roof lighting the opposite planes. The planes of the diagonal cross are rather dark. Through the glimmering cross in the centre of the hip roof Christ Almighty was seen. Outside the hip roof was decorated with suspended or attached symbolics: crosses, rings, rhombes.

Multi-cupola temples were of two kinds: they became multi-cupola when they started to add more cupolas to usual temples other multi-cupola temples were so stipulated. "The stipulated" one was the cathedral of the Holy Trinity on the ditch of 1555-1561 (St.Basil's cathedral). And, for example, in the Kremlin's three-cupola cathedral of the Annunciation of 1489 cupolas were added, and it became nine-cupola after inside lateral altars and galleries were built in 1563.

In the Kremlin of the 17th century a few multi-cupola temples appeared. First two cupolas on Eastern lateral altars were added to the five-cupola cathedral of Archangel Michael; then at the departments the IO-cupola cathedral of St.Alexander Nevsky and the Miracle-Workers of Chernigov was built; 11-cupola cathedral of the Saviour near the tsarinas' palace; 10-cupola temple of the Annunciation and St.Alexius the Metropolitanate in Chudov monastery; gradually even the old cathedral of the Saviour on Bor got nine cupolas; perhaps, the church of the Entrance into Jerusalem near Troitskie gates was also multi-cupola. All these temples with so many cupolas made the Kremlin an unwitnessed town in the whole world or, as it is said in fairy-tales, "the miracle of miracles". The Kremlin in the centre of Moscow looked like a gigantic candle stand shining to the sky with a hundred of golden lights-cupolas, crowned with glittering golden crosses.

In Kitay-gorod there were only two multi-cupola temples: St.Basil's cathedral and the church of the

Hip roof church of the Transfiguration in the village of Ostrov near Moscow. The Middle of 16th century. Reconstruction of M. Kudriavtsev.

Ten-cupola cathedral of the Annunciation and St.Alexius, metropolitanate, in Chudov monastery in the Kremlin (dismantled in 1930s)

Resurrection in Pani, near Bulgakov yard, which had 11 cupolas. In Bely-Tsar's town there were two temples too: the church of the Assumption in Pokrovka of 12 cupolas and an unknown 9 cupola church depicted near the Bely wall by A. Oleary. The most impressive temple near Moscow is the 9 cupola cathedral of the Resurrection of New Jerusalem monastery.

It is considered that Christian symbolics is in the quantity of temple's cupolas. Five cupolas is the symbol of Christ and four Evangelists; 7 cupolas symbolise seven gifts of the Holy Spirit and seven sacraments of the Church; 8 is the symbol of the future age (life); 9 is the nine heavenly reignments (there was Deviatichnaya church in Constantinople); 10 cupolas were usually formed by two five-cupolas of a double temple; 11 cupolas were formed in the same way, but with one cupola between the five-cupolas; 13 cupolas symbolise Christ and the Apostles; 15 symbolise the same, but together with the Theotokos and St.John the Predecessor, 25 cupolas are the symbol of 25 heavenly thrones, the Heavenly Town. But the question about symbolics of Russian multi-cupola temples has not been studied thoroughly yet.

Hip roof-cupola temples are some of the types of hip roof temples. In themthe hip roof rises not from the temple's walls, but from the drum (neck), whichis on the vault. Temples with two or three hip roofs are very impressive. Churches with two hip roofs have not remained till our time. Those were the churches of St. Nicholas Mokry in Zaryadie, St. Nicholas in Sapozhki near Troitskie gates outside the Kremlin, of Sts.Cosmas and Damian in Starye Pani of Kitay-gorod, of St.Hieromartyr Anastasia, deliverer from bonds, of St.Demetrius of Thessalonica in Tverskaya, of St. Elijah the Prophet in Vorontsovo field. The church of the Nativity of the Theotokos in Putinki, which exists now, has three hip roofs. Earlier there were more such temples: of the Resurrection Slovutschee near Kuznetsky bridge, of the Resurrection in Gonchary in Taganka, of ArchangelGabriel in Myasniki, of St.John, archbishop and miracle-worker of Novgorod inthe Kremlin, of the Assumption in Uspensky Vrazhek.

The hip roofs of these temples which were a load for the vault, probably, were the reason of collapse, because of which in the middle of the 17th century some interdiction on construction of all hip roof churches, appeared. After that the stone hip roof moved to Moscow bell-towers. A bell-tower with an open inside hip roof became a real «musical instrument» rising above the town. There were dormers in bell-towers' hip roofs, sometimes at several tires.

Fiery temples were built in Moscow in the 17th century, they began to form theappearance of the town, beautifying its corner, supplanting almost all types of churches. So they should be mentioned specially.

There are no supporting pillars inside fiery temples, – groined, closed orchute vault is installed on the walls, and is decorated with round or keel-likekokoshniks, above which one, more often five cupolas rise, besides, four cor-

Nine-cupola cathedral of the Saviour on Bor (dismantled in 1930s).

Twelve-cupola temple of the Assumption in Pokrovka. (Dismantled in 1930s).

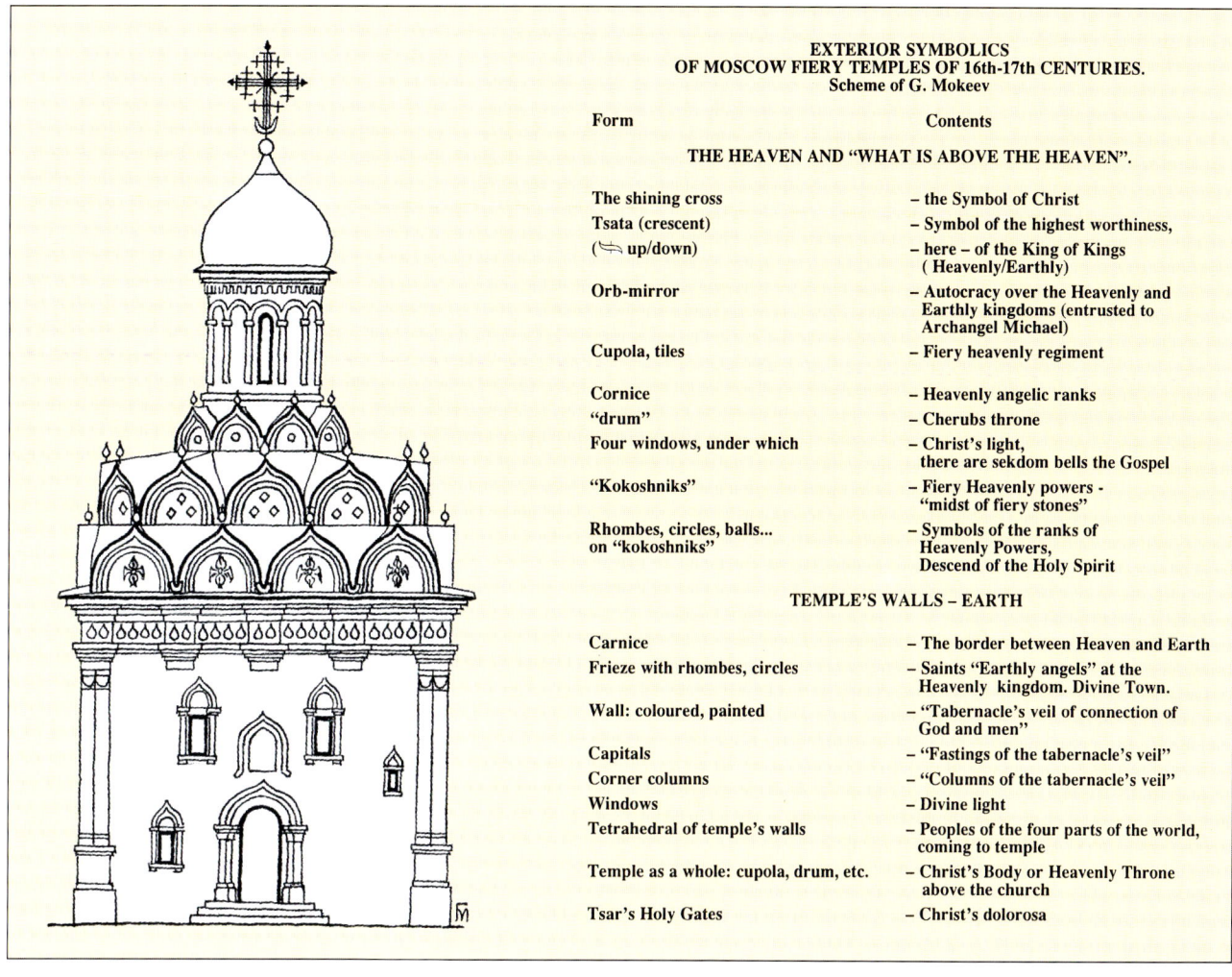

EXTERIOR SYMBOLICS OF MOSCOW FIERY TEMPLES OF 16th-17th CENTURIES.
Scheme of G. Mokeev

Form	Contents
THE HEAVEN AND "WHAT IS ABOVE THE HEAVEN".	
The shining cross	– the Symbol of Christ
Tsata (crescent)	– Symbol of the highest worthiness,
(⌣ up/down)	– here – of the King of Kings (Heavenly/Earthly)
Orb-mirror	– Autocracy over the Heavenly and Earthly kingdoms (entrusted to Archangel Michael)
Cupola, tiles	– Fiery heavenly regiment
Cornice	– Heavenly angelic ranks
"drum"	– Cherubs throne
Four windows, under which	– Christ's light, there are sekdom bells the Gospel
"Kokoshniks"	– Fiery Heavenly powers - "midst of fiery stones"
Rhombes, circles, balls... on "kokoshniks"	– Symbols of the ranks of Heavenly Powers, Descend of the Holy Spirit
TEMPLE'S WALLS – EARTH	
Carnice	– The border between Heaven and Earth
Frieze with rhombes, circles	– Saints "Earthly angels" at the Heavenly kingdom. Divine Town.
Wall: coloured, painted	– "Tabernacle's veil of connection of God and men"
Capitals	– "Fastings of the tabernacle's veil"
Corner columns	– "Columns of the tabernacle's veil"
Windows	– Divine light
Tetrahedral of temple's walls	– Peoples of the four parts of the world, coming to temple
Temple as a whole: cupola, drum, etc.	– Christ's Body or Heavenly Throne above the church
Tsar's Holy Gates	– Christ's dolorosa

ner cupolas are closed (not for the day light, but just symbolical); in theEast one big or three apses of different dimensions are attached, in the Westthere is less high refectory and high, usually hip roof, bell-tower above theentrance.

"In its absolute form" the fiery temple appeared at the end of the 16th century, though it had precursors as four lateral altars of St. Basil's cathedral, two lateral altars of the church of the Transfiguration in Ostrov of the middle of the 16th century, the lateral altars of the Kremlin's cathedral of the Annunciation. Separate forms also appeared on temples of earlier time. For example, the groined vault, which allowed to remove four inside pillars, was, probably, developed and used by Aleviz Fryazin at the beginning of the 16th century, who built in Moscow 12 so called "three-blade" temples. These are the churches of the Nativity of the Most Holy Theotokos in the Kremlin on Seni, of the Annunciation in Old Vaganjkovo, of the Presentation of the Virgin in the Temple in Lubyanka, of St.Prophet Elijah in Kitay-gorod, of St.Vladimir in Old Sadi, etc. The three-blade form of finishing of the temple's facades existed from ancient time in Novgorod, Pskov, but all the temples there had interior pillars.

The tires of kokoshniks also appeared long ago before the 16th century on thetemples of cross-cupola type, and already in the 14th-16th centuries they had three-four tires: these are the cathedral of the Holy Trinity in Pskov, cathedrals of Andronikov monastery and the monastery of the Nativity of the Thetokos in Moscow. The precursing works of this kind were used in the fiery temple.

These temples were born, most probably, by the genius of the "tsar's town,church and other affairs master" Theodore Savelievich the Steed. Certainly, hedid not work alone, but with a group of apprentices of the Regal Stone Department. Construction of such temples began at the time of tsar Theodore Ioannovich with dismantling of the ramshackle and construction on its place by 1588 of the new church of All Saints in Kulishki – the first monument in Moscow in the honour of the victory in Kulikovo field. After it stone temples of St.Nicholas Yavlenny in Arbat of 1589 (not survived), the cathedral of Donskoy monastery of 1593, of the Holy Trinity in the regal village in Khoroshevo of 1598 appeared.

Moscovites liked the temples so much, including patriarchs, tsars, that they were accepted as the samples for further construction. So, after destruction of Moscow during the Troubled Time they spread, like fire, all over the capital during its restoration and further construction. It started from construction of temples-monuments in honour of liberation of Moscow from invaders-catholics: of the Intercession in the regal village Rubtsovo in 1620-1626, of St.Michael, Hegumen of Maleinus of the monastery of the Ascension in the Kremlin in 1625, the cathedral of the Icon of Kazan of the Theotokos in Red Square in 1636-1637. A hundred years before the 18th century, in the capital and near it, up to 300 such temples were built – it is a unique

Fiery temples of Moscow. Diversity of roofs and cupolas. Scheme of G. Mokeev.
а – 15th century in Kolomenskoe, б – the church of John, author of "The Ladder" (Gorokhovets), в – the church of Archangel Michael in Ovchinniki (Moscow), г – the church of St.Alexius of St. Cyril-St. Nicholas monastery, 1685 (Belozersk), д – the church of the Holy Trinity of St.Paisius monastery (Kostroma), е – the church of the Assumption in N.Novgorod, ж – the on-gate church of Novodevichiy monastery (M. Л.; on Pikar), и – the cathedral of Our Lady of the Sign, к – the church of the Tikhvin icon of the Theotokos in St.Alexius monastery, 1680 (M. Л.), л – the church of Sts.Mattyrs Florus and Laurus in Myasniki (M. Л,), м – the ch. of St.Nicholas "Posadskiy" in Kolomna, н – in Bely-town of Moscow, 17th century (ace, to dearly), о – ch. of St. Irene in the Naryshkinys' house (Moscow), п – the ch. of the Resurrection in Gonchary (M. Л.;), р – the ch. of St.Prophet Elijah in Vorontsovo field (M. rc), с – the ch. of the Assumption in Kozhevniki (M. rj), т – the ch. of the Nativity of Christ in Izmaylovo (Moscow). (M.r. means: Mokeev G.Ya., reconstruction).

phenomenon in our and in world's town-building. All the temples were painted and Moscow looked very colourful with them.

Fiery temples are highly symbolic. Their four walls symbolise the people, coming to the church from the four parts of the world. Powerful cornice usually separates "the earth" from "the sky" – heaps of kokoshniks crowned with cupolas. Most of the temples had keel-like kokoshniks (with sharp tops), seldom they were round (wooden ridges made them keel-like too). From the wall edge kokoshniks rose up the vault. The upper tire was, as a rule, from kokoshniks at the bottom of cupolas.

Especially expressive were the temples with a big number of kokoshniks on the walls and tires, but more effective were those with fiery inside lateral altars, such as the churches of the Holy Trinity in Nikitniki, Khoroshovo, Ostankino, of the Intercession in Rubtsovo, of the Nativity of Christ in Izmaylovo, and near Moscow the churches in the villages Markovo, Arkhangelskoe, Nikolo-Yrjupino (the main temples are of two pillars) and others.

The symbolics of "the heaven" was described above in Small Jerusalem which the cathedral of the Assumption presents. In the third row of its kokoshniks angels are shown as heavenly forces. Pictures of cherubs, seraphs and angels can be also on kokoshniks of stone temples. The essence of the pictures, of the architectural form of kokoshniks explain clearly Christian holy writs. "Created (the Lord) His Angels, His spirits and servants like fire" (Prokimen); "God willcome... with incomparable glory in His coming to the glory of Angelic and Archangelic reignments, all of them are fiery flame (St.Ephraim the Syrian. TheWord about God's Advent); "His throne was like the fiery flame" (St.Daniel, VII,9). Finally, the fallen angel was outcast from the heaven from the midst of *the stones of fire* (Ezekiel, 28, 16), "I suppose – from the midst of Angelic reignments", – explained St.Andrew of Caesaria (Comment on the Apocalypse, p.95).

So, the top of the fiery temple represented symbolically the Heavenly Throne from fiery powers (the heap of kokoshniks), on which there is "One Sitting on cherubs" (the Head of the Church).

The appearance in Moscow and then spreading of fiery temples in all Russia was an outstanding phenomenon. Plenty of churches of one type, which were not similar to each other, gave Moscow's appearance the *unity* which cannot be achieved by today's architects, working according to the master plot plans of the city. Fiery temples changed not only the look of Moscow, they were built in the 17th – the beginning of the 18th century first in the nearby, then far away towns of Russia. Architects of all Russia took part in this creation. Wonderful buildings appeared in Kolomna, Vereya, Uglich, Kashino, Yaroslavl, Kostroma and many other towns, which were equal to and sometimes excelled the capital's buildings.

Interior and exterior paintings, ceramic facings, floral and geometric design, endless variations of architectural details, volumes, colour expressed all that seemed to be in Christian symbolics before, which had been developed by

Small Jerusalem of Moscow cathedral of the Assumption. 15th century.

Fiery temples of Moscow. The church of the Life-giving Trinity in tsar's village Khoroshevo. 1598. Architect F.Konj.

Fiery temples of Moscow. The cathedral of the Kazan icon of the Theotokos in Red Square was rebuilt by Moscow government in 1991-1993. Architect-restorator O.I.Zhurin.

Fiery temples of Moscow.
The church of the Life-giving Trinity in Nikitniki. End of 17th century.

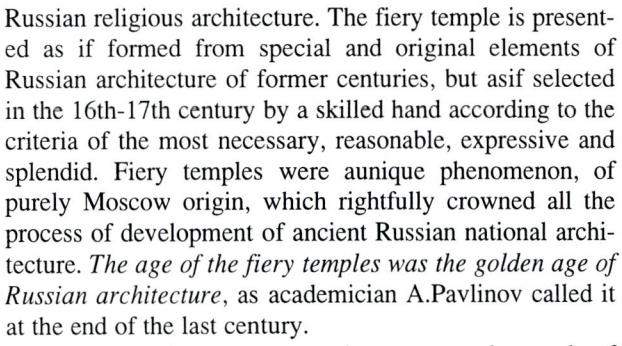

Fiery temples of Moscow.
The church of St. Nicholas the Miracle-worker in Khamovniki.

Russian religious architecture. The fiery temple is presented as if formed from special and original elements of Russian architecture of former centuries, but asif selected in the 16th-17th century by a skilled hand according to the criteria of the most necessary, reasonable, expressive and splendid. Fiery temples were aunique phenomenon, of purely Moscow origin, which rightfully crowned all the process of development of ancient Russian national architecture. *The age of the fiery temples was the golden age of Russian architecture*, as academician A.Pavlinov called it at the end of the last century.

It is interesting to compare the cross-cupola temple of Kievskaya Rus and the fiery temple of Moscow, Moscow Rus, in the sphere of their divine symbolics. Kiev's temple in its ideal was prompted by Greek architects after christening of Russia. It represents a materialised double symbol: the Heavenly Town (its gates) and the Heavenly Throne inside it with Calvary on it. Through the gates (on thetemple's walls)a paradise garden was seen with exotic flora, animals, birds,with its Saints: St.David, St.Solomon (the cathedral of St.Demetrius of Thessalonica in Vladimir, the cathedral of St.Hieromartyr George in Yuriev Polsky, the church of the Intercession at the Nerl, etc.). The temple was built in the centre of an ancient Russian town to venerate the Heavenly Town, the credence, the Holy Life-giving Trinity.

In Moscow and Moscow Rus the walls of the fiery temple stopped expressingthe gates, they symbolised now the Christian peoples of Earth, and the roof symbolised now only the fiery Heavenly Throne with the cupola which symbolised theHead of the Church. The temple was a unified, "concentrated" symbol of the Universe (the lower part was the earthly world, the upper one – the Heavenly Kingdom of fiery stones). It took off the Greek tradition finally and stood in pure ideal born by final development of Russian temple symbolics.

A fiery temple could not occupy the central position in an ancient Russian townand monastery – there was already a cross-cupola temple as the main cathedral. Soa fiery temple became the temple of town settlement, town and village communities,private palaces, mansions.

Tire temples were built at the end of the 17th century. The favourite forms were – one, two, three octahedrons with a cupola on top installed on a tetrahedron. It is the church of Archangel Michael in the Saviour-Andronikov monastery, the church of the Saviour in Zachatievsky monastery, the cathedral of the Veneration of the Holy Cross. In temples, which were three-part in their plans, the influence of the traditional Ukrainian three-part log house temple (log houses – along the main axis) showed clearly. At that time in Kiev I.D.Startsev, D.V.Aksamitov and other Moscow architects worked. Probably, they "brought" "the new" form of the orthodox temple from there.

In symbolical meaning it was as though descending of the "heaven on earth", because the symbolics of tire temple originated from the church under chime (bell-tower) of the Holy Sepulchre in Jerusalem (in Moscow – from the bell-tower of John the Great). Nevertheless, Moscow architects introduced into the temple's architecture the symbolics of the fiery heavenly powers, for example, "thrones". From these "thrones" (in the shape of balusters) pilasters were formed on the walls or corners, window and door casings. The "thrones" were especially improvised in decorative forms of so called "crests" on top of the temple's tires. There is such decoration in a one-tire church of the Resurrection in Kadashi, multi-tire church of Our Lady of the Sign in Sheremetiev yard, the church of the Intercession in Phili, the cathedral of the monastery of the Epiphany...

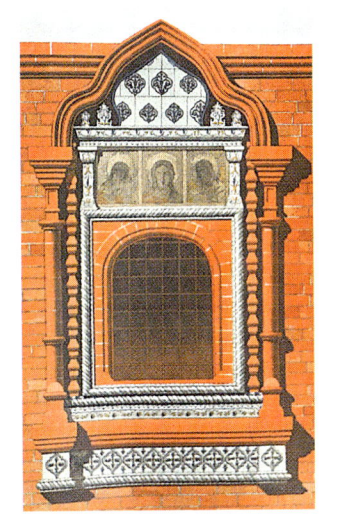

Symbolics of ancient Russian architectural forms: I - Jlsis: 2 - thrones-deisis, 3 - thrones are the symbols of deisis-and heavenly powers; 4 - symbol of the heavenly throne. According to M.P.Kudriavtsev.

It is also characteristic for the temples that more and more orders systems(Corinthian, Ionic, Doric orders) were introduced into their architecture. Appearance of these systems meant the beginning of mastering of the symbols of the "Earthly Church". It was connected with the time of Peter I, who "hacked the window into Europe". Through this window various flows poured into Russia, including architectural ones, in the form of rather late baroque of Dutch-French-Italian-German mixture. The orders systems of the so called Naryshkinsky or Stroganovsky baroque became characteristic for the temples, rich in appearance, at the border of the 17th-18th centuries.

Tire temples are all together the synthesis of the Heavenly and Earthly Circles. Creative work of Russian architectures of the beginning of the 18th century was implemented within the framework of European styles and tendencies (baroque, classicism, Empire-style) prevailing at that time, with replacement in their forms of the heavenly symbols by the earthly ones.

The Centre of the Capital. Zamoskvorechie

Here the picture comes in sight worth the greatest capital in theworld, built by the greatest nation on the nicest place. For the one,who stood in the Kremlin and looked with cool eyes at the gigantictowers, ancient monasteries, majestic Zamoskvorechie, and was not proudof his Fatherland and did not bless Russia, for that one... all greatis alien, for he was robbed mercilessly by nature at his very birth.

K.Batyushkov

The capital centre of a state is a special structural entity, composed ofsocial-state, capital's objects. It usually consists of three parts: the centralkernel, quarters around the "kernel" and objects near the city. "The kernel" issituated in the centre of the main city of the state, is indivisible and compact. Over the city, round the "kernel" there are the quarters of the capital's objects. Other objects are in the countryside. Not only Moscow, but later St.Petersburg, as well as capitals of other countries had this structure.

We shall consider only the kernel of the capital's centre of Moscow of the 16th-17th century, besides that the word "centre" refers mostly to the middle part of the city. The "kernel" included different capital's and general municipal departments. The highest state authority – the tsar and his court – were accommodated in the whole system of the city's and country palaces, the main of which was the Kremlin's palace. The governing of the country was implemented in the Golden, Dining, Respondent Chambers, Tsar's Hall and Faceted Palace. In the Golden Palace the government of Moscow Rus held its meetings – Boyards Duma. The place of tsars coronation, final enforcement of documents, acts, agreements and legal documents, decrees of hierarchs, stars weddings was the cathedral of the Assumption. The place of promulgation of all state acts, as well as all-state celebrations and discussions was Red Square with the Frontal Place (first Lobnya, Troitskaya Square). Tsarinas palaces, the whole system of palaces cathedrals and churches, the monastery of

Tire temples of Moscow. The church of the Intercession in Fili. End of 17th century.

The centre of the capital. The view from the south from Zamoskvorechie.

the Saviour on Bor on the inside square of the regal palace, a whole complex of official and household buildings and yards was directly connected with the life of the tsar's court.

The most important state departments were concentrated not only in the Kremlin, but in Kitay-gorod too. They are first of all Prikazy (Departments) – unique ministries of that time. In the Kremlin they occupied the southern part of Ivanovskaya Square, in Kitay-gorod in Red Square there was Zemsky Department, which governed Russian lands of Moscow state by origin. The other towns and big monasteries were here too. Part of the representations was trade and was referred to the capital's trade centre. Some of the representations were located in Bely-Tsar's town.

Governing of the Church was implemented by the Patriarch, and the most important body of the church power was the Local Council, which gathered for discussionof the most important affairs and election of a new Patriarch. The centre of thispower was the cathedral of the Assumption and the Kremlin's Patriarchy Palace.There were other big church centres in the Kremlin and Kitay-gorod: representations of metropolitanates, eparchs and monasteries. The most important of them were in the Kremlin (Krutitskoe and the Holy Trinity-St.Sergius).

The centres of education and art were under the management of the tsar's andchurch's authorities. The Arsenal Chamber was also under the authority of thetsar's court, which had gunsmiths, jewellers, fretmasters, even icon-

The centre of the capital. The view from the West.

Reconstruction of M. Kudriavtsev.

painters. Moscow Printing Yard, which was in Kitay-gorod, was in the authority of the tsar, but under the church's control. The Greek-Slavic Academy in Zaikonospassky monastery in Kitay-gorod and all monastic schools were under the authority of the Patriarch.

The capital's centre occupied a huge territory and its main part was located in the Kremlin and Kitay-gorod. Along the outside border the Upper, Middle and Lower Rows, as well as Icon Row in Nikolskaya street, had roofed stone rows. This complex of trade rows ended near Moskvoretskie Gates with the Customs Mytny Yard, near Voscresenskie Gates they ended with the Coin Yard, and behind the trade places they ended with the Guests Yard. In Kitay-gorod there were special places for cross kissing – official certification of trade transactions and other agreements.

In Zaneglimenie along the river Neglinka the trade centre consisted of groups of trade rows and stores, divided by church's plots, the monastery of St. Moses and Borovitsky garden. And Voskresensky Bridge to Red Square and Borovitsky bridge in the Kremlin were trading, because there were stores there.

Zamoskvoretsky trade place occupied the square in front of Moskvoretsky, later also in front of Big Stone Bridge. There were stores for gold and silver masters on Kamenny Bridge. On the frozen Moscow-river in winter near the Kremlin's walls there was so called Gribnoy (Mushroom) Market.

Reconstruction of M. Kudriavtsev.

Out of the trade places of municipal importance Lenivy (Lazy) trade place was near Vsekhsvyatskie gates of Bely-Tsar's town and the trade places behind the gates of Kitay-gorod: Lubyanoy, Sennoy and Konevoy.

There were also purely municipal buildings in the centre: the meeting log house in Kitay-gorod, Tiuninskaya log house near St.Basil's cathedral, places of executions in Lobnaya and Lubyanskaya Squares. There were also three important tsar's courts: Konyushenny (Stable), Kolymazhny and Pushechny (Cannon). The first one was in the Kremlin, the other two were in Bely-Tsar's town.

The centre of the city was beautified by the tsar's gardens: terraced ones in the Kremlin, there were also winter gardens and small gardens of tsarina's palace, Borovitsky garden behind the Neglinnaya in front of the Kremlin, Vasilievsky garden in the South-East corner of Bely-Tsar's town, finally Big Tsar's Garden in front of the Kremlin in Zamoskvorechie.

All economic system of the "kernel" of the capital's centre is characterised with diversity of departments, high development, reasonability of its parts location. The Tsar's Palace was connected with the Patriarch's one, both were close to Cathedral Square and directly connected with the Departments, monasteries, representations in the Kremlin. The central public squares were connected in one unit with the main trade places, which allowed people to gather at special places. The same was in other business and trade departments. Near each garden there were town settlements of gardeners (except the Kremlin's gardens), and all the centre was inhabited by those people who worked in it: clerks, diplomats, warriors, etc.

The system of the main ensembles of the capital's centre was unified not only economically, but compositionally too. The integral view of the centre opened from the main four sides: from the southern borders of Zamoskvoretsky trade place (from the line of today's Kadashevskaya quay), from the north – along the valley of the river Neglinka from Kuznetsky bridge, from the west – from the church of St.Prophet Elijah Obydenny and from the east – from the Red Hill.

Most of all, in all its beauty, the centre was admired from the south, where there was the Big Tsar's Garden on the front plan with the following squares surrounding it: Vsekhsvyatskaya, Bolotnaya, with Zamoskvoretsky trade place. To the East and West from these squares the construction of the Upper and Lower Gardeners' Town Settlements began with two churches: one of the Holy Trinity in Bersenevo (of St.Nicholas) and the other of the Nativity of the Theotokos in Endovo (of St.Hieromartyr George).

If to stand in Zamoskvorechie at the beginning of Voskresenskaya street (now the lst Kadashevsky lane), it was possible to see from that place the forceful, with the length of 2,5 km, stone defence wall of Bely-Tsar's town in the West and in the East, of the Kremlin and Kitay-gorod in the middle. This wall united all the southern panorama of the "kernel" of the capital's centre, being as a platform for all the panorama. From this point the tire-like composition of all the ensemble was clear.

The tire-like composition of the southern panorama of the capital's centre was in conformity with the multi-cupola style: the tires not only rise one after another, but also sequentially "go away" from the on-looker. This view, due to which the notion of the "depth", unlimitedness of the city, appeared is like the impression from the view of long big forests. Their own, very sharp silhouette, location at certain "rhythm" stresses even more the presence of many plans of the whole ensemble.

From Zamoskvorechie there were other four places of the best view of the capital's centre – the exits to Zamoskvoretsky trade place of the mains streets: Yakimanka, Polyanka, Ordynka and Pyatnitskaya. From these places the horizontal sight angle at all the Kremlin's ensemble is equal to 45°, i.e. to one of the best angles of perception. These angles' borders include compositionally the main buildings of the southern panorama: gold-cupola cathedrals, the bell-tower of John the Great, the Tower of the Saviour, St.Basil's cathedral.

The view of the ensemble of the capital's centre from the North, West and East have common features with the view from Kadashi. There is also the complication and richness of the silhouette, the composition of tires and many plans in the basis of construction of the ensemble. The centre's main buildings also stand out clearly and accurately.

The ensemble's view from the centre has very clear axis, conforming to the valley of the River Neglinka and directed at the cathedral of the Holy Trinity on the Ditch. There is no dense architecture on the front plan, but as though extended coulissees (on the left there are two big ensembles one after another - Suzdal Representation and Pushechny (Cannon) Yard, on the right – the churches and yards in Petrovka). The temples of the monastery of St.Hieromartyr George and the church of St.Hieromartyr Parasceva of Iconium on Torg rose above the buildings of Petrovka.

From the valley's hollow of the river Neglinnaya there was a view of the wall of Kitay-gorod, which was a certain platform for the complicated silhouette of the architecture with plenty of monasteries and churches. This silhouette also included the Kremlin's towers, the cathedral of the Holy Trinity on the Ditch, to the right from which above lots of golden cupolas of Cathedral Square the bell-tower of John the Great rises to the sky. Here the compositional role of the bell-tower is a little weaker. The role of the cathedral of the Assumption is even much weaker – its five cupolas are mixed with all many cupolas of the Kremlin's cathedral and churches.

The view of the ensemble of the capital's centre from the East, from the Red Hill, was especially interesting because it opened all the three walls of Bely-Tsar's town, Kitay-gorod and the Kremlin. From here the tires and plans of the ensemble were the most complicated. And the walls did not just make the plans outlined, but united them: the wall of Bely-Tsar's town, limiting the front plan, turned to the shore of the Moscow-river and joined with the southern walls' facade of the centre's ensemble. Here it was joined with the walls of Kitay-gorod and the Kremlin.

The view of the capital's centre from the West from the church of St.Prophet Elijah Obydenny had the same contrasting of the architecture of the left shore of the Moscow-river and Zamoskvorechie. Here from the cathedral of

The centre of the capital. The view from the East, from the Red Hill. Reconstruction of M.P.Kudriavtsev.

St.Basil the cupolas were hardly seen, but the temples of Cathedral Square with the bell-tower of John the Great looked an expressive group with lots of cupolas. The wall of Bely-Tsar's town looks very powerful on the left-shore part of the city. All the front plan here is very beautiful with the wall, expressive corner octahedral tower and the near by single tower of seven tops. And above the wall the gates and cells of Alexeevsky monastery rise with three hip roofs cathedral of the Transfiguration.

Making a scheme of location of the ensembles of the capital's centre, directions of its main visual connections and the borders of the zones of panorama perception, it is possible to note that the general composition of this huge complex is triangular on the plan: triangle cape in the mouth of the river Neglinka became the place of location of triangular fortresses of the Kremlin and Kitay-gorod. The main trade places near these fortresses comprise the next such triangle. The dwelling buildings, surrounding the trade places and the fortresses, repeating on the plan the triangle outline of all the complex, opens at the top of the triangle, made by it, along the valleys of the rivers Moscow and Neglinka.

Zamoskvorechie, separated by the river, was always as though opposed to the centre – the Kremlin – and to all the city, so it is worth being considered specially. The opposition happened due to a number of circumstances. First of all the bottom of Moscow natural "bowl" is here – the lowest place of the landscape. During high waters the Moscow-river flooded the bottom, then left on it two parts of the old river-beds and a morass along the way of these beds (now it is a channel). The territory of Zamoskvorechie went down smoothly to the North, into the morass, contrasted there with the hills of the height of 20-30 m behind the river. This contrast of hills and low land was stressed due to town-building: on the hills there was the Kremlin, Kitay-gorod with their high buildings: the bell-tower of John the Great, cathedrals, fortress towers. People always admired this contrast. This contrast also existed in Kiev (the hills and Podol), Vladimir (the same), Smolensk (the hills and Bolonie), even in the Holy Trinity-St.Sergius monastery (Makovitsa and Podol). So, it was favourite with ancient Russian architects.

For the appearance of Zamoskvoretsky settlement absence of strong culminations of height, volume and colour is characteristic. Above the quiet silhouette of dwelling buildings parish churches rose almost equal in height, the majority of which were the most common in the 17th century one- or five-cupola fiery temples with refectories and bell-towers. The bell-towers were either built above the entrance from the west part, or near by. Several

The centre of the capital. The view from the North from Kuznetskiy bridge. Reconstruction of M.P.Kudriavtsev.

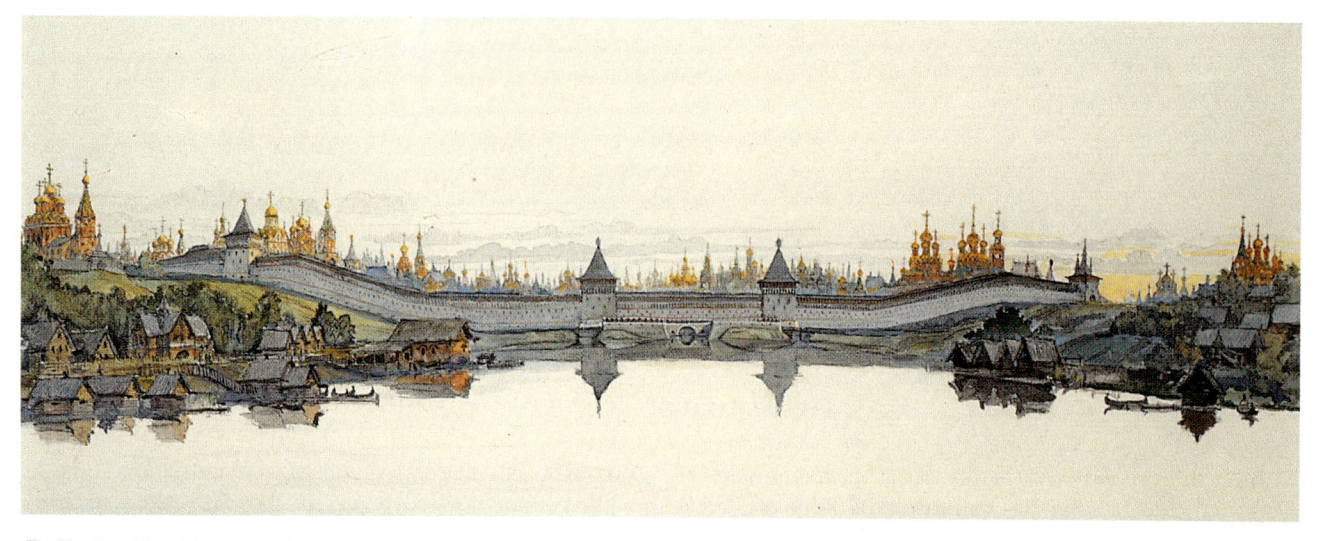

The Northern line of the monasteries-guards. From left to right: Sretenskiy (of the Meeting of our Lord in the Temple), Rozhdestvenskiy (of the Nativity of the Theotokos), Vysokopetrovskiy, Strastnoy (of the Passions). Reconstruction of M. Kudruavtsev.

hip roof and one-cupola tire temples, built by octahedral on tetrahedral, are also known. Besides the churches, a few municipal buildings made Zamoskvorechie unique: they were the above-mentioned Kadashevsky textile and Kadashevsky Brethren yards, well seen behind the river, especially from the Kremlin.

The Tsar's garden in front of the Kremlin occupied the central position in Zamoskvorechie, and near the garden there was Kadashevsky town settlement, which extended from the west to the east, between Yakimanka and Perepelkina streets (Bolshaya Ordynka). The settlement had its own special planning of the streets: nearly all of them were "regular" and went to the north, to the morass and the garden. The settlement's temples and municipal yards were the basis of the composition of all the district.

In the composition of the Eastern and Western parts of Kadashevskaya townsettlement the balance between temple ensembles was observed too at the joint of Zamoskvoretskie streets and the city's centre: Pyatnitskaya, Perepelkino, Bolshaya Polyanka and Yakimamka. There is a couple of churches in the first two streets, connected by Chernigovsky lane: the church of John the Predecessor under the Bor and the one of the Miracle-workers of Chernigov. The ends of the other two streets are marked with the churches of Sts.Cosmas and Damian in Kadashi and of Sts. Joachim and Anna.

The southern plot of Zamoskvorechie was built conditionally symmetrically inrespect of the axis north-south; there are Serpukhovskie gates on the axis in Skorodom, and at equal distance from them there are Kaluzhskie and Kolomenskie gates. In the system of the streets there is the main one Perepelkina (Bolshaya Ordynka), in the west – Bolshaya Yakimanka, and in the east – Bolshaya Tatarskaya. The axis of Zamoskvorechie was especially underlined by the churches of St. Nicholas in Pyzhi and the hip roof church of St.Hieromartyr George the Victory-bearer in Vspolie.

Location of near-shore churches in Zamoskvorechie is also estimated compositionally as symmetrical, in spite of asymmetricity of the river's winding with a sharp backwards bend of the river-bed in the west part. There are three churches in the west on the shore: of St.Nicholas in Golutvin, of the Annunciation (of St.Maron) and of St.Martyr John the Warrior, in the east there were three

Western line of the monasteries-guards. At the front there is Novodevichiy monastery. Reconstruction of M.P.Kudriavtsev.

The Southern line of the monasteries-guards. From left to right: the monasteries of St.Apostle Andrew, of the Don icon of the Theotokos, of St.Daniel, of St.Symeon. Reconstruction of M. Kudriavtsev.

churches too: of the Transfiguration (St.Nicholas Zayaitsky), of St.Cosmas and Damian in Sadovniki and St.Nicholas in Pupyshi. Thus, the composition of Zamoskvorechie was based on symmetry of town-building along the axis north-south. It was understood as symmetrical by ancient Russian architects. And though it is not actually strictly mathematical, but deformed in the plan and composition, it can be easily imagined on an idealised scheme as symmetrical and in this way it is easier to understand.

Monastery Complexes

Moscow's fortified monasteries are divided into two big complexes. The second one is also divided into other four "lines of monasteries", situated on four parts of Moscow, – as though on four ends of a huge cross, in the middle ofwhich there is the city.

Seven big fortified monasteries composed the first big monastery complex. The monasteries were the centre of Bely town and like a chain surrounded the centre of Moscow from north-west and north-east parts. The monasteries were connected with each other with a system of streets-connections and situated almost at equal distances from each other. In spite of expressiveness and richness of monastery ensembles, all their system was not understood as a whole, because it wassituated inside the dense architecture of the city's central part. Alexeevsky monastery was in Volkhonka (where later the cathedral of Christ the Saviour wasbuilt), the monastery of the Adoration of the Holy Cross was in Vozdvizhenka, theMonastery of St.Nicetas was in Bolshaya Nikitskaya street, the one of St.Hieromartyr George was between Tverskaya street and Bolshaya Dmitrovskaya street, the monastery of St.John the Crysostome was between the streets Myasnitskaya and Maroseyka, the one of St.Barsanuphius was between the streets Rozhdestvenskaya and Lubyanka, the monastery of St.John was on the hill between the streets Bolshaya Ivanovskaya and Solyanka. Prevailing in the composition of the surrounding streets and lanes, they underlined the silhouette of the central ensembles of the capital's centre which was seen from the streets of Bely-Tsar's town.

The far west and east points of the system – Alexeevsky and Ivanovsky monasteries – were included right in the

The Eastern lines of the monasteries-guards. From left to right: the monasteries of the Saviour, of the Intercession, of the Saviour-St.Andronicus. Reconstruction of M.P.Kudriavtsev.

kernel of the capital's centre. But if to connect all the seven monasteries with one line, its outline will repeat the triangle of the walls of the Kremlin and Kitay-gorod. And independent from the fact that all the seven monasteries were not percepted all together from any point, except the unique top points, for example, from the Kremlin's towers or from the bell-tower of John the Great, all the system has quite a distinct compositional connection.

This connection is also in the observation of the principle of balance between the flank monasteries. Alexeevsky monastery, standing on the high edge next to the walls of Bely-Tsar's town, was a large ensemble with central hip roof cathedral, three-bay bell-tower, refectory and an above-gate temple. Built on a high hill Ivanovsky monastery had more modest buildings. But the combination of one possible temple's hip roof, hip roof bell-tower, as well as of the hip roof bell-tower of the nearby church of St.Vladimir in Old Sady looked on panoramas as a whole three hip-roof composition, like the composition of Alexeevsky monastery. It is well seen on Meiberg's panorama, who showed a three hip-roof temple in this place.

The clear compositional interconnections of the monasteries making on its location in the city a unified system, also show that Moscow architects were veryefficient not only in the modes of creating harmony of the ensembles percepted together, but of keeping compositional wholeness of ensembles' group, which united speculatively, not evidently.

Fourteen monasteries-guards composed the second monastery complex in Moscow, As it was already noted it falls apart in four lines on the four parts of the city. The eastern line of the monasteries-guards is composed from the monasteries of the Saviour-St.Andronicus, of the Intercession and Novospassky; the southern line is composed of the monasteries of St.Simon, of St.Daniel, of the Icon of the Most Holy Theotokos "Of the Don" and of St-Andrew; the western line is composed ofthe monasteries Novodevichy, of St.Sabbas, Novinsky; the northern line is composedof the monasteries of the Passions, Vysoko-Petrovsky, of the Nativity of theTheotokos and of the Meeting of the Saviour Jesus Christ. The eastern and westernlines were made from three monasteries, the southern and the northern lines – byfour monasteries. The eastern line of the monasteries controlled the river Yauzaand the roads Vladimirskaya and Ryazanskaya; the southern line protected the winding of the Moscow-river and southern roads: Kolomenskaya, Serpukhovskaya and Kaluzhskaya; the western line was all near the Moscow-river, from the place infront of the Setun's mouth to the fall of the Presnya, and guarded the westernroads Smolenskaya, Mozhayskaya and Zvenigorodskaya. The northern line in difference to the others getting during the city's growth inside its fortifications, controlled from the beginning the northern roads: Tverskaya, Dmitrovskaya, Yurievskaya and Yaroslavskaya.

The northern line of the monasteries-guards is divided by the Neglinka intotwo halves: two monasteries are in the west, two – in the east. At the same time, it is necessary to take into account that the Neglinka's valley is directed to the south right at St.Basil's cathedral. The complex was built with very efficient use of the landscape's qualities. For example, bigger ensembles – Vysoko-Petrovsky and of the Passions – are further from the axis than the smaller – of the Nativity of the Theotokos and of the Meeting of the Saviour Jesus Christ. It was conditioned by the location of the edges of the Neglinka's valley and the lines of the closest watersheds where the monasteries were built. So the ensembles are different in dimensions on the plan, including the buildings inside them. In this way the architects achieved the balance of all the complex of the northern monastery line in relation to the valley of the Neglinka.

The southern line of the monasteries-guards is organised a little differently.There is no clear natural transversal axis north-south, but there is a loop ofthe Moscow-river, so, according to the location on the relief's tires and in their dimensions the monasteries alternate: the western monastery of St. Andrew was built nearly on the shore of the Moscow-river, Donskoy monastery was built on the line of the watershed, the monastery of St.Daniel – on the first low terrace, and the eastern one of St.Simon – on the high and steep opposite river bank. Two extreme monasteries – of St.Andrew and of St.Simon – had couples of temples (a cathedral and a refectory) and on-gate churches, and two middle ones – of the Icon of the Theotokos "Of the Don" and of St.Daniel – each had one cathedral and on-gate churches. And all the cathedrals, refectories and on-gate churches of the southern line of the monasteries were one-cupola, which underlined the unity of the complex ensembles.

The monasteries are situated at approximately equal distances from each other,but not quite symmetrically in relation to the axis north-south indicated by theNeglinnaya's valley from the north. The monastery of St.Daniel is nearer to theaxis than Donskoy monastery, however the principle of balance is observed due tocorresponding difference in the sizes of the ensembles: during the construction in the 17th century of the monastery of St.Andrew and reconstruction of other ensembles of the complex the monastery of St.Daniel was increased.

The western and eastern lines of the monasteries-guards were also built withconsideration of the principle of balance, as well as similarity in construction of extreme flank ensembles. Novodevichy and Novospassky monasteries, situated in the southern points of the complexes, are more developed in composition: each has five temples. At the end of the 17th century in these monasteries high bell-towers were built. So, the main "axis of balance" for the complexes is the axis north-south of all the city again.

The common feature of the monasteries of all the complexes of all the linesis the location of the bell-tower or on-gate temple under the chime near the road controlled by the monastery. Thus the subordination of the monastery ensembles to the centre is underlined. The bell-tower of John the Great, from which monasteries bell-towers are connected visually, is in the centre of the Kremlin, i.e. from the military and town-building and compositional points of view – in the centre of the systems of monasteries-guards.

Town-building Composition

The best of all that I have seen in this world, is Moscow anyway.

S.Esenin

All the above-said about the city's location on concrete landscape, about the temples, which made its gold-cupola appearance, about the capital's centre on the hills and Zamoskvorechie on the low land, about the monasteries complexes inside and outside the city can be generalised in *idealised scheme* of town-building composition of the 16th-17th centuries.

The scheme helps to understand the complicated phenomenon, substituting the principle of balance in the composition of the city by the principle of classical symmetry. But without such scheme, with help of only wordly descriptions it is difficult to understand anything in Moscow's composition because it is extremely complicated. It is not by chance that people who tried to do it without knowing Christian symbolics, finally just called everything "chaotic" and thus calmed down, thinking that they had characterised the truth. Only understanding the ideal essence of the complicated architectural composition of Moscow, it is possible to comprehend all the city in all the richness of its appearance. But the scheme also needs some explanation about how it was made.

Moscow's composition, shown in the idealised scheme, keeps its connection with the natural landscape and is quite grounded strategically. In it the centre is underlined very well, in the structure of which the rivers are used organically. The centre's triangle with seven monasteries is within the borders of a conditional square of aristocratic Bely-

Idealized scheme of town-building composition of ancient Moscow of the end of 17th century. On the scheme the following is shown: a – triangle composition from 7 monasteries of 14th-17th century around the Kremlin and Kitay-gorod; b – cross-like composition from 14 monasteries-guards. Scheme of M. Kudriavtsev.

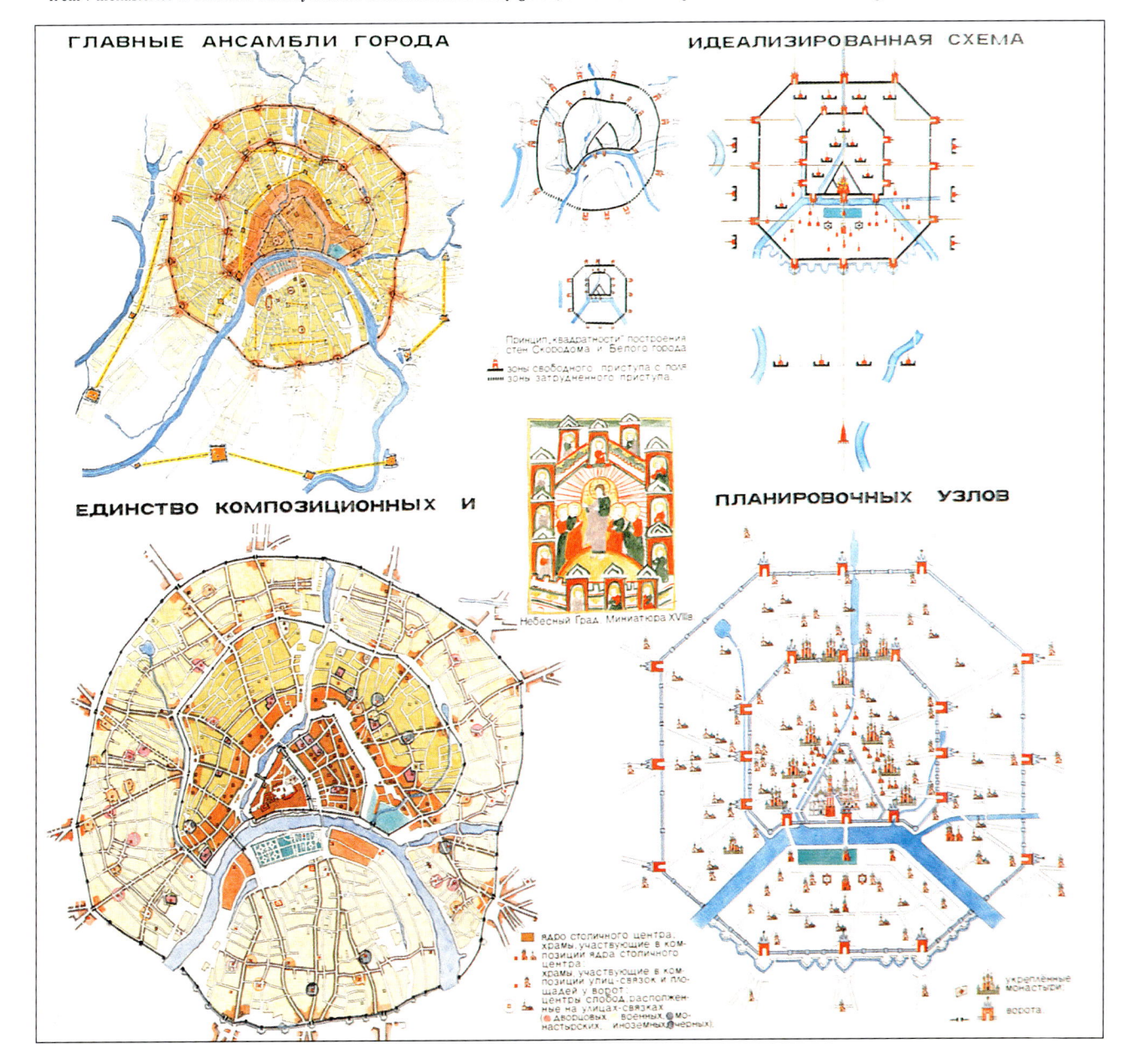

Tsar's town, which is also inside the square with sloped corners of military-handicraft Skorodom.

There is an interesting difference in the imitation of the composition of the axises north-south and west-east with extension of the first axis at a significant distance: it can be stretched from the church of the Holy Trinity in Troitskaya settlement (to the north from Skorodom at the Neglinka-river) through the cathedral of the Holy Trinity (St.Basil's cathedral) in Red Square, further – through the church of the Resurrection in Kadashi and the church of St.Hieromartyr George in Vspolie, Serpukhovskie gates of Skorodom and the church of the Ascension in Kolomenskoe.

The idealised scheme of Moscow's composition, which is the result of the carried out analysis, has a parallel in the ancient Moscow cartography. It is a series of axonometric plans of Moscow known under the name "The plans of Isaac Massa". All of them were done during the Troubled Time, at the beginning of the 17th century upon the order of Massa by a Russian artist. They depict the invasion into Moscow of the Polish and coming into the capital of Marina Mnishek, a false tsarina of False Demetrius I, i.e. they are actually not plans but miniatures -pictures devoted to a certain plot. There is not only axonometry in the picture, but perspective too: we look at Moscow from the south and from top, due to which the city's outlines became oval with straight long parallel parts of the walls from the north and the south, as well as with short straight parts of the walls from the east and the west. If to unfold this figure up to the real city's plan, equalling the sizes of the axises north-south and west-east, as it is on the real plan of Moscow, we shall get a square with rounded corners.

Moscow plan of Isaac Massa, on which the Western and Eastern lines of monasteries-guards are shown, as well as the church of the Ascension in Kolomenskoe on the main Moscow axis North-South.

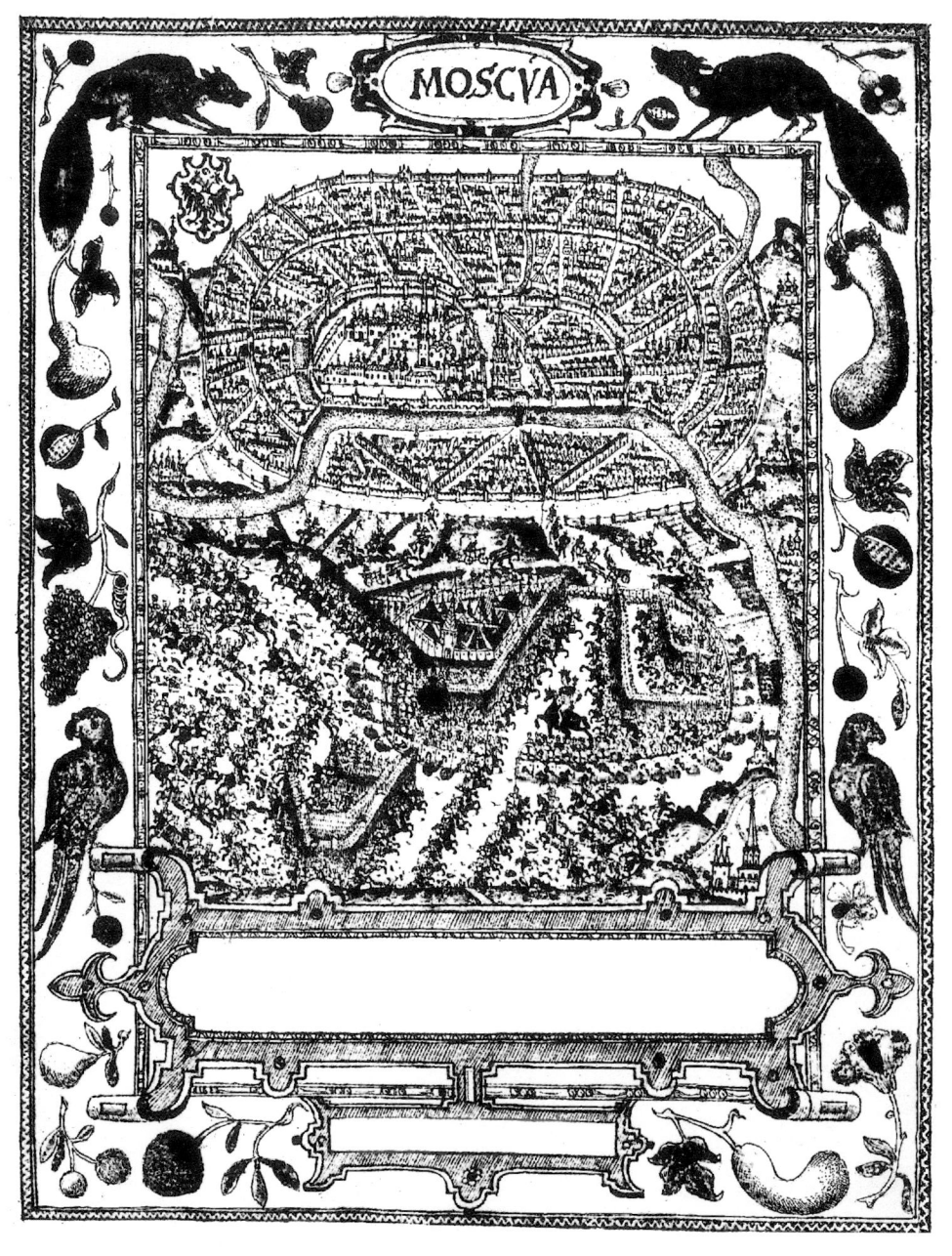

In the geometrical centre of the city there is the cathedral of the Holy Trinity (St.Basil's cathedral) in Red Square and on the left and on the right of it there is the Kremlin and Kitay-gorod. Like the outlines of Skorodom's walls, the walls of Holy-Tsar's town are sham, which, being unfolded up to the exact plan, will have the form of a square with rounded corners.

To the west from the city three monasteries are shown: Novinsky, of St.Sabbas and Novodevichy (the western line). From the east there are also three monasteries of the eastern line, from which the Saviour-St.Andronicus monastery is recognised in the upper one. It is quite possible that the lower (southern) monastery is either Novo-Spassky or Krutitsky metropolitan court. Such interpretation of the picture is grounded on the fact that the monasteries complex is shown right in front of the southern end of Kozhevnicheskaya settlement. The location of the middle monastery conforms to the location of the monastery of the Intercession. However, the monastery of the Intercession was founded at the time of Michael Feodorovich (i.e. later the depicted event), and it got the stone walls even later, at the time of tsar Alexius Mikhailovich. So it is still difficult to make the final conclusion about what monastery is shown here.

Nevertheless, the fact that to the east and west from Moscow an artist of the 17th century showed three monasteries is not less important. It also conformswith the idealised scheme, in spite of the fact that it was made for a little later period. It can mean that at the beginning of the 17th century the idea of "symmetrical" lines of monasteries-guards to the city already existed in some way.

And, finally, on the plan of Isaac Massa the extreme southern point of thecomposition, as it is in reality, is the church of the Ascension in Kolomenskoe, shown in conformity with the real situation not exactly from the south, but to the south-east from the city.

The northern and southern lines of the monasteries-guards are not shown on theplan, as the northern one "drowned" in the architecture, and the southern was intentionally removed in order to show the main plot of the picture. It is possible to say that Moscow was understood by the people of the 17th century as ideally symmetrical in relation to the axis of north-south city, a little deformed by the rivers and concrete landscape. And this is the true approach to the understanding of town-building composition of ancient Moscow.

The composition of each system or complexes of the ensembles of ancient Moscow separately is of no less interest to the history of town-building than thecity as a whole. But it is a subject of special research. Though considerationof each ensemble should begin from finding out its place in town-building composition which is most clear exactly on the idealised scheme.

Geometrical idealisation shows in relief the general structure of the city'scomposition and the unlimited diversity in use of the principle of balance in construction of separate buildings and big capital's ensembles. This principle isat the basis of all Russian architecture. As for Moscow, it is an encyclopaedia of various modes of its application. Comparison of real location of the ensembles with the geometrical idealised scheme underlines that in town-building of ancient Moscow the qualities of natural landscape were used not only functionally, but also for creation of not less beautiful hand-made city's landscape. Specialities of the landscape relief became the integral part of the ensembles making direct influence on their dimensions, silhouette and location in the town-building composition.

The idealised scheme can be considered just the first step on the way to thesolving of the question about the formation of the town-building structure of the capital in the whole compositional conception. A rather important task is explanation of the internal contents of the found out formal scheme. The way to it is in comparing Moscow to the cities of western Europe similar to it in complicity of compositional structure and to the known schemes of "ideal" nation of the internal cities.

The Memorial of Military Glory

Its destiny is to trouble always
The sworn enemies of Russia
To humiliate it, to annihilate
Their malice tried many times.
But for the fear of the enemies,
but for the joy of the country
It is, the great, alive,
And I raise the old call:
May Moscow live for ages!
                                    K.Aksakov

Moscow became the capital of Russian land during the most difficult time-during the Mongolian-Tatar yoke. Accepting the wretched refugees from the ravaged Russian lands, a small town in the forests of bellicose Vyatichis began to develop military force, first becoming *the shield* and then *the sword* of Russia. The victory in Kulikovo field finally moved Moscow to the front edge of fight with enemies.

Moscow moved boyards to itself purposefully, as well as handicraftsmen, merchants from the joined ravaged Russian principalities and lands. It created the all-Russian army, which was located mainly in the capital. In the 17th century the Moscow army comprised nearly one third of all the Russian army. Within Bely-Tsar's town warriors from aristocratic families lived: princes, boyards with their nobility men (troops) and dwellers. It was the main kernel of the army – princely and nobility cavalry. The tsar usually chose the commanders from them. Within the boundaries of Skorodom there were streletskie and gunners settlements: Moscow cavalry troops and foot streletskie troops made reliable support of all Russian troops. Military settlements, concentrated near 12 gates of Skorodom, made four areas of accommodation of the Moscow army in the north, South, East and West. All the plan area of accommodation looked as if it were the Greek cross, because between the ends of the cross there were morasses: flood-lands of the Moscow-river, Kozie morass, the morasses of Oljkhovets.

All the town-building complex, which formed in Moscow – *the memorial of Military Glory of Russia*, consisted of three parts: I – town walls and fortified monasteries-guards; 2 – military departments (Streletsky, Gunners) with the Razryadny (Rank) Department at the head of them in the Kremlin; 3 – vowed temples – memorials of battles, victories,

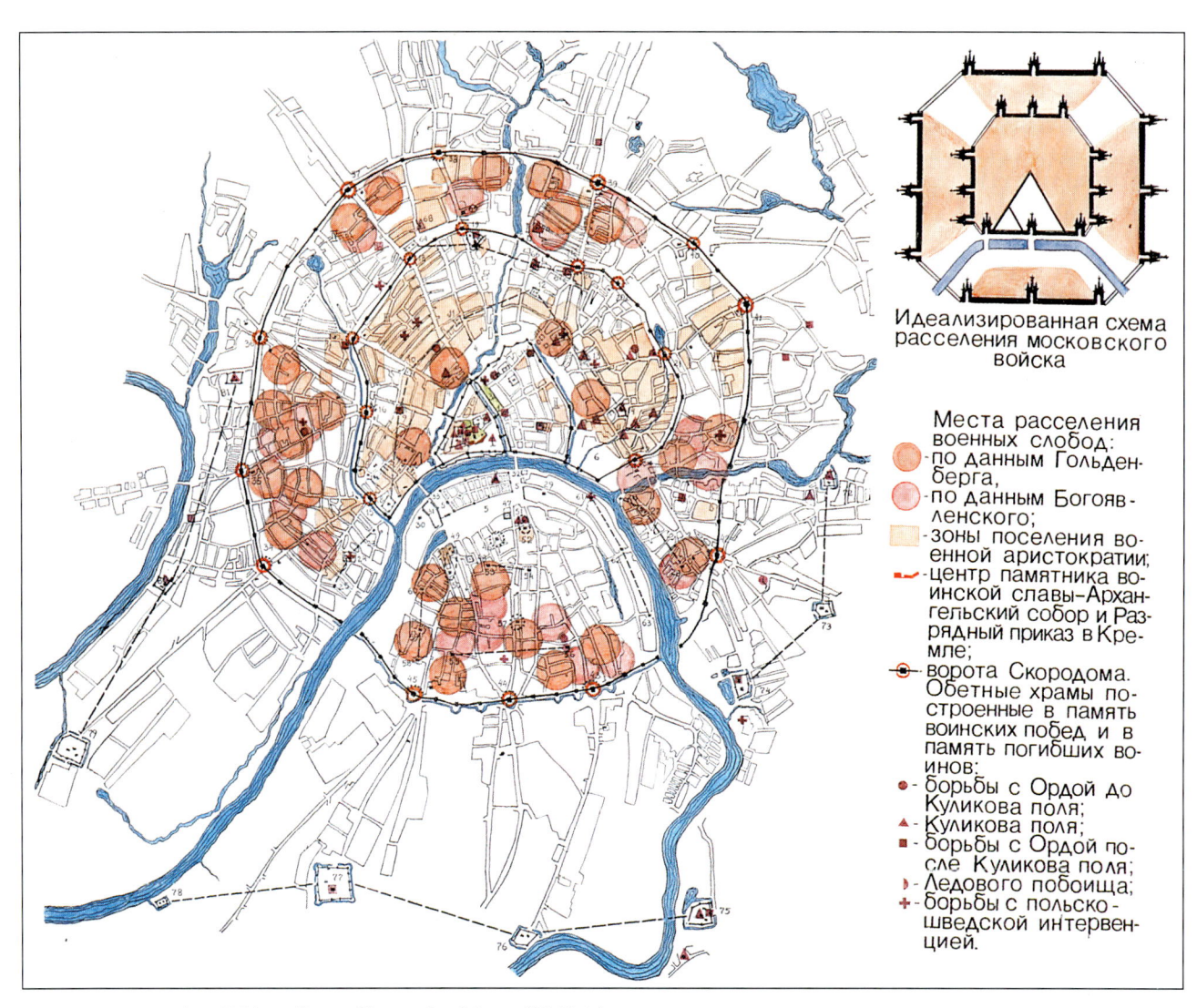

Location of the memorials of Military Glory on Moscow plan. Scheme of M. Kudriavtsev.

disasters. In the 17th century along the walls of the Kremlin, Kitay-gorod, Bely-Tsar's town memorable religious processions of all holy orders and people were made, which began from the Frontal place. Before that in the cathedral of the Assumption a praying service was conducted about protection of Moscow from invasions of enemies and disasters. The same service then ended the religious processions. The same praying services with religious processions were made to many Moscow monasteries.

Plenty of temples are the memorials of accommodation of the Moscow army, evenbuilt for the account of streltsy and gunners. The main of them was the church of St. Nicholas Streletsky in front of Borovitskie Gates of the Kremlin, built in 1682 and ruined in the 30s of our century. In Skorodom and Zamoskvorechie there were the churches of the Holy Trinity in Pushkary (Gunners) of 1657, of St.Sergius in Pushkary of 1684, of the Transfiguration in Pushkary of 1683, of the Holy Trinity in Listy of 1671, of the Ascension ("Big") in Storozhy of 1685, St.Nicholas in Arbat (Yavlenny) of 1589, of the Annunciation behind Tverskie Gates of 1697, of St.Poemen in Starye Vorotniki of 1689, of St.Nicholas in Pyzhi of 1647, of the Holy Trinity in Veshnyaki of 1678, of the Holy Trinity in Zubovo of 1657, of the Icon of the Most Holy Thetokos of Kazan near Kaluzhskie Gates of 1681, of St.Nicholas in Vorobjino of 1690 and many others (the dates are indicated for stone churches, which had been wooden before).

Speaking about memorials of military glory of Russian people in Moscow, it isnecessary to mention that in Russia no obelisks, like in Egypt, no mausoleums, like in Greece, statues and triumph arches, like in Rome, were installed. All disaster or heroic events were marked by installation of chapels or templcs. In them memorable days, events were celebrated annually by prayers, services. Thus, the memory of the event did not disappear, like the history which consisted of such events (temples-memorials were ruined not long ago just like churches).

Plenty of temple-memorials were consecrated to different military events in thelife of Russian people. Nevertheless in a memorial of Military Glory, like in an army, it is possible to find out certain hierarchy structure.

The centre of all the memorial of Military Glory is Red Square and its mainobjects: the cathedral of the Holy Trinity on the Ditch (St.Basil's cathedral) – the main memorial of the victory over Kazan and Astrakhan khanates, final liberation of Russia from Tatar-Mongolian yoke, from the threat of Muslim slavery, and the cathedral of the Kazan Icon of the Theotokos

Temples of Military Glory in Kulishki. From right to left: of All Saints, of Sts. Cyrus and John (of the Holy Trinity), of St.Hieromattyr Patasceva of Iconicum, of St.John the Predecessor. There is the Horse trade place at the front. Reconstruction of G. Mokeev.

and the main memorial of liberation of Moscow and Russian land from catholic expansion.

In its turn the main military memorial building in the capital became the cathedral of Archangel Michael in the Kremlin. Being the burial vault of grandprinces and tsars it embodied the symbol of the Russian army. Almost all princes and tsars depicted on the pillars and walls of the cathedral, are presented not in the scheme, (though they took it before death), but in princely and tsar's clothes. In the painting of the temple the meaning of their earthly way was underlined. On each face not just the life of the depicted governor of the Russian land is shown, but the life of his army. The idea of warriors' heroic deed was fully reflected both in the consecration of the cathedral to Archangel Michael – the Heavenly protector of warriors, and in the paintings glorifying military heroic deeds according to the examples of ancient battles. The temple's coffins are the places of burials of high Russian commanders, the mere names of which refresh in the memory the names of the greatest battles of Russian people with their enemies.

Sometimes several memorials were devoted to one important event. For example, to the victory in Kulikovo field of 1380 the church of the Nativity of the MostHoly Theotokos on Seni and the monastery of the Ascension in the Kremlin, Vysoko-Petrovsky monastery and the monastery of the Nativity of the Theotokos, the church of All Saints were consecrated. The main ensemble of this memorial – Kulishki – is the complex of the temples with the monastery of the Holy Trinity on the place of prayings and burials, which took place before and after the battle with Mamay.

To commemorate the liberation of Moscow from Polish-Lithuanian-Swedish invasion during the Troubled Time of the beginning of the 17th century a lot of temples-memorials were built, earlier buildings became such memorials. Those were the cathedral of the Saviour of Novospassky monastery – temporary the main cathedral of Russia during the conquering of Kremlin by the Polish, the cathedral of the Kazan Icon of the Theotokos in Red Square, the churches of the Presentation of the Virgin in the Temple in Lubyanka, of the Intercession in Rubtsovo, of the Kazan Icon of the Theotokos in Kolomenskoe, of Prophet Elisha, of St-Prophet Elijah on Vorontsovo field, of St.Apostles Peter and Paul in the latest Lefortovo and others.

Donskoy monastery was founded in commemoration of the liberation of Moscow from the attack of the army of the Crimean khan Kaza Gurey in 1592; Novodevichy monastery of 1542 was founded in the memory of liberation of Smolensk, like the temple of the Saviour of Smolensk in 1514 near Moskvoretskie Gates of Kitay-gorod. The church of Chasuble-laying in the Kremlin is the memorial of the saving of Moscow from the attacks of the horde of tsarevich Mazobsha in 1451; the cathedral of the Annunciation in the Kremlin and the church of St.Nicholas in Bolvanka were built (were rebuilt from stone) in the memory of overthrow of the Tatar-Mongolian yoke in 1480; and the inside lateral altars of the cathedral of the Annunciation appeared in the memory about Polotskaya victory in 1566. In the memory for the killed in the battle near Vozha in 1378 St.Sergius founded the monastery at Stromyn near Moscow, after the battle Kulikovo field Demetrius Donskoy founded the monastery and ordered to build the stone cathedral of St. Nicholas at Ugresh. The monastery of the Meeting of Our Lord God Jesus Christ was built in the memory about liberation of Russia from invasion of Tamerlan's hordes in 1395, as well as for the liberation from the yoke in 1480, from attacks of the Crimean Akhmet Guirey in 1521, in honour of seizure of Kazan in 1552. The tradition to consecrate temples to memorable military events was continued in Moscow later too in the 18th-19th centuries.

Here the memorials of special kind should be mentioned too, which were builtin honour of birth or the days of Angels of Russian tsars. It is the insidelateral altar of St.Demetrius of Thessalonica of the cathedral of Assumption -the memory about the first Moscow prince Vladimir-Demetrius Vsevolodovich; the temple of Archangel Michael – the memory about Michael Khorobrit, besides the stone temple in 1333 was also built in the memory of the saving from horrible famine in 1332; the church of St.John the Author of "The Ladder" – the memory about John Krasny – the father of Demetrius Donskoy, the church of St.John the Predecessor in Old Vaganjkovo – in honour of the birth of John (the Terrible), the church of St.Symeon Stylites behind the Yauza – in honour of the tsar's church coronation of tsar Boris Godunov, the church of St.Michael, Hegumen of Maleinus, in the Kremlin – in honour of election and regal coronation of Michael Feodrovich Romanov.

Each memorial was keenly perceived by people first of all because the temple's altar was consecrated to a Saint or church Evangelic holiday, on the day ofwhich the historic event happened. As there were temples-memorials in the capital, it so happened that during a year anniversary of some disaster or victory was commemorated in one of them. In this way people paid tribute to their tragic and heroic history each day.

It is quite natural that military denomination of the city was understood atfirst glance. It was typical for all ancient towns, surrounded by defence buildings. So all the structure of the memorial of Military Glory of Moscow was in organic conformity with the system of the fortress walls. The lines of the monasteries-guards and Skorodom's walls, the gates of which visually pointed to the location of the Moscow army (settlements) – that is the first impression of the memorial. Then sequentially the inside town's walls and monasteries were perceived. The southern town's facade was especially expressive, being repeated if to look at the centre from Zamoskvorechie.

The town-building memorial of Military Glory of Moscow was grandiose not only in its dimensions, but because it embraced 500 years of historical period of thecountry's life reflected in it – from the 13th to the 17th centuries. Embodied in temples' buildings the image of Military Glory combined in one unity with theimage of all the city's ensemble and its main fortifications. It was an integralpart of Moscow's history and life. Time did not leave any documents to us whichtestified to conscious forming of such grandiose memorial. However, it is widelyknown what significance the state attributed to the impression which was made on foreigners by Moscow and its army. The memorial first of all taught warriors-moscovites, as well as all Russian people, self-consciousness and honour. And they remembered the simple wisdom of the ancient said by the Prophet Solomon: *"Do not give away your honour to foreigners, so that they never fill in your forces, otherwise your labour will be in alien home, and you will be finally in despair"*.

Red Square. 17th century. Artist A.M.Vasnetsov.

CHAPTER SIX

The Symbol of Holy Russia

*The capital, ancient and native,
Does not the country know it?
To call it and the Holy Russia
Was called together with it.*
           K.Aksakov

*The great town on the Neglinnaya banks,
The Holy Russia under ancient gown,
The shelter of hospitable kindness...*
           A.Polezhaev

The Heavenly Town Jerusalem. Lithograph from Apocalypse. The 13thcentury. Paris, national library.

About Thee Rejoyceth. Icon of the beginning of XVIth century. Studio of Dionysious.

The Saviour, Golden Hair. 1st quarter of 13th century.

Symbolic picture of Jerusalem. From description of Palestine. 13th century. Padua, seminary's librstty.

The cathedrals of the Resurrection and the Nativity of Christ with the bell-tower of John the Great – the basis of the symbol of Moscow as "The Second Jerusalem"

Plan of Rome. Miniature on parchment. Beginning of 15th century. Brothers Lamburg (1402-1416). Chantil, museum Conde.

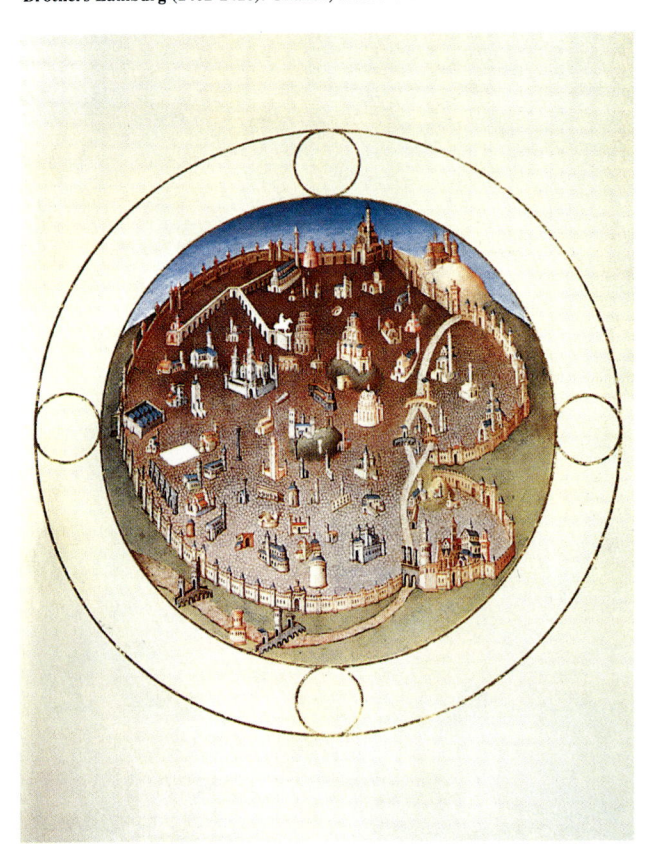

Spasskaya Tower of Moscow Kremlin - the basis of the symbol of Moscow as "The Third Rome".

> *"Today the glorious city of Moscow is standing in splendour, accepting like the sun-rise, Mother of the Lord, Your miracle-working icon. And today coming to it and praying to You with all heart: "Oh, wonderful the Most Holy Theotokos, pray to Christ, Your Son and our God, so that He protects this city and other towns and countries of Christendom from all enemies and salves our souls, for He is Merciful ".*
>
> Feast prayer to Vladimirskaya
> icon of the Most Holy Theotokos

The Greek word "symbol" means sign, token, purpose, heavenly phenomenon...So the symbol is understood widely as any sign having a certain meaning for a certain group of people. So, it means that it is necessary to know the contents and form of symbol. All pagan world worshipped symbols and they were very important in life. Symbols of Christian Middle centuries are also conditional and mysterious.

After christening symbolical ideas of temple, town, even land as God's creation were brought into Russia. And these ideas were comprehended well, even developed. So it is reasonable to speak about some Moscow town-building symbols, which were not just existing in people's consciousness, but embodied in Moscow's structure, its town-building composition. Two symbolical memorials have been already mentioned above: "Synaxis Russia" and "Military Glory", included from the 14th century into the structure and image of the capital. Now four religious-architectural symbols – certain sacred images of ancient Moscow, should be mentioned: "The House of the Most Holy Theotokos", "The Second Jerusalem", "The third Rome" and "The Heavenly Town".

In the centre of Moscow there are still four big famous buildings along one line from the east to the west: the Big cathedral of the Assumption, the bell-tower of John the Great, the Saviour Tower, St.Basil's cathedral. In combination with other buildings of the city these symbolic ones meant the four holy images of the ancient Russian capital. It is not easy to understand and to tell about them. Partially because historical material is scarce or because the images were shown to a different extent; besides, they are presented in mixture with each other, which is found in their close location in the single architectural body.

"The House of the Most Holy Theotokos"

> *Here in the temple of the Assumption.., in the heart of the Kremlin's walls,*
> *Being moved by Your tender image,*
> *So many cruel and stern eyes*
> *Became wet with tears!*
>
> *Elders and monks kneeled in front of You,*
> *The altars were shining full of incense,*
> *Meek tsarinas kissed the ground,*
> *Sullen tsars venerated You...*
>
> M.Voloshin

The image of praying entrust of the city to protection of the Most Holy Theotokos is considered Constantinople. It was done by the city's builder who had accepted Christian belief the Roman emperor Constantine the Great (306-337). Our Regal chronicle has the following: "Again the tsar and the Patriarch and other priests and the whole Tsar's Senate and many people conducted a religious rite... In praying they praised and thanked the Almighty and Life-giving Trinity: the Father and the Son and the Holy Spirit and the Most Holy Theotokos; and *entrusted the city and all ranks of people into the hands of the Most Holy Theotokos Hodegetria, id est the Teacher*, saying: "You are the Mother of the Lord the Most Holy Theotokos being so merciful, do not leave *this city*, which is Your property, but being the Mother to all Christians, *defend, keep and be merciful to us*, educating us at all times... And all the people said "Amen!"*

The protection of Constantinople by the Most Holy Theotokos was always mentioned in prayers, written in books, was reflected in the architecture, art, numismatics... For instance, above the southern doors of the temple of St.Sophia there was a mosaic panel (976-1025), which showed enthroned Theotokos, to whom the emperor Constantine brings the medal of Constantinople, and the emperor Justin (527-565) – a model of the temple of St.Sophia. On Byzantine coins of the emperors Andronicus II and Michael IX Paleloguses (1282-1320) the walls of Tsargrad with Vlakhernskaya icon of the Theotokos inside them are depicted -for She is the city's Heavenly Protector.

After construction in the first half of 11th century by the grand prince Yaroslav the Wise (after christening – George) of huge Christian Kiev, the first Russian metropolitanate Hilarion, also with many people, in 1049 conducted the praying service for sanctifying the city. Then he said, as though addressing the deceased grand prince Vladimir: "Your son George is very kind and faithful... for he built the God's House of His Great Wisdom (the temple of St.Sophia) for the holiness of your town... *And your glorious Kiev* is surrounded with majesty like by a crown, *entrusted your people and the city to the Most Holy Theotokos quick intercessor of all Christians*. And Hers is the church on the Great Gates of the meeting in the name of the first state feast of the Holy Annunciation".

In Constantinople and Kiev sanctifying of the main cathedral of St.Sophia God's Wisdom (Logos) did not contradict the idea of the intercession of the Theotokos. In Constantinople the altar's holiday of St.Sophia coincided with Christmas and was connected with Virgin Mary through the embodiment of Christ. In Kiev the altar's holiday of the icon of St.Sophia – "The Wisdom created her own home" – coincided with the day of the Nativity of the Theotokos. Later in Russia the majority of the main city's cathedrals were consecrated to the feasts of the Theotokos, which had been already done in Vladimir Zalessky. Mentioning the consecration of the capital to the Theotokos, the chroniclers then speak many times about Her help in defence of the city. For example, under 1175, «the people of Vladimir were fighting *for the city of the Theotokos and the Theotokos defended Her city...*»; under 1176: "There was great joy in Vladimir and everyone glorified the Almighty God and His Holy Mother, *quick intercessor to Her city, Who protected it from great disasters* and made Her people stronger and did not allow them to be afraid".

From all Christian holidays, after the holiday of Easter, Russian people began to venerate the holiday of the Assumption, calling it "the Easter of the Theotokos" (15th of August acc. to old style). The Russian man felt the great truth of the feast prayer: "In Your dormition You did not abandon the world, the Theotokos", and felt well that through Her Assumption the Most Holy Theotokos became closer and dearer to believers, for She became the Intercessor for them before the throne of Her Beloved Son, "in the prayers of the Not-sleeping". That is why the main temples of the main Russian cities were consecrated to the Assumption. In the 11th-13th centuries they beautified Galich, Vladimir Volynsky, Smolensk, Ryazan, Vladimir Zalessky.

The Moscow cathedral of the Assumption was built in 1326-1328 already knowing the governing position in Russia of the temple (the chair of the head of the Russian Church, the relicts of the first metropolitanate Peter are here) and of Moscow (the throne of grand princes of the Russian land, the relicts of the first Moscow grand prince Yury Danilovich are here too). Even today the decisive move of the metropolitanate Peter in the direction of extolling Moscow which was small at that time, certainly supported by the prince John Kalita, arouses admiration. Till that time the town was under the heavenly protection of St.Nicholas the Miracleworker, and with the appearance in the Kremlin of the temple of the Assumption the town was entrusted to the Heavenly Mother of God.

But if Vladimir Zalessky was the town of the Most Holy Theotokos, in relation to Moscow there was a certain north-west understanding of the protection through "The House of the Most Holy Theotokos", under "the House" the following was understood: temple, town and its domain. People of Smolensk called the cathedral of Assumption, the town of Smolensk, Smolenskaya land "the House of the Most Holy Theotokos"; the people of Novgorod called their cathedral of St.Sophia, the town of Novgorod, Novgorodskaya land "the House of St.Sophia"; people of Pskov called their cathedral of the Holy Trinity, the town of Pskov, Pskovskaya land "the House of the Holy Trinity"; the House of St.Nicholas" was Izborsk – the temple, the town, the domain. There in the north-west were the "Houses" of Archangel Michael, St.Hieromartyr George, Sts.Cosmas and Damian.

In Moscow the new idea of the *"House of the Most Holy Theotokos"* rooted from the end of the 15th century after Aristotel Feorovanti had built the new Big cathedral of the Assumption. It happened under the influence of people from Novgorod and Pskov. John III in 1478 adjoined Novgorod to Moscow; several hundreds of Novgorod's boyards, merchants, handicraftsmen were accommodated among moscovites and in other towns of the state. The same was done by his son Basil III after taking Pskov in 1510.

This triple notion was often used so that it was difficult to understand about what they talked: about the temple, town or land. Cosmas Minin in 1612 called in Nizhny Novgorod: "Orthodox people! Let us help the Moscow state – let us fight as one for the Russian land, for the House of the Most Holy Theotokos!" And when Novgorod's people's volunteer corpse took on 22 October Moscow's Kitay-gorod by storm, then forced the Polish and Lithuanians to give away the Kremlin, an unknown chronicler of the events summed up: "And so God cleaned *the House of the Most Holy Theotokos of the Universe and of all Moscow Miracle-workers* from unfaithful Lithuanians" (the miracle-workers were also stipulated: "St.Peter, St.Alexius, St.Jonah and St.Philip").

The cathedral of the Assumption in the Moscow Kremlin, in the heart of the Holy Russia, one of the most venerated places of Russian people. There was Vladimirskaya icon of the Theotokos, which was miracle-working, Russian grand princes, tsars, later emperors were coronated in it, hierarchs of the Russian Church were elected. So all the capital, then all Moscow Rus was called the "House of the Most Holy Theotokos" (the "Belt of the Most Holy Theotokos" was called in the 15th-16th centuries the border river Ugra, where Russia was liberated from Tatar-Mongolian yoke).

Architectural embodiment of the symbol of the "House of the Most Holy Theotokos" in Moscow was implemented not only by the construction in the Kremlin's centre of the Big cathedral of the Assumption, but by the construction of plenty of temples sanctified in the name of the Theotokos on the city's territory, consecrated to Her other feasts. The invisible presence of the Theotokos on the Russian land is shown through numerous miracle-working icons. They are the visible signs of the protection of the Most Holy Theotokos of Russian people and state. In conformity with the belief of Russian people from these icons

The cathedral of the Assumption – "The House of the Most Holy Theotokos"

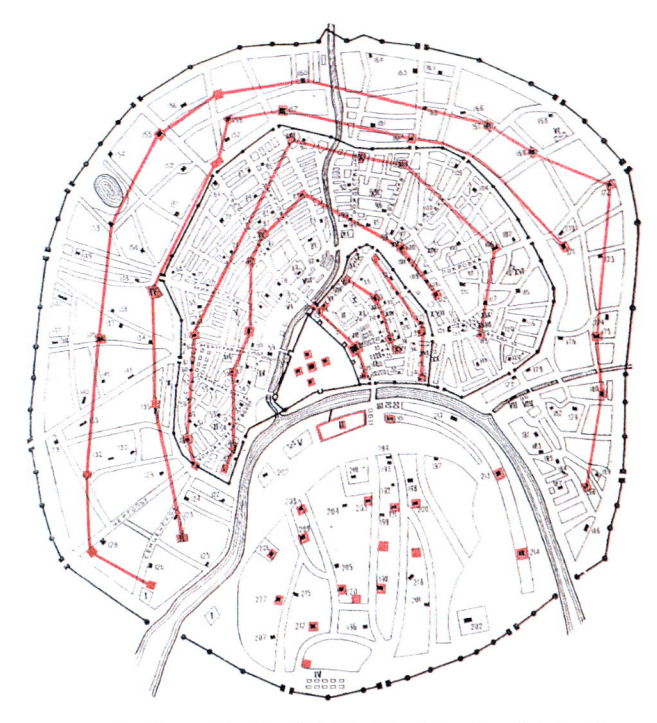

Moscow - "The House of the Most Holy Theotokos". Location of the temples consecrated to the Theotokos on the plan of Moscow of 17th century. Scheme of M.N.Gorodovaya.

numerous miracles are granted: ill people recover, some get saved from troubles, others acquire*) happiness, etc. At crucial moments, which sometimes threatened the mere existence of Russian people, upon zealous prayer in front of these icons, the Most Holy Theotokos really raised the spirit of Russian people, saved miraculously the Russian land from horrible ravages, and Russian people She saved from death. In this connection two exclusively Russian holidays consecrated to the Theotokos, are significant.

One of them is the Intercession. Many times Russian people were granted withprotection of the Theotokos at the most disastrous moments. So the hip roof ofthe church of the Intercession was not just raised in the middle of the cathedral of the Holy Trinity on the Ditch (St.Basil's cathedral), but together with the cathedral in the centre of Moscow. This memorial reminds of the Tatar-Mongolian yoke, about the victory on Kulikovo field, the liberation from the yoke at the Ugra, finally about the liberation after the battles near Kazan and Astrakhan.

The centre of Moscow was also beautified by the cathedral of the Kazan Iconof the Theotokos, besides this holiday also became an exclusively Russian national holiday, consecrated to the Intercessor of Russian orthodox people during the Troubled Time, during the catholic expansion of the West. The words of the Troparion to the Kazan icon of the Theotokos, written during the Troubled Time, are remarkably timely and appropriate:

"Our zealous Intercessor, the Mother of God the Most High, pray to You Son,Christ our God, asking for salvation of everybody, who come to Your powerful protection. Protect all of us, the Most Holy Theotokos, being in sorrows and illnesses, burdened by many sins, praying to You with moved soul and humble heart, in front of Your Holy image with tears and having the undoubtful hope for You that You save us from all evil, grant everybody everything useful and save all, the Holy Virgin, for You are the divine protection of Your slaves".

In the Kremlin the churches of the Annunciation were built at Seni (at passage halls) of Moscow grand princes and tsars, in metropolitanate (patriarch's) Chudov monastery; the church of the Nativity of the Most Holy Theotokos was at Seni of grand princesses (tsarinas). And in the town itself there was an uncountable quantity of temples and inside lateral altars built and sanctified in the name of the Most Holy Theotokos, the Protector and Intercessor, of the miracle-working icons of the Theotokos: Akhtyrskaya, of the Annunciation, Bogolyubskaya (God-loving), Presentation in the Temple, Vladimirskaya, "The Joy of All Who Sorrow", "The Consolation in Sorrow and Grief", Grebnevskaya, Georgian, Donskaya, "The Life-giving Spring", Our Lady of the Sign, Iveron, Korsunskaya, "The Unburnt Bush", "Unexpected Joy", Hodegetria, the Intercession, Rzhevskaya, Smolenskaya, "Of the Passion", Tolgskaya, "Of the Three Hands", "Of Tender Feeling", the Assumption, Ustyuzhskaya, "Assuage My Sorrow", "The Cureress", Feodorovskaya and many others. So, there is nothing surprising that Moscow, being full of such temples and icons to which moscovites prayed each day, was called "the House of the Host Holy Theotokos".

"The Second Jerusalem"

*Like peoples, we shall go to meet Him with love, so that
Christ comes into our Jerusalem today...
We shall clean oursouls with humbleness, so that
through Eucharist the Son of God enters into us...*
St. Cyril of Turov

The tradition to make the town like Jerusalem was also known since the time of christening of Russia. Metropolitanate Hilarion of Kiev said in 1049: "He (St.Constantine the Great) with his mother St.Helen brought the Cross of Jerusalem, glorified it widely and consolidated the belief. And you (Vladimir) with your grand-mother St.Olga brought the Cross from *the new Jerusalem – Constantinople*, installed it all over the country and consolidated the belief".

The Golden Gates of Kiev were built and named like the (gates of Constantinopleand Jerusalem, and Golden and Iron Gates of Vladimir Zalessky – like Jerusalem. But it is not known when this symbolic likeness, when the idea of Moscow as theSecond Jerusalem, established in it.

There is a late news that St.Peter the Metropolitanate prophesied: that inMoscow "upon the blessing of the Almighty and Life-giving Trinity and the Most Holy Theotokos there will be an innumerable quantity of churches and monasteries, and this city will be called the *Second Jerusalem*. It will hold great power, and will be glorified not only in Russia, but in all Eastern, Southern and Northern countries; it will possess many hordes up to the warm sea and cold ocean; its power will be extolled by God from now till the end of the world".

In Sophiyskaya chronicle in the legend "About the taking of Moscow by Tokhtamysh and about the capture of the Russian land" the following is written: "Oh God, the heathen are come into thine inheritance; thy holy temple have they defiled; *they have laid Jerusalem* on heaps..." (Psalm 78). The calling of Moscow as Jerusalem, "New Zion" can be encountered later too. In the famous "Lamentation about the captivity and final ravage of the highest and lightest Moscow state" of the beginning of the 17th century there is the following: "Oh, Christ the King, Oh, the Saviour and God's Word and God... by Him and within him the glorious voice of God's words were speaking, how the town of the Tsar and God and of *the Most Holy Theotokos*, Your great and gloriously reign-

The Frontal place. The procession on "the donkey".

ing *town of Moscow*, the eye of the earth itself, the light of the Universe, stopped shining. Who will give water to my head and the source of bitter endless tears to my eyes? And the daughters of the *new Zion* will cry, the daughters of the gloriously reigning *town of Moscow...*"

In accordance with such ideas Jerusalem symbolical elements appeared in the structure of Moscow, and not just in the names, but in town-building.

First veneration hills began to appear near Moscow, certainly, like the Veneration Hill in Jerusalem. Hegumen Daniel who visited the town at the beginning of the 12th century, wrote about it: "There is *a hill* here near the way to Jerusalem, at one versta from it, there people get off their horses and *bow to the Christian Holy Resurrection*".

As imitation of Jerusalem the Frontal place appeared in Moscow, probably, already at the time of Basil III (1533), though for the first time it was mentioned in 1549. On it after the horrible fire in 1547 and a riot in Moscow John IV (the Terrible) was present at the prayer serviced by St.Macarius the metropolitanate, then he told people about the reasons of disasters in the state. Besides, the Frontal place in Moscow was not the place of execution like in the old testament Jerusalem, but it had Christian meaning of a place sanctified by Christ's salving sacrifice. On the Frontal place in Moscow public prayers were served, from it the tsar's decrees were announced.

In difference to towns and monasteries of Western Europe, where in the 12th-17th centuries symbolic via dolorosa of the Saviour to the Cavalry was marked, the Moscow Frontal place from the time of St.Macarius the metropolitanate was connected with the celebration of the Entry of the Lord into Jerusalem on Palm Sunday.

The tradition appeared at the beginning of the 16th century in Novgorod, then it came to Moscow, St.Macarius the metropolitanate explained to John IV (the Terrible) how emperor Constantine the Great carried out "horse" service: he held by the strings the horse of Pope Sylvester, which he precepted to do in future time. So the young tsar also did this rite, which is confirmed by evidences of foreigners. According to the rite of the middle of the 17th century it happened as follows: "Patriarch taking the Gospel in one hand, and a golden cross in the other, blesses the Tsar with the cross, sits on the donkey. The tsar leads the donkey by the strings, and the Patriarch, sitting on the donkey, blesses people with the cross. They go to the town to the cathedral (symbolic Entry of Christ into Jerusalem). When they enter Spasskie Gates the doorman orders to ring the bells at Kirillovskoe representation and everywhere, and all the way is covered with willow in front of him. They come to the cathedral, willow is put on the bridge in front of the doors of the Faceted Palace, and the Tsar leads the donkey to Cathedral Square..."

In 1532 also at the time of Basil III, near the bell-tower of St.John, the author of "The Ladder", the church of the Resurrection (more exactly of the Renovation of the temple of the Resurrection in Jerusalem) was founded, which was finished only in 1552. In 1555 St.Macarius the metropolitanate and John the Terrible brought into it the altars consecrated to the Nativity of Christ from Miloslavsky yard, *"and arranged the cathedral"*. Even in the 17th century this cathedral was called "of the Resurrection, the one under the bells" (1669).

The cathedral of the Resurrection stood actually in the middle of the large Kremlin square, composed by two squares at its both sides: Cathedral square and Ivanovskaya square. It occupied the central position both on the plan and in the composition, being attached to the bell-tower of St.John, the author of "The Ladder" (later –

The cathedral of the Resurrection in Jerusalem.

The altar of the Resurrection in the bell-tower of John the Great in the centre of the Kremlin.

The chapel of the Ascention in Jerusalem.

of John the Great). Jerusalem symbolics became central in all town-building composition of Moscow. But its forms vaguely reminded of the original, besides they were adjusted for bells. A little time passed and the question of a more exact reproduction of the image arose.

At the beginning of the 17th century tsar Boris Godunov thought of dismantlingthe cathedral of the Assumption and building here the Holy of the Holiest with precious decorations: "Stone, lime, piles, all was ready, and a wooden sample was made *according to the original*, how the Holy of the Holiest was composed; but soon death caught him (the tsar)". "Beyond any measure" they were going to decorate the church of the Holy Sepulchre: "They made stocks of precious stones of many colours with which it was to be covered,.. the handicraft was exquisite amazingly and precious; the mind could not imagine the volume of the temple, eyes could not look at the shining stones and gold".

As Jerusalem temple of the Resurrection was built on the place of real events,according to Christian ethics it *could not be repeated* in other places. So all temples of the Resurrection were built in memory of Renovation (i.e. sanctifying after reconstruction) of the temple of the Resurrection, which took place at thereign of Constantine the Great in 335. So, this temple stood near the bell-towerof John the Great.

In the folk tale "Jerusalem Talk" there are interesting lines: "From that Eastern part the sunrise is shining all over the Holy Russia, which is *the town of Jerusalem Initial*, and in this town there will be the cathedral of St.Sophia God'sWisdom of seventy cupolas, id est the Holy of the Holiest".

If to build in the Kremlin the Holy of the Holiest, but not like the old testament temple of St.Solomon (which was ruined in Jerusalem after its conquering by the Moslems), but as the image of the Heavenly Kingdom, the focus of which on earth is the Holy Sepulchre – Moscow will be as though "Jerusalem the Initial".

People around Boris Godunov were against this plot. The tsar was accused of the intention to destroy the holy thing of Moscow, as well as of pride. The Troubled Time and the decease of Boris put an end to this intention. Probably, the deep essence of what happened was in the fact that there was already the cathedral symbol of the Holy of the Holiest in the Moscow Kremlin. It consisted of the cathedral of the Saviour with the altars of the Resurrection and the Nativity of Christ at the bell-tower of John the Great (the image of the Holy Sepulchre), the cathedral of the Assumption, the altar holiday of which coincided with the feast of the icon of St.Sophia God's Wisdom brought from Novgorod (the image of St.Sophia in Constantinople) and the cathedral of the Twelve Apostles (the image of the Holy Apostolic Church). This sacramental symbol quite corresponded to the wish of Christians to defend their holy things from blasphemy of unfaithful.

In the middle of the 18th century Patriarch Nicon disclosed the symbolic mystery of the capital again, building the monastery "New Jerusalem" close to Moscow andarranging of nearby lands according to the image of Palestine Holy Land. Tillnow these impressive, majestic copies of Holy Places and the Holy Sepulchre beautify the Istra-river near Moscow. The capital remains with the previous holy things – the cathedral of the Assumption, the symbol of the Heavenly Town, the cathedral of the Resurrection "under the bells" near by, reminding of the Jerusalem temple very distantly.

With these two efforts of Boris Godunov in the 16th century and Patriarch Niconin the 17th century of creation in Moscow of not so concealed, but clear to thewhole world symbols, opening the significance of the Russian capital, – two biggest riots, which shook the Russian state to the bottom are connected historically in a surprising way: the Troubled Time of the end of the 16th – beginning of 17th centuries with crashing of the tsar's dynasty, destroying of state order and invasion of foreigners and church dissidence of the middle of the 17th century.

From the holy places surrounding Jerusalem, the Gethsemane Garden and the chapel on the place of the Ascension were embodied most brightly. The Gethsemane Garden is situated along the eastern walls of Jerusalem and separated from them by the valley of Kedron. The Golden and Gethsemane Gates led to the garden. The main Christian holy thing, situated in the Gethsemane Garden, became the Burial Tomb of the Most Holy Theotokos. Behind the Gethsemane Garden to the east, on one axis with the Golden Gates, there is a chapel built on the place of the Ascension, which has a centric octahedral form. The place where the Theotokos was buried is spiritually connected with the Assumption, which is not just the end of Her earthly life, but the beginning of glorifying the Theotokos, the Tsarina of the Heavenly and Earthly Church.

In Moscow near the Kremlin's walls, from the south, separated by the valleyof the Moscow-river, there is the

Big Tsar's Garden (Tsarina's Meadow), where the church of St.Sophia God's Wisdom was. As it was already mentioned the holiday of the Assumption is celebrated on the day of the icon of St.Sophia, and the theological comment of the icon of St.Sophia in Russia connects it not only with the image of Logos-Christ, but with the image of the Theotokos, Church, through Whom He embodied.

Thus, in Moscow, the axis from the Saviour (Golden) Gates to the Tsarina's Meadow (Gethsemane) was directed to the East, not to the South, to Zamoskvorechie. If to prolong the axis further, it will be directed at the church of the Ascension in Kolomenskoe, built also in the form of the centric octahedral hip roof temple.

And though the distance separating it from the Kremlin, is much longer than the distance from the walls of Jerusalem to the chapel of the Ascension, the hip roof of the church of the Ascension in Kolomenskoe was seen well from the Kremlin.

Not only orthodox people, but catholics too understood well the spiritual significance of Moscow, its symbolic transformation. The above-said elements of the structure of the town-building composition testify to a conscious organisation of the city, for instance, according to the image of the world Christian capital of Jerusalem. It was not by chance that a Polish man Maskevich, who was a participant and a witness of the invasion in Moscow of the Polish army with the False Demetrius at the head at the beginning of the 17th century, wrote: "So, we burn it again, as the Psalmist said: I shall sweep about the Town of God so that there will be nothing in it".

How many times the enemies wanted that there would be nothing in it!

"The Third Rome"

There, like Rome lying on the hills,
Rising assemblies of cupolas, adornment of the holy thing,
Moscow is keeping its memorial inside its walls,
As immortal inspiration of descendants.
A.Odoevsky

The place where the conception of "Three Romes" appeared was Italy. In the most ancient variant it was initially the chain of the towns: Troja – Rome - Constantinople. The hero of ruined Troja Eney moved to Lathium, where his descendant Romulus founded Rome. Later the Emperor Constantine the Great, adopting Christianity, founded Tsargrad as close as possible to the holy things of Jerusalem.

Then the Christian comprehension of the concept excluded Troja. ChristianRome took the first place – the first capital of a huge "world" empire, and after its falling out into two parts and the massacre of the West Empire by barbarians, Constantinople became "the second Rome".

The search for the "third Rome" began in 12th century. Usually it happened at the moments of unsuccessful wars, even during the temporary fall of "the second Rome", for example, in 1204 when it was conquered by crusaders, Latin patriarchs exercised their sway over it in 1211-1261. In Europe several centres turned up pretending for this serious and responsible role of the third world Christiancapital.

In the 12th-13th centuries scriptures inform about appearance of "the third Rome" in Germany. It was called the town of Trir, where already during the division of Roman Empire into Western and Eastern sometimes the emperors of the Western Empire lived. In the second half of the 18th century Tyrnovo began to pretend for the role of "the third Rome", the capital of the Second Bulgarian kingdom: here in a big state the tsar's and patriarch's powers united. Perhaps for the same role Kiev pretended secretly, which was built according to the image of Constantinople in many ways (the temple of St.Sophia, the Golden Gates etc.).

But in 1240 Kiev was massacred by Mongolian hordes, at the end of the 13th century (after 1273) the German Empire fell out into small domains, then in 1396Bulgaria was conquered by the Turks, finally, in 1453 the Turks took Constantinople by storm. But the idea of "The Third Rome" did not die. "The Holy Spirit breathes where He wants", so the idea found its roots in Moscow Rus.

The move in 1325 of the metropolitan chair to Moscow from the beginning of exfoliation of the town as the religious and state centre, as the capital of Russia. The reason for development of the idea in Moscow state was the event of 1439. Byzantine Empire which fell down under the Turkish attack, trying to get the support of the Christian countries of catholic Europe, signed at the Florentine Council the act about the autonomy of the Eastern and Western Churches with acknowledgement by the Greek church of catholic dogmas and the leadership of Roman Pope.

The first one who was indignant at the union unequal in rights and turned itdown was Basil II. The Council of Russian Hierarchs called upon the initiative of the grand prince in 1441 deposed Russian metropolitanate Isidore (a Greek by nationality) and elected a new representative of the Russian Church: metropolitanate Jonah became the first autonomous metropolitanate of Russia. Basil II informed the patriarch of Constantinople to this effect: "We, being poor, governed by God, hold it annulled as well as himself (Isidore) and turn down the disaster made by him (the union), like dried grass. Since that very time *we begin to take care of our orthodoxy*, about our immortal souls and the hours of decease, and of our presentation on that future terrible day of the Last Judgement before the Judge with all our secrets daily thoughts and deeds". And in 1453 with the fall of Constantinople "the Greek orthodoxy dried itself out" – as the son of Basil II – John III said.

Final liberation of the Russian land from Tatar-Mongolian yoke directly raisedbefore the Moscow state "the question of comprehension of its historic existence and denomination. Just then the idea of "The Third Rome" was transplanted from Byzantium on our soil" (Macarius Veretennikov). The idea really began to develop quickly, following in parallel the development of historic events: 1473 – the marriage of John III and the Byzantine princess Sophia Paleologus and adoption as the State Emblem the emblem of Byzantine Empire – the double-headed eagle,

1480 – liberation from the yoke, 1498 – John III tries to *coronate* his grand-son Demetrius... At that time in St.Joseph-Volokolamsky monastery a chronology was made according to which the historic development of all the world resulted in Moscow Rus. St.Joseph, the Hegumen of the monastery, made much effort for consolidation of the state and for the purity of orthodoxy.

The idea "Moscow – the Third Rome" became widely known and accepted in Rus atthe Terrible, the son of Basil III, when after 1547 Moscow state became the kingdom. The author of "The Story of the Taking of Kazan" confirms it as follows: "And now the throne and glorious town of Moscow is shining, like the second Kiev – and neither being ashamed nor guilty I should call it, – the *Third new great Rome*, which has been shining during the recent years like the great sun in our great Russian land, in all towns and all people of our country, standing in splendour and being enlightened, adorned with colourful stars and firm in orthodoxy".

Upon establishment of Patriarchate in 1589 in Rus the Oecumenical PatriarchKeremiah confirmed by his signature the role of the Russian land as "The ThirdRome". Other Greek patriarchs and hierarchs, though they had been oppressed anddragged poor existence because of Turks, did not approve of the surpass of thehuge powerful and, which was very important, free state, did not want to giveaway the priority themselves. Anyway the coronation in the Third Rome was now carried out like in the First and the Second Rome (up to 1453). The idea Moscow is the Third Rome played a very important role in the development of Russian autocratic self-conscious, in surpass of Russian centralised state.

Not only orthodox people, but catholics too understood the increasing ecclesiastic significance of Moscow in the world, which actually became the centre of all orthodoxy. The autocratic and religious idea of the ecclesiastic succession of Moscow role of the Third Rome from the First and the Second Romes found its realisation in the town-building structure and in the image of the capital. Comparative research of these cities allows to find out these elements.

When Constantine the Great at the beginning of 4th century transferred thecapital from Rome to Byzantium, the main principles of town-building successionwere two characteristic features of the first capital of the empire: "seven hills" and "Roma Guadrata" (Roman Square) on Palatine Hill. Besides that the streets and squares of the "New Rome" were measured according to the Roman tradition, i.e. according to the ancient Etruscan rules. The architecture of dwelling houses, yards Roman aristocracy moved to the new capital, were exactly copied from Roman palaces.

Seven hills in the landscape of Constantinople, like the Roman ones, weresuch an important factor that they were included into all legends about the foundation of the new town and even became the reason of one of its names "Of Seven Hills". The main hills in both capitals were considered the places of the most ancient citadels: in Rome - the Palatine, in Constantinople – Acropolis Byzantium. On these hills the complexes of emperors palaces were situated. K.P.Kondakov noted close likeness of their planning, composition, functional structure, accordance to the landscape and the capital's buildings.

One of the important symbols was also Hilly, built in Constantinople in Augustan Square in front of the West entrance of the temple of St.Sophia like the Roman gilded Milliary (mile column), from which the distances were measured to all the borders of the Roman, then Byzantine Empires.

But Constantinople was also built in accordance with Jerusalem, with its holy things. So, the temple of St.Sophia, built by the emperor Constantine andthen rebuilt by Justinian, was oriented at reproduction of elements of the Holy Sepulchre. Many Christian holy things were transferred to Constantinople, though in their concrete location there is no intention to reproduce the real topography of Jerusalem and the Holy Land.

At town-building comprehension of Moscow as the Third Rome in the 16th-17th centuries they began to look for the seven hills first of all. There are no concrete documents enumerating these hills. There are no distinct hills in Moscow relief at all, which underlines that imitation of the capital of Rus according to the capitals of Roman empires was symbolical according to this criteria. Still the efforts to indicate seven hills were made and still are made (M.P.Kudriavtsev)

On the Kremlin central hill the complex of chambers and buildings of the royal palace became square on the plan. Perhaps, it had "Roma Guadrata" as theprototype of the Palatine Hill (Palatine Palace of Roman emperors) and the Royalpalace in Constantinople. The Second and the Third Romes had different in the form main cathedrals with different consecrations. However, Moscow cathedral of the Assumption was often called by people as St.Sophia, because on the day of the Assumption (15/28, August) the icon of St.Sophia from Novgorod was also celebrated.

The State Emblem of Russia became the Byzantine double-headed eagle, but onits chest they placed Moscow's Emblem – St.Hieromartyr George the Victory-bearer, killing the dragon. The double-headed eagle crowned all governmental buildings in Moscow: Royal palaces, Departments, business yards, representations, the gate walls of the Kremlin, Kitay-gorod, Holy-Tsar's town, Skorodom, hip roofs of Vsekhsvyatsky (of All Saints) bridge, and, certainly, many buildings of the country royal palaces. All the double-headed eagles seemed to have flown from the buildings of Tsargrad on the shore of the Bosporus to the Regal buildings at the Moscow-river. Patriarch Jeremiah of Constantinople agreed that Patriarchate in Russia was established by the decision of "all the saint synaxis of Russian and Greek *kingdoms*". Thus the transfers to Russia of the ancient Byzantine Emblem was agreed internationally and confirmed and thus the further political pretensions of Russian tsars for the succession of the Byzantine throne were explained.

In the Second Rome the main Golden Gates were built and called like the Golden Gates of Jerusalem. The gates of the Holy Town were glorified because of theEntry of Our Lord Jesus Christ through them before Easter. During the period ofChristianity already since the 4th century in the memory of this event the tradition of portentous entry

Guards banner of the Russian army, which includes heraldic symbolics of Byzantium.

of the Patriarch with crowds of people through the Golden Gates of Jerusalem established. Later in the 15th century Turks closed the gates, but once a year, only on Palm Sunday, they allowed the Patriarch to celebrate the holiday of the Entry of Our Lord Jesus Christ into Jerusalem, then the gates were closed with stones again.

As Constantinople is on the cape, the Golden gates were built not from the East, but from the West of the town and combined with the Seven-towers Castle, reminding of the castle of David in Jerusalem. However, the main gates of Constantinople were used exclusively for triumphant entries of Byzantine emperors.

Such symbols appeared in Moscow too. In the southwest end of Bely-Tsar's town the only seven-top tower was built which resembled the Tsargrad's Seven-tower castle – Heptapergy. And the symbol and function of the Golden Gates was given to Spasskaya (the Saviour) tower and the Kremlin's gates, which acquired double meaning. The first one was connected with celebration of the Entry of the Lord into Jerusalem, the second one – with a triumphant entry of tsars into the Kremlin, like in the second Rome.

Moscow Frontal place in its town-building meaning also combined in itself two traditions: Roman-Byzantian – installation of Milliary on the town's main square – the original centre of the empire, beginning of measuring of all distances and the Christian tradition of regarding Jerusalem as the centre of the Earth, and the place of the Crucifixion as the centre of the Earth. In the church of the Holy Sepulchre, – Daniel described, – there is *the hub of the universe* near the wall behind the altar. A chamber was built over it, on top of which Christ is depicted. And the scripture says: "*I measured the Heaven* with My foot, and *with My palm – the earth*". In "The Book on the Big Drawing" all distances to the towns of the Russian state are given from the Frontal place of Moscow, just like from Roman "Milliaries".

Our Royal chronicler wrote under 1453 about the defence of Constantinople: "The Tsar ordered... the warriors to divide the town's walls, loop-holes and the gates; and so all the people and to install *military bells* on all sides..." In Moscow Kremlin, near Spasskie, Troitskie and Taynitskie gates on its three wallstowers were installed for military (alarm) bells. From these small memorials about the second Rome only Tsar's tower near Spasskie Gates exists now.

In Moscow there were memorials about the second Rome in other places too. For example, one of the main roads – Vladimirka came to Moscow near St.Andronicus monastery near the river Golden Horn. The river was called in the 17th century by metropolitanate Alexius in memory about, the bay Golden Horn in Constantinople. Further on the way to Moscow near the river Yauza there was a Greek settlement. Then, inside the walls of Bely-Tsar's town there was the monastery of St.John the Predecessor, which conformed to the monastery of St.John the Predecessor in Tsargrad, which was near the entrance into the town on the shore of the bay Golden Horn.

From the point of view of the idea of organisation of the Third Rome it is easy to understand the purpose of attraction of so many *foreign specialists* to Moscow, first of all *the masters from the first Rome* (Italians) and the *second Rome* (Greeks, especially, icon-painters, wall-painters). Architects, brick-layers, fretmen, chasers, etc., were invited from everywhere. They were not only Italian and Greek, but also Serbs, Bulgarians, Germans, English, Swedish, Tatars. Like the first and the second Romes, Moscow was built "by people of different hordes". "All tongues" of earth built the capital of the orthodox world. To this respect Moscow, Moscow Kremlin can be compared not only with Rome and Constantinople, but also with Babylon, Alexandria, which were built by thousands of people from different countries.

However, the basic difference of Moscow construction in the 15th-17th centuries was in the fact that its painters and architects were not slaves, captives, but *invited masters*, equal in their position. The third Rome was built on absolutely new, Christian ecclesiastical principles, coming out of the idea of original relationship of peoples and their cultures.

As a result, the idea "Moscow – the Third Rome" led gradually to creation in the centre of the capital of an outstanding complex, symbolising ecclesiastic unity of all the mankind, reflecting the "effort to connect the history of Moscow state with the world's history, to show that Moscow state is the chosen, that it is the subject of "heavenly home-building"; this idea is confirmed by many analogies from the old testament history, the history of Babylonian and Persian kingdoms, monarchy of Alexander of Macedonia, finally, of Roman and Byzantine empires" (O.Podobedova). The Kremlin became the centre of this complex.

In the paintings of the cathedrals and palaces, in utensils and books, collected from various countries, the idea of the union of ecclesiastic revelations of the world was embodied. Like the presage of Christianity the pictures of the Old Testament Greek and Roman poets: Homer, Plato, Aristotle, Vergil and others, then the images of sibyls on

Symbolic samples in town-building of Moscow.
Comparative table of town-building compositions of Rome, Constantinople, Jerusalem and Moscow.

1a. Moscow at the end of 17th century. Scheme of location of the main ensembles.
1b. Heavenly Town. Miniature from the Apocalypse of 17th century.
1c. Idealized composition of Moscow in the image of the Heavenly Town.

Seven Moscow hills: I – Borovitskiy hill, 11 – the holy place Kievets, III – the holy place Ostrov, IV – Red hill (the right shore of the Neglinka), V – Peter's hill (the left shore of the Neglinka), VI – Ivanovskaya (Alabova) hill, VII – Red hill.
1 – the cathedral of the Holy Trinity on the Ditch, 2 – the Frontal place, 3 – Cathedral Square of the Kremlin, 4 – the church of the Resurrection in Kadashi, 5 – Kadashevskiy Textile Yard, 6 – Kadashevskiy Brethren Yard, 7 – the church of St. Sophia the God's Wisdom in the Big Tsar's Garden, 8 – the church of St.Hieromartyr George the Victory-bearer in Vspolie;
Seven fortified monasteries of Bely town: 9 – of St.Alexius, 10 – of the Adoration of the Holy Cross, 11 – of St.Nicetas, 12 – of St.Hieromartyr George, 13 – of St.Barsanuohius, 14 – of St.John the Chrysostome, 15 – of St.John;
Riverain monasteries of Skorodom: 16 – Zachatievskiy, 17 – of St.Nicetas behind the Yauza;
Monasteries-guards of the Western line: 18 – Novodevichiy, 19 – of St.Sabbas, 20 – Novinckiy;
of the Northern line: 21 – of the Passions, 22 – Vysoko-Petrovskiy, 23 – of the Nativity of the Theotokos, 24 – of the Meeting of Our Lord in the Temple;
of the Eastern line: 25 – of the Saviour-St.Andronicus, 26 – of the Intercession, 27 – of the Saviour (Novospasskiy);
of the Southern line: 28 – of the Nativity of the Theotokos-St.Symeon 29 – of St. Daniel, 30 – of the Don Icon of the Theotokos, 31 – of St. Apostle Andrew;
twelve gates of Skorodom: 32 – Tverskie, 33 – Dmitrovskie, 34 – Yatoslavskie, 35 – Stromynskie, 36 – Pokrovskie, 37 – Taganskie, 38 – Kolomenskie, 39 – Serpukhovskie, 40 – Kaluzhskie, 41 – Prechistenskie, 42 – Smolenskie, 43 – Nikitskie; 44 – the church of the Ascension in the village of Kolomenskoe.

2a. Jerusalem. The scheme of the plan in the Middle Ages.
2b. Idealized scheme of Jerusalem's composition.

I – Maria, II -Gethsemane garden. III – the Mountain Olivet
1 – the Holy Sepulchre, the place of the Calvary, 2 – the place of Solomon's Temple "The Holy of the Holiest".
3 – the Burial Tomb of the Theotokos, 4 – the chapel of the Abcm&ion;
Jerusalem gates: 5 – Golden gates ("Eternal Gates"), blocked up, 6 – Purulent gates, 7 – Zion gates, 8 – Jaffa gates (of Bethlehem), with David's Castle near by (9), 10 – Damascus gates, Herod's (Benjamin's) gates, 12 – Gethsemane (St.Stephan's) gates, 13 – New (blocked up),

2c. Idealized scheme of Moscow Kremlin as of the image of Palestine Jerusalem.

I – Cathedral Square, II – Big Tsar's Garden (Tsarina's Meadow); I – ensemble of bell-fries (the altars of the Resurrection and the Nativity of Christ, the churches of the Adoration of the Holy Cross and St.John, the author of "The Ladder"),
2 – cathedral of the Assumption, 3 – cathedral of the Annunciation, 4 – cathedral of Archangel Michael, 5 – ensemble of the royal palace, 6 – the Frontal place, 7 – the cathedral of the Holy Trinity on the Ditch, 8 – the church of St. Sophia the God's Wisdom;
Six gates of the Kremlin: 9 – Nikoickie, 10 – Spasskie (Frolovskie), 11 – Konstantino-Elenskie, 12 – Taynitskie, 13 – Borovitskie, 14 – Troitskie, 15 – Vsekhsviatskie gates of Bely town, 16 – Moskvoretskie gates of Kitay-gored.

3a. Constantinople (Tsargrad). Scheme of the plan of the town of Byzantine period.
3b. Idealized scheme of composition of Constantinople.

I-VII – row's seven hills, 1 – the temple of St. Sophia the God's Wisdom, 2 – Miliy;
the monasteries of: 3 – St.Sergius and St.Bacchus (Martyrs), 4 – Chrism, 5 – Sts.Carpus and Babylas ("of the Holy Sepulchre"), 6 – of the Theotokos Periviepta, 7 – Gastra ("Bethlehem"), 8 – St.John Studit, 9 – St.Diomedes ("Jerusalem"), 10 – St.Andrew "inJudgement", 11 – St.Dius, 12 – the Saviour "of the Choir", 13 – St.John "in Trulle", 15 – St.Panthepoptus (Clairvoyant), 16 – Pantocrator (Almighty), 17 – St.Caeharitomena, 18 – Ten Martyrs, 19 – St.John Calabytes, 20 – St.Antony, 21 – Mother of God Panahranta (the Most Holy), 22 – Emperor's Palace in Vlaherna, 23 – Golden gates and Heptapergy (Castle with seven towers)

3c. Idealized scheme of Moscow inside Bely town as the image of Constantinople – "New Rome".

I-VII – seven hills (see 1a);
The Kremlin's monasteries: 2 – of the Saviour on Bor, 3 – of the Holy Trinity, 4 – of the Ascension, 5 – of the Miracle of the Archangel Michael at Colossae (Chonae); 6 – the church of St.Sophia the God's Wisdom, 7 – the cathedral of the Holy Trinity on the Ditch, 8 – the Frontal place;
Monasteries of Kitay-gorod: 9 – Zaikonospasskiy, 10 – of St. Nicholas-the Greek, 11 – of Epyphany, 12 – of Our Lady of the Sign;
Monasteries of Bely town: 13 – of St.Alexius, 14 – of Adoration of the Holy
Cross, 15 – of St.Nicetas, 16 – of St. Martyr George, 17 – of St.Barsanuphius, 18 – of St.John the Chrysostome, 19 – of St.John, 20 – of the Resurrection in Uspenskiy Vrazhek, 21 – Vysoko-Petrovskiy, 22 – of the Nativity of the Theotokos, 23 – of the Meeting of the Lord in the Temple, 24 – of St. Moses;
Gates of Bely town: 25 – Prechistenskie, 26 – Borisoglebskie (Arbatskie), 27 – Nikitskie, 28 – Tverskie, 29 – Petrovskie, 30 – Sretenskie, 31 – Myasnitskie, 32 – Pokrovskie, 33 – Yauzskie, 34 – Vsettsvyatskie, 35 – Seven-top tower of Bely town, 36 – Toynitskie gates of the Kremlin, 37 – Moskvoretskie gates of Kitay-gorod

4a. Rome. Scheme of the Town in 4th century Anna Domini.
4b. Idealized scheme of composition of Rome.

Rome's seven hills: I – Palatinskiy, II – Kapitoliyskiy, III – Kvirinalskiy, IV – Vaminalskiy, V – Eskvilskiy, VI – Celliyskiy, VII – Aventinskiy;
1 – complex of Emperor's palaces and forums, 2 – Golden Miliary, 3-16 – 14 town's gates, including – Golden gates (15).

4c. Idealized scheme of Moscow inside Skorodom as the image of Rome.

1-VII – seven hills;
1 – complex of royal palaces in the Kremlin, 2 – the Frontal place, 3-14 – twelve gates of Skorodom

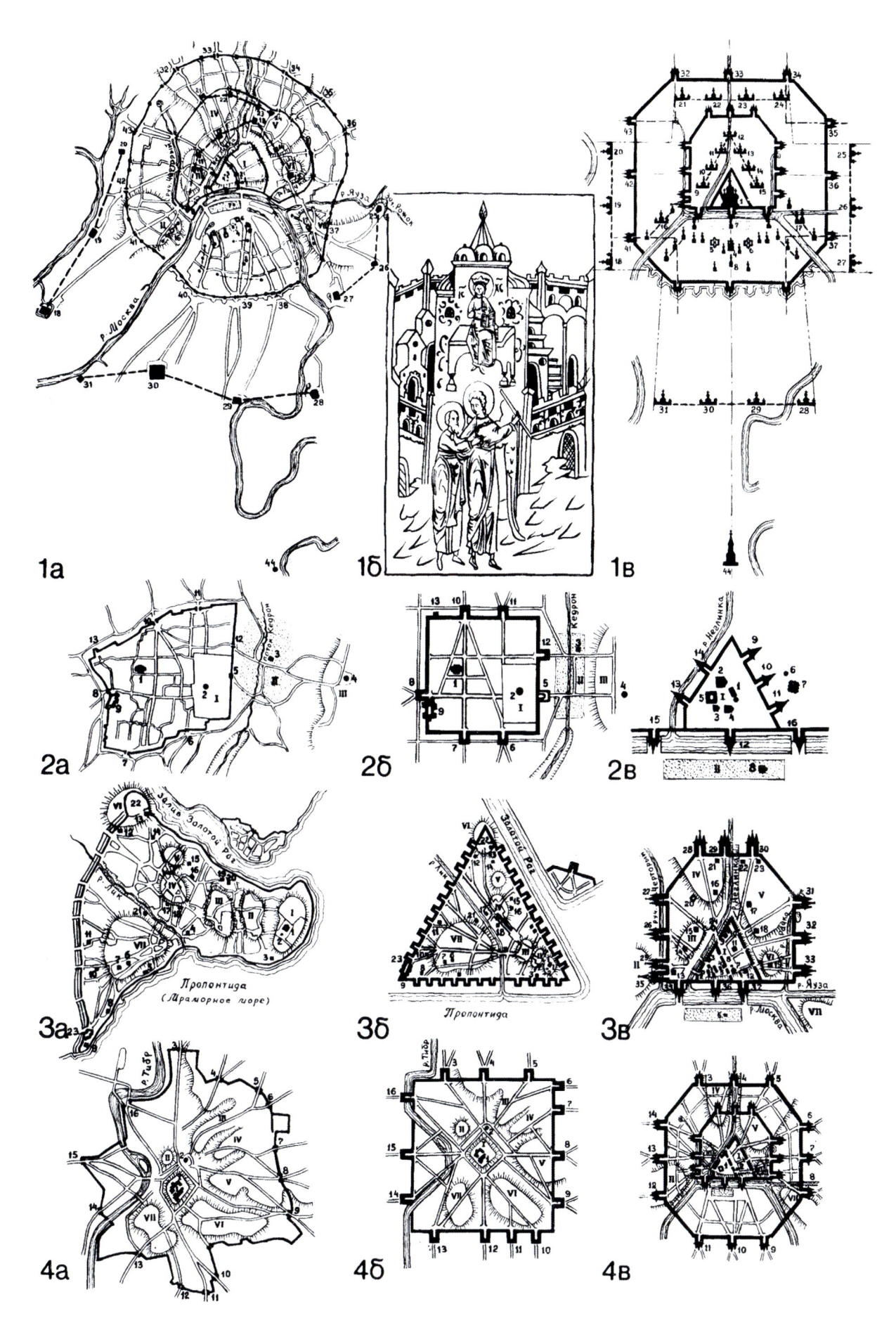

Rome – Constantinople – Moscow. Comparison of structures of the three Routes. Scheme of T. Kudriavtseva

the cathedral gates, meet those who come to the porch of the cathedral of the Annunciation.

In the painting of the Tsar's Palace we see the images of Gideon, St. Joshuathe Son of Nun, Darius I, Alexander of Macedonia... The scientists who did the research of these paintings considered them only from the point of view of military symbolics and political idea of autocracy. However, the choice of concrete historical personalities convinces that the task of the paintings was more significant. These are the images of the creators of the greatest empires in the history of the mankind, which united a great number of peoples and mixed together a great number of cultures. The spiritual idea of unity with the East is in the images of the Byzantine tsar Constantine and his mother Helen in the paintings of the cathedral of the Assumption and St.Ioasaph prince of India in the cathedral's altar.

"The Heavenly Town"

And it was shining as if from the Altar
Between the valleys and the hills,
The heart of orthodox Rus
The sacred autocratic town,
Secular town of Moscow Itself.

And its dense gardens,
And preserved ponds,
Bell-towers, tower-chambers,
The vast sea of roofs.

And in solemn peace,
Towering among them
The Kremlin ancient and majestic,
Our Altar washed in blood,
And expiated in fire.

A. Maykov

In the Holy Script two Jerusalem are mentioned: the Heavenly and earthly. Theyare relate to each other as *the image and the Archetype*. So for Christian spiritual consciousness it was natural to make an earthly town like a town-building icon as the image of the Heavenly Archetype. In the best progressive form this imitation was realised in the town-building structure and image of Moscow. This idea was directly shown, for example, in the icon of the 16th century "The Blessed Regiment", where Moscow is shown as "The Heavenly Town of Zion".

The most detailed description of «Heavenly Jerusalem» is in the last chapters of the Apocalypse of St.John the Theologian. Comparison of its facts with the compositional structure of Moscow, which formed by the 17th century, allows to follow the coincidence of a number of essential features of the structures of Moscow and the Heavenly Town.

"The sacred town of Jerusalem is new... having a great wall and very high, having twelve gates, three gates in the South, three in the North, three in the East, three in the West". The structure of Skorodom's walls fully conforms to this description not only in the quantity of big, as a rule three hip-roof gates, but in their distribution in accordance with four groups of the roads at four parts of the worlds.

The same quantity and location of gates is in the earlier walls of Bely-Tsar's town, surrounding the settlement from the East, North and West, being next to the southern Moskvoretskaya line of the walls of the Kremlin and Kitay-gorod in the south-east tree gates on each side of the world in these stone walls outside Moscow settlement of the 16th century. Moscow was surrounded twice by twelve-gate walls of the Heavenly Town, first by stone ones then by wooden.

"This town has four corners, its length is the same as the width". The length of Skorodom's axis north-south is 4 km 800 m, the axis West-East is 4 km 700 m, i.e. the axises are nearly equal. In the contour of its walls Moscow had more distinct quadrangle than Rome and Jerusalem.

In comparison of Moscow with description of the Heavenly Town of St.John theTheologian it is also important to pay attention to the image of the walls of the town inside the walls: "And the building of the wall of it was of jasper... and the foundations of the wall of the city were garnished with all manner of precious stones". Jasper, according to the comment of St.Andrew of Caesarea, is "a stone of green colour and means Divine nature, always blossoming, life-giving and feeding everybody, because grass grows from any of its seed, thus it is so frightening to its enemies". The wall from jasper means, – as it was often said, – "always blossoming and not fading away life

Title page of the Bible of tsar Alexius Mikhailovich, on which Moscow is presented as the symbol of New Heavenly Jerusalem. 1663

of saints. The town is of pure gold because of the sanctity and honesty of its dwellers".

Each turn of Moscow streets, each cross road and square always had a church. The majority of Moscow churches had golden cupolas, some had green and blue ones. Gold symbolises righteousness, Divine light and Christ, green – jasper – also the-fm! symbolises Christ, blue symbolises the Heaven. The churches of the 17th century are unusual phenomena. V.Nikolsky gives the following characteristics of the general features of Russian architecture of Moscow period: "Aspiration for adornment of the facade parts of a building with different patterns. Architects work over the outside finishing of their buildings like jewellers. A whole number of extremely elaborate decorative forms is created, as well as fretwork of all kinds. But that is not enough: they use patterned tiles of different colours. Architects insert them into the walls, like precious stones, make whole ranges from these tiles, sometimes face all outside walls with them... But that is not all either: they paint outside plastered walls of the buildings with "patterns and herbs".

It is possible to judge about this adornment according to the wonderful painting of the 17th century of the cathedral of the Holy Trinity on the Ditch (St.Basil's cathedral), kept till 1980, according to the fragments of tile walls of the church of the Assumption in Gonchary, uncovered from later plastering, the church of St. Gregory the Miracle-worker of Neo-Caesarea in Zamoskvorechie, the restored tire of Terem (tower-chamber) Palace in the Kremlin, Krutitsky on-gate terem, and the decoration of all Moscow temples and chambers of the 17th century, existing now. The words of St. Andrew of Caesarea fully explain the true meaning of Moscow adornment in the art of the 17th century and especially in the image of the temples, because each church is God's Home, so the ornament of church facade is the symbol of flourishing, the reflection of "Divine nature always blossoming".

In the south, Middle Asia, Middle East and in Jerusalem gardens are considered to be the precious elements of yards, settlements, towns. In this respect ancient Moscow was all full of "precious things" – gardens, and to such extreme volume which was allowed in a huge medieval city. Garden in Rus was called "Ray" (paradise). Such "Ray" was ancient Moscow, being a copy of the Heavenly Paradise.

From the end of the 16th till the end of the 17th centuries, i.e. during one century, nearly 300 fiery temples were built in Moscow and its outskirts. "Kokoshniks" of these temples symbolised the fiery heavenly regiments. Hundreds of "fiery" temple roofs, thousands of "flame-like" cupolas towered over Moscow, over the roofs of its houses, chambers, terems, many green gardens. It was hand made "Earthly paradise" crowned with "the midst of the stones of fire of the mountain of God" (Ezekiel, 28, 16).

At the end of the 17th century another symbolic «plot» appeared. The theme of the heavenly powers was expressed not only in the flame-like "kokoshniks", but in balusters "thrones". Platbands of windows, doors of churches and chambers, edges of walls of tire temples were adorned with "thrones". At this time orders style was spread too, especially of ancient Rome. Combination of Christian heavenly symbolics and classical Roman orders of "empire period" (in the so called Naryshkin's baroque) was the last creative invention of Moscow architects of the themes of "The Heavenly Town" and "The Third Rome". Thus, in the architecture of the monuments of the end of the 15th century a certain synthesis of two town building Moscow symbols appeared, the symbols of the Heavenly and Earthly Churches.

Having described the walls of the Heavenly Town, St.John the Theologian says the following about its midst: "And he showed me a pure river of water of life, clear as crystal, proceeding out of the throne of God and of the Lamb. In the midst of the street of it, and on either side of the river, was there the tree of life, which bear twelve manner of fruits, and yield her fruit every month". In the capital's symbolic structure the Moscow-river was likened to the image of the River of Life. The "either side of the river" is a symbol of the Tree of Life in the form of the terraced gardens of the Kremlin and the Big Tsar's garden in Zamoskvorechie. The image of the Tsar's Garden on Tsarina's Meadow was connected with the idea about the Paradise, about the Tree of Life – Christ, and associated with the icon of the Most Holy Theotokos "The Locked Vineyard", famous in Russia. The icon painted by Nicetas Pavlovets – a master of Moscow Armoury (the second half of 17th century) was especially close in its composition to Tsarina's Meadow. The garden on the icon is regular like the one in Moscow. It is situated on the shore of the River of Life, into which it stands out in the form of a semi-circular plate resembling ambo. On this plate the Most Holy Theotokos is standing in regal garments and a crown, which is put on Her by two Angels. On Her hands She is holding Christ with a scroll in the left hand.

It is likely that the icon is directly connected with that image of the Paradise and Christ and His Mother existing in it – of the Church, which was created by Moscow Tsarina's Meadow with the church of St.Sophia God's Wisdom in it. This huge garden in front of the cathedral of

Krutitskiy metropolitane palace. Tower-chamber with ceramic tiles.

all Russia can be considered as an evident symbol of dedication to the Most Holy Theotokos of the Russian land itself.

Red Square (Troitskaya, Frontal) personified a huge temple not made by man. Inone of descriptions of a religious procession it was said: "And coming to the Frontal place, they install icons there *like at the choir place of the church*". The divine service was conducted under the sky.

The cathedral of the Holy Trinity on the Ditch is in Moscow's geometric centrein relation to the ring of Skorodom. In the 17th century it was sometimes called "Jerusalem", at which already I.E.Zabelin indicated: "Foreign travellers of all time were also amazed much at Moscow wonder, for example, the travellers of the 17th century. Most of them called it *Jerusalem*, saying that it was called so among people too". When the cathedral of the Holy Trinity is considered in the ensemble of Red Square, it is the Credence in the temple under the open sky. But in the centre of such space, which is the town within the limits of Skorodom, the cathedral of the Holy Trinity becomes the symbol-image of the Credence of the Heavenly Town.

On the title page of the Bible of 1663 there is the *plan of Moscow*, engravedfor the tsar Alexius Mikhailovich, surrounded by the scenes from the Old Testament and the Gospel. Under it there is the State Emblem of Russia – the double-headed eagle, on the chest of which instead of the traditional Moscow Emblem – St.Hieromartyr George the Victory-bearer – a portrait of the tsar Alexius Mikhailovich on a steed, killing the dragon with a spear, is placed. The inscriptions on the title-page were taken from the book of St. Prophet Isaiah: above the Emblem – "I established the tsar with the truth and all his ways are true"; above Moscow's plan – "Rise, rise, Jerusalem, and take your strength".

These words of St. Prophet Isaiah mean that the prophecies taken from hisbooks could be the basis of comprehension of ecclesiastic role of Russia and its capital, which appeared in Russian medieval society. The phrase above the Emblem has the continuation: "This one creates my Town". There is an opinion that this was the tsar's pride, who referred the prophecy about the Heavenly Town and Christ to himself and his reign (this supposition is notable itself). However, the symbolics of the Bible's title-page can be understood in a more subtle way, in accordance with the subtle and mysterious symbolics of Christian Moscow and all Holy Russia.

The Russia capital was certainly understood as the image of the Heavenly Townof Jerusalem and built so not just by the wish of earthly tsars, but mainly bythe Providence of Christ the Tsar of the heaven and the Earth. As for the portrait of Alexius Mikhailovich in military rank, killing the dragon, it conforms very exactly to the common opinion, including the tsar's opinion, about tile significance of Russia as the last pillar of orthodoxy.

View from the Kremlin ot the Tsar's Garden in Zamoskvorechie in 17th century. Reconstruction of M.P.Kudriavtsev.

It is the book of St.Prophet Isaiah, which contains the prophecy about thetransfer of the glory of God's people to other peoples: "You will leave your name to my chosen ones. God will kill you; those working for He will be called by a new name". Here it is also said about the transfer of the glory of Jerusalem to *a town with another name*: "The tongues will see your truth, and the kings will see your glory, they will call you by a new name, by which God will call you".

Thus the title page of the Bible of Alexius Mikhailovich can be assessed asa certain result, a certain announcement of Moscow as Hew Earthly Jerusalem – the image of Heavenly Jerusalem.

The number of the previous and further coincidences confirms the idea aboutconscious observation of the prophecies of the sacred books, including the prophecies of St.Prophet Isaiah, during construction of Moscow: the walls of the new town are created by foreigners, "And on your walls, *Jerusalem*, the guards, all day and all night, will not stop saying God's name till the end".

The construction in the 17th century by patriarch Nicon of the monastery «NewJerusalem» near Moscow can be in this case not just the effort to acquire Moscow's glory, but a certain establishment of the same idea by the way of transfer close to the capital of town-building image of the Holy Land, earthly Jerusalem. The monastery is on the way from West Europe to the capital and by its consecration it as though tells the travellers beforehand about the existence further to the south-east of the main symbol of Rus. Such location of temples, for example, of the Entry of Our Lord Jesus Christ into Jerusalem before the town, was traditional in Rus (Novgorod, Suzdal, Kashin, Vereya etc.).

* * *

Ancient orthodox Moscow was built by *all Russian people* during half a centurytogether with people of other Christian nations. People were the creator of aunique city. They were the creative power in this town-building process, fighting at the same time with natural disasters and enemies.

Together with unknown architects, hundreds and thousands builders, it isnecessary to pay the tribute to the remarkable personalities, who made everyeffort to extol Moscow, especially to the tsars and princes: Yuri Dolgoruky,Vladimir Vsevolodovich, St.Daniel (Alexandrovich), John Kalita, John III, John the Terrible, Theodore Ioannovich, as well as the glorified hierarchs Sts. Peter, Alexius, Macarius.

The outstanding town-builders especially should be remembered: Protase, Barma the Faster, Theodore the Steed, who did not just create some holy things, but extremely original ensembles and complexes.

But even from all this Pleiad of outstanding personalities it is necessaryto note creators of Moscow "Symbol of tile Heavenly Town". Tsar, John the Terrible, Macarius the Metropolitanate, architect Postnik (Faster) Yakovlev created the temple under the open sky in the centre of Moscow with the Altar of the Holy Trinity and the Canopy like the Heavenly Town (St.Basil's cathedral). Tsar Theodore Ioannovich, St.Job the Patriarch, architect Theodore the Steed fixed at the end of 16th century the idea of creation of the "Heavenly Town" by the construction of 12-gate Skorodom. Theodore the Steed began then to build in "The Town" with fiery temples.

Combination in the general town-building composition of Moscow of the symbolsand images of the "House of the Most Holy Theotokos", the "Second Jerusalem",the "Third Rome" and the "Heavenly Town" as though shows all the historic way of Christian states and peoples to the purpose of salvation – the Heavenly Kingdom. Moscow included all Russia and all world town-building into this overwhelming symbol.

Golden-cupola Moscow. Artist A.M.Vasnetsov.

CHAPTER SEVEN

The Phenomenon of Holy Russia

In divine revelation of Moscow

Красная площадь — Возрождение общерусского Храма

The Theotokos the Vineyard Secluded. Icon of about 1670. N.Pavlovets.

The Saviour Almighty. Icon. The 10s of the 15th century. A. Rublev.

Synaxis of Moscow Saints. Icon. End of the 19th-beginning of the 20th century

The tree of Russian state. Icon. S.Ushakov.

Adoration of the Holy Cross.
St. prince Constantine and St. tsarina Helen, tsar Alexius Mikhailovich and tsarina Mary Ilinichna. Icon. 1670s

The Throne of the Holy Trinity.
Miniature of the Apocalypse of the Chudovskiy Translation. 1638. (F.Buslaev "Russian Front Apocalypse", l. 12).

Theotokos. Icon. 1675.

RED SQUARE –
THE TEMPLE UNDER THE OPEN SKY

"Though God's Wisdom created and is creating all, however, so that the created was worth the existence, He granted His Wisdom to creatures, so that in all creatures and in each of them there was some likeness and some traces of His Image and the coming to existence is wise and deserving God deed".
St.Athanasius the Great. The 2nd Word on aryans.

In the largest centres of Christendom – in the structures of Jerusalem, Rome, Constantinople, Kiev – it is possible to see the likeness to Heavenly Jerusalem in accordance with descriptions from the Old and the New Testaments. But this likeness was most developed and embodied in the town-building structure and image of Moscow[1].

Probably, two processes of ecclesiastic-symbolic and concrete structural creation of the centre of Ecclesiastical Israel – Russian Holy Land, were going on historically simultaneously. The calling of Moscow as Jerusalem, "God's Town", «New Zion» can be seen in Russian documents already from the 14th century.

But in the Holy Writ Script two Jerusalems are mentioned: earthly Jerusalem, historic, living through times of spiritual ascend and descend of its people, times of ravage, crush of the walls and creation, of gathering holy things and Heavenly Jerusalem – the Town of paradise, abode of salvation prepared by God for people. And it is not by chance that both towns have the same name. They, like all earthly and divine correspond to each other like the image and the Archetype.

As we see, in the structure of Moscow of the 17th century the likening to earthly and Heavenly Jerusalems was realised simultaneously[2] "The Third Rome" – the last pillar of orthodoxy

Heavenly Town Jerusalem. Miniature of manuscript Apocalypse. The 18th century.

The Heavenly Town in the form of cube. Apocalypse of Peter's time. (F.Buslaev "Russian Front Apocalypse", No. 230).

as if marked in this way all the ecclesiastic via of Christ's Church: Alpha and Omega – the Beginning and the End of the via from the First Advent of Christ in Palestine Jerusalem till appearance of the Heavenly Town of Jerusalem.

In Red Square, on the bank of the Moscow-river, in the geometrical centre of the city inside Skorodom in the 16th century the cathedral of the Holy Trinity on the Ditch was built. The fact that it is of the Holy Trinity is very important for understanding symbolic town-building structure of Moscow. The cathedral was called later "of the Intercession" and "St.Basil's cathedral". The first name appeared because the central altar under the high hip roof was consecrated to the Intercession, and this hip roof was usually seen from all points of the town. The second name appeared in the memory of the fool-for- Christ St.Basil, later above his grave the altar consecrated to him was built.

However, according to Christian canon, cathedrals and all churches in general are called according to the main Eastern altar, and in this case it was consecrated to the Holy Trinity. The fact that the cathedral was of and built as the cathedral of the Holy Trinity, is confirmed by the inscription about its construction in Piskarevsky chronicle too: "About the cathedral of the Holy Trinity on the Ditch in Moscow. In the same year by the order of the tsar and grand prince John the vowed church was begun, the one in the honour of taking of Kazan: of the Holy Trinity and the Intercession and seven altars, which was called "on the Ditch". The master was Barma with associates".

Nicon's chronicler writes about "the cathedral of the Intercession", but clarifies that "two years before the church of the Holy Trinity had been founded and the tsar ordered to add to it the church of the Intercession and altars"[3].

V.L.Sneguirev writes about the churches included into the cathedral: "the altar of St. Nicholas was not like the other altars a memorial of some event connected with taking of Kazan's kingdom. As for the other altars, the following was detected: the church of St.Alexander, abbot of Svir, and the Three Patriarchs are the memorials of the victory on the 30th of August over tatar prince Epancha; the church of St.Heromartyr George is the

Apocalypse. The vision of God's Throne and 24 elders.
Miniature from Chudovskiy Translation. 1638.
(F.Buslaev "Russian Front Apocalypse", No.12).

sacrariums and the bell-tower)[6]. There are all reasons to state that the figured cupolas of the end of the 16th century, like more strict and initial cupolas of the cathedral, were golden taking into account the documentary data[7] and the symbolic meaning of the number 25, which was mentioned in the Apocalypse of St.John the Theologian: "And immediately I was in the spirit: and, behold, a throne was set in heaven, and one sat on the throne. And he that sat was to look upon like a jasper and a sardine stone: and there was a rainbow round about the throne, in sight like unto an emerald. And round about the throne were four and twenty seats: and upon the seats I saw four and twenty elders sitting, clothed in white raiment; and they had on their heads crowns of gold". (The Revelation, ch. 4: 2-4)[8].

The painting of the cathedral's walls was well seen until the last restoration on the parvises, in the gallery and the four small sacrariums – it was a floral ornament on white background of the gallery with red columns and with red ornament of the main parts of the adornment (horizontal links of cornices, protruding edges; of the triangles on the octahedrals, etc.). The colour picture is finished with colour tiles – "jasper, sardonyx and emerald" (jasper and emerald, according to St.Andrew of Caesaria, are yellow-green and dark green; sardonyx is orange) and silver-white grooves of white iron. Dressed in "white chasubles", knitted with flowers and precious stones, the richest in the whole town in its forms and adornment, surrounded with shining sunny hales of many golden cupolas, the cathedral of the Holy Trinity stood out in the centre's panorama exactly by the fact that it included all adornments of Moscow churches and chambers.

It is known that in the 16th century the religious procession was introduced in the direction of the cathedral of the Holy Trinity on Palm Sunday. During the religious procession the divine service was conducted in front of the cathedral of the Holy Trinity, and on the Frontal place the lectern was installed.[9] In this way the Frontal place became symbolic like an ambo in front of God's Altar, and Red Square, full of praying people, symbolised a huge and unruinable temple not made by man. The divine service on Palm Sunday took place under the open sky, i.e. directly in front of God. So, in Moscow of the 16th century the most complicated idea for symbolic realisation of the phrase from the Apocalypse was reflected: "And I saw no temple therein: for the Lord God Almighty and the Lamb are the temple of it[10].

The religious procession on Palm Sunday was the reason why the cathedral of the Holy Trinity was called Jerusalem. In ancient Russian icon-painting it is possible to see the expressions of Heavenly Jerusalem on the walls in the form of eight- or twelve-end cross, which is explained by the quantity of 12 gates. On the plan of the cathedral of the Holy Trinity its nine temples comprise eight-end cross, and the surrounding gallery – twelve-end cross. Such likeness of the cathedral's structure to the Heavenly Town of Jerusalem even more fully discloses its

memorial of taking on the 30th of September of Arskaya Tower and the victory on Arskoe field near Kazan; the churches of the Intercession and of Sts.Hieromartyr Cyprian and Virgin-martyr Justina of Nicomedia were built in the memory of the explosion of the town's walls and taking of Kazan on the 1st and the 2nd of October. It is not clear yet the memorials of what event or events were the churches of St.Barlaam, abbot of Chutin and the Entry of Our Lord Jesus Christ into Jerusalem"[4].

In respect of the latter it is possible to suppose that the altar of the Entry into Jerusalem was built in honour of return of our army to Moscow. There is still the icon of the 16th century "The Bellicose Church"[5], in which the Russian army was depicted coming back to Moscow from Kazan all in flame with victory, Moscow was shown as the "heavenly town Zion", i.e. "Heavenly Jerusalem".

Thus, the main vowed cathedral in honour of the victory was of the Holy Trinity, the others were consecrated to different events of the war. Foreign travellers – Paul Alepsky, Olearius, Streis, Corb and others – called the cathedral as of the Holy Trinity and of Jerusalem. In encyclopaedias the church of the Holy Trinity on the Ditch was indicated on the plans of Moscow of the 16th-19th centuries (Peter's charts, Sigizmund, Olearius, Meiersberg and others).

In the 17th century the cathedral of the Holy Trinity had 25 cupolas (9 were the main, 8 were around the hip roof of the cathedral of the Intercession, the other 4 were on the octahedron of the temple of the Entry into Jerusalem and 4 were on the

The cathedral of the Holy Trinity on the Ditch. The plan of the second flee.

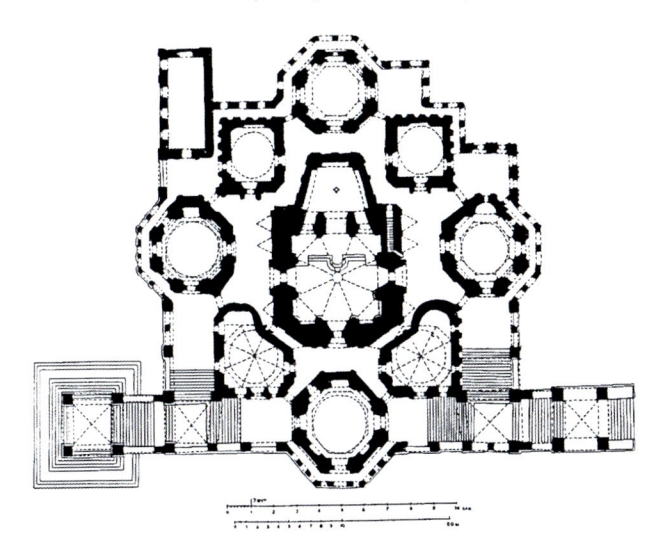

symbolic significance as of the centre of the town-building image of the Heavenly Town. The development of the essence of the complicated architectural composition of the cathedral is based on the axis west-east: from the western altar of the Entry of Our Lord Jesus Christ into Jerusalem through the central hip roof altar of the Intercession – as the symbol of Christ's Church existing in the Heavenly Town and being the Intercessor in front of the Altar of the Holy Trinity, – to the eastern main temple of the Holy Life-giving Trinity, which symbolises God's Altar in the Heavenly Town.

Red Square is a trapezium in its form, being wide to the north-west and more narrow to the south-east, to the cathedral of the Holy Trinity. This visual increase of the perspective results in the visual increase of the cathedral, as it seems to be further than in reality. This impression is also increased by making the adornment smaller to the top of the cathedral and by the fact that from the square it was not seen down to the bottom: in front of it there was the high Frontal place, a dead floor for big cannons and its own stone fence with gates and a house for the cathedral's library. And the opposite row of buildings from Nikolskie gates till the beginning of Nikolskaya street which is fractional and made smaller anyway, is visually decreased, because it seems to be closer as the square is made wider. The significance of the cathedral of the Holy Trinity is also stressed by the fact that it is single on its part of the square, and on the opposite side there are: part of the wall of Kitay-gorod, Zemsky Department, Voskresenskie Gates of Kitay-gorod, the Kazansky cathedral with Coin Yard. All these buildings look subordinated to the cathedral of the Holy Trinity and smaller in their significance than in reality.

Along the second and the third rows of the Kremlin's walls, surrounding the fortress ditch, in the 16th-17th centuries there were some more small churches on the square, which were pulled down at the border of the 17th-18th centuries. The part of the space of Red Square was filled in by tents and counters from time to time, which were for retail trade. In the 17th century according to tsar's decrees the Square was cleaned many times and in 1680 it became free. In this case the historic destiny of the ensemble is quite remarkable showing the way from an imperfect earthly image to its heavenly Archetype.

Planned as the temple under the open sky, as an image of the centre of the Heavenly Town, the square was first like the Old Testament Temple of Jerusalem, full of sellers, whom God dispersed Himself. Only after dispersal of the sellers Red Square fully acquired the portentous beauty of an ensemble like of a temple.

On big church holidays all-town religious processions were carried out in Moscow, many of which began from Cathedral Square of the Kremlin, then they went across Red Square along the town's walls, along its streets and squares, sanctifying with prayers all the town.[11] Just at such moments the likening of the capital of Russia to the Heavenly Town acquired a special spiritual power and reality.

As of all religious processions it was on Palm Sunday (the Entry of Our Lord Jesus Christ into Jerusalem an especially portentous divine service conducted in Red Square, it is important to consider how the ecclesiastic-symbolic organisation of the square-temple under the open sky is connected with this holiday. In a usual temple the praying intercession for people before God's Altar of the Saints especially adored in this temple, is expressed in the icons, placed in the iconostasis and on the temple's walls. On the square-temple this intercession is expressed in consecrations of the churches' altars, included in the square's ensemble.

The main longitudinal axis of Red Square from Voskresenskie Gates of Kitay-gorod in the north-west to the cathedral of the Holy Trinity in the south-east stresses the special symbolic meaning of the square. In the celebration of the church year the days of the Holy Pentecost from the Resurrection (Easter) till the day of the Holy Trinity are for the images of the joy of the future universal Resurrection and adjoinment to God in the eternal life in the Heavenly Town, descend to the new Land. In the centre of Moscow, built as the image of the Heavenly Town, – there is the image of the temple where the Perpetual Easter is celebrated.

On the left from the axis, at the entrance to the square there is the cathedral of the Kazan Icon of the Most Holy Theotokos and the chapel with the especially venerated in Moscow Iveron icon of the Mother of God, brought in the 17th century from the Holy Mount of Athos. These altars, together with the temple of the Intercession of the cathedral of the Holy Trinity, composed the visual image of the intercession for all the Christendom of the Holy Virgin Mary and Her Protection so clearly felt by Russian Land during the days of disasters.

On the right from the axis – from the church on the Ditch near the Kremlin's walls, two temples near Moskvoretskie Gates of Kitay-gorod (behind the cathedral of the Holy Trinity) and the chapels inside the Kremlin's gate towers, consecrated to Russian and Universal Saints, – made the image of especially adored Saints of this unusual temple. Including the consecrations of the altars of the cathedrals of the Holy Trinity and of the Kazan Icon of the Theotokos, all the main ranks of God's saints were gathered here:

Red Square. Scheme of the composition. I – the cathedral of the Holy Trinity; 2 – the Frontal place; 3 – the cathedral of the Kazan Icon of the Theotokos; 4 – Zemskoy Department; 5 – Coin Yard; 6 – the Kremlin's Spasskaya Tower; 7 – the cathedral of the AscenMon; 8 – the Kremlin's Nikolskaya tower; 9 – Trade rows; 10 – Voskresenskie (Iverskie) gates of Kitay-gorod; II – Cathedral library and gates; 12 – blocked up tower.
Scheme of M.P.Kudriavtsev, T.N.Kudriavtseva.

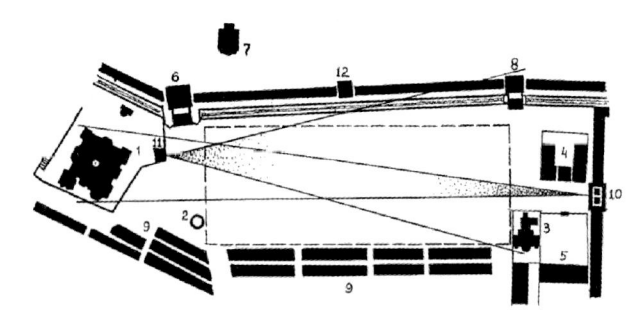

Red Square. Fragment of axonometric plan "Kremlenagrad". 1600-1601.

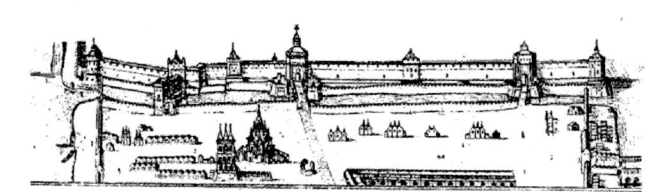

Or the Prophets	– of the Beheading of St.John the Predecessor (on the Ditch, 1670)
Of the Apostles	– of St. Apostle Andronicus (on the Ditch, 1584, 1628) – of St. Apostle and Evangelist Mark (on the Ditch, 1657) – of St. Apostle Andrew the First-Called (the altar of the church of the Saviour of Smolensk near Moskvoretskie Gates, 1514) – of St.Equal-to-the Apostles tsar Constantine and tsarina Helen (Konstantinoeleninskie Gates of the Kremlin)
Of the Saint Hierarchs	– of St.Equal-to-the Apostles Abercius, bishop of Hierapolis (an altar of the Kazansky cathedral, 1636) – of Sts. Gurius and Barsanuphius of Kazan (an altar of the Kazansky cathedral, 1636) – Sts.Athanasius and Cyril of Alexandria (on the Ditch, 1657)

	– St.Nicholas the Miracle-worker, archbishop of Myra in Lycia (St.Nicholas Moskvoretsky, the altar of the church of the Annunciation near Moskvoretsky bridge, 1626)
	– of St.Nicholas the Miracle-worker of Myra in Lycia (near Nikolskie gates of the Kremlin)
	– of St. Nicholas the Miracle-worker, archbishop of Myra in lycia (St.Nicholas Veloretskiy, the altar of the cathedral of the Holy Trinity, 1560)
Priest Martyrs and Martyrs	– Sts. Hieromartyr Cyprian and Virgin-martyr Justina (the altar of the cathedral of the Holy Trinity, 1560)
	– of St.Hierormartyr Parasceva of Iconium (on the Ditch, near Spasskie Gates, 1636)
	– of St.Virgin-martyr Theodosia of Tyre (on the Ditch, 1582, 1657)
Saints	– of Righteous Eudocimus (the altar of the church of the Saviour in Smolensk near Moscvoretskie Gates, 1514, 1687)
Blessed	- St. Blessed Basil, fool-for-Christ (the altar of the cathedral of the Holy Trinity, 1588)
Of the Righteous	– of St.Righteour Alexander of Svir (the altar of the cathedral of the Holy Trinity, 1560)
	– of St.Barlaam, abbot of Chutin (the altar of the cathedral of the Holy Trinity, 1560)
	– of St. Sergius of Radonezh (on the Ditch, 1629)
	– of St.Mary the Egyptian (the altar of the church of St.Apostle Andronicus on the Ditch, 1628)

Besides that there were two altars of All Saints – the altar of the church of the Nativity of the Theotokos on the Ditch and the altar of the church of the Saviour of Smolensk near Moskvoretskie gates.

Besides the altars of the Holy Trinity and the Intercession there were other Holy Altars consecrated to great church holidays in Red Square:
– the Entry of Our Lord Jesus Christ into Jerusalem (in the cathedral of the Holy Trinity, 1560)
– the Epyphany (on the Ditch, 1657)
– the Ascension (on the Ditch, 1472, 1485)
– the Resurrection (on the Ditch, 1657)
– the Annunciation (near Moscvoretskie Gates, 1488)
– of the Precious Wood of the Life-giving Cross of the Lord (the church of the Saviour of Smolensk near Moskvoretskie Gates, 1514)
– the Nativity of the Most Holy Theotokos (on the Ditch, 1547)
– the Nativity of Christ (on the Ditch, 1547)

After the pulling down of all the temples on the Ditch at the border of the 17th-18th centuries all the altars (except the church of the Ascension brought into the church of St.Hypatius in Kitay-gored) were brought into the cathedral of the Holy Trinity. So in the 18th-19th centuries the symbolic structure of Red Square practically was not changed.

It turned out to be impossible to express this complicated image with any conditional schemes. So we tried to explain the symbolic structure of Red Square through the icon-painting images of its altars, connecting them according to the principle reflecting town-building composition of the square's ensemble in idealized form.

The square is bordered at two sides by water: in front of the entrance through Voskresenskie Gates in the North-West it is bordered by the river Neglinka, and in the South-East behind Troitskie gates – by the river Moscow – the image of the River of Life, flowing from under the Throne of the Holy Trinity. The vine, surrounding the square, on the green background is the Big Tsar's Garden behind the Moscow-river, Vasiliev Meadow of Kitay-gorod (on the left) and suspension gardens of the Kremlin's Tsar's Palace (on the right) is the image of all Moscow orthodox people, "God's vine", planted by His hand. People praying on Red Square are the burning Easter candles.

There is an Ambo at the bottom of the Throne of the Holy Trinity (the Frontal place), on which there is a chanlice for water sanctifying with willow. On the left there are the images of the intercession of the Most Holy Theotokos, on the right – the range of the Saints venerated in the temples of Red Square and the images connected with the Kremlin's gates: Nikolskie (of St. Nicholas of Mozhaysk) and Konstantinoeleninskie gates (of Sts.Constantine and Helen).

Research of the modes of town-building realization in Moscow of the image of Heavenly Jerusalem discovers one amazing quality of the city – the main squares and ensembles of the capital's centre are simultaneously connected with various levels of the embodied contents.

The cathedral of the Holy Trinity in Red Square, when we consider it only in the square's ensemble, is a Throne in an open temple, but inside such space, which is the Kremlin with

River of Life and Tree of Life in the Heavenly Town. Miniature from the Chudovskiy Translation. 1638. (F.Buslaev "Russian Front Apocalypse", No. 120).

Heavenly Town Jerusalem. Miniature from the Chudovskiy Translation. 1638. (F.Buslaev "Russian Front Apocalypse", No. 118).

Kitay-gorod, Bely town or the town inside Skorodom, the cathedral of the Holy Trinity becomes a symbol-image of the Altar of the Heavenly Town.

The small Frontal place is also simultaneously a symbol of vetches platforms of Russian towns, "the centre of earth" (like Miliaries of Rome and Tsargrad), an image of Calvary-the Frontal place in Jerusalem and a symbol of the open temple of the Heavenly Town.

The Big Tsar's Garden with the church of St. Sophia God's Wisdom combines together three symbolic levels – of Gethsemanes as a historic place of the land, where the betrayal of Juda was committed, from where Christ's salving via dolorosa began and where the Virgin Mary, Who gave birth to Him, reposed, – of Paradise where the Theotokos – the Tsarina of all the earthly and Heavenly Church and all the Saints in the expectation of the Second Christ's Advent exist, – of the New Land in the image of the Tree of Life, the place of Eternal Life after the Second Advent and the Last Judgement.

This transfer of the ensembles' symbolics from one level to another can be considered one of the most important qualities of Moscow town-building, because it is likely to determine the measure of realization in town-building of orthodox Christianity of an icon of an ideal Paradisiacal town.

The polysemy of the capital's buildings gave rise to involuntary wish to contemplation of the architecture and understanding of the fact that the knowledge of the huge city is not for a humane life limited by time. This polysemy is likely to symbolize to some extent the perpetual contemplation of the Heavenly Town.

300 years passed. The 20th century is coming to an end, by God's Providence, this almost liquidated all-Russian temple under the open sky in the heart of half ruined image of the Heavenly Town is revived. The cathedral of the Kazan Icon of the Most Holy Theotokos, the chapel of the Iveron Icon of the Most Holy Theotokos and Voskresenskie (of the Resurrection) Gates were rebuilt and sanctified. Divine services are conducted in the cathedral of the Holy Trinity on the Ditch. Several times already the religious procession with the Patriarch of Moscow and All Russia Alexius II at the head, with eparchs and Moscow holy orders went from the cathedral of the Assumption, the Kremlin's Cathedral Square through Spasskie (of the Saviour) Gates and Red Square, committing public prayers near the cathedrals of the Holy Trinity and of the Kazan Icon of the Theotokos. A candle began to gleam in front of the town-building image of the Eternal Easter of all Russia.

RELIGIOUS PROCESSIONS IN MOSCOW ARE THE IMAGE OF OECUMENICAL DIVINE SERVICE

A religious procession is a divine service with synodal procession of priests and believers with Christ's cross, gonfalons, icons and other holy things, beginning and ending in God's temple. Religious procession expresses symbolically the Church's via after Our Lord Jesus Christ to salvation. The tradition of religious processions came to Russia together with Christianity from Byzantium, where during the centuries of divine service the traditions and ranges of rituals formed. The religious processions were of monasteries, temples, eparchs depending on who of the clergy men is at the head of the procession. City religious procession was conducted by the bishop. Depending on the reason of the procession, they were divided into feastful, requesting, thanksgiving and ceremonial. According to their frequency they were regular (repeated) and for some event. In the 16th-17th centuries Moscow religious processions had additional important symbolics. To be convinced in their outstanding role, we should consider the history of appearance and development of figurativeness of Moscow portentous processions.

Religious procession around Constantinople with the icon of the Vernicle. F.Zubov. Icon feast of the Vernicle.

Influence of Byzantium on Russian Capitals

Having brought the Cross from new Jerusalem, the town of Constantinople, he installed it all over his land, established the belief.

        Metropolitanate Hilarion of Kiev
        about prince Vladimir who christened Russia.
        The 6th century.

The religious processions of Constantinople were especially famous and significant. Due to them Constantinople was presented not only as the capital of the empire, but the centre of this world, "the centre of the earth", from where oecumenical prayers ascend to God from the earthly Church. The religious procession from the cathedral of St. Sophia of Constantinople was considered oecumenical already because at the head of it the Oecumenical patriarch and emperor were. But the religious processions of Constantinople were so famous because miracles happened upon their requests. In unfavourable circumstances the religious procession gave the last hope for God's help.

In 619 and 626 at the time of emperor Heraclius Constantinople was in cruel siege of hostile ships. To acquire God's help they turned to the main miracle-working holy things of the empire: the icon of the Most Holy Theotokos Hodegetria, the Chesuble of the Theotokos, the Life-giving God's Cross and the Vernicle. Patriarch Sergius with the holy synaxis brought the Holy things during a religious procession along the city's walls. After the procession they committed the public prayer. The patriarch put an edge of the Chesuble of the Most Holy Theotokos into the sea. After the religious procession the enemies were liquidated by a sea storm. In gratitude to the Most Holy Theotokos an Akathist was made[12]. In 677 at the time of emperor Constantine IV Pogonate and in 717 at the time of emperor Leo III Isavr the siege of Constantinople was raised again after taking along the fortress walls of the Chesuble of the Theotokos and the icon of the Theotokos Hodegetria[13]. In 1186 emperor Isaac II Angel took part personally in the religious procession with the icon of the Theotokos Hodegetria around the capital for the sake of its saving from attacks of the enemies[14]. In all these cases, upon firm belief of Christians, the miraculous help was granted to Constantinople upon prayers of the Most Holy Theotokos. As a result it was understood that the miraculous help after eparch's requesting procession around the city with a miracle-working icon can testify to protection of the Theotokos and even to the fact that the city was chosen by God.

Symbolic meaning of a fortress which was called a town in ancient time, was also determined in Byzantium. St.Symeon of Thessalonica wrote that confessing religious procession had to include exit from the fortress: "When we go praying in the city and appeal crying, it means that we defiled the city with our sins. And when we appeal and pray outside the city, thus we express our meekness, state that we are unworthy to appeal from the city in which we defiled ourselves and outraged God and from which, like from the Divine Fatherland, we were moved because of the transgression: we confess that in the city where we have been created and recreated, in which we have been granted with divine sacrifice, being tempted by the snake of sin, we have been corrupted insanely, made ourselves obscene, defiled the holy place; that is why we are placed in a desert, go out into unprotected places, resigning ourselves to the righteous and providential wrath of God".[15] It is clear that in divine service a fortress acquires the meaning of the images of the Church, Heavenly Town, Paradise. The main city's gates become the image of the Holy Gates, the gates of Paradise.

In ancient Russian grand princely capitals like Kiev, Novgorod and Vladimir, the main city's gates like in Jerusalem and Constantinople were called, as it was mentioned above, Golden. However the essence of the enter of the portentous procession with Jesus Christ at the head into the town was emphasized much by the placement above the gates of the church of the Annunciation. As metropolitanate Hilarion of Kiev explains in "The Word about the Testament and Bliss": "If the Archangel gives a kiss to the Virgin here, this city will be blessed... Rejoice, the faithful city. God is with you!" Taking into account that on the Holy Gates in a temple an icon of the Annunciation is placed, a church of the Annunciation on the Golden Gates meant visually the entry of the King of Glory. As for the city it was correspondingly likened to the Church during the religious procession.

The hard time of Tatar-Mongolian yoke put forward the new task: to determine such Russian city which will be the heart of Russian Church and the centre of rebirth of the great country. In this situation many capitals of princely domains for better confirmation of their pretentions use religious processions whenever possible, so that through the likening to Constantinople to confirm that their town had been chosen by God. Requesting and thanksgiving religious processions with locally venerated miracle-working icons of the Theotokos were committed in Novgorod and Pskov, Tverj, Smolensk, Rostov, Kostroma, Yaroslavl, Ryazanj, Murom, Nizhny Novgorod, Pereyaslavl-Zalessky and other towns. Each princely town was looking and found spiritual likening to the rituals of the Ecumenical Tsargrad. If in Byzantium there were miracles from icons only in Constantinople and Athos, in Russia nearly each princely capital got the miraculous help of the Most Holy Theotokos till the 16th century, which was revealed through locally venerated icons. That means that, firstly, by the 16th century all Russian land was established as the domain under the protection of the Theotokos, and, secondly, the new state centre of Rus was to become the capital which did not just prove its similarity to Constantinople, but also which gathered Russian holy things that newly revealed themselves.

Synodal Procession of Russian Church

Through Your holy icon, the Virgin,
The Creator granted miracles to everybody in ancient time,
Saved our town of Moscow from invasion of foreigners,
Always be the protection and intercession, the Theotokos,
Of our land.

        Irmos

Medieval Moscow was not much different from other Russian princely capitals in religious processions till the end of the 14th century. The first indirect news about the religious processions for some events in Moscow are connected with metropolitanate Peter. According to the life description of the Saint, in 1325 moscovites went with religious procession with prince John Danilovich Kalita at the head to meet portentously the Hierarch going out of the fortress gates along Vladirnirskaya road to the field[16]. On the 4th of August, 1326, metropolitanate Peter founded the cathedral of the Assumption in the Kremlin, repeating Byzantine church tradition: "The procession with a cross and singing of psalms was carried out; the Bishop, having called Christ-loving people and having read there a lot of prayers and psalms, girded himself and the first began to bring the stones and making the foundation"[17]. In December 1326 St.Peter the Metropolitanate was buried in Moscow cathedral of the Assumption. Already in 1339 Russian metropolitanate Greek Theognostus asked for the blessing Patriarch John the Cripple of Constantinople to canonize Peter. The Patriarch taught Theognostus in his answer to follow the "acts of the Church venerate and gratify God's hermit with singing and divine eulogies and leave it for the future time to God, Who glorifies those who glorify Him"[18]. By a religious procession Moscow celebrated acquisition of its first Saint and intercessor.

Going to the war, Byzantine emperors, for example Leo Isavr, took a miracle-working icon of the Theotokos with him[19]. Gathering unprecedented in quantity the Russian army against the army of khan Mamay, grand prince Demetrius Ioannovich in 1380 took to Kulikovo field with him the miracle-working icon of the Theotokos, which got the thanksgiving name Donskaya for the help in the overthrowing of the enemy. Following the example of Constantinople a copy of this icon they began to keep in the domestic palace church of the Annunciation as the pledge of the help of the Most Holy Theotokos to Moscow grand-princely house[20]. With this icon thanksgiving religious processions were carried out along the walls of the white stone Kremlin.

The acknowledgement of Moscow as the capital of Russian centralized state was stimulated even better than the victory at the Don, the tragedy which followed it. In 1382 troops of khan Tokhtamysh, having conquered fraudulently Moscow fortress, annihilated the town and massacred all who stayed in it[21]. Grand prince Demetrius Ioannovich, who gathered troops in Kostroma during the massacre, encountered the difficult task of recreation of Moscow. Announcing the recreation to be the affair of all Russia, Demetrius Ioannovich, and then his son Basil Dmitrievich, organized mass move to the capital of "the best people" of many Russian towns. Expatriates brought not only their property, but their holy things too – copies of locally venerated miracle-working icons, bells. The first who began to collect the holy things of all Russia were John Danilovich Kalita and Symeon Ioannovich the Proud already, but at the end of the 14th century this phenomenon became of mass character. In future the collection of holy things and best people in Moscow became the favourite deed for Moscow governors.

In 1395 another menace of Moscow ravage appeared from Tatars. The khan of the Golden Horde Timur-Aksak-Tamerlan, who was already known by his conquering wars in India, Persia and Zakavkazie, ravaged Ryazanskaya land and went with a big army to the border of Moscow domain at the river Oka. In such cases they usually appealed to the locally venerated holy thing for help. For Moscow it was the icon of the Theotokos "Donskaya" that had been glorified recently. However now Moscow was a gathering of representatives from different towns, so it was decided to appeal to the All-Russian Holy Thing. "Grand prince Basil Dmitrievich after the council with metropolitanate Cyprian and boyards, precepting everybody to fast and confess and pray hard, ordered to bring from Vladimir to Moscow the miracle-working icon of the Mother of God from there"[22]. "When they were coming closer to Moscow with the miracle-working icon of the Most Holy Theotokos, then all the town went out to meet it, metropolitanate Cyprian with crosses and icons and candle-stands with candles, bishops, archiimandrates, hegumens, priests, deacons, with psalms and prayers, and with them princes and boyards, princesses and boyarynyas, husbands and wives, boys and girls, old people, teenagers and babies, orphans and widows, poor and cripples, monks and nuns, all ages of masculine and feminine sex, from babies to adults, all the great quantity of Christians met the icon far from the town in the field; and when they saw the miracle-working icon of the Most Holy Theotokos, all of them fell on the ground in tears praying and crying with all their hearts, thus appealing to Her with raised hands: "Oh, the Most Holy mother of God! Save us from invasion of unfaithful, threatening to ravage Your property, protect the princes and people from all evil, defend this town and all towns and countries, where the name of Your Son and our God is glorified and Yours... And thus gratifying for a long time they went to the town with the icon of the Theotokos and installed it in the cathedral of the Assumption"[23]. On that very day the Tatars army turned back and went away.

So, on the 26th of August, 1395, the confessing religious procession with metropolitanate Cyprian at the head went out from the town's gates and on Kuchkovo field there was the divine service in front of the icon, and the praying was accompanied with everybody's bowing to the earth at each request.

Like the thanksgiving religious procession in Constantinople metropolitanate Cyprian of Kiev and All Russia together with grand prince of Moscow Basil Dmitrievich established the memorial annual religious procession[24]. At the same time it was not supposed to take away miracle-working icons from other towns at first. They usually made copies from them and returned them back with religious procession. Finally the Vladimir Icon of the Theotokos was brought to Moscow only on the 23rd of June, 1480, when the requesting religious procession of moscovites was consecrated to saving from invasion of the army of khan Akhmat[25]. After defeat of Tatars, in the memory of the praying meeting, grand prince John Vasilievich III and metropolitanate Gerontius the second annual procession was established in honour of "The Meeting of the Vladimir Icon of the Most Holy Theotokos"[26]. In 1401 another Holy thing was brought to Moscow. Archbishop Dionysius of Suzdal brought from Tsargrad the shrine with "God's Passions" in 1382, which means "the Saviour's blood and parts of things left after His passions – of the crown of thorns, stick, spear etc."[27]. From Tatars massacre the shrine was hidden inside the wall of the cathedral of the Nativity in Suzdal. In 1401 "The Passions of our Lord Jesus Christ were brought to Moscow; they were met honourably with crosses by all holy orders and all the town"[28].

In 1449 the copy of Ovinovskaya Icon of Assumption, the intercessor of the town of Galich, was met in Moscow with a religious procession.[29] In 1456 – they were saying farewell to the Smolenskaya Icon of the Theotokos Hodegetria: "They went with the miracle-working icon of the Most Holy Theotokos that was followed by the Metropolitanate and all the Saint Synod, then by the Grand Prince with his children, other princes and boyards, great quantity of military people and all people of the glorious town of Moscow. The Grand Prince saw it to the church of the Annunciation, which is in Dorogomilovo, from there they returned back praying"[30]. In Moscow a copy of the miracle-working icon was left, that was returned to Smolensk.

In 1496 the miracle-working icon of the Most Holy Theotokos "Tender Feeling" was met from Novgorod and in 1508 it was returned. A copy of it was made and left in Moscow[31].

In 1518 a religious procession to the monastery of the Meeting of Our Lord Jesus Christ met the miracle-working icons of the Saviour and the Theotokos from Vladimir. It was a copy of the Vladimir icon, that had been brought from Moscow and glorified with miracles in Vladimir. The icons were returned by another road and on the place of the memorable praying a church was sanctified with the altar in honour of the Vladimir Icon, which was famous according to the lateral altar as the church of St. Martyr Nicetas in Basmanniki: "The holy icons were brought to Moscow from Vladimir because they became delapidated during many years. They were met by Metropolitanate Barlaam with crosses and all holy orders in the monastery of the Presentation of the Theotokos in the Temple, and people met them outside the town, behind the settlement. Grand Prince Basil Ioannovich ordered to install them, adorned them with gold and silver, and released them back to the glorious town of Vladimir, seeing them with Metropolitanate Barlaam and all holy orders and all people behind the settlement. And on that place to which they saw them they built a new church in the name of the Most Holy Theotokos, of Her honorable and glorious Meeting. And seeing off those holy icons Metropolitanate Barlaam sanctified that new church and conducted the Divine liturgy there with all holy orders. And releasing the holy icons to Vladimir, seeing them off the Grand Prince with his boyards and people returned behind the monastery of St.Andronicus with psalms and many prayers"[32]. Moscow was growing, so prince Basil Ioannovich had to go out of the town "behind the settlement" even behind the monastery of the Saviour-St.Andronicus in 1518.

In 1540 the miracle-working icons of the Theotokos of Rzhev and the Life-giving Cross were met and seen off, and on the place of the praying the church of the Rzhev Icon of the Theotokos was sanctified[33]. John the Terrible and all the successive tsars continued to collect Holy Things in Moscow.

Besides many Moscow churches and monasteries kept copies of miracle-working icons of all ends of Russia. For example, in Sretenskiy monastery, in the iconcase, a copy of the miracle-working Tolgskaya icon of the Theotokos was installed, the main holy thing of Yaroslavl. To avoid any doubts there was the inscription on tile icon's copy: "The true image and size of the miracle-working icon of the Most Holy Theotokos in Tolgskiy monastery..."[34]. It is not difficult to imagine that the synodal Moscow religious procession, into which all monasteries and churches brought out their Holy Things, became a portentous icon procession of all Russian church, in which all dwellers of Moscow state were convinced.

The Image of the Procession of Saints

The Heavenly Regiments rejoin gloriously serving the miracle-working icon of the Theotokos, and call to spiritual joy all people on earth, and indicate it as salvation of the world and protection of all Russia.

The service to the appearance of the Tikhvinskaya Icon of the Theotokos. The 17th century.

People's belief in the effect of the requesting religious procession was really unlimited. When in summer 1518 during the Fast of the Sts. Apostles Peter and Paul it started raining heavily, "Grand Prince Basil Ioannovich of all Russia told the Metropolitanate of all Russia to pray to God and our Saviour Jesus Christ and His Most Holy Mother, the Theotokos Mary and Russian Great Saint Miracle-workers for God's mercy, for the sun's warmth, for stopping of the rain with the Bishops, archimandrites, hegumens and with all holy orders; and to all people, orthodox Christians he precepted the fast and prayer with true repentance and tears. And it so happened that the dark sky cleared promptly, it became sunny and warm. As for the reigning autocrat he and the Hierarch gratified and thanked the Lord Jesus Christ, His Most Holy Theotokos and Saint Russian Miracle-workers"[35]. It is especially characteristic of religious processions of Moscow state the combined gratifying of "Our Lord Jesus Christ, the Most Holy Theotokos and Saint Russian Miracle-workers".

Teaching scripts of that time tell about the people's conviction of the synodicy of church praying: "It is possible to pray at home, but it is not like in church, where there is the synaxis of Angels, people, and God Himself"[36]. Speaking about people's idea of religious processions attention should be paid to a very important characteristic feature of the tales about miraculous visions. In Byzantium the visions have only Jesus Christ, or only the Theotokos, or only one saint, who appeared to give instructions to the worthy ones about what to do in order to get Divine help. For example, Greek empress Zoe, the wife of emperor Leo the Wise, saw in illness a dream, that she would recover after the Belt of the Theotokos was put on her[37], some elder got the instruction to put the Belt of the Most Holy Theotokos into water to get saved from hostile ships[38], St.John Damascene and elder Athanasius on the Athos saw the Theotokos and got instructions from Her[39].

In Russian tales about visions there is an absolutely new quality, the tales of the time of establishment of Moscow state. The Heavenly help very often turns out to be the synaxis divine service of the Heavenly Regiments and Saints, carried out for Russian land. Novgorod's chronicle of 1439 contains the tale about the vision of Aaron the sacristan of the cathedral of St. Sophia about how the Saint "before deceased archbishops came inside the cathedral by the former door which opened itself, and went inside the altar through its doors, then went out one by one and stood in front of the Korsunj Icon of the Most Holy Theotokos and sang prayers for many hours"[40].

The Divine service is even brighter in the later variant of the tale about the miracle of the Vladimir icon of the Theotokos in 1395. During the time when the saving religious procession took place in Moscow, which met the miracle-working icon, khan Timur-Tamerlan (Temir-Aksak in Russian chronicles) saw in his dream the appearance of the Theotokos in shining light, accompanied by the procession of saint hierarchs with crosiers and She ordered him to leave the borders of Russia. The procession of saint hierarchs with the Most Holy Theotokos at the head sent away the invaders from Russian land: "On the day when the miracle-working icon was brought to Moscow, sleeping Temir-Aksak saw a horrible dream: a high mountain and from the mountain saint hierarchs were coming with golden crosiers in hands precluding him to commit the evil. And again he saw above the saint hierarchs in the air the wife in crimson chesubles with plenty of regiments precluding him to commit the evil"[41]. According to Christian symbolics the high mountain is the Heavenly Kingdom[42], so, the religious procession in the tale was coming out from the Heavenly Town.

Finally the most convincing Moscow religious procession was described in the tale about the miracle of 1521 (the text of the tale dates back to the end of the 16th century). "At the beginning of the 16th century, during the invasion of Moscow by

Feast of the Entry of the Lord into Jerusalem, veneration of the image of the procession of the righteous into the Heavenly Town at the Last Judgement. Drawing of Meierberg.

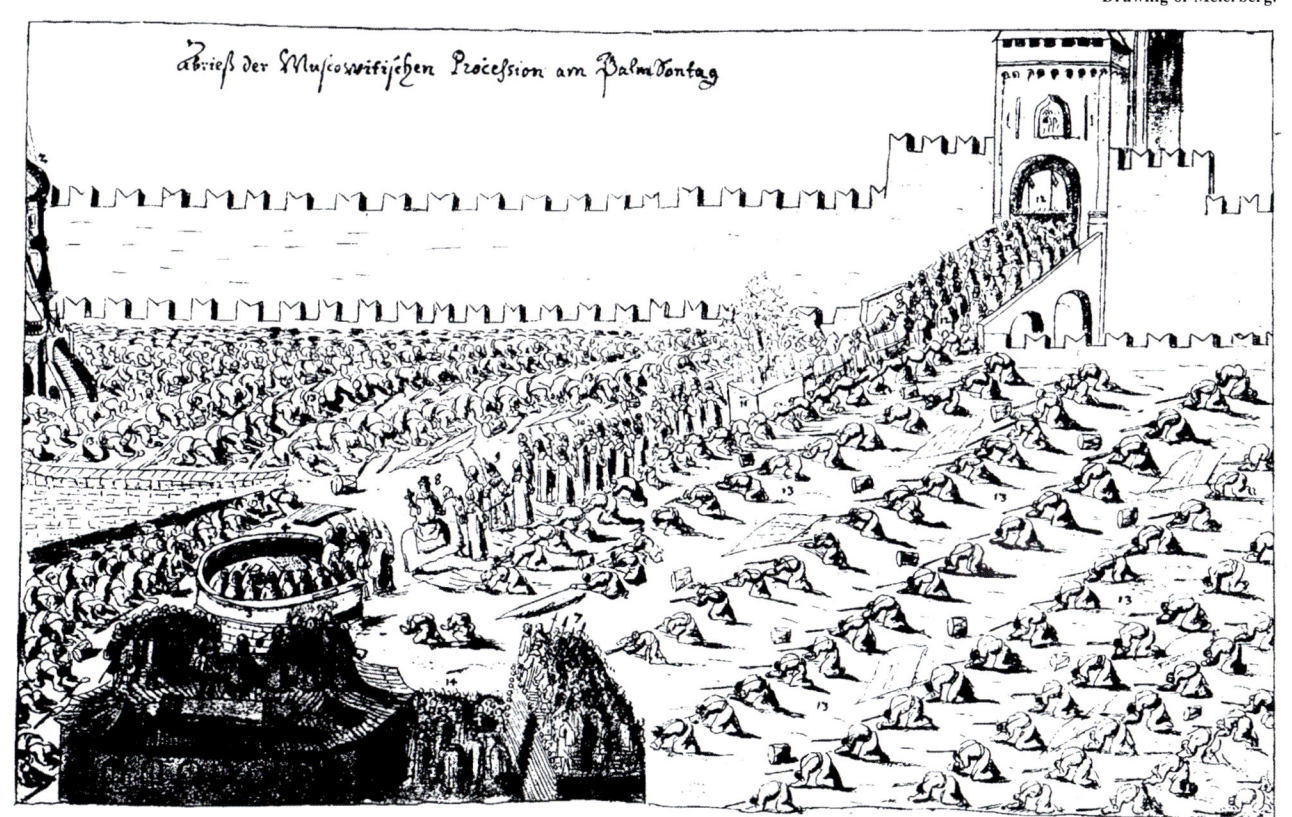

Mekhmet-Guirey, moscovites were in deep grief and prayed. At that time an elder-nun of the convent of the Ascension, which was in the Kremlin near Frolovskie gates (now the Saviour's), who was blind, after praying hard, got down to spiritual contemplation and was granted with spiritual vision. She saw that from the Kremlin into the Frolovskie gates big quantity of priests and deacons went in, among whom there were many metropolitanate and bishops, including those of Moscow: Peter, Alexius and Job and saint hierarch Leontius. They were bringing the miracle-working icon of the Theotokos "Vladimirskaya" and other icons, crosses and gonfalons. They were met at the Frontal place by Righteous Barlaam of Chutin and St.Sergius of Radonezh who asked the hierarchs why they were going out of the town and heard that they were doing it at God's will because of the town's indecency. Then St.Barlaam and St.Sergius fell down at the feet of the hierarchs with prayer and tears asking them not to leave the town to the enemies. The hierarchs heard their prayer and sang prayers with them in front of the on-gate icon of the Saviour and then they returned to their place, and the Tatars soon ran away behind the borders of Moscow state"[43].

In this important tale we can single out all necessary specialities of the confessing religious procession, which was carried out by Russian saints praying for Moscow state. Firstly, clergy men went out of the town's gates with miracle-working icons, with hierarch at the head. Secondly, the repentant praying of St.Sergius the Hegumen of Radonezh and St.Barlaam of Chutin. Thirdly, the praying at the future Frontal place in front of miracle-working icons and tile on-gate icon of the Saviour.

The New Town of New Constantine

In the Third Rome, id est on Russian land – the bliss of the Holy Spirit will shine.
PSHL.T. I. Collection of years.

In 1439 Patriarch Josef II of Constantinople and the last Byzantine emperor Constantine Paleologus agreed at the Florentine Council to pass on to the catholic confession. The shaken gonfalon of orthodoxy was immediately undertaken by Moscow: "Today the Church of Tsargrad wavered, renounced our orthodoxy"[44]. In 1448 without agreement with the patriarch of Constantinople the Synode of Russian archbishops and bishops elected St.Jonah (Odnoushev) as the metropolitanate of Moscow, who had been the archbishop of Ryazan before[45]. For certification of this decision they addressed the patriarch of Jerusalem, not of Constantinople. The new situation was reflected in Moscow religious processions at once.

In 1451, when Moscow was sieged by the troops of Tatar prince Mazovsha, following the tradition of Constantinople, metropolitanate Jonah organized requesting religious procession along the town's walls with the copy of the Vladimir icon of the Theotokos and other icons. "Saint metropolitanate Jonah ordered all the holy orders to sing prayers in all the town, and all the people to pray to God and the Most Holy Theotokos and to the Great Miracle-workers Sts. Peter and Alexius... and the Tatars on the same night ran away from the town, having heard the great noise in the town, thinking that the Grand Prince had come with a big army"[46]. This time the rules of prayers were sung near each fortress tower "all over the town".

If in Kiev and Vladimir religious processions went out of the town through the Golden Gates, in Moscow the Kremlin's Frolovskie Gates became the Holy Gates in 1462, which led to Red Square. In 1462 "on the 27th of July the stone church of St.Athanasius was sanctified in Moscow on Frolovskie Gates with the lateral altar of St.Hieromartyr Panteleimon, the church was built by Basil Dmitriev, the son Ermolin"[47]. In 1464 the same Ermolin built the altar of St.Hieromartyr George on Frolovskie Gates, with fretwork, in 1466 – the altar of St.Hieromartyr Demetrius. It is important to add that in the 1460s the Kremlin walls, which had been built in 1360 by Demetrius Donskoy, were repaired again and again, for example, in 1462 the town's wall was renovated with stone from Sviblovo shooting tower to Borovitskie gates[48]. What stimulated such hurried spiritual extolment of religious procession through Frolovskie Gates? It was evident that soon they would have to build new walls, however, grand prince John III Vasilievich and metropolitanate Theodosius wanted to emphasize immediately the succession of Moscow from lost Constantinople, which was now renamed into Istanbul. The selection of the Saints, blessing Moscow religious procession through Frolovskie Gates, is interesting. St.Athanasius the Great was famous for his firm belief in the fight with aryans. Now the main and firm defender of orthodoxy was Moscow. Sts. Warriors George and Demetrius were the Heavenly Protectors of emperor house and, so of the Byzantine army. It is known that according to the Russian tradition Sts.Boris and Gleb conformed to their paired icon, so the appeal to Sts. George and Demetrius established Moscow as new Constantinople. The Saint Warriors were called for the religious procession to see Russian troops off to the defense of orthodoxy.

On the initiative of the same grand prince John III Vasilievich in 1491 Italian architect Pietro Antonio Solari built new Frolovskaya Tower from red brick. Now the likeness to Constantinople was reflected in another way in it. In Golden Gates of Constantinople the inside passage was composed from two arches which were increased in the direction of the city. The same design was repeated in the new Frolovskie Gates, which expressed Golden Gates of Constantinople in exterior. The correctness of such understanding was confirmed by metropolitanate Zosimas in 1492 in the Paschalia on the eighth thousand years: "And now God glorified the Grand Prince John Vasilievich, faithful and Christ-loving, shining in orthodoxy, the tsar and autocrate of all Russia, new tsar Constantine to new town of Constantinople-Moscow"[50]. For the reliefs of Sts.George and Demetrius near Frolovskie Gates in the monastery of the Resurrection in 1527 the church of St.Hieromartyr George the Victory-bearer was built from stone

Religious procession along the Kremlin's walls.
Miniature of I Osterman's volume. L.352 ob.

Religious procession on Cathedral Square. Podea. 1498.

with the lateral altar of St.Hieromartyr Demetrius of Thessalonika[51].

At the end of the 15th century on Cathedral Square in Moscow some church rituals were repeated, which had been carried out before exclusively in Constantinople. In the 14th and the 15th centuries in Constantinople each Tuesday an unusual ceremony took place, which was described by Russian pilgrim Stephan Novgorodets: "On Tuesday we went to the icon of the Most Holy Theotokos which was painted by St.Evangelist Luke... That icon is brought out each Tuesday. It is a surprising scene: then all people gather there, and people from other towns come. This icon is very big, with skillfully made setting framework, and the singers, walking before it, sing beautifully, and all people exclaim crying: "God, be merciful to us!" They put the icon on the shoulders of one man, he spreads his arms as if crucified, so that it is frightening to look at him, and he even does not understand, where the icon carries him. Then another man takes it, and the same thing happens to him, then the third and the fourth, and they sing with deacons wonderfully, and people appeal crying: "God, be merciful to us!" It is an amazing scene: seven of eight men install the icon on the shoulders of one man, and he, by God's will, walks as if without any load"[52]. In the State Historical Museum there is a podea, which was knitted in 1498 in the workshop of grand princess Helen Stephanovna, on which Moscow religious procession was shown, which took place in 1498. In the centre of it there is a deacon carrying on belts a frame with the icon of the Theotokos Hodegetria. Before him and at his both sides there are two monks, one with a cross, the other with a bowl with tidy water. On the left and on the right from the icon sacramental fans with seraphs are carried. Metropolitanate Symeon incenses the one who carries the icon, the metropolitanate has a nimbus around his head. On the right the metropolitanate is followed by hierarchs and boyards. On the left, before the hierarchs there are three men with crowns. They are grand prince John III Vasilievich, his son Basil and beardless grandson Demetrius. John III Vasilievich and Demetrius are shown with nimbuses. Very big umbrellas are carried above the groups of the grand princes and hierarchs. On the left, in the first row, behind the singers with sharp-edged hats, waving their hands in rhythm, after the monks there are the princesses Theodora and Eudocia in round hats, from under which their hair came out. Between them there is Helen Stephanovna, and the last one on the right – their mother is, Grand Princess Sophia[53]. So in 1498 in Moscow on the holiday of the Entry of our Lord Jesus Christ into Jerusalem the icon of the Theotokos Hodegetria was brought around Cathedral Square of the Kremlin, like it had happened in Constantinople. In the same way at the time of John III Vasilievich on Cathedral Square they began to celebrate the New Year on the 1st of September.

Ecumenical Annual Divine Service

In the courts of the Lord's house, in the midst of thee, O Jerusalem. Praise ye the Lord.
                                                    Psalm 115.

In 1547 John IV Vasilievich was crowned, which gave the opportunity to metropolitanate Macarius to create the rules and rituals of the system of annual town's divine services of Moscow. Celebrations of the New Year, the Nativity of the Theotokos, Adoration of the Holy Cross, the Intercession, Chrismas, Epyphany, Triumph of Orthodoxy, the Annunciation, Entry of the Lord into Jerusalem, the Good Friday, Easter, Mid-Pentecost, the Ascension, the Holy Trinity Pentecost, Procession of the Holy Life-giving Cross, the Transfiguration, the Assumption became all-town church rites of seven Moscow cathedrals. Most of the rites contained religious processions, at the head of which there was orthodox tsar and Russian metropolitanate supposing that soon he will become the patriarch. Besides that there were religious processions in honour of especially venerated icons and Sunday summer processions from the week of All Saints till the week of the Adoration of the Holy Cross. In this presentation the town's service had the character of continuous ecumenical praying about salvation of the Church, coming out of "the centre of earth". Metropolitanate Macarius as if revives the ancient tradition of Constantinople of praying to God on behalf of Ecumenical Church, but he does it at the qualitatively new level. The above-said presentation did not destroy the traditional understanding of Moscow religious procession as the procession of Russian Church to salvation. But now Russian Church with all its Saints was as if at the head of the ecumenical procession after God to Salvation.

For the rite of the New Year in the centre of Cathedral Square a platform was arranged, from where the hierarch blessed three times the four parts of the world with a cross, while in front of him the archideacon incensed each time[54]. Metropolitanate announced: "Hear us, God, our Saviour, the hope of all the ends of the earth... As for our faithful tsar, you approved, God, to possess the weapon of truth, crowning him with the weapon of good-will, raise his hand, protect him with Your wings. Subdue to him all the barbarian tongues, who want to fight with us... Bless the crown of years with Your goodness, soothe the hostility of the tongues raising against us, accept all of us into Your Kingdom due to prayers of the Most Holy Theotokos the Virgin Mary and all Your Saints"[55]. As John IV soon was going to the war against Tatars, metropolitanate Macarius tried to include into the prayers biblical grounds for the victory of the orthodox tsar over the unfaithful, which remained in the rite of the New Year for a long time after: "Like the Jewish bodies fell rightfully in the desert, as they did not follow You, the Lord of everybody, so now disperse the bones of the evil-minded and unfaithful... Help our faithful tsar to fight against the unfaithful, like You helped David, as they came to Your places and defiled holy things, but You grant the victory, our Lord Jesus Christ, for You are the victory and laudation of orthodox people"[56]. It is important to note that metropolitanate Macarius, appealing to God, calls Russia "Your places and the holy thing".

On the platform of Cathedral Square the places for the tsar and hierarch were arranged. On the holiday of the New Year when the tsar and the hierarch sat down on their places the authorities came to the tsar and bowed to him twice", then the participants of the religious procession bowed once to the hierarch[57]. In order to confirm the significance of orthodox tsar for the Church and its rites, we can present the written application to John IV in 1548 of monks of the Athos Serbian Hilendarskiy monastery, who call him "the autocratic great tsar of Moscow, the only true tsar, the white tsar of Eastern and Western countries, who is the tsar to all orthodox Christians; the sacred, great, pious kingdom; the Christian sun, shining in the East and North and lighting all under the sun; the establishment of seven synodal pillars, the second Constantine and defender of divine churches, the Christian gonfalon on which the holy cross is installed for the enlightening of orthodox people"[58]. About the placement at the front flank in divine services of orthodox tsar the rule of washing on the Good Friday testifies, which was described in the Regal Book. In Moscow relics of many Saints were kept, following the example of Constantinople, in the domestic church of the royal palace. On Friday of the Passion week the metropolitanate "with the authorities and holy orders of all cathedrals go to cathedral of the Annunciation to the holy relicts and at that time the bells ring"[59]. According to the picture in the Regal Book the procession from the cathedral of the Assumption to the royal palace was very different. At the head of the procession of the priests of seven cathedrals metropolitanate Macarius rode sitting sideways on a donkey as though continuing the Entry of the Lord into Jerusalem. On top of the picture the riding metropolitanate Macarius is shown coming closer to the porch of the cathedral of the Annunciation, from where the staircase led to the royal palace. The artist especially stresses the big donkey ears, perhaps because the role of the donkey was played by a white horse with ears made from cloth and bound to it, as it happened later.

The royal palace meant a town as it is shown on the engraving by a symbolical wall, behind which the procession went. The next scene is shown in the middle of the picture. In the Golden Chamber of the Palace metropolitanate Macarius invites tsar John IV to go after the holy relicts of the cathedral of the Assumption.

Then the hierarch distributed on the porch of the cathedral of the Annunciation shrines with the holy relicts to the authorities, he himself took "the Cross – Life-giving Cross on his head" (i.e. a plate with a cross on it)[60]. "And they walk slowly and portentously from the cathedral of the Annunciation to the cathedral of the Assumption; archdeacons and deacons incense with many censers before and at both sides of the holy relicts and the bells ring at this time". The procession from the royal palace goes in the picture from the porch of the cathedral of the Annunciation. Before that in the middle of the cathedral of the Assumption a big table was installed with silver chances and prepared water. (People responsible for the water are seen in the background, at the table, on the picture from the Regal Book.) Near the table a platform for the metropolitanate was installed, covered with a carpet, at the corners of the table 4 silver candle stands were installed. Here the hierarch installed "The Life-giving Tree Cross" on the table. Further Macarius received the holy relicts from the authorities and gave them to tsar John IV. "The tsar coming after the holy relicts to the cathedral... kisses them" and puts them on the plate, on the table. In the picture, on the right, there is metropolitanate Macarius and tsar John IV, carrying the shrines with the relicts. "They sanctify the water with prayers and psalms". The metropolitanate hallows the water with the cross and all in the cathedral sing: "Save, God, Your people" three times. Then he wets the relicts of the saints in the water, distributes to the tsar's court 4 cups and 4 cups to his own yard, then to the boyards and all the people, which takes a long time". So the rite was carried out in 1552, when during the Passion week Poemen was ordained as the archbishop of Novgorod, about which the Regal Book informs: "Tsar and Grand Prince John Vasilievich of All Russia and metropolitanate Macarius brought in the holy relicts and prayed to God and then released Poemen to Novgorod, where he came on the day of St. Nicholas". After decease of Macarius the rule was changed on the wish of John IV. John the Terrible, editing the Regal Book, wrote the resolution: "This is not needed for the tsar to carry himself (the holy relicts)". Further descriptions of the rule inform that the tsar kisses the holy relicts, but does not take them. The procession of the metropolitanate on the donkey was also stopped, which was carried out just to invite the tsar.

Installation of the Holy Cross and the ambo in the middle of the Kremlin's Cathedral Square is shown on Moscow icon of the 16th century from the tsar's church of the Ascension in Kolomenskoe. The plot of the icon is the following: "Constantine the Great, having tried in many accidents the power of Christ's Cross against enemies, felt the wish to find the real Christ's Cross. Soon after the Ecumenical Council of Nicaea with this intention he hurried to Jerusalem with his mother, tsarina Helen. The Pious intention of this righteous wife was a success. An old Jew Ruda, knowing, according to a verbal legend, about the place where the Cross was hidden under Venera's pagan place, offered to undig its foundation. Helen and other Christians were extremely happy when they found three crosses there. The miracle settled the question, on which of the three crosses the Saviour had been crucified. Patriarch Macarius of Jerusalem ordered to attach the three crosses to a dead man. Two of them had no effect, but after the touch of the third one the dead man came back to life. Thus they became sure that this one was Christ's Life-giving Cross. Innumerable inflow of people because of this event did not allow each one to kiss this precious holy thing: so many just wanted at least to see it. Patriarch Macarius, in order to satisfy this sacramental request, went up to a high place and installed the Holy Cross and thus blessed the people... St.Cyril, being tile bishop of Jerusalem, 25 years after the acquisition of the Lord's Cross told about this event to his listeners as to the witnesses of it"[61]. In the lower part of the icon the finding of the Lord's Cross during the digging of the Golgotha in Jerusalem led by Saint Tsarina Helen, transfer of the found crosses and acquisition of the Lord's Cross from them according to the miracle of resurrection of a dead man are shown. In the upper part of the icon the action takes place in Jerusalem, the new one, – in Moscow. It happens against the background of the cathedral of the Assumption in the Kremlin, the royal palace, which is on the left, and the bell-tower of John the Great on the right. From the main Red Porch, which is near the Faceted Palace, Saint Tsarina Helen comes down. Surrounded by Moscow boyards in "golden" vestments, in the middle, on the ambo Patriarch Macarius of Jerusalem, metropolitanate Macarius of Moscow and young tsar John IV Vasilievich install the Lord's Cross together. From the left side bishop Cyril of Jerusalem points at them. The moment of installation of the Lord's Cross is presented as the triumph of establishment of the new Christian kingdom, the second Byzantium – Moscow kingdom. Succession of Moscow from Tsargrad and Jerusalem is directly shown by the delivery from Saint Equal-to-the-Apostles Tsarina Helen and hierarchs Macarius and Cyril of Jerusalem of the highest Christian ideals into the hands of tsar John IV, who has been just crowned, and to metropolitanate Macarius of Moscow. Attention also should be paid to the emphasized conformity of the names of the acting people in Jerusalem and Moscow: the mother of the first tsar of the Great Christian Empire in Jerusalem – Saint Equal-to-the-Apostles Helen, and in Moscow – Helen Glinskaya; the Ecumenical hierarch in Jerusalem – patriarch Macarius of Jerusalem, and in Moscow –

Ablution of relics by metropolitanate Macarius and John IV. Sheet from the "Regal Book" with correction of the text by John IV.

Adoration of the Holy Cross. The upper part of the icon of the church of the Ascension in Kolomenskoe. Museum of Sergiev Posad.

metropolitanate Macarius of Moscow. After decease of St.Macarius the Adoration of the Holy Cross on Cathedral Square was substituted by the divine service in the cathedral of the Assumption.

The victory of the orthodox tsar over Kazan khanate and communication of the subdued to orthodoxy inspired the construction of the cathedral of the Holy Trinity (of the Intercession), which is on the Ditch, which became the new and unrepeated building determined for Moscow religious procession. As a historian of architecture F.F.Gornostaev supposed: "Metropolitanate Macarius takes close to heart the expressiveness of the ecclesiastic glory and advises the tsar to build a cathedral with the altars of the "vowed" temples, which is more worthy of the great event, – triumph of all Russia. Probably, the leading idea of the general planning of the unusual forms of the temple also belonged to metropolitanate Macarius... Into one line from the East to the West three altars are grouped sequentially: the Eastern – in honour of the Life-giving Trinity, the central one -of the Intercession and the Western one – in honour of the Entry of the Lord into Jerusalem. The person who was the chief of the construction attributed the main importance to these altars... The third main place, in the row from East to West, was given to the Entry of the Lord into Jerusalem, evidently with the purpose to make this altar, and so the cathedral itself, the place for the special spiritual feast – the procession "on the donkey" on Palm Sunday from all the Kremlin's cathedrals. With this purpose the ladders near the altar of the Entry of the Lord into Jerusalem were built so that the religious procession could walk directly into the temple without having to turn to other altars. The special importance of the altar of the Entry of the Lord into Jerusalem, as it is seen, gave it the significant place. It was not by chance that the foreigners (who visited Moscow in the 16th-17th centuries) called the cathedral of the Intercession as Jerusalem, the church of Jerusalem, as it was called, according to their words, among people[62]. The wide ladder of 4 metres led the religious procession up, which came from Frolovskie (the Saviour) gates of the Kremlin inside the temple of the Entry of the lord into Jerusalem. Another ladder of the same kind led the procession in the direction of the Moscow-river.

The cathedral of the Holy Trinity (of the Intercession) was built in the form of an octahedral star, the symbol of "the eighth age", the Heavenly Town, which adorns the Theotokos on the icons. Besides that, the ensemble initially had 25 cupolas, which symbolized God Almighty and 24 elders in the Revelation of St.John the Theologian, and was the image of the Altar of the Holy Trinity. The central temple of the Intercession not only glorified Orthodoxy for the victory over "the unfaithful", but also presented the Heavenly Town as "the house of the Most Holy Theotokos"[63]. The hip roof – canopy of the central church spread the protection of the Theotokos over the whole country. Crowned with golden cupola octahedral hip roof according to the symbolics of the 16th century meant the Throne of Jesus

Christ as the Most High Judge at the Last Judgement, which stands on many Heavenly Regiments. According to the analysis of N.I.Bronov, the cathedral, built in the shape of a cross, in the 16th century was seen as situated in the centre of the Earth and blessed all the Universe with the cross [64].

The Rite at the Frontal Place

The Frontal place is the Paradise.
The inscription on the installed cross of the 16th century.

The first chronicle mention of the Frontal place dates back to the time of John the Terrible: in 1549 from a wooden platform tsar John IV addressed the people[65]. The name indicates the different meanings of this town's ambo. The Frontal place is the Golgotha near Jerusalem, where Jesus Christ was crucified. According to the legend, inside the hill "the forefather Adam was buried and his head was sanctified with the blood of our God Jesus Christ, the New Adam"[66]. If the cathedral of the Holy Trinity (of the Intercession) in Red Square was built as the image of the Heavenly Town, and in front of it at the wish of John the Terrible the Frontal place was built, then in the tsar's opinion it was the Frontal place which was the best ambo for the anointed by God to address the people.

For tsar John IV the Jerusalem location of the Frontal place behind the main gates of the fortress-town was important. The proof to it is the fact that the picture of Golgotha was included into Russian State Seal. Among the emblems of Russian domains Golgoatha was shown the first as the symbol that Russian land was the symbol of salvation of the Church. On the frontal side of the state seal of 1577 there is an inscription around the picture of Golgoatha: "The Cross grants the ancient property"[67]. On the other side of the seal there is also the Golgotha with the circular inscription: "Christ's gonfalon is the laudation of Christians".

On usual days tsar's deacons announced loudly state decrees from the Frontal place. But soon it acquires the key symbolic role in Moscow religious processions. The religious procession showed by the exit from the temple the expulsion of the mankind out of Paradise. While the procession was walking the Church of the Old Testament transferred into the Church of the New Testament of Jesus Christ, and return of the procession into the temple meant the coming of the Church into the Heavenly Town, transfiguration of the Church into the Church of the Saints upon the Last Judgement[68]. The Frontal place became the image of the result of the procession of the Church.

The idea of the special role of the Russian Church in preparation for the Last Judgement was developing since the end of the 15th century, when in the event of the 7000 anniversary since the creation of the world the end of the world was to be expected, according to the prophecy of Byzantium historians because the world that had been created during 7 days was to exist for 7000 years, because for God "a thousand of years is like one day"[69]. Expectation of the Second Advent of Christ up to the 18th century became then the feeling characteristic for all the Russians:

Your age, poor damned man,
Is expiring
And the end is coming
And the Last Judgement is getting ready[70].

As, according to the explanation of elder Philotheus: "All Christian kingdoms fell down because of the unfaithful; only the kingdom of our tsar exists due to Christ's bliss"[71], then "the kingdom chosen by God" shall give to God at the Last Judgement the Church and Christ's belief as the unchanged holy thing kept in purity of orthodox rituals[72]. From this understanding of the special role of the Russian Church the expectation of Christ's Second Advent came out, which was not frightening, but joyful.

Preparation of the Russian Church for the meeting of God gradually entered the ritual of Moscow religious processions. Metropolitanate Macarius and tsar John the Terrible prepared almost everything necessary, so that the expected triumph of Russian Church at the Last Judgement acquires visual symbols in town's divine services. The ecumenical praying from "the centre of the earth" reflected this idea. At the time of metropolitanate Macarius and tsar John IV in the centre of Cathedral Square on the platform during the rites consecrated to the New Year and the Last Judgement they began to install the tsar's and metropolitan places, each one under a canopy. Boyards and priests bowed to earth to the orthodox tsar, sitting in the armchair, as to the image of the Almighty. But in order to express how the orthodox tsar gives to the Saviour the protected Church, a patriarch was needed. Establishment of patriarchate was the last important factor that finalized the process. In the above-mentioned rites of the New Year and the Last Judgement on Cathedral Square another, the highest Tsar's place appears. In it, under a high marquee the tsar's bell was, which made the loudest image of God's voice.

Eschatologic expectations at the end of the 16th century also influenced the appearance of the separate flat bell-fry, which was remade as a bell-tower, placed in front of the temple as the gates in front of the Heavenly Town. The form of the bell-tower meant that above the tetrahedral of the earthly Church the octahedral Throne of the Most High Judge stands. "God's voice" coming out of the marquee and calling to the divine service was presented as the image of the trumpet voice calling to the Last Judgement, to the main divine service of the Great Eparch Jesus Christ.

Russian ecclesiastic legends added the image of Golgotha with its presentation as the place of the coming Last Judgement, explaining it so that where the Saviour gave His blood for people's sins, He will manage the judgement there[73]:

And Archangel Michael, the father, will descend,
And he will install the throne in the centre of the earth,
He will sound the golden trumpet:
Get up all, alive and dead,
Old and young be at the end of years![74]

It is interesting that Golgotha as the image of Salvation was placed on the reverse side of Byzantine icons for religious processions. In the 8th-9th centuries in Byzantium apocalypses of Pseudo-Methodius "The Vision of Daniel about the Last Time" and some others were created. In them the saving from invaders was entrusted to the tsar, who was to establish peace everywhere and in "the centre of the earth", on the Golgotha in Jerusalem, to return to God the symbol of tsar's power – diadem[75]. The Frontal place was included into the iconography of the Last Judgement as the image of God's Throne, where Angels bring out the Cross. The Last Judgement is understood by orthodoxy first of all as the divine service of the Heavenly and earthly powers in the glory of the Great Eparch. During orthodox divine service the installed cross was brought out being laid on the plate. So in the icons of the Last Judgement from the monastery of St.Hieromartyr Catherine on Sinai (the 12th century) and the cathedral of the Assumption in the Moscow Kremlin (the 15th century) there is the installed orthodox cross for divine service lying on the throne-Golgotha. Such cross on the Frontal place in the centre of the Last Judgement was depicted by Andrew Rublev on the frescoes of the cathedral of the Assumption in Vladimir at the border of the 15th century.

As soon as the Patriarch was elected, in 1599 on the order of tsar Boris Godunov and the blessing of patriarch Job the Frontal place was "renovated from stone with fretwork, the doors were from iron rails"[76] already like divine services, and the church legend, which was not mentioned above by chance, told that from this place Sts.Sergius of Radonezh and Barlaam of Chutin during the religious procession of the Saints entreated the Saviour and the Most Holy Theotokos not to leave Moscow without their protection (the procession of 1521). In all town's religious processions the Frontal place was the symbol of salvation and the symbol of the Last Judgement. Such understanding of the Frontal place did not disappear with time. To this effect the intention of Moscow merchants testified at the beginning of the 19th century to install on the Frontal place under a canopy the carved wooden cross made by G.S.Shumaev[77]. During the religious processions the patriarch was always accompanied by

The Last Judgement. Fresco of the cathedral of the Assumption in Vladimir. A. Rublev.

the orthodox tsar and boyards to the Frontal place. Here, near the cathedral of the Holy Trinity (of the Intercession) the first rule of the procession was carried out with praying canons to the Holy Trinity and Archangels. The symbolic contents of the service at the Frontal place is shown by Russian spiritual poems with description of the beginning of the Last Judgement:

> *Then God's Angels will descend from the Heaven,*
> *They will bring down God's Throne to the earth*
> *As well as the Life-giving Cross,*
> *That they will install on the Frontal place,*
> *Where God suffered and was crucified*[78].

The coming of the Last Judgement was expressed by the authors of the poems as the religious procession of the Heavenly Regiments to the Frontal Place: "The Angelic Powers will come down from the Heaven, bringing the horrible token on the Throne, that is God's Cross, where He was crucified by Israelits, and the Angelic Regiments will stand around the Throne and trumpet in a frightening way; before them there will be a frightening thunder... and then bringing down God's Cross, they will install it on the place, where He suffered the crucifixion at His own will". The Heavenly procession was to be expressed by the religious procession from Frolovskie (Spasskie) gates: "They go to the Frontal place with gonfalons, sacramental fans, lanterns and crosses, then with images, also before the Patriarch they carry the installed cross on the plate and the Gospel on the podea, and in front of the image deacons walk with two candles, and archipriests, walking, sing irmoses eulogy prayers". "When they come to the Frontal place they install the icons like at the church choir place, the Vladimir icon of the Most Holy Theotokos is installed in the middle of the other icons, in front of it they read prayers and incense, the images that are usually installed in the altar are put behind it with the sacramental fans at both sides, the gonfalons stand at the Frontal place, they do not come up the Frontal place".

It was allowed only for patriarch or tsar to go up the Frontal place. "After coming to the Frontal place the Patriarch reads the first rule of prayers to the Holy Trinity and Archangels, then the ektinia and blesses with the cross to the four sides, the deacons sing "God be merciful to us!" three times at each blessing, then he blesses the tsar with the cross, sprinkles the holy water"[79]. At the tsar's blessing with the cross all who were present crossed themselves and bowed to the Frontal Place. This significant scene presented the image of the triumph at the Last Judgement, to which the orthodox tsar took the protected in the purity of rituals and belief Russian Church (the religious procession) and deliveries to the Saviour, the image of which was the patriarch.

If in the West they traditionally repeated on Good Friday the Via Dolorosa of the Saviour to the Calvary, the Moscow religious procession of the 17th century was all directed to the future, to the Heavenly Town and God's Throne, the image of which was the cathedral of the Holy Trinity (of the Intercession) and the Frontal place in Red Square.

Feast of the Entry of the Lord into Jerusalem. 1636. Drawing of A. Olearly.

Forty of Forties –
The Image of the Concluding Procession

*They have seen thy goings, o God;
even the goings of my God, my King, in the sanctuary.*
Psalm 67.

Patriarch Job transferred synods of priests into the forties. Forty priests were symbolically enough for synodal fullness of town's religious procession, and now the town's religious processions could be made by the forties in turn. It allowed to divide Moscow processions into big, average and small. In small processions one, two forties, in average processions – three or four forties, in big processions – all the forty of the forties took part. With time attitude to some regular processions changed, then they transferred from one category to another. For big, average and small processions in the cathedral of the Assumption in the Kremlin big, average and small gonfalons, crosses, censers and other utensils were specially kept. The names of the utensils for different processions were transferred even to the icons: "In the procession they carry the small gonfalon, small crosses, and the image of the Most Holy Theotokos, painted by St. Peter the Miracle-worker, is small, and they do not carry big miracle-working icons"[80]. "Big" is not referred here to the size of the icons, but to the type of the procession. Big Moscow religious processions began with two processions which gathered at Cathedral Square. Tsar's palace played the role similar to that of the palace of Byzantine emperors. The religious procession of the priests of palace churches was led by the tsar accompanied by boyards. The procession went out of the palace down to the square through the portal of the porch of the church of the Annunciation. From the cathedral of the Assumption the procession of priests of all Moscow cathedrals with the patriarch at the head went to meet it halfway. In the middle of Cathedral Square, in "the centre of the earth", patriarch blessed the tsar and the processions joined together and went again to the cathedral of the Assumption from where they went to the feast.[81] Historian Malinovsky, describing the utensils of the cathedral of the Assumption, informs: "Two zions, which were called jerusalems before, were both from silver... Both zions were brought out to religious processions: small was used in small processions, the big – in the big processions"[82].

Patriarch Job in the "Tale about Life of Theodore Ioannovich" noted "the beauty and majesty of all the reigning town, the big stone town's walls and gilded and wonderfully adorned divine churches and tsar's majestic and splendid two-roof and three-roof chambers"[83]. He compared Moscow figuratively with Heavenly Jerusalem, saying that tsar Boris Godunov "adorned the town splendidly and generously like a bride: he built plenty of wonderful stone churches and chambers which are amazing to look at"[84]. In the Revelation St.John says: "And I John saw the holy city, new Jerusalem, coming down from God out of heaven, prepared as a bride adorned for her husband"[85]. The patriarch could not speak more openly, because he was speaking about the sacrament of image, which appeared during town's divine service of "the reigning town" of Moscow.

In 1604 Patriarch Job ordered to all eight church forties to be in Moscow, which conformed to the symbolics of the Heavenly Town. It is not difficult to see in it the embodiment of the idea of the future triumph of Russian Church. The image of big Moscow procession, uniting eight forties, acquired the triumphant character of the image of the ideal Church. People began to call the synodal Moscow religious procession at once by the apt name "forty of forties". "Forty of forties" (the synaxis of forties) is the sacred image created by Russian people for the conclusive triumphant procession of the Heavenly and earthly Churches after their adjoinment at the Last Judgement, which was described many times in visions[86].

In 1591 by the procession around Bely town with the miracle-working Donskaya icon the attack of the Crimean khan Kazy-Guirey was precluded, for which tsar Theodore Ioannovich gratified the Most Holy Theotokos in front of Her Vladimir icon, calling Moscow "the lot of the property" of the Theotokos: "Thank You, Oh, the Most Holy Virgin Theotokos, the immutable Intercessor of Christians, as You have shown today Your great mercy to us! As You protected in ancient time the reigning town of Constantinople from the proudest Persian commandor Khozdroy, and as You protected the lot of Your property in ancient time, this reigning town from invasion of the evil-doing khan Temir-Aksak by the procession of Your Most Holy Icon, so today You showed to us Your great mercy and generosity. You saved us and our town gloriously and beyond hope from the invasion of the damned barbarian"[87]. In 1599 Patriarch Job and tsar Boris Godunov began the construction of the "new Jerusalem temple the Holy of the Holiest", according to the image of the biblical one, on the Kremlin's Ivanovskaya Square. From this grandiose project only the unfinished bell-tower of John the Great is left with the memorable inscription under the dome in the memory of the reign of Boris Godunov[88].

Processions of the Troubled Time

Ye that fear the Lord, bless the Lord. Blessed be the Lord out of Zion, which dwelleth at Jerusalem.
Psalm 134.

The Troubled Time, the trials of which were taken by moscovites as the punishment for unworthy behaviour and forgetting of Christ's testaments, gave outstanding examples of repentant religious processions in Moscow. On the 3rd of

The Heavenly Town. Miniature from the Cosmography of Cosmas Indikoplov.

June, 1606, the holy relicts of tsarevich Demetrius were met, which were brought from Uglich. "They went out to meet the Saint with life-giving crosses, candles and candle-stands, and the pious tsar and grand prince Basil Ioannovich (Shuysky) with all synod, as well as the mother of the Saint the pious tsarina Martha, all holy orders, all husbands and wives of the reigning town, young and old, where the monastery of the Meeting of the Lord is with the Vladimir icon of the Theotokos. After singing of proper prayers, the tsar was happy greatly about the coming of the Saint to his fatherland"[89]. "When the holy relicts were brought into the town and put on the divine place called the Frontal, a lot of miracles were granted to those who asked with belief... Then the holy relicts were brought to the church of Archangel Michael"[90]. On the 20th of February, 1607, on the holiday of the Triumph of Orthodoxy priests, deacons and parishioners of eight forties with their holy things gathered near the cathedral of the Assumption, where patriarchs Job and Germanus served the praying rite. From the amho archdeacon Olympius read on behalf of the people the petition to patriarch Job with confession and prayers, and then the absolutory chart of the hierarch. In turn the moscovites of all forties came with the absolution to the blessing of the patriarch and kissed his right hand.

On Sunday after the 22nd of October, 1612, "archimandrites, hegumens, all holy orders, all Christ-loving regiments, all orthodox people of boyard and commandor prince Demetrius Timofeevich Trubetskoy gathered in the church of the Kazan Icon of the Most Holy Theotokos behind Pokrovskie (of the Intercession) Gates, and commandors and warriors of prince Demetrius Mikhailovich Pozharsky gathered in the church of St.John the Merciful in Arbat. Taking the holy crosses and miracle-working icons they went to Kitay-

The meeting of tsar Michael Fedorovich. Miniature from "The Book of the Coronation of the Great Tsar and Grand Prince Michael Fedorovich". Fragment.

gorod followed by many warriors and people of Moscow state singing gratifying prayers to God. They all gathered at the Frontal place and served the praying... Archbishop Arsenius of Galasun went to the Frontal place with all holy synod carrying the miracle-working Vladimir icon of the Most Holy Theotokos and holy crosses and other divine icons... And singing prayers they went inside the Kremlin with great quantity of people"[91]. On the 2nd of May, 1613, a religious procession of moscovites went behind Troitskie gates to meet newly-elected tsar Michael Feodorovich Romanov. During the praying "innumerably many people with wives and children with happy tears and raised hands gratified God with all heart"[92].

On the 14th of June, 1619, a religious procession through Nikitskie gates behind Zemlyanoy town met metropolitanate Philaret, who was coming back from the Polish captivity. This event made such impression on people that they composed a historical song about it:

> *From the glorious stone town of Moscow*
> *Not the beautiful sun was rising,*
> *But the orthodox tsar went out*
> *To meet his father Hierarch Philaret Nikitich*[93].

Meeting each other the tsar and the metropolitanate bowed to the earth to each other. Soon metropolitanate Philaret was approved to be the patriarch and headed the gratifying religious procession to the Frontal place.

The meeting of the relicts of St.Demetrius, tsatevich. Icon of the 17th century.

The meeting of metropolitanate Philaret Nikitich with tsar Michael Fedorovich. Miniature from "The Book of the Coronation of the Great Tsar and Grand Prince Michael Fedorovich".

Spasskie Gates and the Image of the Entry of the Lord Jesus Christ Into Jerusalem

This gate of the Lord, into which the righteous shall enter.
Psalm 117

Enter into his gates with thanksgiving, and into his courts with praise.
Psalm 99[93]

Having coped with the consequences of Moscow ravages of the Troubled Time the Romanovs encountered difficult problems. How to continue extolment of Moscow, remaining faithful to the previous sacred idea, but to take into account the lessons of hard years. The construction in the centre of the Kremlin of the grandiose cathedral with the temple of the Holy Sepulchre, as patriarch Job and tsar Boris Godunov wanted, did not conform to the economic and political situation of that time. In the conditions of limited means it was required to make a new building, connected with town's divine service, of the first priority. They found out that the new is the well-forgotten old. In order to extol a town it is enough to extol the main fortress gates. It is possible to make out of town the image of temple, making Holy Gates out of the fortress ones. Temple's gates "are called the Tsar's (Holy) ones, because through them in the Holy Sacrament the King of Glory and the King of Kings passea"[94]. During town's divine services with religious processions through the Kremlin's Frolovskie gates the Saviour passed figuratively, so they should be made Spasskie (the Saviour's). The main content was reflected in the icon of the Saviour, reminding about the miracle of 1521: "The image was painted not on a board, but on the stone wall. The Saviour is shown standing. He blesses with His right hand, in the left hand He is holding the Gospel open on the words: "the Lord said to the Israelits who had come to Him: I am the Door". At both sides of the Saviour there are Sts.Sergius and Barlaam kneeling to Him, and above there are two angels, one with a cross in his hand, the other – with a spear. Above the image, in the triangle icon-case the Holy Life-giving Cross is painted with two Angels holding it"[95].

The above-gate icon from the inside part of the gates was not less important: "From the side of the Kremlin, above the passage, the Pechera icon of the Theotokos was painted. Above the head of the Theotokos the Vernicle was painted. At both sides of the Mother of God there are two great Moscow hierarchs Sts. Peter and Alexius. The Pechera icon shows the Theotokos on the throne installed on the ambo. On Her knees She is holding Jesus Christ, Who is blessing the praying. Already since the time of St.Alexius the Metropolitanate of Moscow this image was the seal of Moscow metropolitanates, and then of patriarchs. A chapel was built with the image of the Intercessor of Moscow hierarchs, which was painted on the wall, next to the domestic church of metropolitanates built in 1485, which was known as the church of Laying of the Chesuble of the Theotokos or the Laudation of the Theotokos. The icon revealed itself as miracle-working (it was liquidated during the Soviet time), miraculously protecting the temple from being destroyed in the 17th century, about which written collection of the 17th century informs: "There is the image of the Most Holy Theotokos of Pechera on the throne with Sts.Peter, Alexius, Sergius and Nicon, standing near by; on the wall painting on the church of the Laudation of the Theotokos, in front of the Western gates of the cathedral of the Assumption. There were many miracles from it, it did not allow the church to be destroyed, when it was built in 7187 (1679)". Placing the icon-intercessor of patriarchs and metropolitanates of Russia above the fortress gates made the town the symbol of patriarch's throne.

The Saviour's Town is the Heavenly Town, the Paradise. So the interior part of the arches were painted with floral ornament – the image of "paradisical garden".

At the border of the 16th-17th centuries Frolovskie gates were a high square fortress tower, crowned with a small wooden tower four-slope hip roof. On the order of patriarch Philaret Nikitich and tsar Michael Fedorovich in 1674-1625 Cristopher Galovey and Bazhen Ogurtsov built on top of the existing square tower a cube, in the centre of which there was a pillar finished by an octahedral hip roof. The place of the additionally built cube is marked with a white stone ribbon. At this section twelve windows begin, three ones at each side, which fully conform to the description of Heavenly Jerusalem, which also has the form of a cube.

On Spasskaya tower the walls of "the Heavenly Town" are finished with flame-like arches; – ancient symbols of heavenly powers. There are also white stone lions here – the symbols of regal souls in the paradise. The central pillar symbolized the Throne of God Almighty in the Heavenly Kingdom. It is characteristic that above it there was the same canopy like above the tsar's place, for example, the place of John the Terrible in the cathedral of the Assumption. The image of the "Eight age", i.e. the Heavenly Kingdom and God's Throne, was the octahedral hip roof. As the Saviour is the Lord of time, at the foundation of the central tower a clock was made. It is interesting to note that in the clock of the 17th century from the top, from the sun, an immovable ray-hand came down. Ray usually symbolized the Descent of the Holy Spirit on icons. It was the clockface that moved around – which was the image of the Universe.

Archdeacon Paul Aleppskiy informs of the important details in 1655, which make to remember Godunov's project: "Above the gates there is a huge tower, built highly on stable foundation, on which a wonderful town's iron clock was famous in the whole world for its beauty and design and for the loud sound of its big bell... At the celebration of this Christmas, because of devil's envy, the squared timber inside the clock caught fire, and the whole tower was on fire together with the clock, the bells and all their accessories, which during the fall ruined by their heavy weight two vaults made from brick and stone... And when the tsar (Alexius Mikhailovich – *G.R.*) looked at a distance at this wonderful burnt tower, the adornments and the weathervanes of which were disfigured and tile various and skillfully fretted

"Paradisical" painting of Spasskie Gates of the Kremlin. Drawing. The 19th century.

stone statues fell down, he cried a lot"⁹⁶. According to the information of deacon John Timofeev tsar Boris Godunov planned the construction of the cathedral "the Holy of the Holiest", adorned with golden statues of twelve angels. It is possible to see the Angels on the gates of the Heavenly Town, for example, in the creation of Shumaev. So, it is possible that the cathedral of Godunov also was to represent the image of the Heavenly Town, crowned with images of twelve angels in twelve gates.

I.E.Zabelin comments: "It is curious, that among the figures and balusters, which still adorn Spasskaya Tower, as the archdeacon mentioned, there were also skillfully made statues, which were mentioned in domestic evidences too. In 1624, on the 6th of October, on the order of tsar Michael Fedorovich outdoor clothes were made for four statues, for which 12 arshins of English broad-cloth of different colours were used; and these statues shall be, as it is said in the entry, on Frolovskie gates. Thus, these statues were, probably, installed at four corners of the gates already during the first arrangement of the tower according to the idea of Golovey. However, according to the Russian tradition they were dressed in broadcloth caftans (long tunics with waist-girdle), probably, with the idea to hide their idol-like appearance and make them look like alive people"⁹⁷. As the symbol was, as we understand, the cube of the Heavenly World, the four figures in the corner arches, cried over by Alexius Mikhailovich, were to be the symbols of the Evangelists (such compositions adorn Gospels). From far distance it was difficult to distinguish the stone sculptures from the surrounding arches, and in order to make the symbolically important statues more vivid they were dressed in coloured clothes, and not because the statues had been made without clothes as some scientists stated.

It was important that the primary finishing of Spasskaya Tower had the State Emblem of the "reigning town of Moscow", fixed by Meierberg: a double-headed eagle in two crowns with St.Hierormartyr George on the chest is holding the Calvary, above which from a big crown an eight-end Cross rises.

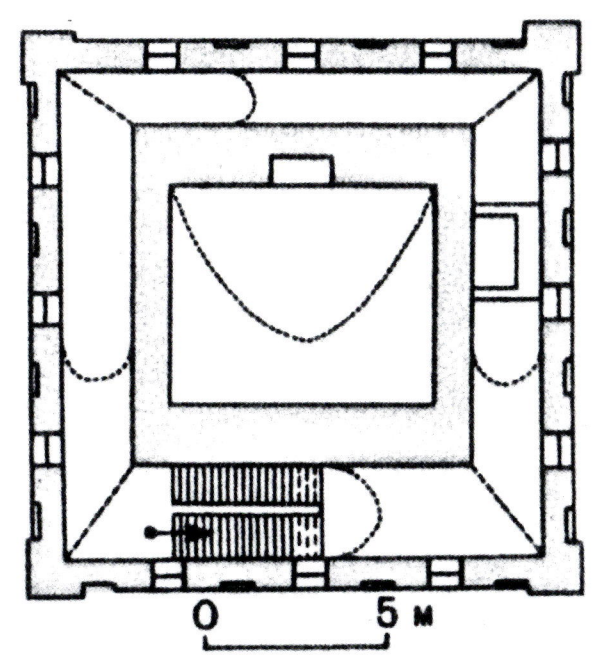

It is undeniable that the outstanding construction was to be in the centre of town's divine services. That is why the significance of one of the main Moscow church holidays, the Entry of the Lord

The plan of the fifth tier of Spasskaya Tower with 12 gates – symbol of the Heavenly Town.

Adornment of Spasskaya Tower. 1624

Spasskaya Tower. Miniature front "The Book of the Coronation of the Great Tsar and Grand Prince Michael Fedorovich". Fragment.

Clock of Spasskaya Tower. 1662. Drawing of Meierburg.

into Jerusalem, is even bigger. The reason for the new architectural accent of the town's ensemble of Moscow can be the idea that the feast of the Entry of the Heavenly King into Jerusalem was related to the transfiguration of the Romanovs into the tsar's dynasty chosen by God. For better fullness of the image of "the King of kings and the Lord of the reigning" it was shown both by the tsar and the patriarch in holiday clothes. The entry of tsar Michael Feodorovich and patriarch Philaret Nikitich by the painted with paradisical floral ornament Spasskie gates into Jerusalem meant that the Romanovs had been chosen by God as the royal family. The entry was shown by the Romanovs as the visual sign of the mysteriously inspired God's selection, because in conformity with God's will Michael Feodorovich had been elected unanimously and Philaret Nikitich was approved to be the patriarch in conformity with God's choice by patriarch Theophanes of Jerusalem, who happened to be in Moscow, to the effect of which patriarch Philaret wrote to the other patriarchs: of Constantinople, Alexandria and Antioch. Gradual changes in the rule of the service on Palm Sunday in the 17th century are connected with this circumstance too.

As the colleagues of the mission of the duke Johansen, the prince of Denmark, testify in 1603 "the procession on the donkey" of patriarch Job was not much different from the rite established by metropolitanate Macarius, though at that time it also made such impression in quantity and brightness that foreigners in 1605 called Frolovskie gates the gates of Jerusalem. When the procession went back before it tsarevich Theodore Borisovich went, "holding a bunch of willow; from time to time he broke a branch and threw it on the road... The tsar went two steps further before the patriarch's horse, having bound tile string round the left hand, in the right hand he was carrying the sceptre, and in the left hand he had the usual regal staff"[98]. After the building of the additional superstructure of Spasskaya Tower the culmination moment of the triumph was transferred by the Romanovs from the temple of the Entry of the Lord into Jerusalem to the Frontal place, where the above-said rites of big religious procession had been already served. "In 1636 on Red Square wooden columns were upholstered with red cloth from the Frontal place to the bridge, which leads to Spasskie gates"[99]. The procession in 1636 of patriarch Ioasaph and tsar Michael Feodorovich was described by Adam Oleariy. "In front of everything they were carrying a tree, on which apples, dates and raisins were hung... then priests followed in white expensive ephods, they were carrying gonfalons, crosses and icons, installed on long poles, and sang; some of them were with censers with which they were incensing towards people... The tsar was walking dressed in rich

Angels at the gates of the Heavenly Town. Fragment of the cross. The 18th century. G.S.Shumaev.

Eagle. Emblem of Moscow made on top of Spasskaya Tower. 1662. Drawing of Meierberg.

clothes and with the crown on his head. He was supported by two most noble tsar's councils, by prince John Borisovich Cherkasskiy and prince Alexius Mikhailovich Ljvov. The tsar himself was leading the patriarch's horse by a long string. The horse was covered with a horse-cloth, with long ears like the donkey's. The patriarch was sitting sideways, he wore a white round hat adorned with very big pearls and on top of it there was also a crown. In the right hand he held a golden Cross adorned with precious stones and blessed people were crowding around. At these blessings people bowed and prayed crossing themselves"[100]. After a short praying in the church of the Entry of the Lord into Jerusalem the Patriarch went to the Frontal place, from where blessed the tsar and people with the cross. Then the procession entered through Spasskie gates.

In future years they tried to increase even more the significance of the procession from the Frontal place through Spasskie gates. For this the procession "on the donkey" was carried out only from the Frontal place to the cathedral of the Assumption. The Frontal place was arranged beforehand with rich velvet and cloth, near by a willow was installed – "a big tree adorned with artificial green leaves, flowers and fruit: apples, pears, raisins, dates, figs and even nuts"[101]. The procession from the cathedral of the Assumption was carried out as usual: "The procession stopped near tile cathedral of the Intercession, facing the East. The tsar and patriarch went into the altar of the Entry of the Lord into Jerusalem. The tsar was accompanied at that time only by the people of the highest ranks, the others stopped at both sides of the Frontal place. The tsar put on regal clothes at the porch of the cathedral: the cross, diadem, tsar's cap etc. Instead of the staff, which he used during the procession, he was given tsar's crosier forged with gold"[102]. This action allowed to include into the rite of the procession the sending by the patriarch from the Frontal place of two people after the donkey and reading of the conversations of the Saviour with the disciples, and the reading of the Gospel was announced by the archdeacon, and the patriarch only pronounced the words of Jesus Christ. The procession from the Frontal place got the character of the procession from the Mount of Olives. "Coming to Spasskie gates, the patriarch stopped before the icons of the Saviour and the Theotokos, painted on the gates, and read the prayer about the town. At that time the chime sounded both in the Kremlin and in all Moscow"[103]. It is surprising that in Moscow of the middle of the 17th century the entry into the sacred Spasskie gates acquired the image of the Entry into the Heavenly Town during the Last Judgement. Such symbol was vaguely reflected in all religious pro-

cessions through Spasskie gates, but on Palm Sunday this symbol was brighter and more complete. When the procession stopped in front of the gates all who were on Red Square fell down on the knees and all was quiet. The orthodox tsar in feast clothes led the saved Church in the person of the patriarch into the Holy Gates of the Heavenly Town, about which all Moscow bells announced immediately and joyfully.

Transfiguration of Moscow into the image of Jerusalem, which happened during the town's services at the time of the Romanovs' reign, was even clearer due to the arrangement in the cathedral of the Assumption of the image of the Holy Sepulchre inside a forged chamber, into which soon the acquired in Persia God's Chesuble was laid. "When a few days later after tile image of the Holy Sepulchre had been arranged the ambassador from Persia arrived in Moscow and presented the tsar with the miracle-working Chesuble of the Saviour Jesus Christ"[104].

"The Town of Moscow" in Ecumenical Processions

You protect the town of Moscow, venerating You, the Saviour, and in long prayers glorifying You, the Most Merciful.

The service to God's Chesuble

During more than 40 years Spasskaya Tower was the only one from additionally built Kremlin's towers, being the image of the Tsar's (Holy) Gates of the fortress-temple during the divine services. The statement about its renaming into Spasskaya in 1658 is not correct. For example, the decree of 1654 already called it Spasskaya. By the decree of 1658 tsar Alexius Mikhailovich forbade the use of other names of many fortress gates, except those connected with the Heavenly protection[105]. All passage towers of Moscow fortresses were consecrated to the Heavenly protection. For this on the outside wall, and very often on the inside one, on-gate protecting icon was placed. Paul Aleppskiy informed: "There are more than 15 gates in the White wall, which are called according to the names of different icons, which are installed on them. All these on-gate icons have a wide round tent from copper and tin for protection from rain and snow. There is an icon-lamp in front of each icon which is lowered and raised by a rope; the candles are lighted by streljtsy, who stand near each gate with guns and other weapon"[106]. The icon-lamps were burning day and night, and the holy images indicated the way in darkness.

In 1621 from the week of All Saints till the week before the Adoration of the Holy Cross 15 Sunday evening religious processions were made by Moscow forties to the cathedral of the Assumption. From the cathedral of tile Assumption, according to approximate data, 36 regular religious processions were carried out on church feasts before the liturgy. From them 17 were held inside the Kremlin, 12 went through Spasskie Gates and served the religious rite at the Frontal place, 3 went through Troitskie Gates and 2 – through Tayninskie (Water) Gates. To them the religious processions should be added which were connected with some event, for example with sending troops to war.

The religious procession presented a praying, divided into rites. While walking they were singing complines to the Holy Trinity, the Theotokos, Archangels or Saints, Who were commemorated in pairs during each rite. During singing the compline at each stop the corresponding Gospel was read, the request was said accompanied by incensing and the hierarch said the final prayer with cross blessing, thus the rite was over. The Saints, mentioned during the rites, were chosen in connection with the event, as well as with the place where the procession stopped near the church or town's gates. Depending on the duration Moscow religious procession contained from one to seven rites. When the procession went out into the street all bell began to ring and finished it when the procession left it. The procession stopped near each church or monastery, the hierarch kissed the icon or the cross, which were brought out of the church, blessed people with the cross and sprinkled with holy water. At the final point of the procession, "in the monastery the hierarch is met by the hegumen with brothers near the Holy Gates with chime, the priest with the cross and the deacon with the censer. The hierarch prays in front of the gates and says: the final prayer, the parish prayer according to the rule, during the prayer mentions the Saints of his temples and of this monastery and temples, and blesses himself, the authorities, the monastery's hegumen, the priests and deacons, who are in ephods, with the cross and tile brothers he blesses with his hand. And then he enters into the monastery"[107]. If at the head of a religious procession the patriarch was, then when it came back through Red Square he rose again on the Frontal place and blessed people with the cross. As it was mentioned above, the entry of the procession through Spasskie Gates finalized symbolically the history of the world showing the entry of tile righteous into the Heavenly Town.

The processions around Moscow fortresses had most of the rites. The Kremlin with Kitay-gorod were passed around on the feast of Mid-Pentecost, Bely town – always on the day of All Saints and sometimes on the day of St.Prophet Elijah or of the Meeting of the Vladimir icon of the Theotokos. Since 1660, on the 22nd of October, the feast of the Kazan icon of the Theotokos, the procession went along the walls of the Kremlin and Kitay-gorod, Belytown and Zemlyanoy town. At the gates the religious procession stopped. In front of the on-gate icon they carried out either the rite of the religious procession, or the praying about the town. In the second case the hierarch read a short prayer with a request about the town to the Holy image. During the singing of prayers the on-gate icons, gates passages and cannons were sprinkled with holy water.

In the 17th century establishments of Russian eparchs in the Kremlin's cathedral of the Assumption were finished by religious processions around Moscow fortresses. According to people's idea, the eparchs, who had just been established or already finishing their priestly service, had most of God's bliss. So moscovites always tried to get the blessing from a just ordained hierarch. For the same reason the towns of Moscow domain got support of Divine protection by the blessing of newly ordained patriarchs, metropolitanate, archbishops and bishops. Accompanied by deacons, boyards and streltsy newly ordained eparchs, sitting on the "donkey" and holding the Gospel and the cross, on the first day rode around the Kremlin and Kitay-gorod, on the second day – Bely town, on the third – Zemlyanoy town[108].

In 1636 Adam Oleariy described the religious procession on Red Square on the 22nd of October to the newly built cathedral of the Kazan Icon of the Most Holy Theotokos. Before the procession the square had been swept. Plenty of sellers offered wax candles. At the head of the procession three red and white banners were carried. After 4 round images of cherubs the eparch's icon-lamp was carried. A huge cross with orbs at the ends was carried by 8 priests. 100 priests and monks were carrying icons. The big Kazan icon of the Theotokos was carried covered with a cloth by two priests for the sake of sacrament. After the silver cross adorned with diamonds, which was carried on the dish four people of patriarch's choir followed. The patriarch walked in feast vestments under a blue canopy supported by two metropolitanates. In front of him two big candles were carried. Tsar Michael Feodorovich walked under a red canopy supported by the most noble boyards. At the end of the procession the tsar's red chair was carried.

During the reign of Theodore Alexeevich the town-building ensemble of Red Square was finished by building of the main Holy Gates of Kitay-gorod. "There are two passage gates in Kitay-gorod built again, which were named before as Neglinskie, they must be named now and always as Voskresenskie, not Neglinskie"[109]. By this name Red Square was officially recognized as the place of symbolic triumph of the Resurrection at the coming of the Last Judgement. Two hip roofs of Voskresenskie (Resurrection) gates were symbolic eparch's double crossed candles of the Great Eparch Jesus Christ inviting to the Great service on Red Square. Above the passage of Voskresenskie gates there was the icon of the Resurrection. It is interesting to note that the image of the Last Judgement as the patronizing image of Moscow was repeated outside the last passage gates of Moscow built in the 17th century. In 1692 it was placed above the passage arch of Sukharevskaya tower.

During the last third part of the 17th century worldly splendour first unnoticeable, then more and more vividly began to prevail over the spiritualness of religious processions. The Council of 1667 adopted the decision that in Moscow there would be six forties of priests, coming out only of the quantity of priests and not following the symbolic grounds. At the time of Theodore Alexeevich hierarchy of boyards clothes was introduced for church feasts. On the main church feasts and big religious processions boyards were to

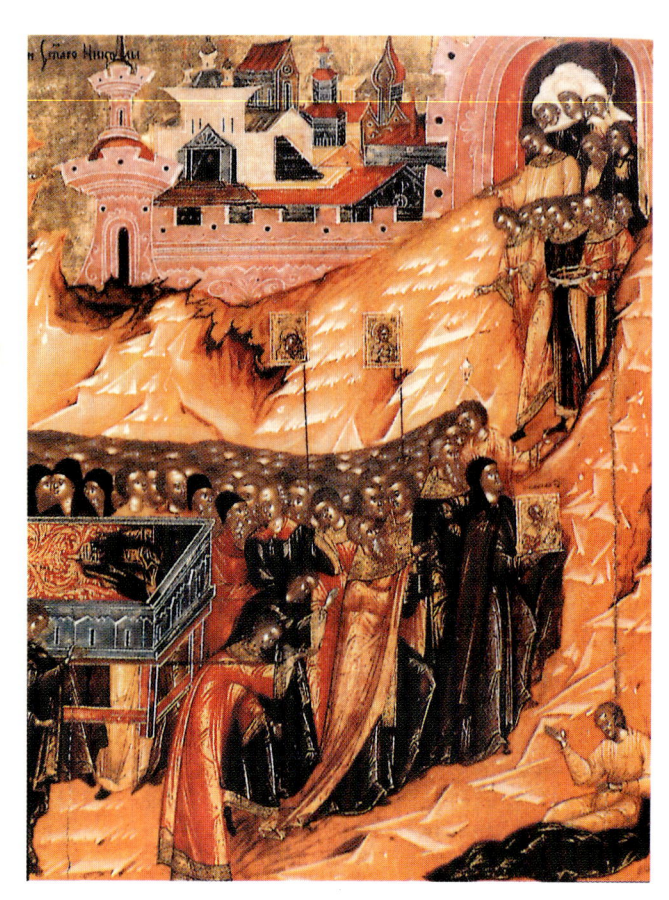

Meeting of eparch's religious procession in the monastery. Icon fragment. The 18th century.

put on golden clothes, on average ones -"velvet", and on the other feasts and Sundays – clothes from silk or moire. The brilliant procession of boyards sometimes eclipsed priests with icons. In 1680 sanctifying of banners with holy water turned out to be a continuous military parade of troops of different kind at the Moscow-river, which took more time than the religious procession on the day of Epyphany. During the rites on Cathedral Square and the Moscow-river the tsar's place was substituted by a complicated colourful construction with five mica cupolas and windows. After 1682 the rite of the Last Judgement was stopped. In 1689 tsar Peter I stopped the rite on Palm Sunday. After death of Patriarch Adrian in 1700 the symbolics of Moscow religious processions as of ecumenigal service ceased to exist.

"It is Common Knowlege That the Earth Begins From the Kremlin"

> *When the Son of man shall come in his glory, and all the holy angels with him, then shall he sit upon the throne of his glory: and before him shall be gathered all nations.*
> The Gospel according to St. Matthew, 25. 31-32.

That was already the ancient Russian capitals Kiev, Vladimir and Novgorod that were looking for the grounds to present Russian land as sacred for Christians. In the 15th century the taking of Constantinople by Turks (1435), final liberation from the Tatar-Mongolian yoke (1480) and the coming of "the eighth thousand" from the creation of the world (1492) defined the theological idea of Russia, partially known under the name "Moscow – the Third Rome". In it Moscow is considered to be the last third capital of the fourth ecumenical kingdom of the world's history, prophecied in the Bible. Russia's eschatologic task was to keep orthodox belief and Church up to the Last Judgement, the coming of which was constantly expected during the "eighth thousand" of years. From here comes the peculiarity of the Russian idea about the Second Advent of Christ, from the conviction that for keeping the Church, founded by Christ Himself as for their main deed on the earth, the righteous shall get the reward of triumphant entry into the Heavenly Town. From the end of the 15th century Moscow town-building was closely connected with town's services. Both were devoted to the proving of Russia's worthiness to be the last orthodox kingdom and the image of the coming Last Judgement.

Tsar John III Vasilievich was to build the cathedrals, palace and fortress according to the sample of Constantinople. However it was not by chance that the Kremlin's Frolovskie gates were built urgently right by 7000 from the creation of the world, because in that year the Advent of Christ was expected. It makes to see in Frolovskie gates both new Golden Gates of Constantinople and the image of gates of the Heavenly Town, through which the righteous will enter, which had already vaguely appeared. Grand prince John III Vasilievich established the celebrations of the New Year on the 1st of September, the Entry of the Lord into Jerusalem and the Last Judgement as town's divine services with religious procession on Cathedral Square of the Kremlin. For such rites Cathedral Square was arranged as an ambo of the temple-Universe.

Basil III Ioannovich continued the construction of the Third Rome, using work of Italian architects. The Kremlin with newly-built Kitay-gorod was understood from the beginning as similar to medieval Palestine Jerusalem, which became wider in comparison to the time of Christ's Via Dolorosa. So in the 16th-18th centuries the Kremlin together with Kitay-gorod always comprised necessarily one church forty, though in the quantity of priests it sometimes exceeded several others taken together.

The coronation of John IV Vasilievich allowed metropolitanate Macarius to create the rites and rituals of the system of the annual town's divine service of seven cathedrals of Moscow, directed at glorifying of the ecumenical tsar of the last ages. Canonization of a big quantity of Russian Saints and the miraculous help from the icons of the Most Holy Theotokos in different towns of Russia allowed to speak about Moscow state as about "the property of the Most Holy Theotokos" and Russia of Saints, which quickly changed in people's consciousness into Holy Russia. Taking into consideration the idea of salvation of the Church by orthodox kingdom, metropolitanate Macarius and tsar John IV built the cathedral of the Holy Trinity (of the Intercession) on Red Square as the image of the Heavenly Town, the mysterious sign in the shape of the star of the Most Holy Theotokos, sanctifying from the centre of the world all the Universe. It was established to carry out religious processions on the feasts of the Entry of the Lord into Jerusalem and the Intercession. The images of the Second Advent of Christ influenced all the activity of tsar John the Terrible. According to research of historian Yurganov, even oprichnina (military units) of John the Terrible was an effort to create an unusual image of the Last Judgement in space and time, in which he assumed the role of the image of the Judge.

Tsar Theodore Ioannovich built another fortress around Moscow – Bely town, according to the documents of the 16th century – "Tsar-town". The name reflected the merit of "the reigning town of Moscow" as the capital of the last orthodox kingdom. The religious procession around Tsar-town with Patriarch Job at the head was the request to God "about peace in the whole world".

The project of Patriarch Job and tsar Boris Godunov of construction in the Kremlin of the cathedral of "the Holy of the Holiest" with the Holy Sepulchre was not realized. They only managed to build the bell-tower of John the Great and the stone Frontal place. The rite at the Frontal place during each big religious procession with the reading of the Gospel to "the Holy Trinity and Archangels" became the commemoration of the coming scene from the Last Judgement, where the orthodox tsar gave to the Lord in the image of the patriarch the kept Church and received the blessing with a cross.

Patriarch Philaret Nikitich and tsar Michael Feodorovich built in 1624 a superstructure on Spasskaya Tower of the Kremlin consecrating it to the Saviour. On the on-gate icon the Saviour holds the Gospel open on the words: "the Lord said to the Israelits who had come to Him: "I am the door". Through Christ like through Spasskie Gates the righteous will enter into the Heavenly Kingdom. The significance of the Entry of the Lord into Jerusalem increased. The entry of the tsar and patriarch through Spasskie Gates showed the cherished image of the Last Judgement: the orthodox tsar in feast clothes presented the salved Church in the person of patriarch into the Holy Gates of the Heavenly Town.

Tsar Alexius Mikhailovich built superstructures on the other Kremlin's towers. On the cover of the personal copy of the Bible of Alexius Mikhailovich Moscow was depicted as New Jerusalem, and the tsar himself – as the defender of Orthodoxy. During the celebration of the Entry of the Lord into Jerusalem Red Square was adorned and arranged like a temple under the open sky. On the Frontal place covered with velvet, a lectern with icons were installed, the patriarch with archdeacons read the feast Gospel. The cathedral of the Holy Trinity (the Intercession) was transferred into an altar, and Spasskie Gates – into the Holy Gates of the temple. In 1680 tsar Theodore Alexeevich finalized the ensemble of Red Square with building the superstructure on two-hip-roof Voskresenskie gates. This temple was consecrated to the Resurrection during Christ's Second Advent. Two hip roofs of the gates like eparch's two long crossed candles invite the Great Eparch Jesus Christ to carry out the Last Judgement.

From the end of the 15th century till the beginning of the 18th century eschatologic expectations defined all the organization of life of Russian people. Prince Kurbskiy in his correspondence with John IV calls: "Let us raise our heads to the Living in the Heaven, from where we expect Him, our Saviour, for our salvation is coming... for the time of revenge is close". John the Terrible in his turn, as the ground of the oprichnina, quotes the prophecy of St. Isaiah about the last time, for instance: "During the last time the mount of God's house will be put at the head of the mounts and will tower above the hills, all the peoples will come to it. And many peoples will come and say, come and rise to the mount of God, into the house of Jacob's God, He will teach us His ways, we shall follow His ways; for from the Zion the testament will come, and God's Word – from Jerusalem". Metropolitanate Macarius during drinking the "cup for health" prayed for "the long-year health and salvation" at the coming Last Judgement of tsar John IV.

Synodics of the end of the 16th century taught negligent priests: "Such are not priests, but hirelings and bribetakers, who will dare to say to God on the day of the Last Judgement: These are my children, but who do not pray properly for their souls". Abraham Palitsyn cried for Moscow burnt in 1611 like for burnt earthly Jerusalem, which was predicted for the time of implementation of Apocalyptic events. Without knowing the eschatologic idea of Moscow kingdom even the name of old-believers (staroobryadtsy) can not be understood fully. Being in opposition to patriarch Nicon, they believed that, if not to keep old rituals, in which they saw embodiment of the Church, there will be nothing to give to the Judge Jesus Christ at the Last Judgement for justification of Russian people. But patriarch Nicon also believed it necessary to the Church to God with the initially established rituals, and those were Greek rituals according to Nicon's opinion. In New Jerusalem near Moscow built by him he also got ready for the coming Last Judgement, to the effect of which he left the inscription: "Today He will resurrect me from the dead too, by the Holy Spirit He will recreate me and make me new; He will give us, according to God's will, a blissful builder and teacher, who will die and resurrect in Christ too; thanks God forever, amen".

Together with this official state documents do not contain direct indications of theological grounds of Moscow construction. But they are not to be there, because Moscow authorities and church hierarchs addressed God, not descendants in their deeds. The construction connected with the town's service was a certain praying, request to God about realization of the cherished plans and about granting of bliss through God-like images. Infringement of the church "rule about secrecy" would have ruined all hopes. Receipt of divine bliss as the highest ideal of piety should be concealed. (Thus, mercy as the image of God's bliss should be concealed). In order to keep the blissful concealed power the main miracle-working icons both in Byzantium

Religious procession with the miracle-working Kazan icon of the Theotokos. 1636. Olearius.

and Russia were carried during religious processions under podea and opened only at stops at implementation of the rite of the procession.

The custom of closing the image possessing Divine bliss explains the rule about the title of abbreviation: "Title of abbreviation shall be written above God's and the Theotokos' names; all Christ's divine names and those of the Theotokos, St.John the Predecessor, St. Prophets, Apostles, hierarchs, martyrs hierarchs, saints, righteous, blissful, blessed, pious tsars and tsarinas, princes, princesses, eparchs, bishops, priests, teachers. Passions of Saints and all and any holy name shall be written in concealed way; so any fallen name shall be written fully and openly, which are: fallen angels, false apostles, false prophets, evil spirit, antichrist with his predecessor, evil-minded tsars, teachers, priests, gods, churches with idols, passions which are casualties and the like". If the concealed power of bliss must be kept and protected, the negative essence must be revealed to God's light, disclosed and evident to everybody, thus weakening the evil power living in it.

Moscow town's divine service and town-building ensemble of Moscow centre of the second half of the 17th century represented together a surprisingly interesting phenomenon of Russian orthodox culture, which created unique spiritual and artistic images of the Resurrection during the Second Advent of our Lord Jesus Christ in the centre of the world at the Frontal place. The blissful beauty of the symbolic centre of the Universe warmed people's soul for a long time. Being put aside into depths of social consciousness, it suddenly breaks through in the poems of the poet of the 20th century who was very far from Christianity V.V.Mayakovckiy, which were written above in the title. But the most surprising is that millions of Russian children now also comprehend these lines as a norm, without any explanations from adults.

1. Kudriavtsev M.P. Moscow – the Third Rome. M., 1994, p.173-230
2. The same, p. 196-224.
3. PSRL, v. XIII, p. 251.
4. Snegirev V.L. Monument of Architecture St.Basil's cathedral. M., Stroyizdat,1953, p.32.
5. The other name of this icon "The Blessed Regiment...", 1552-1553, Collection GTG.
6. Sobolev N.N. Project of Reconstruction of the Architectural Monument – St. Basil's Cathedral in Moscow// Architecture of the USSR, 1377, No. 2, p. 42-48.
7. Kapitokhin A.A., Yakovlev I.V. The Cathedral of the Intercession (St.Basil's Cathedral). M., 1970, p. 3, 16.
8. By the word "the Sitting" St. Apostle John defines tile Holy Trinity. Already after the analysis of the essence of the symbolics of the number of cathedral's cupolas documentary confirmation of gildering of the figured cupolas was published. See Kapitokhin A.A., Yakovieva I.V. (73).
9. Zabelin I.E. Home Life of Russian Tsars in 16th and 17th Centuries, part 1. 2nd Issue, supplimented. M., 1872, p. 349-354.
10. Apocalypse, 21; 22.
11. Georgievskiy G.P. Feast Divine Services in Ancient Moscow. M., 1896.
12. Collection of Akathists. T. 1. M., 1993, p. 4.
13. Fast Trinily Service of the beginning of XVth Century. RGB, F. 178, m. 3143, 11. 235-236. Quotation according to: Karabinov I. Fast Trinity Service. Spb., 1910, p.39.
14. Byzantine Historians. V. 4. Nicetas Honiat. SPb., 1860, p. 496-497.
15. Benjamin (Krasnopevkov). The New Testimony. T. 2, SPb., 1899, p.464.
16. Life of St.Peter the Metropolitanate of Moscow. PSRL. V. XXI. Part 2, p.404-424.
17. Benjamin. The above works. V. 2., p. 302.
18. Golubinskiy E.E. History of Russian Church. V. 2, semi-volume 1. M., 1900, p. 151.
19. Poselyanin E. The Theotokos. Full Illustrated Description of Her Earthly Life and the Miracle-Working Icons Consecrated to Her. SPb., reprint: Kiev, 1994, p. 234.
20. Legend of Ancient Chronicle Stories about the Miracle-Working Image of the Most Holy Theotokos, called "of the Don"... RGADA, f. 181, op.1, part. 1, d. 327, 1. 5.
21. PSRL. V. XXIV, p. 151-154.
22. Golubinskiy E.E. The above works. V. 2, semi-volume 1. M., 1900, p.333.
23. PSRL. V. VIII, p. 67.

24 Ambrose (Ornatskiy). History of Russian Hierarchy. V. VI. M., 1815, p. 290.
25 Golubinskiy E.E. The above works. V. 2, semi-volume 1, p. 333.
26 Prayer-book. H., 1658, p. 30.
27 Golubinskiy E.E. The above works. V. 2, semi-volume 1, p. 334.
28 PSRL, V. VIII, p. 74-75.
29 Ambrose. The above works, V. V, p. 447-450.
30 PSRL, V. VIII, p. 144-145.
31 Poselyanin E. The above works, p. 451.
32 The Rite-book of the Moscow Cathedral of the Assumption and Processions of Patriarch Nicon. Edited by Golubtsov A.P. M., 1909, p.8-9.
33 Historical and Archaeological Description of the Church of the Rzhev Icon of the Theotokos near Prechistenskie Gates. M. 1888.
34 The Main Inventory of Sretenskiy Monastery of 1908. TsIAM.f. 1184, op. 2, l.223.
35 Tatitschev V.N. History of Russia. V. VI. M.-L., 1966, p. 118.
36 Levshin A.G. Historical Description of the Main Russian Cathedral of the Assumption in Moscow... M., 1783, p. 261.
37 Poselyanin E. The above works, p. 94.
38 Pilgrimage of Stephan Novgorodets. Memorials of Literature of Ancient Russia. Book 4, M., 1981, p. 34.
39 Poselyanin E. The above works, p. 102.
40 PSRL. V. III, p. 239.
41 Levshin A.G. The above works, p. 116.
42 Bulanin D.M. Translations and Messages of Maximus the Greek. Not-published texts, L., 1984, p. 158.
43 Nikolskiy K.T. About the Services of Russian Church, Which were in the Previous Printed Books for Divine Service. SPb, 1885, p. 74.
44 Quotation acc.to: Kartashev A.V. Essays on the History of Russian Church. YMCA-PRESS.Paris, 1959, M., 1991. V. 1, p. 369.
45 Ambrose. History of Church Hierarchy. Scripture. TsIAM, f. 421, op. 1, d.7757, 1. 236.
46 PSRL. V. XXIII, p. 155.
47 PSRL. XXIII, p. 157-159.
48 PSRL. XXIII, p. 158.
49 Big Orthodox Theologic Encyclopidic Dictionary. SPb, 1913. M., 1992, V. 1-2, p. 269.
50 Kartashev A.V. The above works. V. 1, p. 389.
51 PSRL. V. XIII, p. 46.
52 Memorials of Literature of Ancient Russia. Book 4, p. 28-41.
53 Mayasova N.A. Medieval Embroidery. M., 1991, p. 60.
54 Church Rites. M. 1630. GIM. p. 9.
55 Prayer-book. M. 1624, L. 681-687.
56 Church Rites. X. 1630. p. 14.
57 Prayer-book. M. 1624, l. 681-687
58 Kartasilev A.V. The above works. V. 1, p. 440.
59 Church Rites of Moscow cathedral of the Assumption... p. 115.
60 As above, p. 117.
61 Jeremiah. About the Great God's and Theotokos' Feasts. Kiev 1835, p.84-87.
62 Gornostaev F.F. Essay of Moscow Ancient Architecture//Travel Book around Moscow, published by Moscow Architectural Society for the members of Vth congress of architects in Moscow. Editted by Mashkov I.P., M., 1913, p.LVI- LVIII.
63 Lebedev L. Patriarchate Moscow. M., 1955, p. 299-350.
64 Brunov N.I. St.Basil's Cathedral in Moscow. The Cathedral of the Intercession. M., 1988, p. 217-219.
65 Batalov A.L., Vyatchinina T.N. Role and Significance of Jerusalem Sample in Russian Architecture of XVIth-XVIIth Centuries//Architectural Inheritance. No. 36. M., 1988, p. 26.
66 Uvarov A.S. Collection of Small Works. V. 1, M., 1910, p. 67-68.
67 Soboirva N.A. Russian Prints. M., 1991, p. 210-214.
68 Bulgakov S.V. Table Book of a Priest.M., reprint, 1993, p. 631.
69 Psalms. 89.
70 Memorials of Literature of Ancient Russia. Book 8, M., 1986, p. 554.
71 Malinin V.N. Elder Philotheus of Eleazaroc Monastery and His Messages. Kiev, 1901, p. 524.
72 Kartashev A.V. Recreation of Holy Russia. Paris 1956. M., 1991, p. 32-39.
73 Pokrovskiy N.V. The Last Judgement in the Memorials of Byzantine and Russian Art. Odessa, 1887, p. 53.
74 Dove Book: Russian Folk Spiritual Poems of XIth-XIXth centuries, M., 1991, p. 244.
75 Brandes V. Byzantine Apocaliptic Literature as the Sourse of Study of Some Aspects of Social History//Byzantine Time Table. V. 50. M., 1989, p. 116-122.
76 PSRL. V. 34, p. 202.
77 TsIAM, f. 789, op. 19, d. 1602, 1. 75 ob.
78 Sakharov I.P. Songs of Russian People. Part 1. SPb., 1838, p. 152, 158, 162.
79 Rites of Moscow Cathedral of the Assumption. p. 186.
80 Rites of Moscow Cathedral of the Assumption. p. 195.
81 Rites of Moscow Cathedral of the Assumption. p. 186.
82 Malinovskiy A.F.Moscow Review. Composed by Dolgova M., 1992, p.28, S. 28.
83 Memorials of Literature of Ancient Russia.Book 9. M., 1987, p. 82-90.
84 As above. Book 9, p. 88.
85 Revelation. 21. 2-10.
86 Antony. About the Ordeals of Righteous Theodora and Other Visions of Gregory -the Disciple of Righteous Basil the New. M., 1907, p. 70-78.
87 Memorials of Literature of Ancient Russia. Book 9, p. 108.
88 Batalov A.L., Vyatchinina T.N. The above works, p. 36.
89 RIB T.13. SPb, 1891, p. 584.
90 As above, p. 169.
91 Tale of Abraham Palitsyn. M.-L., 1955, p. 236.
92 Book about Election to Reign of the Greet Tsar and Grand Prince Michael Fedorovich. H., 1856, p. 31.
93 PLDR, V. 9, p. 538-539.
94 Benjamin. The above works. V. l., p. 30.
95 Bartenev S.P. Moscow Kremlin in Ancient Time and NOW. V. 1. M., 1912, p.126.
96 Zabelin I.E. History of the Town of Moscow. M., 1905, p. 189.
97 As above, p. 189.
98 Foreigners about Ancient Moscow (Moscow of XVth-XVIIth centuries). Composed by; M.M.Sukhman. M., 1991, p. 155-157.
99 Nikolskiy K.T. The above works., p. 78.
100 Oleariy A. Detailed Description of the Journy of Golshtinskoe Embassy to Moskovj and Persia... Translated by Barsov P. M., 1870, p. 90-93.
101 Zabelin I.E. Home Life of Russian Tsars in 16th-17th centuries. Part 1. M., 1872, p. 351.
102 №3 above, p. 350.
103 Lyubetskiy S.M. Ancient Moscow in Historical Relation to Home life of Russian People. M., 1872, p. 216.
104 Cyprian the Metropolitanate of Sarsk. The Divine service for the Laying of the Lord's Chesuble. M., 1625.
105 PSZ. V. 1. SPb., 1830, p. 418.
106 Foreirners about Ancient Moscow. S. 325-327.
107 Rite of the Novgorod Cathecdral of St.Sophia. Edited by Golubtsov A.P., M., 1899, p. 22.
108 Nikolskiy K.T. The above works, p. 3-13.
109 Rpmanyuk. Moscow. The Losses. M., 1992, p. 54.

The Militant Church. Middle of the 17th century. "God Blessed Army". Moscow is portrayed as the heavenly

Panorama of the Kremlin and Zamoskvorechiye (district at the opposite

Zion under the protection of the Virgin – Mother of God is meeting the triumphal army returning from Kazan.

to the Kremlin bank of the Moscow River). Reconstruction by A.Malinov.

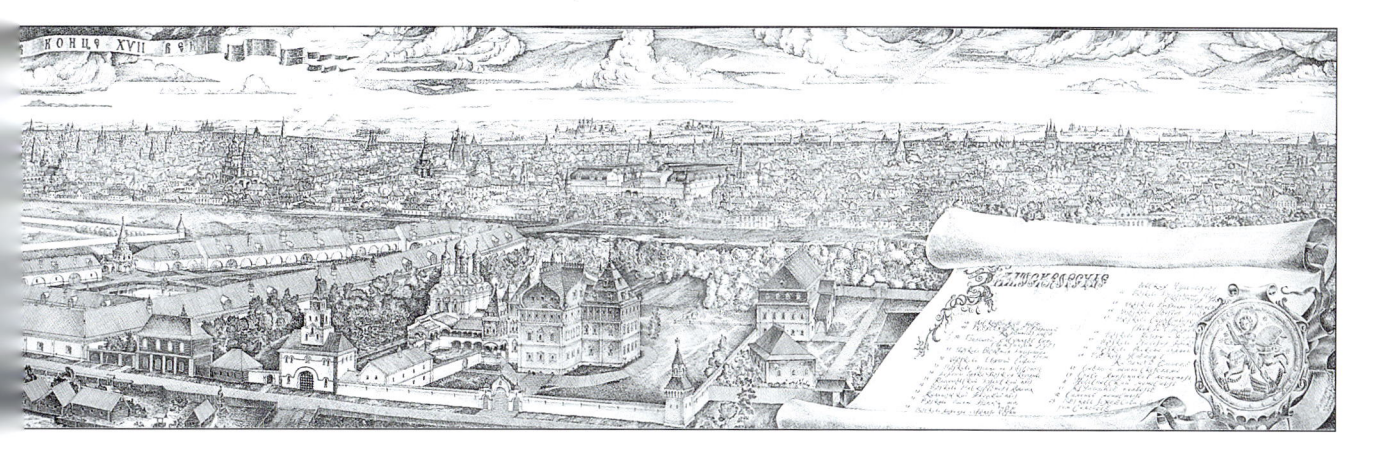

Pillars of the Russian Orthodox Church. The Cathedral of the Assumption of the Moscow Kremlin. The Interior.

Pillars of the Russian Orthodox Church. The Cathedral of the Assumption of the Moscow Kremlin. The Interior.

The Russian State Emblem.

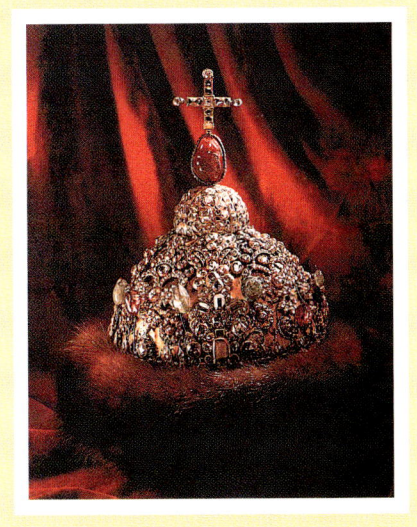

Diamond cap of Peter I.

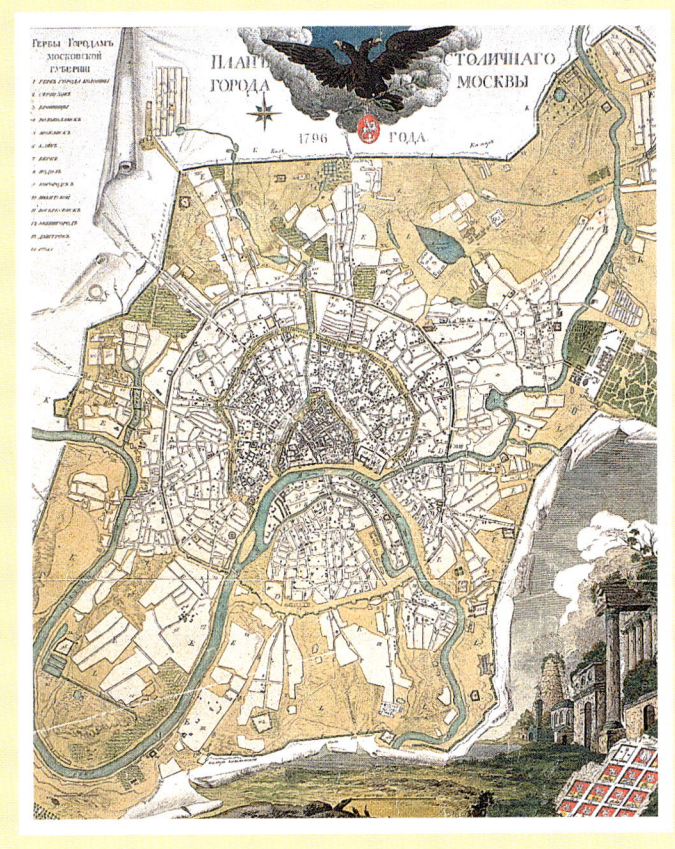

Plan of the capital city of Moscow. 1796.

BOOK TWO

Images of Moscow
of the 18th - beginning of the 20th century

Krasnye gate, built for the coronation of Elizabeth Petrovna. The middle of the 18th century.

Church of Sts. Apostles Peter and Paul inWew Basmannaja
(1705-1717, the bell-tower of 1740-1744).

Textbook on artillery of the early 18th century with a picture of the Kremlin and bastions.

Moscow panorama. Fragment. Triumphal entry of the Russian army in Moscow after the victory near Poltava. Print of A. Zubov. 1710.

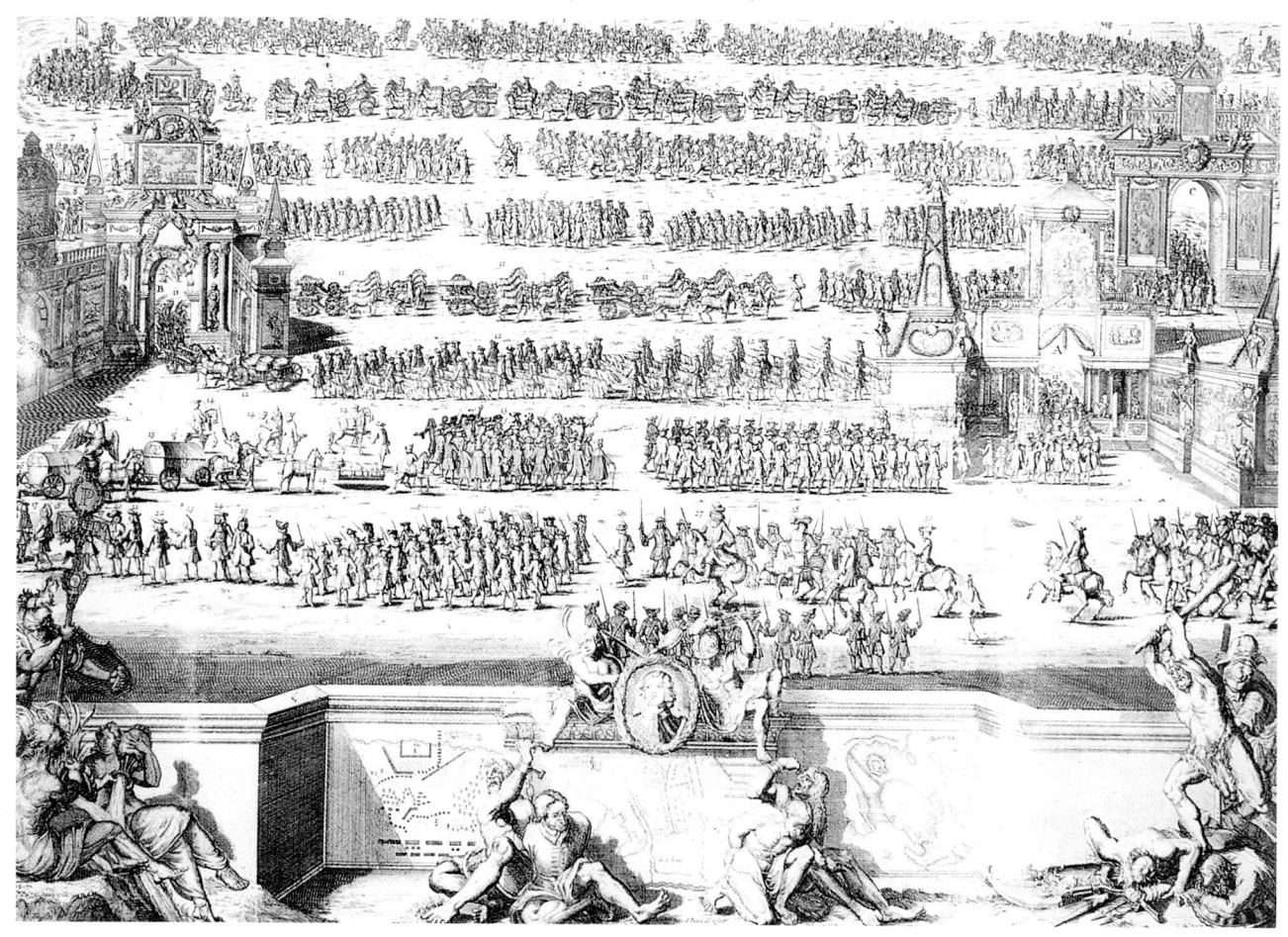

Tsar Peter I (1682-1725). Unknown artist. 2nd half of the 18th century.

Cathedral of Christ the Saviour (1839-1883, architect K.A.Ton) and the memorial to Alexander III (sanctified in 1912, sculptor A.M.Opekushin).

Introduction

TWO CENTURIES IN THE ARCHITECTURAL HISTORY OF MOSCOW

Moscow panorama. Artist D.Indeytsev. 1850s.

The time about which this book will tell, is the most interesting epoch in the national history and in the architectural history of Moscow. The theme "Architectural images of Moscow" is a separate case of more general problems in the history of Russia, of Russian culture, home architecture, and finally, – in the architectural-townbuilding history of Moscow, for this comparatively short period of time, which was full of sudden changes.

The theme of this book is the images of Moscow. The word "image" was used in plural form because of the authors' principal approach to the interpretation of town as an independent architectural body. Town is a changeable and complex phenomenon, especially if it is so large and multi-functional, having the history of many centuries, like Moscow. In difference to creations of other types of art, creations of architectural art are not comprehended separately, as something significant by itself. They always exist in the context: in the natural or architectural landscape, surrounded by the buildings of the same or some other time, in the system of the space of the street or square. So the image of town of certain period is the interrelation of newbuildings with historical surroundings. The second reason of multi-compositional character of images of any town, including Moscow, is the heterogeneity of social structure and different types of culture of the estates inhibiting it. This aspect is even more important for Russian architecture of that epoch, which will be the subject of consideration in this book. Peter's time and so-called Peter's reforms began an abrupt cultural division ; its traces have not been eliminated till now. It does not mean, however, that all the different world views got an adequate and wide expression in the architecture. Sooner it is on the contrary. The nature of architecture – the most state art of all – is such that it represents mostly official ideals and values, significant for the state ideology. Ideals and values, which are different from those officially adopted, often cannot get or do get the expression which is far from showing how they are really spread. So even indirect ways of expression of the multiple nature of architectural culture are more important.

The phenomena, which historically ceased to exist or lost their Importance in the system of the prevailing opinions, and most important – their material equivalents, which expressed by means of architecture the most complicated state concept, did not and could not disappear in a moment. They continued to keep their previous meaning for the majority of people of our country. Besides, they did not lose at once their significance even for the carriers of the new world view – active creators of new Russia and new Moscow. At the same time, since Peter's time the place of the traditional values and the structure representing them in the system of the prevailing culture changes abruptly. What was recently secondary, now is undergoing the process of fast extolment. All the state policy in the sphere of architecture is subordinated to the consolidation of new values and creation of material carriers of these values. Different aspects of state policy, defining the general picture of artistic novelties, are expressed, and perhaps, most purposefully and on a larger scale in architecture, because only it is easy to understand by all plies and estates. State policy is realized in the establishment of the principally new, in relation to all Moscow of the time before Peter, town-building concept, in appearance of new types of buildings, in the new artistic orientation and in turning to the inheritance, which was outside the framework of the habitual cultural and ideological preferences. Thus another range of questions is defined, which shall be touched upon in this book in more or less detail, i. e.: life of pre-Peter's tradition in Moscow of New Time, Moscow – the second (ancient, historical, national) capital of Russia,

Moscow panorama. Artist D. Indeytsev. 1850s.

Moscow and Petersburg, Moscow and the province, Moscow and the destinies of the historical towns in new Russia.

Peter's reign – the beginning of epochal change in national history and culture

A reader, who has taken the first volume, cannot miss the difference in the contents of each of the two books, which is clear even after reading the Contents. Consideration of the contents and the look of the city from the Christian position prevails in the first book, the second one considers the state and social, and only partially the Christian orthodox view point. It is connected with the global, enveloping all aspects of life, change endured by Russia during the pre-Peter's time, which made the impact on and defined further ways of Russian history and culture.

It was expressed differently in art and culture. It was shown in the creation of the independent ramified sphere of secular art. In appearance of newgenres, unknown in Russia before, for example, entertainment regal and nobility mansions, secular painting, historical and mythological painting, historical, mythological and portrait sculpture, sculptural and architectural monuments, town-building in the European meaning of the word – organization of, the so-called significant space of the settlements, turning roads into streets as expressive and meaningful space. On the basis of the most obvious acts it becomes evident that the main attention of the state policy in the sphere of art is paid to creation of secular art. In this sphere the orientation to the Western culture was definitely striking. Practically all the afore-said genres of art were created anew, as though transplanted on Russian soil. But the repetition failed. Adoption is also a creative process. The one which is in conformity with one's own needs is comprehended and considered as necessary for Russian culture. Besides, European samples get into different context and are superimposed on the traditions which are different from European ones. Simultaneously under the influence of new requirements, new values and images the character of those types and genres of art, which were famous in Russia before Peter's reforms, but which also live through significant transformation, change. All types of art connected with church are meant – churchmusic, buildings of temples and monastery ensembles, paintings of temples and icon-painting, as well as town and village dwelling. For example, it was since Peter's time that an ancient portrait becomes the portrait as it is understood now standing.

The degree of dependence on West-European samples and radicality of innovations depend on the circumstances of double nature – social and geographic. Change of forms of life, getting to know new cultural and artistic values, in other words the degree of deviation from the traditional cultural norms and the knowledge of European norms of culture and life is in proportion to the closeness to royal surroundings. I. e. it depends on estate affiliation. The farther from the royal court the more traditional the culture and way of life remain even those of the nobility. Merchants, peasants and craftsmen remains carriers of traditional culture for a long time.

Something similar to the spreading of the new culture in the social life is going on in the area of geography too. Novelties appear and are implemented most actively and successively in the capital, first in Moscow, and then after the move of the royal court to Petersburg – in both capitals.

The ways of development of culture, architecture of Russian capitals, all types of settlements in the vast space of the empire in general go in one direction – the direction of Europeanization. However, the degree of the Europeanization of the modes of life in different regions of Russia, in different in its place in the hierarchy of types of settlements is also different. The most successive realization it got in the capitals, then in the province and district towns, least of all it was realized in the peasant settlements.

Europeanization remains the token of the state policy in the sphere of architectural and town-building activity in Russia till the middle of 1820s – 1830s. Then the new change comes. In its radicality it can be compared to the change undergone by it during Peter's time, but opposite in its essence. The official policy in the area of culture and art changes. Like in 18th – the first quarter of 19th century (this period in the history of Russia is usually called Peter's time) new phenomena got their expression most early, successively and on a wider scale. The essence of the second change can be characterized by the notion – the national renaissance. It was accompanied by turning to the traditional (national and orthodox) values. From the time of the reign of tsar Nicholas I they get independent meaning. The change of direction of the cultural policy is accompanied by the change of the artistic orientation at the people's (peasant) and orthodox culture of Ancient Russia. This turn was realized within the framework and on the basis of the high culture which rooted by that time and partially penetrated in the lower people's one, the culture of the European type and so could not become direct continuation of the process interrupted during Peter's reign. However it meant the end of a big period in Russian history, marked by the supremacy of the European cultural orientation. In difference to Peter's reforms, which was the process of one direction – from the top to the bottom, the turn of 1820s-1830s included several processes directed at each other; official and non-official kinds of high culture of educated classes from the top to the bottom – and traditional people's one – from the bottom to the top.

From the second quarter of 19th century, from the time of coronation of tsar Nicholas I, the values, represented by the national traditional culture, and it is likened to the orthodox culture and the people's (peasant) culture, become, if not unconditionally supreme, then equal insignificance in any way to the values embodied by the European culture. The carriers of the Europeanized culture are the nobility and the state (represented by the same nobility). The carriers of the national renaissance – together with the state and the educated class which includes now the intelligentsia (raznochintsy – intellectuals not belonging to the gentry in 19th century Russia) and educated merchants, becomes the third estate and even peasants. The process envelopes actually the whole society. As for architecture and first of all Moscow one, from 1830s-1840s

Moscow panorama. Artist D.Indeytsev. 1850s.

and especially after the abolition of the serfdom and realization of town's reform which introduced municipal self-governing, the social power defining the development of the ancient capital the change of its image, renovation of the town's midst, become the merchants, to be more exact – the trade-industrial class.

The change of Moscow image during the time covered by the second book of the first volume, was depicted by an author of one of pre-revolution issues. At the beginning it is "Moscow of the Greek Representation and Nicon, schismatic elders and Habakuk, German settlement and Peter the Great. Thus ancient Moscow, royal, boyards' and monastic, official and of settlements, is changed by new Moscow – of 18th century. For us that Moscow which was new at certain time, became old long ago. The old Moscow of 18th century, not royal, but landlord's residence... a landlord`s mansion with the Noble Assembly in its center, with Moscow rural peasants in periphery, with Penza and Tambov peasants in its basis and with the granted chart in its heart. Moscow, which burned down during Napoleon's invasion and resurrected after his disappearance to sing and dance, banquet and play cards as before... until the bigwigs of boyards went away and the other bigwigs came from Taganka and Zamoskvorechie and remade Moscow-mansion into Moscow-factory and trade bureau, Moscow of trams, factory chimneys and illuminated advertisements. From people's depths other vivid powers came and turned the capital of slave-owners and Voltairianism with serf theaters and stables into the capital of Russian enlightenment with museums and classrooms, theaters and universities. Now Moscow is Moscow of Kljuchevskiy and prince S. Trubetskoy, of Ermolova and Shaliapin, Shtcukin and Stanislavskiy"[1].

Character of Legal Relations of the Government and the Church of 18th - Beginning of 20th Century

As it is known, Russia took the model of relations between the government and the church from Byzantium. This theory was later called the "symphony of kingdom and priesthood"; its essence was stated in the VIth novel of emperor Justin and his Code (6th century), as well as in Epinagogue of emperor Basil of Macedonia (9th century). After christening of Russia in 10th century this model of relations was accepted by Kiev princes and metropolitanates, and later, in 13th-14th century, legal stipulations of the VIth novel and other legal definitions of the "symphony" were included into the 42nd chapter of Slav Helms Books, into all the system of Russian law. This model of government-church building predominated formally till the end of 17th century, though in practice it was infringed by the government, which often oppressed church power.

During the time of Peter I the balance between the government and church powers was upset. Though at the beginning of his reign Peter issued the manifesto about religious tolerance, the first in the history of Russia, in which he guaranteed freedom of public and private religious services, including in the army[2] – during next years he assisted actively in repressing freedom of belief in Russia and making religion the state one: abolition of patriarchate in 1703, development of Ecumenical regulations, adoption of a number of antireligious laws and acts and, finally, creation in 1721 of the Holy Synod – all this made religion the state ideology and reduced priests to officers of a rather low rank.

Only in the middle of 19th century in the sphere of the government-church organization some changes started taking place, which can be regarded as movement in the direction of contractual-legal relations between the Russian Emperor and some confessions. An example of this can be the conclusion of an agreement ("concordat") between the top state power of Russia and the Pope's Throne on 22nd of June, 1847[3]. By that time Vatican accumulated rich experience of conclusion of concordats and conventions with the leading European states and large regions: for instance, on 15th of July, 1801, an agreement was signed between Napoleon and Pope Pius VII, on 5th of June, 1817 the concordat of the throne with Bavaria was concluded, on 16th of March, 1851, – with catholic Spain, on 19th of August, 1855, – with Austria etc. Russia was not an exception. However, Russian-Vatican concordat did not last long: in the autumn of 1866 the diplomatic relations were broken, from 22nd of November of that year the emperor signed the Decree abolishing the validity of the concordat on the territory of Russia[4].

At the end of 19th – beginning of 20th century the church-government relations were formally regulated by the laws of the Russian empire. But there was a visible unequality here between the legal status of Orthodox Russian Church and other confessions. Orthodoxy received, according to Article 8 of the Main Laws of Russian Empire[5], the status of the supreme religion: however, there was no document regulating the legal status of Orthodox Church, because it was considered to be the part of the state administration and was actually controlled by a secular officer – an ober-procurator of the Holy Synod. Heterodox confessions had their own bylaws of ecumenical affairs published in Volume XI of the Code of Laws of Russia: such bylaws were developed for Catholics, Protestants, Armenian-Gregorian church, Karaites, Israelits, Moslems, Lamaits and Pagans. Thus, the "supreme" orthodoxy turned out to be legally deprived of any rights and strongly subordinated to the government, the rights of heterodox confessions were also infringed. The wellknown decree of Nicholas II "About Consolidation of Beginnings of Religious Tolerance" of 17th of April, 1905[6], did not clarify the situation, it extended the limits of freedom of belief of Russian citizens, but did not specify the legal basis of relations of the government to religions, and in some points it sharply contradicted the Main Laws of Russian Empire. It is characteristic that representatives of the supreme church were the first who spoke against the decrees: the latter got a significant assistance of the government, but paid with its dependence on the tsar and responsibility for mistakes of the supreme power.

Prime-Minister P. A. Stolypin and the first Russian Parliament – State Duma -tried to correct the situation. On 6th of March of 1907 Stolypin introduced on behalf of the Ministry of Interior Affairs seven projects, which were to change the

Moscow panorama. Artist D.Indeytsev. 1850s.

valid national confession law in accordance with the top decrees of 17th of April and 17th of October, 1905[7]. Among them there were law projects about heterodox societies, as well as about the attitude of the government to separate confessions[8]. They contained, though not evidently, the seeds of contractual-legal relations between the government and the church, but the latter, however, remained quite free. Only in three years the State Duma, the third one, could consider these offers: May 22, 1909, the Prime-Minister presented law drafts to the deputies which were accepted with understanding[9]. But none of the drafts became the law: some of them were rejected by Duma, others – by the State Council or by the tsar. Relations between the government and the church became worse meanwhile.

After the revolution in February 1917 the parties began to get a bit closer. The Provisional Government issued the decree "About Liberty of Conscience" on 14th June, 1917, which did not make any of confessions particularly dominating and actually made religion a free affair of each indivuae[10]. The ober-procurator's office was liquidated and in August 1917 it was substituted by the ministry of confessions with the famous theologian and historian A. V. Kartashev at the head.

On their part, the leading Russian confessions made their own demands. On 15th August, 1917, Synaxis of Orthodox Russian Church was opened portentously, which besides all considered a number of church-legal matters, as well as adopted on 11th December, 1917, the definition "About Legal Status of Orthodox Russian Church"[11]. This definition was the sign of synaxis strengthening of Russian society in efforts to achieve the "symphony" between the government and the church. For the first time independence of the church from the governmental power in religious doctrine was declared and main eight spheres of interaction of the government and the church were stipulated: agreement of the state and church law, state veneration of the church calendar and holidays, guarantees from profanations and abuse of national holy things, apostasy, questions of marriage and divorce, problems of people's education, ecumenical education of military men, matters concerning church property and governmental subsidies for the church, in the definition which contained 25 articles. A number of provisions of this definition contradicted the practice of statebuilding in the USSR in 1920s, other points grew out of date, but the general significance of the document is underestimated even now – it was the first effort to establish free, good-will and equal relations between the church and the government. Doctor of political economy N. N. Bulgakov, who presented the project, supposed that the latter created "some gap between the church and the government but relations of union were still kept"[12]. The church made it clear that it was an equal partner, an ally of the government, but did not intend to undertake extreme commitments before the government, wishing to keep distance to some extent.

Town Actions and Orthodox Traditions

Moscow town life, according to experience of 17th century, was regarded by Muscovites as a continuous chain of religious processions. From the Kremlin cathedral of the Assumption big religious processions were conducted headed by the Patriarch and tsar, when holy orders of all Moscow church forties (by 18th century y there were six of them) went, average religious processions consisted of three or four forties and little ones – from one-two forties. Each forty also conducted local religious processions, that went with Holy Things around all the territory. Here monastery processions, processions in commemoration of fires and disasters, processions with locally venerated icons and in honor of altar consecration holidays also should be added.

Europeanization of way of life carried out by Peter I and his environment, changed the praying appeal of town actions to God into a ceremony of glorifying the emperor and humiliating his enemies. Besides the nobility ingrafted by Peter, other plies of society also expressed their disagreement with the changes. Those who disagreed, were unanimous in their wish to keep the old town way of life, but they were very different in their attitude to Peter I. Old believers regarded the tsar as antichrist. People's cheap popular prints depicted him as a cat imitating the title: "Cat from Kazan, mind from Astrakhan". Family relations between Peter and the Swedish Catherine were expressed by a print: "How Baba-Yaga (a witch in Russian folk tales) is fighting with a crocodile". The pictures were sold in big quantity near Spasskie gates of the Kremlin.

Merchants who became rich during Peter's reign were inclined to call him: "The Father of the Fatherland". They felt to be obliged to substitute boyards in construction of temples, adornment of icons and making church rituals splendid.

In 1699 a religious procession during water sanctifying, conducted near the river Neglinnaya, was visited by Peter I. Instead of following the cross being dressed in ragal clothes, he went together with a regiment and a chorus as the captain of Preobrazhenskiy regiment. Near "Jordan" a bridge was made, on which a German hireling of Peter I stood and held a white royal banner with a double-headed eagle embroided with gold. The banner-carrier inclined the banner several times which at settling of the cross down into water, was sprinkled with the saint water.

Already at the time of patriarch Adrian Peter's teacher deacon Zotov had the nickname of "patriarch Kokuyskiy" (after the name of the German settlement Kokuyskaya of that time). He took part in clown processions dressed like patriarch and even send his messages to Muscovites which parodied not only patriarch's messages, but also those of known prayers.

Peter I tried to substitute religious processions with theatrical ones. In January of 1722 celebration of Nishtadskiy peace treaty led to an enormous fancy-dress procession in Tverskaya street through a specially installed triumphal gates. In front of it a motley marshal was riding, after him the head of "all the most drunk assembly" "prince-pope" I.Buturlin rode in big sledge. At his feet a made-up Bachus showed off, who held a big cup in the right hand and in the left hand – a bowl with wine. After several sledges crowned Neptun, with a long gray beard and a trident in the right hand followed. His sledge was arranged like a shell. Prince Menshikov and his suite, dressed like abbots, were sailing on a boat decorated with a gilded figure of Fortune. Emperor Peter himself commanded a battleship under sail installed on runners. The ship which stood out due to the royal flag, had plenty of wooden and 10 real cannons, out of which

Moscow panorama. Artist D.Indeytsev. 1850s.

they fired from time to time. All the masquerade train consisted of 60 sledges. Together with it regiments were going through the triumphal gates.

An author, who was an old-believer, accompanied his story "About the End of the World" with drawings of the procession

Celebration of water sanctifying in 1699.

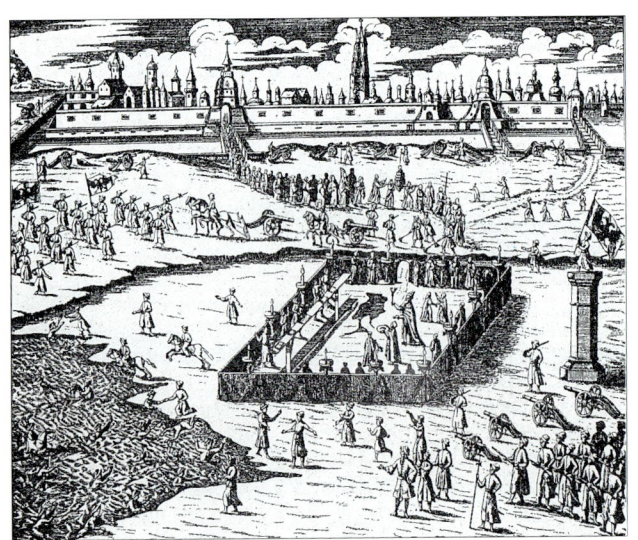

of Peter's soldiers which had an inscription from the Bible, from Prophet Isaiah: " Thy country will be eaten by strangers". After St. Petersburg had become the capital the dismissed deacon Dokukin exclaimed in horror about Moscow: "My heart is aching so much seeing the devastation of New Jerusalem and people in unbearable sorrow".

The tradition of gala fancy-dress processions was continued in January 1763 by the famous masquerade entrance into Moscow through Krasnye gates of empress Catherine II. The theatrical performance arranged under the leadership of A. P. Sumarokov and F. G. Volkov according to the poem of M. M. Kheraskov with participation of Moscow students, got the name of "The Triumphant Minerva". New traditions showed that Peter I and his successors saw Russia not as the Holy Land, but as new Roman Empire.

New leaders of the Holy Synod did not have the basic knowledge of home rituals. When in 1843 a religious procession was established in St. Petersburg from the cathedral of Kazan Icon of the Theotokos to the Lavra of St. Alexander Nevskiy, they had to ask Moscow priests for explanations about how to conduct religious processions[13].

In the middle of 18th century the locally venerated religious processions so loved by Muscovites, were just persecuted. In 1767 the Holy Synod ordered: "Usual Religious processions, conducted at free will by Moscow churches, except those which were held from the cathedral of the Assumption, which are not blessed by the Holy Synod or by a eparch, shall be canceled forever". By the end of 18th century by efforts of Moscow metropolitanate Platon, who had been earlier the law teacher of the throne heir Paul Petrovich, favor of top church authorities to processions from the cathedral of the Assumption was restored, which were all-town ones. In 1800 metropolitanate Platon issued a table of Moscow religious processions, in which the actions of clergy men of each church concerning organization of a procession were clearly defined. As the next step, merchants demand to renew divine services in Red Square. In 1804 on initiative of Moscow merchants it was supposed to install on the Frontal Place under a closed canopy the Holy Life-giving Cross from the monastery of the Candlemas, made by G. S. Shumaev. The memorial was to become the center of divine services, revived in new quality, to which religious processions were to gather.

G. S. Shumaev worked from 1717 till 1755. The carved Cross was placed in a case of size (7.3m x 4.27m x 1.20). The main Crucifixion with the Theotokos and St. John the Theologian at both sides as though flew in the air in the center of cube of the universe under the model of Divine Town Jerusalem and above three temples-monasteries. The background consisting of buildings of earthly Jerusalem was painted with bright green, blue, pink and orange. The composition was finished on the right and on the left by vertical stripes with scenes from the Old and New Testaments. At the top there was a model of Divine Jerusalem with high mirror walls, in the 12 gates of which figures of Angels flew. At the bottom the constructions of the earthly town are transferred into a high Zion from three temples-monasteries, an image of earthly Church uniting the earthly world with the Divine one. Two-tier constructions stand out in the direction of an on-looker. At the sides of their bottoms and at the sides in the bays tormenting of souls in hell is shown. The Cross is a program creation about the Christian image of the World and an ideal town, showing how keepers of traditional culture learned to express the long loved orthodox ideals with the help of new expressive means.

Moscow mascarade in 1722.

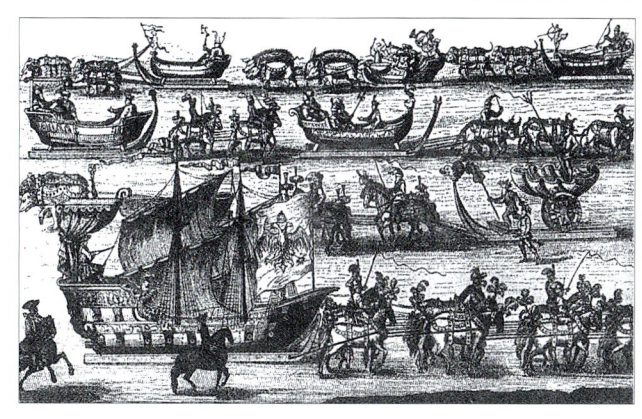

Restoration of Moscow, burnt by the French in 1812, became an all-national affair. Everything connected with ancient Moscow now stirred up pride and tender feelings in the aristocracy. In such situation in 1813 a new regular religious procession around the Kremlin was established. By this deed each year Moscow purified itself from all accumulated foul and was sanctified.

Philaret, who was elected Moscow metropolitanate in 1821, acquired great authority by comforting people in December 1825 (the rising of the Decembrists), He paid much attention to religious processions, having established the position of taxiarch – a supervisor of the order of a procession. Upon his blessing Moscow society of gonfalon-carriers was established, which consisted from eight divisions: of the cathedrals of the Assumption, Archangel Michael, Verkho-Spasskiy on Bor and the Annunciation; of the church of the 12 Apostles; of the Chudov monastery and a little later of the temple of Christ the Saviour. Splendour-lovers from different estates, who had entered the society, put on caftans (long tunics with waist-girdles) embroidered with gold or silver lace, and carried the Kremlin's holy things during town processions.

Those who took part and watched a religious procession in 19th century comprehended again its deep symbolic meaning. Though the Moscow religious procession was not understood as Ecclesiastical divine service any more, when in 17th century all the town was transfigured into an image of the Church, but now "a religious procession represented as though a movable temple ... The religious procession inspired all who took part in it to pray unanimously, warmly and vividly. Here as though one wide and swift flow of prayer is formed. Some people, meeting a religious procession stop, raising their thoughts to God, and become participants of the prayer themselves. Others, being fair from the procession, hearing the chime announcing the religious procession, try to participate cordially in the general prayer, and thus, a praying sacrifice favoured by God is brought from the whole town ".

Fragment of Shumaev's cross. The Entry in Jerusalem.

Fragment of Shumaev's cross. Side part.

Crugifixion with the intercessing. Fragment of Shumaev's cross.

Moscow religious procession in 1892. Print according to Gribov's photo.

Religious procession around the Kremlin in memory of Moscow liberation in 1812.

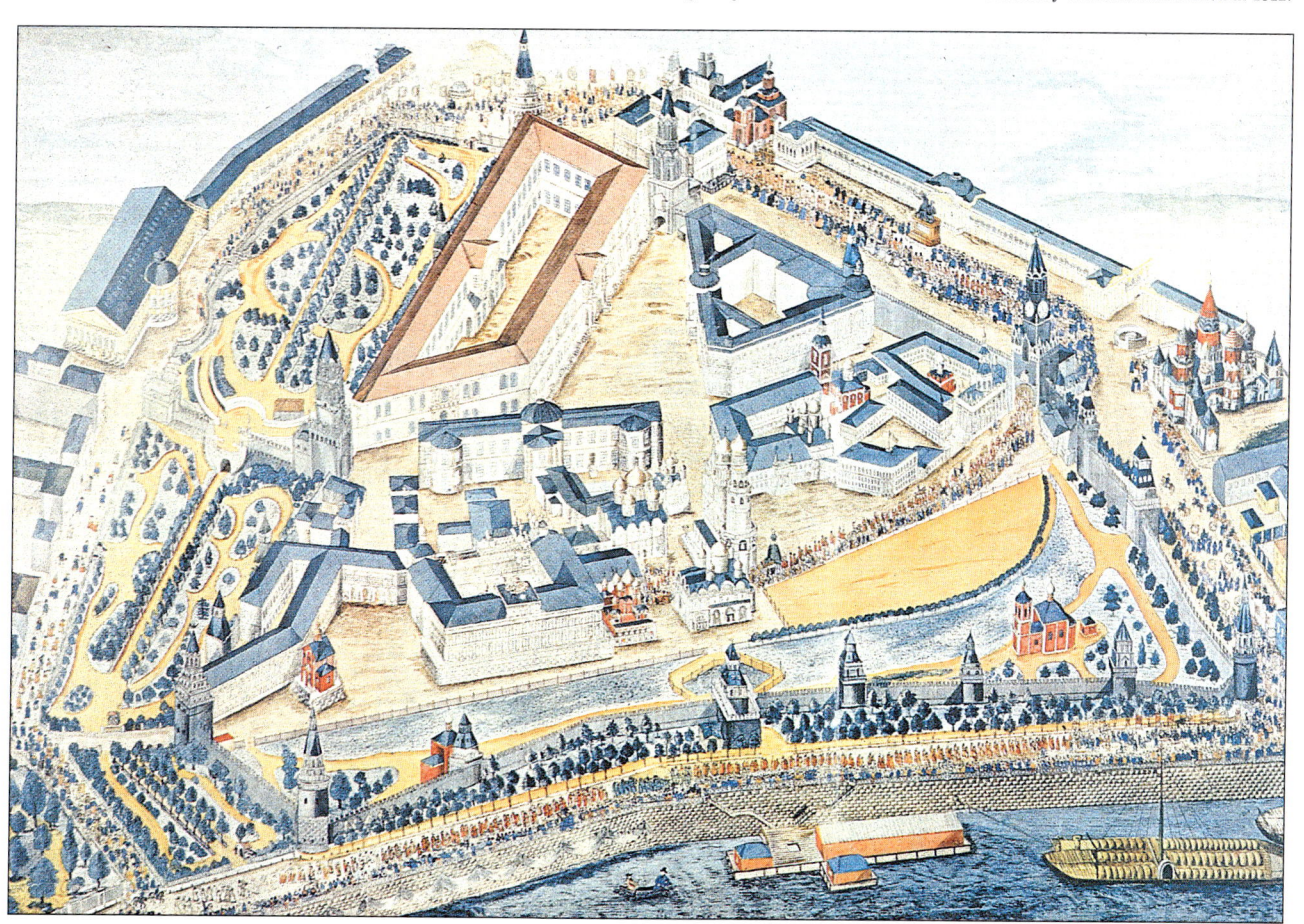

The opportunity to ring the bell granted on the Easter day led in 19th century to a pious merchant tradition: "On Great Thursday Moscow merchants gathered in the Kremlin after the Mass, on the porch of the temple of St. John the author of "The Ladder", which is under the belltower of John the Great. They agreed upon the amount of a contribution upon sortition. The contribution was very big – hundreds of roubles. Here they collected these contributions from each one who wanted. They cut coupons according to the quantity of the contributors, from them they wrote on twelve coupons the word "chime", rolled them, mixed and put into the visored cap of one of the merchants. Then they called a poor boy or girl to draw lots. They drew out the twelve lucky lots and went away, presenting the one who had drawn lots with such a sum that he or she with all his or her family ceased being poor at once. The rest of the money was donated for charity. And the twelve lucky men were those who would ring for all Moscow the big Kremlin bell before the Bright Matins".

Constantine Pobedonostsev commented: "Orthodox Church is adorned with its people... In it all is united, all is comprehended by people and all is held by people". People's orthodox traditions defined the church-respectable character of Moscow of 19th century.

---

[1] Moscow in History and Literature. Comp. by M. Kovalevskiy. M., 1916, p. 4.
[2] Manifesto of Peter the Great of 16th April 1702. 1910 //Full volume of laws of Russian Empire. 1st works. From 1649 to 18th December 1825. In 45 volumes – V. 4: 1700-1712 (published in the book: V. A. Fetler. Liberty of Conscience and Tolerance. SPb., 1909, p. 13-14.
[3] Full text of the concordat was published in the language of the original and in translation into Russian in the book: Acts and Charts about Organization and Management of Roman-Catholic Church in Russian Empire and Polish Kingdom. SPb., 1849, p. 193-207.
[4] About Russian Concordat. See: Popov A. The Last Destiny of Pope's Policy in Russia. 1845-1867 // European News. 1867. 3; Tcshebalskiy P. K. History of Russian Concordat // Russian Vestnic. 1871. 4.
[5] Code of the main state laws. Chapter 81 "About Faith" // Code of laws of Russian Empire. 1876-1917. In 121 volumes. V. 1, part 1. SPb., 1906.
[6] The Highest Inscribed Order to the Governing Senate of 17th April 1905 "About consolidation of Initials of Faith Tolerance" // Law acts of transitional time: 1904-1906. SPb, 1907, p. 47-51.
[7] Stolypin P. A. "We Need Great Russia..." Full collection of speeches in the State Duma and the State Council. 1906-1911. M., 1991, p. 53.
[8] About Heterodox Religious Societies. Law draft introduced by the Ministry of Internal Affairs of Russia to the State Duma // State Duma. The second convocation. Review of the activity of the commissions and divisions. SPb., 1907, p. 541-547.
[9] Stolypin P. A. Decree. Works, p. 209-219.
[10] About Liberty of Conscience. Enactment of the Provisional Government of Russia of 14th July 1917 // News of the Provisional Government. 1917. July. 109.
[11] About the Legal Status of Orthodox Russian Church. Definition of the Holy Synaxis of Orthodox Russian Church. 11th December 1817 // In the book: Theologic News. Issue of Moscow Ecumenical Academy. In book №1. Sergiev Posad. 1993, p. 145-147.
[12] Quoted acc. to; Odintsov M. l. Government and Church in Russia. 20th century. M., 1994, p. 48-49.
[13] PSZRI. 8779.

Red Square in Moscow. 1801. Artist F. Alexeev.

CHAPTER ONE

The Second Capital of Russian Empire

Sign of the order of St. Andrew the First Called. Late 18th century.

View Of Voskresenskie gate of Kitay-gored and the Kremlin from Tverskaja street. Water-colour of F.Ya.Alexeev's studio. Early 19th century.

Empress Anna Ioannovna (1730-1740).

Empress Elizabeth Petrovna (1741-1761).

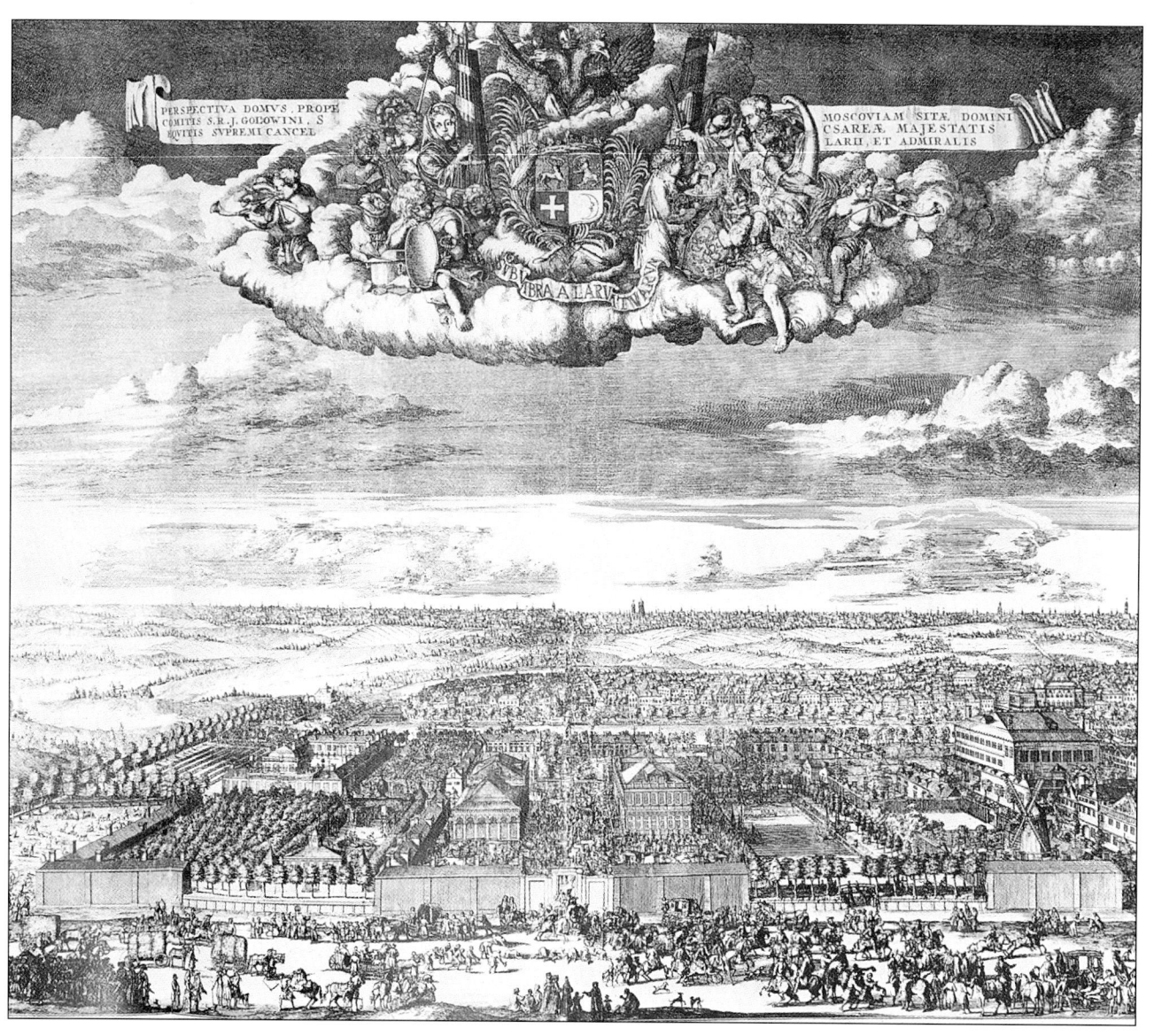

F.A.Golovin's estate in the German settlement at the Yauza and Moscow panorama of the early 18th century. Print of de Vitte.

Arrival of Elizabeth Petrovna and the court from Petersburg to Moscow, behind the Yauza, to Annengof. 1744.

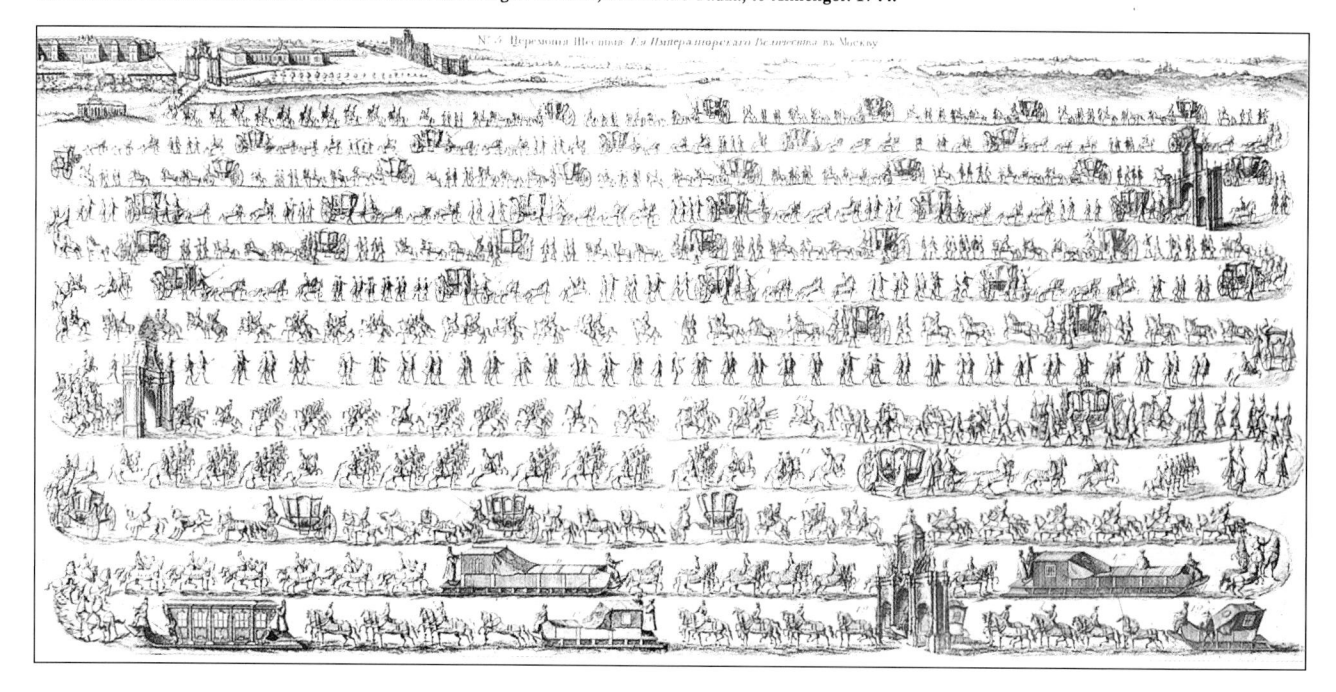

The concept of reign of Peter I and his father Alexius Mikhaylovich is approximately in the same ratio as naryshkinskaya architecture and petrovsky town-building in style. Or, if to consider European town-building, the ratio is like the first national stage of Renaissance and the second one – Italianized, based on order architecture. Many historians are inclined to think since recent time that it is reasonable to consider both reigns as a whole. The reasons for this are in the effort made by Alexius Mikhailovich to reconsider the relations till that time between the church and the government, to put the government above the church and to make the church subordinate to the government. The Council of 1667, which upon the wish of Alexius Mikhailovich sanctioned dismissal of patriarch Nicon, " established a formal limit of the previous form of management. Here is the boundary from which a new stage of the Russian state system began, which was later consolidated in the Empire of Peter I"[1]. By 1660s the sources of the process appeared, which led the son of Alexius Mikhaylovich Peter to cancellation of patriarchate and establishment of the Holy Synod. And though Alexius Mikhaylovich settled singularly local tasks, his actions created a political and psychological precedent of organised, certified in legal order subordination of the church to the government. An important fact was that dismissal of Nicon went out far "behind the framework of formal relations between the church and the government. It was an effort to make a state system out of sufficient part of public life, which had been before within the sphere of influence of the church and sanctified by it. The process also made an impact on everyday life, which had been based before mainly on the traditions and experience of the previous generations" [2].

Russia before Peter's Time

All aspects of architectural activity get into the sphere of unusually extending space which is subject to state regulation. The state policy in the sphere of town-building, which had implied before Peter's time organization of all the space of the capital (the space of the streets and squares of public importance and the space of an individual – building of houses), was just one case when the government assumed the functions which are not typical to it. "The Instructions to Moscow Mounted Wardens", issued on 17th April 1667 by Alexius Mikhaylovich, stipulated supervision of implementation by the capital's inhabitants of obligatory rules in their everyday life. It stipulated when and how many times they should heat stoves, where and how they should be installed etc. The first signs of special care about splendour and beauty of town space are referred to the same time. Decrees prohibit to sell on holidays (except for food sale). Decrees were issued which prohibited food sale near the Trinity Gates and the building of the Judgement Department. A number of decrees was directed at clearing out Red Square from stores, motivated by the fact that "those unsanctioned trade points in Red Squared caused much inconvenience". All the decrees had one characteristic feature: the care about the splendour of the land space. Its essence is in the appearing sacralization of the state, all expression of which the architectural organization of town space became. Development of ideas about an ideal organization of a city and new contents go on parallel and result in increase of importance of the land space, its likening to divine space, and then its supremacy over the divine one. Symbolics and meaning of this process in the spheres of architecture and art have much in common with the process of subordination of the church organization to the state structure. One of its expressions was the prohibition to build above dwelling houses, including

View of the Kremlin from Zamoskvorechie. Print according to S.I.Makhaev's drawing. 1760s.

stone ones, wooden chambers: "henceforth no wooden house construction shall be built on chamber construction by anybody, and provided some one builds henceforth any rooms or garrets with high ceilings, their wooden construction shall be broken". The prohibition to build high chambers, born only by fire protection purposes, entailed disappearance of one of the brightest and original specialities of ancient town dwelling buildings. It significantly changed the characteristic image of the ancient Russian town. It objectively contained the sources of the new ideas about the beauty of a Russian town with its low buildings, as it seems to us now. After checking it turns out to be a rather late phenomenon which appeared together with the idea of the absolute state power.

The same consequences were the result of the process which dates back to 1st September 1685, also directed at fire protection: "About henceforth covering of chamber constructions with deal, then with earth above it, and then with turf". It was repeated a lot later during Peter's time. Besides its practical importance the decree shows the above-mentioned progress in the mentality of the state power. In it the change of the state function showed itself again, which gradually strengthened itself by power that ruled every aspect of human life without exception. The same decree gave rise to all-penetrating regulation, including regulation of construction activity, which changed radically the look of medieval Moscow during 18th century. The new look and new-buildings of Moscow appeared during realisation of purposeful state policy. The city's look changed during implementation of decrees: they stipulated clearing up of places, especially important from the point of view of the new substantiality, from buildings "low" in their functions – also trade ones and dwellings. The decrees stipulated the dimensions, materials and design of the most mass type of buildings – the dwelling ones and, finally, the general principles of planning and organization of land space. Implementation of the decrees which were issued one after another created conditions for changing of the capital's look, essence and structure, which had been formed naturally and historically for centuries.

Town-building policy of Peter's reign

In 1699 Peter I issued a decree about adoption of the calendar which is valid in Europe, that started the counting of years from the Nativity of Christ.

The calendar from creation of the world, valid in Russia, was cancelled. Coming of the new 18th century became a significant boundary in the history of Russia and Moscow. Anyway the government and the tsar did all to make the new 1700 – the first in the new century – a symbol of beginning of the new history of Russia. Besides, in the year that started the century according to the European calendar, Peter changed the day of the New Year. In ancient Russia it began on 1st September. Peter established the new date, valid in Europe – 1st January. With Peter's participation a detailed plan of celebration of the New Year was developed for Moscow. It was stipulated in the legislative order " 1st January to congratulate each other with the new year and the new century as a sign of merriment and to do the following: when on Big Red Square fireworks and shooting are started, then at the aristocratic yards Boyards, Heads of outskirts, officers of Duma and chambers, people of military and merchant rank, each at one's own yard must shoot three times from small cannons, if there are any, and let off a few rockets. . . and in large streets, where space allows, from 1st to 7th January every night fires from brushwood or thatch must be burnt", and on these days houses were to be decorated with fir-tree, pine and juniper branches. The holiday ritual included together with portentous divine service secular forms of celebration, which had started to become traditional – arrangement of triumphal arches, "fiery funs" of fire-works, shooting from guns during a week. New Year celebrations ended on the day of the Holy Theophany with a large religious procession to the Jordan [3].

Thus Peter declared and defined in the ritual of the new, mostly secular holiday the supertask of his reign – Europeanization, re-creation of the country according to the European sample. On 4th January, 1700, he issued the decree forbidding to the privileged plies of society to wear Russian dress and ordering address "in the Hungarian manner", clothes of "Hungarian, French and Saxon style". The decree was hung on Spasskie and other Kremlin's gates. Here tailor's dummies were placed in "sample" dresses. Variants of this decree were issued several times. In 1700 and 1701 decrees were also issued directly concerning the character of building in Moscow, which originated from the general program understood as Europeanization. First of all it was orientation at stone buildings. Poor people, who could not afford to build stone houses, were ordered to build cobhouses.

From the time of Peter's reign the tradition to give wooden houses the look of stone ones was started and spread widely in Russia for more than two centuries. The striving to make Moscow buildings of stone was stimulated not only by the wish to keep it safe from fires . The "stone" look of a house acquires valuable essence and is regarded as one of forms of Europeanization of the country. The decree of 1701 "About building in Moscow on burnt places of stone houses for well-off people and cobhouses for those who are not well-off", which repeated the decree of 1700 that did not keep to our time, stipulated to build new houses according to the Western style. Samples of the houses were demonstrated in Pokrovskoe. Attention is attracted by the similarity of measures undertaken to expedite Europeanization and the symbolic character of these measures. "Model" dresses, like model houses, are exhibited for public observation as patterns that were to be followed absolutely. However, Peter's impatience broke against double resistance. Against the town-building reality, that had been formed for ages, and against silent resistance of people faithful to traditions and suspicious of novelties.

All the above-mentioned decrees were to settle concrete problems. At the same time they contained some elements testifying to the formation of a new system. Its fundamental signs accompanied by appearance of the idea about town as a whole body, were first fixed in the decrees of 1704-1705. According to A. A. Musatov "The new epoch in Russian town-building actually began on 28th January, 1704, by the issue of the nominal decree "About building in Moscow, the Kremlin and Kitay-gorod of stone houses, about their location near the streets and lanes, and not inside the yards and about the obligation of the owners to sell their yards if they cannot build stone houses". The essence and great importance of the decree were, according to the scientist, in the phrase: "These stone buildings shall be built along the streets and lanes, and not in the middle of their yards, with good skill"[4]. Decrees of future years were directed at confirmation of two main theses of the decree of 1704 – first at the turning of Moscow centre – the Kremlin and Kitay-gorod, and then Bely gorod, and, finally, all Moscow into the stone European town. With this purpose as the main and general principle the regularity – geometric correctness of forms of streets and squares and location of buildings along the streets, is proclaimed.

In 1705 the decree "About the building of stone houses and stores in Kitay-gorod and the prohibition to begin such construction in other parts of Moscow" was issued. In the same year a grandiose programme appeared of pavement of all Moscow streets with stone, and in 1705-1706 a number of decrees was issued to this effect. On 12th May, 1709, the decree "About construction in the Kremlin and in Kitay- gorod of stone buildings for people of all ranks, and about non-beginning of construction in Bely and Zemlianoy gorod before the construction of the above-mentioned parts of the town" was issued. The latter decree testifies to the existence the wooden Moscow into a stone town of European type.

It is important to point out that formation of new hierarchy of values did not reflect itself in the hierarchy of territories. The importance of the historical centre in the Kremlin is bigger than the importance of the new one forming on the shores of the Yauza. The last town-building action in Moscow, connected with the construction of defence structure, confirms it. When the threat of Swedish invasion arose, only the districts of the historical centre – the Kremlin and Kitay- gorod, were bounded with bastions in 1707-1708.

After the victory at Poltava, which had become a crucial point in the history of war with the Swedish, Peter's attention was again directed to Moscow. On 19th May, 1712, the decree "About prohibition of construction in Bely gorod of wooden houses" was issued, and in a week on 26th May – "About covering of stone buildings and cobhouses in Moscow in Bely gorod with tiles and turf", on 25th May – "About construction in Moscow, in Kitay and Bely gorod of stone buildings and cobstones along the line, and about punishment for non-implementation of this decree by deprivation of a yard". Stone chamber construction was stipulated "from this decree of His Majesty Tsar, for the interest of His High Majesty and for the best way for it, and the construction shall be carried out along the lines of the streets and lanes like the buildings of other European countries".

These decrees are a valuable evidence of the role of Moscow in development of the new town-building concept connected with absolutization, even sacralization of the role of the government. They also confirm that during the first ten years of existence of Petersburg the attitude to Moscow as the capital remained. All the most important town-building measures of all-state scale were conducted in Moscow. Here all novelties were also tried. Due to the first efforts of transformation of Moscow on the new grounds understanding of planning as a unified organization of town territory appeared. New methods of design appeared: the plan became primary, not the volume of a house or a complex of houses (of the Kremlin, monastery ensemble, transport gates, town walls), they believe that it is necessary to create a town plan on the basis of initially stated geometrically correct forms. The concept of an ancient Russian town and first of all a capital town as the Heaven Town, earthly Jerusalem, Third Rome, the idea of Moscow as the house of the Theotokos concentrated attention on the divine space and the volumes which made the earthly space meaningful and structural. In this system street did not have an independent architectural importance, remaining a transportation or pedestrian road. As soon as the role of the master of life on the earth was undertaken by the government, organization of the earthly space becomes most important. The open space of wide squares and straight wide streets with houses located along the red line, subordination of the composition and the look of their facades to the space and direction of the street become the symbols of the new values. It is impossible not to point out the alliance of the methodology of regular town-building, born in Moscow and authoritative in its essence, which ordered to build houses "along one line" according to universal rules in any conditions, for any towns, on any relief, and the idea of a regular government ruling all aspects of private life, including the daily schedule (time and frequence of heating stoves), character of buildings, clothes, outer look (the notorious shaving of beards).

Creation of Petersburg, as it was noted, did not change the attitude to Moscow at once. For more than ten years it still implemented its capital's functions, it still had the first priority in town-building ideas of Peter. At the beginning the Moscow status was not influenced by the transfer of the court to Petersburg in 1712 either, i.e. its transformation into the official capital. The turn came only in 1714. On 7th July the decree, prohibiting construction of new "stone houses in Zemlianoy gorod and behind Zemlianoy bank in Moscow" was issued. Then on 9th October, 1714, the decree "About prohibition for several years to build stone houses in all the State, including Moscow, followed.

But already on 24th January, 1718, emphasizing its special importance, a new decree was issued, which cancelled the prohibition and actually repeated the decree of 1704: "About construction in Moscow, the Kremlin and Kitay- gorod of stone buildings along the streets, not in the yards, and about pavement of streets with raw stone". The stone construction was cancelled in all Russian in 1714. The permission to renew it in 1718 referred only to Moscow. This date can be considered as an expression of acknowledgement of Moscow as the capital, but already the second capital.

Recognition of the fact of existence in Russia of two capitals, developing parallelly, adding to each other and opposing each other, was demonstrated by the "Instruction of Moscow head office of the city police". The office became the first state body in the history of Russia that controlled all the town construction, arrangement and sanitary state of the city. The instruction included all the previous Moscow experience of transformation of an ancient Russian town into a regular one. It allows to see in it the first conscious effort made in Russia to realize reconstruction of a historical town with principles of regularity with orientation at European experience and trying to make or to give it a look of a stone town. All these requirements together make that ideal at which, beginning from Peter I, Russian town-building is oriented. The issue of the Instruction demonstrated the importance of Moscow, and mainly, its special mission, different from Petersburg. Since the time of becoming the capital Petersburg was built with principles of regularity according to European samples. Moscow was to be transformed on the basis of new principles. It made Moscow an example that was to be followed by all other historical towns . The Moscow status as of the second capital made it the capital of a province.

The first point of the Instruction stated: "It shall be controlled that all dwelling houses, in case of new construction or their reconstruction, shall be made in conformity with the decree along the streets in one line, and no house shall stand out of the line (in order that with time all streets and lanes should be equal)". The other points of the Instruction stipulated creation of entire buildings, liquidation of waste land, construction of buildings in such a way that it was possible to build new ones next to them. The Instruction was important because it reflected a new level of consciousness, which made it different from the first decrees of 17th-beginning of 18th century, directed at solving of concrete tasks only. In the Instruction the utilitarian requirements are inseparable from the idea about an ideal town. It testified to the appearance during Peter's time and existence till the middle of 19th century of an ideal notion about a regular town founded on reasonable principles, about a Utopia, implementation of which became the purpose of the state policy the sphere of town-building.

**Moscow. Temporary triumphal gate.
Built in 1709 in honour Of the victory near Poltava.
Architect I.P.Zarudny. Printed by A.F.Zuhov. 1711.**

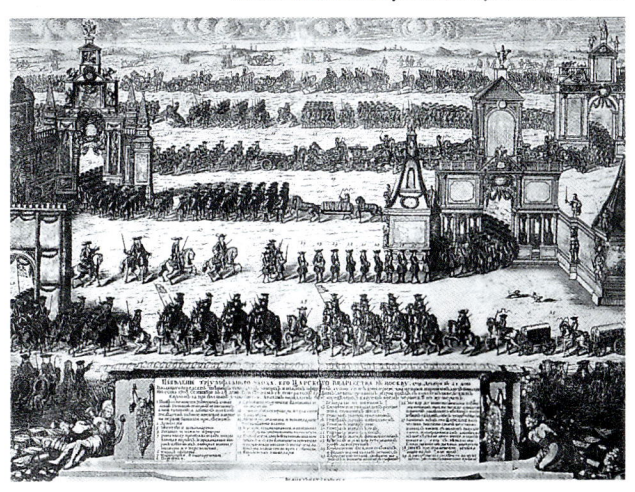

"Moscow – the Third Rome". Reconsideration of the Traditional Formula in the Light of the Imperial Idea

State decrees of the beginning of 18th century aimed at the change of the planning of town's parts that had burnt during fires, construction of stone houses and cobhouses in accordance with the new artistic ideals and new samples was only one way of changing of Moscow look, connected with realization of the state idea. The second way were the new secular holidays – antipodes of church ones, for instance, of religious processions. Such holidays became the gala "in-comings" that in a way reminded in their rituals of religious processions and even pretended to substitute them or at least to be equal to them. The first "in-comings" in Moscow were organized in honour of military victories, but very soon other events were celebrated in this way, those that were regarded as being of state importance. Construction of triumphal gates, connected with the holiday ritual, and organization of "fiery funs" – fireworks, referred to this kind of holidays.

In 1696 for the occasion of taking of the Azov – the first big victory of the Russian regular army and fleet, which had grown out of Peter's fun regiments and flotillas, the first secular celebration was organized, based on the system of contents and ideas new for Russia. Celebration of the victory was marked with a gala – procession through all Moscow of victorious troops that had entered the city from the South. The culmination moment of their meeting was their passing through the triumphal gates near Vsesviatskiy (Big Stone) bridge. They were a decoration leaned against the first transportation arch of the double hip roof bridge.

In February 1697, during Shrovetide, the taking of the Azov was celebrated in Moscow widely for the second time, when an enormous crowd gathered in the village Krasnoe this time. Constructions raised especially for this holiday, of temporary character, depicted the Azov with towers, gates and minarets ("highwatch-towers"). In the real space of a grandiose theatrical decoration the troops that had returned from the Azov, reproduced the conquering and bombing of the Turkish fortress. The battle action was added by a fire-work that lasted from the midnight till the morning and in which Peter himself took the most active part. A decoration on a specially arranged ice-hole on the Krasnoselskiy pond depicted Neptune floating on a sea-horse. Behind him on an ice land there were triumphal gates with a wall of fiery rockets. Then a huge triumphal column raised with an inscription – "victory" and an allegoric picture of Nica on the throne. At two sides of the column there were shields with a picture of the eagle – a symbol of Russia, that engaging the Turkish crescent with rockets (it was that machine operated by Peter). There were also transparencies here with battle scenes of the siege of the Azov by the Russian army and fleet, triumphal "pillars" or "trophies" – obelisks and pyramids.

The triumphal gates (of about 11 m high and 13-15 m wide) were adorned with paintings and sculptures made by the masters of the Armoury with John Saltanov at the head. For the first time in the decoration of an arch Peter was likened to antique gods and heroes. The fact of construction of a triumphal arch was unprecedented for Moscow and Russia, as it had formed as a separate type of building in Ancient Rome and was reborn during the New Time to immortalize great deeds, first of all military victories of the emperor. New was the fact of immortalization and glorifying of the emperor's earthly deeds with the help of the means established in pagan Rome and reborn in European countries.

Together with this already in the first triumphal gates there was the likening of a tsar to Christian saints and their inclusion in panegyrical compositions, that was widely spread in the first half of 18th century. Like his father, Peter was often likened to St. Constantine the Great. Rebirth of his cult during Peter's time got double meaning: together with the traditional Christian meaning the imperial one was actively emphasized. Combination of Christian symbols and allegories with antique pagan ones, that was Introduced for the first time widely into triumphal genres of art of Peter's time is a distinctive feature of baroque art. In difference to baroque classicism with its strict rigorism and orientation at neatness of style allows use of only antique characters, mythological and allegorical plots. As for the triumphal gates in honour of the Azov's taking, at their both sides there were pyramids entwined with plants, that glorified the "bravest marine and field warriors". The pyramids were connected to the gates with huge bright pictures with battle scenes;the same scenes adorned the tower: "the occasion of the Azov's taking was made on the tower, also in front of the tower and at its both sides all was painted in a picturesque way, all that had happened near the Azov"5 .

Gala entries into the capital with construction of triumphal gates and organization of fire-works became a tradition during Peter's time. Celebrations were often arranged, enveloping all the capital, and most important, were the first action and material symbol that changed its look and traditional symbolics. The New Year fire-work of 1700 was already mentioned. In 1702 in honour of the victory of B. P. Sheremetiev near Erstfer on Red Square a "triumphal arch" and a gallery-hall were constructed, where Peter gave a banquet to the military estate, that lasted all night. The celebration ended with a three-hour fire-work. In the same 1702 on the occasion of taking Nienchance a gala procession of troops through three triumphal gates took place. In the next 1703 celebration with construction of four gates for march of troops was conducted in connection with the taking of Nienchance, Koporie, Ingermanlandia and the foundation at the mouth of the Neva of the fortress Saint-Petersburg. One gate bordered with Voskresenskie (Iberon) gates of Kitay-gorod, the second gate was in Nikolskaya street in front of Zaiconospasskiy monastery, the third one was ear lljinskie gate, the fourth was built in Miasnitskaya street by A. D. Menshikov near his own house. Near Riazanskoe representation on a majestic pedestal under a canopy a portrait of tsar Alexius Mikhailovich and an icon of the Theotokos were placed, in Red Square a high tower crowned with the state flag was built.

On 14th December, 1704, on the occasion of taking of Derpt and Narva again a gala entry into the capital took place, to which construction of already seven triumphal gates was timed, they were decorated with "pictures of Mars, Hercules, Bellerophon, Neptune, Juno, and simultaneously – an allegoric Nadezhda (Hope) was holding the labarum of St. Constantine the Great". The next "entry with triumph" in Moscow took place on 19th December, 1705; for it Peter ordered "to rebuild the previous triumphal gate and to make a pyramid".

In 1709 with special splendour the victory near Poltava was celebrated. For the celebration in the ancient capital eight triumphal gates were built: near Serpukhovskie gates, near Kamenniy bridge, in Red Square at the beginning of Nikolskaya street, at Chistiye ponds near Miasnitskaya street at the yard of prince A. D. Menshikov, in Miasnitskaya street at the expense of the Stroganoffs, near Riazanskoe representation, near Zemlianoy town in the place of the most recent Red gate. The celebration lasted for ten days from 21st December, 1709, to 1st January, 1710. On the first day a ceremony of portentous entry of Peter in Moscow took place, the procession stopped near each triumphal gate. Public celebration which had started in the morning, continued in the evening with the light of illumination and fire-works. The tenth day ended with an enormous firework.

By the end of 1700 ideas and forms of a secular celebration had formed, which included gala processions of troops and fireworks. The route of holiday processions was defined, they usually began in the Kremlin, and after Petersburg had been made a capital – they began near Tverskaya piquet. The route always included the Kremlin, from where a procession went to the new centre of Moscow – Preobrazhenskoe. The Triupmhal gate was installed in the main points of Moscow historic structure, at the places of crossing of the main streets with fortress walls; in

Tverskaya street near the gates of Zemlianoy and Bely towns, near the Nikolskie gate of the Kremlin, in Miasnitskaya street near the gates of Bely and Zemlianoy towns (the present square of Krasnye (Red) gate). Thus, the spatial organization of a secular celebration was fixed by the main points at the places of crossing of radial main roads and circles of fortress walls. The Triumphal gate, which was constantly renewed, practically became a permanent element of town buildings. They became the backbones of the new secular town-building construction, born by the cult of the tsar and the state, enveloping and symbolically uniting all the city with the secular idea of triumph and state power. Thus their principal difference from religious processions. Due to celebrations of Peter's victories in Moscow the basis of the new secular architecture, new town-building principles and new secular symbolics of a capital town formed. More than that, during these celebrations the basis of the secular art of Russia of the New Time as a whole formed.

Peter's reign passed under the sign of novelty. Secular holidays and the triumphal arches and fire-works that decorated them became one of the brightest expressions of pithy and artistic innovation. During the time of Peter I the new acquired the meaning of valuable character. It was "a synonym of good, valuable, worth to be followed, and "the old was understood as bad, subject to breaking and liquidation. People of Peter's epoch imagined Russia as "some reborn into a new form" creature or as an off-spring. In the "Eulogic Word about the Poltavskaya Battle" Theophanes Prokopovich glorified "Russia, reborn, powerful and absolutely grown up".

All these images were summed up in one idea – a miraculous and full transfiguration of Russia under emperor Peter's power. Kantemir found a synthetic form:

> *"those are the wise who do not take Peter's*
> *orders off their hands, thus we have become already,*
> *the new people".*

The Image of "new Russia" and "new people" became an original myth that had appeared at the beginning of 18th century already..."

View from the Kremlin of Nikolskie triumphal gate and the Arsenal (1702-1736, architects M. Choglokov, M. Remezov, Kh.Konrad, D. Ivanov). Print according to M.l.Makhaev's drawing.

But such position, as scientists note, is not unique in Russia and is not characteristic only for Peter I. This idea was characteristic for the whole 18th century and the fist quarter of 19th century – i.e. from the reign of Peter I to the reign of Alexander I. But to make it possible for the tsar to influence events in his state and to transform it radically, the understanding of the state and the tsar's personality should have been changed. Alexius Mikhailovich already became an absolute ruler. According to the words of a contemporary, he "rules the state at his own will", and "Peter could not overdo him much in this respect". But before Peter autocracy had been abstract, i. e. autocracy of a tsar, not a concrete person. Completion of absolutism formation, which happened during Peter's time, included transfer to personified absolutism – dictatorship of concrete absolute. Peter was not just an autocrat who used absolute power. He not only "is obliged to give anybody an answer for his

Gala arrival in Moscow for the occasion of celebration of the victory near Poltava in 1709. Print of A.F.Zubov.

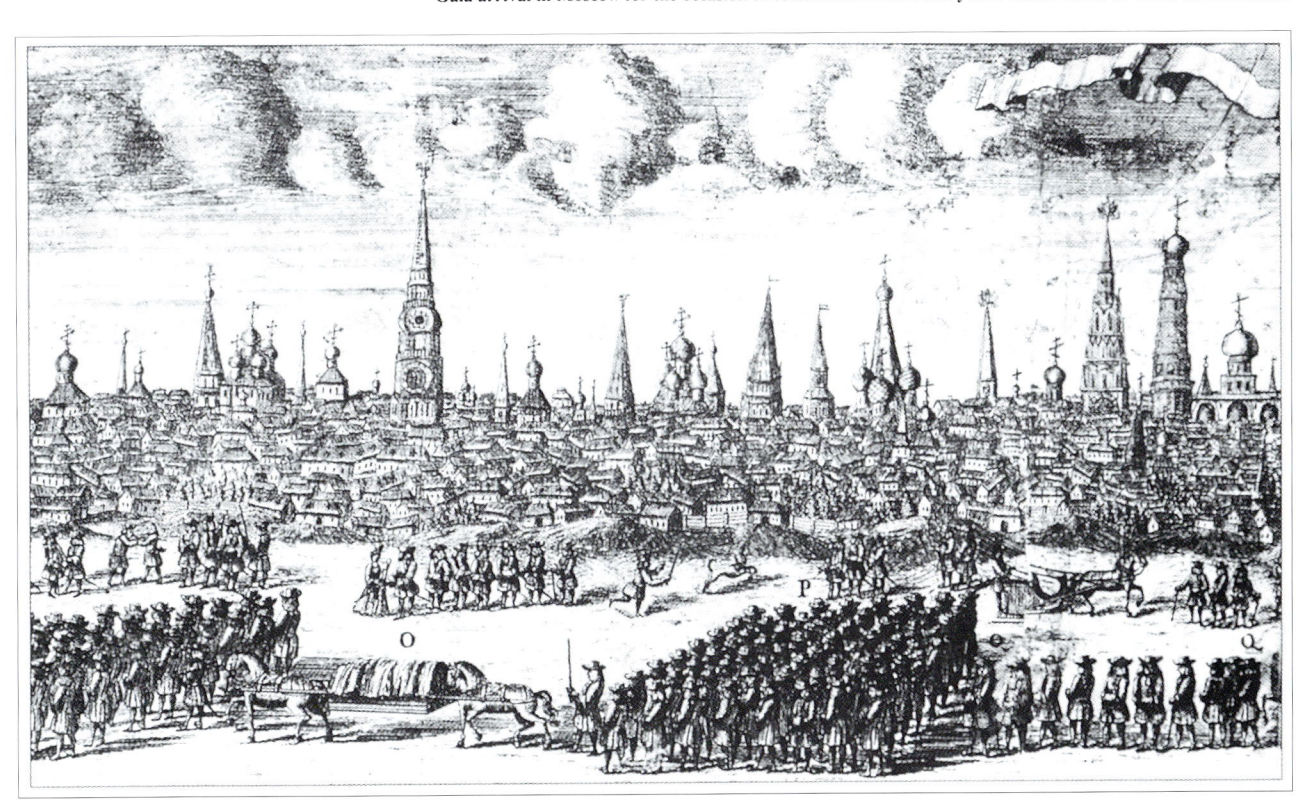

deeds, but has force and power to rule his states and lands, like a Christian tsar, duly and of his own will". Following the example of European states. Peter created the personality cult step by step and purposefully. He received the name of a "father of the Fatherland" and an emperor of All Russia, which were credited to him by right".

Creation of another version of absolutism, different from what it had been before – a personal one, personified, and such type of absolutism had formed in Europe of the time of Renaissance with a typical idea, dating from the epoch of Renaissance, of power personification, required the attitude towards the person of a tsar, which had been strange for Russia till then. The new notion about him was to form the new influence events in ideology, new system of view points. It was to consolidate, legalize and to reason the cult of a concrete ruler, that very tsar. An example to follow was found by Peter in contemporary Europe and Ancient Rome, partially in orthodox traditions and patriarchal views prevailing in Russia. The symbol of Peter's reforms and new Russia, which was being created (or just created) by him, became the title of emperor and renaming of Moscow kingdom into the Russian empire. As analogues he could take the Roman empire, Byzantium, Holy Roman Empire. The title of the "father of the Fatherland", simultaneously adopted by him, could be comprehended and used as an original Westernized analogue of the traditional patriarchal character. In the ideology of Peter's time (and this is typical for the culture, ideology, mentality of baroque and remained during the first half of 18th century) there is orientation at the orthodox ancient Russian tradition and European one existing in two entities of contemporary experience and antique inheritance mostly of Ancient Rome, the traditions which closely interacted in the same phenomena, or sometimes existed separately prevailing in some separate sphere. Peter's understanding of the emperor's title was connected with the orientation at Western European culture. He was the first who changed the old Moscow rule to address tsars by their Christian names and father`s names and began to name himself like kings and emperors of Western Europe and Christian spiritual fathers by the name and Peter the First, thus emphasizing the beginning of "counting of a certain historical period" [6].

The cult of the tsar's personality, introduced by Peter, getting in Russia the character of apotheosizing, created other relations than before between him and the church and the state. The victory of kingdom over priesthood, gained by Alexius Mikhaylovich, acquired during the time of Peter I corresponding organizational forms. It resulted in creation in 1721 of the Holy Synod instead of the cancelled patriarchate, the first became fully subordinated to the tsar and in essence it was one of the departments of the new bureaucracy. The personified autocracy, consolidated by Peter, made him an official ruler of the state's destiny, and his reformatory seemed to be fully in conformity with the new ideal of personified power and required a new regulated state structure. The tsar, a certain tsar, a concrete person became a personification of the state; praising of a tsar was comprehended and represented praising of the state. And on the contrary. Glorifying of the state, its well being, was associated with deserts and virtues of a tsar and connected with his name. The notions of a tsar and the state became synonyms and could substitute each other.

This part of the official conception of Peter's reign was expressed in the triumphal arches. They also represented one of the options of reconsideration of the traditional Ancient Russian formula – Moscow – the Third Rome in new rituals and arrangement of secular holidays. In the conception of the Third Rome, from the two components of this formula – imperial and Christian – for Peter, as it was mentioned, the first one – imperial – was important. That was the reason of his orientation at the first – Ancient Imperial Rome and the appearance of one of the brightest expressions of the imperial idea – triumphal processions and triumphal arches. In Moscow this idea got spatial-architectural embodiment, enveloped all the city, included two Moscow centres – the new and the old ones, and even symbolically extended on all Russia and its new capital Petersburg. With that the transformation of Tverskaya street into the main road was connected, as it opened or closed the way from one capital to the other and united them.

Fire-works and triumphal gates, the tradition of which appeared in Moscow, creations of program new art and embodiment of the new aesthetic ideal confirmed the idea of l. E. Grabar, that Peter's architecture and Russian architecture of New time were born in Moscow.

The move of the court to Petersburg did not change the attitude to Moscow as to the place of immortalization and celebration of the most important state events. In 1712 in Moscow there was a fire-work on the occasion of the wedding of Peter and Catherine I. In both capitals fire-works in honour of the Nativity of Christ, during the Shrove and on the New Year were arranged annually. As a result there was an original mixture of notions. Sacred became secular, worldly values turned into sacral ones, and both became state ones in an original way. Important events in the imperial family (weddings, coronations, Angel days, births of babies) were raised to the level of the state ones and celebrated together with religious holidays (like Christmas), holidays born by the Europeanization (the New Year), people's ones dating from pagan Rus (Shrove-tide). Together with that royal days were celebrated: holidays of the imperial family became secular ones (free days) and simultaneously church ones accompanied with gala divine services. Such was the influence of the traditions of antique paganism, reborn by Europe, on execution of the orthodox ritual, which went on together with likening of the mighty of the earth to antique gods. The established tradition gave rise to new analogies at the time of Peter's successors – Catherine I, Anna Ioannovna, Elizabeth Petrovna, Catherine II.

Likening of an empress to antique gods, for instance the likening of an empress to Minerva and other female deities of antique pantheon, was usually associated with Catherine II as most widely spread in her time, dated from the reign of Elizabeth Petrovna. The triumphal gates, built in 1742 in Petersburg in honour of gala entrance of Elizabeth Petrovna into the capital after the coronation in Moscow, were crowned with a statue of Minerva that symbolized the empress, lower there were together with eight angels – eight Greek gods.

Celebration of events of Peter's family life, accompanied by arrangement of fire-works in Petersburg and Moscow, raised them to the level of events of state importance and gave start to another tradition. That tradition existed during all 18th century and was developed further after Peter's time. In 1725, after Peter's death, a "gala entry" into the ancient capital and construction of triumphal gates had forthcome the coronation of Catherine I; during the coronation celebrations a fire-work was arranged. Besides political reasons of celebrations – military victories and conclusion of peace treaties, coronations, the emperor's birthday, events of the emperor's family life – events of cultural life were also celebrated in 18th century. In 1753 in Moscow a grandiose fire-work was arranged in honour of opening of the first university in Russia.

The usual location of triumphal gates in Moscow was kept while there was the custom of building of temporary triumphal structures. Succession was kept also in architecture and contents of the style of the gates situated in a certain place. Krasnye gates, that were changed successively in 1722, 1724, 1727, 1732, 1742, repeated each other in composition, contents and character of the adornment, though they were raised on different occasions.

Antique motif in triumphal constructions of Peter the Great in Moscow

On 20th August, 1696, after the Azov victory, tsar Peter wrote to deacon Vinius to Moscow: "Min Her Vinius"... I offer more in some case. It said: "The labourer is worthy of his reward", as, to my mind, it will be better to receive

Moscow fire-work in 1744.

Mr. Generalissimo and other gentlemen, who worked so hard, with triumphal gates built in their honour: as for the place on this occasion, to my mind, a bridge across the Moscow-river will be convenient for it, or something which is better"[7] – it was the first mention about triumphal gates in Russian history. The message shows undoubtfully that the initiator of the construction was the tsar himself. It was also mostly he who developed the order of celebrations. His letter is known where he mentioned use of cannons during celebrations, as well as that he "on the way to Moscow went forward with little suite and stayed in the village of Kolomenskoe in the expectation of the troops and construction of triumphal gates and other signs of victory; meanwhile he occupied himself with establishment of the order of the portentous entry for his commanders and army"[8]. Certainly, deacon Vinius did great service in the real construction of the gates (his answers to Peter's orders about construction of gates testify, on the one hand, that he understood well what the tsar asked him for, on the other hand – about creative attitude to his task), however, the leading role of Peter in integration of the idea itself is evident.

How did these first Russian triumphal gates look like? One of the most profound Peter's biographers I. Golikov described them as follows: "At the entrance of the stone bridge triumphal gates were built according to the style of ancient Roman triumphal gates with the following adornments: on their right side there was a statue of Mars that had a sword in its right hand, and a bucker in the left one with the inscription: by Mars' bravery; at its feet there were slaves, tatar Murza with a bow and a quiver, behind him there were two chained tatars... On the left side there was a statue of Hercules on the same pedestal holding his usual club in the right hand a green branch with the inscription regarding Hercules' force in the left hand. At his feet a pasha of the Azov in turban and two chained Turks lead..."[9].

Their central part was adorned as follows: "A double-headed eagle under three crowns raised above the pediment among banners, lances; above it cannons, balls, bombs and marine ships were painted... Flying Glory held laurels in one hand and an olive branch in the other. There was an inscription under it: "The labourer is worthy of his reward". In the centre of the gates a green wreath hang, from which two gilded trellis with large inscriptions went down. One had the inscription: "Coming back of tsar Constantine with victory", the second one – "The victory of tsar Constantine over the evil tsar Maxencius of Rome". On the vault of the gates it was written in three places: "Came, Saw, Won" (which was not quite right, because the siege of the Azov fortress lasted for two years). The above-mentioned inscriptions are extremely informative for us, they testify to the innovative character of the construction. Really, here for the first time in Russian architecture the figure of Glory appeared (though just painted) and was not abandoned for three centuries already; military accessories were introduced in architectural construction and occupied, as it is known, an important place in the decorum of Russian classicism, and direct and reasoned historical analogies were given – Peter's Azov victory was compared with the victories of Constantine the Great and Julius Caesar ("came, saw, won" – the famous Caesar's message to Rome informing about the Pontic victory over Pharnak). The high authority of the metaphors chosen, perhaps, by Peter himself, is amazing, as they included Russian contemporary history not in the periphery of European one, but in its most important events. Here, certainly, the ambitious inspiration of that time, crucial in the history of the state, revealed itself – the inspiration to create a new society more open to the world.

It is possible to see in the triumphal celebration, the first in Peter's life, on the occasion of the Azov, an original dialogue of a young tsar with his friends and teachers, including those from the German settlement, his really royal gratitude expressed in the language of antique historical symbolics common for them. It is also evident that Peter wanted to make Lefort glad in this way with the results of European knowledge achieved by him. Thus it can be explained that he plotted out independently the Azov's action, its symbolic and semantic arrangement, as well as it was Lefort who was in the centre of the procession, he was honoured like a "generalissimo", though his share in the Azov's victory was quite small. As for Peter, he participated in it nearly like an on-looker, or to be more precise, like a producer watching with partiality the show made by him – and, probably, listening to the reaction of the audience (the future emperor was walking in front of Preobrazhenskiy regiment in a simple officer's full-dress coat after Lefort's carriage)[10].

The semantics of the carriage's design, in which the "general-admiral" was sitting solemnly, was close to the gate's semantics – "an open triumphal carriage made like a sea shell, it was not possible to see the wheels: they were covered with Tritons and other sea monsters, it was shining with gold. . ."[11] It is not difficult to guess according to this description that Lefort himself symbolized, riding in the carriage, nearly Neptune itself – the ruler of the seas, which was a rather clear hint at the connection of the victory with the sea pretentious of the powerful country and, perhaps, was to flatter the Swiss.

That comparison of Peter's deeds and the deeds of Caesar and Constantine, first made here, should be mentioned especially. His thorough knowledge of life of famous Roman men is evident (anyway, the famous inscription "Came, saw, won" was used in Caesar's Pontic triumph, who won a quick victory). It was expressed not only in the visible parallelism of their political actions (they were also interested in the plans of the capitals' development, were occupied in a wide legal activity, patronized science and art etc.), which ran through all his life, sometimes, perhaps, intentionally making a cult of it.

Probably, Peter could not remain indifferent to such facts of minor importance at first sight: "They say, he (Julius Caesar – *M. N.*) was tall, of light complexion, well-built, with a rather full face, black and vivid eyes. He was remarkably healthy: only at the end of his life he began suddenly to faint and got overwhelmed by fear at night, and twice during lessons he had bouts of falling sickness", or: "During a military march he was walking in front of the army, sometimes he was riding a horse, bare-headed regardless of heat or rain"[12]. (Did not these latter lines induce Peter to walk in front of Preobrazhenskiy regiment at the Azov's celebration?). Peter's unvariable interest to Caesar's life was confirmed by the fact that upon his order Julius messages were translated into Russian, telling about his military marches.

Numerous personal parallels connected (especially In future) life of Peter (the Great) and Constantine the Great – capital punishment of the first born sons, hard fate of the first wives, the change of years counting, foundation of the capitals called after their names, finally, even the establishment of the Academies reveals some similarity[13]. We should pay attention to it at least because that parallelism of the deeds of Caesar, Constantine and Peter was expressed in architecture, in any case, the appearance in Russian architecture of the construction of the new type – triumphal arches, was absolutely connected with it. It is also important to mention that constant comparisons of Peter with Constantine the Great canonized by the church, as well as with St. Apostle Peter, testify that "sacralization of Peter began already during his life", which was also expressed in the semantics of triumphal processions.

Peter's biographer, assessing those magnificent celebrations, explained simple-heartedly: "...The great tsar entered his capital portentously after each victory, and this was not because he loved such showing off of magnificence, or wished to extol himself with his victories, like ancient Romans did, but only in order that such performances, arranged as often as possible, induced love in the hearts of his servants to glory and to his new establishments". This consideration, certainly, had some good sense, however, it is supposed that not only due to it the triumphal processions easily became a fully established tradition of the first half of 18th century. Probably, people enjoyed the noisy, colourful and, it seems, merry processions (for example, an entry of triumphal troops into the city was usually accompanied by a chime of many bells [14]. Its culmination became a divine service in the cathedral of the Assumption). And at the same time they were more relaxed, close in their character to Shrove-tide and Christmas-tide celebrations; music, songs, jokes, a spontaneous conversation found their place here.

The motif of changing dresses common for ancient church and public processions, should also be emphasized here. Characteristic for Shrove-tide and Christmas-tide rituals of Ancient Russia, it obtained during Peter's time a special meaning – a so called playing a tsar was widely spread. During Peter's time the role of a tsar or a patriarch was often performed during his fun processions by his noble men (the triumphator during the Azov's celebrations was Lefort, the prince-Caesar was F. Yu. Romodanovskiy, the prince-pope was P. l. Buturlin). B. A. Uspenskiy considers "playing a tsar" to be indirectly connected with the likening to the Deity[15]. One of expressions of this Russian medieval tradition, genetically connected with the ritual "procession on a donkey", made till 1696 by the patriarch on Palm Sunday and imitating Christ's entry into Jerusalem, was the triumphal procession in Moscow in 1709 after Poltavskaya victory, during which Peter himself was in the image of Christ[16].

If in the first Azov's gates historical parallels between Peter and antique foreimages were reasoned in some way, beginning from the gates of 1703 his expressions as gods (Mars, Neptune) and heroes (Heracles, Agamemnon, Perseus) became traditional. The tsar became the main character of semantic-symbolic plot of the gates, acting among the other numerous chanters of antique mythology – Juno, Clio, Phoenix, Triton, Aeolus, Diana, Ceres, Cerberus, Jupiter, Europa, Palladium, Fortuna, Pan, Porphyrion, Bellona, Halcione, Medusa, Phoebe, Marsy, Apollo, Mercury, Tezey, Fury, Saturn, Janus, Globe, Bacchus, Ariadne, Castor, Pollux and others[17]. The flow of new symbolics that poured into Russian public conscience, made it necessary to explain at that time why on the triumphal gates there "were no images from the divine scripts, but from marine stories, told not by saints, but by historians or poets". Comments of Josef Turoboyskiy, given to this effect in the book "The Glorious Triumph of Livonia's Liberator..." (1704) are quite remarkable. Turoboyskiy stated in favour exactly of such semantics of triumphal constructions the following: "As it is not a temple or a church created in the name of some Saint, but a political, i. e. civil praise of those who work hard for the wholeness of their Fatherland and with their labour, assisted by God, defeating enemies from ancient time (like tsar Constantine in Rome defeated Maxencius) in all political, not barbarian peoples, so that the praised and honoured virtue grows..."[18] Not limiting himself by this reference to the traditional nature of such celebrations, reasoning about a possibility of such "worldly" comparisons, he wrote that they were characteristic for the holy texts too: "we see in divine scripts too... numerous divine images of Christ Himself; either the life-giving tree, or the water-giving stone, or the Iamb, the ox, and others". The evident vacillation of borders between the worldly and the church, visibly demonstrated by Turoboyskiy, makes us pay more attention to the problem of secular and religious contents in the triumphal gates of the beginning of 18th century.

Church "tsar's" gates (holy gates) and triumphal gates (also "tsar's" – the tsar passed through them) had something similar not only in their name, those were the gates for "the righteous souls", it was not by chance, for example, that "traitor Yakushka" was led by a group of soldiers in the Azov procession not through the Triumphal gates, but through the next to it access of Vsekhsvjatskiy bridge. In front of the Triumphal gates they stopped, went out of the carriages, alighted from the horses, took off their hats in front of them and listened to the welcome speeches of ecumenic and civil people with reverence . The fortress town gates were of the same sacral nature as of a de-fence from devils, near the gates temples or chapels were often built, and above the lock of the gate's arch, as a rule, an icon-case was installed with a venerated icon. Coming through the town`s gates a wayfarer took off his hat and crossed himself.

Triumphal gates were often adorned with plots and inscriptions from the Holy Script, however, even on those gates, where secular semantics prevailed, there were symbolic images of ecclesiastical content. For example, on the top of the picture "Triumphal Gates of Nobleman Stroganov", finishing the central part of the gates, a pelican is well seen, that tears his bosom with his beak and feeds his nestlings with his blood, – it is one of the most ancient metaphorical images of Christ, that quite naturally occupies the highest central place. About the special sacral meaning of the gates the following fact also testifies – after the speech of Rjazanskiy metropolitanate Stephan Javorskiy, made near the gates raised in the honour of Poltavskaya victory, by clergy men, "on skilfully made clouds from the gates' vaults" a few lads in white and with wings like Angels, "were descended, "they sang a spiritual song seemly for the celebration". Certainly, there was much from theatrical performances in such

Triumphal gate of eminent man Stroganov.

realistic expression of a special status of triumphal gates, however, due to their special plot they cannot be referred just to entertainment actions. Besides, the gates were generously decorated with fir branches, candles, flowers, artificial fruit, which also made them a sacred thing adorned for a religious holiday.

Some symbolic likeness of triumphal gates to iconostases is a specific Russian feature not typical to semantics of Roman triumphal arches, but there is a rather original understanding of antiquity in it, which was characteristic for the border of 17th-18th centuries. "Antique mythology was not understood by Russian people as something real... The audience of 18th century associated pagan antique gods first of all with the first centuries of Christianity". Association of antique history in commonplace consciousness with the pre-history and first centuries of Christianity made the process of wide adaptation of mythological and historical antiquity easier and more understandable for wide masses besides that this figurativeness was expressed by many kinds of art (painting, architecture and literature). This cultural basis, which was rapidly introduced into architectural creation, prepared already during the first ten years of 18th century a new formal and symbolical architectural language, which was embodied most brightly in the phenomenon of Russian classicism. In metaphorical meaning the triumphal gates of Peter's epoch were the gates into the world of West-European culture, which they began to understand widely in Russia.

State-Imperial Idea in Development of Moscow

The second centre appeared in Moscow. It was located not only behind the borders of the historical centre – the Kremlin, but also behind the borders of Moscow of that time, the border of which went along Zemljanoy bank – near the Yauza, in the German settlement, in Preobrazhenskoe. The monocentric structure of Moscow became double-cenrtic. The old centre kept the importance of the all-state and religious centre. The new centre also acquired the importance of an all-state, as well as a military one. There was also the main royal residence. Triumphal arches and routes of portentous processions were fixed in accordance with these two centres. The Kremlin and Preobrazhenskoe mark the beginning and end of the route. Appearance of a new centre behind the borders of the historical one and even behind the borders of the town was not an exclusive speciality of development of the Russian capital during the period crucial for the country. There were analogues to it in creation of new royal residences in France (first Tuilrie near Paris itself, then Versailles, Escoreala in Spain).

Peter had his predecessors in Russia itself too – his father and grandfather. This phenomenon was noted by S. M. Soloviev already in the last century. He noted the efforts of "tsars to free themselves, at least for some time, out of the Kremlin's smallness to the vastness of the country-side. During the time of tsar Michael the village of Pokrovskoe became such a place of stay, during the time of tsar Alexius it was Izmaylovo, then Preobrazhenskoe which was so closely connected with the German settlement during Peter's time. In consequence of the above 17th and 18th centuries saw a new Moscow, Moscow washed by the river Yauza, in difference to the old one washed by the Moscow-river and Neglinnaya"[19].

Peter's centre at the Yauza grew out of fun exercises of the future tsar. There were headquarters of the first fun regiments here, that later became the basis of the Russian regular army and got their names after the local villages Preobrazhenskiy and Semenovskiy. There also was the fun town-fortress Preshburg. It was not the only fun town around Moscow, they appeared everywhere where Peter lived for a comparatively long time: in Semenovskoe, in Voskresenskoe at Presnja, in Kolomenskoe, in Losinaya (Sokolnicheskaya) woods. But Preshburg's role in Preobrazhenskoe was special. It was 500 m from royal chambers and born the name of a "table town". Its front gates which represented a high octahedral hip roof tower looking at three sides, just like a similar tower of the meeting house on Stromynskaja road, historians connect with the appearance of the first secular memorial in the capital – Sukharevskaja tower. Its historical significance is in the appearance of the idea itself of a secular architectural memorial – a principally new phenomena for Russia. Connection of the composition of this memorial, being far from European prototypes, with the composition of the gates emphasizes the limitness of the process of formation of secular art for Russia itself and Moscow.

Peter's Moscow bounded by the Yauza, was created as a new secular centre of state life. Here regularly planned settlements for Preobrazhenskiy and Semenovskiy regiments first appeared. Here at the General Court the Tsar's Duma gathered, where such departments were focused, which were connected with the tsar's, i. e. military service. Here a special medical body – a military hospital (1706-1707), not connected with monasteries, was first built in Russia. Also here after reorganization of governmental bodies from 1711 the Senate was located. The German settlement with its straight streets and houses situated along the red line became the prototype of architectural innovations in the capital and in Russia"[20].

Construction of palaces in Moscow, signifying separation from the Middle Ages and transfer to the art of the new time, dates from 1690s and from the point of view of the territory it was also connected with the new centre at the Yauza. 1690s was the time of Peter's official strengthening on the throne. Two huge complexes were built at the Yauza according to the program – estates of the closest like-minded associates of Peter – F. Lefort (1691-1699) and F. Golovin (from 1702). It is significant that the construction, program in its novelty, was conducted on behalf of Peter's closest confederates. At the beginning he himself did not dare to build openly his official residences in the forms contradicting the traditions of old Moscow architecture, and used the palaces of his associates for state receptions. This practice remained later in Moscow and Petersburg. Only in 1700s in Moscow and in 1710s in Petersburg that role was assumed by prince A. Menshikov in his construction.

Composition of the estates located on both banks of the Yauza – Lefort's estate was on the right bank and Golovin's one was on the left bank – took into account the impression they made if they were looked at from the water, like the ensembles of old Russian estates, including royal ones, for example, the famous Kolomenskoe estate. However, in the old estates before Peter's time the main meaning and the centre of the composition was the church. Churches defined the general view and the panorama of an estate. They were taken into account when estate's composition was made and the views of it were open from the most favourable points. Chambers were of subordinative character in respect of the church. Regarding the estates at the Yauza, an absolutely opposite phenomena happened there. The main role – from the point of the meaning and the composition – was attributed to the palace and the entertainment park.

Novelty in the plot complied the novelty in composition, architecture and style. Palace buildings got representative symmetrical axis composition. Order got an important meaning in the building's look. Entertainment-representation function of the estate changed the planning and the look of a park. Like in the city (in the city it was in an ideal, in the park – in the reality) the regular planning of an estate and ponds of geometrically right form were realized.

The composition of Lefort's ensemble was created taking into account the point of view from the river and from the opposite bank. The ensemble of Golovinskiy palace, the construction of which was started later than Lefort's one, had even more evident features of an entertainment estate. Its representation functions were defined at once after the end of the construction – in 1703. Peter received an envoy of Ludovig XIV there.

At the end of his reign Peter began construction of a new residence in Lefortovo, now already under the influence of what he had seen in Europe, as well as the experience of creation of the Summer garden and countryside residences near Petersburg. In 1722 he bought the estate from Golovin's heirs. Upon his order the big regular park with channels was re-arranged. At the corners of the stalls the emperor instructed to build various "Hermitages", pavilions Echo. Grotto. In the cascade, arranged in the park and reminding of the one in Petergof, a statue of Samson was installed like in the residence in Petersburg – a memorial of the victory over Sweden (lion is the Swedish State Emblem). The regular park ensemble with plenty of sculptures, summer-houses, complex symbolics of an ensemble of developed European style, was well-developed, though it was created in many cases of temporary materials (statues were carved from wood, garden pavilions were covered with linen above the deal and painted) not by chance. The contents of the ensemble are explained by the date of the construction. It was started in a few months after conclusion of the peace treaty with Sweden, favourable for Russia, Peter's official acceptance of the titles of the Emperor and the Father of the Fatherland, the change of the official country's name to the Russian Empire and the naming of the head of the state as Peter the First and Peter the Great.

Judging by the kept descriptions, rebuilding of Golovinskiy estate was to make new Petergof out of it, a memorial to Peter, the empire, new Russia and to make it equal in its architecture to the most powerful royal courts of Europe. The change of the cultural and political orientation in the second half of Peter's reign was accompanied with the change of the architectural and painting orientation. There was a turn from the sample of the architecture of burgher Holland to the architecture of royal France. New Golovin's estate and a number of other similar undertakings near Moscow were to become memorials of this turn. The fact of rebuilding of Golovin's estate and grandiosity of the plan illustrated another thing too. The new interest to Moscow and the effort to make it though the second, but the capital of Russian Empire, promptly raising an imperial residence conforming to the country's new name.

The estates, created according to Peter's order in compliance with the new ideas and ideals, initiated the new type of palace-like and rich estate dwelling both in the city itself and in Moscow country-side. Preobrazhenskoe initiated much of what later was spread in both capitals and in Russia. This district was the first planned according to the principles of regularity as a straight one with streets situated in chess order and rectangular quarters. The houses in the streets were built with "continuous fasade", reminding of burgher houses and Dutch and German towns. Here street lamps appeared for the first time in Russia. As a result, the statement that Petersburg was born in Moscow, becomes clear, because Moscow was the first place for introduction of Peter's novelties, including those in the architectural and town-building spheres. The spatial localization of the novelties – Yauzskaja Moscow, Preobrazhenskoe – seems to be natural. "Preobrazhenskoe" (of the Transfiguration) "or Preobrazhensk, as it was called during Peter's time, became in full meaning of the word the capital of transfiguration of Russia, while it was started in Moscow". Like "from Preobrazhenskie entertainments a magnificent and powerful organization of all the state appeared, which was called the Empire... from Preburg near Yauza St. Petersburg turned out and flourished near the Neva".

Thus historical and architectural – town-building importance of Yauza's territories was outlined. Here new Russia was born. Here Petersburg was born. But here also new Moscow was born, Petersburg in Moscow, Petersburg before Petersburg or, quoting the words of I. E. Zabelin: "For the rest of Moscow the German settlement in general was Petersburg of some kind, where Europe predominated, all educated and, mainly, all foreign which since that time in all cases was thought of as the gauge both for private and social life".

The general idea of Peter's reign was reproduced in Moscow again and again in various spheres of architectural and town-building activity, on different territories.

Rebuilding of Moscow's historical centre was started from the change of the ancient sacral centre into a secular one, to say more precisely from consolidation of secular aspect in it. From the moment of its appearance Petersburg was formed not only as the administrative centre of Russia, but also as the military capital. However, a new military capital of new Russia was turning up in Moscow too. And not only in Yauza's Moscow, but also in historical Moscow – in the Kremlin. Here, after another devastating fire of 1701, Peter ordered to begin construction of Arsenal (Zeughaus) on the place of the former Zhitnicheskiy yard and dismantled estates of the Trubetskoys and the Streshnevs. It was supposed to be not only a depot, but a storehouse of military trophies and old armament, i.e. a museum. First the construction was headed by Moscow architects, among whom M. Choglokov, the builder of Sukharevskaya Tower, was the leader. According to the initial project, the building's fasade, turned to the city, had no windows, and the building looked like a continuation of the Kremlin's wall. But inside, following the gauge of the famous refectories of the monastery of St. Simeon in Moscow and the Lavra of the Holy Trinity-St. Sergius, it was supposed to paint the walls with pictures of columns entwined with vine and to adorn richly the entrance with fretted sculpture. The symbolics of the decoration of a new secular building of new type was symptomatic. Vine is a symbol of Christ. Christian symbolics of the decoration, taken from temples to a secular building, sanctified with the authority of the highest values the emperor's undertakings, a symbol of which was to be the Arsenal. The history, already known after the triumphal arches, – new ideas and ideals were sanctified with an address to Christian symbols, repeated itself.

The traditional motif of the decoration was in combination with the new understanding of town space and composition of a building. It was expressed in extension of huge homogeneous wall surfaces, solidity of geometrically strict volume, which was so different from the multiple volume of ancient Russian architecture, and regular rhythm of double windows, showing the signs of the way of thinking characteristic for regular construction of fasades. Simultaneously with the works of the Arsenal's construction, in the same 1702 the building of the Ambassadorial Department was reconstructed after the fire.

In the Northern part of Red Square outside the Kremlin in 16th century already a new administrative and social centre began to be formed. The CoinYard (1697) and the General Chemist's on the place of the former Zemskoy Department (about 1700) referred to the first. The second included the "Comedy Chamber", the first public town theatre in Russia, built in 1702-1703 near Nikolskis gates. A huge wooden building equal in its height to the Kremlin's wall (13 m), in its square was twice as large as the court theatre of Alexius Mikhaylovich in Preobrazhenskoe. The theatre on Red Square was understood by people of traditional culture as a devilish act and an abuse of the sacred place: Muscovites did not visit the theatre. In 1706 it was officially liquidated.

In Red Square "Kazanskaja austeria" was built next to the General Chemist's, which combined the functions of a restaurant, a hotel, a place of public meetings and an education department: here a free lunch was served to each one who read an issue of the "Vedomosti", – the first Russian newspaper that was started from 1st January, 1703.

In Red Square, near Spasskiy bridge across the ditch near Spasskie gates, where book sale had been concentrated since ancient time, the first Russian public library appeared too. Its creator was a book seller, publisher and an engraver, the author of "Brjusov's Calendar" V. A. Kiprianov. The fasade of the building, European in its look, was decorated with allegorical sculptures "Science" and "Education"[21], also new to Muscovites in their meaning.

As a whole, Moscow, as it was already mentioned, kept its traditional look. It was a wooden town. Mostly the dwellings were of two types. The boyard estate was a well-developed ensemble of dwelling and economic constructions, situated in the yard inside the fence. The second type – a settlement dwelling house, – cubic volumes of settlement houses were situated along the perimeter of the quarter.

Peter's decrees were motivated by the wish to make an estate house closer to the street and to make it an active element of organization of street space. Large Moscow estates, which had been formed in 17th century, began to acquire the features of regularity in 18th century. For instance, the faзade of the house of deacon Abercius Kirillov, turned to the river, on Bersenevskaya quay, got a triple symmetrical composition and Europeanized decoration reminding of Menshikov's tower. Along the red line economic constructions were placed out, they got architectural treatment and symmetrical composition. Most early the new modes in dwelling buildings were found in large estates constructed in the streets which became the main ones. Such streets are Tverskaya, which went out to the road to Petersburg, the streets connecting the Moscow historical centre with the Yauza, and the streets close to the Yauza and Peter's Moscow of Yauza.

Temples of Peter's Reign

Location of temples of Peter's time and their symbolics were closely connected with the creation of new town-forming centres, and not only inside Moscow, but in Russia too, in other words, not only with Yauza's Moscow, but with Petersburg too. Both, as it was mentioned above, predetermined the location of the triumphal arches at the cross points of the spatial-planning structure of Moscow. The same circumstance predetermined increase of importance and turn to the main ones a number of Moscow streets. Now those streets were connected symbolically and in their contents with the realization of the state idea and the cult of the tsar and the state that was created on purpose.

There was succession and tear away in Peter's actions in respect of the closest ancestors. The first Romanovs created Yauza's Moscow to the north-east from the capital – a country centre-residence. Peter's residence was built near by, but not in the same place. In connection with this the streets leading from the Kremlin to the north-east were made the main ones. During the time of Michael Fedorovich and Alexius Mikhaylovich they included Iljinka, situated in front of Spasskie gates, then Pokrovka, Old Basmannaja and Pokrovskaya.

During Peter's time the main were also the streets leading to the north-east from the Kremlin, but others: Nikolskaya street going from the Kremlin's Nikolskie gates, the Mjasnitskaya, New Basmannaja. Besides, New Basmannaja was included by Peter specially for connection with the new centre. The change of location of the route happened not only because of Peter`s' wish to express the novelty of the conception of his reign, but because of appearance of the new capital – Petersburg. The routes leading from Petersburg to Moscow and in the Kremlin, and from the Kremlin to the new centre of the ancient capital, crossed near Voskresenskie gates of Kitay-gorod and Nikolskie gates of the Kremlin at the beginning of Nikolskaya street. An eloquent confirmation of it was the construction of one of the most brilliant program palace buildings of Peter's reign – the house of prince Gagarin with its strictly symmetrical composition of a whole volume, clear division of the faзade into floors, frontality of the composition, hierarchy of the faзades, with taking out of the main one on the red line of the street, presence of orders. There was a number of features in the building's architecture, which during Peter's time acquired the character of signs and became the symbol of new values. Gagarin's house was in Tverskaya, on the way of tsar's corteges, not far from Voskresenskie (Iberon) gates. Both routes, along Tverskaya to the Kremlin and out of the Kremlin to the Yauza, became original "tsar's" roads. The route from the Kremlin to the Yauza was architecturally arranged as an important independent pithy and structural component of Moscow town organism already during the time of Michael Fedorovich and Alexius Mikhaylovich. The importance of the axis connecting the Kremlin with the new royal estates (Pokrovskoe-Rubtsovo which was the residence of Michael Fedorovich, and Izmaylovo which was the residence of Alexius Mikhailovich) was emphasized by the consecration and architecture of the temples. The route to Pokrovskoe-Rubtsovo was opened by the cathedral of the Intercession at the beginning of Iljinka, now more known as the cathedral of St. Basil – the temple-memorial of the taking of Kazan. It was finished by the temple of the Intercession in Rubtsovo. Two more temples of the Intercession were situated along the route – at the beginning of Pokrovka. After the residence of Alexius Mikhaylovich was built in Izmaylovo where the way led along Pokrovskaya road past Rubtsovo, a monumental cathedral of the Intercession was built in it. Remembering about the symbolics of temples of the Intercession as about the special protection of Russia by the Theotokos and about one of interpretations of Moscow as the house of the Most Holy Theotokos, the importance of the meaning of the symbolics of the system of the temples of the Intercession, created in 17th century, becomes evident.

Peter not only used, but renovated this tradition. The renovation was in the construction of temples consecrated to his Saint Protector, which was one of the ways of the tsar's glorifying. The new contents were consolidated by traditional means: with the help of temple architecture and, for instance, by consecration of the temples. Peter tried to make both capitals, first the ancient one, then the new one, a town of St. Peter and a town of emperor Peter. A whole system of temples consecrated to his Saint protectors, was built. A town of St. Peter was Rome – the capital of the catholic world. In this way the capitals of Russia in their importance in the orthodox world were compared with

Church of the Holy Trinity in Kapeljki. (1708-1712; did not keep till now). Photo. Late 19th century.

the importance of Rome in the catholic world. But the same consecration could be as a denomination of Rome as the capital of the empire of the same name. The same meaning in the similar system of comparisons was received by Moscow – the capital and till 1712-1714 the main symbol of new Russia in the process of Europeanization.

Not only the similarity, but also the comparisons in the consecration of stone Peter's temples in Moscow and Petersburg are significant. All three temples in Moscow were consecrated to the emperor's divine protectors – Peter and Paul. They seemed to fix the angles of a vast spatial triangle which included a wide region of Peter's Moscow – Yauza's Moscow.

The main church of the new centre near the Yauza was built in Lefortov's settlement near the royal residence and the ensemble of hospital buildings. The second was built on the hill near the Yauza's fall into the Moscow-river on the water route from the Kremlin to the new governmental centre. And finally the third one was built in the square of Mjasnitskie gates near Triumphal gates at the beginning of New Basmannaja. The theme of divine protection was continued by creation of a sacrarium of Sts. Apostles Peter and Paul in the wooden church of the village Preobrazhenskoe and installation in temples that already existed of sacrariums of the same Saints in the royal village Pokrovskoe-Rubtsovo, thus emphasizing the succession of ideals of reign of all the Romanovs.

In Petersburg the secular-imperial aspect of consecrations of the main temples was even more evident. Petropavlovskiy and Isaakievskiy cathedrals were built opposite each other on both banks of the Neva. Isaakievskiy cathedral was built in the name of the Saint on whose day the future emperor was born. In Russia the day of physical birth was always less honoured than the spiritual one, and the fact of consecration of the cathedral to the Saint's name connected with the day of his physical birth, only emphasized the worldly striving of symbolics of temple-building during Peter's time. It is significant that Peter built a temple and immortalized the fact of his birth in the new capital, Petersburg.

In Moscow Peter did not take the risk to immortalize the fact of his physical appearance to the world, an act which is more characteristic to Protestants and strange to orthodoxy, limiting himself only to the opportunities given by the symbolics and likening of the names of his divine protectors.

But the tradition took roots. Besides even in Moscow it was embodied in consecrations of double kind: in temples of the same name as the emperor's that he got after christening, and in the temples consecrated to the Saints, whose veneration coincided with the emperor's birth day. Consecration of temples started new contents of temple-building which became also a way to glorify the tsar. It also helps to find out an original parallelism of undertakings of all-state scale in Moscow and Petersburg, whether it was construction of temples of imperial residences. The parallelism, which would become a rule and would be strictly observed till the reign of Nicholas I.

The law of Peter's time was directed at the change of principles of planning of town streets and the look of dwelling houses, but new Moscow was characterized first of all by temple architecture, especially outside both centres – the Kremlin's and the Yauza's. New temples of Peter's time created in the town with a historically complete pithy structure, a new one. Rising above and dominating over ordinary buildings, they emphasized the territory of the new centre and two royal roads leading to it – a land road and water route, by their unusual forms.

It is hardly possible that a number of temples was built along two roads by chance. The choice of the place for them was motivated by the same purpose as celebration processions, – creation of a unified holiday space, which would allow to feel the territory of Moscow as a whole, united by a general idea and opposing the contents and spatial organization of Moscow before Peter's time. In this system secular buildings and temples added to each other.

The beginning of the tsar's road from the Kremlin to the Yauza was fixed by a number of secular and church buildings. Among them there were triumphal arches near the Kremlin's Nikolskie gates, near Nikolskaja street and the cathedral of the Kazan Icon of the Theotokos which immortalized the end of the Troubled Time and the accession to power of the Romanovs' dynasty. There were the following buildings raised in Nikolskaja street; at the beginning of the street there was the church of the monastery of the Epiphany (1693-1696) created at the border of the rule of Sophy and Peter, at the end, near Nikolskie gates of Kitay-gorod, there was the church of the Vladimir Icon of the Theotokos built at the expense of the royal family in 1692-1694. These creations of Naryshkinskaja architecture – of the last stage of ancient Russian architecture (before Peter's time) were added by the church of Zaikonospasskiy monastery (1701-1709) raised on the opposite side from the monastery of Epiphany, the first fully belonged already to Peter's time according to its architectural peculiarities. The first Russian highest educational body was located in the monastery – Slav-Greek-Latin Academy; according to the special Peter's decree in 1719 its ensemble was added by teachers cells. Further in Mjasnitskaya street, near Menshikov's estate (on the place of today's post office) there was the most important memorial of Peter's reign: the church of Archangel Gabriel – Menshikov's tower. In 1711-1715, despite the prohibition of stone building, the church of St. Nicholas in Derbenev was built in the part of Mjasnitskaya street which was situated in Zemljanoy gorod, – the fact which clearly testified to the importance attributed to the look of the royal road. Finally, behind the gates of Zemljanoy town, in New Basmannaja the above-mentioned church of Sts. Apostles Peter and Paul was built, and in the street itself the church of St. Nicholas in Mjasniki was built (1711-1737).

The church of Archangel Gabriel embodied the most characteristic particularities of Moscow architectural school of Naryshkinskie temples – tier-like structure with characteristic location of the octahedral or octahedrons on the tetrahedron with the new clearly expressed striving to Europeanization. It showed in the sequence of use of order forms, sculptural decoration of Western type, installation of a spire on top of the building with an angel holding a cross.

The tower-like architecture taken by Peter's time from Naryshkinskaja architecture and the striving to attribute pillar-like look to buildings remarkable in their height, both to church and secular ones, was associated with triumph and was to express the victory of new ideas. This tendency had appeared in earlier buildings connected in style with the architecture before Peter's time, including in Peter's fun fortresses near the Yauza and in rather serious buildings – Sukharevskaja tower and the Main Chemist's. The group of temples represented by Menshikov's tower belongs to the same direction.

Menshikov's tower belonged to the temples of ancestral lands – it was built on the prince's yard land. Its tower- and tier-like style reproduced the most characteristic compositional particularities of Naryshkin's temples of ancestral lands. These particularities give the idea that the novelty and originality of Menshikov's tower, created according to the order of the man from the tsar's closest environment, is as program as that of its predecessors Naryshkin' s temples.

The pillar-like style of Naryshkin's temples acquired original forms in Menshikov's tower due to the top of the high building (first there were three octahedrons on its tetrahedron, not like now) with a spire. Examples for the temple finished in 1707 were buildings of Holland and Germany. First Menshikov's tower was 3.2 m higher than the highest building of Moscow – the bell-tower of John the Great in the Kremlin. After its construction had been finished the tsar's decree was issued prohibiting to build temples higher than the bell-tower of John the Great. The only exception made for Menshikov's tower – the place for it was chosen near the road to the Yauza's centre – makes to think that the originality of the look and hugeness of the dimensions, which were always associated with the importance of the building, were not accident, that the real customer and inspirator of this unusual temple was Peter himself.

The following facts can be indirect confirmation to this effect, besides he role of Menshikov himself in Peter`s closest environment. It is known that Peter widely expressed the basic ideas of his reign in architecture through the buildings of his closest associates. In connection with this the palaces of Lefort and Golovin were mentioned above already. It is also possible to remind about Menshikov's palace in Petersburg, which was the place for Peter's gala receptions. D. Tresini, a first-hand participant of the construction of Menshikov's tower, in the year of its finalization was sent to Petersburg. There according to the architect's project right upon his arrival the construction of Petropavlovskiy cathedral was started (of Sts. Apostles Peter and Paul, the consecration shows the importance attributed to the cathedral) in the city which had been founded only four years before. Petropavlovskiy cathedral was to become and really became the capital's main building, its symbol and the symbol of new Russia. Peter hurried the completion of the bell-tower of Petropavlovskiy cathedral crowned with a high spire. It became the main pithy point of the city's composition. The spire and pillar style of Menshikov's tower were its prototype among the others. The spire of Menshikov's tower, it can hardly be an accident either, specified in many ways peculiarities of Petersburg school. The spires of temples and secular public buildings became a certain sign of Petersburg of the first third of 18th century. M. Lomonosov wrote about them as about a characteristic feature of the new capital. In Moscow, and it was hardly by chance either, the temples situated along the road from the Kremlin to the Yauza, were notable for their spires.

Besides Menshikov's tower the church of St. Nicholas in Mjasniki was crowned with a spire. The bell-tower of the church of St. Prince Vladimir in Old Gardens was finished with a spire. Probably, the use of such an active in its pithiness element was connected in the latter case with the likening of Peter spread in panegyrical literature to St. Vladimir, and his reforms – to the Christening of Russia.

Composition of the majority of temples of Moscow school was based on the schemes and the character of connection of volumes which were traditional for 17th century. All of them repeated a three-part structure of a parish temple with a bell-tower, refectory and the temple Itself. A relatively small quantity has a more archaic cubic volume of the main temple's part dating from the middle of 18th century – the church of St. Martyr

Church of Archangel Gabriel (Menshikov's tower) near Mjasnitskaja street (Telegrafny lane, 13). (1701-1707, architects I.P.Zarudny, F.Fontana, B.Skala)

Cathedral of the monastery of St.Barsanuphius. (1692-1730; did not keep until now). Photo of the early 20th century.

Monastery of the Don Icon of the Theotokos. Northern wall with the on-gate church of the Tikhvon Icon of the Theotokos. (1713-1713). Photo. Early 20th century.

John the Warrior in Yakimanka street, the church of the Epiphany in Kudrino. Majority combine the three-part style of a parish church with a bell-tower, refectory, the church itself with the altar, situated along the axis from the West to the East, with the tower- and tire-like style of the main volume coming from Naryshkin's prototypes in the shape of an octahedron or octahedrons on the tetrahedron (the churches Zaikonospasskiy monastery and the monastery of St. Barsanuphius). The on-gate church of the Tikhvin Icon of the Theotokos of Donskoy monastery repeated the tower-like centric compositions of four-petalled Naryshkin's temples.

It is significant that the above-mentioned, as well as other churches having evident signs of novelties, were built either according to the project certified by Peter himself, like the church of St. Martyr John the Warrior in Yakimanka street,

Church of Martyr John the Warrior in Yakimanka street (1709-1717).

which immortalized, as the legend says, the victory over the Swiss near Poltava, or for the money donated by Peter I and Catherine (the church of the Holy Trinity in Kapelki), for the money donated by the members of the royal family (tsarina Proskoviya Fedorovna and tsarina Catherine lvanovna: the church of the Tikhvin lcon of the Theotokos of Donskoy monastery), or according to "the project of Peter himself (the church of Sts. Apostles Peter and Paul in New Basmannaya). Due to order elements, new Europeanized decoration, new forms of cupolas, verticality of the building as a whole and the separate elements of the multi-tire composition, these temples represented the new conception of the universe, strange to 17th century.

1730s-1750s.
Town-Building Ideas during the Reign of Anna Ioannovna and Elizabeth Petrovna

After Elizabeth I died in 1727 the Russian Empire seemed to return to the traditions of Ancient Russia. For five years, from 1727 to 1732, Moscow acquired the status of the first capital. The royal court moved to Moscow. In 1728, during the reign of Peter II the decree was issued cancelling Peter's enactments which tried to turn Moscow architecture to European way: "In the Kremlin, Kitay-gorod and Bely gorod, – it stipulated, – both stone and wood shall be used for construction, at one's own discretion in the streets and yards constructions shall be covered with shingles or deal... windows shall be made according to the house proportions... without asking for the police permission, so that there shall not be a burden or insolvency, and the drawings shall be taken from he architect only by those who want it".

But two years later the young tsar died. And Anna loannovna who took the throne, continued Peter's I ideas, translating the notions of an ideal town, which was a regular town of European type during the reign of her predecessor, into the language of practical acts. Elizabeth Petrovna did the same. In otherwords, the second third of 18th century in Moscow – was the time of active realization of Peter's ideas. In 1731 Anna loannovna's decree was issued "About Making of Moscow Plan". "As there is no accurate plan for Moscow, our residence, and houses are not built in order: taking it into account we ordered to make an accurate plan for all Moscow, big and small streets" [22]. In the decree the cause and effect of the connection between the beginning of the new big town-building affair and the status of Moscow as the tsarina's residence was unambiguously stated. An "accurate" plan was to amend the situation: the "disorder" in construction of houses at that moment and to prevent such a situation in future. I. Mordvinov developed it until 1734, and after his death in 1734 – I. Michurin. It was the first in the history of Moscow precise, base on geodesic parameters, plan. It was not only fixing. It also contained project proposals for regulation of the net of Moscow streets. Many streets, especially in the central part, were drawn as straightened and widened, not corresponding to their real tracing. At the same time, in 1730s-1740s a new town border of Moscow was determined. In 1732 for customs tax collection a wooden wall was built with posts on the roads, embracing a large territory and extending along the city's perimeter for 35 verstas. In 1742 the wall was substituted by a ditch with a bank which got the name of Kamer-Kollezhskiy. As it appeared due to economic, not defence requirements, it was not cancelled after the inside customs borders were liquidated in 1754 and remained a material expression of the city border separating the city and the country worlds.

Making of the plan fixed final strengthening of the attitude towards the city, which had been formed during the reign of Peter I, as one whole of a new type. Symbolic interpretation of this wholeness, characteristic for Ancient Russia, which was expressed mainly in the proportion of contextually important volumes, first of all of temples and monasteries, with the walls and towers of Moscow "towns", was added with the new wholeness of planometric quality. Contextual architectural unity of the city was unthinkable outside the correct, fixed in the regular volumetrical-spatial structure of planning of earthly space. The government made efforts directed at making the space, acquiring its own value, regularity. Organized according to the principles of regularity, it was the embodiment of the idea of the state system. The old system, based on organization of the space with the help of the compact vertically oriented volumes of temples, bell-towers, tower-like civil buildings with hip roofs, was added with another one rationally organizing the longitudinal space of streets and squares. That circumstance forced to make the new plan of Moscow not only a fixing one. Fixing the contemporary situation it simultaneously expressed the notion of what should be in reality. The part of the road from Petersburg to Moscow, going along the territory of the ancient capital along the First Tverskaya-Yamskaya and Tverskaya streets, was remarkable with its wideness and straightness, as well as Varvarka, Pokrovka, New Basmannaja, Pokrovskaya and other streets, leading to the new centre at the Yauza. By 1739 the composition of the plan of Moscow was finalized.

The ousting of the dwelling buildings, which had begun in 16th century during making of the Kremlin a symbol of the Russian State system, was completed by the middle of 18th century. From that time the Kremlin became the place for the buildings of all-state importance . The wooden emperor's palace was built in the Kremlin – Winter Annenhoff, which was later moved to the Yauza. It was located in the north-east part of the Kremlin. Thus the new role of Tverskaya street and symbolic importance of this end of the Kremlin, expressing the peculiarities of the geopolitical structure of the Russian Empire with its two capitals, was emphasized. During the time of Elizabeth Petrovna the same conception was shown otherwise: she built a palace in the traditional place – on the socles of old Aleviz's palace (according to the project of F. Rastrelli) and simultaneously near the Winter Annenhoff according to the project of Rastrelli too – a new palace near the Yauza was built.

Approximately in the same direction the buildings in Kitaygorod were changed. In difference to the Kremlin – the all-state centre – Kitay-gorod became the public and educational centre of Moscow and the district of prestigious buildings. In Kitay-gorod, and not only in the main streets, but also in Zarjadie, an unexpectedly big percentage of stone houses of noble people was fixed in documents.

In 1742 a special decree was issued, regulating the width of streets and lanes: "About the construction of houses in Moscow according to the plan and about the supervision that the streets were 8 sazhens of width, and the lanes 4 sazhens of width". A number of decrees testifies to the increase of pithiness of open space, directed at creation of squares with the new idea – open, built in only along the perimeter. The decree stipulated: "The stores in the Rukovishniy and Oil rows shall be broken to enlarge the space". Local tasks were settled in conformity with the general idea about an ideal town as of a settlement with regularly planned wide streets and lanes and open wide squares. In 1753 the decree was issued "About prohibition in future to build in Moscow squares and about breaking of the buildings situated in them"[23]. In 1750 the first cemetery outside Moscow was arranged – Lazarevskoe. In 1758 in continuation of this decree another one was issued: about prohibition to bury the dead in the temples situated along the royal land road along the usual route of the emperor's cortege from the Kremlin to the palace near the Yauza. It became possible to reflect in the construction law the new ideas about the proper arrangement of the town and to take into consideration the empress' psychological peculiarities, who was afraid of death and its memory, only during the absolutism with its belief that it was possible to realize an ideal arrangement of earthly life with the help of the government and the tsar.

During the time of Anna Ioannovna and Elizabeth Petrovna the new norms of European town-building stopped being only declarations in Moscow. They were realized rather successfully in constructional practice due to their support of organizational measures. A "team" of the architect with a group of assistants was established at the Policemeister office. For realization of any constructional undertaking a special permission was required, which was issued only when there was the plan of house ownership. If the submitted project did not correspond to the new rules the architect developed a new project in accordance with the new requirement of "regularity".

Peter's idea about the entire building of Moscow streets remained unrealized. However, streets turned gradually into architecturally expressive space created in conformity with the new artistic norms, due to the undertaken organizational measures in the second third of 18th century. Three main ways of organization of a street fasade were developed. The first way was the location of houses along the red line of a street, which belonged to all estates, were universal. Being a successor of the houses of settlement people it was spread after Peter's time when European and artistic norms took root in construction of rich estates of the nobility and merchant houses. The other two ways belonged to rich noble houses. To them, as it was already mentioned, belonged the estate with a house situated inside the lot, in front of which there was a front yard oriented at the street and corresponding to its direction, at which the house's main fasade looked. The street line was fixed by the gates, railing and symmetrically situated at the sides of the central building lateral outbuildings. The third was the corner type of house, architecturally fixing crosses of streets, it had been tried during construction of public buildings: stores, chemists' with richly decorated cornices and columns (the drug store at the corner of Povarskaja street and Merzljakovskiy lane, the store of merchant Medovstchikov in Kitay-gorod)[24], before it was used during construction of city estates.

Stores, cook-shops, pancake-shops, cafйs were an integral peculiarity of Moscow city landscape. According to their location they were closer to the main points of the city plan – to the gates of Bely and Zemljanoy towns – covering some space of adjoining streets. A number of streets of Zemljanoy town – Arbat, Tverskaja, Sretenka – had a very intensive trade in 17th century already. In the middle of 18th century Arbat and espe-

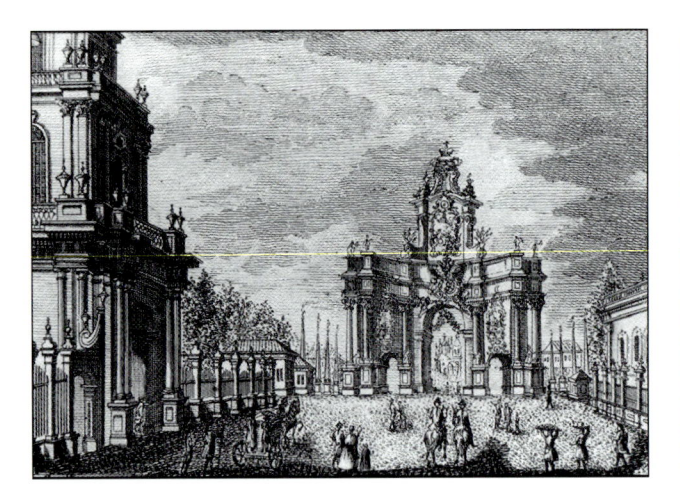

Triumphal gate built for the coronation of Catherine II in Tverskaja street near Zemijanoy bank (1763, architect K. Blank).

Triumphal gate built for the coronation of Catherine II in Tverskaja street near Bely town (1763, architect K.I.Blank). Print according to M.I.Makhaev's drawing.

cially Sretenka were nearly entirely full of stores; everywhere, except Kitay-gorod, the stores were wooden.

In Moscow in the first half of 18th century already there were a lot of manufactories. Manufacturing buildings were situated most often near rivers on the lots of owners. There were a lot of factories in densely built in districts too. The silk factory of A. Miljutin with stone buildings which remained till now, was located in Miljutinskiy lane, and the cloth factory of A. Babushkin was between Old and New Basmannaja; there were factories even in Kitay-gorod. Dwelling houses for the workers of the Cloth Yard, situated, near Vsekhsvjatskiy bridge, were built in conformity with the sample project, similar to the same projects of Peter's time, developed for Petersburg by architect D. Trezini.

All the above-said confirms that since 1730s the slow transfiguration of Moscow began on new grounds which expressed the notion about an ideal town and ideal midst of a capital city. They were associated with a regular town, European town, stone town. Reflecting the new values and ideas about ideal midst of a town as of a festive and triumphal, connected with triumphal processions, celebrations, the emperor's corteges, a new zone system was formed. Ousting of small properties from the centre to the outskirts was going on together with the ousting of nobility estates and other dwellings out of the Kremlins. Along the "tsar's" roads – in Tverskaja, along the streets leading to the Yauza, the streets close to the Kremlin, districts of prestigious estates were formed. Chains of country estates with huge regular parks stretched from Vorobjovskiy palace on the hills of the same name to the centre along the bank of the Moscow-river, as well as on the banks of the Neglinnaja and Yauza. Nobility estate construction embraced in a semi-circle the Kremlin and Kitay-gorod from the West, North and East. In the first half of 18th century during realization of the new town-building conception a new zone estate principle formed, ousting the previous functional, settlement one.

In 1730-1750 the squares near the triumphal arches formed too, which occupied permanent places at the crossing of the walls of Bely and Zemijanoy towns with radial highways. The most brilliant ensemble fixed the exit of the road outside Zemljanoy town and the beginning of New Basmannaja – the road to the Yauza specially built by Peter. The ensemble had started to form already in 1700 near the future stone Red Gates, and at the end of Mjasnitskaja near the church of the Three Saint Hierarchs of 17th century wooden triumphal arch was traditionally installed. Visually and spatially that compositional main point was connected with another one – with the church of Sts. Apostles Peter and Paul at the beginning of New Basmannaja.

During the time of Anna Ioannovna a bell-tower was built near it, which became a new orienting point. During the time of Elizabeth Petrovna the pithy aspect connected with glorification of the state and the tsarina, got a new development. One of the biggest secular buildings in baroque style was built in the square – Zhitniy Yard (Zapasniy(stocks) Palace), where food stocks were kept for the court. In 1753 the church of St. Martyr Sebastian was built at Zhitniy Yard – Moscow analogue of Petersburg cathedral of St. Isaac. Like Petersburg analogue the temple in Moscow was consecrated to the Saint, on whose veneration day empress Elizabeth Petrovna was born. Its future history testifies to the pithy significance of this place and the importance of the meaning of the consecration of the church. After Catherine II had taken the throne the church was reconsecrated in honour of Hieromartyr Januarius – on the day of his veneration Catherine II was born who changed Elizabeth Petrovna on the imperial throne.

It was the wooden gates that later got the name Krasnye, empress Elizabeth rebuilt from stone in the memory of her coronation in difference to all the others. Is it not the proof of the special importance of the ensemble in the system connected with the ideas of the state's majesty and glorification of the tsar?

Something of the kind happened in the square that started to form in the same 1730-1740 in the place of the crossing of Tverskaja street and the walls of Bely town, where a traditionally wooden triumphal arch also was built. At the corner of Blagovestchenskiy lane and Tverskaja street there was the church of the Annunciation. In order to emphasize the artistic and contextual importance of this space, upon the order of Anna Ioannovna in 1732 a new octahedron was built on the church. And in 1750 upon the initiative of Elizabeth Petrovna on the red line of Tverskaya street a high separate bell-tower was built.

Temples of 1730-1750

The latter two examples were the proof that, excluding the utilitarian construction (stores, pubs, saunas), which were close to the places where big roads and gates crossed, and ordinary buildings, the most artistic and contextually important construction (palaces, estates, temples) was located along the tsar's roads connecting Tverskaja post with the Kremlin, the Kremlin with the new centre at the Yauza. In this way as though a town appeared inside the city, Moscow inside Moscow, the look and buildings in it were governed by the expression of the new state idea, represented by two types of baroque buildings – temples and palace estates.

Extremely intensive construction of temples in 1730-1750 is especially amazing. High multi-tier bell-towers were raised together with new temples or with existing temples, were built in the monasteries above the main gates. The bell-towers which seemed to be not high enough got superstructures, as they were situated at the points important from the view of town-building.

In such a way the look of the church of St. John the Theologian in Big Bronnaja was changed, situated near Tverskaja street and the monastery of the Passions, the place where triumphal gates were raised traditionally, actually in front of the church of the Annunciation. Its bell-tower got a superstructure of two new tiers of octahedrons. The same happened in the district of Tverskaja, but on the opposite side. In Malaja Dmitrovka in Putinki at the church of the middle of 17th century a new high bell-tower was built. A new bell-tower of the church of Great Martyr George on the Krasnaja hill instead of the wooden one that burnt during the fire of 1737, was built near the crossing of Tverskaja and Mokhovaja, near the Kremlin.

Temples and new high bell-towers were built even more intensively in the streets leading to the new centre at the Yauza. In difference to the time of Alexius Mikhaylovich and Peter, who preferred each of their highways, – the first, presumably, was Pokrovskaja highway, the second – Preobrazhenskaja, during the time of Anna Ioannovna and Elizabeth Petrovna all streets became the place of intensive stone construction which started from Red Square and led to the north-east: Mjasnitskaja, New Basmannaja, Pokrovka, Old Basmannaja, Pokrovskaja, Varvarka, Soljanka, where the tsar's land road crossed the water one. In the streets of the zone of Peter's highway (Mjasnitskaja – New Basmannaja) the church of St. Nicholas in Zvonari (1760-1762) in Rozhdestvenka was built; the bell-tower of the church of the Transfiguration in Pushkari (did not keep) got a superstructure in 1753 of two tiers (a tetrahedron and an octahedron); at the corner of Kuznetskiy bridge and Big Lubjanka in 1746 the church of the Entry of the Most Holy Theotokos into the Temple was built (did not keep); in the first half of 1750s not far from Lubjanskaja Square and Iljinskie gates in Mjasnitskaja the church of Holy Martyr and Archdeacon Euplus was raised; in the same street a new bell-tower at the church of St. Nicholas the Miracle-Worker was built (1737; did not keep), the church of the Transfiguration in Spasskaja (did not keep), the bell-tower of the church of Sts. Apostles Peter and Paul in New Basmannaja (1745-1746).

Pokrovskaja road of Alexius Mikhaylovich acquired the former importance at the time of Elizabeth Petrovna and was added not less actively with new temples and bell-towers (the church of St. Nicholas the Miracle-Worker was renovated and a new bell-tower for it was built in Klenniki, near Iljinskie gates in Maroseyka; in Pokrovka the following was built: the church of the Resurrection in Barashy (1740), the church of St. John the Predecessor in Kazennaja settlement (Pokrovka, 50); outside the borders of Zemljanoy bank in the continuation of Pokrovka the church of Martyr Nicetas in Old Basmannaja (1750-1751) was built.

Construction in the area of the water route along the Moscow-river and the Yauza was as active as at the tsar's land roads. Bell-towers were built for the churches of St. Nicholas the Miracle-Worker in Golutvino (Golutvinskiy lane, 14), of Martyrs Cosmas and Damian in Kadashi, of Beheading of St. John the Predecessor in Chernigovskiy lane, at the beginning of Pjatnitskaja street (1759); of the Resurrection Slovustchee in Monetchiki (1750; did not keep); of Sts. Cyprus and John in Soljanka (1765-1771), of St. Nicholas Zajaitskiy near Raushskaja quay (1745-1759; did not keep), the bell-tower of the church of St. Nicholas in Podkopai at the corner of Podkopaevskiy and Podkolokolniy lanes (1759).

Especially many majestic temples with high bell-towers here built along the banks of the Moscow-river and the Yauza. A garland of four temples was built at the fall of the river-Moscow into the Yauza, as though fixing the main point and the crossing of the roads leading to the Yauza's centre not only from the top – from the Kremlin, but from the bottom – from Novospasskiy monastery – the burial-vault of the Romanovs, from Krutistkoe representation -the residence of Moscow metropolitanates, from the royal residence in the village of Kolomenskoe, These were the churches of St. Nicholas Zajaitskiy with a huge bell-tower situated on the bank of the Moscow-river at its turn near the Yauza's mouth, of St. Nicholas in Pupyshi (1730s), of Martyr Nicetas (Big and Small Vatin lanes) near the entrance from the Yauza's bridge; the church of the Holy Trinity, situated near the same bridge, in Serebrjaniki with a high bell-tower. Further along the bank of the Moscow-river, lower from its fall Into the Yauza new bell-towers of the church of the Assumption in Gonchary (the middle of 18th century) and the church of the Holy and Life-giving Trinity in Luzhnetskaja were installed; the churches of the Transfiguration in Maly Bolvanovskiy (2nd Novokuznetskiy lane, 10; 1755) and of St. Nicholas the Miracle-Worker in Kozhevniki (1724, the bell-tower dates from 1730s) were built.

The imperial state idea, born during Peter's time, was consolidated by the means of temple architecture, i. e. by the means characteristic for Russia of the time before Peter. Peter I was striving to emphasize the individuality of his time, its difference to the previous age: new highway, new architectural forms. During the reign of the two empresses loyalty to Peter's ideas was accompanied with orientation at the reign of Alexius Mikhaylovich, equally evidently expressed by the means of temple building, and more widely it was oriented at the traditions of Russia before Peter's time. Thus the equal intensiveness of the construction along the land road to the Yauza. Appearance of two temples consecrated to Martyr Nicetas at the royal highways looked as a declaration of loyalty to Russia before Peter's time and to the heritage of the first Romanovs. Using the symbolics of consecrations boyard Nicetas Romanovich Zakharjin-Yurjev, the grand-father of Michael Fedorovich, the first tsar of the Romanovs family, in 16th century founded the monastery of Martyr Nicetas in the place of the church of Martyr Nicetas near Yamskoy yard. After the Romanovs took power, the monastery became an original symbol of the reigning dynasty and a memorial to its ancestor. In the middle of 18th century the churches consecrated to this Martyr near the Yauza's bridge and in Old Basmannaja, at the royal road of Alexius Mikhaylovich in Izmaylovo and Pokrovskoe-Rubtsovo, were renovated and actually built anew, thus they acquired the importance of the memorials of the dynasty fore-father, like the temples of Sts. Apostles Peter and Paul, built by Catherine and Elizabeth, turned out to be certain memorials of the representatives of the Romanovs dynasty of the imperial period.

Zamoskvorechie became another district of active temple construction – the areas of Pjatnitskaja and Ordynka. It was a natural phenomenon and it was connected with the fact that in the middle of 18th century for the first time merchants became temple-builders together with the tsar (tsarinas) and the nobility. The empresses' policy, especially that of Elizabeth Petrovna, with their attention to the ancient capital and traditions of Ancient Russia, could not fail to gain the respect of the merchant estate as the representatives of the traditional culture.

Temple architecture of Moscow is the brightest expression of originality of Moscow architectural school, which became an independent phenomenon in respect of Petersburg school during Peter's reign already.

New characteristic features appeared in the temple-building, which at that time represented most brightly the originality of the schools of two capitals. The most characteristic feature of Moscow school is the closest connection with the traditions of the time before Peter, dates from the first quarter of 18th century. At the same time the ways of development of architecture of Moscow and the province became similar, which made Moscow, as it was already mentioned, the capital of the province in difference to Petersburg opposing with its successive adherence to Europeanization both Moscow and the province.

Petersburg and Moscow schools demonstrated two ways of transfer of the architecture from the Middle Ages to the New Time. Moscow school showed gradual, smooth rooting of European traditions into ancient Russian ones. It happened in two ways. By the

Church of Martyr and Archdeacon Euplus in "strelka" of Mjasnitskaja and mijutinskiy lane (did not keep -tmnow) and Chertkov's house in Mjasnitskaja (rebuilt). Print, showing the buildings of the "tsar's road" of the first half of the lath century.

way of changing of the look and volume-spatial composition of temples under the influence of European samples, first of all of the order decoration, keeping at the same time the traditional types of construction of volumes and compositional schemes. All the great variety of Moscow temples of 1730-1750 can be divided into three types dating from 17th century. They have much in common with Peter's temples and belong to the type of the parish temple. The first type is extended from the West to the East and consists from a bell-tower, refectory and the temple itself which is cubicle and without pillars, with an altar. The second type has the form of a ship – extended along the longitudinal axis two-tier temple uniting in one volume both winter and summer churches. The third type combines the features of a patrimonial tower-like temple of Naryshkin's baroque with its traditional scheme of an octahedron on tetrahedron on the foundation which is cross-like on its plan, with a three-lobe scheme of a temple with a bell-tower, refectory and the temple itself, extended along the axis East-West. The first two variants – cubicle and ship-like are re-presented by single constructions. The type of a tower-like temple absolutely dominates in its quantity and has a variety of the scheme of an octahedron on a tetrahedron. This characteristic feature is common for the buildings of the reign of Anna Ioannovna and Elizabeth Petrovna. Together with this older temples of 1730s were closer to Peter's traditions. The order of canonical forms and proportions was used in the constructions of Elizabeth's reign, dating from 1740 – beginning of 1760s, and there were a lot of columns together with pilasters. Plastic art of compact volume of bell-towers was added with the rich plastic art of columns.

The ascendancy made by the vertically oriented temples of Elizabeth's time, creating the impression of ponderous richness and power of the composition, was intensified by the way of their location in the system of the streets. Most often temples were built on the corner plots. Temples and bell-towers looked at different streets, usually at a street and at a lane organizing the space of both. Other schemes more seldom were used – a bell-tower and a temple were situated parallel to the street or a bell-tower and a temple were situated perpendicularly to the street. However in all three cases a bell-tower was preferably situated on the red line.

All Moscow bell-towers of the middle of 18th century is a brilliant and original phenomenon of Moscow architectural school, and besides bell-towers, at the temples of 1730-1750 a new type of on-gate monastery multi-tier bell-tower was formed and also widely used.

Church of Rts. Joachim and Anna in Big Yakimanka (1634-1689, on-gate bell-tower of 1751; did not keep till now).

Without exaggeration bell-towers can be considered one of the most impressive creations of architecture of Moscow baroque. In them its characteristic features were embodied most fully. It was a genetic alliance with the traditions of ancient Russian architecture. Multi-tierness and verticalism combined with accurately articulated volumes of a building and naturalness of their interchange. The combination of an octahedron on a tetrahedron was mostly spread. The types of bell-towers composed from volumes equal on their plan – square and octahedral – that were built during the time before Peter, could be also encountered.

Synthesis of ancient Russian and European traditions is seen especially clearly in the monastery bell-towers on gates. Bell-towers were installed above the gates which became a huge pedestal, increasing the height and emphasizing the verticalism of the composition, height was associated by Russian and other people with beautiful and important things from ancient time. Till 18th century bell-towers were usually situated inside monasteries, making together with the temple or with a group of central temples the semantic and compositional kernel of the monastery or the Kremlin's ensemble. Its most important buildings were raised in the centre, and the composition, though not geometrically correct, was built centrically: the dimensions and importance of the buildings were increased from the periphery to the centre. The group of the central buildings, freely situated in the middle of the monastery territory, was created calculating on the round movement and the look from many points. The main buildings were notable for their compactness and picturesqueness of high volumes which gave many different combinations when being looked at from various points. In difference to the main ones, the secondary components of the monastery ensemble – cells, had the frontality of extended faзades and even rhythm of regularly repeated elements. At the border of 17th-18th centuries the tendency to create two centres of the monastery ensemble, based on spatial interaction, appeared. There was still the main temple or a group of temples in the centre. Opposite them there was a huge vertical bell-tower on the monastery gates, situated excentrically, which was often sufficiently higher than the temples.

Earlier than somewhere else on-gate temples and bell-towers of the new type appeared in Moscow monasteries. Temples and bell-towers of that kind have one surprising common feature. All of them were created upon the order of the royal family. The famous bell-tower of Novodevichiy monastery, built according to the sample of John the Great and competing with it in height, has one peculiarity indifference to the Kremlin's building: the bell-tower was built out at the monastery wall. On-gate temples and the bell-tower of Novodevichiy monastery with their emphasized verticalism represent the tendency, synthesized in two creations of Peter's time – on-gate bell-tower of Vysokopetrovskiy monastery, created for the expense and upon the order of the Naryshkins, the family, to which Peter belonged according to the mother's line, and the on-gate church of the Tikhvin Icon of the Theotokos of Donskoy monastery, in different ways.

The bell-tower of Vysokopetrovskiy monastery is a tetrahedron installed on the gates, there are two octahedrons and an octahedral neck of the cupola on the tetrahedron. Volumetrical composition of Tikhvinskaja church, which took from Naryshkinskie temples the four-lobe plan and multi-tier composition, was added with an order decoration.

The bell-towers of 1730-1750 inherited from the end of 17th – beginning of 18th centuries the general scheme of composition of the volumes, but surround them with developed order compositions. A structural characteristic feature of bell-towers is in the volume placed on each other and gradually decreasing, which makes the silhouette of the buildings characteristically stepped. The same feature allowed to make ancient Russian composition look like a composition built according to the rules of classical order. It was possible because each tier of a bell-tower was interpreted as a separate volume based on order proportions. Due to the use of freely placed columns and plenty of cornice protuberances the look of the bell-towers acquired volume and plasticity, triumphality and power.

Monastery bell-towers of 1730-1750 can be undoubtedly called the tsar' s ones. All of them were built in the monasteries connected in one way or another with the reigning dynasty or the dynasty of the Rjurikovichis. The first one was built in 1732 on the main gates of the monastery of St. Daniel, founded by St. Prince Daniel of Moscow, and partially repeated the composition of the bell-tower of Vysokopetrovskiy monastery. One of the most famous monastery bell-towers in Donskoy monastery, the construction of which was started at the time of Anna Ioannovna in the year when she took the throne in 1730, according to the project of D. Trezini, which allows to connect it with the empress' order. From the time of Sophia's reign Donskoy monastery became a traditional place of construction upon the orders of the royal family for more than half a century. The new cathedral of the monastery was founded under the vow of Peter's sister Catherine Alexeevna; Tikhvinskaja on-gate bell-tower was built by tsarina Praskovja Fedorovna and tsarina Catherine Ioannovna. The works, which were stopped because of the move of the court of Anna Ioannovna to Petersburg, were renewed according to the project of A. P. Evlashev at the time of Elizabeth Petrovna. The donations in the monastery made by the empress, and consecration of the church in the bell-tower to her Saint protectors Prophet Zacharias and Righteous Elizabeth, testify to the fact that she took part in completion of the construction.

The bell-tower of Novospasskiy monastery is even more grandiose with the height of about 72 meters and having three tiers; there was the burial-vault of boyards Romanovs in the socle of its cathedral.

In 1744 in Vysokopetrovskiy monastery upon the order of A. K. Naryshkina the church of Tolga Icon of the Theotokos was built in the memory of the saving of Peter in the Lavra of the Holy Trinity-St. Sergius during the riot of strelitzs; in 1753-1755 the church of Sts. Apostles Peter and Paul, the protectors of Peter, was built above the Southern gates. Thus Vysokopetrovskiy monastery became an original memorial of Peter, made in a town-building way.

The policy of Anna Ioannovna, connected with return to the traditions of the time before Peter, was continued by Elizabeth Petrovna not only at the level of ideas, but concrete construction undertakings. They included, together with Donskoy monastery, the monastery of St. John the Chrysostome (Zlatoustinskiy) which was near Mjasnitskaja at Peter's road to Preobrazhenskoe. The monastery was renewed due to donations of Anna Ioannovna and of other donators. And during the reign of Elizabeth Petrovna and upon her order the bell-tower was raised. In it, like in the bell-tower of Donskoy monastery, the church of St. Prophet Zacharius and Righteous Elizabeth was made.

In 1730-1750 Moscow architectural school was different from Petersburg one by the absence at that time of five-cupola temples of cathedral type which prevailed in construction in Petersburg. There was only one exception in Moscow – the five-cupola church of Hieromartyr Clement in Pjatnitskaja, built like temples in Petersburg. The consecration of the sacrariums to Hieromartyr Clement, the Pope of Rome, and Hieromartyr Peter, archbishop of Alexandria, on whose veneration day the palace coup d`etat took place, which led Elizabeth Petrovna to the throne, and to the Transfiguration (Preobrazhenie) after which the guards regiment was called, that took part in the coup, give the idea that the look and the type of the temple were to express the same contents as the consecrations of the sacrariums – to glorify and immortalize the accession to the throne of Elizabeth Petrovna. Besides that in Petersburg, soon after the accession to the throne of Elizabeth Petrovna upon her order in memory of that event the construction of the five-cupola cathedral of the Transfiguration with the same consecration of the sacrariums was started.

The construction of temples in 1730-1750 was extremely extensive in Moscow. The data which kept till our time is amazing. According to the data which is far from being complete, more than 30 churches were named as new during those years.[25]

Wonastery of the "Don" Icon of the Theotokos. The Western wall with the on-gate bell-tower (the construction was started in 1730, architect R.Shedel; 1750-1753, architect A.P.Evlashev). Photo. Late 19th century.

Novospasskiy monastery. The Western wall with the on-gate bell-tower (1759-1784, architect I. Zherebtsov). photo. Late 19th century.

The town-building stage of 1730-1750 connected with the ideas of Peter's reign, notably corrected the look and image of Moscow. During this period Moscow continued to develop evolutionary. The novelties corrected, but did not change radically its look and structure. The Moscow ensemble and panorama were still formed by the temples which were added with a big quantity with new multi-tier bell-towers. Being brought on the red lines of the streets, to the banks of the Moscow-river and the Yauza, they enriched a sufficiently typical Moscow silhouette, increasing the usual scale and dimensions of the main structures, emphasizing in orthodox Moscow the imperial-orthodox Moscow.

Two Tendencies in the Civil Architecture of Moscow

Temples represent the type of buildings which dominated in quantity and were the leaders from the architectural point of view in 1730-1750. During the reign of Anna Ioannovna and Elizabeth Petrovna they shared that role with palaces.

The words said by V. Kljuchevskiy about that time "The state was closed in the palace" were not an exaggeration. They reflect the real situation. The royal palace at that time was immeasurably bigger than just a place where a monarch lived. The palace was the focus and symbol of the state and its power. The tsar's residence symbolized the state. So Rastrelli's words were not occasional: "The building of the stone Winter Palace is built just for glory of all Russia". Just for glory of all Russia in Moscow at the Yauza the Summer and Winter Annerhof were built, in the name of the same idea near the latter after transfer of the palace to the Yauza the residence of Elizabeth Petrovna was created.

The palace and temple as creations of art served the only thing. The function of the temples of the first half of 18th century was not limited to their religious purpose only. The temples consolidated actively the idea of the state power, glorifying with their majesty, height, huge dimensions, and often with their consecrations, the tsarinas and the state. In temples Europeanization was going on naturally as a process of assimilation of novelties, gradually transforming traditional structures, palace architecture and civil architecture in general were developing in another way – as a process of placement. Formerly types of palaces and estates were substituted with new ones, taken from the West, transplanted on Russian soil as a finished and whole phenomenon. But an absolute repetition, a replica of Western culture failed. A repetition even of Petersburg failed in Moscow. Moscow tradition, Moscow context gave an unrepeatable originality to Europeanized "isles" of buildings in the ancient capital. Traditional norms made an impact on the interpretation of European schemes. But nevertheless the process of development of the civil and, including the palace construction of Moscow was the opposite of the temple-building. In temples ancient Russian ways and schemes were modified during assimilation of European novelties. In the palace and a civil construction it was different: West-European ways and schemes during the process of their realization in real practice were transformed under the pressure of the national sense of form, space, ideas about the beautiful.

Yauza's Moscow lived during the time of Anna Ioannovna and Elizabeth Petrovna through the second birth. Here Annenhof appeared, the imperial residence, which according to the first plot of empress Anna Ioannovna was to excel the imperial residences near Petersburg. At the beginning of the reign, striving to consolidate her position on the throne, Anna loannovna demonstrated in all possible ways her adherence to Moscow, primordial Russia before Peter's time. A symbolic gesture full of deep meaning of new attention to Moscow was made. For two years (1730-1732) Moscow became the place of stay of the imperial court. In the sphere of temple-building Moscow was allowed to follow the traditional way of natural renovation of the inheritance of Naryshkin's and Peter's architecture. In it Anna Ioannovna, and later Elizabeth Petrovna followed Peter's policy, who did not allow to repeat in Moscow the policy of orientation at Western, which means heterodox, prototypes, accepted in Petersburg as a rule. Palace architecture was another thing. It had to go through the radical and irrevocable Europeanization during the time of Anna Ioannovna and Elizabeth Petrovna.

The palace in Annehof was designed by the future first master of Petersburg baroque Rastrelli, who was young at that time. He created a very long wooden two-storey building with a symmetrical three-lobe faзade which was extended for more than 200 meters and looked at the Moscow-river. Versailles was the prototype of the main characteristic features of Annenhof composition: undivided and equal in height main faзade from the river-side, on the opposite side there was a nearly closed front yard with a regular park adjoined to it with a complex system of ray-like alleys crossing at the right angle. In its turn the palace in Annenhof with its turn of the fasade calculated on panorama look, extension of volumes equal in height, with extended central part, rich adornment anticipate the main creations of baroque of the middle of 18th century – the palaces of Peterhof and Tsarskoselskiy (Tsar's village) near Petersburg.

After Elizabeth Petrovna came to power the period of intensive construction started again at the Yauza. Near the ensemble of Anna Ioannovna a new palace-park complex was built which kept the importance of the imperial centre, acquired by this district at the time of Peter. The organizing point of the new ensemble was the palace created again according to Rastrelli's project. The church of the Resurrection appeared between the new palace and the palace of Anna Ioannovna as a separate building (the only case in the country imperial residences of the first half of 18th century). In order to make the access road portentous, according to

M. Zemtsov's project a bridge, situated on the main axis of the main faзade of Elizabeth's palace oriented at the Yauza, and triumphal gates were built. Here also a throne hall, opera house, an illuminated theatre and a Senate building were raised.

Annenhof, created under the influence of European royal residences and imperial residences near the new Russian capital, in its turn, gave rise to recreation and actually to new creation of estate ensembles near Petersburg. The importance of Annenhof was especially big for Moscow. Around the estate-palace complexes of Anna and Elizabeth on both banks of the Yauza and in adjoining streets appeared an entire parade zone with estates of European type, with extended fasades of palaces oriented at the river, with vast regular parks – of count M. G. Golovin (between Nemetskaja and Voznesenskaja streets, now Radio and Baumanskaja), of Demidov, Tshcerbatov, Bestuzhev-Rjumin. Estate construction was spread in Moscow too.

Not far from Bozhiy house in the district of Bozhedomskie streets in the middle of 18th century count Saltykov built a luxurious estate and a regular park; for prince Trubetskoy on the Moscow-river bank estate Neskuchnoe (Not Dull) was built with a regular park according to the project of the best Moscow architect of Elizabeth's time D. V. Ukhtomskiy. High-born nobility – the Golitsyns, the Dolgorukovs, the Lopukhins, the Apraksins, the Vorontsovs, the Shakhovskiy and others built rich estates near the historical centre, in the streets of Bely and Zemljanoy towns. For Vorontsov a huge estate was created with a palace turned with its fasade and the front yard at Rozhdestvenka, and with a large park going down to the river Neglinnaja (now street Neglinnaja). Near the palace also upon his order the church of St. Nicholas in Zvonari was raised. Rich estate palaces were built in the main streets too. In Pokrovka the palace of the Apraksin-Trubetskoys was built. Near the future Tverskoy boulevard inside the yard there was an estate house of Yakovlev, in Big Nikitskaja, also inside the yard there was the palace of Vorontsov-Veljalminov. The combination of town and village landscapes, plenty of gardens near the nobility estates characteristic for Moscow, which romantic people so admired, probably dates from the middle of 18th century.

House facades of merchants and artisans in Zamoskvorechie, in Zemljanoy town, were always built along the red street line and according to principles of baroque. They were different from palaces, except for modest dimensions, also with fasades without orders (the merchant houses along Alexeevskaja or Taganskaja streets, the house of watch-maker Anju at the beginning of Mjasnitskaja street). Civil dwelling construction was the branch of Moscow architecture that was the closest to the architecture of Petersburg. The palaces of Anna Ioannovna and Elizabeth Petrovna in both capitals, being the example that was followed by high-born noble families, were built according to the project of one and the same architect – Rastrelli. Besides that, Petersburg of the middle of 18th century was built in not only with "entire

Summer Annenhof. General plan of the palace and the Upper park. (1730, architect F. Rastrelli).

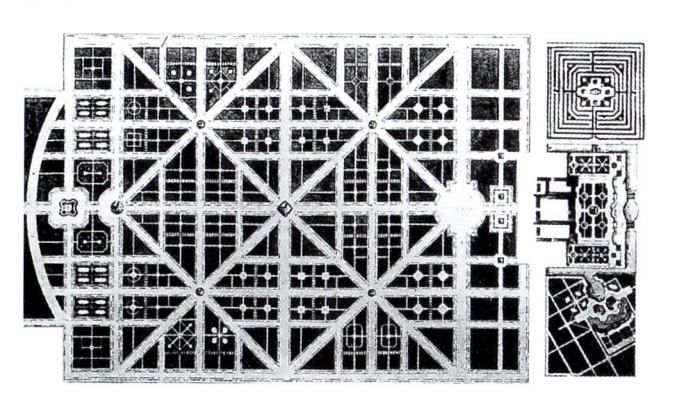

Court hall at the Winter Palace of Elizabeth Petrovna in Annenhof. Print from the coronation album of 1744.

fasades". The district of palace-estate construction in Fontanka can be compared with the districts of the Yauza and the Neglinnaja in Moscow.

In the architecture of the time of the reign of Elizabeth Petrovna there was a unique concentration on the idea of Jerusalem, which had been popular already in Ancient Russia, but acquired its actuality again only during the reign of Nicholas I. Upon the empress' order the tumbled down hip roof of the temple of the Resurrection in New-Jerusalem monastery near Moscow was reconstructed. Upon her order in the outskirts of Petersburg, not far from the Lavra of St. Prince Alexander Nevskiy founded by Peter, the monastery of the Resurrection was built, more known under the name of Smolnyj. The prototypes of the main monastery buildings – the cathedral and the unbuilt bell-tower – were well known. They were the cathedral of the Assumption in Moscow Kremlin and the bell-tower of John the Great. The idea of the Third Rome, recomprehended through Jerusalem, permeated the architecture of the time of Elizabeth Petrovna. Pillar-like bell-towers of kremlins and monasteries – of John the Great, the bell-towers of New-Jerusalem, of St. Josef of Volokolamsk, of Novodevichiy monasteries come from the temple of the Holy Sepulchre (of the Resurrection) in Jerusalem. All of them, together with already mentioned temple and bell-tower of Donskoy and Vysokopetrovskiy monasteries, to some extent were the prototypes of the bell-towers of 1730-1750 – both of monasteries and temples. Jerusalem aspect of contents of the bell-towers in combination with the imperial idea can explain the mysterious project of Ukhtomskiy, known as the project of Voskresenskie gates, where the type of a multi-tier bell-tower with columns decorating each tier combined with features of a civil building. Elizabeth tried to create her own "New Jerusalem" near Petersburg; the one which existed near Moscow was restored by her. She tried to continue Jerusalem theme in Moscow. Again an original double character of conformities appeared, based on the consecrations of the buildings situated on Red Square (one of the sacrariums of the cathedral of the Intercession on the Ditch was consecrated to the Entry into Jerusalem, the gates of Kitay-gorod had the name of Voskresenskie (of the Resurrection). All the above-said allows to understand the logic of Ukhtomskiy's idea, which led the architect to designing of Voskresenskie gates like Moscow bell-towers. Semantics of the names (Voskresenskie gates), semantics of the place (on the crossing of the two royal roads: to the Kremlin and out of the Kremlin, in front of the bell-tower of John the Great and the church of the Entry of Our Lord Jesus Christ into Jerusalem), the towers of old Voskresenskie gates induced the architect to turn to the compositional schemes having sacral meaning while projecting a secular building. In the art of baroque such phenomenon was ordinary. Christian plots were widely used in triumphal gates.

Something of the kind can be seen in another grandiose project of D. Ukhtomskiy, which was not realized, – Invalid and Hospital houses. Projecting a complex of a secular denomination, the architect turned again to the scheme spread in the cult architecture, this time – to the scheme of a monastery ensemble. The Invalid and Hospital houses were to be built in the winding of the

Moscow-river to the south from the monastery of St. Simon. The new complex was planned as the compositional centre of the district, which got a regular planning due to the presumed works. All the composition was successively centric. The ensemble of Invalid house, which was to be situated in the geometric centre of a new district, was surrounded by streets which crossed at the right angle; four ray-like avenues met in it. Construction of a huge five-cupola cathedral was planned in the middle of the square, in the geometric centre of the Invalid house itself. The plan of the ensemble originated from the monastery plans, brought to the clear geometric planning of Donskoy monastery. The cross-like outline of the ensemble with four nearly closed squares of hospital buildings and almshouses had much in common with the cross-like plan of Smolnij monastery.

---

1 Lebedev L. Patriarch Nicon. // Theologic works. 1982; Musatov A. A. Town-building development of Moscow of Peter`s Epoch. M., 1994. Dissertation... in RGB, p. 16. Summary of notions about a town during the reign of Alexius Mikhailovich, Sophia and Peter I, represented in the main law of that time, is based on the material of this dissertation.
2 Musatov A. A. The above works, p. 17.
3 Vasiliev V. N. Ancient Fire-Works in Russia. M., 1972, p. 20-21
4 Musatov A. A. The above works, p. 56-74.
5 As above, p. 16; Rovinsky D. A. Review of icon-painting in Russia Spb, 1903, p. 179-180; Iijin M. A., Vygolov V. P. Moscow Triumphal gates of the border of 17th-18th centuries//Materials about the theory and history of art. M., 1956, p. 107-108.
6 Grabar I. E. History of Russian Art. V. 1. M., published by Knebel, 1909
7 Letters and documents of emperor Peter the Great. V. 1, 1688-1701. SPb, 1887, p. 109.
8 Golikov I. I. Addition to the Deeds of Peter the Great. V. IV. M.,1790, p. 192.
9 As above, p. 192-193.
10 Golikov I. I. Addition to the Deeds of Peter the Great. V. IV. M.,1790, p. 203.
11 As above, p. 197-198.
12 Gay Svetoniy Trancvill. Life of Twelve Caesars. M., 1988, p. 32, 37.
13 Golikov I. I. Comparison of qualities and deeds of Constantine the Great, the First of Roman Christian emperors, with the qualities and deeds of Peter the Great, the first All-Russia. emperor, and events during the reign of both emperors. Parts 1-2. M.,1810.
14 Golikov I. I. Additions to the deeds... V. IV, p. 206; V. XVI M., 1795, p. 222;
 Golikov I. I. Deeds of Peter the Great... P. 2, p. 158.
15 Uspenskiy B. A. Tsar and an impostor: imposture in Russia as a cultural and historical phenomenon. M., Nauka, 1982, p. 211.
16 Uspenskiy B. A. The above works, p. 221, note 23.
17 The list was made on the basis of the description of the gates installed for Poltava's triumph (Golikov I. I. Addition to the deeds. V. XVI, p. 146 -209.
18 Panegyric literature of Peter's time. Under edition of 0. A. Derzhavina. M., 1979, p. 154.
19 Solovjev S. M. History of Ancient Time. M., 1964. V. XII, p. 7-8. Quoted according to: Guljanitskiy N. F. Yauza's Moscow// Architectural inheritance. Issue 34, M., 1986, p. 34. The analysis of town-building phenomenon of Yauza's Moscow in this article belongs to him too.
20 As above, p. 32, 39. Musatov A. A. The above works, p.130-131.
21 Bondarenko l. A. Red Square. M., 1991, p. 89-91.
22 Musatov A. A. The above works, p. 96.
23 Musatov A. A. The above works, p. 174.
24 P.G.Palamarchuk. Forty of Forties. M, 1995, Volume 3. PP.205-206.
25 V.V.Kirillov.A Russian City of the Barocco Epoch, Issue 6. M.,1983. P. 154.

Northern part of Red Square. On the right – the cathedral of the Kazan Icon of the Theotokos. Coin Yard (1732-174n, architect P. Geyden), two-tower Voskresenskiy gate, on the left – the building of the Zemskiy department. Water-colour of F. Alexeev's studio, 1800-1802.

CHAPTER TWO

Nobiliary Capital of Russia

View at Mokhovaja street with P.E.Pashkov's house (1784-1788). Print according to G.Delabarfs drawing, 1797.

Big emperor's crown. 1767.

Orb. 1762.

Throne armchair of emperor Paul 1. 1797.

Empress Catherine II (1762-1796). Artist A. Antropov.

Emperor Paul I (1796-1801). Artist V. Borovikovskiy.

Cathedral square in Moscow Kremlin. Water-colour of F. Alexeev. 1800s.

View on the Kremlin and Stone Bridge. Water-colour of F. Alexeev. Early 19th century.

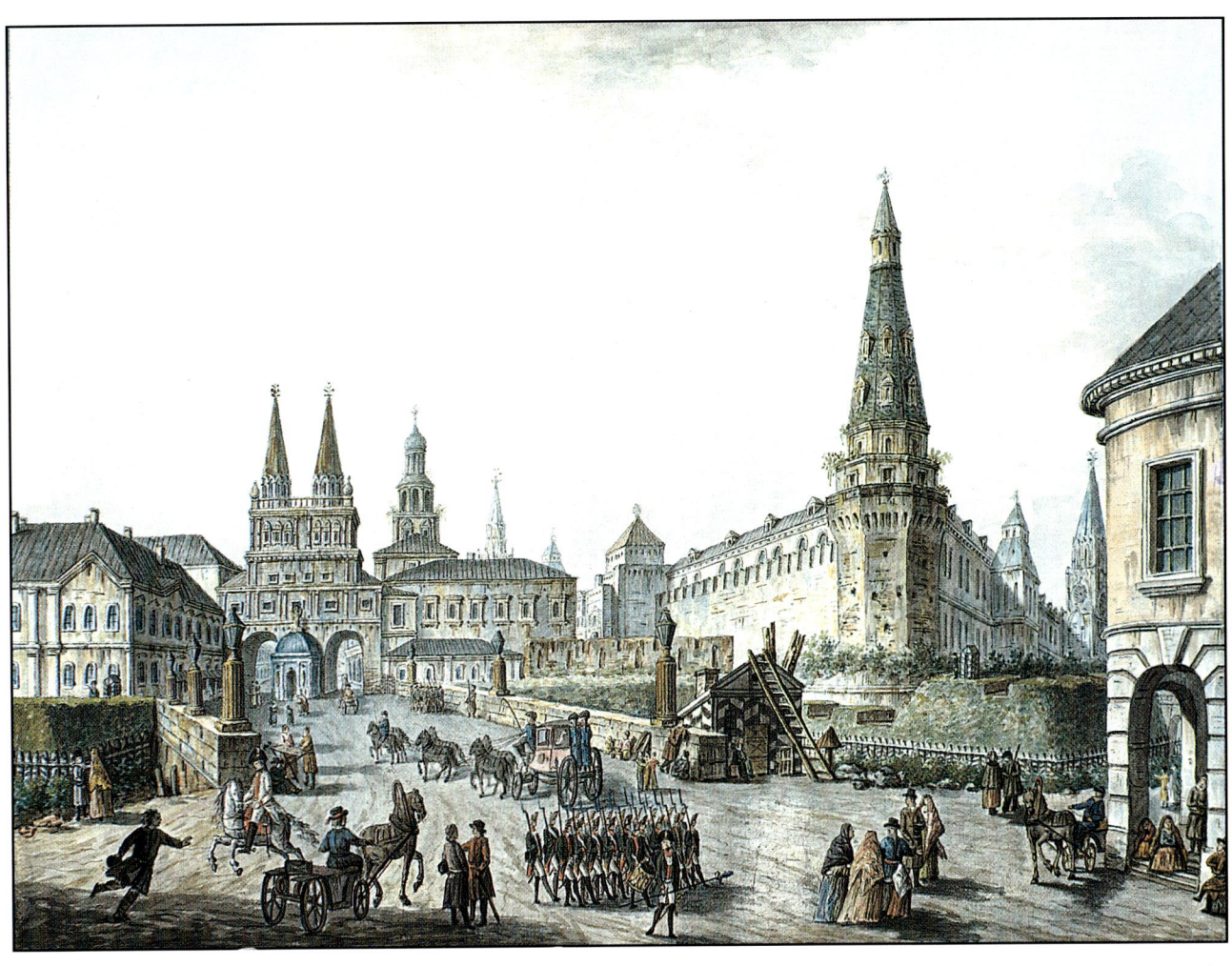

View of Voskresenskie and Nikolskie gates from Voskresenskaja square. Water-colour of F. Alexeev's studio. 1800-1802.

Podnovinskoe outdoor fete (Novinskiy boulvard). Colour print according to G.Delabart's drawing. 1797.

Moscow panorama. View from the Kremlin of Zamoskvorechie and Tuition House. Print according to Delabart's drawing. 1797.

In Russian history and in history of Moscow the period of time, covering the end of the 17th – the first half of the 18th centuries, was the time of a great crush. At the same time this period is a whole thing. It was during that time when notions about an "ideal town" of a new type, which had been gradually forming, were realized first in the architectural and building practice of Moscow, then in that of Petersburg. However, beginning from the 1730s the situation changed. The initiative either came from Petersburg, or the town-building activity was developing parallel in both capitals.

The second half of the 18th century represents a new period in regard of the first half of the century. Like the one which was already considered, it covered about three quarters of the century (1760-1830) and fell into two stages, conditionally called the second part of the 18th century and beginning of the 18th century or Moscow after the fire. The duration of each stage is different. The second half of the 18th century chronologically covered the first ten years of the next century too. The second stage is much shorter and is connected with restoration of the ancient capital after Napoleon's invasion.

Moscow and Petersburg – Two Capitals of Russia

Moscow of the second half of the 18th century can be characterized in different ways from architectural and town-building points of view. If to take into account the prevailing architectural style, it was Moscow of classicism, as it was called in Russia, and in Western Europe it was called – neoclassicism. It was Moscow of nobility, if to take into account the main customer and the type of buildings characterizing the look of the ancient capital. But rightfully it can be called Kazakov's Moscow after the name of the leading architect. I.E.Grabar gave a comprehensive characteristic of the genius, whose name became a symbol of individuality of Moscow architectural school of the second half of the century. "The greatest architect in Moscow and in all Russia in the 18th century was Kazakov, Bazhenov's contemporary and colleague in the Kremlin's palace. This mysterious man, who had got his education in Moscow from prince Ukhtomskiy and who had never been abroad, was such an architectural genius, that he can be compared only with the giants of Renaissance. Starting his activity during the reign of Elizabeth, the epoch of the most unruly baroque, he gradually passed all steps of classicism, including Alexander's one, but at the same time he remained absolutely individual, he followed first of all his own way and created his own "Kazakov's style", which determined all further development of Moscow architecture... During all the reign of Catherine and Paul, as well as during the first ten years of the 18th century, in Moscow no important building was constructed without Kazakov, who either built it himself, or made drawings according to which others built, or just gave advice that was highly appreciated by his contemporaries... He created a school of numerous students who built in all Moscow and a sufficient part of Russia with houses of Kazakov's style which inspired architects during nearly a whole century"[1].

At the end of the 17th century and a century after travelers admired the picturesque location of the ancient capital, plenty of verdure, a lot of churches and chambers. According to the words of English captain D.Perri, Moscow of Peter's time "occupies a large space of land, where even in the middle of the city each important person has his own garden and outside yard belonging to his house. When a traveler approaches the city, the latter appears to him with plenty of churches, boyard and nobility houses, belltowers, cupolas... But the houses were all built from wood... and have nothing imposing in their appearance. The walls and fences between the houses and streets are also wooden, and the streets themselves, instead of being paved with stone, are covered with wood..."[2].

In the second half of the 18th century Moscow remained the city of temples and palaces. However, it is more true to say: of palaces and temples. The first word defining its appearance, is the palaces, the second is the temples. It is already a European city. And at the same time, the city is not just Russian, but of purely Moscow individuality. Painter Vige-Lebren admired Moscow of the end of the 18th century: "This abundance of palaces, public

Moscow panorama from the terrace of the Kremlin Palace of Zamoskvorechie and the Big Stone Bridge. Print according to G.Delabarfs drawing. 1797.

memorials of wonderful architecture, monasteries, churches, mixed with country views and village buildings, presents a really magnificent view. This mixture of splendor with village simplicity makes some magic impression"[3]. K.N.Batjushkov wrote about the "wonderful contrast of city and village views", nearly word by word repeating what the French woman had said. Then this characteristic would be repeated nearly by everybody who would try to express his impression of Moscow: "Here the picture opens which is worth the greatest capital in the world built by the greatest people in the most pleasant place"[4]. The characteristics of those who wrote about Moscow were precise. For the first time in the history of Moscow palaces together with temples, ousting them, occupied a high point of the hilly relief, not only in the country in Lefortovo, but within the borders of the historical city in the area of Mokhovaja, Volkhonka, Prechistenka, Alexeevskaja, on Shvivaja hill.

Impressive changes in the look, structure and building in Moscow of the second half of the 18th century connected with the reforming activity of Catherine II are their architectural equivalent and material expression. Each successive ruler compared the conception of his reign with the activity of the first emperor of Russia. The reign of Catherine II was not an exception. Together with this it was more than the time of the reign of her predecessors oriented at the reforming enthusiasm of Peter's reign. Catherine's reign was permeated with the striving for reasonable reorganization of the state structure, laws, management, architectural and town-building activity.

In 1762 and 1763 the decrees were issued which determined the destinies of the capital cities for nearly a whole century. In 1762 not long before the decease of Peter III, he managed to issue the decree "About the Liberty of the Nobility", which freed the nobility from the obligatory state service. After the decree had been issued large construction of nobility estates began which changed sufficiently the architectural-spatious environment of Russia and made the estate of classicism the synonym of Russian estate in general. The same decree made Moscow a capital of retired and not working nobility in difference to Petersburg – the capital of serving nobility – military men and officials. A few months later after the issue of the first decree already during the time when Catherine II was on the throne the decree was issued about creation of "Commission for Stone Construction in St. Petersburg and Moscow". A year later after a devastating fire in Tverj and the decision to replan it on the basis of regularity a decree was issued which extended the principles of regularity, that had been applied only to Tverj before, on all towns of Russia. Implementation of the decree "About Making Special Plans for All Towns, Their Buildings and Streets, for Each Domain Separately" was entrusted to the Commission for Stone Construction in Petersburg and Moscow. Soon another decree appeared, which influenced much the conception and predetermined the look of public centres of towns: "About construction in All Towns of Stone Public Buildings". The general land survey that started from 1762 was also connected with the issue of these decrees. During its conduct hierarchy and borders of town territories of different rank were established. Each town was divided into three parts according to their hierarchy: the town itself, suburbs and pastures – the lands which were not subject to construction. Moscow borders were limited by Zemljanoy town, the suburbswere limited by Kamer-Kollezhskiy bank.

Introduction everywhere into practice of obligatory construction of towns in accordance with a preliminary made general plan enforced by law consolidated finally the regulating role of the government in town and private life. The plan was to be followed during location of a building in respect of a street on the owner's plot, in a quarter. The look of a dwelling house was to correspond to the norms of the style accepted as the supreme too. A project could not be realized without consideration and certification of the construction authority. For this a well-off builder was to use the services of an architect, those who were not well-off were to use sample projects.

Consolidation of the role of the government was accompanied by derogation of the role of the church and religious indifference especially clear during the reign of Peter and Catherine. The effort to limit the church construction is seen already in the number of documents of Peter's time. The emperor prescribed: "... not to build more churches than required"[5]. Catherine, sharing the conception of educated absolutism, followed the example of the kings of the leading European countries. Her contemporaries Prussian king Frederick II the Great, Austrian emperor Josef II, Swedish king Gustavus III, important statesmen of Spain, Portugal, a number of Italian states, having in consideration the necessity of stable state newer, believed that it was exactly the government who was to meet the requirements of time realizing the improvements useful for people. From their point of view, the government was supreme, the church subordinative. At the beginning of her reign the empress acted like the Austrian emperor, who closed the monasteries, where the monks were not occupied in teaching or looking after ill and poor people, using their property for arrangement of parish churches. In 1764 in Russia by the empress' decree so called staff was established: monasteries were transferred to the government sponsorship. As a result the quantity of monasteries in Russia became twice less than before. "According to the staff of 1764 from 953 great Russian monasteries more than half of them were closed, – only 222 of them were left on the staff list and 161 were extra, on their self-support; then more than 40 monasteries were closed while staff lists were introduced in Malorossija and Belorussia. By the beginning of the 19th century there were only 452 old and newly opened monasteries"[6].

The government which acknowledged itself responsible for realization of a reasonable home policy, for the first time undertook the obligation, which had been the prerogative of the church before, to take care of all who needed help. In connection with this state construction of charity (alms, hospital houses) and educational buildings was started.

The reforming policy, actively conducted during Catherine's time, directed at the reasonable reorganization of the state governing, was accompanied by the work of making of a new code of laws ("Order to Compose New Law", 1767), reorganization of the administrative structure of Russia ("Establishment about Management of the Domains", 1775) and towns ("Chart about the Rights and Priviliges of Towns", 1785). The purpose of the reforms was to intensify development of towns, making administrative centres of them, centres of trade development, industry and culture.

The new direction of the home policy required in its turn development of a new town-building program. In towns, first of all in capital ones, construction of public buildings first of all was started, the public buildings of different denomination, which were to satisfy the needs born by the reforms – charity, educational, administrative. The construction of public buildings was accompanied by construction of rich dwelling houses stimulated by the decree about the nobility liberty. All this defined the unprecedented rise of civil construction. The process, that had been started during the time of Peter, entered a qualitatively new phase.

Catherine's reign was similar to Peter's also in a new "discovery" of European culture, this time antique. Russia got to know a discovery of antiquity for the second time after Renaissance, through which the whole Europe lived, and a new rebirth of principles of the ancient in art, connected with it. Simultaneously with the change of the esthetic ideal, expressed by Winkelman in the words "the noble simplicity and quiet majesty", little by little change of styles was going on. Classicism appeared. Accuracy of recreation of antique samples rapidly increased.

Ideals of enlightenment, inseparable from classicism, changed the character, but did not change the essence of geopolitical orientation of Russia. It was still represented by the conception of Moscow being the Third Rome. During the reign of Catherine II the balance of its two aspects – imperial and Christian – which was established during the reign of Elizabeth Petrovna, outlived itself. Again, like during the time of Peter I, the state aspect won. The Christian-orthodox aspect moved to the second place. However the notion about the grandeur and power of Russia was still connected with the notion about it as about the great orthodox power. Due to this the Greek project of Catherine II appeared. Its essence was in the effort to extend the borders of Russia up to Constantinople, to return the first Christian capital to the lap of orthodoxy, to see new Constantine – the son of Paul I and the grandson of Catherine II – on the throne in Constantinople, to install a cross on the great holy thing of the Christian world – the church of St. Sophia, which was turned by the Turks into a mosque. The striving to realize the dream forced Catherine to lead constant wars with the Turkey.

But then Russian towns were recreated on the principles of regularity in the name of Russia's grandeur and glory. Recreation of towns was started from the capitals and the towns situated on the way connecting the capitals. Recreation of the capitals was started in the 1760s from recreation of their centres. The Neva and the Moscow-river were bounded in granite. In Petersburg construction of two memorials to Peter – sculptural (the famous Copper Horseman) and architectural (the new five-cupola cathedral of St. Isaac according to the project of A.Rinaldi) – was started nearly simultaneously. "Following the example of European towns" in accordance with the program developed by Betskiy, the squares of Petersburg built in with new buildings were adorned with "monuments" "in memory of Russian deeds". Petersburg was the first Russian city, for which the Commission developed a plan (in November of 1763 a competition was announced), works of creation of the central square of the new capital – Dvortsovaja (Palace) – were started.

In 1760s works of radical rearrangement of the centre were started in Moscow too.

Idea "Moscow – the Third Rome". Projects and Practice of Recreation of the Historical Centre.

According to the plot which Catherine II had in the middle of the 1760s, it was supposed to create in Moscow a grandiose memorial to the reign. In symbolical and at the same time understandable form it was to express the novelty and reasonability of the ideas by which Russian Minerva, Russian Palladium, Northern Semiramida, as the empress was usually called, was governed in her wise ruling. V.I.Bazhenov's project of the Kremlin palace is meant here: the author himself called it rightfully the project of the Kremlin's reconstruction.

The idea of N.A.Evsina about connection between the undertaken effort of creation of new laws in Russia under the management of Catherine II, or, as they said then, between the activity of the Commission and the idea of creation of a new grandiose palace, construction of which was to change cardinally the historical centre of the ancient capital with its Kremlin[7], seems extremely fruitful to me. In any case the concurrence of the dates when the Commission was called on (the 14th of December, 1766) and when the idea to create a new Kremlin palace appeared was hardly accidental. It is possible to suggest several arguments in favour of this view. Synodal laws were to be substituted by the new code of laws, were adopted in the Kremlin in 1649. Work on the new code of laws was also started in the Kremlin. Catherine's actions were similar to those of her predecessors. In order to immortalize reforming on the basis of Reason in the state, where the law and enlightenment reigned, and reorganization of domains and reconstruction of towns on the principles of regularity became a visible embodiment of sensible rearrangement of the huge empire, it was necessary to raise a palace, which was to be bigger in its dimensions two times than the dimensions of one of the most impressive memorials-symbols of Elizabeth Petrovna – the palace in Tsarskoe (Royal) village (the length only of the central part of the palace's facade turned in the direction of the Moscow-river, was to be more than 600 m, the total length was to be 1200 m, as for the length of Tsarskoselskiy palace, it was 326 m)[8]. The height of the four-storey palace designed by Bazhenov reached 30-40 m (10-storey house).

Plenty of publications about the project of the Kremlin's palace of V.I.Bazhenov, and most important the character of work make to touch upon only one aspect – the contents, and to analyze from this point of view the document, which was known to scientists well and long ago, – "Word about the Foundation of the Kremlin's Palace", announced by V. Bazhenov, but composed, taking into consideration the fact that it was published in the works of A. Sumarokov, by him. However, in this case it is not important

Project of the Kremlin Palace. Fayade at the Moscow-river (1768-1775, architect V.I.Bazhenov). Lithograph according to N.I.Chichagov's drawing from the palace model. 1827.

who the author was, but the contents of the palace's program, fixed in the "Word", which represented a clearly specified multi-aspect system.

Russia's pretention to be similar to the great empire of the ancient and the city of St.Peter – Rome, first stated by Peter and confirmed by Catherine II, was expressed during Catherine's reign in respect of Petersburg by the projects of the centre made by A.V.Kvasov and I.E.Starov. The same purpose in respect of Moscow was pursued in the project of the Kremlin's palace.

"The Word about the Foundation of the Kremlin Palace" began as follows: "The Eastern Church celebrates the renovation of Tsar-Grad; for pious Constantine transferred the throne from the Tiber's banks into Byzantium and adorned the latter with splendor, and sanctified divinely that place. Today Moscow is renovated. You, great Catherine, in the middle of the bloody battle, among all the plenty deeds entrusted to you by God, did not want to forget about adornment of the capital city"[9]. Renovation of Moscow was compared to the construction by Constantine the Great of the new capital of Roman Empire, the Russian empress was compared to the first Roman Christian emperor. There were two considerations behind the traditional for Ancient Russia and recomprehended in Peter's Russia comparison of Moscow and Constantinople. Emphasizing the ancient Russian source of the idea, which made to take the decision about construction of the eighth miracle of the world exactly in Moscow, Catherine, like her predecessors, rolled on the traditional sympathies of people to the ancient capital and dislike of the new one. Simultaneously in the same way she emphasized the connection of her reign not only with Petersburg, but also with pre-Peter's period in Russian history, accentuating the legacy of her stay on the throne which was constantly worrying her. According to the traditional comparisons, Moscow is not only the Third Rome, but also New Jerusalem; "To your Zion come the inhabitants of the multi-national dwelling to seek your assistance".

Catherine's deeds, "Russian Minerva, renovating the Kremlin and Moscow", were compared with the deeds of "Northern Zeus who created Petrople", i.e. with the deeds of Peter the Great. Due to Catherine's undertakings the banks of new Zion – the Moscow-river would "be adorned like the banks of the flow made out of a swamp into the purest streams of the Neva and having in Petrople the name of the Great Tsarina!". Catherine's channel is meant here, which good arrangement, cleaning and fortification of the banks were conducted during the empress' reign.

Accentuating the similarity of Catherine's deeds with the deeds of Peter I in both capitals, the author of the Word likened the future palace to one of the "seven miracles of the world"- Artemis temple in Ephesus (the 4th century A.D., architects Hersiphron and Metagen). New Ephesus temple called in Roman manner the temple of Diana – the Kremlin's new palace – was built for the glory and devoted (it was specially mentioned in the Word) to "God's vicegerent in Russia shining not only with her virtues, but with dignity too".

All great tsars from the time of John Danilovich, as it is further said in the "Word", "extended and adorned Moscow". Catherine II continued the deeds of Moscow tsars. "She excelled with her victories glorious Russian Monarch John, grand-father of the tsar of the same name, and now she is striving to excel him in adornment of Moscow".

The palace, which was presumed to be raised according to the rules of the "great ancient and contemporary"[10] (Italian, French) architect, was not built because of the tragedies which happened in Moscow (epidemic of plague) and ominous signs: one of counterforts and a wall of the cathedral of Chernigov Icon of the Theotokos came down, the counterforts in front of the cathedrals of the Annunciation and Archangel Michael settled down[11]. The counterforts – grandiose wooden supports were constructed in connection with preliminary construction works – demolishing of the "decrepitudes", which precluded the beginning of the construction works. They included the old building of the Departments constructed at the end of the 17th century, the Kazennyj (Official) yard, built in 1483, several temples and the Kremlin wall along the Moscow-river, between Petrovskaja and Blagovetschenskaja towers (of the Annunciation), the towers "Taynitskaja" and Bezymjannye situated near it[12]. As people were angry with demolishing the holy things of Moscow the construction of the Kremlin's palace was stopped.

The fact that Bazhenov mentioned in the "Word about the Foundation of the Palace" ancient buildings in Moscow which he admired, should not create illusions in regard of the system of values adopted in the second half of the 18th century. Certain good qualities were acknowledged in ancient Russian and other types of not classical (not antique) architecture. In the general hierarchy, however, they were given the secondary importance in comparison

View of the Kremlin hill.

with the classical, antique inheritance. In the name of its rebirth the grandiose works of Moscow renovation were undertaken. There should not be any illusions either in regard of Bazhenov's attitude and that of her crowned customer to the Kremlin's ancient things. The lithograph made by N.I.Chichagov in 1827, and the perspective-reconstruction of the Kremlin's palace made by K.K.Lopjalo already in 1960, evidently show that, if it was realized, the unique panorama of the ancient Kremlin would have disappeared forever, and the quay of the Moscow-river would have become some copy of Palace quay in Petersburg.[13]

Provided that Bazhenov's project was realized, the look and the structure of the building inside the Kremlin which was planned to make a regular ensemble with a developed system of parade squares connected with straight wide avenues, would have changed as radically as the panorama from the Moscow-river side. Bazhenov designed a trapeziform administrative house similar to the Arsenal and symmetrically to it in the Northern end of the Kremlin, between them along the axis of Troitskaja tower he planned a diamond-shaped square and in front of the Arsenal – a polycircular one. At the crossing of the avenues constructed from Nikolskaja tower to the South and from the diamond-shaped square (to the East a round square was planned, and further to the South the biggest and most portentous Oval square was planned). It was the main object in reorganization of the radically changed inside space of the Kremlin.

By Bazhenov's project not only the panorama of the historical centre of the ancient capital was to be destroyed. The Kremlin's structure and hierarchy of its inside space was to be absolutely changed. The Oval square was to acquire the importance of the compositional and contextual centre. From it wide and straight avenues stretched like rays to Spasskie, Nikolskie and Troitskie gates. The avenue leading from the Oval square to Nikolskie gates promised to be the most gala. It went out to the Kremlin's wall to the South from Nikolskaja tower. For this it was also presumed to dismantle a part of the Kremlin's wall from the side of Red Square, and to accentuate the place where Petersburg road leading to the Kremlin ended, with triumphal gates.

Large open spaces, geometrically right squares and streets, which made the designed environment drastically different from the real one, crowded and not regular, symbolized the reasonability of the state structure reorganized on the regular basis. In the new spatial system born by Bazhenov's project the cathedral square with the cathedrals of the Assumption, Archangel Michael and the Annunciation, connected with the Oval one, looked accidental and strange. Ancient holy things, enclosed into the frame of new houses, were isolated from the system of open space and did not arrange it. As for the other Kremlin's buildings with the monasteries of the Ascension and Chudov, Patriarch chambers with the cathedral of the Twelve Apostles, Chamber-rooms and plenty of other buildings, their existence just like the historically formed planning were simply ignored as an inheritance of "a dilapidated poor town". They as though did not exist for Bazhenov. It was presumed to construct the system of straight highways and regular squares by the way of surgical interferences.[14] For a new rational organization and immortal values embodied by classical buildings in the spirit of rebirthed antiquity there was no past as an independent value.

What Greece and Rome could give birth to in ancient time,
The Kremlin want to include inside itself now.
Diana's temple in Epheus was excelled by the beauty of
The gorgeous buildings of the Kremlin's court.[15]

Such was the conception of a reasonable organization of the new centre of the ancient capital, expressed by the official government's policy in the sphere of architecture. The same was the point of view of the poets glorifying this event and the creation of V.I.Bazhenov in poems. G.R.Derzhavin responded to the project of the Kremlin's palace with an ode with the famous name: "For the occasion of bringing down Moscow Kremlin for construction of a new palace in 1770 by architect Bazhenov at the author's departure from Moscow to Petersburg":

Farewell, the capital city, the majestic creation
Of wonderful ancient time, Moscow, the shining of Russia!
Sparkling cupolas and proud heights,
Ages ago you were created as a wonder.
For the last time I see you and measure the roofs with my eyes
And I am surprised by it and horrified,
I am in doubt, but believe,
If it is possible for coffins to fall apart, to rise
And flourish in the previous beauty more wonderfully?
For such strongholds to fall and be recreated,
Nature must-so to say, be applied!
But what is not possible if Deity wants?
Bazhenov! Begin, nature will give way.[16]

The deity, that in the name of creation of the eighth world's wonder did not stop at demolishing Moscow Kremlin was Russian Minerva, Catherine II.

There was an inscription on the foundation board: the new palace is raised "for the glory of Russian Empire, honour of its age, adornment of its city, for fun and pleasure of its people".[17]

Scientists compared many times the Kremlin's system of squares, created by Bazhenov, to the forums of the greatest empire of the past – Ancient Rome. Besides that, N.A.Evsina noted the similarity of the Oval square with the competition projects of the square of Ludovig XV in Paris, indicating that the album of these projects bought by I.I.Shuvalov, was delivered to the Academy of Art and that Bazhenov, creating the project of the Oval square, like Starov designing Dvortsovaja square in Petersburg, oriented at the

Plan of the Kremlin. End of the 17th century.   **Reconstruction Project of the Kremlin of 1767 by V.Bazhenov.**   **Reconstruction Project of the Kremlin of 1797 by M.Kazakov.**

Senate square in the Kremlin (1776-1789, architect M.F.Kazakov).
Water-colour of F.Ya.Alexeev's studio. 1800-1802.

Oval square in front of the cathedral of St. Apostle Peter in Rome and at French projects awarded with Grand Pris.[18] Thus the idea of Moscow-the Third Rome expressed itself in the architecture of Russia.

But the form of the Oval square and its developed system of memorial-triumphal constructions with an obelisk surrounded by four columns with a figure of Glory in the geometrical centre of the square corresponded at least to the other two not less known and contextually important prototypes. They include the forums Troyan and Augustus. In them the initial form of the forum's plan in the shape of an extended rectangle was made more complex with semi-circles, which created inside this strut spatial system a relatively separate transversal oval composition. Three rays of avenues joining at the Oval square of the Kremlin, also likened the planning of its Eastern part to the famous three-ray style of Versailles and Petersburg.

Finally in the project of Bazhenov the experience of Rome reconstruction in the 16th-17th centuries was brilliantly reconsidered, which was expressed in construction inside the ancient town of a system of straight wide highways, among which there were the famous three rays joining in the square del Popolo. The square centre was fixed by an obelisk constructed according to D.Fontana's project in 1589. The new facade of the gates of the front entrance road along which numerous pilgrims arrived in Rome along the Flemish road, was made by Bernini in 1655.

The example of reconstruction of Pope's Rome, inspired by the idea to give the city the look worth of the capital of world Christianity and international pilgrimage centre, was, probably, on Bazhenov's mind. In any case "the trident cut inside the city's body from the gates of Flammeneous road", which became "as though "Rome's spinal column"[19], generally accepted in the town-building of Western Europe method of surgical interference into the historically formed tissue of the city, and the mode itself turned out to be spiritually close to the reconstruction of the historical centre of the ancient capital undertaken by Bazhenov in Russia. Orientation at concrete samples and for instance such different presence of samples of Ancient and Pope's Rome was natural for the project, the purpose of which was creation of a central ensemble in one of the capitals of the Third Rome and the eighth world's wonder.

Ten years later the second effort of the Kremlin's renovation was undertaken. In 1776 P.N.Kozhin who was the head of the "Stone-building department" in Moscow prepared a special report which reflected another attitude to the Kremlin than Bazhenov's – more careful and respectable. It stipulated creation of "regular" squares in front of Troitskie and Nikolskie gates and construction of palace buildings with "the best facades according to the rules of the most up-to-date architecture" instead of Bazhenov's project that was not realized. New buildings were to be placed in such a way that "a rather excellent view of many parts of the city and of the river itself" opened; they were "to be seen from everywhere and to compose quite a beautiful view".[20] A square near Borovitskie gates was to be created too and Ivanovskaja square was to be made regular. It is possible that this report was connected with two realized M.F.Kazakov's projects. For instance the administrative reform conducted in 1775 and issue of the decree "Establishment about Management of the Domains" coincided with the beginning of the construction of the Senate in the Kremlin in 1776. Two departments – of the nobility rights and judicial – were transferred to Moscow. By the Senate's governmental building testifying to the capital functions of Moscow, the originality of its capital status was emphasized at the same time: Moscow was the capital of the nobility society.

For the construction of the Senate's building an inconvenient plot between the Arsenal and Chudov monastery was selected. Kazakov solved the task brilliantly designing a building that was triangular on its plan with cut angles and three yards. There was a temple-like rotunda of the front hall understood as the temple of Justice, inside the medium one on the main axis. The architect managed to create a regular triangular square near Nikolskie gates. At the same time he managed to find such a position for the cupola of the Senate's main hall (Kazakov installed it on one axis with the Senate's tower), that these two vertical accents brought regularity into the space in front of the Kremlin's wall fixing the transverse axis of Red Square. Kazakov also introduced elements of regularity in the ensemble of Ivanovskaja square: according to his project a small, but representable building of Epoch's yard with a corner rotunda was built.[21]

Twenty years later in 1797 in connection with preparation for the coronation celebration and the necessity to arrange the palace for Paul's stay in it, Kazakov had to make a plan of the Kremlin's renovation again. He also was to raise the grandiose building of the Manege.

Designing the building, which was to determine the Kremlin's look from the side of the Moscow-river in many ways, the architect tried to keep "as much as possible the old important buildings" and to stipulate simultaneously "as much as possible spatial squares and passages".[22]

It was a principally different approach to the Kremlin's renovation in comparison with Bazhenov's – the way of regulation, of careful attitude towards old buildings and introduction with the help of new elements of features of symmetry, accuracy and openness in the appearance of the historically formed ensemble and, which seems most important – agreement of what already existed with the newly designed. Kazakov stipulated the making of the palace, designed by Rastrelli, as one part (the right one) of the three-partial, symmetrical classical composition with a six-column portico under a triangular pediment and a cupola on the drum in the centre. On the opposite end of the edge of the Kremlin's hill not far from Spasskie gates Kazakov designed the building of the

View of the Kremlin from Stone Bridge.

Manege. As a result the group of the cathedrals with the bell-tower of John the Great became an original spatially developed axis of the Kremlin's main facade. Trying to increase symmetry and balance of the ensemble renovated with the help of new buildings, Kazakov designed on its main axis coinciding with the bell-tower of John the Great a portentous lone staircase coming down to the Moscow-river.

Insistence with which in the second half of the 18th century the projects of the Kremlin's reconstruction were developed and the construction in 1774 of Prechistenskiy palace from the houses of the Golitsyns, the Lopukhins and the Dolgorukovs, situated near the Kremlin in Volkhonka, for Catherine's arrival for a gala celebration of the honorable peace with Turkey, testified that Moscow returned to the historically formed monocentric structure. A turn appeared in 1750 when after another fire Elizabeth Petrovna did not start to renew the Winter palace in Annenhof, concentrating her attention on the construction of the country residence in Tsarskoe village. Upon the order of Catherine II, and then of Paul too in Lefortovo on the Yauza's bank the palaces were built. But they were just the country residences without pretentions to be the town and even state capital centres. For this purpose the Kremlin was denominated. The grandiose Bazhenov's project signified return to the Kremlin of its initial importance and the only capital centre for Moscow. The same fact was confirmed by the works in the Kremlin, divided by twenty years and connected with the construction of the Senate and the Eparch's house in the 1770s, renovation of the Kremlin's palace and with non-performed projects timed for the coronation of Paul I in 1797. The same was testified by the documents. It was stated directly in one of them: "The centre of Moscow is the Kremlin".

Reconstruction of the Historical Towns on the Principles of Regularity and the Architectural and Town-building Destiny of Moscow. The Plan of 1775.

By the decree of the 11th of December, 1762, the "Commission for Construction of the Capital Cities St.Petersburg and Moscow" was to make plans for both capitals. The necessity of a new plan for Moscow was reasoned by the fact that "due to its very old buildings it is out of order now". In its turn the Commission made the resolution to "compose a plan of all Moscow places, according to which a general one should be made of the city and the outskirts". In conformity with this resolution engineer-topographer Gorikhvostov made in 1763 a geodesical plan of Moscow which fixed the domination of stone buildings in the Kremlin and Kitay-gorod.

Till 1774 it was the only affair implemented by the Commission for stone construction in Moscow. The only design proposal concerning the territory outside the Kremlin, became Bazhenov's project of the Kremlin palace and its surroundings developed together with the first option. Trying to emphasize the town character of the palace which went out of the Kremlin's walls, Bazhenov offered to make even and face with stone the banks of the Moscow-river, construct a bridge across it from the central part of the palace to the Tsarina's meadow situated in front of it, to make out of the Neglinnaja, flowing near the Northern walls of the Kremlin which were still bounded by bastions of Peter's time then, a correctly planned channel with the banks faced by stone. It was offered to make out of Red Square an open accurately planned space and free it completely from the buildings making an oval with trade places at the round ends.

However, only after the devastating fire in 1773 composition of the plan moved from the dead point. On the 14th of March, 1774, the decree was issued "About Establishment in Moscow of a Special Department under Control of the Commander-in-Chief for Composition of the Main Plan and the Project for Improvement of Construction in Moscow". The above-mentioned P.N.Kozhin was appointed the chief of the department. The department's architect N.N.Legran was entrusted to "compose" the plan of Moscow, accentuating that "the city of Moscow from the most ancient time was founded so reasonably that each place had its own borders and fortifications.., and there was no, and is not now, only regularity in the buildings and the streets".[23]

The idea about the necessity to preserve the historically formed plan of Moscow in its main structural particulars and to correct inaccuracies in the name of regularity permeated Kozhin's report. The first realization of this idea became the Kremlin's reconstruction made in 1770 according to Kazakov's project. Before revolution of 1917, and partially after it, all generations of Moscow architects were governed by the principle of regulation of the historically formed plan of Moscow formulated in the middle of the 1770s. The method of substitution of the plan's existing structure with a new one, designed by Bazhenov for the Kremlin's reconstruction, i.e. the method of restructuring for complete regularity, was not accepted in Moscow. However, it became a guide to action during replanting on the principles of regularity of Russian historically formed towns. During the period from 1760 to 1830 they lived through the process of total reconstruction according to new regular plans. The above-said allows to understand Moscow uniqueness and how it was different from Petersburg which in ten years after its foundation was built in on the principles of regularity. And from historical towns of Russian province, for which new regular plans were made taking into account, conditionally speaking, Bazhenov's method and approach, used by him during designing the Kremlin's palace, where the initial point was the ideally correct geometrical (regular) scheme which practically did not take into account the existing planning and buildings.

In this case the principles are meant, not Bazhenov's concrete proposals for good arrangement of the territory surrounding the Kremlin. All of them were included into the plan of 1775 and finally were realized. The Commission recommended to Legran to pay special attention while making the plan to regulation of the streets and quarters and cleaning of space for squares in proper places. Achievement of regularity in constructions, i.e. their design in conformity with the norms of classicism was also included then in the task of the architects.

In the plan of 1775 special attention was paid to the territory inside the Garden Ring, first of all to the arrangement of the public space next to the Kremlin and to the main elements of the city structure. Differences in the notions about an ideal town in the first and the second halves of the 18th century are evident. For the first half the beauty of a regular town was in the architecture of new Europeanized buildings brought out or corresponding to the red line, in direct wide streets. Simultaneously (and this was inherited from town-building before Peter's time) a town as an artistic body was understood as a system organized by volumes of supporting constructions – the Kremlin, monasteries, temples and bell-towers. In understanding of the creators of Moscow plan of 1775 – managers of the Commission, people conducting the town-building policy and people who realized it (architects) a town created on the principles of regularity was a unified rationally planned system of nubile architecturally organized open spaces of streets and squares. A square as an independent artistically and contextually significant space appeared in Russia in the second half of the 18th century. The system which turned up and formed during the first half of the 18th century in Moscow, and then in Petersburg, acquired in the second half complete definiteness. Its characteristic fundamental peculiarity, without which there could not be any system, – the priority of plan. It was exactly the plan, which was later filled in with quarters, plots, buildings, composed the initial element of design. It was a full opposition of the system of ancient Russian and medieval town-building as a whole with its priority of town-forming element – the Kremlin, monastery, cathedral, estate. Streets and squares of a medieval town were always something born, not giving birth to. In regular town-building the initial, giving birth, element is always a plan. It is made as though on an empty place, subordinating to itself the real situation, leading all to an ideal scheme. The government prescribes what should be built, what is beautiful and important, takes care of introduction of all, which expresses the state idea and serves to glorification of the state. Thus the attention paid to the open organized space of streets and especially squares – the most important town-building element.

View of Serebrjanicheskiy bath-house. Print according to Delabart's drawing. 1797.

The new town-building conception was represented also by the project plan, the first for Moscow. Besides the utilitarian purposes it pursued the ideological ones even more – consolidation of spiritual values officially accepted as the most important ones. Together with the traditional trade and temple squares (often temple-trade, like Red Square) in the second half of the 18th century in Moscow new squares appeared – the places of focus of public and administrative buildings. On the basis of a secular square a new administrative-public type of a city centre formed. In it temples already occupied not the main, but one of the main places.

The Moscow plan, which was to make its streets regular, intensified the rational principle of its naturally and historically formed structure. The streets radiating from the Kremlin were strengthened and accentuated and the planning and town-building importance of ring streets was also intensified. A semi-circle of parade squares around the Northern part of the Kremlin and Kitay-gorod was designed. It went along the flow of the Neglinnaja-river from the today's Theatrical Square till its fall into the Moscow-river near the Big Stone bridge. In front of Peter's bastions at the beginnings of the radial streets at the Kremlin it was supposed to create five squares. The largest one, called Big, was to be in front of Big Nikitskaja street, a little bit smaller one was to be near Tverskaja street, near Voskresenskie gates.

According to the plan of 1775 the second ring was to be created in the place of the dismantled walls of Bely town and a boulevard ring was to be arranged there. Along the perimeter of the ring creation of twelve squares was designed in the place of its crossing with the radial highways or where several streets of Bely and Zemljanoy town met near the future boulevards: between Ostozhenka and Sivtsev Vrazhek, at Arbatskie gates, near Nikitskie gates, there were two of them near the monastery of the Passions – in front of it and behind it till Petrovka, between Petrovka and at Petrovskie gates and Neglinnaja, at Sretenskie and Mjasnitskie gates etc.

It was planned to make a ring highway out of the semi-circle of the front squares around the Kremlin and Kitay-gorod by the way of adjoining to the Moscow-river of modern Kitaygorodskiy passage and arrangement of a quay along the walls of Kitay-gorod till the Yauza's mouth and along the Kremlin. For implementation of this offer all the buildings situated on the bank of the Moscow-river and being next to the gates of the Kremlin and Kitay-gorod, were demolished; the streets which led to the bank were made wider. Kazakov, who directed this work, also created the project of construction on Moskvoretskaja quay of long warehouses for the goods supplied by the river. It was planned to face the quay with raw stone, to arrange accesses to the river for people and transport.

By 1800 arrangement of the Kremlin's quay, and by 1804 arrangement of Moskvoretskaja quay was finished. Along them trees were planted, and in 1791 on Moskvoretskaja quay a boulevard appeared which was the first in Moscow. In 1796 creation of Tverskoy boulevard between Nikitskaja and Tverskaja streets was started, which became the beginning of the Boulevard Ring.

Arrangement of front squares along Neglinnaja, according to the plan of 1775, stipulated making a channel faced with stone out of it with green quays. The plan also stipulated water-supply development of the Moscow-river, organization of navigation, arrangement of proper harbour and a bread market on the square surrounded by barns. For this purpose in Zamoskvorechie it was supposed to dig a by-pass canal making an island out of a part of Zamoskvorechie, built in by port-trade buildings and warehouses.

Realization of the plan was started soon after its signing. In 1779 the "Commission for organization of water works in the capital of Moscow" was created, at the head of which engineer-general Bauer was, the author of the project of the first Moscow (Mytitschinskiy) water-pipe. Creation of the water-pipe solved two most important problems: the city was supplied with pure water, and the Neglinnaja, as it was stipulated by the plan of 1775, became a canal with banks faced with stone. In 1804 it reached Kuznetskiy bridge.

Realization of the plan encountered interconnected difficulties of dual character. The territories allocated for the squares in conformity with the plan, were mostly occupied by stone and wooden buildings. For purchasing out and for move of their owners big sums of money were needed, especially in the centre. All this made Moscow governor-general in 1786 come out with a more local and simultaneously though more modest, but real program. Its realization took half a century till 1812.

Red Square in the late 18th century. Print of G.Delabart according to G.Gutenberg's drawing. 1795.

Inside "Bely town, Kitay and Zemljanoy town" Brjus offered to "... leave those squares which already were, or to make... without touching (private) constructions or lands". There was only Red Square left, separated from the Kremlin wall by a ditch at that time. A long and narrow square was made along the wall of Kitaygorod (today's Old and New Squares). In front of the Kremlin in Zamoskvorechie, on the Island which appeared due to construction of the water-line, on a so called "Swamp", creation of a trade square was supposed, "where it was possible to place up to 2000 carts". It was also supposed to create a number of trade squares in other parts of the city.

With liquidation of the double-centric structure the role of Tverskaja street increased rapidly, the street finalized the way from Petersburg to Moscow and the Kremlin. On its axis during the second half of the 18th century a net-work of squares unique in its density, was formed: Triumphaljnaja square at the Triumphal gates at the border with Zemljanoy Bank, Strastnaja (of the Passions) square at the border of Bely town (in the place of today's Pushkinskaja square) and near Okhotny Row at the beginning of Tverskaja street. Later according to Kazakov's plan of 1792 another square appeared – in front of the house of the governor-general. Brjus offered to create other three squares at the crossing of radial highways with the gates of Kamer-Kollezhskiy bank – near Serpukhovskie, Kaluzhskie and Krasnye gates. Out of five squares stipulated by the plan of 1775 along the bastions of the Kremlin wall upon Brjus' offer only two were left – in Mokhovaja and near Okhotny Row. The considerations stated by Brjus in 1786 got the highest approval and their long and hard realization began.

During the 1780s the first regular squares of Moscow renovated centre were formed. They had to free the space of the future square of Okhotny Row from existing buildings. According to the plan besides the dwelling houses also two churches – of Great Martyr Parasceva of Iconium and Great Martyr Anastasia – were to be demolished. The church of Great Martyr Anastasia was demolished, but the church of Great Martyr Parasceva of Iconium was saved by solicitation of metropolitanate Platon. Something of the kind happened during construction of Iljinskaja square in Kitay-gorod. A church was also demolished there. In the second half of the 18th century in Russia it became possible to demolish temples for town-building purposes. For the first time it happened in the Kremlin, during preparation of construction of the Kremlin's palace according to Bazhenov's project.

In the Southern part of the square of Okhotny Row freed from buildings stone trade stores were built with arches on the facade. On the opposite side according to Kazakov's project Dolgorukov's house was built for the Nobility Assembly. A columned portico adorned the facade of the building turned to the newly created square. Mokhovaja (in future Manege Square) was built in with trade stores with arcades. Near it according to Kazakov's project the building of Moscow University was raised. In the same street on the high hill behind the transparent fence one of the best buildings of Moscow classicism raised – the house of Pashkov.

On the opposite side of Tverskaja street at the wall of Kitaygorod (behind Okhotny Row) Voskresenskaja square began to form, which was next to Iverskie gates. Its Northern part was also built in with stores with arcades on the facade. On the opposite side, the closest to Red Square, a building of offices appeared with a portico in its centre. The squares spatially connected with each other – Okhotny Row, Voskresenskaja and Mokhovaja street and square made a belt of parade buildings which met a walker or rider going from Petersburg to the Kremlin.

In front of the Kremlin in Red square at the end of the 18th century they managed to create what Bazhenov could not realize in 1760-1770 – something like ancient Roman forum or the streets of glorified antique Palmyra arranged with a continuous row of columns. Northern Palmyra, so Petersburg was usually called, in other words an ideal ensemble of classicism, was created in Moscow in front of the Kremlin in the second half of the 18th century. Two wide П-shaped buildings ("crampons") of trade rows were constructed around Red Square with high arcades and portentous 10-column porticos in the centre of each house on the transverse axis of the square. The Square's longitudinal axis was oriented at the Frontal place; the transverse one which continued Nikolskaja street, had the Kremlin's tower and the cupola of the recently built Senate's building at its end. As a result Red Square became a closed space isolated from ancient Russian buildings and

The house of Moscow governor-general (1778-1782, architect M.F.Kazakov).

regularly built around with use of order forms. Ancient buildings turned out to be ousted outside the square which embodied the ideals of classicism in itself most consistently.

In Moscow during a few dozens of years an ensemble of the centre of a capital city (Petersburg of the second half of the 18th century did not know anything equal in its completeness) based on the principles of classicism with its ideals of regularity and symmetry was created for the first time in Russia. Its originality was in the developed spatial structure with a whole system of squares and streets, in the unity of the classicism ensembles with the ancient complexes of the Kremlin and Kitay-gorod.

After the fire of 1773 Tverskaja street, which led to the above-described ensemble, became a parade one being entirely built in the style of classicism. Tverskaja street of the end of the 18th century can be rightfully called Kazakov's street. According to the architect's projects along all the street public buildings, estate complexes, rich houses of palace type were raised. The house of Dolgorukiy was at the corner of Okhotny Row and Tverskaja. Behind it, also along the street's red line, there was the house of Musin-Pushkin, then the house of the University's boarding-house. Its corner part in the shape of rotunda fixed the turn of the street; the main building of the boarding-house was moved further inside the plot. The house of Golitsyn, built in the 1760s, raised in front of the boarding-house on the opposite side of the street behind the railing of the front yard. Next to it Kazakov built a wing with a rotunda at the end face that was in concordance with the boarding-house rotunda on the opposite side of the street. Further behind it, also on the left side of the street there was a house of Commander-in-Chief (governor-general). Kazakov designed the building and the square. The architect presumed to construct not very high buildings around the square, which would be connected with railings, and finalized the side opposite the house of the governor-general with a semi-circle colonnade. Kozitskaja's three-storey house was raised on the right side of the street not far from the triumphal gates according to Kazakov's project.

P.F.Bortnikov took an important part too in creation of the new classical look of Tverskaja: he aligned the passages, constructed new ones, he was the first who developed a number of hauhe facades for one- and two-storey houses for Moscow, destined for construction along the street red line.

Other streets oriented at the Kremlin or situated near it – Big Nikitskaja, Vozdvizhenka, Znamenka, Volkhonka, Mokhovaja – became as nobiliary as Tverskaja, being built in with large landlord houses with vast estate parks. There were also all the three types of nobility houses: houses with front yards open in the direction of the street, houses situated along the street red line and corner houses with rounded corners and cupolas, which fixed the crossings architecturally and in town-building way. At the beginning of Vozdvizhenka (building No.2) Rumjantsev's house was behind the railing of the front yard, behind it at the corner of the street and lane there was Sheremetjev's house with a rounded corner and cupola above it. Talyzin's house with a pilaster portico stood out on the red line in front of it.

Big Nikitskaja street entirely built in with the houses of the highest nobility – count Orlov, princess E.R.Vorontsova-Dashkova, the princes Golitsyn, Menshikov, Gagarin, Potemkin-Tavricheskiy, represented the same interchange of three types of rich houses.

Tverskaja street. View: the side of the Kremlin.
Lithography. The middle of the 19th century.

Iljinka street in Kitay-gored with the houses of merchants Kalinin and Pavlov (architect M.F.Kazakov).
Water-colour of F. Alexeev's studio. 1800-1802.

Moskvoretskaja street in Kitay-gored.
Water-colour of F. Alexeev's studio. 1800-1802.

The main streets of Kitay-gorod acquired a whole classical look, which were, however different from the nobility streets of Bely town with their trade colouring. Big stone three-storey merchant houses with stores filled in the front of the street. Stores were created everywhere after the decree of 1769 allowing the merchants to keep them on the ground floor of dwelling houses. Galleries of arcades of trade stores were the characteristic feature of big merchant houses regardless if they were built according to the principle of a rich nobility house with columned portico under a triangular pediment in the centre (the houses of Kalinin and Pavlov) or had an orderless, though rather monumental facade (the house of Khrjatschev, both houses in Iljinka). Entire buildings without interruption also appeared in Moscow in Kitay-gorod for the first time. Also here a monumental guest yard, which occupied a large Quarter, was raised.

The second district of merchant buildings, also unique in its integrity and simultaneous creation at the end of the 1770s-1780s," formed in Zamoskvorechie on Kadashevskaja quay together with the laying of a water way. It was similar to Iljinka with the mode of buildings situation as an "entire facade" unique for Moscow. But they were absolutely aligned buildings. Front blocks of narrow, extended from the North to the South plots which inherited their shape from the settlement of the time before Peter, went out to the street red line. Two-storey houses and stores with arch passages into the yard, with smooth orderless facades represented an integral look of merchant Moscow of the second half of the 18th century born during realization of the plan of 1775, the look which was sufficiently different from respectable Iljinka and more spread one.

Round Kaluzhskaja (Oktjabrjskaja) square, oval Serpukhovskaja (Dobryninskaja) square, trade rows in Taganskaja square triangular on their plan, German market with arcades became expressive ensembles in the style of classicism. New trade squares surrounded two-storey strict houses, the same as in Kadashevskaja quay, with smooth facades and arcades of stores on the ground floor. During the last ten years of the 18th century wooden stores were substituted with stone ones which occupied entirely the street red lines, in the trade streets Sretenka, Arbat. Thus, in the second half of the 18th century together with nobility streets, the look of which was characterized with big nobility estate houses, trade ensembles and even streets were formed with stores on the ground floor and modest orderless facades.

Correct Architecture and the Style "Gothically" Incorrect.

During the reign of Elizabeth Petrovna the "anti-Peter" and "anti-Petersburg" moods in rejection of forced measures used by Peter during Europeanization, were expressed in different spheres of culture including architecture. The most important fact is that the wish to return to some traditions of the time before Peter appeared not only in the society that was in opposition against Peter's novelties and not only in the society of traditional culture. It appeared in the highest plies of the society too, in the society which deserted the traditional culture. In Petersburg it acquired the form of corning back to the type of a five-cupola temple traditional for ancient Russian architecture. By the decrees of Elizabeth Petrovna the type of basilica temple with a spire on the top was ousted step by step from construction as strange to Russian temple-building. In Moscow, where continuity of traditions of the border of the 17th-18th centuries was preserved, it was not necessary to conduct such a policy. Moscow's turn in expression of such moods came in the second half of the 18th century. Moscow and Petersburg seemed to have changed places. It was Moscow, not Petersburg, which became the place of realization of the undertakings which expressed national principles in architecture. But different time and different motives defined different forms in which the principles were materialized coming from the interest and respect to the history and culture of the Fatherland. They were expressed in the ancient capital noticeably influencing the look of its historic centre – the Kremlin, Kitay-gorod. This phenomenon, which remained absolutely strange to Petersburg, together with Moscow was spread in historic towns of Central Russia. It is amazing that it turned up during the period when the classical inheritance and ideals of regularity-were most appreciated. However, highest values were associated with them. There were secondary values too in the hierarchy developed by classicism so strictly. They were in concordance with what was of local importance – man's private life, with landscape colouring, history of a separate nation and its culture. In construction or types of architectural creative work, corresponding to that kind of context, it is possible and even necessary to use other planning and style modes different from classical – irregularity of landscape planning, asymmetry, skills inherited from the culture occupying a lower step of hierarchy: peasant art, medieval, Eastern styles belonging to this or another nation – Egyptian, Chinese, Japanese, moresque etc. The country, and partially town nobility estate is the main place of expression of a private man's self-consciousness (naturally a noble man), his understanding of the world, his place in the history and in the world, his deserts before the history and the state. In the second half of the 18th century artistic planning of an estate landscape park was practiced together with the regular one here.

Finally there was another circle of ideas and moods, especially actual for Russia since the time of Peter's reign: interest in the national culture, in what later was formed as public movements known under the names of Slavophilism, occidentophilism, official national movement, in the problems defined as East-West, Russia and Europe, Moscow and Petersburg. Long before these problems were comprehended and formulated, they had become the subject of the government's policy in architectural and town-building; sphere, getting in the 18th century their dominating expression in Petersburg and in Moscow in turn, and from the time of the reign of Nicholas I – both in Petersburg and in Moscow.

There was another reason – architectural and artistic. It was the idea about the necessity to design a building in the style conforming to its denomination and character of the environment into which it was included. A.T.Bolotov, one of the most famous writers about estate ensembles, formulated this generally accented rule, mentioning that only an artistic landscape or only regular planning of parks was not necessary: "A straight alley in front of a house has nothing unstately in itself; so it can be in all its regularity here, because its regularity will correspond to the buildings' regular architecture".

For reconstruction of the infringed conformity the wall, dismantled because of the foundation of the Kremlin's palace, was quickly and thoroughly restored and the view at the Kremlin from Zamoskvorechie became the most important element again, defining the look and contents of Moscow historical centre. The main idea of the Proposal about the Construction inside the Kremlin, which was contemporary to the plan of 1775 and probably written by P.N.Kozhin who was the head of the Special or Separate Department of the "Commission for Stone Construction in Petersburg and Moscow", was summed up in the statement about the necessity to conduct the construction inside the Kremlin in accordance with its ancient look and original "Gothic" architecture of the buildings.

In difference to the time of Elizabeth Petrovna, when the prescription to build temples according to the gauge of the cathedral of the Assumption in Moscow Kremlin was formulated as construction of temples in "Greek style" (orthodoxy was called Greek religion in the 18th and sometimes in the 18th centuries yet), Kozhin, who lived during the reign of Catherine II, called ancient Russian buildings "Gothic". In the second half of the 18th century Russian was not associated with orthodox, like in the previous case, but with ancient, before Peter's time, with temporary and ethnic factor, not confessional. During that time in Russia any variant of European medieval architecture was called Gothic, including the ancient Russian one. The most educated people of the second half of the 18th – beginning of the 19th centuries, trying to define originality of constructions, created before learning about the European tradition, called them Gothic. V.I.Bazhenov, makingthe famous speech at the foundation of the Kremlin's palace in 1768, called Sukhareva tower "Gothic". The author of the famous "History of Russian State" N.M. Karamzin referred to the greatest memorials of ancient Russian architecture – the cathedral of St.Basil and the monastery of St.Simon in Moscow – as Gothic constructions. P.P.Svinjin, the organizer of the first expedition for study of Russian antiquities, used the epithet "Gothic" in regard of the wooden palace of tsar Alexius Mikhailovich in the village of Kolomenskoe near Moscow, which was considered the eighth world' wonder. The "cathedral of St.Demetrius, of Gothic architecture, built during the time of the first Russian princes" was mentioned among the other most important memorables in the "Topographical description of Vladimir's domain". It was hardly the lack of education. The general meaning of the term and its accordance to the nationally original architecture with local colouring expressed in their own way the complex of ideas which presented themselves so brightly in the cult architecture of baroque of Elizabeth's time. Inclusion of ancient Russian architecture into the rank of a Gothic one and the use of this term itself were the proof of Russia's Europeanization, its communication with European culture. In this way the identity of Russian and European cultures was confirmed. The notion about Europeanization of modern Russian culture was transferred to its past. The growth of national self-consciousness, giving rise to the proud feeling of antiquity of our own culture allied with the culture of European nations, was expressed in Russian "Gothic" of the second half of the 18th – beginning of the 19th century.

It was paradoxical that the architecture which had never existed in Russia before became the sign and symbol of Russian: there were no analogues to Romanic and Gothic architecture in the architecture of Russian medieval time. Russian "Gothic" of the second half of the 18th century was a local variant of Europe-wide movement for Gothic Renaissance. "Gothic" became the first national branch in Russian architecture, developing in the context of architecture of the New time, which keeping its characteristic fundamental peculiarity of order architecture – retrospectivity, turned demonstratively and openly to the antipode and antagonist of antique tradition – to medieval architecture. For the first time within the framework of the New time medieval architecture acquired the importance of a tradition not only actually, during a real designing, but in program, i.e. of inheritance not connected genetically with the architecture functioning during a certain historical period, but corresponding to it with certain artistic and contextual peculiarities and becoming an example to be followed due to it.

The author of the project of the Kremlin palace, creator of Moscow plan of 1775 and his correctors were governed by the wish to arrange "according to the perfect rule" the "delapidated and poor town", which "because of its ancient construction was not in proper order". Those were Bazhenov's words during the foundation of the Palace. Pre-Petrine architecture in difference to the classical one was not referred to the category of "correct", i.e. based on rules.

A characteristic feature of correct architecture is that it is of wide importance. The rules of this architecture are to be observed always, everywhere, in everything. "Correct" architecture, according to Bazhenov's words, is never out of fashion like clothes: "it is subject to fundamental rules, not fashion". This hierarchy caused Kozhin's proposals for the Kremlin's renovation. He believed that the new building of the emperor's palace "was to be constructed with the best facade according to the rules of the newest architecture", and the reception hall constructed next to the old palace turned inside the Kremlin, should be built with "Gothic facade which will correspond to other buildings around them". Modern blocks, to his mind, were to be at a distance from the ancient buildings, which were to be guarded carefully, especially "the square in front of the Red porch" (Cathedral square). The royal palace built according to Rastrelli's project, which "was not in concordance with the ancient facades", was to be closed, according to Kozhin's proposal, by Gothic facades, corresponding to "other constructions around them": "as though renovating the building in this place, which was rather eminent in ancient time that is Golden, Dinner and other chambers".

This understanding of esthetics and way of thinking in the second half of the 18th century, i.e. the necessity of correspondence in style of a newly raised building to the buildings surrounding it or the landscape (in a park) caused the use of the Gothic style in Moscow Kremlin.

The second circumstance which determined the choice of style, was in building's denomination and the system of values represented by it, and for Moscow, like for any other town there was the choice between classicism and Gothics. In the language of architecture the Kremlin palace, Senate, numerous civil buildings expressed the idea of nationhood, Russia's majesty, sensibility and education, i.e. the highest values of the time. So they could be constructed only in the style, which according to the categories of ethics and esthetics of Education, represented these values – in the style of classicism. The Gothic style was left for temples, bell-towers, monastery and fortress towers, railings, gates, i.e. for the types of buildings, denomination of which coincided with ancient ones or corresponded to the antiquity of their construction.

Exactly such circumstances can be seen in the Kremlin. During renovation of the look of Moscow historical centre together with "correct architecture" "the incorrect Gothic style" was used.

The process of renovation included two oldest Moscow monasteries – Chudov, founded in 1365 by metropolitanate Alexius and turned in 1744 into the department of Moscow metrorolitanates, and of the Ascension (a convent), founded in 1387 by Grand Princess Eudocia, the wife of Demetrius Donskoy. In 1780

Senate square in the Kremlin.
The Armoury (1806-1809, architect I.V.Egotov), Arsenal and Nikolskaja tower.

Zachatjevskiy monastery. The cathedral and the bell-tower (1800s, architect M.F.Kazakov (7) and M.M.Kazakov) and the hospital church of the Holy Spirit (1844-1850, architect M.D.Bykovskiy). Photo. Late 1870s-early 1880s.

upon the order of metropolitanate Platon a new entrance into Chudov monastery was constructed in Ivanovskaja square according to M.F.Kazakov's project. Its "Gothic" porch in the shade of a portico, four columns of which supported lancet arches and gabled roof towers, became the centre of the regulated space of the square with an eparch's house (also according to Kazakov's project).

The design and construction of "Gothic" buildings were especially active during the first ten years of the 19th century. It was a certain highest point of Gothic expressions in Moscow architecture of the classicism epoch. The beginning of this period were the renovation works in the Kremlin for the coronation of Paul I. Architect N.A.Ljvov in difference to Kazakov designed the palace, renovated for the coronation celebrations, in two variants – classical and Gothic. The classical variant was implemented and even not completely. During the first years of the new century during reconstruction of the Fun Palace in the Kremlin in order to make it the Commandant block I.V.Egotov used Gothic elements in the finishing of the facades too.

In 1806-1809 the Arsenal Chamber was built – the first special museum building in Moscow, the design of which was also entrusted to I.V.Egotov. First the building of Sytnyj yard was planned to be adjusted to it by the way of giving it "Gothic" forms. But then, taking into consideration the importance of the Arsenal Chamber, it was decided to construct a special block, placing it in the square in front of Nikolskie gates and near Troitskie ones giving it a classical look. In 1806 L.Ruska rebuilt Nikolskaja Tower, crowning it with a "Gothic" hip roof and adorning with "Gothic" details. "The Kremlin wall is our Palladium" – N.M.Karamzin wrote. Kremlin Nikolskaja tower was the closest to Voskresenskie gates of Kitay-gorod where the road connecting both capitals, ended. The renovated look of the tower emphasizing its "Gothic" style, was an embodiment of Moscow antiquity and the status of the first capital.

Construction of the Arsenal Chamber and the superstructure of Nikolskaja tower increased sufficiently the gala look of the northern Kremlin part near the road to Petersburg. Renovation projects of Kitay-gorod towers in Gothic style bounding Red Square, were, probably, connected with renovation of Nikolskaja tower, being designed by Egotov during the years before the fire, and by A.N.Bakarev – after the fire. These projects were not realized. But the North-Eastern part of the Kremlin, close to Petersburg road, was enriched with a majestic building, which occupied a dominating place in the ensemble of Spasskaja square in the Kremlin. According to K.I.Rossi's project in 1809-1818 the church of Great Martyr Catherine in the monastery of the Ascension was built – a monumental building with a cupola on a wide drum, with lancet Gothic forms of windows, portals and towers above the columns of the facades and the drum. The church which had been there before, was dismantled for town-building reasons, trying to increase regularity of the Kremlin South-Eastern Part, which appeared due to construction of the new porch in Chudov monastery and Eparch's house according to Kazakov's project. It was decided "to remove it as at the entrance it closed from sight the splendour of all Kremlin in general and of other buildings on the same line".

Emphasizing the antiquity of Kitay-gorod wall, in 1802 a new church in Gothic taste was built in the place of the delapidated church of St. Nicholas "Mokryj" not far from it. The central parts of its smart facades got pediments of lancet outline, and the bell-tower got lancet arches (architect A.N.Bakarev).

In 1804-1808 in Zemljanoy town the cathedral and bell-tower of Zachatjevskiy monastery were built in Gothic style (architect M.F.Kazakov). The five-cupola cathedral was rare for the second half of the 18th century with a square drum, extremely rare for Moscow, under the central cupola and the same hip roofs under the lateral cupolas. The bell-tower of the traditional type (a tetrahedron on an octahedron) was near the cathedral making the central group of the buildings. Further in Moscow outskirts behind the borders of Kamer-Kollezhskiy bank a number of complexes connected with old believers, was built – the coreligionist monastery of St. Nicholas near Preobrazhenskiy frontier post, the complex of Preobrazhenskiy and Rogozhskiy cemeteries. The buildings implemented in Gothic style, emphasized the adherence of zealots of "ancient piety" to old orthodox traditions. "Gothic" of these complexes was different in contents from "Gothic" of contemporary secular constructions and orthodox temples, it was closer to the Greek manner of temples of Elizabeth Petrovna, where the implementation in old traditions was dictated by the religious idea.

Nobility Estate in Moscow.

When Karamzin wrote: "Moscow will always be the true capital of Russia", – he connected the capital status of Moscow mainly with the nobility.

Together with the Kremlin, with ancient and new temples Moscow look of the second half of the century was characterized by nobility estates in many ways. It was already mentioned that the radial streets of Bely town close to the Kremlin, such as Big Dmitrovka, Tverskaja, Big Nikitskaja, Vozdvizhenka, Znamenka, Volkhonka, Prechistenka, the streets which connected the historical Moscow centre with the new one, became noble ones built in by landlords estates. Large dimensions and splendour of their buildings made the nobility estate of the second half of the 18th century one of the brightest characteristic features of Moscow look, most expressively representing its concrete historical originality. The territory occupied by the estates was not limited by the streets ending at the Kremlin in the West and North. Those were the places where large nobility estates mostly concentrated, where behind each facade of the main house looking at the street there was an estate complex with a park and economic constructions. Rich nobility estates appeared in all parts of the city. Contrasting with residential buildings of relatively modest dimensions and architecture, they dominated in the street ensembles.

Due to rich nobility houses Moscow acquired the features of a European city and at the same time managed to preserve its originality of a unique Russian, especially Moscow colouring. The rich nobility city estate of the second half of the 18th century was an absolutely Moscow phenomenon, partially characteristic of domain towns of Central Russia, for those places, where the nobility were represented as an independent estate. From the time of establishment of the Commission for Stone Construction in Petersburg and Moscow and creation of Petersburg plan development of dwelling buildings and the look of both capitals went on in different ways. Though there were paying houses in Moscow, they did not determine its look. They did not represent the leading type of dwelling houses either.

The third type of Moscow estate house – a corner one – was added to two types which was formed in 1730-1750 already: a house with an open front yard extended along the street, and a house standing out on the red line of the streets. Red lines of the plan of 1775 stipulated rounding off corners. This mode accentuated the unity of the buildings standing out on the place of crossing of two streets, a street and a lane, and at the same time emphasized the town-building main role of a crossing as the place of their intersection. There were plenty of variants of plastic decisions of architectural treatment of corner rounding off: from a slight rounding to a rotunda emphasized by decorative protuberances. At the end of the 18th century the type of a large landlord house with a corner rotunda appeared. It was often surrounded by freely installed or adjoining columns or pilasters.

The corner rotunda did not only accentuate the architectural and town-building importance of a crossing. Its raised part became simultaneously the compositional centre and the axis of a house symmetry, in accordance with which the adjoining lateral parts of a house were designed (Jushkov's house, Mjasnitskaja 21; V.P.Razumovskaja's house, Maroseyka 2/15; V.P.Razumovskiy's house, Vozdvizhenka 8).

There was another sign of the town-building function of rich dwelling houses, which had been exclusively the function of temples. Estate houses were raised on tops of the hills (Pashkov's house on Vaganjkovo hill in Mokhovaja, Tutolmin's house on Shvivaja hill). They were situated in such a way that their most gala central part with a portico finalized the perspective of the street (Musin-Pushkin's house in Razguljay). The latter mode was used not only during designing of landlord houses. Governor A.A.Prozorovskiy offered to adorn the stores which were built in Volkhonka at the end of the 18th century, with a columned portico which would finalize the perspective of Lenivka street from the side of Stone bridge (the bridge was on the axis of this street then). The governor thought it was necessary that a portico "would make the bridge an adornment".

Repeating spatial planning schemes of baroque houses, rich nobility classical houses were their antipodes from the point of view of style. Whether they were constructed deeply inside the yard, or on the street red line, the compositional centre of two main longitudinal facades oriented at the street and the front yard, was inevitably the central protruberance – a rizalit adorned with a portico under a triangular pediment. Nobility houses of the second half of the 18th century were huge. Most often they had three storeys. A portico occupied tile height of two storeys. It could be columned or pilaster, consist of 4, 6, 8 columns. The first rizalit storey made as a pedestal, was most often an open arcade, more seldom it was a wall treated with rustic.

The composition of buildings was successively hierarchy. Its

Mjasnitskaja street. On the right – I. Yushkov's house (late 1780s-beginning of 1790s, architect V. Bazhenov (7), yard of the Post to the left. Print of the middle of the 19th century according to I. Sharlenlan's water-colour.

Yauzskiy bridge and Shapkin's house (later T.l.Tutolmin's house). Print of F.Lorie according to G.Delabarfs picture. 1797.

characteristic feature was strict symmetry, emphasized centre, sequential subordination of the secondary to the main. The simplest, most evident and spread expression of hierarchy of composition was that it consisted of three parts. Composition of an estate complex, which consisted of three parts, had the main house accentuated in height and dimensions and lower blocks of wings. Symmetrical axial composition of the main house itself was of three parts. Its central part was often higher than the lateral. The lateral parts looked independent though subordinated to the central. Subordination of storeys along the vertical was successively kept. The second storey was usually the main. It excelled the others in its height, height of windows and richness of decoration. If it was a corner variant of a house its facades were built according to the same symmetrical scheme, where the corner part was treated as a curved rounded off portico. The similarity of the front and corner compositions was finished by a cupola crowning the rotunda and belvederes of the houses situated in the street system.

In difference to baroque portico with freely installed columns was widely used in classicism. It was a contextual and compositional centre of a building. Its iconography and sense come from abuttal facades of antique temples. Similarity to temples of the leading types of classical buildings was one of the characteristic features of the style. This similarity was of special type. Antique temples of peripteral or pseudo-peripteral type, for corner houses – antique temples-rotundas, were the prototype of rich classical houses.

Similarity to temples, likening to antique temples and, on the one hand, decrease of the notion of the divine down to prophane, and, on the other hand, extolment of prophane, worldly to the divine, resulting from it, was connected with the general character of culture of the New Time. Likening of the emperor to gods and antique characters was mentioned in the first chapter. It resulted from the world view of the time and was represented in creations of all types of art: literature (in poetry, odes), ballets, dramatical ballets, operas, cantatas, sculpture, gala portraits. Likening of Catherine to antique goddesses and such word-combinations as Russian Minerva, Russian Palladium, Northern Minerva were usual for the hearing of an educated man of the 18h century. The system of similarities used for glorification of monarchs, was extended to their "loyal subjects" In Petersburg upon the order of Paul I a monument to A.V.Suvorov was built, in which the Russian general was represented as the god of war Mars.

The composition of the most gala palace ensembles with a belvedere (a cupola on the drum) above a columned portico repeated also the scheme of the Pantheon of ancient Romans.

Pantheon was the temple of all gods in Ancient Rome, losing its first religious importance, it acquired an allegorical meaning in European architecture of neo-classicism of the 18th century. The same thing happened to it as to gods and characters of antiquity, to whom emperors and great people of the New Time were likened. Pantheon became the synonym of the temple of Glory. Such was one of architectural interpretations of this extremely significant idea for the world understanding of the second half of the 18th – beginning of the 19th centuries. Allegorical interpretation of the word "temple" was formed simultaneously with esthetics of classicism. It was applied to the buildings of big public importance.

In the architecture of classicism a rich nobiliary house did not belong to the rank of a private dwelling. Similarity to a temple was to express the high civil predestination of the owner's activity. That was why a rich house in the architecture of classicism was among the constructions defining the system of architectural style, together with palaces and temples. As for baroque architecture it is possible to speak about palace-like temples and public buildings. As for neo-classicism, such definition is not possible. It will be closer to the truth to say that social enthusiasm was a characteristic feature of the architecture of palaces and temples. The reason for generally used word-combinations referring to theaters, museums, educational institutions, stock-exchanges is seen in it too: temple of muses, temple of art, temple of knowledge and even temple of trade.

Structural and artistic forms of the main temple types of antique world acquired a symbolic character and a new life in the architecture of neo-classicism. Two architectural elements – a portico and a cupola (the portico of Parfenon, crowned with the cupola of Pantheon as A.I.Hertzen said) – most widely used on facades of buildings of the second half of the 18th – beginning of the 18th centuries, were the carriers of temple similarity and an original analogue of allegorical characters in painting, sculpture, theater and literature.

Cupola, portico and colonnade symbolically combined in themselves the forming beginnings of two main types of antique temples – the Greek-Roman peripter and Roman Pantheon.

The association connecting a civil building with a temple, was generally significant and generally accepted in the second half of the 18th century. G.R.Derzhavin called his new house constructed according to M.A.Ljvov's project, "temple-like" ("To Ljvov"), Naryshkin's house "similar to temple" ("About Naryshkin's Decease"). In the ode "About Decease of a benefactor" (I.I.Betskiy), the poet wrote, explaining that under his supervision "the splendid building of the academy of art, the monument of Peter the Great, hermitage theatre, the Neva's quays, the railing of the Summer Garden" were built:

"Whether we look at the huge buildings,
At the temples of muses, at Palladium's temple,
At the shore, at Peter's house, at the garden,
And stones will speak about you!"

The Academy of Art, the Hermitage Theatre were likened by the Root to the "temple of muses, Palladium's temple" symbolically, stylistically and contextually.

The temple-like house of the nobility estate represents an architectural analogue of the monuments or portraits depicting tsars or people of the nobility estate as gods and character of antiq-

The estate of Batashov in the Taganskaya street.
(1798-1800, architects R. Kazakov and M. Kiselnikov).
Photo. Early 20th century.

uity. Moscow nobility raised plenty of temples in their honour. Rich merchants tried not to fall behind them. A temple-like building was raised for merchant Gubin according to M.F.Kazakov's project in trade Petrovka street in front of Vysokopetrovskiy monastery. Another Kazakov's chef-d'oeuvre, called "golden rooms" for the luxury of its interior, was constructed for a descendant of the merchant Demidovs family near Lefortovo.

In classical Moscow, in spite of the triumphant march of the regularity principles, the opposite artistic, landscape principle did not die. A splendid view opened from the parks and windows of the houses situated on upper lands, especially along the banks of the Moscow-river and the Yauza. From Tutolmin's house on the top of the Shvivaja hill, which was one of the most famous of the border of the 18th-19th centuries, the Kremlin and the panorama of the Moscow-river were seen. From the park of Batashov's house, the main facade of which looked at International street and

View along the Yauza of the Tuition House. Print. Early 19th century.

the park one looked at the Yauza, a beautiful view opened of the river with its slope bank. On this bank along Vorontsovo field almost continuous gardens came down to the river. The churches united, brightened, spiritualized the landscape.

The churches seen from the yards, were also a characteristic feature of Moscow architectural landscape. For instance, from the park, situated on the upper land behind the main house in the estate of rich merchant V.I.Venevtsov in Taganskaja street "a wonderful view of Moscow opened: of the gardens of Vorontsovo field, the Yauza's banks, lanes situated below and the church of St.Symeon Stylites". In the splendid combination of town and village landscapes, composing a characteristic feature of Moscow landscape, both were appreciated. Picturesque views opening out of the windows of a house or from a park, were considered as a separate merit, and it was always specified during a sale or lease of a house. "The view out of the windows of the ground floor is most beautiful, Vorobjevy hills and Novospasskiy monastery are seen, and, in one word, all Moscow lands". "The location and the view from the garden excels the best of Moscow country-side".

The space of a town estate is always designed as a whole composition, architecturally organized, regular, symmetrical. The architecturally organized space of the gala yard, composed by service blocks and decorative walls, is outlined from the plots of irregular form. They were included into the practice of classicism as a mode of correction of the incorrectness and irregularity so unpopular that time. As Moscow houses were not always built anew, an accurate geometrically correct symmetrical composition usually appeared as a result of additional structures, adjoining buildings, inclusion into the general ensemble of decorative walls.

Ideas of Enlightenment and Construction of Public and Administrative Buildings in Moscow.

The intensity of Europeanization of Moscow look increased rapidly in the second half of the 18th century due to plenty of variants of its introduction. Construction of public and administrative buildings, which became extremely different in their composition and volume, was to become very important in this process. Never before so many new types of buildings had been introduced simultaneously into the practice of Russian town-building. Many of them implement their former functions till now.

Since then the government became the main factor of education spreading, and first of all the secular one. The government undertakes charity functions – construction of hospitals, alms houses for sick, old and chronic invalids, houses care of orphans and illegitimates. The first social-representative departments appeared, though only nobiliary – the Noble Assembly, English club. A stationary theatre was built.

The zenith of absolutism and nobiliary monarchy coincided with the time when trade-market relations began to appear, for instance, of trade agriculture and growth of trade. In the second half of the 18th century it gave rise to construction in towns of large trade squares with warehouses and trade rows. Their characteristic forms with arcades on the ground floor defined the specific look of many central squares and streets of Moscow. Finally, the domain and town reforms, conducted in the second half of the 18th century one after another, were accompanied by appearance of new types of administrative buildings. Architecture of such constructions and ensembles became the carrier of the state idea. Moscow, remaining a domain city together with Petersburg, implemented certain capital functions. This, for instance, resulted in construction of the Senate building in the Kremlin. Appearance in the architecture of domain and rural towns of buildings of the domain government, official chamber, department of public care, court hall etc., was directly connected with the reforms of 1775 and 1785. At the expiration of the century, in 1797, Paul I issued the decree about liberation of houses from lodgment and construction of special buildings for accommodation of military troops located in tows – barracks. As a result, another characteristic type of buildings and complexes appeared, which defined in many ways the look of a number of districts.

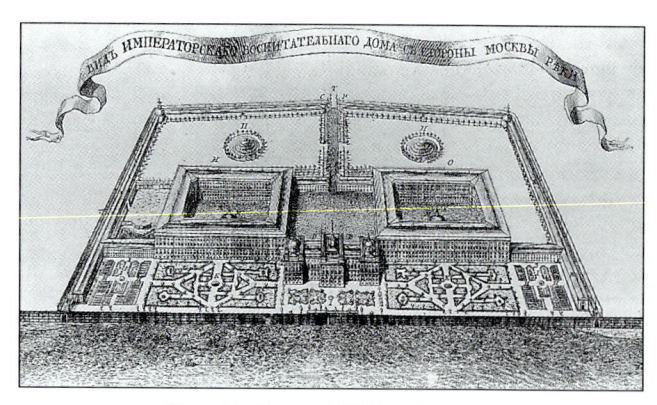

View of the Emperor's Tuition House from the Moscow-river (1763-1767, 1781-1784, architect Yu.Felten (?). Print.

The state importance of the new types of public buildings was expressed in the regulation and replanning of the lands where they were situated. So new squares appeared in front of the Senate in the Kremlin, in front of the house of the governor-general in Tverskaja street, in front of Peter's theatre, in front of the military hospital in Lefortovo, in front of domain offices. Parade-grounds were created in front of barracks.

Together with palaces public buildings began to occupy the places and to assume the functions which belonged to temples. In 1730-1750 the way from the Kremlin to the Yauza became the focus of extremely intensive church construction. Catherine II who was on friendly terms with encyclopaedists and shared their ideas and belief in the reason, began renovation of Moscow at once after taking the throne with construction of three buildings, the purpose of which was rather symbolical and expressed the conception of her reign. She intended to rebuild the Kremlin and to make the Kremlin palace a symbol of her stay on the throne, which was to change radically the look of the historically formed centre and actually annul, annihilate the function of Moscow as the centre of orthodoxy (from the point of view of town-building art, context and the look of the city). This undertaking was to be supported by the other two, not less grandiose buildings which were to change cardinally the panorama of the Moscow-river on the most important part of the water variant of the tsar's road from the Kremlin to Lefortovo – from the Kremlin to the Yauza. The building of the Educational Hospitium was constructed on the Kremlin's left bank, which was huge even for our days and seemed gigantic at the end of the 18th century, and on the opposite right bank, nearly in front of it the building of Crigs-commissariat was constructed. In combination with the new Kremlin palace they were to form a new look of the banks of the Moscow-river. The construction of the Educational hospitium and Crigs-commissariat began before the

Panorama of the Kremlin and the Moscow-river with the view of the Tuition House and Zamoskvorechie. Print according to G.nelabarfs drawing. 1797.

construction in the Kremlin. Petersburg-European principle of their location on the quay, applied in Moscow for the first time during the construction of these buildings, was to be continued in the Kremlin palace. They were to form a new look of the panoramas developing in the Moscow-river banks and make them super-Petersburg ones.

Administrative buildings, educational institutions and structures, representing social functions of the nobility, were constructed in the centre of the city on the newly created grounds. Official and charity buildings were constructed in the outskirts, outside Zemljanoy town. And not only for the account of the government, but the first private benefactors. A hospitium was raised for the account of count Sheremetjev behind Zemljanoy bank, between Sretenskie and Mjasnitskie gates. Golitsynskiy hospital was built for the account of Golitsyn outside Kamer-Kollezhskiy bank, on Kaluzhskaya road. Pavlovskiy hospital appeared near Serpukhovskaya frontier post of Kamer-Kollezhskiy bank, a huge complex of the military hospital appeared in Lefortovo, a Widow's House appeared behind Nikitskie gates of Zemljanoy town.

Especially intensive construction was conducted in the area of Bozhedomskie streets, where old squalid houses were. The first big secular educational charity centre formed here at the border of the 18th-19th centuries, which was absolutely unique because of the concentration of representative public buildings. In 1802 Moscow Institute of Catherine's Order – one of the institutes of nobiliary maidens – was built in future Ekaterininskaya square (now the square of Communa). Two years later in 1804 at this Catherine's Institute Petty bourgeois department for maidens of other estates was created, and for it in 1809-1811 a special block was built according to D.Gileardi's project (N.Bozhedomka, 4, now Dostoevskogo street). In 1806 near it a hospital for poor people was opened, built by I.D.Gileardi according to the project of A.A.Mikhaylov-2 (Bozhedomka, 4). A huge house of I.A.Osterman-Tolstoy, situated not far and burnt in 1812, was adjusted for an ecclesiastical seminary in the 1830s.

In 1775 by a decree of empress Catherine II together with Catherine's alms house Catherine's hospital was established in the building of the former Karantinnyj yard (Quarantine) in 3rd Petty Bourgeois street (today Tschepkin street, 61/2). After its move to the former house of Gagarin near Petrovskie gates it was called Staroekaterininskaja, and Cagarin's house was adjusted for a hospital which got the name of Novoekaterininskiy (1786-1790, M.F.Kazakov).

In 1792 army barracks, the first in Moscow, were built for the account of the citizens near Pokrovskie gates in Pokrovskiy boulevard. A little later, in 1809-1811, an enormous complex of Khamovnicheskie barracks was built according to M.M.Kazakov's project with a large parade-ground in front of them.

Making a separate town-forming factor out of educational and hospital buildings and appearance of whole districts with educational-charity functions in Moscow outskirts became a characteristic speciality of Moscow functional and planning structure in the second half of the 18th – beginning of the 20th centuries. Developed separate complexes appeared notable with their gala architecture and big dimensions on the background of modest dwelling buildings of outskirts. But it is important that the appearance and specialization of such districts, their localization on Moscow map found their source from the complexes or buildings constructed at the end of the 18th – beginning of the 19th centuries. That was the destiny of all suburban territories, where separate buildings or whole complexes of educational-charity denomination – Big Kaluzhskiy, Metschanskiy, Sokoljnikov, Lefortovo – appeared during the period of classicism.

The names of the first Moscow institutes and hospitals – Paviovskaja, Ekaterininskaja, Mariinskaja (after Mary Fedorovna, the wife of Paul I), Alexandrovskiy – testify that the unique in their denomination and outstanding in their dimensions and look buildings were a way to glorify and keep grateful memory of the reigning people. This phenomenon in its sense and form was similar to the way to glorify tsars and memorable events of their reign, which was established in the practice of temple-building in the 18th century, with the help of consecration of newly built churches and

The hospitium of count Sheremetiev near Sukharevskaja square. 1794-1807, architects E.S.Nazarov, D.Kvarnegi). Engelman's lithography according to O.Kadors drawing. 1830s.

The Moscow University in Mokhovaja street (1789s, architect M.F.Kazakov). Water-colour of M.F.Kazakov. Early 1790s.

bell-towers (churches inside bell-towers) to the divine protectors of Russian tsars. Public buildings: serving social well-being, a symbol of the age of Enlightenment, simultaneously became an original memorial, immortalizing and glorifying educated absolutism and enlightened monarch.

Army barracks were designed according to another scheme – a scheme of a rich house situated along the red street line. The difference was only in the fact that very long blocks with multi-columned porticos were created for barracks. Ensemble of a number of barracks consisted of several blocks, for instance, Khamovnicheskie – from three, situated on one line along a large parade-ground.

Demidov's house ib Gorokhovaja street
(the late 18th century, architect M.F.Kazakov). View of the park. Water-colour.

All the above-said about temple similarity of rich houses is right for public buildings too. Here also compositions with columned porticos under triangular pediments dominate. But only in the buildings of mature classicism. Buildings of old classicism (Educational Hospitium, Crigs-Commisariat) with their facades without orders are distinguished with their exaggerated dimensions, original aggressiveness in consolidation of the new ideals by the way of contradiction of the newly raised buildings to surrounding buildings – enormous extent, height unusual for that time (four storeys). The building of the Educational Hospitium war designed with three central rizalits flanked at the sides with two colossal "squares" – blocks square on the plan with internal yards (only one left "square" was built).

Christian Universalism of the State Policy and Temple Architecture

During the period considered in this chapter three emperors reigned (Catherine II, Paul I and the beginning of the reign of Alexander I). With all heterogenity of political conceptions their attitude towards the Church and especially to temple architecture was similar. The uniting principle was the belief that it was necessary to subordinate the Church or in any case that the government should be supreme. As Catherine said, "church power must be absolutely subordinated to her". The opinion of Paul I was notable with original Christian universalism: his dream was to unite churches under the power of the Russian emperor and to create original European-wide Christian theocratic monarchy on the basis of Catholicism and Russian autocracy. Following these ideas he thought it possible to undertake obligations of a master of catholic Maltese order. In the view of Alexander I at the beginning of his reign the ideas of Christian universalism prevailed too. After the victory over Napoleon they became a policy directed at the uniting of European Christian kings for the fight with atheism the result of which was the French revolution.

Khamovnicheskie soldier barracks (180s, architect M.M.Kazakov). Photo. The 19th century.

Kuznetskiy bridge. Print. Early 19th century.

So the Holy union of Christian monarchs was created upon the initiative of the Russian emperor.

The state policy of all three Russian tsars was similar in Europeanization and concrete-historical interpretation of the Christian idea characteristic of the epoch of Enlightenment. For it the confessional aspect, as for Russia – orthodox aspect, was not defining. As a consequence of such views which could not hut were shown in the real practice, for the first time in Moscow temple architecture general European tendencies prevailed. In her time Elizabeth Petrovna made much effort purposefully trying to turn temple architecture of Petersburg to Moscow path, pressing for rooting of the five-cupola temple of cathedral type and multi-tier bell-tower, traditional for pre-Petrian Russia and spread in the contemporary Moscow architecture, in the new capital.

In the second half of the 18th century the situation was quite opposite. Moscow and Petersburg as though changed places. The idea of time was expressed not by Moscow individuality, but by Europeanization adherence of Petersburg. For the first time Moscow temple architecture turned to "Petersburg" path, i.e. for the first time the types and forms of heterodox European temples prevailed. As a whole this phenomenon was European-wide. Something like that happened in European countries in the 17th – first half of the 18th century. For all European countries, catholic and Protestant, architecture of the temples of Italian Renaissance and baroque and French classicism became an example to follow, many times renewed and varied. In the second half of the 18th century in Russia Moscow type of architecture development, i.e. Moscow provincial, was finished absolutely. Europeanization enveloped the last area of the high style architecture, where direct connection with the architecture of pre-Petrian time was kept and where Europeanization went on organically, by natural historical way of gradual reforming of traditional volume-spatial structures and forms. The impulse which changed the situation was given by the capital, as always. After Moscow European-wide types of temples began to penetrate and spread in the architecture of the Russian province.

However, the turn of Moscow temple-building to "Petersburg" path did not make it a copy of Petersburg. The development went on (and irrevocably already) in one direction, but along parallel tracks.

In comprehension of European samples Moscow temple-building showed bright inventiveness and clear preferences. In their turn they were determined by correspondence and non-correspondence of the types of heterodox temples to traditional Moscow orthodox, adaptability of European prototypes to the most spread pre-Petrian types of temples – cathedral cross-cupola type and parish with its three-parts structure and a bell-tower and refectory extended-along the axis West-East and a temple itself with an altar. A cubic one-cupola temple with a refectory and a bell-tower, i.e. with a full list of premises for a parish temple, was most spread in Moscow, or in its shorter variant – without a refectory, but with a bell-tower. The basilical type of temple, which returned into the practice of temple-building in Petersburg after decease of Elizabeth Petrovna, remained strange to Moscow.

From two types of temples – cathedral cubic and parish – in Moscow of the second half of the 18th century, like in 1730-1750, the second type prevailed. Both of them were successively connected with the ancient Russian tradition, but adjusted, as it was mentioned, to European norms, especially the cathedral type, which was indistinguishable from its European prototypes.

Bell-towers of classicism continued the traditions of a multi-tier style of ancient Russian and baroque bell-towers. Their orders on each tier come from baroque too. But their forms and successiveness were evidently Europeanized. The composition of an octahedron on tetrahedron nearly disappeared. The compositions of two or three tetrahedrons decreasing to the top, a cylinder on one or two tetrahedrons, round bell-towers of two or three cylindrical tiers prevailed.

The parish type of temple in difference from the cathedral type, like in 1730-1750, was spread widely in Moscow. Its variants were extremely numerous: the church of Great Martyr Barbara in Varvarka street (1796-1804, R.R.Kazakov, the church of the Iberon Icon of the Most Holy Theotokos (R.Ordynka, 39, 1792-1802), the church of Holy Martyrs Boris and Gleb in Povarskaja (1799-1802, did not keep), the church of St.Nicholas the Miracle Worker in Mjasniki in Mjasnitskaja street (1780s, did not keep), the church of Great Martyr Demetrius of Thessalonica on Strastnaja square, at the corner of Tverskoy boulevard and Tverskaja street (1791, did not keep), the church of St.Nicholas the Miracle Worker in Khlynov (Khlynovskiy line end, 1781-1788, did not keep) and others.

Temple-rotundas, being round on their plan and cylindrical volume, belong to absolutely new types brought by Europeanized consciousness into the practice of orthodox temple-building. Temple-rotundas, spread during antiquity, attained a new life in Europe since the time of Renaissance. Baroque and classicism created their versions of rotundal churches. In Russia temple-rotundas, single in the first half of the 18th century and spread in its second half, were connected with symbolics of a circle.

A circle – one of the most spread elements of mythical and poetic symbols of various origin and meaning. Most often it expresses the idea of the highest perfection, unity, infinity and finality. Circle combines itself the ideas of unity and infinity of space and time. Circular models of the Universe united two circular movement of the sun: horizontal (annual, circular movement around the axis of the world tree) and vertical (daily movement of the sun determines the vertical flatness of the world tree, including the variant of the anti-tree, another world, abyss). Both circular movements were rather often supported (as it happened during antiquity) by mythological objects placed around, "for example, by Zodiac signs or some deities (pantheons with 12 members, for instance, Olympic gods form some contemplative circle, putting them in order; compare round dance, i.e. the same circle with Apollo in the centre, in the idea about Muses); so it is not accidental that a circle is a symbol of pantheon as a whole and a symbol of separate gods".

Rotunda became in civil buildings of classicism, created upon the orders of "earthly gods", a symbol of power and god-likeness. In civil architecture this process got the meaning of extolment (sacralization) of the worldly. In cult architecture the opposite process happened: decrease of the sacred and simultaneously likening of Christian temples to pagan antique. Christian temples were built like antique ones (temples with porticos, temples-rotundas) and at the same time like centrical and rotundal temples of catholic Europe, which recomprehended antique samples. Exactly the temples of the New Time, including the Russian ones, were meant by

A.I. Hertzen, who saw "Pantheon on Parthenon" – a combination of two symbols of antique temple-building – a portico under a triangular pediment and a cupola on a wide cylindrical drum. But in the architecture of classicism Pantheon was recreated literally too: a rotunda with a cupola and a columned portico in front of the main entrance. Such was, for instance, the competition project of the cathedral of Christ the Saviour in Moscow (D.Kvarnegui), the same were some temples constructed in the province according to N.A.Ljvov's projects.

Some temples of rotundal type were built in Moscow according to M.F.Kazakov's projects. The church of St.Metropolitanate Philip, which was built as a domestic church of metropolitanate Platon (2nd Metschanskaja street, 1777-1788) reproduced both antique prototypes. Its outside volume cylindrical on the plan with two porticos at the sides (from the West a refectory and a bell-tower of the 17th century adjoined the church) repeated the volumetric composition and the outline of the plan of Pantheon in Rome; its interior volume with a round dance of columns reminds of ancient Roman temple-rotundas. The church of St. Martyrs Cosmas and Damian in Maroseyka represented a complicated combination of four cylindrical volumes – a temple, the main altar and two altars-cylinders in the refectory which served as a winter temple (1791-1803).

The church of the Holy Spirit in Lazarevskoe cemetery (1782-1786, is put down to V.I.Bazhenov) surprisingly combines in itself the type of the Russian three-part parish temple with European types of some of its parts. The temple itself represents a rotunda crowned with a cupola on a wide drum. The Western facade of the temple reproduced the scheme of a two-tower temple with two bell-towers, spread mainly in Central Europe. The church of the Assumption in Mogiljtsy, placed on the crossing of Big and Small Vasiljevskiy lanes and the lane of Ostrovskiy, also has two towers and also is put down to Bazhenov, belongs to the classical type of a parish temple.

Emphasized frontality of two-tower temples remained strange to Russian tradition of temple-building with its adherence to an all-round facade style. On the contrary, rotundal temples with their rich and multi-ply symbolics and plasticity close to the Russian feeling of form, were spread widely in Moscow. Besides, rotundas could be used "purely" (a church could have a cylindrical volume), or as a false rotunda, when a low cubic volume of a church was crowned by a cupola, equal to it in diameter, on a high drum (the church of the Ascension on Gorokhovoe field, 1790-1793; the church of St.Symeon Stylites, 1798, which makes the impression of a temple-rotunda).

The church of Hieromartyr Philip, metropolitanate of Moscow and All Russia in 2nd Metschanskaja street (1777-1778, architect M.F.Kazakov). Photo. 2nd half of the 19th century.

The bell-tower of the monastery of St.Andronicus (1795-1799, architect, R.R.Kazakov).

"The of Kremlin buildings and environs" B.Loris engraving made after the drawing of J.Delabart. 1796. The veiew of the enbankment near Kitay-gorod wall constructed in the year of 1790 after the project of M.F. Kazakov, as part of the contontinnous passadge along the Moscow-river bank. All the buildings along it were torn down and stone shop houses were attached to the Kitay-gorod wall.

The esoteric, mystical part of classicism, composing its concealed ply of spiritual life, was embodied most brightly in the temples which are triangular on their plan. But a triangular is a too hard corner form, and in Moscow architectural school (exactly the Moscow one, Petersburg analogues are not known) triangular temples were designed with rounded corners: the church of Great Martyr George the Victory-bearer in Vspolje (M.Nikitskaja, the corner of Georgievskiy lane, 1777-1788, did not keep), the church in the village of Vinogradovo near Moscow. There are plenty of meanings of a triangular, but all of them are summed up in the idea of trine. Many of them were presented in the description of A.L.Vitberg of the first project of the cathedral of Christ the Saviour, accepted for construction: the trine entity of God, trine essence of man, created according to the image and likeness of God (spirit, soul, body), three main stages in the life of Christ: Nativity, Transfiguration, Resurrection.

The plan of the church in Clinitschi is close to a triangle or a circle inserted inside a triangle – a rotunda with three semi-cylinders (did not keep). Its unusual plan and similarity to the church of Great Martyr George in Vspolje and to the church of St. Martyrs Cosmas and Damian.

Due to the complexity of its plan (octagon, four protuberances of which make a cross with a rotunda inserted in it) the church of St.Symeon Stylite can be included in the list of cross-type temples. Their quantity is comparatively small: the church of the Nativity of the Theotokos at Strelka in Soljanka street, the church of the Beheading of St.John the Predecessor in Kazennaja (Official) settlement (1794-1801, M.F.Kazakov). However, the unusual plan and volume of the latter also make to presume the presence of a secret sense in it, most possible masonic symbolics.

The temple of the Beheading of St.John the Predecessor, which did not keep till our time, was one of masterpieces of classicism. The grandiosity of simple and expressive forms are impressive, the power of which was emphasized by the smooth walls with rustic masonry up to all the bight of cross-like protuberances and not a very high cupola of the rotunda, as though growing out of the cross-shaped volume.

Temples of the second half of the 18th century, like rich estate houses, were spread around all the city's territory. It is even more difficult to find out the tendency of their location than that of nobility houses. But still one speciality shows itself illustrating how complicated the spiritual life of Moscow was and what different flows of thought intersected and found their expression in temple-building. Not far from Rogozhskiy Frontier Post, in the district of Preobrazhenskoe cemetery and on the way to it at the end of the 18th – beginning of the 19th centuries the most grandiose temples were built in the ancient capital. Their dimensions, the splendour of decoration, monumentality, even some gigantism of forms are explained by specific features of their location near the places of concentration of Moscow old believers in the district of Rogozhskoe and Preobrazhenskoe cemeteries – certain nestles of old believers. In the hope to return them in the lap of the orthodox church temple construction was conducted in these places with special splendour the church of St.Martin the Confessor in Big Alexeevskaja street in Taganka, 1782-1793, R.R.Kazakov; built after the fire of 1812 already the church of St.Sergius of Radonezh in Rogozhskaja (Nikolojamskaja street, 59, 1818),the bell-tower of the monastery of St.Andronicus (1795-1799), built according to the sample of monastery bell-towers of the middle of the 18th century with their huge dimensions and powerful columns of tiers (it was supposed to build it higher than the bell-tower of John the Great, but by a special decree of Paul I its height was decreased).

Strict volumes and order forms of Moscow temples, palaces and public buildings, realization of the plan of 1775, which gave regularity to the look of Moscow streets without reducing the unrepeatable national colouring, added strictness of European style to Moscow look, making it a unique city in Russia. Moscow, and it should be pointed out, is the only historical city which did not get a new regular plan. It was just regulated. In it Moscow repeater, but already at the scale of the whole city, the speciality, represented by the temple architecture in the first half of the 18th century: pre-Petrine architecture of the 17th century and after-Petrine temple architecture of the first half of the 18th century were connected with direct succession, new tendencies just corrected the traditional schemes, which were not substituted with new ones. The same happened to town-building development of Moscow. The city was developing on the same structural-planning basis, but the reality brought natural corrections, dictated by needs of time, in it.

---

1 Grabar I.E. History of Russian Art. V. 1. M., PH. I.Knebel, b.g., p. 38, 40.
2 See Savarenskaja T.F., Shvidkovskiy D.O., Petrov F.A. History of Town-building Art. The Last Years of Feudalism and Capitalism. M., 1989, p. 123, 125.
3 See Nikolaev E.V. Classical Moscow. M., 1975, p. 13.
4 As above, p. 21, 13.
5 Golikov I. Deeds of Peter the Great. V. V. M., 1788, p. 109. Quot.acc.: Bunin A.V., Savarenskaja T.F. History of Town-building Art in 2 Volumes. V.T, Issue 2nd. M., 1978, p. 368.
6 Znamenskiy P. Quot.acc.: Talberg N. History of Russian Church. Reprinted Issue of St.Job Pogaevskiy. Jordan. ville. N.Y., 1959. M., p. 576, 621-622.
7 Evsina N.A. Architecture of the Epoch of Catherine II. M., 1994, p. 49.
8 As above, p. 48.
9 Sumarokov A.P. Word on the Foundation of the Kremlin Palace //Snerirev. Architect V.I.Bazhenov. M., 1937, p. 183. Further the above issue will be quoted, ps. 183-185.
10 Evsina N.A. The above works, p. 47.
11 As above.
12 Chernov V.G. and Shishko A.V. Bazhenov. M., 1949, p. 44, 65.
13 Bondarenko I.A. The above-said works, p. 100, 113.
14 See the "Plan of the Kremlin Palace", published in the book of Chernov V.G., Shishko A.V., positioned above the existing Kremlin buildings, p. 51.
15 As above, p. 45.
16 Chernov V.G. and Shishko A.V., the above works, p. 45.
17 As above.
18 Evsina N.A. The above works, p. 48-49.
19 World History of Architecture in 12 Volumes. V. 7. Western Europe and Latin America. The 17th – first half of the 19th centuries. M., 1969, p. 60-61.
20 Moscow Architectural Memorials. The Kremlin. Kitay-gorod. The Main Squares. M., 1985, p. 293-294.
21 Vlasjuk A.I., Kaplun A.I., Kiparisova A.A. Kazakov. M., 1957, p. 286.
22 Savarenskaja T.F., Shvidkovskiy D.O., Petrov F.A. The above works, p. 194.
23 RGADA. Quot.acc.: Budylina M.V. The above works, p. 135.
24 GIM OPI. Quot.acc.: Boris A.G. Romantic Direction in Architecture of Moscowof the Second Half of the 18th – Beginning of the 19th centuries. M., 1988. Dessertation... of candidate of architecture in RGB, p. 69.
25 Moscow Records. 1813, p. 1881; the same, p. 1856 etc. Quot.acc.: Nikolaev E.A. The above works, 126.
26 Toporov V.N., Meilakh M.B. Circle //Myths of Nationa of the World. V. 2.M., 1988, p. 18-19.

The Okhotny Ryad (hunters' market place) Square nearby the Nobles Assembly (former Dolgorukov's Palace reconstructed in 1784-1787 by M.F.Kazakov). Lithography made after drawing by Dits. Middle of the 19th century.

CHAPTER THREE

Burnt and Revived Moscow

The square of the tverskaja frontier post
with the triumphal gate according to O. Bove's project.
Lithography of F. Bends. 1840s.

Illumination of Theatre Square for the occasion
of the coronation of Alexander II
and the opening of the restored Bolshoy Theatre
on 6th of August, 1856.
Lithography according to V.S. Sadovnikov's drawing.

Emperor Alexander I (1801-1825). Master D. Evreinov.

Red Square. Spasskaja Tower with two chapels of 1805 and 182n. Colour lithography of A.Durand. 1842.

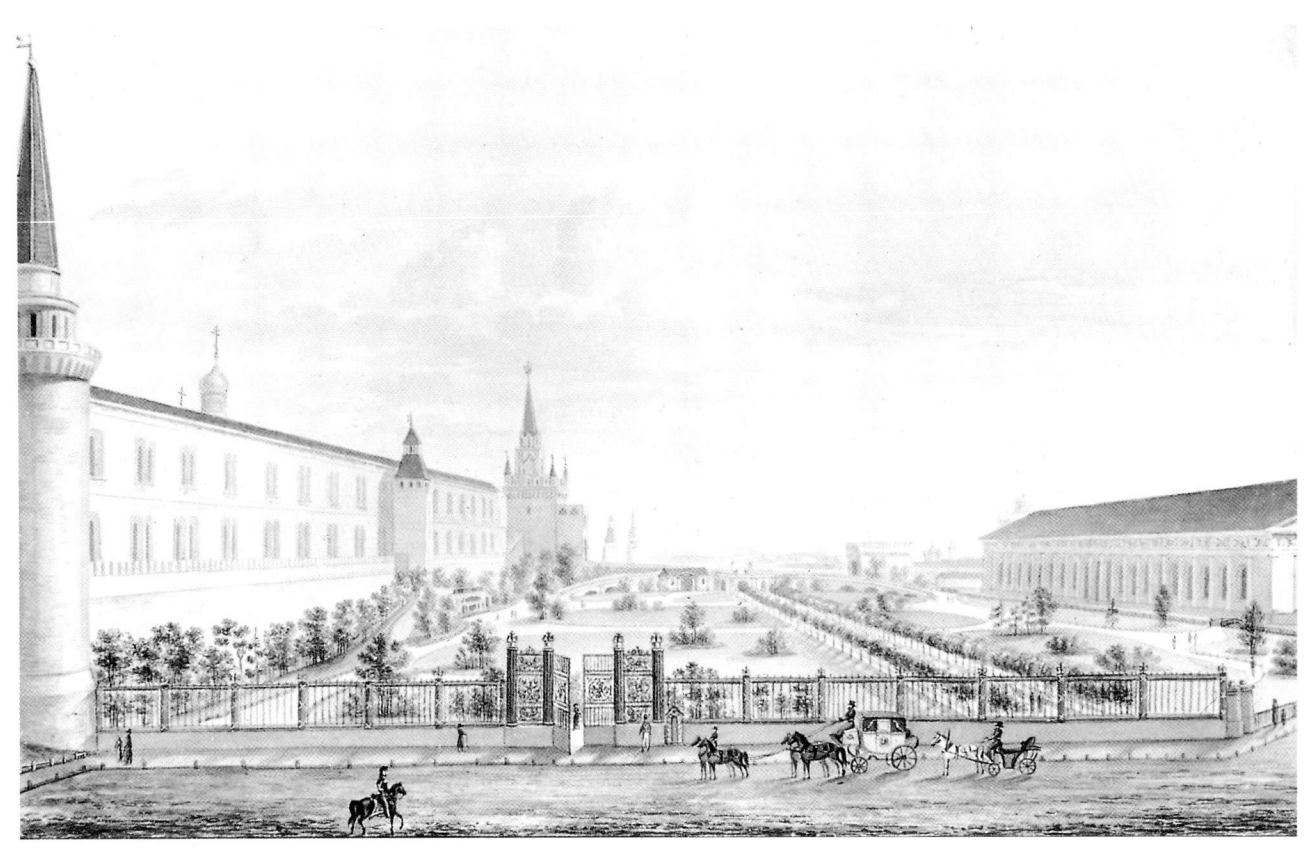

The Kremlin (Alexander's) garden. Sanctified on the Angel's day of AlexanderI. Drawing from nature by N.Chichagov. 1827.

Tverskoy boulvard. View from Nikitskie gate jt the monastery of the Passions. Lithography of O.Kadol. 1825.

View at the Kremlin, Kitay-gorod and Zamoskvorechie front the Shvivaja hill.

Armenian gymnasium after it had been turned into Lazarevskiy Institute of Eastern Languages. 1316. Drawing on a stone by Shmidt. Middle of the lath century.

Departure of emperor Alexander I from Moscow. Adam's lithography according to Kurtina's drawing.

Moscow Synodal printing house. New block (leu-1815, architect I. Mironovskiy).
A. Frolov's print according to I. Lavrov's drawing. Early 19th century.

View of the Kremlin from Zamoskvorechie. Water-colour of D.Kvarnegi. 1797.

When on 2nd of September, 1812, the troops of the French army of Napoleon approached Moscow, from the Poklonnaja Hill a view of a wonderful city opened in front of his generals, which they had not seen before in any European country: "From there we suddenly saw thousands of bell-towers with golden cupolas. The weather was splendid, and all this was shining and burning in the sunlight and seemed innumerable sparkling balls. There were cupolas like balls, installed on a steeple of a column or obelisk, and then it reminded of an aerostat hanging in the air.

The Moscow-river is flowing among light meadows washing and impregnating all around, it suddenly turns and flows in the direction of the city, runs through it, dividing it into two parts and thus separating from each other plenty of houses and constructions; there are wooden, stone, brick houses here; some were built in Gothic style, mixed with modern, others represented a mixture of distinctive signs of each separate nationality. Houses are painted in very different colours, church cupolas are sometimes gold, then dark, leaden and covered with slate. All this together made this picture unusually original and various, and big terraces near palaces, obelisks near the city gates and high bell-towers in the manner of minarets, all this reminded, and really represented a picture of one of stone towns in Asia, which existence it is difficult to believe and which seem to live only in the rich imagination of Arabic poets"[1].

In a week after entrance of Napoleon's army in Moscow, this fabulous city, which amazed the French so much, was destined to become enormous smouldering ruins. The grandiose fire in Moscow left by its inhabitants, enveloped most of the city's districts, in the centre and in periphery; Lefortovo and the German settlement were burning, many streets were burnt out completely. "Moscow – one of the most beautiful and richest cities in the world – does not exist any more" – so it was written in Napoleon's bulletin.[2] According to ober-policemeister's report of 20h of January, 1813, in Moscow more than 70% of the city buildings were burnt: 6532 houses burnt out of 9158. 123 churches were damaged.

The exit of the French army out of the ruined Moscow on 10th of October, 1812, was accompanied by a deafening blow. Upon Napoleon's order the Kremlin was mined, and only the pouring rain and courage of Muscovites who stayed in the city and took up timely measures prevented the implementation of the insane plan of total ruining of the ancient capital. The national holy things were kept in the Kremlin – the cathedrals and John the Great. However, the damages were serious: the Arsenal and Philaret's attached house were blown, the palace was damaged, the Faceted Palace, the Senate; the Water Tower was ruined to the foundation, the Kremlin walls were ruined in five places.

Moscow that played a crucial role in Napoleon's defeat, burnt and ruined, but that did not surrender to the enemy, became the symbol of Russia and the immortality of its people.

"Moscow... How much in this sound is blended for the Russian heart! How much is stirred up in it!" – these words, said by A. S. Pushkin, were actually carried on by Russian people through all successive generations.

Rebuilding of Moscow after the fire became a great patriotic, national and state deed of all Russia. At once after the banishment of the enemy the inhabitants began to return to Moscow in a continuous flow. Hundreds of masters and builders came here from village's, spontaneous reconstruction of dwelling houses was started throughout the city.

Restoration works were going on extremely intensively: Muscovites, who stayed in the city during the fire and those who came back to it after the retreat of Napoleon's army, badly needed shelters. The city was built rapidly.

The restoration works had a most important meaning. Moscow was being restored with the idea that the city which rose from ruins should be more beautiful, orderly, "correct", regular, than before. So, together with construction of dwelling houses, great importance was attributed to improvement of the planning and reconstruction of the centre, which was to fully express by means of architecture the national patriotism overwhelming Russia and historical importance of the victory.

The devastating effect of the fire of 1812 created real conditions for implementation of full scale reconstruction of Moscow on the basis of the principles of regularity. It was dictated by the notions dominating in classicism about an ideal capital city and capital's centre as a memorial of the victory in the greatest war, which entered the history of Russia under the name of Patriotic.

Getting down to reconstructive and restoring works, the officials and architects followed two principles connected with each other: to immortalize the history and give Moscow a look of a modern well-arranged city. These principles became basic in the wide-scale architectural and town-building transformations of the ancient capital.

In February 1814 Moscow Commander-in-Chief count F.V.Rostopchin sent to Alexander I to the Army in the Field, which was on the close approaches to Paris then, "projects of squares, stores and views of the Kremlin with new constructions", accompanying them with the words: "I would like very much that these projects will be certified by You in Paris itself and that the new plan of Moscow will be one of tile memorials of Your glory". [3]

The emperor Alexander I, being in the Army in the Field in Europe, during the first months after liberation of Moscow already gave the order about the city's restoration. On the basis of it on 18th of February, 1813, the Senate issued the governmental decree about establishment of the special Commission for Construction in Moscow, the purpose of which was to render

Burnt Moscow. Water-colour of an unknown artist. Early 1810s.

assistance to people in construction of dwelling houses and putting in order the city's buildings. But soon the Commission's functions were expanded. It led all the after-fire construction not only in restoration, but in reconstruction of the city.

The events developed as follows. In February of 1813 Alexander I entrusted the architect of the royal court V. Geste to design a new plan of Moscow. The author of projects of replanning of many towns in the South of Russia on the basis of the principles of regularity characteristic for classicism, during development of the plan of Moscow reconstruction considered it necessary to preserve the original beauty and majesty of Moscow historical centre. Putting his geometrical plan on the alive tissue of the city, he did not only leave the Kremlin and Kitay-gorod untouched as the architectural and compositional kernel of the city, but also made a number of proposals for disclosure and exposure of its leading importance in the city. Geste's proposals were developed by the Commission for the Construction, which was entrusted from the beginning with implementation of the plan developed by the architect. Later the Commission was entrusted to make a new plan, more real and realizable in those conditions, on the basis of Geste's plan.

The project plan of Moscow of 1817 followed and continued in many aspects the "projected" plan of 1775, which was not fully implemented.

There was the principle of development of the historically formed structure of the city in its basis, its organic combination with regular plans of classicism. The plan included both the city as a whole and its separate town-building units, squares, streets, buildings.

Moscow centre was considerably expanded by the way of creation around the historical new gala area – of squares, public buildings, and a green belt of boulevards on the place of the walls of Bely town. After the fire of 1812 the works for exposure of the concentrical and circular structure of Moscow were continued. The second highway in respect to Boulevard Ring, bounding Moscow, was created parallel to the restoration of the buildings. In the place of Zemljanoy town Garden Ring was laid out. This highway got its name due to front gardens, which the owners of the houses were obliged to arrange, in order to decrease the excess width of the street and at the same time to make it comfortable and green. During the period from 1816 to 1830 the new street was laid and the construction in it began. From the freed space which was 60 meters wide only 21-25 m were alloted for the street; approximately the same space was occupied by the front gardens at each side.

Together with construction of the new ring highway – today's Garden Ring – wide scale works were conducted in all Moscow territory to increase the rationality and correctness of its plan: the existing streets and squares were regulated, made wider and aligned. The restored and newly built houses acquired a new look. "Hollow" space of suburbs (vacant land and pastures) were planned with straight streets; creation of a number of new squares of utility use was stipulated.

After the fire of 1812 the bastions around the Kremlin and Kitay-gorod, built during the time of Peter I and which existed more than a century, were razed to the ground. Hue to the fire and opportunities which appeared for wide replanning, the works for making Moscow a regular city, based on classical European norms, entered a new phase, much more radical than the previous ones. One of the conditions of this change was understood, as it was mentioned above, as turning Moscow from a wooden town in stone one. During the restoration works renovation and construction of new wooden buildings inside Bely town was prohibited. The owners of the houses, who could not afford to construct stone buildings, moved outside Bely town to Zemljanoy town or farther on.

Like the liquidation of the bastions another town-building decision made a significant influence on the look and structure of Moscow centre: encasement of the river Neglinnaja into a pipe, which had flown approximately along the direction of modern Neglinnaja street, near the Kremlin's walls and had fallen into the Moscow-river near the Big Stone Bridge. Implementation of this project increased the level of comfortability and created favourable preconditions for construction of new gala ensembles of the centre.

Important changes happened during the after-fire period not only in the centre, in the Kremlin and Kitay-gorod. The functional, social and town-building structure and the look of each part of the city changed. The process of ousting of dwelling houses out of Kitay-gorod, which began in the second half of 18th century, first of all of rich nobility estates, became especially intensive after the fire. The trade function of Kitay-gorod became increasingly stronger, and merchants' properties became more and more numerous. The social structure of Bely-gorod had also changed. Out of the district of mainly big landlords estates it began to turn into Moscow cultural centre. This process, like many others, was begun in the second half of 18th century, by the construction of the University in Mokhovaja, Peter's theatre in future Teatraljnaja (Theatre) square and the building for the Nobility Assembly in Okhotnyj Row. Construction of the new building of the Bolshoy Theatre was accompanied by creation of one of the most majestic ensembles of the after-fire Moscow. Near the University building, restored after the fire, Pashkov's house was adjusted for its needs, a number of other large public buildings and ensembles was created.

New construction of nobility estates gradually left Bely town. Now it was concentrated in Zemljanoy town and first of all in its south-west and western parts. Here the majority of such buildings was constructed, which were associated with the most spread notion about the after-fire Moscow as of the city of nobility mansions – not big nobility dwelling houses of one or two storeys, often with an attic, with a columned portico under a triangular pediment, with smooth walls, scarcely decorated with stucco moulding. Boulevard Ring, the streets of Zemljanoy town – Prechistenka, Ostozhenka, Big and Small Nikitskayas, Povarskaja with the nearby lanes, Arbat lanes – that was the place of concentration of the most famous Moscow mansions.

The north-east, eastern and south-east parts of Zemljanoy town, as well as the district outside Zemljanoy town were inhabited mainly by merchants and artisans. Here the houses are more modest, there are more houses of merchant and petty bourgeois types with fазades without orders. Zamoskvorechje also became a merchant area. The buildings of Sophiyskaja quay were especially gala, the quay situated on the Moscow-river bank opposite the Kremlin. The beauty and expressiveness of its ensemble combined the traditional, purely Moscow spatiality, picturesqueness, plenty of verdure with classical strictness of fазades, clear volumes of houses, representativeness of porticos. As a result another historically concrete variation of the typical for after-Petrine Moscow combination of freedom and picturesqueness with regularity, expressive fазades and frontality, born by the new idea about a city beauty, was formed.

The striving to the integrity and beauty of buildings had program character and was achieved by the hardest reglamentation and strict control of the construction. The construction of each house which was restored after the fire or newly built, was controlled, as well as of a wing or a service block, including railings and gates, if they stood out to the red line of the street.

The architects' duties included certification of the projects presented by the owners, their amendment in accordance with the "rules", supervision of the buildings' foundation, because exactly during foundation the correspondence of a building with the street and the city was determined. The architects and their assistants, who were state employees, managed to implement a huge volume of work only due to the fact that the majority of buildings was not designed anew. The architects mainly corrected and amended the faзades chosen by the builders in accordance with their taste and financial capabilities out of the projects, which were offered in the albums of sample faзades of dwelling houses, issued in 1809-1812. O. I. Beauvais was at the head of all the work in the city, connected with faзades.

The choice of faзades architectural decorations happened in a similar way. Sample elements of gypsum decorations, made in special work-shops, were used for decoration of houses. Variability and uniformity were the main principles of construction in Moscow, which turned into a gigantic construction site for ten years after the French had left it.

Burnt and unmercifully ruined during the stay of Napoleon's troops, Moscow rose from ashes. And though the after-fire Moscow inherited principles of classicism from the second half of 18th century, after the restoration it appeared to be anabsolutely new city in respect to the city of that time, beautiful and whole as before, but new. Only its Moscow character was not changed, which from the time of Peter's reign always included adaptation of Europe-wide norms through national traditions, preservation of the national feeling of space and form.

New Ensemble of the Centre.

The most significant change of Moscow look, restored after the fire, concerned the city's centre. Its reconstruction began from Red Square, the concentration place of trade and social life. Being historically connected with the Kremlin and the cathedral of St. Basil, for a long it had formed with them the architectural and compositional centre of the city, staying a link between the Kremlin and Kitay-gorod. In the second half of 18th century in conformity with the decree of Catherine II about arrangement of squares in Moscow, Red Square turned out to be fully isolated from the Kremlin, the cathedral of St. Basil and ancient buildings in the northern end of the Square, due to the fact that it was built around from all sides with stores with two-tier arcades in front of them. During the fire of 1812 and the blowing off of the Kremlin nearly all the stores at the Kremlin wall were destroyed, and on the opposite side of the square they partially burnt. During the period of the enthusiasm after of the victory in the Patriotic war, an interest increased in all national, Russian, primary importance was attributed to Red Square with the Kremlin wall in it. Preserving the memory of the history in itself, it was to become again the city's central square, and its historically formed ensemble was to respond to the requirements of the new time and enter the life of the revived Moscow.

In the "highest" instructions of Alexander I, sent from Paris, and in the "comments" of Commander-in-Chief count Rostopchin, the reconstruction of Red Square and composition of faзades of new Trade rows were prescribed to be under "special" control. And special attention was paid to "opening of the Kremlin" by demolishing of a number of stores along the Kremlin wall, liquidation of the ditch and bank and arrangement in this place of a boulevard to the Moscow-river; instead of demolished the stores it was offered to allot the place for them around the walls of Kitay-gorod, which remained intact because "for their long age they deserve respect and make the part of the town, which they bound, majestic".

The "wonderful building of the church of St. Basil, freed from small constructions, was also kept untouched, the building was offered to be "built around with counterforce to support the foundation of that building".

The historical memorials of the Square's northern part were restored after the fire – Voskresenskie gates, the cathedral of the Kazan Icon of the Theotokos and Offices, which occupied the former Coin Yard and the Main Chemist's.

It was instructed to "shape with a majestic building" the part of Red Square, which was opposite the Kremlin, where there were stores before the fire too – Trade Rows.

I. Beauvais was entrusted with the task to make the project of new Trade Rows. Soon all construction works connected with reconstruction of Red Square, were handed over to him. The architect had a complicated town-building task: to include a modern building into a historically formed ensemble of the square which was in the process of restoration and reconstruction.

Taking into consideration the wide understanding of the town-building role of Red Square as of a link between the Kremlin and the system of central squares planned in the new Moscow centre and situated in a semi-circle around the Kremlin and Kitay-gorod, Beauvais emphasized its gala importance.

Liquidating a number of stores and the former defence fortifications, Beauvais showed the leading importance of the Kremlin wall in the square's ensemble. The boulevard arranged In their place, connected the wall and the square even more, and the passages to the Moscow-river and Voskresenskaja square opened it in the direction of the city.

The cathedral of St. Basil became the dominating part of the square again, freed from recent buildings and surrounded with the counterforce and a terrace. The multi-tower complex of the cathedral dominated the square due to its spaciousness, concentrated verticals, sharp dynamics of its forms, and together with Spasskaja tower, the highest vertical of the ensemble, counted on its volumetric contemplation in foreshortening, like a powerful finale completed the leading theme of the composition of the square – the Kremlin towers interchange. The tower tops of the historical buildings on the northern side of the square, opposite the cathedral of St. Basil, were comprehended like an echo of this chord.

Beauvais included new Trade Rows – buildings of other stylish and forming qualities – into this ensemble built on the basis of interior harmony and picturesque balance of architectural volumes – irregular principles of ancient Russian town-building.

It was started by M. F. Kazakov: by taking out of the cupola of the Kremlin Senate to Red Square he anticipated geniously the future gala ensemble of Moscow central square. New Trade Rows, being in conformity with modern idea about a town public building, remained compositionally subordinated to the Kremlin in the square ensemble. The square extent, strict rhythm of the wall and verticals of the Kremlin Towers determined the composition of the new Trade Rows.

Trying, first of all, to create the square ensemble, Beauvais actually designed the faзade of the Trade Rows, which covered

**View of the Kremlin with Troitskie gate from Vozdvizhenka street.
Lithography. Middle of the 19th century.**

"View of Red Square in Moscow in Kitay-gorod from Voskresenskie gate". Herds' lithography according to O. Kadors drawing. 1825.

the constructions of different time of private owners and did not correspond to the interior structure of the building.

The Middle and Lower Rows were built in the same forms – with these buildings of whole quarters Red Square was connected with Kitay-gorod.

Implementing the instruction "to make a project for proper decoration of the upper part of the square and for demolishing of the stores around the church of St. Basil", Beauvais made a plan, faзade and estimations of the counterforce and the terrace around the cathedral, and by 1817 he reported to the Commission about the fulfilment of the construction.

By this time nearly all construction works in Red Square were over. Only Nikolskaja tower remained destroyed.

In spring of 1817 during making of the projects for reconstruction of the Kremlin walls and towers, Beauvais paid special attention to Nikolskaja tower which stood out in Red Square, it was badly damaged during the explosion of the Arsenal. In difference to the other towers, which Beauvais planned to reconstruct in their previous design, the architect wanted to make Nikolskaja tower "in an open place higher and wider than the previous one with a stone steeple and better faзade in concordance with Spasskaja tower".

This project was not fulfilled. And architect Sokolov, who was entrusted with the work to control the reconstruction of the Kremlin wall and towers, in summer of 1817 reported to the Commission that Nikolskaja tower was reconstructed "without making it wider, but as it was before, stone, sculptural and with adjustment of stucco moulding, with cleaning and finishing of the old remaining walls". The architectural decoration of the tower, which existed before the fire, was changed only a little.

Later, in 1821, at both sides of Spasskie gates small stone chapels were built according to Beauvais project, because "the old ones did not correspond to the tower faзade and could make an absolute ugliness in such a well seen and open place".

The ensemble of Red Square was finished by construction of the memorial to Minin and Pozharskiy – the first Moscow sculptural monument, it was made by L.P.Martos. Together with temple memorials – the cathedral of St. Basil and the cathedral of the Kazan Icon of the Theotokos this monument was to emphasize even more the ideological and moral importance of the city ancient square.

The memorial was installed in the centre of the square closer to the Trade Rows, so that Minin's raised hand pointed directly to the Kremlin, for the defence of which he had called Russian people 200 years ago (in 1930 the memorial was moved closer to the cathedral of St. Basil).

The composition of the memorial was expected to show its contents in the successive change of aspects during movement along the square. But, like the Trade Rows, the memorial had the main faзade too – frontal, conforming to the central axis of the Trade Rows. Fixing in this way the transversal axis of the square, it emphasized even more the compositional connection of the building with the Kremlin.

In the images of the national heroes Martos could find such lofty simplicity and monumentality, which were found in the classical architecture of the Trade Rows. The group of the memorial was comprehended well from the far points of the big square due to laconicism of its language and quietness of its outline.

The gala opening of the memorial on 20th of February, 1818, was accompanied with a military parade and led to a real national celebration.

During reconstruction after the fire Red Square acquired a spatial design, which has remained till our time. After the recon-

Theatre Square. View from the Bolshoy Theatre of Kitay-gorod. Tonolithography of Geacote and K. Bashelie according to Bronin's drawing. Middle of the 19th century.

struction of the beginning of 19th century it became the biggest and most beautiful square of Moscow again.

"And today, – as the Guide-book of Moscow of 1831 informed – Red Square is one of the remarkable places of the capital... For a long time it was not filled in by a shout of a punished criminal, there are not any public meetings here any more, but there are many people here too: from morning till evening we can see colourful crowds of people here... New Trade Rows have good form, especially covered with the colonnade of 1815, they are an excellent outside decoration of the square... These Trade Rows make Red Square very beautiful".[4]

In spite of the significant dimensions, Red Square was not sufficient for the centre of the city that had grown up so much. So in the system of the gala square which surrounded the Kremlin and Kitay-gorod, according to the plan of the Commission for the constructions in front of the building of Peter's theatre, which burnt in 1805, it was supposed to create a new square, "the first in its arrangement and spatiality". So the first regular square appeared in Moscow, created according to a plan developed beforehand. Its location near Red Square, and at the junction of the radial streets – Petrovka and Big Dmitrovka and in the semi-circle, surrounding the Kremlin and Kitay-gorod, was extremely convenient.

Creation of a square here was stipulated already in the project plans of Moscow of 18th century. In the initial projects of the Commission for constructions, like in the plan of Moscow of architect Geste of 1813-1814, the square was outstanding in its dimensions, but it was extremely large, shapeless, and the building of the theatre looked accidental in it. In the projects of Moscow planning of 1813, 1816, 1819 it is possible to see how the plan of the square crystalized: from an irregular square coming from the traditions of an ancient Russian town, through ideal schemes to a geometrically correct plan, conforming to the city's scale and connected with its historically formed structure. Final projects of the square and a new Big Peter's Theatre appeared as a result of a number of competitions and endeavours of many Moscow and Petersburg architects and engineers.

However, the historical documents testify to the fact that the initial ideas both of the square and the theatre belonged to Moscow specialists, and first of all to architect O.I.Beauvais. They became the basis of further developments. Only at the last stage of the designing, when preparation works on raising the foundation for the theatre began under the leadership of Beauvais, and one of the buildings in the square – "a structure nearly finished (probably, Senate's printing-house), according to which like according to a sample other buildings bounding the square, were constructed", architects of Petersburg Academy of Art were also entrusted with the task to participate in the construction. Besides, they were provided with the projects of the theatre and buildings of the square, developed by Moscow architects Beauvais and Lamoni. Documents testify to this effect too.

Upon certification of the project of Petersburg professor A. Mikhaylov Moscow governor-general D. V. Golitsyn found it "on its part, made according to the projects of architects Beauvais and Lamoni".

Beauvais was occupied with amending and finishing Mikhaylov's project, adapting it to the local conditions. The project of the theatre and the square signed by Beauvais, was certified by his majesty on 10th of November, 1821. At the same time D. V. Golitsyn noted that "some ideas of professor Mikhaylov helped much Moscow architect Beauvais in making the project of the theatre's building, approved by the emperor".[5]

According to the project approved at the highest level Teatraljnaja square got a shape of an extended rectangle bound-

The Bolshoy (Peter's) Theatre.
G. Arnou's lithography according to Vivien's drawing. 1830-1840.

ed by four symmetrical buildings and divided by a passage into two equal parts.

On the longitudinal axis fixed by Sophiyskaja tower of Kitay-gorod wall, inside the square the building of Peter's theatre was located freely. In order not to destroy the correct geometrical form of the square a public garden (flower market) was laid out an angle to the wall.

Teatraljnaja square was open in the direction of Kitay-gorod and Red Square at the cathedral of the Intercession and the Kremlin's Spasskaja tower seen far off, and was connected with it through the neighbouring Voskresenskaja square planned simultaneously with Teatraljnaja (Theatre) square.

Thus, here the initial idea of the Commission for Construction was realized, which presumed already according to the plan of 1813 to connect this square with the old centre – the Kremlin and Kitay-gorod and to connect it with all the squares situated around the walls of Kitay-gorod. Orientation of Theatre Square across the ring of these squares made it the main one, holding all the composition of the city centre.

At the same time, in difference to the previous projects real needs were taken into consideration. In suite of the fact that during realization of the project dimensions of the square were significantly decreased, it was 355 m long and 177 m wide and after Red Square was the largest in Moscow.

The buildings, surrounding Theatre Square, of the same type in their look, with horizontal extent of their faзades and plane walls, limiting its space with their faзades, created a beautiful background for the theatre's majestic building. In one of the square's buildings, constructed by architect Elkinskiy according to the project of Beauvais for merchant V. Vargin, in the leased part of the house on 14th of October, 1824, the Fiscal Drama Cast gave its first performance, commencing the existence of the famous Maly Theatre.

Opening of Big Peter's Theatre took place on 6th of January, 1825, and was the biggest event in the cultural life of Moscow. More than ten years later, in 1838 the last empty plot of land was bought and a dwelling house and a bath-house of merchant Chelyshev were built (in the place of today's hotel "Metropol"). Thus, the ensemble of Theatre Square was completed, though the project of planting of greenery was not realized.

The biggest and most expressive building in the square was the freely standing inside it the building of the theatre, surrounded with passages at all sides. Its strict volume dominated all the space of the square and the surrounding buildings. Emphasized horizontals of articulations, rustic, strict plastic frieze girdling the upper and lower parts of the building making softer the severe blind walls, gave a quiet majesty to a little heavy volumes.

"Now let's admire this beautiful square. Look at this white wall of Kitay-gorod, at these buildings seen behind its, and your eyes will not know where to stop, – tells the Guide-book of Moscow of 1831, – . . . right in front of you behind the wall among plenty of cupolas rising steeples of Synodal Printing-house are seen, there is the church of the monastery of Theophany near their wonderful old architecture; their hell-tower and the cupola of the church of the Greek monastery are closer; to the left there is a row of long roofs of the buildings, finished by the view of the renewed ancient church of the Holy Trinity in the Fields. All this is covered by the wall of Kitay-gorod with an exquisite turn. . . Look to the right and the picture of Kitay-gorod and the Kremlin becomes even more splendid: you see the beautiful faзade of the offices and behind them in a charming mixture the guilded cupolas and crosses of the churches, pyramidal steeples, crowned with eagles on fiscal buildings and the towers Spasskaja and Nikolskaja, and, finally, above all of them the pillar-like bell-tower of John the Great". That was the picture of ancient Moscow which could be seen coming to the first regular square in Moscow.

The transversal connections of Theatre Square were not less important with the semi-circle of the squares around the Kremlin and Kitay-gorod: "to the left near the clean boulevard and the wall a street goes up to Loubjanskaja square; big private buildings, composing the opposite side of the street, make a wonderful perspective"... From the other side ". . . behind the faзade of the Senate's Printing-house you can see the long extent of Okhotny Row, the five-cupola temple of Great Martyr Paraskeva of Iconium. . . and at a distance Mokhovaja street". 7

In it a visual connection of new ensembles with the historical monuments of the city architects-classicists caught one of the characteristic features which determined the wholeness and individuality of the Moscow image.

The ensemble of Theatre Square in Moscow with the buildings of the Bolshoy (Big) and Maly (Small) Theatres was the fullest and most successive in recreation of the scheme of ancient Roman forum, brilliantly presented at the beginning of the 19th century in the system of the central squares in Petersburg. In Moscow it was interpreted otherwise than in the northern capital, but not less expressively.

The after-fire Moscow gave its contextually important and architecturally perfect version of the formula "Moscow is the Third Rome", which kept its viability at that time. Like Petersburg, remembering the pretension of the ancient capital to be new Rome, Moscow architects, creating the system of gala squares of the renovated centre, oriented at the forums of ancient imperial Rome.

Another remarkable speciality of Theatre Square. As a known researcher of Russian architecture Z. Taranovskaja noted, – it was " the first theatre ensemble in the world history of architecture".[8]

The Bolshoy Theatre embodied the traditions of Russian theatre buildings, on which the predecessors and contemporaries of Bove worked – J.Toma de Tomon, G.Quarenghi, C.Rossi. Together with the Alexandrinskiy theatre built by Rossi (1828-1831) it became the top of Russian theatre architecture and was among the best European theatres of its time. As well as the ensemble of the square of the Alexandrinskiy theatre in Petersburg, created according to Rossi's project, the ensemble of Theatre Square with the Bolshoy Theatre became the biggest achievement of town-building art. Turning of a public theatre into the main building of the city central square was in accordance with the national ideals of that time, reflected the Renaissance of culture and art revived after 1812. "Erudition, love of art and talents were undoubtfully on Moscow side", – A. S. Pushkin wrote.

Not much remained till our time from the Bolshoy Peter's Theatre of Mikhaylov-Beauvais: the fire of 1853 and reconstruction of the building by architect A. Kavos changed its look in accordance with the taste of the new stylistic epoch of eclecticism. Even less was left in today's Theatre Square from its previous ensemble either. Only the building of the Maly Theatre,

Fire in the Bolshoy (Peter's) Theatre.
1853. Lithography according to Ernie's drawing

reconstructed by architect C.Ton in 1838-1840, reminds about its initial look.

Arrangement of the garden at the foot of the Kremlin wall was one of constructional undertakings, which changed significantly the look of the centre of Moscow which rose from ashes. Its gala opening took place on the day of Angel of the emperor on 30th of August, 1821. In this way the memorial sense of creation of the garden was emphasized: it became simultaneously a memorial to Alexander I and a memorial to the victory in the Patriotic war of 1812, won by Russia during the reign of this tsar.

Alexandrovskiy, or, as it was called then, Kremlevskiy garden, was very important for a proper and comfortable arrangement of the city centre and became a favourite place where Muscovites walked. The garden was laid out near the Kremlin wall from

Voskresenskie to Borovitskie Gates in the place of a deep ravine, where the river Neglinnaja flowed till its encasement into a pipe in 1817.

During 1820-1821 the first most gala part of the garden from Voskresenskie to Troitskie gates was designed, so called the Upper garden. It was designed as a park, in which strict axis planning was combined with winding paths, grouped with flower-beds and bushes in a picturesque way, with romantic ruins and architecture of small structures.

The main entrance into the garden was designed from Voskresenskaja square, due to which the Kremlin garden was connected through Voskresenskaja square with Theatre square and its verdure was in concordance with the verdure of the square's public garden.

The fountain made by sculptor I. P. Vitali, built in 1835 in Theatre square, was oriented at the gates of the Kremlin garden. Finishing beautifully the ensemble of the square, it emphasized its spatial connection with the architectural and compositional centre of Moscow. The dynamic space of the garden, extended along the Kremlin wall, was not closed: from the opposite side behind Borovitskie gates it had an exit in the direction of the passage near the Moscow-river and connected with the verdure of the boulevards, bounding the Kremlin walls. It was accentuated also with the gates and railing installed here, similar to the gates of the Upper garden (demolished in 1872).

Along the outside border of the garden a small ditch was digged and a small iron railing was installed. Bounding the territory of the garden, it opened it in the direction of the city, to Neglinnaja street, which at that time went from Voskresenskaja square to the Moscow-river.

The side entrance into the garden designed along the axis of Nikitskaja street connected the Kremlin with the city very well: Nikitskaja street, which at that time reached the garden, as though continued along its transversal alley and was finished by a beautiful grotto in the shape of ruins, situated near the Middle-Arsenal tower of the Kremlin.

Four Doric columns were adjusted in the grotto's arch, which supported a heavy entablature with a triglyph frieze and a parapet.

The strict clearly drawn order forms combined contrastly with a conglomeration of stones, which reproduced an ancient Cyclopian masonry. In this construction the romantic effort to combine the classics of Moscow with architectural antiquity showed as a characteristic feature of Russian art of that time. Arrangement of the grotto was finished on 18th of October, 1820.

The forms of a small fountain arranged in the verdure of the garden, were inspirated by antique motives too.

The ramps were especially admired by Muscovites – the semi-circular declivious slopes into the garden from Troitskiy bridge, which, according to the words of contemporaries, represented "something especially majestic" and together with the arch under the bridge finished beautifully the perspective from the side of the main entrance (did not keep).

From here, from the upper part of the bridge, like from other places, "pictures of the Kremlin garden" opened – a surprising view of Moscow showed on lithographs, prints and descriptions of contemporaries. "In the Upper garden a wonderful view is opened by the Kremlin wall, corner tower, Troitskie gates and the Arsenal rising above the wall, on the other side there are huge buildings (the University, Pashkov's house are meant – Z. P.), from which the only exercise House was especially different, – the Guide-book of Moscow of 1831 noted. – In the second one the view... of Troitskiy bridge, near Troitskie gates, the wall, from which the Ordonans-House was seen, which was a mixture of ancient and new taste. In front of it there was the church of St.Nicholas the Miracle-worker in Sapozhok, the street Vozdvizhenka and private houses of good most recent architecture. – In the third one the wonderful Stone Bridge, part of the quay, Zamoskvorechie and the splendid Vorobjevy hills".[9]

In this Kremlin's openness to the city, in the dialogue of the Kremlin ensemble with the buildings and architectural landscapes surrounding it, which was created by the new spatial setting of the Kremlin – Alexandrovskiy garden, the whole image of Moscow formed, unrepeatable with its beauty and expressiveness.

During the last years of his life Beauvais, who headed earlier all the works on creation of Alexandrovskiy garden, prepared, according to the words of contemporaries, a project of genious construction in the garden of a system of ponds and cascades, using Mytischinskiy water-pipe which went under the Upper garden. "On Sundays boats and motor-boats could sail on the ponds with music and singers, and in the evening with illumination of the garden and the ponds on appointed days it could be possible to switch on lamps, prepared for such occasions, behind the cascades... Water falling from the top would present a splendid view... In winter ice-skating would be allowed... at the sides of the ponds several galleries would be arranged".[10]

In the panorama which opened out of tile Kremlin garden, two important buildings of the after-fire Moscow were notable. It was the building of the Манйге and Moscow University, reconstructed by D. Gilardi, constructed by M. F. Kazakov in the end of 18th century.

The building of the Manege was constructed in 1817 upon the order of Alexander I for the celebration of 5 years of the Victory for troops review, training and parades, but understood both by the contemporaries and the creators wider than its functional denomination – as a memorial of military valour and honours of Russia. Its freely installed volume with a wide step of semi-columns, raised oh a high massive socle, with an enmhasized horizontal of a powerful Doric entablature had a significant scale corresponding to its location in front of the Kremlin and in the area of gala buildings of the city.

The building was constructed by engineer L. Carboni according to the project of engineer A. Bethencourt and had a unique

Troitskie gate, Koutafia tower and the Manege
(1817, engineer A. Betankoir, 1925, the sculptural decoration of O. Bove).
Tsurov's lithography according to Kiktorg's drawing. 1838.

Loubjanskaja square. View (yp Iljinskie gate from Sophiyka street.
Lithography. Middle of the 19th century.

system of erection trusses, which covered a vast space nearly 45m wide without supports, which was, according to the comments of contemporaries, a "miracle" of the construction practice of that time.

Stucco mouldings of the Manege design like military emblems in methods of frieze, made according to Beauvais' drawing, increased the ideological importance and plastic contents of the construction. They were in concordance with the similar reliefs of the frieze of the nearest Grotto of the Kremlin (Alexandrovskiy) garden, which, as it was mentioned above, also became a memorial of the Victory in some way. The garden had an especially gala look also due to the cast iron gates of the main entrance with elements of ancient Roman martial emblematics in decoration.

From the opposite side from the Kremlin the Manege looks at Mokhovaja street with its gala buildings turned to the Kremlin with monumental constructions. Here in the centre of intensively constructed Moscow, during five years the University burnt in 1812 was.

With great artistic tact D. Gilardi, one of the best architects of the after-fire Moscow, approached reconstruction of the old building. Preserving as much as possible of the main volume, Gilardi with amazing mastery changed the character of the main fasade looking at the Kremlin, in accordance with the stylistic speciality of the architecture and town-building requirements of his time. Instead of the exquisite beauty of Kazakov's creation, Gilardi, following development of style, gave the University a new look, complying with the created ensemble of the centre. Enlargement of the central portico with fluted columns in the

Mokhovaja street. View from Okhotny Row of Znamenka street.
Photo. Early 20th century.

style of early Greek Dorics, contrasting smoothness of the walls and the powerful plastics of the portico, – changed the scales, emphasized the importance of the building in the city space of Moscow centre.

The main theme of the University architecture – "The triumph of science and art" – was with great skill developed by Gilardi in the images of nine muses personifying different types of art. The beautiful bas-relief of the fasade was devoted to them, which was made from marble by sculptor G. T. Zamaraev.

On 5th of July, 1819, in a splendidly finished assembly hall – with unique interior of Russian classicism -a gala opening of the University took place. A chorus sang "Renewal of Minerva's temple" by professor A. F. Merzljakov. The leit-motif of the speeches and poems was the pride and joy because of success in the quick revival of the city:"... Like a hill out of a fog, Minerva's temple rose, rich with glory and gifts".

In 1816 the governor-general of Moscow wrote to the minister of education: "Moscow, which recently was in ruins devastated everywhere, today... is renewed in all respect and with the best success, assuming splendour, excelling even that one, in which Moscow had been before the tragedy...

Public Buildings

The University building, which had become "new", located on the other side of Nikitskaja street, was constructed upon the order of the Pashkovs as a city estate in 1790 according to the same scheme with a front yard, like the old building according to the project of M. F. Kazakov. After the city had obtained it in 1833 it was changed like the old one: the compositional basis remained the same, but the fasades acquired stylistic specialities characteristic for the architecture of classicism of the first third of 19th century. The former manege of the Pashkovs' house was remade too, it was turned into the church of Martyr Tatiana (1835, E. D. Tjurin); its semi-rotunda surrounded with a colonnade acquired an even more gala and monumental look.

As a result in Mokhovaja street in front of the Kremlin, not far from Alexandrovskiy garden an ensemble of two University buildings similar in composition appeared.

Another ensemble of buildings of the University printing-house was formed at the border of Holy town, at the corner plot of land, coming to Strastnoy boulevard and Dmitrovskaja street. In 1816-1817 the first building on the boulevard was reconstructed for the editors' block (architect K. P. Sobolevskiy, with participation of F. P. Bouzhinskiy). In 1821-1827 according to the project of A. G. Grigorjev in Big Dmitrovka a block of the printing-house was constructed. Both buildings were situated along the red line. The composition of the first one with a portico raised on the colonnade of the lower storey came from rich houses and public buildings of the second half of the 18th century, the second one – with its orderless smooth fasade is similar to contemporary merchant and petty bourgeois houses, while the central part, though accentuated with a very wide rizalit, reminds about the modes more characteristic for mansions. In construction of public buildings all range of compositional modes, typical for city estate, dating to the 18th century, was used.

The ensemble of the buildings of the Tutorial Council, built in Soljanka street, reproduced the spatially developed type of an estate complex with the main house brought out on the red line with two wings. All the buildings, connected by a railing (with lions on the gates), were constructed with their lateral sides to the street and so looked as compact laconic volumes (1823-1826, D. Gilardi, A. G. Grigorjev). The central one was distinguished by its height, by the raised on the arched pedestal gala six-column portico above the triangular pediment and cupola, i. e. with all attributes typical for the palaces of the second half of the 18th century, but interpreted in accordance with the artistic norms of the after-fire time much more laconically and monumentally.

During designing of public buildings, especially hospitals, alms houses and educational institutions the estate scheme of a rich palace-like house with a front yard and a block extended along the street, remained most popular. Architects followed it designing buildings situated within the borders of Bely town and in the outskirts, including those which were outside Zemljanoy town. Lazarevskaja Armenian Gymnasium (later Lazarevskiy Institute) belonged to the first, representing this variant with really classical successiveness and fullness. In the depth of the front yard there was the main block extended along the street. It was notable with its dimensions, the height (2,5 storeys), representativeness of the look and gala symmetrical composition with a six-column portico in the centre and two rizalits with three-part arch windows at the edges. The main block was flanked with wings turned at the street with their narrowed fазades, brought on the street red line lower blocks (2 storeys) and more modest in

Tutorial Council (1821-1826, architect D.I.Giljardi, A.G. Grigoriev). Lithography of P.A.Bishebois according to G.-Dits's drawing. Middle of the 19th century.

architectural decoration (porticos from four pilasters). A railing with the gates in the centre, the pylons of which were decorated with figures of lying lions, separated the front yard from the street.

The same scheme was recreated, though being situated in the outskirts on the opposite sides of Moscow, Nabilkovskaja almshouse (1828-1836, A. G. Grigoriev (?), Protopopovskiy lane, near the 1st Mestchanskaja street) and the First City Hospital (1827-1833, O. I. Beauvais), constructed near Golitsynskaja hospital and according to its scheme. Both in Nabilkovskaja almshouse, in Golitsynskaja and the First City Hospitals there were churches situated in the central part of the

House of artificial mineral water of H. Loder near Ostozhenka street. Lithography. Late 1820s.

building, emphasized with a columned portico and crowned with a cupola. The mode of construction of the new hospital near the existing one and according to the same scheme reminds of creation of the University building ensemble in Mokhovaja street. A splendid architectural and artistic ensemble was created then beyond the Garden Ring in Big Kaluzhskaja street, which was then a far away outskirts. Due to construction of the second building similar not only in its composition, but in its purpose to the first one too the specialization, the new large scale and gala character of the buildings in this suburban street, were established. Like the Boulevard Ring the Garden Ring became the place of extent of representative buildings.

In the waste land near the Moscow-river (today's Krymskaja Square), in a corner plot of land coming to Sadovaja and Ostozhenka streets, an ensemble of an absolutely another type was created – Victuals shops – military food ware-houses. It was constructed by architect F. M. Shestakov according to a sample Project of V. P. Stasov. Three two-storey blocks, situated along the perimeter of the plot, represent a splendid example of the "functional" architecture of the after-fire Moscow, which was spread when ware-houses and all kinds of industrial buildings were designed. Architects of that time, trying to create highly artistic utility buildings, risked for the first time to diverge from stereotypes, which connected the beautiful in architecture with modes and forms, which were stereotypes for public and palace buildings. Three blocks were connected with a railing, on the gates of which military accessories (compositions of helms, shields, swords) were placed instead of traditional lions. Monumentality, laconism and large scale of orderless faзades were accentuated by inclined walls – a detail taken from Egyptian architecture, which was popular during that time, and the same "Egyptian" doors extending to the bottom. This ascetic ensemble, which was closer to the architecture of the northern military capital – Petersburg – with its strict spirit, remained a unique phenomenon in the architecture of the after-fire Moscow.

Construction of Temples

The cathedral of Christ the Saviour – a memorial of the victory in the Patriotic war of 1812 – was to give a special colouring to the image of revived Moscow both from ideological, symbolical and town-buildings points of view.

The idea of creation of a temple-memorial to the glory of Russia, which was to excel all temples in the world that existed before, appeared already during the war: on 25th of December, 1812, on the day of the banishment of the enemies out of Russia, the "Highest" manifesto was promulgated.

"In order to keep the immortal memory of that unexampled effort, loyalty and love to the Faith and the Fatherland, with which Russian people extolled themselves during those hard times... We intend to create a temple in the name of Christ the Saviour in Our City of Moscow".

In 1816 Alexander I chose out of the works presented for the competition, the project of artist A. L. Vitberg, which impressed the emperor with the depth of the religious plot, which was in harmony with the idea about Christ the Saviour, that had been suggested by him. "It is necessary that each stone of it (of the temple – Z. P.) and all together spoke about the ideas of Christ's religion..." – Vitberg exclaimed, "...A temple in the name of Christ the Saviour! It is a new idea. Before this time the Christian world built its temples in the name of some holiday, some Saint; but here a comprehensive idea appeared..."[11]

This extraordinary idea to consecrate a temple to Christ the Saviour of the Christian world and to devote it to the memory of Russian soldiers, who died in the patriotic war, – resulted in the complicated religious and philosophical plot of the project (triplicity and integrity of the complex were to express three main stages of Christ's life – the nativity of Christ (the temple of the body), the Transfiguration (the temple of the soul) and the Resurrection of Christ (the temple of the spirit). Resides that, the low temple was devoted to the memory of the soldiers who died in 1812 – here their bodies were to be buried and memorial boards with their names were supposed to be placed.

However, a concrete place for construction of the temple-memorial was not found at once.

Alexander I, who arrived in Moscow in the same year, did not accept Vitberg's proposal to built the temple inside the Kremlin on the slope of the Borovitskiy hill near the ancient memorials, believing that "it is not decent to destroy the ancient Kremlin, and the building itself would be out of place among the Byzantine buildings of the Kremlin".

The emperor proposed to build the temple on the Shvivaja hill, a high steep bank of the Moscow-river at the fall of the river Yauza into it, well seen both from the near and far points of the city.

Vitberg, however, rejected this proposal. Agreeing with all the positive qualities of the place, which according to Vitberg's words, "occupies a pictoral view, from which the Kremlin, Zamoskvorechje and the part of the city leading to the monastery of St. Andronicus, were seen near each other as if presented on a plate", he supposed that there was not "enough space for the required square of the temple", besides, for that purpose was necessary to demolish a big quantity of good reconstructed houses.

Vitberg, convinced Alexander I that except the Vorobjovy hills no place would do for such construction either from the contextual symbolical, or the historical, or the town-buildings points of view. The temple would be situated between two memorial roads – Smolenskaja road, by which the enemy entered the city, and Kaluzhskaja road, by which they retreated from Moscow; from the Vorobjovy hills there was a wonderful view of Moscow and, on the other hand, it would be possible to observe the memorial freely from the side of the city.

The foundation of the cathedral of Christ the Saviour on 12th of October, 1817, on the fifth anniversary of the banishment of Napoleon out of Moscow, resulted in a nation-wide celebration: with a religious procession, divine service, water sanctifying, a military parade (a temporary wooden bridge was built across the Moscow-river), in the presence of Alexander I and his family and a grate crowd of people. The first stone on the place of the foundation was laid by the emperor himself.

However, for the reason that Vitberg did not have any experience of real construction, big ravines, difficulties in delivery of construction materials and getting the working force, as well as some doubts in implementation of such a grandiose plot delayed the preparation works for a long time. And the project itself, in which the romantic and religious ideas were expressed in abstract classical forms, aroused doubts.

Examination of the earth of the Vorobjovy hills, conducted by Moscow architects and engineers, showed that construction of a temple here was not possible, because the earth was subject to the ruinous impact of melting snow and pouring rain each year, which created huge ravines on the hills slopes and the earth was full of water springs.

However, the commission came to the conclusion that there was a reliable plot of land for the foundation of "the great building" higher from the foundation of the temple, on the top of the Vorobjovy hills, in the southern end: "this earth is not less durable than the best places which were considered the most convenient for construction till now", but it was necessary to exclude the low part of the complex, along the slope of the hill, and instead of the staircase to make sloping roads with several turns up to the level of the bridge across the river".

Exclusion out of Vitberg's project of the low part of the temple broke the main idea of the memorial, the romantic-symbolic sense of which was, perhaps strange to architects-classicists who were the members of the commission.

Soon the place for construction of the cathedral of Christ the Saviour was reconsidered. In 1831 the design of the cathedral was entrusted to C.Ton in the centre of Moscow, on the bank of the Moscow-river near the Kremlin. But it was already a memorial of the new world-view epoch, with new forms of expression of patriotic ideas connected with the Patriotic war of 1812.

In its volume the construction of new cult buildings occupied a sufficient place in the very intensive construction of the city revived after the devastating fire.

Churches and bell-towers, ancient and contemporary, retained their functions of the main orientation points, town-building accents, making an independent compositional-spatial and contextual system in the volumetric-spatial structure of the after-fire Moscow. Combination of ancient memorials-dominants with ordinary buildings situated along the street red line, nearly fully renovated after the fire, added individuality to the look of the revived city.

More than 100 churches burnt in Moscow during the fire, many of them were not reconstructerd until certification of the new plan of the city in 1817. Only a few churches were dismantled: as for the most of them, they were reconstructed in their former appearance or new temples were built on the old foundation.

Special attention was paid to the churches, which occupied an important position in the new plan of Moscow in regard of the town-building aspect. The church of the Ascension turned out to be such a church ("Big Ascension") in Tsaritsynskaja (Big Nikitskaja) street, in the place of its crossing near Nikitskie gates with the new highway of the Boulevard Ring. In 1820 – the time of development of large scale town-building works in Moscow – upon the conclusion of the Commission for the Construction this church "attracts special attention among the other unfinished buildings".

Its construction, which was started at the end of 18th century near an old stone church with a bell-tower of 17th century damaged during the fire and being subject to demolishing, by 1820 was far from being finished (only the refectory with two sacrariums were built (as historians found , A. S. Pushkin got married in one of these sacrariums) and the socle of "the real" cold church was brought out).

Complicated and tiny forms of the main temple in the old project did not correspond to the aesthetic taste and stylistic specialities of the architecture of the New Time. The governor-general wanted to build on this place a temple "in the manner of the cathedral of the Transfiguration in St.Petersburg", which was built at that time according to the project of V. P. Stasov (a monumental five-cupola cathedral alien to the traditions of Moscow architecture).

Resistance on the part of clergy men and parishioners, who wished to build the church according to the old project, insistence of Moscow architects who proved that it was impossible to build such Petersburg temple, led finally to creation of an absolutely laconical cubic volume, crowned with a plane cupola, with dominating large smooth walls. The contrasting combination of the rich plastics of its porticos and the smoothness of the walls (the upper windows were made later) made the stern look of the temple especially expressive and humane, which is the main good quality of the building.

Together with the similar cubic temples in classical style churches of a more traditional three-part type were built. In 1830s in the suburbs of the city, mainly on the grave-yards, such buildings of the leading Moscow architects appeared like the church of the Resurrection "Slovutschee" in Vagankovskoe cemetery (1824), the church of the Holy and Life-giving Trinity in Pjatnitskoe cemetery (1830) – both were constructed by architect A. G. Grigorjev; the church of the Holy Spirit in Danilovskoe cemetery (1832) of architect F. M. Shestakov and a little later the church of the Theophany in Elokhovo (1835-1845) of architect E.D. Tjurin.

Temple cupola-like rotunda was one of the kinds of cult architecture in Moscow in 1820-1830. Being widely spread in Moscow classicism in 18th century, they were changed because of stylistic specialities of its time.

It is possible to see it most clearly in the example of the rotunda of the church of the Icon of the Theotokos "The Joy of All the Afflicted" in Big Ordynka street – the building of O.I.Beauvais (1832-1836).

By construction of the rotunda – the main part of the temple – of the church of the Transfiguration Beauvais finalized the construction of the old church of late 17th century, started by V. Bazhenov in 1782-1790 – a bell-tower and a refectory with two sacrariums consecrated to St. Barlaam, abbot of Khutin, and the icon of the Theotokos "The Joy of All the Afflicted" (in honour of the miracle-working icon in this sacrarium all the temple was called so).

Beauvais did not imitate his great predecessor, remaining an architect of his time.

In Beauvais' rotunda – this late creation of the master, the strict rhythm of geometrical clear forms dominated, the contrast of big smooth walls with a rich ornament, which substituted the soft plastics of Bazhenov's facades.

The archy window with an order insertion, a favourite motif in classicism, often used by Beauvais , got here the character of a plane decorative detail. Big semi-circular arches of windows framing, supported by pylons, add monumentality to all the building by their enlarged scale.

The splendid, finely painted ornament of acanthus leaves, palmettes and lockets covered the wide vaults of arches, the friezes of the rotunda and the drum; contrasting with the background of the wall, it emphasized the gala look of the building. Rhythmic repetition of round forms and lines, successively conducted both in the general composition of the rotunda and in the details and elements of the decoration, added wholeness and harmonic completeness to its look. This theme was played up skilfully in the interior of the rotunda too, one of the most perfect in Moscow cult architecture of late classicism.

Beauvais' rotunda became a new important dominant in the buildings of Big Ordynka street, one of the interesting and original streets of Zamoskvorechje in respect of architecture and art.

The round forms of the rotunda complied to the open space of the front yard of the estate of merchant A. A. Dolgov, making an original ensemble in the buildings of the street. The gates of the railing with its open-work cast iron grille opened in front of the temple, opening the near and far away point for its obser-

Church of Martyrs Florus and Laurus in Zatsep.

vation. The cathedral of the Holy Trinity in the monastery of St. Daniel is on the list of important cult buildings of late classicism in Moscow, at the end of the 20th century the cathedral was to become the main temple of the residence of the Moscow Patriarchate.

One of the main merits of architects of Moscow school of classicism – the ability to include a new building in a historically framed ensemble – showed itself in construction of this temple. The cathedral of the Holy Life-giving Trinity with the sacrariums of St. Alexius the Man of God and the Conception by St.Anna of the Most Holy Theotokos was built in 1833-1838 according to the project of O.Beauvais at the expense of parishioners: nobility people, the Kumanins – Moscow merchants of the first rank, and Vicula Shestov, a commercial advisor of the first guild, with his brothers.

By the time when the cathedral of the Holy Trinity was raised the ensemble of the monastery of St. Daniel dating from the end of 13th century, had already been formed. It was composed mainly by the buildings of the 17th – the middle of the 18th centuries, which substituted the ancient dilapidated buildings which had been here. Following the tradition of raising of buildings of classicism in the city historical environment, the temple was constructed in such a way that it did not suppress with its monumental order forms, but only completed the historically formed ensemble of the monastery, ad-ding a more significant scale to it and making it more expressive.

The planning and volumetric-spatial design of Troitskiy (of the Holy Trinity) cathedral war determined in many ways of its rather complicated location in the irregular space of the monastery – in an open central square to the right from the Holy Gates. This predetermined the creation of the freely installed volume intended for the round observation. Beauvais designed a cross-cupola centric construction with similar composition of the faзades, finished with a cupola. Wide and high staircases leading to the Doric porticos, added to the stern and closed, at first sight, building, openness and democratism. The cathedral looked with its eastern one-apse faзade at the western part of the central irregular square, where the main monastery dominants were situated (the Holy gates with the above-gate church of St. Symeon Stylites and the church of the Saint Fathers of the Seven Ecumenical Councils, the buildings of the first half – the middle of the 18th century). The porticos, more expressive in respect of the town-building aspect, were situated on the side faзades of the cathedral and were not the main theme of the ensemble, being observed during the movement around the temple. In difference to the vertical volumes of the other buildings of the monastery, the cathedral was not high and was designed in emphasized horizontal proportions (extended along the transversal axis of the building along the square). At the same time, the cupola on the high drum, not connected very much with the main volume of the temple, at first sight, was in harmony with the verticals of the other buildings, and the classical cubicles on its drum, which were not characteristic at all for a Moscow temple, brought additional scale and make the cupola more complying to the baroque tops of the architectural dominants of the monastery.

Simultaneously with Troitskiy cathedral the parish church of the Resurrection "Slovutschee" was built according to the project of F. M. Shestakov behind the walls of the monastery, close to it in style. Being visually connected with Troitskiy cathedral, it "supported" with its forms Beauvais' building in the style of classicism and matched the monastery with the city buildings.

Ben-tower of the monastery of the Nativity of the Theotokos (1835-1836, architect N. Kozlovskiy) and the church of St. Nicholas in Zvonari (1762-1781, architect K. Blank). Photo. 1880s.

Church of the Intercession in Krasnoe village. Photo. 1880s.

Additional constructions of Moscow temples evidently prevailed over new constructions. Most often new refectories and bell-towers were additionally built at the old buildings of the temples. But this phenomenon was prevailing only from the point of view of the typology of church construction itself. From the point of view of the territory the construction of church buildings, their reconstruction and additional construction, were going on homogeniously in all the territory of the ancient capital, bounded by the Camer-Collezhskiy bank. The Kremlin was the only exception, where reconstruction work was going on at that time.

The bell-towers of the after-fire Moscow represented not only the spread, but most traditional type of church construction. The types of bell-towers which were characteristic for the second half of 18th century, prevailed: two, three or four tiers of tetrahedrons; tier-like bell-towers, where tetrahedrons with cut corners or cylindrical volumes rose above the low tiers of tetrahedrons. Only one bell-tower is known, all the tiers of which consisted of cylinders – it was the bell-tower of the church of St. Spyridon in Spiridonovka street.

Refectories of Moscow temples, which were constructed additionally at more ancient buildings together with bell-towers or without them, belonged to two variations. One of them repeated the style more spread in the second half of the 18th century: not high extended volumes with rounded corners, independence of which was accentuated by a portico of columns and pilasters, situated in their centre (the church of the Resurrection "Slovutshec" in Uspenskiy Vrazhek street; the church of the Smolensk Icon of the Theotokos at the corner of Smolenskaja street and Pljutschikha street and others).

A new variation – a refectory with right angles and a bell-tower block cut inside its volume – was a harder and more lapidary combination of its volumes. Both variants of refectories were used not only in additional constructions at the existing temples, but during full renovation or new construction. The first type included the refectory of the church of the Holy and Life-giving Trinity in Vishnjaky, built in 1815-1826, at the corner of Pjatnitskaja street and Vishnjakovskiy lane; the second type included the refectories of the churches of the Icon of the Theotokos "The Joy of All the Afflicted" in Kolomenskaja-Yamskaja settlement (today's Dubininskaja street); of the Resurrection "Slovutschee" in Danilovskaja settlement (Sredniy Starodanilovskiy lane, consecrated in 1837); the church of Sts. Athanasius and Cyril in Aksakov lane (No.35); the same was the refectory and its connection with the bell-tower of the church of St. Nicholas in Tolmachi (both these parts of the temple were built according to the project of F.M. Shestakov, 1833-1834).

There wan certain naturalness in various compositions. Creation of compositions inclined to the modes and schemes spread in the second half of the 18th century, took place during the first after-war years; appearance of new compositions, those, which some scientists would like to define as of the Empire-style, took place in the second half of 1820s and in 1830s years. The same naturalness was found in the composition of the temples themselves.

Well proportioned volumes of extended pillar-like form were created due to the fact that the diameter of the cupola was equal to the side which was square on the church's plan (for example, the church of the Seventh Ecclesiastical Council of the Saint Fathers near Novodevichiy monastery in Big Tsaritsynskaja street, 1813-1818; the church of St. Nicholas in Koteljniki in the First Koteljnicheskiy lane, 1822-1824, O. Beauvais).

Through a strange coincidence no church crowned with a cupola without a drum, remained, they belonged to the type which spread widely in Moscow exactly during the after-fire period. The contrast between the heavy lapidarity of the temple's volume and the well-proportioned bell-tower with its rising volume was especially expressive in such buildings (the church of Rzhev Icon of the Theotokos in the modern street Gritsevets; the church of St.Tychon, bishop of Amathus, near Arbatskie gates

Church of the Theophany in Elokhovo (1837-1845, architect E.D.Tjurin). Photo. 1880s.

in Arbatskaja square; of the Resurrection "Slovutschee" in Malaja Bronnaja street; of the Holy Trinity in the Fields; of St. Sophia in Sofiyka; of St. Nicholas "Moskvoretskiy" in former Moskvoretskaja street). The churches of the Ascension "Bolshoe" in Bolshaja Nikitskaja street or of St. John the Theologian "Under the Elm" on Novaja square belong to the type of church, most spread in the second half of the 18th and beginning of the 19th centuries, with a cubic volume crowned with a cupola on a drum. They are different from earlier temples with emphasized strictness and geometric volumes, big heroic dimensions.

The construction of big five-cupola temples of cathedral type was a new phenomenon in temple-building in Moscow in early 19th century, For the first time they appeared in the ancient capital after the middle of the 17th century, if not to take into account only one exception, which only confirms the general rule – construction in the middle of the 18th century of the church of Hieromartyr Clement, pope of Rome, in Klimentovskij lane.

Under the influence of the cathedral of Christ the Saviour, approved for construction, and of the cathedral of St. Isaac in 1830s in Moscow two huge churches of cathedral type were built – one in the district of Yauza's Moscow, in Elokhovo – the church of the Theophany, the second, as monumental as the first one, church of St. Sergius of Radonezh in Rogozhskaja zastava, in Nikolojamskaja street. Construction of the latter and specialities of its architecture were the result of the same considerations as those which in their time gave life to the composition and character of the architecture of the church of St. Martin the Confessor and the bell-tower of the monastery of St. Andronicus – the nearness of the district of old believers in Rogozhskaja zastava and the complex of Rogozhskoe cemetery, with monumental buildings of witch orthodox temples were to compete. Besides that, orientation at the ancient Russian inheritance showed in the latter temples built in the style of classicism, like in the baroque temples of Petersburg of Elizabeth's time, the orientation comprehended within the framework of general European style like it was in the architecture of baroque. Probably, it was one of the ways, in which the turn to the national roots and the nationality and the transfer from the Christian universalism, characteristic for the second half of the 18th century – beginning of the 19th century, to understanding of the value speciality of orthodoxy, began to appear from the time of certification of the new project of the cathedral of Christ the Saviour.

Triumphal Arch.

In the 18th – the first half of the 19th centuries, before railways appeared, entrance into the city was controlled at frontier posts. An ensemble of a frontier post consisted of guards premises, situated at tile sides of a road, and the road itself was usually flanked by columns in the shape of obelisks. In this way the majority of the city frontier posts of the second half of the 18th – beginning of the 19th centuries looked. The same was Tverskaja frontier post (zastava).

The patriotic war of 1812, its importance in the history of Russia and Moscow got a different expression in various buildings of Moscow. The memory about them was consolidated in creation of sacrariums and a cycle of icons consecrated to the biggest events of the war which happened on the days of veneration of the Saints or the holidays, on which these events happened. It was consolidated in the construction of the temple-memorial, devoted to the banishment of the French out of Russia – the cathedral of Christ the Saviour (its project was certified in 1832), in creation of Alexandrovskiy garden, the Manĭge, the memorial to Minin and Pozharskiy, finally, squares-forums – Teatralnaja and Red Squares. But besides the cathedral of Christ the Saviour and the church of Great Martyr Paraskeva of Iconium, besides the ensembles and buildings, the architecture and decoration of which were contemplated as memorial ones, a special memorial civil construction was raised in the after-fire Moscow -the Triumphal arch. The place for them near Tverskaja frontier post was not chosen by chance. The special importance of Tverskaja street and Petersburg highway, as the final and starting points of the road connecting both capitals, was mentioned many times.

The idea of construction in Moscow of the Triumphal arch as a memorial of the Victory belonged to emperor Nicholas I. In April of 1826 during the coronation celebration in Moscow he expressed the wish to build a Triumphal arch in the capital, like the one which was raised in Petersburg during that time: architect V. P. Stasov renewed the wooden Triumphal arch of G. Quarenghi near Narvskaja frontier post, using durable materials, the arch was built in 1814 on Peterhof road for the meeting of the glorious Russian army, coming back from Europe, and which became a symbolic embodiment of the Victory of Russian armoury in the Patriotic war of 1812 for many years.

Exactly because of this in the project of the Moscow arch the compositional scheme of this construction was used, at the basis of which Titus' arch was, one of the best memorials of Ancient Rome. It was a one-bay arch, with six pairs of columns, supporting a complicated entablature, crowned with a high attic with a sculpture group of Glory on a chariot.

The initial project was certified by the highest authority on 4th of November,1827. However, the accidental installation of this monumental construction in the outskirts, outside the city environment, near the frontier post marked by two obelisks and the houses of cordeguardians did not comply with its denomination of a memorial to the Victory. In connection with this Moscow military governor-general prince Golitsyn submitted a proposal to the Commission for Construction: "Before giving the order to build the arch, I suppose it is necessary to offer the Commission for Construction in Moscow a drawing and a project showing how it would be better and more convenient to arrange the direction of the highway to Tverskaja street and in what way to arrange this street, so that . . . the entrance corresponded to the splendour of the above-said gates".[12]

Thus composed "Offer of the project of the square for the Triumphal arch instead of Tverskaja frontier post" stipulated creation of a gala square constructed on a regular basis of classicism, as well as regulation and comfortable arrangement of all the neighbouring territory. The Triumphal arch with new cordeguards were to become the centre of the composition.

On 17th of August, 1829, a gala ceremony of foundation of the memorial took place. A bronze foundation board was laid into the foundation of the arch, the board had the following inscription: "Upon the order of now successfully reigning Emperor Nicholas Pavlovich, who assented during his stay in Moscow in 1826 to express his Most High will that a Triumphal arch will be arranged in front of Tverskoy entrance as a sign of commemoration of the victory of the Russian soldiers in 1814 and reconstruction of the capital city of Moscow with splendid memorials and buildings, as it was destroyed in 1812 during the invasion of the Gauls and twelve (as it is indicated in the source – Z. P.) tongues, this Triumphal arch was founded".[13] The construction of the Triumphal arch was appreciated by the Muscovites as a big national affair. The means, required for the construction, exceeded significantly the sum allocated by the government. So they were additionally remitted both from the City Duma and from citizens. Opening of the arch took place in five years – on 20th of September, 1834 – on the twentieth anniversary of the end of the Patriotic war. Though, as count Buturlin remembered later, "metropolitanate Philaret who was invited to sanctify the arch, refused to do it for the reason that he would have had to sanctify mythical gods, goddesses and the like".

For the facing of the arch made in brick, tatarovskiy white stone was used. The other parts – columns, entablature, sculpture – were made of cast iron. The contrast of colours and variation of materials, complex entablature and rich Corinthian order, lofty structure of the sculptural decoration – all this contributed to the impression of gala elated mood and heroic character of the image. The sculpture, an organic part of a memorial's artistic image, opened its ideological contents in allegorical forms. Figures of antique soldiers were placed between the columns, the entablature was finished skilfully by allegorical women figures – Firmness and Courage, supporting the vertical row of columns; the figure of the trumpeting Glories above the arch were full of surprising grace, the Glory's chariot crowned the composition – six horses with a winged goddess holding laurels. This magnificent equestrian statue was cast according to Beauvais' drawing, the author of the project. All the huge volume of the sculptural decoration was implemented by the sculptors I. Vitali and I. Timofeev.

Tile beautiful bas-relieves in the piers are interesting – "The Banishment of the French" and " Liberated Moscow". In these relieves, similar to antique ones, the Kremlin wall, the bell-tower of John the Great, Moscow Emblem, figures in Russian national costumes were shown, and the antique warriors had beards, ancient Russian hauberks, lances and helms with sharp tops. The ideals of classicism of state patriotism and the immortality of antique samples were changed and substituted in Russian art by the ideas of the national character and the national.

An original decision to this respect was found by Beauvais, building into the rich ornamental bas-relief frieze of the order the military armour and the emblems of thirty six domains of Russia, the inhabitants of which participated in the Patriotic war of 1812, as well as the monogram of emperor Nicholas I, on whose initiative this memorial was created. The inscription on the attic was approved by Nicholas I. It stated: "To the blessed memory of Alexander I, who raised from ashes and adorned with many memorials this capital city with his fatherly care, during the invasion of the Gauls and twelve tongues with them, burnt by the fire of 1812, 1826".

And it should be mentioned that experts and connoisseurs of Moscow architecture thought that "The Triumphal arch with its cold and gala beauty was far from the traditions of Moscow classicism".

The Triumphal arch was connected with two small cordeguards made in the style of Moscow mansions of the after-fire Moscow, by small grilles installed in a semi-circle. Being turned wiith their Doric porticos in the direction of the street brought out forward to the city, together with the arch they created a three-part composition and not only created with their ensemble a gala entrance into the ancient capital but finished beautifully the perspective of the city main street – Tverskaja, going from the Kremlin.

Contrast combination in the ensemble of big and small orders, characteristic for Beauvais, allowed the Triumphal arch to be in harmony both with the large space of the city and with the small buildings of the street, introducing it organically into the structure of the city.

Construction of the Triumphal arch turned out to be a big town-building event: a new regular square was planned, spontaneous buildings around the frontier post were demolished, "for the symmetry" the square on both sides was built around with houses having similar forms of fasades designed by Beauvais. Along Camer-Collegeskiy bank the houses were also constructed along the "projected" lines. The open canal coming to the new square, was substituted with a stone one with s brick vault.

Simultaneously with the square the Petersburg road was well arranged, the square and part of the road were paved, trees were planted at both sides, alleys were arranged, bridges and passages, which composed "continuous splendour" up to Peter's Palace itself. Tverskaja-Jamskaja streets were planned too: they were made of 10 sajens wide, with side-walks, paved, bordered at one side with barriers for street trade. It was presume to build beautiful houses and stores on the other side of the street.

The Triumphal arch together with the square composed a city ensemble which initiated a comfortable arrangement of a large territory.

Moscow Mansion and City Estate.

Moscow mansion of the after-fire period was as bright and unrepeatable national phenomenon as a rich nobility house of Kazakov's school in Moscow in the second half of the 18th century.

Dwelling buildings of the city, almost completely renovated after the fire, was one of the sights of the architecture of the after-fire Moscow. This capacious notion acquired in the home architectural knowledge the character of a term. The idea about the specialities of Moscow architecture and the look of the after-fire Moscow was connected with it. The term "after-fire Moscow" with its complicated and various content can be compared with the definition of Petersburg of early 19th century as "Pushkin's", and if to speak about Moscow of the previous period, it can be defined as "Kazakov's Moscow".

When they say, that the look of the after-fire Moscow was defined by a mansion, they mean that the character of the leading type of a dwelling house was changing. Reconstruction of Moscow after the fire resulted mainly in reconstruction of its dwelling houses. "...Moscow streets, due to 1812 are younger than Moscow beauties, still flourishing with roses", – Pushkin wrote.

The Moscow mansion was the main house of a city estate. The change of the definition of the leading type of a building reflected the change of the character of the architecture. The main builders in the ancient capital of the beginning of the 19th century became the middle and small gentry and rich merchants. It does not mean that the construction of large estate complexes with front yards and rich houses of palace type, brought out to the street red line. But the type of a rich dwelling house, which formed in the second half of the 18th century, continued to exist as though under its own momentum. The after-fire period did not introduce principal changes neither into the planning of the estate ensemble, nor into its composition. Only stylistic specialities of buildings' architecture, the character of the order and adornment changed.

On the contrary, the Moscow mansion, though taking the specialities of small nobiliary houses of the second half of the 18th century, grew into an independent type, and due to clear individual features and wide spreading it became not only a new, but a mostly spread type of dwelling buildings.

At the same time in the after-fire Moscow the construction of estates with rich houses of palace type was sharply reduced. The majority of them was the result of additional construction or reconstructions of buildings and estate ensembles, started during the after-fire period, or reconstruction of the complexes of the 18th century. Those were the estates, situated in the prestigious streets: tile former estate of L. K. Razumovskiy (later – the

N. Gagarin's house in Novinskiy boulvard (1817, architect O. Bove; destroyed in a bombardment during the second world war). Photo. Early 20th century.

English club), the estate of A. N. Soymonov in Bolshaja Dmitrovka near the Garden Ring, the estate of Lopukhina near Chistoprudny boulevard, which in 1816-1822 acquired the look characteristic for the early 19th century.

However, the houses of palace type were constructed again during that time too in the districts of especially intensive estate construction – most often in boulevards and in radial streets. The examples of it can be the houses, standing in the depth of the front yards, of general A. A.Tuchkov in Ostozhenka street (architect A. C. Grigorjev), of S. S. Gagarin in Povarskaja street, the estate in Volodarskiy street, 16.

According to the palace scheme with a front yard in front a house or just in the depth of a yard buildings of mansion type of relatively modest dimensions, were constructed. Sometimes, like in the case of the famous property of N. S. Gagarin in Novinskiy boulevard, an estate ensemble in decreased size recreated the classical estate scheme mostly not of a city, but country type – the main house with semi-circular wings in the depth of the yard. One of the wings was only decorative and built only for the symmetry of all the composition, being only a decorative wall connecting the mansion with two outbuildings brought out to the street red line. The compositional scheme of a riche estate house was used too: the central part was accentuated by an attic with a semi-circular window decorated with figures of flying Glories at the sides . The chamber style of this small ensemble was combined with the representativeness and monumentality typical for the architecture of that time.

The former thoroughfares of Bely and Zemljanoy towns, turned into gala highways, became the place for construction of about most famous and remarkable representative ensembles. It was the Lunins' estate (Nikitskiy boulevard), the above-said house of N.S. Gagarin in Novinskiy boulevard, the house of Z. Rjasovskaja in Prechistenskiy boulevard, the house of architect F.K. Sokolov in Pokrovskiy boulevard, the Usachevs' house in Zemljanoy bank.

The type of estate complexes with houses brought out to the street red line, certainly, prevailed during the after-fire time. That was the reason why Moscow was called the city of mansions.

The third type of estate house, spread in the second half of the 18th century and situated on a corner plot, war mostly changed. The houses with rounded corners and, mainly, with the faзades made symmetrically in relation to the corner part, which got the role of a portico, were rare. The cases when this composition was used, were practically singular. A rounded corner stopped being the compositional basis of a building, each faзade was made independently in conformity with the stylistic norms of the after-fire Moscow, when each faзade got its own finished composition. As for the building's configuration, it was usually taken from the old building, as it was, for example, during the construction of the house of merchants Zaborovs in Yauzskaja street. This novelty was typical for all corner buildings regardless if the estate was located in a nobility district (Steingel's house in Gagarinskiy lane) or in a merchant one (the above-said house of the merchants Zaborovs in Yauzskaja street, 1).

Such buildings were in the new districts of prestigious nobility constructions, in the main "nobiliary" streets of the after-fire Moscow. In Prechistenka street one of the most famous Moscow mansions – Khrutschev's house (Prechistenka, 12; the corner of Khrutscevskiy lane) had two similar gala faзades with porticos in the centre of each, which were, however, significantly different in the composition. The same phenomenon was encountered in the old "nobiliary" district of Bely town near Maroseyka (the house of I. V. Lavrentjev, Sverchkov lane, 4; the corner of Devjatkin lane) and in the merchant districts of Zamoskvorechie behind the Yauza. In the corner house in 1st Golutvinskiy lane (No.8/10) the faзade in this lane was adorned with a pilaster portico, which accentuated the higher central part (the 2nd floor and the attic), and the faзade in the 2nd Golutvinskiy lane was made plane as it was spread in construction of merchant houses. The same was the house of merchant H. G. Popov in Ljalin lane, 10; the corner of Barashevskiy lane.

A.S.Sytin's house (Sytinskiy lane, 5). 1806.
Before-fire mansions, which became a sample for many similar buildings of after-fire period.

With this universalism of the initial scheme of Moscow mansions: a symmetrically constructed street faзade with the central part accentuated by a portico or a rizalit, or a rizalit with a portico, they are remarkably different. The simplest mansions – one floor with seven or nine windows on the faзade with a columned portico (four or six columns, sometimes pilasters), finished with a triangular pediment. The same houses were often built, but with an attic, where portico's columns occupied not only the height of the ground floor, but of the attic, houses with attics crowning the terraces of balconies, were spread in the same way. There were often two-storey houses too, when a portico was raised on the archy socle or the standing out part of a rizalit of the ground floor. A variation of this composition was a two-storey house with an attic, where portico's columns and pilasters were situated at the height, of the second floor and the attic.

Absolute majority of mansions was constructed on the basis of the above-mentioned schemes. Smarter, less strict compositions, were also spread. The faзades of the mansions with porticos in the centre are meant, the columns of which supported not the straight beam of the architrave, but the arcade. This mode was found on the mansions of nobiliary districts in Arbat and Prechistenka lanes (the above-mentioned house of Steingel in Gagarinskiy lane, 15; the house of A. G. Tschepochkin in Spasopeskovskiy lane, 6) and in merchant Zamoskvorechie (the house in Bolshaja Poljanka street, 53 and on Kozmodemjanskaja quay).

Another novelty not known in Moscow before the fire: construction of absolutely similar houses near each other, the mere identity of which allows to see a relatively small part of a street as a compositional centre of the street space adjoined to it. This mode was used during designing of big three-storey buildings of palace type (houses 16 and 18 in Pjatnitskaja street) and small one-storey mansions (the houses in the same street 44 and 46). It was used during construction both in different properties and on one plot (the houses in Rozhdestvenskiy boulevard, 13 – two-storey ones, with a four-columned portico of the second floor, connected by a fence with the gates in the centre).

Merchant houses represented a whole number of variations too. Buildings were constructed so that they could not be distinguished from mansions: a faзade coming out on the street, with columned and pilaster porticos or with a decorative composition. Houses with orderless faзades were equally spread, their faзades had three-part compositions with accentuated height, a rizalit and a decoration of the central part. The houses situated in crowded trade places with stores on the ground floor, as a rule, were built with two storeys (the second floor was used as a dwelling). They were notable for their long extent and equal distribution of accents.

The type of a petty bourgeois house with its architectural specialities was close to the most modest type of a merchant house

The Taneevs' house in Small Vlasjevskiy lane. 1820.
Wooden mansion built according to one of sample projects of dwelling houses, published in 1809-1812.

with a store on the ground floor (a rustic ground floor, window openings without casings and decorative elements, a smooth orderless facade, equal distribution of accents). These modest faзades, the simplest in their composition, had the prototypes in wings of rich houses in their most modest variant.

However, regardless of the specialities of the composition of separate buildings and even of making Moscow buildings look more "city-like" during the after-fire period (the quantity of the houses brought out to the street red line increased sharply), construction in both capitals was developing in opposite directions. In Petersburg within the city borders a tendency appeared to increase the height of buildings up to maximum dimensions allowed by the construction law of the Northern capital. In Moscow, on the contrary, the quantity of floors and dimensions of the leading types of buildings including a Moscow mansion, during the after-fire period showed a stable tendency to decreasing, combining in itself in a surprising way a chamber style with big dimensions and laconism of separate buildings.

In difference from Petersburg, where "a house became the city's function in the sense of town-building, in Moscow, on the contrary, a separate estate remained primary: *the city as a whole was as though a function of the latter*". In this speciality of buildings of the after-fire Moscow the ancient Russian town-building traditions with its primacy of volume in respect of the space cannot be missed, transformed by the requirements of regularity and the world view of the New time. Separated buildings allowed in Moscow, relative freedom in the choice of height and the dimensions of buildings conditioned the domination of estate buildings and, which was most important, its visual signs were kept, which were expressed in relative independence of the composition of each estate provided its main buildings were brought out to the street red line. Due to it and also due to the fact that separate buildings were situated freely at a distance (often at a considerable distance from each other) a feeling appears of independence and significance of each building and also of its inclusion into the ensemble of the street and concordance with its direction and width. This connection was in the frontality of the compositions, in their openness to the street, in subordination of the mode of location of buildings in respect of the direction and width of the street.

During all the 19th century the Moscow city landscape preserved the chamber and partially patriarchal character which had established during the after-fire period. The location and not big dimensions of Moscow buildings made Moscow an antipode of Petersburg – the most "city-like" city of Russia, which lived through the process of expedited and often forced "urbanization" due to the decrees of 1760s.

In the after-fire Moscow many specialities remained viable, which were characteristic for its buildings during the period of classicism of the second half of the 18th century. Due to the picturesqueness of the relief with big differences of heights and plenty of far away points (both were taken from ancient Russian town-building with its characteristic choice of a place for a town, specifics of location of accentuated buildings) mansions and petty bourgeois houses were contemplated in the architecturally organised space of the city not only as a plane, forming the space, but as a volume too. It is not possible to neglect the "forty of forties" of Moscow churches which rose in sacred places and fixed from the point of view of the contents and the compositions most important places of the spatial structure of the ancient capital. For the look of a Russian historical town, which Moscow was, the contrast of the ideal world of classicism and the naturally and historically formed city landscape was rather important. Classicism always was opposed the problem of "the natural", on the one, and "the correct", "more perfect than the nature itself", on the other. Depending on a concrete case, it was settled differently in the forms and the modes, but synonymously in the essence – according to the principle of the contrast and contraposition.

In the estate ensemble it was shown as a contrast between the geometrical rightness of the space near the house and "the natural" picturesqueness of the park. The contrast between the ideal space of the world of streets and squares, front yards, faзades and city panoramas opening from a building or a street, estate yard or a garden, from the windows, a belvedere, an attic, corresponded to it, Contraposition and opposition of the regular and picturesque, gala and ordinary or landscape space, their coexistence, but no merging, is the general law of classicism, its ideal line, because life is always richer than a scheme. Everywhere when it was possible, architects of classicism tried to introduce "order" and "correctness" into the spontaneously forming city landscape. It was organized like a composition of a classical picture or a scenic platform interpreting it as a background bounded by new buildings. The same happened during organization of the views opening from separate buildings, streets and squares, from park pavilions and from park paths of Moscow city estates. In difference to Petersburg the after-fire Moscow was called, not by chance, the city of mansions. Placed along the red line, they did not join together in "an entire faзade" according to Petersburg sample, but were located separately from each other. Not high fences between them with various gates together with the verdure of the gardens made the streets picturesque, and well observed free volumes of the houses brought spatial freedom into it, which was a distinguishing feature of Moscow buildings, its unrepeatable individuality. This picturesque architectural landscape of Moscow appeared because each mansion subordinated to the regular buildings of the street, being the main house of a city estate, preserved in a simplified form all the features characteristic for it. They were especially evident in relatively big estates.

Such estates include the estate of the Lunins in Nikitskiy boulevard a bright example of Moscow Empire, a gradual creation of D. Gilardi (1814-1818,1822).

It is difficult to imagine now that this ensemble, adorning one of the main city highways, is a part of an old city estate, hidden by these gala buildings. It still has the dimensions of the Poutjatins' old estate known from the second half of the 18th century. It is important to mention that during rebuilding of the estate, burnt in 1812, Gilardi created an absolutely new composition – he brought out the main house out of the depth of the plot and turned to the street line, the new gala highway of the Boulevard Ring.

It is also essential that in the asymmetrical composition of three buildings standing out on the highway, different in height, extent of the faзades and the character of the plastic development, Gilardi created an ensemble which was surprising in its freedom and picturesqueness; he opened the beauty not only of the harmonical interconnection of separate classical buildings, but more complicated and fine contemplation of them from different points while approaching the house along the boulevard. By this mode Gilardi, an unsurpassed master of classical architectural forms, anticipated the specialities of the ensembles of romanticism, the next stage of development of Russia architecture.

In 1829 according to the project of D. Gilardi the estate of the Usachevs was built near Zemljanoy bank, probably the only ensemble which from the very beginning of its creation got the name of "estate". At the same time, no other estate of Moscow was connected with the city in so many ways. With a surprising mastery the features characteristic only for a city building as a part of a street ensemble, combines in its composition with development of the traditions of Russian town-building art: in the composition of the park situated on the high picturesque slope of the river Yauza, in the opening of the ensemble in the vast space of the city, on the picturesque river banks, at the distances on the other side of the river and high dominants of the memorials. In this dialogue of the ensemble with the architectural landscape of the city, surrounding it, the whole image of Moscow was formed unrepeatable in its beauty and expressiveness. Besides the mastery use of the system of order modes of classicism – from the monumental portico of the main house to the lyrical pavilions of the park – add a surprising wholeness to the ensemble.

A city estate defined in many ways the look of the after-fire Moscow. It made a great influence on the individuality of the Moscow architectural school of that time, and in a wider sense – stimulated the formation of the national school of Russian classicism, which was acknowledged world-wide.

[1] Labom E. Intrusion into Moscow. Quoted after: Kovalevskiy M.N. Moscow in the history and literature. M., 1916, p. 232.
[2] Bulletin of Napoleon I No. 20. Quot. after: History of Moscow. M., 1953. V. Ill, p. 109.
[3] Correspondence of emperor Alexander Pavlovich with count F. Rastopchin. Ouot. after: Fire of Moscow. After the memoirs and correspondence of contemporaries. M., 1911, part 1, p. 97.
[4] Moscow, or historical guide-book of the famous capital of the Russian State. M.,1831, part Ill, p. 270-271.
[5] Journal of Fine Art. SPb., 1825, book 2, p. 78-81.
[6] Moscow, or historical guide-book of the famous capital of the Russian State. M.,1831, part Ill, p. 108.
[7] As above, p. 131.
[8] Taranovskaja M. Z. Carl Rossi. M., 1980, p. 155.
[9] Moscow, or historical guide-book of the famous capital of the Russian State. M.,1843, p. 108.
[10] Moscow domain records. 1843, p.520.
[11] Notes of academician Vitberg, the builder of the cathedral of Christ the Saviour in Moscow // Russian antiquity. 1872. Vol.V., p.180.
[12] CIAM, f. 163, op. 2, d. 41, 1. 1.
[13] Quot. after: Sobolev N.N. Triumphal arches in Moscow // Old Moscow. M., 18I4, p. 68-69.

The Khrutschevs' house in Prechistenka street (1814, architect A.G.Grigoriev (?); today A. S. Pushkin' s museum).

CHAPTER FOUR
Two symbols of Moscow

Military parade in Ivanovskaja square. Artist V.S.Sadovnikov. 1851.

Moscow panorama. I.I.Sherleman's print. 1850s.

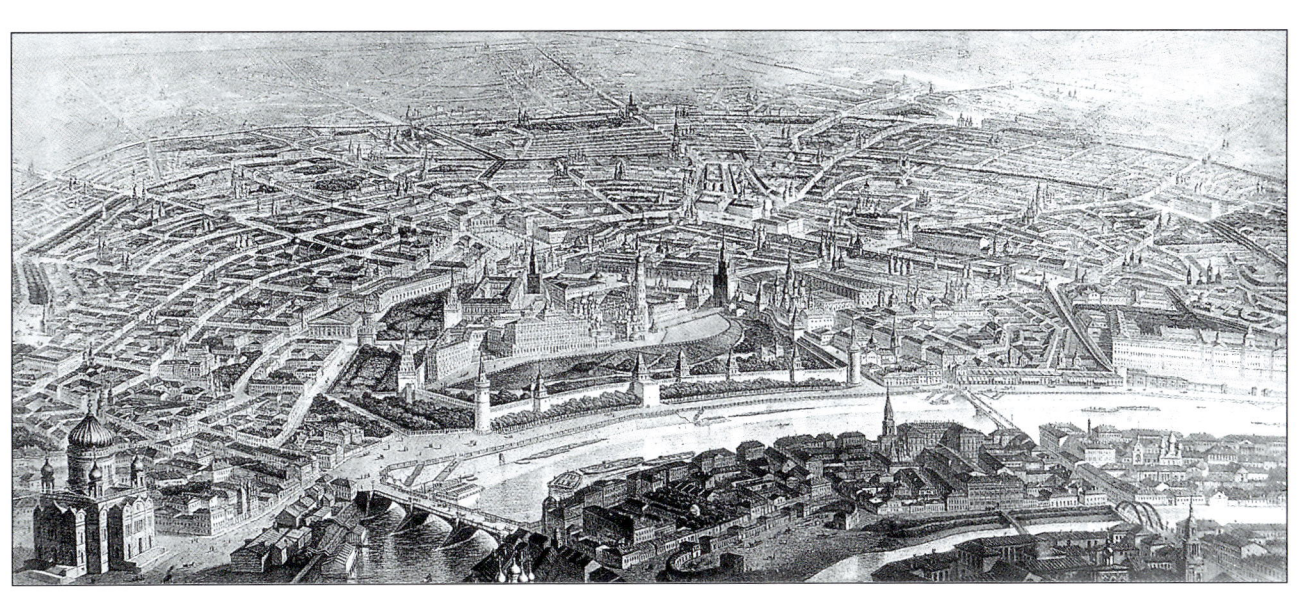

Emperor Nicholas I (1825-1855).

View of the Kremlin from Big Stone Bridge. There is the Kremlin Palace (1838-1849, architect K. Ton) and the Armoury (1841-1851, architect K. Ton). Lithography. 1896.

View from Voskresenskaja square (of Alexander's garden and the cathedral of Christ the Saviour. Lithography of A.Rudnev. 1860s.

View from the Kremlin 9f- the cathedral of Christ the Saviour (architect K.A.Ton, project of 1832, construction of 1839-1858). There is the Armoury on the right. Photo of I. Bartschevskiy. Early 20th century.

Nikolaevskiy (Petersburg) railway station in Kalanchevskaja square (1844-1851, architect K.A.Ton). View from Krasnoselskaja street.

Cathedral of Christ the Saviour. View from the Kremlin quay. Lithography of A.Rudnev. 1867.

Nikolaevskiy railway station and the customs house in Kalanchovskaja square. View from the Garden Ring. Lithography of Datsiaro from I. Sharleman's drawing. Middle of the 19th century.

Pokrovka street. There is the church of the Assumption in the foreground (1696-1699) and the church of the Holy Trinity "In Grjazi" behind it (1868, architect M.D.Bykovskiy). Photo. Late 19th century.

"Panorama of Moscow and its envipons", made from the bell-tower of John the Great. Lithography. Moscow – Paris. 1847.

Historical epochs and periods do not always have clear limits. Their determining in architecture is especially difficult. But anyway some dates are invariably thought of as the turning. For the history of Moscow architecture such turning years were the second half of 1820s – the first half of 1830s.

Here each detail is important. Moscow remained the city of the high nobility, the city of waste lands, gardens and vegetable gardens, full of contrasts between big buildings and village landscapes. But some principal novelties appeared which were very important architecturally and contextually.

The idea of "Moscow is the Third Rome" showed a surprising ability for transformation. It not only found a new life in Russia in the 18th – beginning of the 19th century.[1] It was revived and renewed in 1830-1860 in Moscow. It retained its viability, though gradually fading away, in the outskirts of the Empire – in Siberia, in the Far East till the beginning of the 19th century.

Tsargrad and Manchester.

Nicholas I, who took the throne at the end of 1825 after decease of Alexander I, was in the full sense an autocrat and a statesman. During all the emperor's or synodal period (which was the same) the reality was of such kind that it deserved the characteristic of the Landed Synod of 1917-1918: "for the emperor's period one shouldspeak not about orthodoxy, but tsaredoxy"[2].

Each Russian monarch, including Nicholas I, thought it was necessary to leave an architectural town-building memorial about his reign and to imprint his understanding of the historical destiny of Russia. The imperial state idea dominated in all town-building undertakings. Thus was the Greek project of Catherine II and her ideas about recreation of the centres of both capitals. Thus were the projects of Paul I, inspiredby the theocratic idea and non-acceptance of the ideals of the Great French revolution. They were similar to the state policy of Alexander I: creation of a system of squares-forums in the Russian capitals and turning of Petersburg's centre into not only a symbolical copy of the centre of Ancient Rome, but into the memorial of the Victory over Napoleon, who wanted to turn Paris into new Rome and into a memorial of his victories, including over Russia. And only during the reign of Nicholas I a certain return to the idea of "Moscow is the Third Rome" happened in the interpretation which was typologically similar to the ancient Russian one with its orientation at the second Rome – Constantinople and domination of the religious aspect over the state one. It was accompanied by the revival of the idea of Moscow – New Jerusalem. A turn happened which was cardinal since Peter's reign. In the ecclesiastical sphere it was connected with the renaissanceof orthodoxy; the sources of the religious renaissance of the turn of the 19th-20th centuries come from it.

The reign of Nicholas I was marked with creation of an original state version of the official policy in the area of architecture, where, like in the conception of Elizabeth's reign, autocracy was inseparable from orthodoxy, and both of them were inseparable from the revival of an ancient Russian architectural tradition. However, in difference to the middle of the 18th century the third necessary component of the architectural and town-building program of Nicholas I in accordance with appearance of new spiritual values was the nation. The renovation program of the centre of Moscow, following after the after-fire program, was determined by the complex of these ideas: the construction of the grandiose cathedral of Christ the Saviour, the complex of the Kremlin Palace with the Armoury and restored chambers and temples, renovation of the sacral space of both capitals, revival of the ancient Russian, orthodox tradition in temple construction, which meant the national Russian architecture then.

A number of symbolical likenings allowed to comprehend not only the centre of Moscow, but all the space of the ancient capital not only as Tsargrad, but as "Russian Zion", New Jerusalem.

Revival of the importance of not just Christian, but exactly orthodox aspect of the conception of "Moscow – the Third Rome", which in its turn was understood in the sphere of architecture as an expression of the Russian national idea, coincided with the coming of the new 19th century. Not only the chronological 19th century is meant here, which starred in 1800, but the 19th century as an independent historical period.

In Europe the historical 19th century began earlier than the chronological. It began in 1789 by the Great French revolution. For Russia the transition from the 18th century to the 19th was longer and, most important, of many stages. The frames of mind born by the Great French revolution did not pass by the Russian society and the Russianart either. But an especially strong impact was made on them by two turning events of Russian history – the Patriotic war of 1812 and the revolt of the Decembrists. The reaction to them was fixed in the formula of the official ideology of Nicholas' reign: "orthodoxy, autocracy, nation". The history was shown in it as a result of the interaction of orthodoxy, autocracy, nation.

N.A.Berdjaev wrote: "All revolutions were finished with reactions. It was inevitable. In any spiritual reaction to a revolution something new appears... the third, different from what was in the revolution, and from what was before the revolution... the main importance of the French revolution should be seen in the fact that in the early 19thcentury it gave rise to the catholic movement and the romantic movement, which inspired all the ideas of the 19th century... French catholicism of the 19th century was new, post-revolutionary catholicism... Shatobrian's christian romanticism was also a new post-revolutionary phe-

"Panorama of Moscow and its environs", made from the bell-tower of John the Great. Lithography. Moscow – Paris. 1847.

nomenon. The turn of "the reactionaries" of the early 19th century to the past and search for their roots in the medieval time was a creative turn and a creative search"[3].

The same thing happened in Russia. Orthodoxy of the 19th century was post-Decembrists orthodoxy. The turn to the medieval roots of the Russian culture was also new post-Decembrist. In Russia it was K.A.Ton who expressed this turn in architecture. According to his projects the program buildings, which were most important not only in Moscow, but in Russia, were constructed. With them the new period in renovation of the centre of the ancient capital, the new period in development of Moscow and Russian architecture, was connected.

The name of Ton became a common noun. For contemporaries Ton became a synonym of an architect, in whose workshop "the process of the world history was performed". The essence of the process was compared with revival of the nationality: "the highest purpose of the Russian art of our time is the nationality". The new turn in the art connected with the name of Ton, was the turn to the nationality and the nation. Ton'screation embodied the necessity understood as the most actual and burning, "to acquire our own nationality in art, our own character, which, keeping all its originality of invention and implementation, was striving towards the general harmony with European art"[4].

The national revival in architecture is inseparable from the religious and in 1830-1850 was related mainly with temple-building. It was fed from other sources and was connected with other tendencies in the spiritual life, than with "unofficial" types of art – literature, music, even in painting. Architecture continued to be a state-wide affair, was regulated and controlled by the government.

So, when they speak about Ton as about the father of the revival of the national in architecture, first of all the projects of his temples are meant. I.I.Svijazev wrote: he "created... the Russian church architecture". "I say straightway "Russian", – Svijazev continued, – because since long time Ton comprehended and was imbued by his spirit with the basis of this architecture"[5]. Ton became the first architect of the New Time in Russia, in whose creative work the first place was occupied by temples, if not in quantity, but in their importance. It became possible due to the fact that a certain revival of temple-building began in the middle of the 19th century. Not the quantity of constructed temples increased, though it was a fact. But the temple became the style-creating type of buildings. New tendencies in architecture were expressed more fully in it. Appearance of styles of the New Time in Russia was connected with the civil architecture before that time. Only in the romanticism the stylistic turn appeared and expressed itself earlier than ever in town-building and in genres relatively secondary for the classicism, connected with the ideal of a private man – in the estate and dwelling interior.

Thus, the most fundamental re-assessment of values since the time of the reign of Peter I, showed in art.

Revival of the nationality in architecture acquired the form of the revival of the orthodox temple type (i.e. an ancient Russian temple). It was conditioned semantically by the fact that Russian history, historical acknowledgement of Russia in the official and Slavophil doctrine were comprehended now through orthodoxy. Berdjaev wrote: "Russia's mission is to be the carrier and the guard of the true christianity, orthodoxy. It is a religious vocation. "The Russians" are defined by "the orthodoxy". Russia is the only orthodox kingdom and in this sense, the kingdom of the Universe like the first and the second Rome. Extreme nationalisation of the orthodox church happened on the basis of it. Orthodoxy turned out to be the Russian belief"[6].

Russia's national individuality, which had Byzantine roots, was defined by orthodoxy, according to the official ideology and Slavophils. Thus was the origin of the term "Byzantine style". The phenomenon itself, which was called by this term, its essence and the ways of expression in architecture were never occasional. All three aspects were interconnected and mutually conditioned. Romantic philosophy, aesthetics, historiosophia connect the individuality of each national culture with the individuality of its sources. In this context it becomes evident that the individuality of the Russian culture was conditioned by the fact that before Peter's time it belonged to Byzantine culture. The genetic roots of Russian culture demonstrated clearly its difference from the European one. But the same fact, emphasizing the uniqueness of Russian culture, testified clearly that it had much in common with the great cultural tradition, especially respected in Romanticism – with the ancient Greek branch of antique culture.

By the mouths of romantics Russian culture announced itself through Byzantium, the first heiress of Ancient Greece. Byzantium was called not only the second Rome, but new Greece, Constantinople – new Athens. Russia got the orthodoxy from Byzantium. The roots of Russian temple architecture came from Byzantium, as well as of the sphere of cultureconnected with the orthodoxy. The idea of "Moscow – the Third Rome" came from Byzantium. Belonging to the Byzantine cultural tradition, opposing Russia to European countries, emphasized the uniqueness of its culture – the quality which acquired the first priority in the system of values dominating in Europe of the 19th century, which appeared together with romanticism. The definition of Russian culture as Byzantine, by the use of the term itself, disclosed its special place in the culture of Europe: its inseparability and sovereignty.

But the term "Byzantine" did not emphasize only the originality of the sources of Russian culture. It was regarded simultaneously as an indication of the speciality of the Russian idea as the idea of orthodoxy.

"Panorama of Moscow and its environs", made from the bell-tower of John the Great. Lithography. Moscow – Paris. 1847.

Exactly this – the inseparability of the national idea from the confessional, the confessional as a symbol and expression of the national, unification in one notion of two most important symbols and values of romanticism pre-determined the appearance of the term "Byzantine" for the definition of that variation of Russian style in Russian art, with which Ton's name was connected.

Calling the Russian style "Byzantine", those who used this term were mistaken least of all in respect of the identity of the style, created in Russia in the middle of the 19th century, with the style of Byzantium. But the clear feeling of the Byzantine roots of the national culture, new rise of the national self-consciousness, renovation of Moscow, large scale of temple-building in Byzantine style, the adherents of which, I would like to emphasize it again, did not connect it in any way with direct copying of Byzantine constructions, – all this gives the reason to see in the intensively renovated Moscow in 1830-1860 – the Third Rome and the second Constantinople – Tsargrad.

New attitude to Moscow as to new Tsargrad brought in a new meaning in the city's look. Together with the traditional admiration of the city and village views combined in it, the admiration of its individuality, unsimilarity with other towns appeared. Till that time all town-building works in Moscow were inspired by the wish to amend the "incorrectness", irregularity of its planning, having a program character with orientation at European architectural practice. Since that time, though the regulation of Moscow plan still remained the supertask of town-building works, another tendency appeared in them – the effort to emphasize by the new construction its individuality and originality, to support and develop what was and became the history already. The task to continue and develop Moscow historical look was invariably connected with ancientpre-Petrine Moscow during 1830-1900.

For Zagoskin Moscow became the symbol of all national, an embodiment of all most characteristic and original. "Go up the bell-tower of John the Great in summer, look around, and you will not see the city in front of you, but a boundless green sea, poured around with buildings... it is not a praising trick, but the most true expression of the reality. Excluding the centre of the city, where buildings are mostly entirely everywhere you will seldom see a house without a small garden at least or without at least some bushes of acacia or elder. Everywhere there was some strange mixture of city comfort with village simplicity. There are flower gardens, vegetable gardens, ravines, hills, whole fields everywhere... This makes Moscow a true representative of all Russiawhich was not similar to all the Western states in the same way as Moscow was not similar to all European cities... to splendid Petersburg, to smart Berlin, to Paris, to any European city. It is wonderful with its own, unborrowed beauty"[7].

The beautiful in the aesthetics of romanticism is associated with picturesque, varied, unexpected, contrasting, and most important – national. New "discovery" of Moscow as the national historical capital of Russia, begins with romanticism. Zagoskin became one of its first praisers. "Like a thousand of sun rays join into one point, goingthrough a kindling glass, all separate features of our national face join in Moscow into one national look... in Moscow you will find the union of all elements composing the private and official life of Russia, this huge colossus, in which Petersburg is the head and Moscow the heart". Zagoskin does not stop admiring the panoramas, which enchant "with their luxury, beauty and surprising variety. The shallow Moscow-river and the tiny Yauza are not remarkable as rivers at all, but they have such picturesque banks". The picturesqueness of Moscow planning – its incorrectness and irregularity are comprehended now as the source of beauty of the Moscow architectural landscape. They add constant changeability to the picture opening in front of a traveller. At the entrance into Moscow from the side of the Vorobjovy hills "like in a magic opera the decorations constantly changed on this wide stage: at each turn, on each bending, of the hills Moscow got a new look"[8].

But this is one image of Moscow, which in half a century after Zagoskin made the author of the photo-album devoted to Moscow temples, to give it the title: "Moscow is Russia's Temple, and the Kremlin is the altar of this Temple"[9].

Simultaneously in 1830-1850 in the shadow of Moscow-Tsargrad another Moscow was developing – trade and industrial. Its representatives began to press the nobility from the height of the economic life and well-being and this was shrewdly noticed by A.S.Pushkin already in 1830s. He wrote: "Moscow, having lost its aristocratic glamour, is flourishing in other aspects: industry, strongly patronized, came to life and wasdeveloping in it with an unusual force. Merchants become rich and begin to inhabit the chambers left by the nobility. On the other hand, the enlightenment loves the city, where Shuvalov organized the University upon the outline of Lomonosov"[10].

Moscow turned into the centre of the intensively forming industrial district, specializing in textile production. Intensity of the development of the textile industry, growth of the quantity of factories and the rate of this growth give the reason to compare Moscow with Manchester – the industrial capital of England.

The essence of the crucial turn which happened during these years, was defined best of all by poet P.A.Vjazemskiy:

Here is a miracle – the landlord's chambers,
With the coat of arms, by which the noble family was crowned.
Huts on "hen's feet" near by.And a garden with cucumbers.
Poetry near trade, Manchester broke into Tsargrad.
Boilers steam with stench.
Paradise of sweet bliss and working hell.

"Panorama of Moscow and its environs", made from the bell-tower of John the Great. Lithography. Moscow - Paris. 1847.

Turning of Moscow into the focus of Russian industry, into Russian Manchester was noted by Zagoskin together with Pushkin and Vjazemskiy: "...in Moscow our artisan industry flourished... there are 198 different plants, 884 factories, artisan workshops,in total 4071, in Moscow. In them there are 70,209 workers, which is more than one fifth part of all Moscow inhabitants. It seems, after that Moscow, if it were not the ancient capital, could be rightfully called Russian Manchester (it was written in 1840)"[11].

Cathedral of Christ the Saviour

In 1832 the decree of Nicholas I was issued about renewal of construction of the vowed temple-memorial in the name of Christ the Saviour in Moscow. Breaking ground for the cathedral took place in 1839 during the gala celebration of the 25th anniversary of the entry of the Russian army into Paris. In 1858 the preliminary construction of the cathedral was finished. The scaffoldings were taken off, and the cathedral became an integral part of Moscow centre.

The cathedral of Christ the Saviour became a stage in the history of development of the ancient capital, in the history of Moscow architecture and in the history of the architecture of Russia. By the construction of the cathedral the turn in development of architecture in the direction opposite to the one which composed the main sense and inspiration of the regular architectural and town-building policy in the 18th – first quarter of the 19th centuries, began. In it the striving to continue and develop the individual features, which had been initially characteristic for the ensemble of the ancient capital, showed.

The change of the program of the cathedral of Christ the Saviour, conditioned by a significant consolidation of historicism and the wish to turn into a memorial of Russian history and a national temple-memorial, found its reflection also in the change of consecration of its sacrariums. The cathedral's sacrariums, designed by Vitberg, reflecteda complicated symbolics of its structure and the idea of the trine – God, man, likening of man to God. Or, quoting the words of Vitberg, represented "the ecclesiastical idea of a live temple" of man, his body, soul and spirit, following the words of Christ: "Know ye not that ye are the temple of God, and that the Spirit of God dwelleth in you?". So thesacrariums of the Temple were consecrated to three main events in Christ's life – the Nativity, the Transfiguration and the Resurrection.

Orientation at the classical inheritance and the striving to surpass the greatest of the temples of the catholic world – the cathedral of St.Peter in Rome – reflects the Christian universalism characteristic for the time of Alexander I. In Vitberg's project it was expressed in the consecration of the sacrariums and in the interpretation of the cathedral of Christ the Saviour as the cathedral which belonged to all the Christian world.

In the project, approved for the construction by Nicholas I, the opposite conception that the cathedral of Christ the Saviour belongs to the orthodox world and the wish to interpret it as a memorial of the event of universal importance, prevailed, but the event which took place within the borders of the history of Russia, the results of which were determined by the participation of Russia. So the central altar of the temple was consecrated to the Nativity of Christ. On that day the outcome of the war with Napoleon was finally decided. His troops left Russia. Two other sacrariums were consecrated to the Saint protectors of emperors Alexander I and Nicholas I – to St. Prince Alexander Nevskiy and St.Nicholas the miracle-worker. By this consecration the memorialimportance of the cathedral was emphasized. During the reign of the first of these emperors the events of the Patriotic war took place and the idea of creation of a temple-memorial appeared, during the reign of the second emperor this idea was realized. Already in the change of the consecrations of the sacrariums the new interpretation of the historical event was seen and the new attitude to the form of its immortalization. The vowed and memorial temples in Ancient Russia were usually consecrated to those Saints or holidays, on the day of which this or that memorable event happened. Applied to the cathedral of Christ the Saviour it seemed even more grounded and corresponding to the ancient tradition, and the manifesto about construction of the cathedral of Christ the Saviour was added by another one, issued in 1814. "The 25th of December, the day of the Nativity of Christ, shall be since now the day of thanksgiving celebration called in the church: the Nativity of Our Lord, God and Saviour Jesus Christ and commemoration of liberation of the church and the Russian Power from the invasion of the Gauls and with them twelve tongues".

The change of the program of the cathedral of Christ the Saviour resulted in the change of its location. It was decided to build the memorial to the greatest event in Russian history close to the Kremlin which invariably retained the importance of the historical symbol of Russia.

The place for the cathedral of Christ the Saviour was chosen by Ton. He, in his turn, followed the ideas of the competition conducted between Moscow architects and marked by its unanimity in the striving to change the location of the temple approved by Alexander I, choosing a new place for it, directly connected with the historical centre of Moscow – with the Kremlin[12].

Due to the lucky opportunity to arrive in Moscow Ton could, being based on his own observations, to present for the choice of the emperor three variants of the project of the temple's location in the city. All of them had something in common with the proposals of Moscow architects in the closeness to the historical centre of the ancient capital and the direct alignment with the Kremlin. Nicholas I inspected together with the architect all three places determined by him: behind the EducationalHouse, where there was the church of Martyr Nicetas "On Krucha" on the other side of the Moscow-river (the variant of O.I.Bove on the Shvivaja hill), in Tverskaya street in the place of the convent of the Passions – "one of the most high places of Moscow" (today it is Pushkinskaya square, a public garden with the cinema "Rossija", the variant similar to the project of F.M.Shestakov) and, finally, the place of the monastery of St.Alexius, which was near the Kremlin near the Big Stone bridge. The emperor preferred the latter.

In the variant offered by Ton, all the advantages of the place which could be chosen for the temple by his predecessors, were luckily combined: location on the high bank of the Moscow-river in direct closeness to the Kremlin and directly aligned with it. In February of 1832 because the previous place of the temple's location wascancelled a further acceptance of competition projects was stopped. And on 10th of April, 1832, the Holy Synod and Moscow military governor-general D.V.Golitsyn received from Nicholas I the instruction: "In the blessed memory of emperor Alexander I, inspired by the feeling of adoration and gratitude... ordered to construct in Moscow a Temple in the name of Christ the Saviour, a memorial which must be worth the greatevents of that time and the heart of the great Tsar.

In 1817 this temple was founded on the Vorobjovy hills, but insuperable obstacles, stopped the undertaking. Another, more convenient and proper place had to be chosen: such place was accepted by Us as the place occupied now by the convent of St.Alexius, as it is in the centre of the city and by its position is similar to the first place".[13]

The successful choice of the new place for the cathedral of Christ the Saviour, very Moscow like in its character – on the high bank of the Moscow-river, near the Kremlin, with the views opening at it and from it, the symbolical meaning of the connection between the temple and the Kremlin, are noted by everybody.

The churches which were in the place of the future cathedral, and then the cathedral of Christ the Saviour were an integral part in the panorama of the Moscow-river banks, whether it was the views from the Yauza and the monastery of St.Simon or from the opposite side – from the Entertainment Garden, the Vorobjovy hills or Zamoskvorechie. From the opposite side and along the Moscow-river the cathedral of Christ theSaviour was always seen together with the Kremlin and in direct connection with it. It was favoured by another, than today, location of the Big Stone Bridge, near which the temple was constructed. The old Big Stone bridge and the new metallic bridge, which changed it in the middle of the 19th century, were situated in another place different fromtoday's one, constructed in 1930s. It was higher by the flow of the Moscow-river on the axis of the street Lenivka. But most important, it was in a principally another alignment with the quay, as the bridge floor was situated on one level with its surface and was not partially closed by the bank span, like now. The space of the quay was seen asone whole, like a gala avenue. The cathedral finished the perspective and at the same time looked like an integral part of the quay which spread at the foot of the Kremlin and continued behind the cathedral of Christ the Saviour. A great merit of the place, chosen by Ton, was the splendid view at the Kremlin with the cathedrals, towers and the bell-tower of John the Great, which opened from the cathedral of Christ the Saviour and was very important for its symbolics and contents.

In the location of the cathedral of Christ the Saviour and its dimensions another additional aspect could be seen, specifying, significantly its contents and symbolics. Its location shows even more similarity with another Moscow holy thing – the cathedral of the Intercession (the cathedral of St.Basil), constructed in the middle of the 16th century in the memory of the subjugation of Kazan khanate. Symbolical similarity of the locations of both cathedrals was to emphasize the symbolical similarity of the meaning of the two temples as the memorials of military honour.

The symbolics of the dimensions is also extremely important. The grandiosity of the cathedral of Christ the Saviour and

View of the cathedral of Christ the Saviour and the Kremlin quay. Photo of I.F.Bartschevskiy. Early 20th century.

its undominating role in relation to the surrounding buildings, which at the moment of the designing remained one- or two-storey, was not a mistake, but a considered mode. Not complying in its dimensions to the nearest buildings, the cathedral of Christ the Saviour complied in its dimensions to the city and its biggest ensembles. By the contrasting dimensions the main idea of the project was achieved – hierarchy of the meanings. Incomparability of its dimensions not only with the dwelling houses, but with numerous Moscow churches and bell-towers is a symbol and an expression of its special ideological importance. The symbolics of the dimensions of the cathedral of Christ the Saviour shows itself in the relation between its height with the height of one of most famous holy things and the highest building in Moscow – the bell-tower of John the Great. In difference to Vitberg, whose dream was to surpass the main temple of the catholic world, the cathedral of Christ the Saviour, constructed according to Ton's project, was oriented at the national holy things. The bell-tower of John the Great, the description issued after the sanctifying of the cathedral of Christ the Saviour, said, "can be installed under the biggest cupola of the temple". It was the first and the only case in Moscow, if not

Comparison of the dimensions of the cathedral of Christ the Saviour and the main historical holy things of Moscow: the church of Christ the Saviour in Bor, the cathedral of the Assumption and the bell-tower of John the Great. N.V.Dmitriev's scheme. 1851.

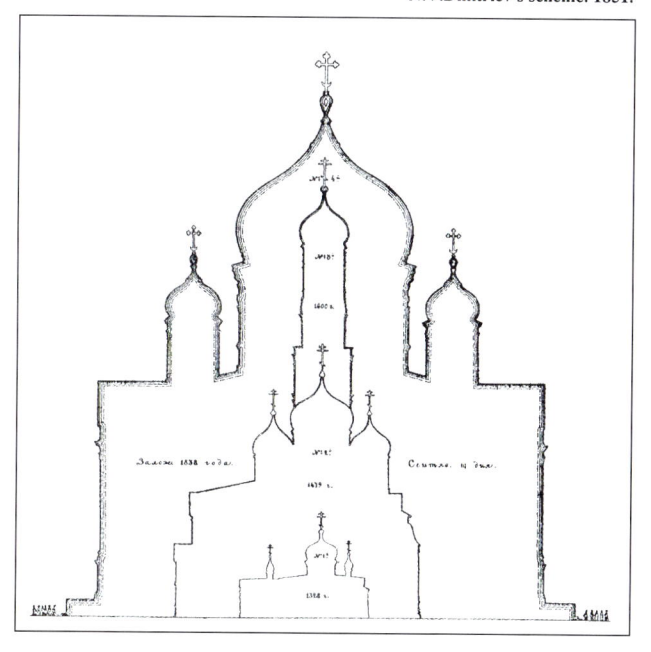

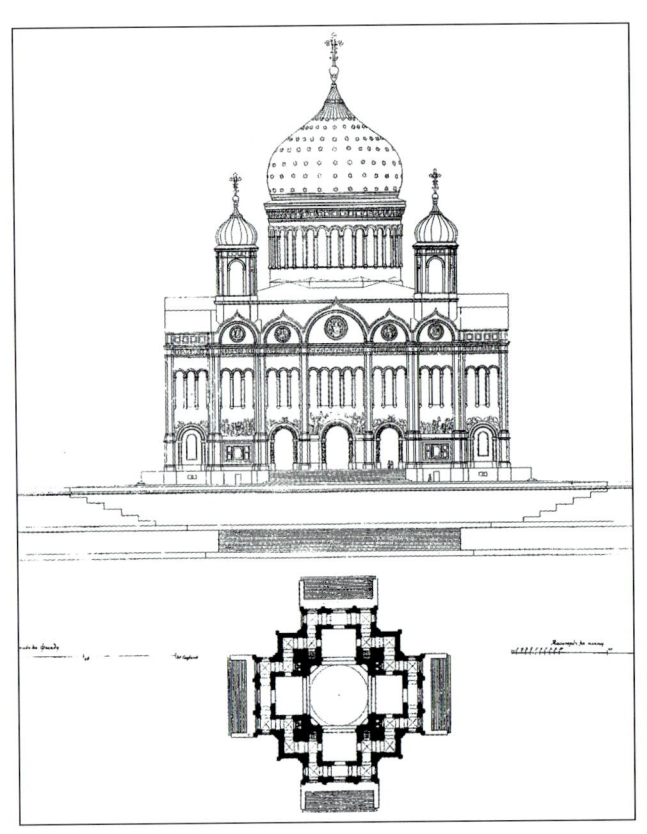

Project of the cathedral of Christ the Saviour (1832, architect K.A.Ton). Initial variant.

to take into account the burnt top of Menshikov's tower, when the emperor allowed creation of a temple higher than the bell-tower of John the Great.

Making corrections in the views and panoramas of Moscow, the cathedral of Christ the Saviour made even more influence on the nearby territories. It finished the perspective of Mokhovaya street, Manage square, Alexandrovskiy garden, Sivtsev Vrazhek, Prechistenka, Ostozhenka, Vagankovskiy lane and some others. From the side of Antipievskiy lane there was the Ionic portico of the Museum of Fine Art on the background of the cathedral of Christ the Saviour.

The cathedral of Christ the Saviour was designed by Ton in Russian style according to the type of an ancient Russian church. It repeats its most characteristic spatial planning and structural specialities – cubic volume, entire facade, five cupolas, four pillars supporting the central cupola, each vault covering.

The wish to make the cathedral of Christ the Saviour the main cathedral of Moscow and even Russia, is seen in the forms and dimensions of the composition. It was expressed in the features of the temple likening it to all the main cathedrals of the Kremlin Cathedral Square at the same time – to the cathedral of the Assumption (archature belt), to the cathedral of the Annunciation (keel-like outlines of the vaults), to the cathedral of Archangel Michael (the cells of the "kokoshniks" at the bottom of the central cupola), as well as to the cathedral of the Intercession on Red Square (the forms of the cupolas and the same location in respect of the Kremlin). In this way the cathedral of Christ the Saviour symbolically combines in itself the significance of all the main temples of Moscow.

A number of specialities of the cathedral of Christ the Saviour, which made it similar to the church of St.Sophia in Constantinople, testify to the fact that it assumed the role of the main temple of the orthodox world, thus symbolizing the historical destiny of Russia, expressed in the formula "Moscow – the Third Rome". One of these specialities is the plan of the building in the form of a Greek cross. In publications of 1830-1840 it was said about the church of St.Sophia: "it was built in the form of a cut nearly square cross... the main part of it was occupied by the cupola".[14] Descriptions of the cathedral of Christ the Saviour give the same speciality. They note that the plan of the church in the form of a Greek cross "was given to Russia by Byzantium during the time of prince Vladimir of Kiev. All ancient Russian churches werebuilt according to this plan"[15]. Other specialities of the cathedral of Christ the Saviour were also taken from the church of St.Sophia in Constantinople: three roundabout galleries; two of them, situated one above the other, bounded the main volume of the temple, the third was sooner a balustrade, was at the bottom of the cupola's drum; thegalleries were not very evident in the outside look of the building; a huge cupola; a wide use of marble and revival of golden backgrounds in the interior painting.

The location of the cathedral of Christ the Saviour was also similar to the location of the church of St.Sophia in Constantinople, the place from which Christianity came to Russia. It was situated "in the most convenient place, in one of the best parts of Constantinople. It was built at the height of the main city of Byzantium, behind the hill which leads to the sea by the angle of seraglio"[16]. The cathedral of Christ the Saviour was also built on one of the highest hills, in the most beautiful place on the bank of the Moscow-river (an analogue of the sea in Constantinople), turned in the direction of the Kremlin and the Kremlin palaces.

The system of the signs which make one see in it another great christian symbol – New Jerusalem – was also successively presented in the cathedral of Christ the Saviour. Like the idea of "Moscow – the Third Rome" it was also the permanent theme of the architecture both of ancient Russia and partially of the New Time. The effort to make thecathedral of Christ the Saviour similar to the Holy Sepulchre in Jerusalem was shown already in A.L.Vitberg's project. The semantics of the project, which corresponded in its structure to the trine entity of God, three main events in Christ's life – the Nativity, the Transfiguration and the Resurrection, trine nature of man (body, soul and spirit), were also expressed by the idea that the low underground temple was a symbolic grave of the warriors who died during the war. As a result, another analogy appeared – of the warriors' heroic deed to the heroic deed of Christ, and of the low temple to the Holy Sepulchre in Jerusalem.

The idea about Moscow as new Jerusalem and about the cathedral of Christ the Saviour, founded on the Vorobjovy hills, as about the new temple of tsar Solomon, ran through the "Song about the gala foundation of the cathedral of Christ the Saviour in Moscow", pronounced in the Society of amateurs of Russian philology at the Moscow University by professor A.Merzljakov. In it Alexander I was analogized to Solomon, Moscowwas analogized to Jerusalem, the Moscow-river – to the river Jordan, Vorobjovy hills – to the Tabor, the woods on the Vorobjovy hills – to the woods on the mountain Olivet, revival of Moscow out of ashes was compared with the Resurrection and the Transfiguration of the Saviour, and the future temple – with "the ladder to the heaven".

The analogy of Moscow – New Jerusalem was also based on the coincidence of the dates, which was interpreted also symbolically. "Everybody remembers, – the author of the "Historical description of the celebration during the foundation of the cathedral of Christ the Saviour", – that on this date (12th of October – the day of the temple's foundation on the Vorobjovy hills according to the project of A.L.Vitberg – E.K.) the French left Moscow in the night... On this day the church venerates the Jerusalem icon of the Theotokos"[17]. Already during the reign of Alexander I the tendency to comprehend historical events in analogy with the events of the Christian history appeared. It was mentioned in the description of the ceremony of the temple's foundation: "The tsar went like Moses on the mountain".

What looks a single sign of the appearing tendency in the first quarter of the 19th century, in its second quarter, during the reign of Nicholas I, acquired a systematic character. The history of construction of the cathedral of Christ the Saviour was analogized to the history of construction of the Jerusalem temple.

During the time of the Old Testament the realization of David's idea to raise a temple of God, was left to his successor on the throne tsar Solomon. "The same was in Russia, – metropolitanate Philaret said at the ceremony of the second temple's foundation, – the idea of Alexander I was destined to be realised by his successor Nicholas I".[18]

In historical works of the 18th – the first quarter of the 19th century and in works of art of the same period the emperors from Peter I to Alexander I were analogized mainly to gods and heroes antique history. During the time of Nicholas I this tendency lost its significance and stopped being used at all. Its place was occupied by another system of analogies. The construction undertakings, being of state importance, concerning the change of Moscow look and turning it into the national and orthodox capital were oriented at, analogised and were associated with the deeds of Justin, the builder of the church of St.Sophia in Constantinople, of Constantine the Great – the builder of the Holy Sepulchre and of Solomon, the builder of the Jerusalem temple, making to remember home monarchs too with their programs of renovation of Moscow centre: John III, John IV and Boris Godunov.

There was a multi-ply system of analogies in the cathedral of Christ the Saviour, letting to compare Ton's creation with two main holy things in Jerusalem – the temple of Solomon and the Holy Sepulchre. Like in Vitberg's project for the Vorobjovy hills, the cathedral of Christ the Saviour was built over a symbolical grave of the warriors who died in the war with the French and in gratitude to all who brought in a sacrifice within one's power in the name of saving of Russia from foreign invaders. In its structure the cathedral of Christ the Saviour also reproduced the scheme of the Holy Sepulchre surrounded by a gallery with sacrariums consecrated to the Saviour's Passions.[19]

Multi-figure relieves of the western facade represented symbolically the history of creation of the cathedral of Christ the Saviour, the construction of which began and was nearly over during the time of Nicholas I, as the history of the reign and construction of the Jerusalem temple by Solomon (sculptor A.V.Loganovskiy).

The fact that the development of the temple's program, including the design of the sculptural decoration of the facades, belonged to one of the initiators of the religious revival and an adherent of revival of the national art in Russia metropolitanate Philater, testifies to the importance of the cathedral.

The unique composition of the iconostasis of the cathedral of Christ the Saviour in the form of a hip roof temple was like a temple inside a temple, which was conditioned by the uniqueness of the program which was to make it similar to the two main holy things of Jerusalem. The liturgical models of the temples, which in this or another way corresponded to the idea about Divine Jerusalem, were taken as the basis of the composition of the iconostasis of the cathedral of Christ the Saviour. A special symbolical importance was acquired in this context by the "models made from unperishable materials – gold, silver, precious stones and pearls... because in corresponding sacramental texts or in liturgical poetry holy things are compared with treasures or were built from precious materials. So the real liturgical ciboria from gold and silver were like the Holy Zion – the dwelling of God and were the icons of Divine Jerusalem."[20]

A direct prototype of the iconostasis of the cathedral of Christ the Saviour were the precious models of the temples known under the name of Jerusalems, and which is most important – big and small Jerusalems, made upon the order of John III in 1486 for the cathedral of the Assumption in Moscow Kremlin. Jerusalem is a vessel "for Eucharistic bread in the form of the Holy Sepulchre and at the same time of Jerusalem of theOld Testament, corresponded best of all to the varied symbolics of the bringing and installation of the gifts"[21]. The vessels from the cathedral of the Assumption, which were structurally and symbolically analogised to the prototype – the cubiculum and the rotunda of the Jerusalem church of the Holy Sepulchre, reflected the autocratic strivings of John III, when as a result of his marriage to Sophia Paleologus and after thefall of Constantinople, Russia became the main orthodox guardian of the Holy Sepulchre, and the tsar himself was honoured with the epithet "new Constantine" and characterised as the holder of the reigns of the holy divine throne of the ecclesiastical church".[22] The name of Constantine the Great combined two main orients of Moscow state, accumulatingpower, – comprehension of one self as the successor of Byzantium, acceptance of its mission to be the centre of orthodoxy and simultaneously – the succession from the Jerusalem Holy Sepulchre.

The succession from the Jerusalem church of the Holy Sepulchre was one of the main points of the program of the main cathedral of Moscow metropolitanate, built by John III – the cathedral of the Assumption[23]. Thus, the direct orientation of the facades and the interior of the cathedral of Christ the Saviour and the holy things kept in it,connected it not only with pre-Petrine Russia and the national and autocratic idea of Moscow and Vladimir, connected with it, but with the other component of the official triad – with orthodoxy, which was embodied in the cathedral of Christ the Saviour by the orientation at the Christian-wide holy things connected with Jerusalem.

The iconostasis of the cathedral of Christ the Saviour in the form of an octahedral chapel, crowned with a gilded hip roof, the white marble parts of which were adorned by an ornamental decoration from colourful enamels, repeating in their forms the jerusalems of the cathedral of the Assumption, recreated the ideas about Divine Jerusalem, inspired by sacramental texts, as the city from gold and precious stones, whichwas at the same time a temple and a bounded paradise garden – the vineyard. The real specialities of both Jerusalem temples, known according to descriptions and pictures, were also recreated in the specialities of the iconostasis of the cathedral of Christ the Saviour. In this way the contextual and compositional kernel of the cathedral of Christ the Saviour – its iconostasis was symbolically analogised to the cradle of Christianity, turning into an icon, an image of Divine Jerusalem.

Insistent analogy of the cathedral of Christ the Saviour to the cathedral of the Assumption makes one see in the built cathedral the revival of the Jerusalem-Constantinople ideology characteristic for the Kremlin central ensemble. Id est, behind the revival of the orthodox ancient Russian look of the temple there was the analogy of its contents to the contents of the temples, which were its prototypes, especially to the main one – of the Assumption. There was also an analogy to the interpretation of Moscow as the House of the Theotokos. The symbolics of the cathedral of the Assumption was as though doubled due to the analogy to it of the temple-memorial – the cathedral of Christ the Saviour.

Recreation in the iconostasis of the cathedral of Christ the Saviour of the jerusalems of the cathedral of the Assumption, like the archature belt on the facades, testified to the fact that the new orthodox holy thing of Russia was built as the image of Constantinople, the capital of Byzantium, of the capitals of the great principalities of Ancient Russia – Vladimir and Kiev, which was also the cradle of Christianity in Russia. Equal-to-the-Apostles emperor Constantine the Great and Equal-to-the-Apostles grand prince Vladimir of Kiev, who followed his example, like the city of Vladimir later, consecrated the capitals of their principalities to the Theotokos by construction of cathedrals of the Assumption. Moscow cathedral of the Assumption in the Kremlintestifies to this effect too. The construction of the cathedral of Christ the Saviour and the symbolics of its architectural forms confirmed that Moscow and Russia still remained the House of the Theotokos for ecclesiastical and theological consciousness.

There is also another aspect of the formula of "Moscow-the Third Rome" in the cathedral of Christ the Saviour, representing the idea of state power and majesty of Russia. It was expressed in a double way – in the form of the analogy to Roman memorials – to Pantheon and the cathedral of St. Peter in Rome, and in the alignment of a number of characteristic features of the cathedral of Christ the Saviour at the similar characteristic features of the cathedral of St. Isaac in Petersburg.

The temple-memorial of the victory in the Patriotic war of 1812, the temple of nation-wide importance, constructed in Moscow, was destined to become the main and the biggest temple of the ancient capital. It this way it was made equal in its importance to the cathedral of St.Isaac, which became the main temple of Petersburg after certification of Monferran's project. Many things in the cathedral of St.Isaac anticipated the cathedral of Christ the Saviour – huge dimensions, cubicle forms and squatness of the main volume, equivalent facades, closeness to the Neva and orientation at the panorama of the Neva bank, finally, the memorial-contextual meaning of the temple itself – asymbol of the whole epoch and a memorial of its creator and initiator Peter I. But the difference between the two buildings was equally essential. The cathedral of St.Isaac, in difference to the cathedral of Christ the Saviour did not open either conceptually, or stylistically, but closed, summed up the results of a long period in the historyof Russian architecture, though many of its features – memorial essence, grandiosity of the dimensions, the way it was included into the city environment, were intended to acquire a new life in constructions of the Byzantine style after their sanctifying by the authority of the new holy thing – the cathedral of Christ the Saviour – the main temple not only in Moscow, but in Russia. The cathedral of St.Isaac was the last big construction of Peter's time in Russian history, the last memorial connected with the ideals of state honour, the cathedral of Christ the Saviour was one of the first memorials representing the state-national idea; in it the idea of the state honour was inseparable from the ideals of orthodoxy and the nation.

Conception of the Capital City Centre in 1830-1850

Simultaneously with the construction of the cathedral of Christ the Saviour the construction of a new emperor's palace and a new depository of national antiquities began – the Armoury. During the construction of these buildings large-scale works were undertaken for restoration of the ancient cathedrals and the royal chamber. The works in the Kremlin were the second, together with the cathedral of Christ the Saviour, main component of the ensemble of Moscow historical centre, renovated in the national spirit during the time of Nicholas I.

Both grandiose construction undertakings opened a new period in development of Moscow, following the after-fire period, and in the renovation of its historical centre. Due to its look and a favourable location new buildings united organically with the pictures and views, which personified Moscow and its historical individuality traditionally.Finished in the rough form in 1858, when the scaffoldings were taken off it, the cathedral of Christ the Saviour became an integral part of the historical centre which became much wider. Amending its look the new cathedral changed it in the traditional direction. It was traditional not in respect to classical Moscow of the second half of the 18th – beginning of the 19th centuries, but to ancient pre-Petrine Moscow.

The town-building of the l9th century, being oriented at the preservation of the basis of the city plan, developed the traditions of pre-Petrine Russia, where the town-forming element was not the plan, but the volume or a system of volumes of unique constructions. Spatial structure of the city ensemble was renovated for the account ofan extremely intensive construction of new temples, bell-towers, monasteries.

However, during the renovation of Moscow city centre the romanticism was based, and not less wider than on the inheritance of Ancient Russia, and the widely understood Byzantine tradition, and baroque style continues town-building traditions of classicism and not only Moscow one, but of Petersburg, recomprehending them and adapting to its own program and needs.

The construction of the Big Kremlin Palace and the Armoury was conducted in 1838-1852 according to the projects of K.A.Ton (the facades and the general design), F.F.Rikhter (detailed projects of the interiors), N.I.Cichagov (interior arrangement), F.G.Solntsev (the drawings of the parquet floors and the front doors). In the design of the Armoury N.I.Chichagov and V.A.Bakarev took part together with the main authorof the project Ton.

The Big Kremlin Palace, oriented by the main facade in the direction of the Moscow-river, created the kernel of the developed ensemble. It included in its composition the ancient Terem palace (from the North), the Armoury and the dwelling rooms of the emperor's family, with which it was connected by a passage (from the West), the Faceted Chamber (from the East), nine churches and seven yards. In the composition of the low storey, interpreted as a basement typical for ancient Russian constructions, Ton repeated the outlines of the basement of the ancient palace of Moscow princes, which existed here. In the composition of the upper part of the facade the architect recreated the composition of three upper tiers of the Terem palace, which got a superstructure in 1637. The central part of the new building, crowned by a dome, had a double as the upper floor of the Terem palace. The casings of the windows of the Big Kremlin Palace were the main element of the decoration of its facades – were created according to the sample of the casings of the Terem palace. Preservation of the ancient monuments, the wish to follow their forms, their inclusion into the new ensemble as an organic part were part of Ton's program, like dismantling of the Kremlin wall and liquidation of the historical panorama from the side of the Moscow-river were the part of Bazhenov's program.

The change of the state policy in the architectural and town-building area turned out at once when Nicholas I accessed to the throne. One of the first emperor's decrees dated by 7th of January, 1827, the heads of the domains were obliged to make the survey of the ancient monuments, the first in the empire, to collect the data about their use: by the same decree their demolishing was prohibited. A little later the Synod published the decree which allowed to construct new churches in the place of the old ones only under the condition that the architectural style of the previous building was preserved.[24]

Historical monuments (the Terem palace, a group of ancient temples and monasteries) were not less important in the ensemble of the Big Kremlin Palace than the new building. The symbolical importance was acquired not only by the views at the Palace and the museum and their connection with the Kremlin, but by the view from the Palace and the Armoury looking at Moscow. From the main facade of the Palace and the railing in frontof the Armoury, from the windows of the gala halls the wide panorama of the river reaches opened with the cathedral of Christ the Saviour, seen in combination with the Kremlin's towers – and this was also the creator's idea.

The function of the emperor's palace was radically recomprehended. The Big Kremlin Palace was not only the embodiment of the state idea, but the interpretation of the government as an integral part of the national history of people. The Big Kremlin Palace, remaining a Palace, became an original variation of a museum and a monument at the same time, a symbol of connection of the tsar and the state, embodied by him, with the history and life of the people, like the cathedral of Christ the Saviour, planned as a temple-memorial, not losing its initial religious function, acquired the importance of the temple of the nation, a temple-museum. The tendency to attribute museum features, the striving to make architecture an expression of the idea of the national and historical development was a general sign of the architecture of the romanticism and historicism. But the wish to turn a national museum into an integral part of palace rooms, adding to the emperor's palace a status of an original monument of the national history belonged to the specialities of the architecture of the romanticism in those countries, where the government and the monarch still retained the influence on thedevelopment of the artistic process, including the architectural one, i.e. in Germany and Russia.

The composition and specialities of the architecture of the Big Kremlin Palace showed the inclination to colossal dimensions and a specific union of the traditions of the regular and ancient Russian town-building, characteristic for that time.

Big Kremlin Palace and the Armoury. View from Cathedral Square. Lithography according to D.Indeytsev's drawing. 1850s.

Following the ancient Russian tradition and the ensemble which existed before, Ton designed the complex of the Palace with the Armoury and dwelling blocks, which were picturesque and asymmetrical.

The building of the Armoury was not the first construction specially raised for placement of its treasures. The first one was built on the eve of the Patriotic war of 1812 according to the project of architect I.V.Egotov. The classical forms of its facades and interiors in 1830 did not correspond already to the new contents of a national museum. After the new building of the Armoury had been constructed according to Ton's project, the previous one was adjusted for the army barracks.

In the two main components of Moscow centre, renovated in 1830-1850, according; to the words of a contemporary, "the same task of the national system was solved... in the first the artist thought how, constructing the temple, to comply it with the general original character of our ancient capital, with the character of its forty of forties of churches... in the project of the palace he was guided by the same idea in respect of the character of the spared tsar's chambers"[25].

The presence of the state component in the conception of the official national system makes one emphasize in the composition and the contents of the Big Kremlin Palace the analogues hardly mentioned in the descriptions of the cathedral of Christ the Saviour. The analogising of the palace to the palaces of Roman Caesars and Greek (Byzantine) emperors, of Moscow not only to the second Rome – Constantinople, but to the first – the imperial, of the Kremlin – to Capitol, of the Kremlin hill – to the Capitol hill sounded to full extent[26].

The main components of the renovated centre – the cathedral of Christ the Saviour and the Big Kremlin Palace symbolized by their compositional unity the contextual unity of different aspects of the official doctrine "Moscow – Third Rome" and the official national system. At the same time in each of them one of the aspects was accentuated. The Byzantine roots of Russian culture were emphasized in the cathedral of Christ theSaviour, its national individuality was emphasized in the Big Kremlin Palace.

The cathedral of Christ the Saviour, the Kremlin with the new complex of the Big Kremlin Palace and the bell-tower of John the Great dominated above Moscow. They were seen "from far away and nearly from all Moscow roads, especially from South-Eastern, Southern and South-Western". The leading idea of Nicholas' reign got in this way the town-building embodiment not only in the dimensions of the centre of the ancient capital, the panorama of the Kremlin bank, but in the dimensions of all the city, in the city panoramas, which opened while approaching Moscow.

The construction of the cathedral of Christ the Saviour and of the Big Kremlin Palace initiated in 1830s the realisation in both capitals and in the province of the official policy, which became nation-wide, of returning to Russian settlements of the individual national look, which was lost, as it seemed at that time, during the realization of the program of Europeanization in Russia in the l8th – the first quarter ofthe l9th centuries. The national renaissance in the architecture during the period of romanticism was inseparable from the religious renaissance. The official ideology of the 18th – beginning of the 19th centuries, and there was not any other then, had the form of the state, imperial idea. During Nicholas' reign the autocracy (the imperialidea) was one of the three components of the official ideology, the other two were the orthodoxy and the national system. Besides, the national system was the structural and contextual beginning in this trine union. Autocracy and orthodoxy were comprehended as the forms of existence and expression of the national system. Adherence to theidea of autocracy in the centre of Moscow, renovated by Nicholas I, was symbolized by the complex of the Big Kremlin Palace, the symbol of orthodoxy became the cathedral of Christ the Saviour, sanctified by its authority construction of temples in Russian style developed at once after certification of the project in 1832. The state policy in thesphere of architecture for the return of the Russian look to all types of settlements was realized in the middle of the 13th century in the wide scale of church construction, in the renovation of the historically formed system of verticals.

Renovation of the Verticals System

1830-1860 were the period of certain renaissance of temple architecture.

Designing and construction of the cathedral of Christ the Saviour and the impulse given by it to the intensive construction of temple and monastery complexes in Moscow, which were new in the spirit – was the most distinctive characteristic speciality of town-building development of the capital during the period, which began after the one which we usually call the after-fire Moscow. Moscow is the focus and the cradle of Russian culture, thus this program can be defined. The changes made in the look and the scale of Moscow historical centre by the construction of the cathedral of Christ the Saviour, the Big Kremlin Palace and the Armoury, the bell-tower of the monastery of St.Simon entailed renovation of the historically formed system, of verticals and silhouette of Moscow, added in many cases by new accents, which were to emphasize monumentality of the previous buildings, to support what was begun, and most important, to embody the new town-building idea directed at expression of the new spiritual values, concentrated in the notions of orthodoxy, national system and nationality, by the means of architecture.

The systematic and total character of the renovation of the verticals system give the reason to see in this activity a considered town-building idea. The temples and monasteries situated along the flow of the Moscow-river, forming the panorama of

Monastery of St.Simon with a new bell-tower. Photo. 1880s.

Moskvoretskaja street. Photo. 2nd half of the 19th century.

the river valley, i.e. "exterior" ensembles, were rebuilt and renovated first of all.

After the construction of the bell-tower of the monastery of St.Simon and the cathedral of Christ the Saviour had been started, the bell-tower of St.Nicholas Moskvoretsky was built very close to the Kremlin and the cathedral of St.Basil in Moskvoretskaya street which led from the quay of the Moscow-river to Red Square (1857, arch. N.D.Korinskiy). A new church of St.Nicholas "Krasny zvon" ("Beautiful Chime") was hunt in the former Jushkov (Nikolskiy) lane in the place of the church dismantled in 1858. On the opposite side of the Moscow-river on Sophiyskaya quay according to N.I.Kozlovskiy's project (1862-1868) the bell-tower of the church of St.Sophia was built; Ivannovskiy monastery was completely renewed according to M.D.Bykovskiy's project near Solyanka street (1861-1878). The churches were reconstructed and a number of bell-towers was built in the streets leading to the centre of Moscow, and in the mainpoints of the city ensemble (the bell-tower in the former monastery of the Adoration of the Holy Cross in Vozdvizhenka street (1848-1849, P.P.Burenin), the bell-tower and the fence of the former monastery of the Passions in Strastnaya square (1849-1855, M.D.Bukovskiy), the bell-tower of the monastery of Martyr Nicetas in Big Nikitskaya street (1868, Bykovskiy), the chapel of Great Martyr Panteleimon near Nikolskiegates (A.S.Kaminskiy, not survived). New temples and bell-towers were built in Arbat, Tverskaya, Pokrovka, etc. Many new temples and bell-towers were raised then in Moscow suburbs: in Krasnoselskaya, Yakimanka, Shabolovka and other streets, in Dorogomilovo and Old Tolmachy, "in Three towns", etc. During 30s-60s years of the 19th century the Kremlin was surrounded by a new ring of verticals and thus the historically formed structure of the plan within the limits of Boulevard Ring was as though renovated. Developing and strengthening the signs of regularity, Moscow town-builders revived the traditions of ancient Russian town-building and of the time of baroque.

A number of churches and bell-towers of 1830s still had the forms of classicism (the church of St.Sergius in Rogozhskaya, 1835, F.M.Shestakov), the bell-tower of the monastery of the Nativity of the Theotokos (l835, N.I.Kozlovskiy), the church of the Theophany in Elokhovo (E.D.Tyurin). But in the cult construction classicism surrendered most quickly. The destiny of the bell-tower of the monastery of St.Simon is very illustrative. In 1832 E.D.Tyurin offered to build a new bell-tower in the style of classicism on the line of the previous one, but in the centre of the Southern monastery wall, instead of the dilapidated bell-tower which was in the depth of the monasteryterritory near the cathedral of the Assumption. However, using the offered place, in l835 the bell-tower was constructed according to K.A.Ton's project in Russian style.

Combination of traditions of different kind, advocated by the eclecticism, resulted in a revival of the mode used in the helltowers of baroque churches and in above-gates monastery churches. It was a combination of picturesque ensembles of ancient Russia with facade representativeness of Moscow bell-

Church of the Holy Trinity in Grjazi in Pokrovka street
(1868, architect M.D.Bykovskiy). Photo. 1880s.

Church of Martyr Nicetas in Old Tolmachi
(1858, architect M.D.Bykovskiy; did not keep till now). Photo. 1880s.

Strastnaja (Pushkinskaja) square with a new bell-tower of the monastery of the Passions (1849-1855, architect M.D.Bykovskiy) and the church of Great Martyr Defnetrius of Thessalonica at the corner of Tverskoy boulvard. Lithography of G.Geakote and Sh.-K.Bashelie according to I.I.Sharleman's drawing. Middle of the 19th century.

towers of 1730-1750. A bell-tower was brought out to the monastery wall and installed above the entrance gates, which meant replacement of the main accent outside the monastery. Due to colossal dimensions and expressiveness of expressive silhouette a bell-tower became not only the centre of the ensemble. The role of the wall which was on one line with it, changed, out of a secondary element it turned into the main facade of the complex and a colossal socle – a foot of a vertical dominant, emphasising its good proportion.

The composition of the bell-towers which were widely built in Moscow in 1830-1860, showed a qualitative difference from the bell-towers of 1730-1830. The order was excluded from the bell-towers designed in Russian style. The classical type of a multi-tier bell-tower with round tiers disappeared. The type of a hip roof bell-tower with the characteristic combination of the volumes of an octahedron on a tetrahedron, which completely disappeared out of Moscow architecture in the 18th – the first third of the 19th centuries, was revived. The type of a multi-tier bell-tower with tiers in the shape of octahedrons or octahedrons on tetrahedrons, which first appeared at the turn of the 16th-17th centuries (the bell-tower of John the Great) and represented by the famous bell-towers of Novodevichy monastery and the monastery of St.Joseph, abbot of Volokolamsk, was revived.

The same synthesis of regularity and picturesqueness was in the complexes of Strastnoy (of the Passions) (1849-1855), Ivanovskiy (1859) and Nikitskiy (of Martyr Nicetas) monasteries, reconstructed according to M.D.Bykovskiy's project. The bell-tower of Strastnoy monastery with its hip roof had nothing in common in its look with the building which existed in this place before. And nevertheless, the five-cupola combination repeated twice in the composition of the bell-tower, connected it rhythmically with the five-cupola composition of the ancient cathedral and the picturesque composition of the monastery ensemble. The expressive silhouette and statuesque volume showed that

Bykovskiy understood the power of the artistic influence of the plastic forms spread in ancient Russia. At the same time the architect showed a free mastery in the skills of regular townbuilding (the towers placed widely and the accentuated smoothness of the walls on the low tier and on the adjoining blocks transferred the accent from the volume of the bell-tower on the square in front of it. Again the architectural dominant "was transferred" from the depth of the monastery to the gala city space in front of it. The function lost by the group of the volumes inside the monastery, was assumed by the bell-tower: which radius of influence was much wider. The classical pathos of space was also used, though the mode of its expression, like in all simultaneous buildings, was not the plane, but the volume. The turn to various sources allowed Bykovskiy's creation to become the main element in the square's ensemble and simultaneously the vertical dominant of the big area from the square in front of the house of the governor-general to the Triumphal arch and from Petrovskie gates to Nikitskie gates.

So, the temples and bell-towers constructed in Moscow in 1830-1860, were different by the speciality found during consideration of the projects of E.D.Tyurin, K.A.Ton and M.D.Bykovskiy – the merging of the modes of regular and ancient Russian town-building. The purpose to create vertical accents was combined with gala arrangement of the street space, characteristic for regular town-building.

An interest to renovation of the complexes, connected with the dynasties of the Romanovs and Ryurikovichis and with the

View of the Kremlin and Kitay-gorod. There is the bell-tower of the church of St. Nicholas "Moskvoretskiy" in the centre (1857, architect D.N.Korinskiy; did not keep till now). Photo. 2nd half of the 19th century.

great events which happened during their reign, was revived in the cult architecture in 1830-1860. The monastery of Martyr Nicetas, the founder of which was a fore-father of the future father of the dynasties, was renovated. The monastery of St.Simon, connected with the memory about Kulikovskaya battle and about Moscow grand prince Demetrius Ivanovich Donskoy, was renovated. The monasteries of the Passions and of the Adoration of the Holy Cross were renovated. Ivanovskiy monastery was built anew.

The idea of "Moscow – New Jerusalem", represented in Moscow architecture only during the reign of Elizabeth Petrovna, was revived. It was one of the main contextual aspects not only of the cathedral of Christ the Saviour, as a separate building, but spread its influence on all the ensemble of the centre of the ancient capital. The orientation atJerusalem images and Jerusalem samples, realised in the practice of the ancient Russian architecture, could be seen in Moscow at the level of town-building too. For example, the highest hill after the Kremlin hill was chosen for the cathedral of Christ the Saviour on the Moscow-river bank, like for the Jerusalem temple built on the mountain Moria; like tsar Solomon, Nicholas I, after he had accessed to the throne, constructed a splendid royal palace not far from the cathedral and many other buildings.

The history of construction of the bell-tower of the monastery of St.Simon according to K.A.Ton's project, is understood in another way in connection with this. As it was mentioned above, the source of its multi-tier composition were the bell-towers of John the Great and of Novodevichiy monastery. The bell-tower of John the Great is theonly object of the idea of Boris Godunov, realized during his reign, to create "The Holy of the Holiest" in the Kremlin – a new cathedral of the Resurrection like the Jerusalem church of the Holy Sepulchre[27]. The name "The Holy of the Holiest" corresponds to the understanding of the Jerusalem church of the Holy Sepulchre as of "The Holy of the Holiest" of the New Testament, which transfigured and renovated the Old Testament temple[28]. The location of the bell-tower of the monastery of St.Simon in relation to the Kremlin like the bell-tower of Novodevichiy monastery repeated the principle of location of the cathedral of Christ the Saviour in relation to the cathedral of St.Basil. Probably, the similarity in the principles of the location made to reject Tyurin's project, made in the style of classicism, and to give the preference to the Byzantine style of Ton's project. Due to it the idea of "Moscow – New Jerusalem", which was spatially and symbolically embodied in the structure of the renovated centre, acquired completeness and purelyarchitectural organization in the city-wide scale.

The national idea of orthodox revival (new orthodoxy was like a reaction to the Russian revolution of 1825 – the revolt of the Decembrists), embodied in the ensemble of the ancient capital, became an integral part in the ecclesiastical movement of 1830-1840 with the address to the inheritance of Ancient Russia and to the programs called "Moscow – the Third Rome and New Jerusalem", which was typical for it. And the works of Ton in Moscow in Russian style, remaining an expression of the ideas and ideals of the after-Decembrists period in the history of Russia, simultaneously, like the philosophy of Slavophils, the class of the orthodox icon painting of the Academy of Art and a number of other similar phenomena in the art of 1830-1860, include the sources of Russian religious renaissance of the silver age, which was brightly embodied in Moscow temple architecture of the early 20th century.

New Regular Ensembles

Till the present time it had been about the tendencies in the architecture and town-building of Moscow, connected with the address to the ancient Russian tradition. But this was only one, though the brightest side of the architectural and town-building activity. The program universalism of eclecticism, the first stage of development of which was represented by the architecture of the romanticism of 1830-1850, allowed to remainfaithful to the norms of regular town-building and to the classical orientation, traditional for the architecture of the 18th – the first quarter of the 19th centuries. All depended on a concrete building. Thus, the tendency appeared which can be called as the interconnection of style and genre. In the town-building undertakings connectedwith the construction in the Kremlin and with design of temples, orientation at the ancient Russian samples prevailed. In construction of country estates and cottage construction different styles were used, mainly "Gothic" and Russian. In the civil construction in towns orientation at the samples of classical architecture dominated.

The address to the inheritance of different epochs and styles in many ways depended on the denomination of the designed objects and the place of their location. First this circumstance was mentioned when Moscow buildings of the second half of the 18th century were described. Though in the middle of the 19th century during the period of romanticism the choice of the past styles increased sufficiently, the limits importantfor that time were valid. During creation of dominating buildings, which organized large space, the town-building of 1830-1860 was oriented at the inheritance of Ancient Russia of the first half of the 18th century. During creation of the "internal" local ensembles of the streets and squares the town-building of the same years continued the tradition of classicism, recomprehending and renovating it.

Moscow classicism chose an original system of connection of the internal ensembles with the historical centre. The connection of the ensembles of the after-fire Moscow with the ancient kernel of the city, their orientation at the Kremlin, openness in direction of the Kremlin were generally acknowledged. But this also means another thing. The main buildings of the squares, from the main point of view of the ensemble, were directed not at the Kremlin, but away from it. The connection-opposition, typical for the ensembles of the after-fire Moscow, was created, due to which Red Square and Theatre Square retained their completeness and independence in relation to the Kremlin. It is hardlypossible to doubt the determining importance of the Big Theatre in the ensemble of Theatre Square. If it is so, the main thing in the look of its ensemble will be the view in the direction of the theatre, opposite the Kitay-gorod wall. The same can be said about Red Square. The University and the upper trade rows looked at the Kremlin. But in both cases these accentuated buildings, the expressiveness of the symmetrical composition of which, if did not provide the predominance of the centrifugal orientation over the centripetal, it made it quite appreciable. The main thing for the ensemble of each square was the view not at the Kremlin, but from it.

The town-building works of 1830-1860, developing the principles of regularity, were concentrated on the traditionally important territories of Moscow – the area of Tverskaya street and in the centre, which became wider after construction of the cathedral of Christ the Saviour.

The works on proper arrangement of the area connected with the entry from Petersburg into Moscow, were developed earlier and more intensively. The part of the road, which was behind the city line from Tverskaya frontier post to Peter's palace, and the part adjoining Tverskaya from the side of the city – 1st Tverskaya-Yamskaya streetand the neighbouring streets were arranged. Implementation of these important town-building works stimulated creation of new gala ensemble of Tverskaya frontier post with the Triumphal arch (1829-1834).

During three-four years the territory adjoining Tverskaya post along Petersburg highway became unrecognizable. A regularly planned district of country houses in different styles grew, exactly in the country-side construction, first in estates, then in cottage villages many styles were used. The type of settlements, which was the first in the Moscow region, did not keep. But rarely unanimous descriptions of contemporaries remained. In the "Guide-book from Moscow to St.Petersburg and back" it was mentioned that in all the territory from Tverskaya frontier post to Vsekhsvjatskiy bridge "Gothic merged with the whims of the recent mode, Asia with Europe, Greek and moresque styles, stone with wood... it was a whole town of country cottages".[29] And here is the testimony of M.P.Zagoskin: "Creation of the park also belongs to our time... it is a trine highway with two boulevards, occupied from both sides by country houses, which, beginning from the frontier post, extended to the park itself; these are clean and joyful houses,which crowd around the palace; it is a toy, a summer theatre, and entertainment...", "...from the bank itself (Camer-Collezhskiy – *E.K.*) and further to Vsehsvjatskiy bridge there are cottages, houses, gardens, colourful, beautiful, Gothic, fantastic,... the outskirts worthy of our ancient capital – it is a fascination, the most charming phenomenon of labour, intellect, art, richness".

Creation of public parks in both capitals was a token of time too. They were designed according to the sample of estate ones, but initially they were stipulated to function as public ones. In Petersburg they included Ekaterinhof and Pavlovsk, in "Moscow – Peter's park and Sokolniki.

In 1838 the designing of two big city ensembles was started. One of them – the main entry into Moscow along Petersburg road – was mentioned already. The second big work was the designing of Bolotnaya square. Moscow military governor-general prince D.V.Golitsyn presented to the clerk for special duties architect M.D.Bykovskiy an offer about construction "the main street from the entrance into Moscow on the way from Petersberg, as well as in Tverakaya-Yamakaya settlement and Bolotnaya square, in the way corresponding to the honour of the capital".

The work began after all Tverakaya-Yamskaya streets had been put in order. The main attention was turned to the highway street – 1st Tverskaya-Yamskaya. First in the place of the wooden stores and corn-chandler's shops, which had been in this street "to the left from the entrance front Petersburg into the capital", it was presumed to makethere a boulevard, "but after better consideration it was found out that the Triumphal arch would remain aside in this way and the implementation of this project would be ugly". So, in order to keep the town-building importance of the Triumphal arch, it was decided to make the buildings in the street more expressive and significant, without changing the street line, in order to add beauty and gala style to such an important part of the capital: "to build stone two-storey houses with proper facades on the existing line of the corn-chandler's shops, like the houses of coachmen, built on the opposite side, then the Triumphal arch will stay in its place and in the middle of the street. If stores are arranged in this street, their entrances shall be from the street behindthese houses". For the main governmental highway, built in with small houses of coachmen, arrangement of stores seemed to be not quite representative and they were transferred to side streets, including 2nd Tverskaya-Yamskaya street.

The Second Tverskaya-Yamskaya street was also reconstructed very much. The instruction was issued: "In the place of today's dilapidated yards, which are entire and can be dangerous in case of a fire, new, though wooden, houses should be built with considerable breaks (distances), and the houses, that should

Nikolskaja street. View in the direction of Red Square. Middle of the 19th century.

be demolished in order to make the breaks, shall be transferred to those streets, which lead to Tishina and Gruziny" (to Tishinskaya square and Gruzinskaya street – *E.K.*).

By 1842 the arrangement of the streets adjoining Tverskaya frontier post, was over. Only after that in the same year the construction of flour shops in Bolotnaya square and addition to it of a look of a whole architectural ensemble, was started. The work was conducted rapidly: the construction committee tried to reduce to the least the losses of the sellers and by "the breaking of old stores to improve the "indecent" look of this part of Moscow, caused by the old stores".

Creation of the new ensemble, making a worthy background for the Kremlin and the constructed cathedral of Christ the Saviour, increase of the level of comfort in Moscow, creation of favourable conditions for support of the appearing trade-industrial upsurge and the striving to make Moscow, even just architecturally, the national capital of Russia – all this was revealed in the new concept of the square ensemble, which was new in relation to the after-fire Moscow.

The work in Bolotnaya square was a continuation of the arrangement of the By-pass canal and construction of its stone quays, which had been begun upon D.V.Golitsyn's initiative too in 1833, i.e. at once after the manifesto about the construction of the cathedral of Christ the Saviour had been issued.

The complex which extended along the quay of the Overflow canal for nearly half a kilometre, consisted from a long block of stores which was square on the plan and two semicircular blocks at its sides. As a result an original composition was created with an oval gala yard-square turned in the direction of Bolotnaya square and the canal. Bykovskiy's general compositional plot was in successive relation with the complex of Red Square, which was similar to it in its denomination and location. In Bove's project the symmetrical-axial composition with a clear centre attracted attention. The main thing in Bykovskiy's composition, though it was symmetrical, was the rhythmic of alteration of two main elements: one-storey stores accentuated by pilasters and porticos' triangular pediments and two-storey houses with Bykovskiy's favourite correlation of apertures, strange to classicism, – downstairs there was one rectangular door, upstairs there were three archy windows, divided by columns. Bykovskiy changed the places of the main and the secondary in classicism. The architect used the order composition and order forms for relatively secondary elements. For the main, accentuated elements of the ensemble, which the two-storey stores were, the motifs, which were far from canonical order ones, were used. The centre of each block was not much accentuated and instead of the gala static symmetrical composition of classicism a dynamic composition appeared, based on the rhythmic ofa complicated alteration of two main elements. Four two-storey houses were

Kuznetskiy bridge. Lithography. Middle of the 19th century.

situated in the centre of a long rectangular block, two were at its ends, two were at the ends of the semi-circular blocks and two were at the sides of the entrance, which was in the centre of each of them.

The stores in Bolotnaya square showed the mastery of Bykovskiy – architect, classical sources of his education and at the same time, marvellous creative braveness.

The stores in Bolotnaya square were designed in direct closeness to the Kremlin and the cathedral of Christ the Saviour. So, the definition of the character of their connection was the task of first priority and importance for the designer. Bykovskiy turned out to be in the situation like Bove was when he designed the Upper trade rows in Red Square and Theatre square. However, the ensembles, designed by Bykovskiy and Bove, were in quite the opposite alignment with the Kremlin and Kitay-gorod.

For Theatre and Red Squares the main most advantageous point of view, from which both new buildings and the square looked a complete whole, was the point of view from the Kremlin. In Bykovskiy's project the opposite mode was used. The back facade of the complex, made identical to the main one, looked at the Kremlin. The main point of view at Bolotnaya square was at the Kremlin and the cathedral of Christ the Saviour. Both of them could not be seen from Bolotnaya square and contemplated otherwise than in combination with the blocks of the stores. Visually the stores were situated at the bottom of the main buildings and ensembles of the historical centre of Moscow. The thesis, coming out from the aesthetics of romanticism, about the necessity to create the new in direct connection with the existing was not just a declaration for Bykovskiy. It was embodied in the master's creations, determining not only the compositional and stylistic innovation of his buildings, constructed on the basis of the classical tradition, but also the novelty and originality of town-building decisions. In this case Bykovskiy was Ton's like-minded person and a successor of Kazakov's tradition.

Bringing out of the main buildings and complexes to the Moscow-river, the intensive process of renovation of the river panoramas was accompanied by intensification of arrangement of the Southern, Zamoskvoretskaya part of the territory of the ancient capital. In 1835-1836 at the Moscow-river and the Overflow canal dams were made. In 1830 the wooden Vysokopyatnitskiy bridge across the By-pass canal on the axis of Pyatnitskaya street which led to Red Square, was substituted by the first metallic bridge in Moscow – from pig iron. In 1859, in a year after the cathedral of Christ the Saviour had been freed from scaffoldings, the first metallic bridge across the Moscow-river, the Big Stone Bridge – was built.

In 1842 the "Commission for Construction in the "Town of Moscow" was liquidated, which reflected, on the one hand, the increase of centralization in architecture and town-building and, on the other hand, understanding of the role of technical progress in construction. The authority of all the architectural and construction affair was concentrated for more than twenty years (in 1865 the Technical and Construction Committee at the Ministry of Internal Affairs was established) at the Main Department of the Ways of Communication and Public Buildings. During this period Mytitschinskiy water pipe-linewas fully improved by engineer Delvig and water building near Babjegorodskaya dam was constructed in 1853-1858. The previous renovation of the water line in 1830-1835 was accompanied by construction of five fountains, which were a colouring speciality of Moscow squares. Sheremetevskiy fountain was near Sukharevskaya tower in Sukharevskaya square, Petrovskiy fountain was in Theatre square, Voskresenskiy fountain was in the square with the same name near the entrance into Alexandrovskiy garden and Varvarskiy fountain wasin Varvarskaya square. Nikolskiy and Petrovskiy fountains were adorned in 1835 by bronze sculptures made by I.P.Vitali.

The estate scheme with a front yard open in the direction of the street was used in 1839-1840 during construction of the Agricultural school according to the project of Bykovskiy. But Bykovskiy used another type of estate ensemble too – with the main block brought out to the street red line. Thus were Gorikhvostskaya alms house in Big Kaluzhskaya street, the hospitium of A.A.Akhlebaev in Warm lane in Khamovniki, the complex of buildings of the community of sisters of mercy of the icon of the Theotokos "Assuage My Sorrow" in Hospital square.

In Moscow during that time the private, houses were reconstructed, adjusted or constructed in Sretenskaya, Pyatnitskaya, Khamovnicheskaya, Yakimanskaya parts (the end of 1830s – beginning of 1840s), at the end of 1840s – beginning of 1850s – Arbatskiy in Stolovy lane and Sutschevskiy in Seleznevskaya street. The main block of a private house (the main from the point of view of its compositional role, in Sretenskiy private house the stables looked at the street) was always situated on the street red line. Symmetrical location of the street blocks added gala look to an ensemble. In the middle there usually was the big volume of the main block with a characteristic fire-tower inthe centre and wings or lower blocks at the sides. The economy houses were usually placed along the perimeter of the land plot at the back side.

All public houses of 1830-1860 in Moscow showed the speciality stated during the description of the stores in Bolotnaya square: the rhythm in the architecture of romanticism substituted the accentuated hierarchy of classicism. The successive subordination of the secondary to the main disappeared. The composition of facades became rhythmic, based on the interaction of several elements. All variants of axial and symmetrical compositions were interpreted as though in a softer form. But at the same time they were included into a more complex rhythm of the whole, accentuating not the self-sufficiency and completeness of a separate building, the main axis of which was perpendicular to the main axis of the street as though forming its inter-

Big Yakimanka street. Buildings on the left side. Middle of the 19th century.

Big Yakimanka street. Buildings on the right side. Middle of the 19th century.

Pogodinskaja hut (1856, architect N. Nikitin).

rupted rhythm, but the coulissesform and frontality of the facades subordinated to the street, the composition of which formed the general facade of the street run through by even rhythm. This speciality was characteristic both for public and dwelling buildings. The new conception of the personality, new idea of the system of the highest values, new idea of the beautiful, which was so brightly expressed in the description of the district near Tverskaya frontier post, was behind it.

It is most difficult to define the changes, which took place in the civil construction in Moscow. It was although classicism operating with the modes typical for its simplest genres – for the dwelling houses of merchants, artisans, clergy men. It was orderless architecture with equal distribution of accents on the facades, without representative compositions with an accentuated centre and a gala portico. If an order was used, it was in an intimate, not heroic variant proportionate not to the building as a whole, but to its separate elements, most often to the sizes of the window or to the height of the floor.

At the same time, this common style without expressive features of Moscow architecture had clear signs of local individuality, which made it different from Petersburg and provincial architecture. Stylizations of baroque and rococo were used rather widely in dwelling buildings in Petersburg. The compositions, which made the facades of the dwelling houses similar to Florentine palaces, were spread in Petersburg. In Moscow there were just separate elements taken from the architecture of the facades of Italian palaces. At the same time in Moscow the above-mentioned original "negative" compositions with accentuated side parts and the neutral central one, introduced into the practice by one of the best Moscow architects of the second third of the lath century M.D.Bykovskiy, were often used.

The disappearance of porticos was the most characteristic feature of the composition of the facades of the dwelling and public buildings in 1830-1860, which influenced the change of the look of Moscow streets and especially the central ones. The look of the houses in the area of Lubyanka street can be well illustrated not only by the house of M.N.Golitsyn, but by the comparison of pictures of Kuznetskiy bridge, Tverskaya and other streets of the beginning and the middle of the 19th century. The street, the look of which was defined at the beginning of the century by porticos of nobility houses, creating big accents and clear rhythm, was sharply changed. It was as though built in with an entire extended building with even rhythm of windows. The wholeness of the construction was emphasized, but its heroic scale disappeared.

The type of a small rented house with two floors and one, two or four flats on the floor, prevailed in Moscow together with mansions. Continuing the tradition of a dwelling house of the first quarter of the lath century, they did not have the visual features of bidermeier with even distribution of accents, empha-

sized wide development of the composition, neutrality and coulisses style, orderlessness.

The mania of remaking of facades and liquidation of porticos everywhere was characteristic for 1830-1860 in the same way as superstructures with the purpose of adding symmetry and regularity to the facades and arrangement of columned porticos were typical and spread in the second half of the lath century. The liquidation of porticos was motivated by artistic considerations. The requirement "to remove columns for a betterlook" accompanied numerous remakings of facades. Order, columns, porticos, which stopped being the symbols of the highest spiritual values, were not looked at as the beautiful, artistically expressive and lost the importance of the significant element of a building composition.

At the end of 1850 with cancellation of the obligatory construction according to sample facades, new, but single at that time, dwelling houses in Russian style appeared. It was a simultaneous process "from the bottom to the top" and "from the top to the bottom". Merchant Kokorev , an "economic Slavophil" presented a house in Russian style tohis friends and like-minded person historian Pogodin. It was the famous Pogodinskaya hut, constructed in 1850 according to N.V.Nikitin's project. In 1857-1859 according to the project of architect F.F.Rikhter the chambers of the boyards Romanovs were restored, but actually built anew upon the emperor's order, in Varvarka street, anticipating the coming of Russian style in the second half of the 19th century into the civil architecture of a Russian town and into the ancient capital of Russia too.

Industrial Construction

In 1830-1850 Moscow was not just a city with developed industry, but had its own specialization, becoming the all-Russia centre of textile industry. Textile factories made 94% of the total quantity of Moscow enterprises and at the beginning of 1840 occupied more than 1300 buildings. In 1853 in Moscow 866 industrial enterprises operated,bounding the historical centre from the West, South and East, being situated, mostly, in a semicircle along the flow of the Moscow-river and the Yauza. However, such quantity of industrial buildings did not influence the look of the streets and quays, because they, as a rule, were situated on the owners' plots in the depth of the yards. The houseof the Ryabushinskiys, situated in Golutvinskiy lane, can be a characteristic example. The Moscow mansion, typical for the early 19th century, – two-storey with an attic, adorned with a portico from four pilasters under a triangular pediment, stood out to the red line.In 1846 in the territory of the estate a three-storey building, of a factory was built. Ten years later V.M.Ryabushinskiy asked for the permission to build "in the garden on the waste land a stone four-storey dwelling block

12 sazhens long, 6 sazhens wide, in which it will be quite convenient to install the looms which are at the factory". In answer the permission was received to construct the building and to place in it fifty looms, usual machines in the quantity of forty one, four warping machines, three hundred and fifty five working machines for adults and sixty bobbin machines; one hundred and eighty sazhens of fire-wood, obliging him, Ryabushinskiy, by his signature to substitute the latter with peat".

In 1830-1860 Moscow was still a city built in freedom. According to statistics, vegetable gardens in the pre-reform Moscow occupied 1/6 part of the city space, gardens occupied 1/2. So on the majority of the land plots there was enough place for construction of three- and even four-storey factory blocks. During the period of industrial overturn the intensive industrial construction influenced the look of the city only indirectly. Democratization of life showed in the change of the look of dwelling and public buildings, in the composition of which the composition of merchant and petty bourgeois houses was reconsidered and renovated. Where earlier big nobility estates prevailed – in Pokrovskaya, Sutschevskaya, Taganskaya, Lefortovskaya parts, now the main quantity of manufacture enterprises was situated. More private properties appeared in the East, North-East and South-East of the capital, which being divided into smaller parts, were transferred to soldiers' wives and petty bourgeois wives, producing a small quantity of products. Due to the transfer already by 1830s of many nobility properties into the hands of merchants, the quantity of their stone houses increased by 1/5 in comparison with the pre-fire Moscow. Even bigger increase was seen among the petty bourgeois. And thoughmerchants, like the nobility, made in Moscow only 4-5% of its inhabitants, merchants, already in 1830-1850, i.e. before the abrogation of serfdom, held in their hands the main levers of the economic life of the ancient capital: whole sale and retail sale and industry. The main districts where merchants lived were Zamoskvorechie and Rogozhsko-Taganskiy at that time.

The role of merchants increased and the first signs of their influence on the culture and the look of the ancient capital could be seen in the above-mentioned use of the modes of dwelling buildings of the third estate on the dwelling buildings of the nobility and public buildings, the turn of the specialities of the dwelling buildings, which had been secondary recently, into style-making.

At the same time, in Moscow of 1830-1850 the specialities of the after-fire Moscow were retained, but mostly of town-building than stylistic character. Mostly one-storey buildings were constructed at distances, which was typical both for dwelling ant public buildings. There was even a tendency to decrease the height of dwelling buildings in comparison with the second half of the 18th century, when a rich nobility house usually had three floors, and simultaneously there was increase of the height of temples and bell-towers. There was also an indirect influence of merchants in it and, in a wider sense, – an influence of carriers of the traditional culture, on whom absolutism was based then, turning the enlightened into unenlightened.

There was another side of turning Moscow from a nobility city into a merchant city – the sphere of economic, practical activity. Besides, together with the original concealed forms of Moscow transformation there were demonstrative, open forms, which attracted attention of contemporaries. They influenced noticeably the look of the central streets and city's suburbs and became the subject of heated discussion. The new types of buildings are meant, connected with development of new forms of trade, enterprise, transport, practical activity.

The appearance of shops with large shop-windows, which gradually supplanted the traditional stores was mentioned above already. But besides the shops there were other phenomena similar to them. The novelties in the character of trade and the look of the trade buildings were mentioned in the "Essays about Moscow of 40s" of I.T.Kokorev. Hewrote: earlier in Moscow "there were simply stores and rows, which were overflown with goods; a few years passed and shops ousted the stores nearly into dirt; 10 years more passed and now, wherever you look, there are depots everywhere: a baker has a depot of biscuits, a tobacco-worker has a depot of cigarettes... Then passages, galleries, small bazaars appeared".[30] Exactly these buildings – passages, galleries, exchanges, railway stations became the first visual impressive signs of the turn of nobility Moscow into merchant one, and the appearance in Tsargrad – the third Rome of characteristic signs of Manchester, a merchant capitalist city.

This turn happened with support of the government and especially of the municipal authority. The first initiator of trade-industrial novelties in Moscow became the family aristocracy. In 1830-1840 the work of the numerous Golitsyn's family was especially active in this respect. Not all their projects were realized. However, their importance is as symptomatic as the importance of the unrealised projects of the 18th century. At the same time their difference was striking. In the 18th century representative, serious projects, directed at glorification of the state – triumphal arches and palaces – appeared and were not realized, in the 19th century – there were trade buildings which seemed too new and not worth occupying gala public squares.

In 1835 upon the initiative of the governor-general prince D.V.Golitsyn, architect Bykovskiy, a like-minded person and a laborious assistant of the head of the city in the affair of turning Moscow into the centre of Russian trade and industry, made a project of a bazaar in the manner of Pale-Royal in Paris. A building of the type of a roofed market with an inside yard and a large inside space, made due to the use of wooden pillars of a frame. Their large space contrasted with the stern closeness of the facades.

Several years passed and upon the initiative of another Golitsyn – Michael Nikolaevich, according to Bykovskiy's project an arcade was constructed, the first in Moscow and in Russia, more known under the name of Golitsyn's gallery.

It was planned as a palace of trade and as an important public building, but absolutely different from its predecessors. According to the sample of an antique temple the famous Petersburg Exchange was built. Moscow building was based on other prototypes. It was built according to a sample, which was not known till that time in Russia and finished with the luxury inside and outside, which was not known during construction of trade buildings till that time. "All the window and door casements shall be made in bronze, the windows shall be large, the gallery floor shall be from marble and in general all the exterior and interior finishing shall be made according to the sample of the best Parisian passages and galleries".

Golitsyn's gallery did not keep. At the beginning of 1910s it was rebuilt for Golofteevskiy passage and then demolished; now there is the new block of the Central Universal Shop (Supermarket) (CUS) in its place.

The gallery was open on 15th of February, 1842. Nearly at the same time with this event a book was issued, which described enthusiastically the type of trade buildings, which had not been seen in the country till that time, "Arrangement of this gallery is an absolutely new thing. At its sides it has the shape of a huge ship with one small house on its bow and one on the stern, between which there is a roof from green-house frames instead of a deck with glass through which light comes into the gallery; they are covered with a wire net and in case of a thunder storm or heavy hail, they are immediately covered with wooden shutters".

Golitsyn's passage, like passages in general, demonstrated the preliminary stage of artistic mastery of the interior yard and interior quarter space. For the regular town-building it was not a subject for artistic arrangement, was considered as utility one, lower than public gala space of the streets and squares. The new type of a trade buildings made the inside space an object of the art of architecture. A passage represented a variation of a roofed street with shops at both sides. The choice of the place was symptomatic in this case of the first passage. It occupied the place of a lane, retaining the meaning of space, connecting two streets – Petrovka and Neglinnaya.

All important projects of big trade buildings and complexes (including Bolotnaya street) appeared upon the initiative or were

Gallery with the shops of prince M.N.Golitsyn.

actively supported by the municipal authority. Due to their construction the streets, adjoining the central squares of the Kremlin and Kitay-gorod, were turned into trade ones out of the nobility dwelling streets.Thus was the destiny of Kuznetskiy bridge, Lubyanka, Petrovka and Tverskaya. Designing of trade complexes and buildings, connected with expression of economic power of merchants, more than other showed the conflict of relations between the state power, on the one hand, and the municipal authority and merchants, on the other hand.

The history of creation of the Exchange in Moscow, founded on 1st of July, 1836, according to the project of M.D.Bykovskiy, represents a long opposition between the emperor and Moscow merchants. The will for self-consolidation made the merchants to look for a place for the Exchange near the Kremlin in Red Square. They offered to build it either in front of the monument of Minin and Pozharsky (in the place of the future mausoleum), or in the place of the former Offices and the future Historical Museum. Their purpose was to create an Exchange, "huge and magnificent, which could be a monument too".[32] The merchants did not agree to the offer to place the Exchange behind Iljinskie gates in the place of the Apple Row, where later the Polythechnical Museum was built. But the emperor rejected all the pretensions for construction of the Exchange near the Kremlin. Finally the merchants had to agree with the emperor's insistence to find a place withinthe boundaries of Kitay-gorod, and, most important, to give up the wish to construct it "in the large and majestic style", because "with all the effort to find an appropriate and convenient place..." was not possible "as the City part is crowded". An authorized representative of Moscow merchants had to agree also to the variant of construction, which had been initially rejected by them, "of one exchange hall: without any other accessories in front of the former house of Alexeeva" in the place of the Fish Row.[33]

The certified project of the Exchange was, probably, one of the first, if not the first project of a public building in the spirit of romanticism. Its composition was a direct contrast to the temple-like exchange in Petersburg, to public buildings of classicism and even to the preliminary project of M.D.Bykovskiy, though in the facade composition the traditional classical symmetrical-axial three-part composition and division into socle, main and crowning parts were kept. The place of a gala columned portico in the centre was occupied by a light transparent gallery on thin pig iron posts. The place of the standing out rizalit was taken by recessed space of a loggia-gallery, the place of a pediment was taken by an attic, crowning the main volume of the building. Not the central, but the side parts of the building were accentuated, in the form of massive archy porches. Due to them and to the three-part composition, which was simultaneously finished and subordinated to the direction of the street, not a big volume of the Exchange was not lost on the background of G.Quarenghi's grandiose Guest Yard with its even rhythm of columns of the gigantic order.

In 1830-1850 together with the Exchange square in Moscow another square of new type appeared – of the railway. In 1844 the construction of the big railway, the first one in Russia, which connected Moscow and Petersburg, was begun, and in 1851 it was finished. On 16th of August, 1852, by the train, by which the emperor and two battalions of Preobrazhenskiy and Semenovskiy troops travelled, the direct transportation was opened. The railway stations in both capitals, which nearly repeated each other (in Petersburg the building was a little bigger, in Moscow a complex of three building' was planned) were designed by K.A.Ton.

In order to avoid inconveniences caused by the railway: infernal din and smoke, the place for a railway station was chosen in Moscow in the suburbs of the city – in Kalanchevskaya square.

The railway station belongs to the type of dead points: the railway finishes at its building. In the centre from the side of the square the main entrance was arranged, to the left and to the right there were the pairs of the gates leading to the platforms. The platforms were covered by a single roof on pig iron thin columns.

The railway station in Moscow was designed as the central building of the architectural complex, which started a gala construction in a waste square. At both sides from the railway station symmetrically in relation to it the buildings of the customs house (to the left) and a dwelling house for the employees (to the right, was not realized)were designed.

The customs house was secondary in relation to the railway station, designed in Renaissance style or in the Renaissance version of bidermeier. It was a three-storey building, but architecturally, following the composition of the railway station, was dividedinto two main tiers – the first rustic floor with archy windows, repeating the rhythm of the archy windows of the railway station; the second and the third floors were united by plane pilasters. Their even rhythm repeated the rhythm of the columns of the building.

The plainness and significantly big neutrality of the composition of the facade testify to the subordination of its building to the building of the railway station.

Kalanchevskaya square was to become the focus of the railway junction, which began to be formed in 1850-1860 in Moscow. In 1862 Yaroslavskiy railway station was built near it, continuing the red line of Kalanchevskaya square, started by the construction of Nikolaevskiy (Petersburg) railway station. Soon in the same square, but on the opposite side, in 1862-1864 the third building of the railway station appeared – Ryazanskiy (in 1894 it was renamed into Kazanskiy). During the same time, in 1860s behind Pokrovskaya (Abelmanovskaya) frontier port Kurskiy railway station was built and not far from it Nizhegorodskiy railway station was built with the stations for passengers and cargo (in 1890 it was placed in the right wing of a new building of Kurskiy railway station). The initial cycle of construction of Moscow railway stations was finished by the opening of Smolenskiy (Brestskiy, Belorusskiy) railway station in 1870.

The social-economic changes in Moscow life got their purely architectural expression in 1870-1890, declaring about them-

Exchange in Kitay-gorod in Iljinka (1835-1836, architect M.D. Bykovskiy). Lithography. Middle of the 19th century.

selves for the first time approximately in ten years after the abrogation of the serfdom. But then in 1830-1860, in spite of the fact that "Moscow is the focus of Russian trade, that for our empire it is the shop both of home and foreign products, that... its influence is felt even in many foreign countries", the definite influence on their look was made by the state policy with its program of the official national system. Construction in the city was defined mainly by the state policy and officially accepted values. The social-economic side of town-building expressed it self much weaker and less successively. New types of buildings born by economic development and the first railway boom did not yet become determined in Moscow look. In 1830-1860 new types of buildings were not the leading ones yet.

---

1 Lotman Yu.M., Uspenskiy B.A. Echo of the conception "Moscow – the Third Rome" in the ideology of Peter I (about the problem of the medieval tradition in the culture of baroque) // Artistic language of the medieval time. M., 1982, p. 237.
2 Acts. The Holy Synod of Russian Orthodox Church. M.-Pg., 1918, b. II, is. 2, p. 351.Quot.: Uspenskiy B.A. Selected Works in 2 volumes, V. 1. Semyotics of the history.Semyotics of the culture. M., 1994, p. 111.
3 Berdjaev N.A. The Philosophy of inequality. Letters to the enemies of on-socialphilosophy. Berlin, 1923, p. 13-14.
4 From the publisher // Art newspaper. 1837, No. 1, p. 9.
5 Svijazev I.I. Practical drawings for arrangement of the church of the Entry of the Theotokos into the Temple in Semenovskiy Regiment in Petersburg, made by architect E.I.V. and professor of architecture of the Imperial Academy of Art and a member of different foreign academies Constantine Ton. M., 1845, p. 3.
6 Berdjaev N.A. Russian idea. The main problems of Russian thought in the 19th century and in the early 20th. // About Russia and Russian philosophic culture. Philosophers of Russian after-October emigrants. M., 1990, p. 81-86.
7 Zagoskin M.N. Moscow and moscovites // Full collection of works. v.7. M., 1898, p. 4, 12, 24.
8 As above. V. 5, p. 5, 12, 25.
9 The album was made by photographer N.S.Matveev at the end of 1890s.
10 Pushkin A.S. Full collection of works, v. X.
11 Zagoskin M.N. The above works, 116.
12 See, in detail from the history of design and construction of the cathedral of Christ the Saviour in the book: The cathedral of Christ the Saviour in Moscow. Text E.I.Kirichenko. Composition of G.A.Ivanov. M., 1992.
13 Braykovskiy A.A. Description of the cathedral in the name of Christ the Saviour in Moscow. Guide-book for the visitors of the cathedral of Christ the Saviour at the present time. M., 1882, p. 61; M.N.V-v., Survey of the cathedral of Christ the Saviour. M., 1882, p. 8.
14 Sophiyskaya mosque and the mosque of Ahmed in Constantinople // Artistic survey. M., 1837, v. III, p. 86.
15 The cathedral of Christ the Saviour in Moscow // Journal for the disciples of the military-educational institutes. 1851, v. XCIII, No. 369, p. 102.
16 Mosque Sophiyskaya and mosque of Ahmed in Constantinople,, p. 87.
17 Sokolov P. Historical description of the celebration which took place during the foundation of the cathedral of Christ the Saviour on the Vorobjovy hills at the Highest presence of His Imperial Majesty Tsar Emperor Alexander Pavlovich... 1817, on 12th of October. M., 1818, p. 1, 2.
18 Mostovskiy M., The above works, 39.
19 Full orthodox theological dictionary. V. 1. M., p. 1059.
20 Sterligova I.A. Jerusalems as liturgical vessels in Ancient Russia// Jerusalem in Russian culture. M., 1994, p. 46.
21 As above, p. 48.
22 As above, p. 52.
23 As above, p. 54.
24 Decree of 7th of January, 1827. "The tsar emperor wished to order me to collect immediately the following data in the domains: 1) in what towns there are ancient castles and fortresses and other buildings of antiquity and 2) in what condition they are. At the same time the will of His Majesty is to prohibit most strictly to demolish such buildings...4 (RGIA, f. 797, op. 3, d. 10028, sh. 1). Decree ofthe governmental Synod of 22.11.1840, No. 1422. (RGIA, f. 797, op. V, 1843-45, d.3220, 9, sh. 2).
25 Dmitriev N. Essay about Moscow Kremlin in the architectural aspect // Moscow Domain Records. Part two. Unofficial. 1849, No. 50, p. 502.
26 As above, p. 432.
27 Batalov A.L. The Holy Sepulchre in the plot "The Holy of the Holiest" of Boris Godunov // Jerusalem in Russian culture., p. 156.
28 Batalov A.L., Vjatchanina T.NN The above works, 25.
29 I.D. (Dmitriev V.I.). Guide-book from Moscow to Petersburg and back, informing historical, statistical and other facts... M., 1847 (printed from the issue of 1839), p. 2-3.
30 Nikolaev E.V. The above works, 174.
31 Quot.: Sivkov K.V. Moscow in the first half of the 19th century // Teaching of history at school. 1947. No. 2, p. 27.
32 Naydenov N.A. Moscow Exchange. M., 1883, p. 10.
33 The words of D.V.Golitsyn in favour of the necessity of construction of the Exchange in Moscow. Ouot.: Naydenov N.A. The above works, 3-4.

CHAPTER FIVE

Merchant Moscow

Illumination of the Arsenal tower on the coronation day of Alexander II. Artist V. Sadovnikov. 1856.

Announcement about the coronation of Alexander II in Red Square. Artist V. Sadovnikov. 1856.

Emperor Alexander II (1856-1881). Artist A. Harlamov. 1874.

Emperor Alexander III (1881-1894). Artist I.Kramskoy. 1882.

The building of Moscow City Duma in Voskresenskaja square (1890-1892, architect D. Chichagov). Colour post-card. Late 19th – beginning of the 20th centuries.

Tverskoy boulvard. The memorial to A. Pushkin (1880, sculptor A. Opekushin, architect I. .Bogomolov). Photo. End of the 19th century.

The Historical Museum in Red Square (1875-1883, architect V.O.Shervud, A.A.Semenov). Photo. 1880s.

Moscow panorama from the Shvivaja hill. Photo. Late 19th century.

Square of Iljinskie gate and the chapel-memorial to the heroes of Plevna (architect V. Shervud). Photo. Late 19th century.

Kuznetskiy bridge. Photo. Late 19th century.

View of Tverskaja street behind the house of the governor-general. Photo. Late 1880s.

Loubjanskaja square after the construction of the Loubjanskiy passage and the substation of the electrical tramway. Photo. Early 1910s.

Loubjanskaja square. View 9t the Teatraljny passage before the construction of the Loubjanskiy passage. Photo. Late 19th century.

The memorial to Alexander II in the Kremlin
(sculptor A.M.Opekushin, architect N. Sultanov). Chromolithography.

The Synodal printing house. Restoration and the new block near
the wall of Kitay-gorod (1870s, architect A.Artleben).

Nikolskaja street. Slav Bazaar (1870s, architect A.Veber). Photo. 2nd half of the 19th century.

In the second half of the 19th century approximately in ten years after the abrogation of the serfdom all the tendencies, which had appeared earlier in the social and economic life of Moscow and in architecture, became absolutely definite. In 1830-1860 merchants conquered the leading positions in the economic life of the city. Beginning from 1850 and especially in 1860s the main customer of the most significant constructional undertakings of all-Russian, city-wide and local scale, were the merchants. For their account and upon their initiative industrial enterprises were built, works connected with arrangement of the city were conducted. For the account of the merchants Hospitals and alms houses, gymnasiums, high and secondary schools, specialized schools, museums, exhibitions, theatres, libraries were built. The sphere of the social order and charity went far beyond temple-building. The city of the second half of the 19th – beginning of the 20th centuries was created at the expense of the merchants. In the second half of the 19th century merchants together with Slavophils influenced most of all the development of the architectural style, to say more exactly, the style of object-spatial arts, in all the wide sphere enveloping architecture and applied arts. The role of merchants during that period can be compared with the role of the government in 1830-1850 and resulted in the same thing – spreading of the Russian style.

Moscow – Merchant Capital of Russia

The unusual character of the cultural and historical mission of Russian merchants was determined by the originality of the history of the New Time. The merchants initiated the process of synthesis, merging of European education with the roots of Russian national system, Russian life and Russian culture. It was the activity of the merchants in all its variety – in the sphere of economy, trade, enlightenment, construction, charity made it possible to spread the culture of European type outside the framework of the nobility.

One of the expressions of materialization of this process became in the middle of the 19th century the union of the nobility Slavophils, which was unique for all the history of Russia and was the intellectual centre of this movement, with Russian merchants who lived through the period of increase of the national self-consciousness. Slavophils were represented by A.S.Khomjakov, brothers I.S. and K.S.Aksakov, brothers I.V. and P.V.Kirevskiy, Yu.Samarin, I.A.Koshelev, professors M.P.Pogodin and K.D.Kavelin, writer V.A.Sollogub, artists G.G.Gagarin, A.E.Beideman, M.N.Vasiljev. Among the most remarkable representatives of the first generation of the enlightened Moscow merchants – F.V.Chizhov, V.A.Kokorev, I.F.Mamontov, K.T.Soldatenkov, P.I.Gubonin, A.K. and V.K.Krestovnivs, K.V.Rukavishnikov, S.M. and P.M.Tretjakovs, the brothers Shilovs, T.S.Morozov, P.P.Maljutin, I.A.Ljamin.

It is characteristic that both Slavophils and the merchants who joined them, were mostly Muscovites. The attitude to Moscow as to the national centre and the keeper of traditions, its official status of the second, ancient historical capital, all its way of life and environment, which made one see in it the embodiment of Russian individuality, naturally, turned Moscow into the focus of the movement for revival of the national culture, into the capital of Slavophilism. And equally naturally, due to development of textile industry and the formation of Moscow railway junction already since 1860s – into the capital of Russian merchants. The economic program of Slavophils turned out to be identical to the interests of Russian merchants. They spoke for the state policy of protection of home industry, imposing of proteotionist duties, development of railways, extension of engineering education. As for merchants, the religious and moral principles of Slavophilism, respectful and interested attitude to their business activity, could not be strange to them. The merchants made the efforts to be and really became an independent social and economic force and, being educated at the contemporary level, represented a practical embodiment of the Slavophils' ideas in real life.

Acquiring such special features of the nobility life as making collections, protection of arts, becoming the main customer of construction works, the merchants brought the traditions, criteria, point of view of the cultural environment that brought them up, into all the undertakings, which were "nobiliary" by origin. The growth of self-consciousness of the third estate, supported by the growth of its economic power, beginning from the middle of the 19th century, got a wider and more variable echo in the sphere of culture. The essence of the merchants activity in this sphere was in one thing: in the striving to reflect, emphasize, support, make more evident the cultural and historical roots of merchants, to show their connection with folk culture.

The merchants became protectors of Russian style, and the closer to the end of the 19th century the more evident it was, they were the customers of constructions in Russian style. They were the first who began to collect the objects of Russian folk art, which became one of the main sources of revival of Russian art which was seen in 1830-50s.

What was said does not contradict the above described fact of protection by Nicholas I of Russian style and the official policy in the sphere of art during the reign of this emperor. In 1830-1850 Russian style was applied in temple building. The following stages in development of Russian style were connected with the efforts and initiative of merchants – its spreading in the civil architecture and in the applied art in the second half of the 19th century.

In the "Guide of an Architect around Moscow", published by the second congress of Russian architects in 1895, in a short essay about construction activity during the last 25 years the appearance in Moscow of buildings in Russian style was especially mentioned: "In this respect Moscow gave an example to other towns"; hope was expressed that "revival of Russian architecture, begun by Moscow, will progress".[1]

Thus was one of the expressions of the qualitative transformation, which happened in the second half of the 19th century and turned Moscow into the all-Russia capital of merchants. It was stated by everybody who wrote about Moscow of that time. The formula itself belonged to P.D.Boborykin. He wrote: "What is Moscow? The capital or a domain town?.. It should be better to regard it as the central domain city or, better to say, the type of what large points of regions of the Russian land can be in future, which were a little separated. The framework of a domain town is in everything here". However, what was associated with and represented the capital status of Moscow (Moscow of aristocracy, nobility and clerks), was, from the point of view of Boborykin, "only one fifth of the capital". Near it and, so to say, under it another kingdom was developing – economic. And in this sense Moscow was the most important centre of Russia, and not only for Russia. Exactly in this Moscow is the real capital! Not a city in general, but a "city" in a special Moscow meaning, i.e. the one which was bounded by a wall and adjoined the Kremlin (Kitay-gorod – E.K.) – the central body of Russian productivity. It feeds the city economy too; but its importance is not limited by this domain town, but by all the empire. It is a huge world, the successor of the multi-million productivity... In future it will be the capital of the industry of all Russia of a special kind and of trade like New-York became the capital of all American states in these aspects... by the end of the 19th century the trade-industrial Moscow became simultaneously Manchester, London, New-York".

The merchants became a real social force, when, upon the definition of Boborykin, when making Moscow not only like Manchester, but like New-York and London, it reached the heights of culture. "In Moscow there is evidently the pulse of Russian scientific and social thought and artistic endeavours... Giving way to Petersburg as the political centre, Moscow should be considered at least equal to it in the aspect of Russian thought and Russian culture. At the same time Moscow is the focus of Russian industry and trade. Moscow is the place of merchants of all Russia (the biggest industrial and trade companies, wholesale warehouses are here, providing all Russia with goods, banks, exchanges etc.), a huge industrial centre, in which all the main types of processing industry are represented.

With its 10 railways Moscow also occupied the first place in Russia, as the biggest railway junction of the most important railway lines. All this put Moscow to the first place in the state, near the official capital – Petersburg".[2]

Together with Petersburg Moscow in the second half of the 19th century was the biggest city in Russia, the second after the Northern capital in the quantity of inhabitants and the first in the speed of increase of inhabitants.

In the second half of the 19th – beginning of the 20th centuries in Moscow and Petersburg the phenomenon of a big city, characteristic for that time, showed itself most fully for Russia. Its distinctive speciality – concentration of a sufficient mass of inhabitants on a comparatively limited territory. Exactly big cities grew especially quickly due to the inflow of people from villages during the general growth of towns at that time. In 1882 the percent of newly arrived people in relation to the indigenous population reached 73,3% in Moscow. Before the first world war it decreased, but not much, to 72.4%.[3]

During three quarters of the century from 1830 to 1902 Moscow had 305631 inhabitants, in 1902 the population was more than a million, making 1059923. But the growth was not smooth. Its highest point was in 1864-1871 after the abrogation of the serfdom and forming of Moscow railway junction. In 1864 in Moscow there were 364148 people (not more than thirty years later), and seven years later a sharp leap happened. By 1871 the population was nearly twice bigger, reaching 601969 people, i.e. increased by 93%. This figure is especially impressive in contrast with 1830-1864, when Moscow population increased during ten years nearly by 5,5%. Later the growth of population, though it remained high (20-25% during ten years), and Moscow was one of the most dynamically developing cities of the world and Russia (in the speed of growth it left Petersburg behind and was competing with New-York), the speed of growth of its population did not reach the level of the years of reforms even during the first world war.

By the end of the 19th century during thirty years which passed after the time of the abrogation of serfdom, Moscow look changed sharply, as well as the character of its constructions, town-forming factors. The geography and specialization of the districts of the most intensive construction became different. At the beginning of 1860s the construction was concentrated mostly in the centre. While Moscow railway junction formed the main place of attraction of people, the territories near the railway stations became the location of the new industrial and dwelling construction. Thus the natural – factor the first factories were placed, mainly, on the river banks and near the ponds, near big water resources, – was added with another factor, which had not been known before – railway construction.

During 1860s the main points of the radiuses of Moscow railways were put into operation and Moscow railway junction was formed. The location of the railway stations determined the geography of construction of factories, plants and dwellings for their employees. Near the railway stations industrial complexes, not known before the reforms, were formed and grew quickly. New dwelling quarters grew around them as quickly. The rapid growth of capitalism showed itself in extension of traditional trade districts and transformation of the functional structure of the city centre.

Descriptions of Moscow of the second half of the 19th century attract attention by rapid urbanization and appearance of a new customer as a result of the radical social and economic changes. "The great reforms and first of all the abrogation of serfdom and introduction of the city self-authority changed most radically the conditions which specified the economic and cultural life in Moscow. Since then the village, estate Moscow became a thing of the past irrevocably, rapidly becoming the type of a modern city... with construction of Rjazanskaja, Kurskaja, Nizhegorodskaja, Brestskaja, Yaroslavskaja railways the importance of Moscow as of the centre of a large industrial region became especially evident and grew each year".

As a contemporary said, "so many new elements, which had not been allowed before and had no right to exist", at once appeared in the society, that all the way of life, impregnated with serfage relations and serfdom spirit, changed unrecognizably.

The estate Moscow, which lived for the account of Penza and Tambov souls, transformed quickly into capitalist Moscow. A new powerful class appeared on the scene, which had managed to accumulate a great economic force in the silence of patriarchal corn-chandler's shops.

The importance of Moscow as the centre of the national culture, under the token of which architecture of the ancient capital developed in 1830-1850, was valid in the second half of the century too. But the tendency of turning Moscow into Russian Manchester acquired a qualitatively new character and scale. Moscow turned, according to Boborykin's words, also into Russian London and New-York, into the main junction of Russian railways, and due to it – into the main centre of all-Russia internal trade and the kernel of the Central (sometimes called Moscow) industrial region.

The look and character of Moscow after the reforms changed more radically than in any other town of Russia, not excluding Petersburg. The contrast between the habitually not high buildings and the new huge buildings was especially acute.

The reasons were not only in the fact that the factors which influenced architecture most actively, concentrated in Moscow. It was only one side of the matter. The second was in the patriarchality of Moscow look, its spatiousness, in the plenty of waste land and gardens inside the city, in buildings with not many floors in the first half of the 19th century.

Together with the intensive construction in Moscow the rapid increase of the speed and volume of construction, with appearance of new types of buildings due to rapid urbanization, growth of dimensions and the quantity of floors of buildings in Moscow already in 1870s another tendency characteristic for big cities of the world -a rapid growth of suburbs in comparison with the centre – which showed itself fully at the end of the 19th – beginning of the 20th centuries, began to appear. Movement of people first out of the centre to the suburbs, and then to the country-side began. The city centre gradually turned into a business one, full of life during the day time and empty at night.

City Reform of 1870s

After the decease of Nicholas I the epoch of hard state regulation, centralization and control of architectural and construction activity stopped. All life in the country developed in the direction of democratization and increase of the rights given by the local authorities. The city reform belonged to the most significant during the epoch of the great reforms. The right of leadership and control of the construction policy in the city was transferred to the city authority. An exception were a few objects of state importance – railways and a number of public buildings of all-Russia significance – unique hospitals, high educational institutions, state banks etc.

The administrative reform influenced the development of Moscow and other towns in the same direction as new phenomena in the economic life: the townforming, artistic, contextual importance of the factors of utility character increased rapidly. The utilitarian, practical became an independent, and not only material, but also spiritual value and the changed town-building policy, was connected with the new conception of the city centre and the change of architectural style.

Up to the reign of Nicholas I the main functions of any town, including the capitals, were the administrative and trade. The architectural and town-building conception, contents and symbolics of the main ensembles and their artistic expressiveness were determined by the administrative function, raised to the level of the state idea, and in the capitals – by the state conception of this or that reign. In 1830-1850 the habitual situation remained. But the sense given to the traditional forms of state policy, began to change. A historical town, and first of all, the ancient capital, was comprehended as a phenomenon of the national culture, connected with the past by its roots, expressing the national ideals and serving the national interests. During the reign of Nicholas I the national system was comprehended first of all as a spiritual aspect, as orthodoxy.

In the second half of the 19th century this notion retained its viability. But material values became equally important. The change of accents was expressed in the change of the denomination of civil buildings, forming the centre of the city. Now it was not only temples, palaces, administrative buildings, but first of all – museums, theatres, the buildings connected with the idea of people's power and self-authority. The role of educational institutions and hospital complexes and their quantity increased rapidly. Moscow became generally acknowledged as the national-economic centre of trade and industry, as the railway junction. Accents in town-building policy changed. The social-utilitarian aspect became of the first priority now in comparison with the spiritual-state aspect. The state idea, which traditionally prevailed in the 18th – beginning of the 19th centuries, transformed in 1830-1850 into the idea of the official national system, and in the second half of the 19th century – in the idea of people's power and self-authority. The ideas of the national system and the nationality during the period of flourishing of science, enlightenment, art and folk art, which were the embodiment of the national system in the second half of the 19th century, predetermined another renovation of Moscow centre in 1870-1890.

Eight years earlier than other towns of Russia, in 1862 Moscow and Petersburg got the right for self-authority and the post of the city governor.

The administrative organization of the country, inseparably connected with the prevailing system of values, was significantly democratized. The leadership of the construction activity concentrated in the cities and was determined by the policy of the local authority. The government lost its ability to realize its interests in the town-building activity, understood as the propaganda of the state idea and the extolment of the state by the means of architecture. The abrogation in 1858 of the obligatory construction of dwelling and public buildings according to the sample projects, certified by the highest authority for all Russia, deprived the government of the function of the centralized rule and control of construction activity.

The reign of Alexander II was not called the time of great reforms for nothing. During that time the system of values, which had been gradually turning up during the reign of Nicholas I was established legally and organizationally. Simultaneously with implementation of the city reforms the end of the epoch came, when some were to design and the others were to chose from the designed by the architects only what was worth the highest approval. The system of organization of design, construction and control of this and that, enforced since the time of Peter I, was liquidated.

The main object of the government regulation and control in Russia till the middle of 1820s was the civil construction. Exactly with it the new ideals and values, which appeared simultaneously with Russian Empire, were connected. Cultural re-orientation had begun from the civil architecture in Moscow during the time of Peter I. The new look and often new denomination of civil buildings was reflected and accompanied in appearance of new notions and new Europeanized forms of life. First for Moscow, and then for Petersburg first sample projects were created. They were the dwelling houses not by chance. The government assumed the right to regulate the private right of a separate man. From the second half of the 19th century during the reign of Catherine II the use of sample projects was extended, projects of administrative and public buildings appeared. In the construction according to sample projects the Russian authorities saw the guarantee against appearance in the streets of the towns of buildings constructed not according to the "rules" of architecture, created in conformity with the norms of general European style. The custom of construction according to sample projects existed in Moscow for a century and a half.

An absolutely opposite situation was formed in the sphere of temple-building. The first album of sample projects under the name "Collection of plans, facades and profiles for construction of stone churches" was published only in 1824. i.e. more than a century later than the projects of dwelling houses appeared. Already only this fact is an undoubtful proof of what was considered the most important object of reforming in Russia of the New Time.

The first album of church sample projects, like the projects of all civil buildings that had been made till that time, were created in accordance with the norms of classical architecture. While the conception of "unenlightened absolutism" or of official national system was forming the government began to pay more attention to the role of the church in the life of the country and to the temple architecture. The break had appeared by the end of the reign of Alexander I, and the issue of the first album of temple sample projects testified to this effect. But only the reign of Nicholas I signified the end of the epoch of total Europeanization and the turn to the traditional cultural values, to the fatherland national and folk tradition. And this meant first of all the end of the epoch of Christian universalism and the turn to orthodoxy. During the time of Nicholas I three albums were issued with church sample projects – in 1838, 1841 and 1844. But most important, by the projects of each album construction of temples in Russian style was made obligatory.

Crystallization of the ideas of the national system and the nationality, as the main spiritual values and the crisis of the autocracy as a political doctrine coincided. Their result were such phenomena, which were at first sight far from each other, like spreading of church construction according to sample projects in Russian style, cancellation of the obligation to construct dwelling houses according to sample projects and the city reform. All of them brought sufficient changes into the look of towns of Russia, including Moscow.

The crisis of the autocracy idea was accompanied by decrease of the government power in the economic and spiritual spheres. Architecture was not an exception in this respect, though here the retreat happened later than in other kinds of art – in literature, music, painting. During the reign of Nicholas I only architecture was under control of the government, and in the second half of the 19th – beginning of the 20th centuries only one of its spheres was controlled – temple-building. And not everywhere, but in the outskirts of Russia – Western, Eastern, South-Eastern, where for different reasons it was especially necessary to consolidate orthodoxy and the national system as the basis of the autocracy. As for the both capitals, in them the leadership of the government of the architectural and town-building activity became a fact of history. The rejection to regulate and control the architectural and stylistic part of construction meant in its essence the rejection of the hard regulation of private and public life, which was characteristic for the earlier period.

It is even difficult to imagine now that the cancellation of the obligatory sample projects during construction of dwelling houses was understood by contemporaries as liberation of a person from the strict and detailed governmental guardianship. The possibility to create a project of one's own house in accordance with one's own taste became a symbol of personal freedom. Free-thinkers of the time of Nicholas I called Russia the facade empire and Petersburg – its capital. Rejecting the leadership of the contextual and stylistic part of architecture, the government retained only the leadership over development of wide-scale programs, important for the country, like development of the net-work of railways, leadership over the construction connected with migration etc.

Till now, following how from one reign to another Moscow look changed and the conception of the centre of the ancient capital, it was necessary to emphasize the connection of town-building works with the personal position of the tsar and the state conception of the reign. Nothing of the kind happened during the reign of the last three emperors. They did not make influence on the planning and the look of Moscow, did not interfere into its construction. The ancient capital was not an exception, the same thing happened in Petersburg and the province. Development of architecture was not going on as a natural historical process. The tsar was still one of the biggest customers, but as a private person.

One of the many results, though extremely characteristic, of the loss of the all-importance of the official ideology, was the expiration of the type of an emperor's palace as a residence of the head of the state. Including the reign of Nicholas I the emperor's palace always belonged to the most evident symbols of the reign. The last symbol of autocratic Russia became the Big Kremlin Palace in Moscow.

The ideas of the reign of Alexander II and his successors expressed themselves in architecture in another way. No tsar of the second half of the 19th – beginning of the 20th century left such memorials in Moscow about his reign as it happened during the reign of all Russian emperors from Peter I to Nicholas I. The ideas of the time were expressed in the architecture by other people and means. The exception was only the beginning of the reign of Alexander II. The architectural and town-building policy of his father still lived as though under its own momentum in the construction undertakings of the emperor in 1850-1860.

On the order of Alexander II the above-mentioned restoration was conducted (and actually the designing) of the chambers of the boyars Romanovs in Varvarka street. The project, made by F.F.Rikhter, ideologically and artistically continued the restoration of the ancient chambers in the Kremlin, which became an integral part of the ensemble of the Big Kremlin Palace. At the same time it cannot be compared with its predecessors neither in town-building, nor in contextual importance.

Alexander II also tried to create a new official gala residence. The choice of the place for it is very illustrative – Kolomenskoe near Moscow was the favourite estate of the Rjurikoviches and the Romanovs before the imperial time. Creation of a new emperor's residence here meant successiveness of the dynasties and the connection of new Russia with pre-Petrine Rusj. A competition for the best project was announced. The necessary condition was to design the palace in Russian style and its look in accordance with the pre-Petrine buildings which existed here.

The idea was not realized. After that the emperor undertook any construction works in Moscow or near it. With expiration of the state idea, the stimulus, which made the Russian emperors to undertake big construction works in Moscow, disappeared. The tsar became one of the private customers and this changed the geography of construction of the emperor's family. It was conducted mainly in the South of Russia – in the Crimea and the Caucasus.

In the second half of the 19th – beginning of the 20th centuries Moscow and Petersburg did not lose the capital sense of their architectural and town-building programs and undertakings. But the changed contents resulted in disappearance of the former parallelism in development of both capitals. Each of the city authorities realized their own plans.

The essence of the plans was determined by the new prevailing spiritual and ethical values: the belief that the government lives and functions in the name of man and for man, and not man for the government. The ethics of service to the government was ousted by the ethics of service to people. Increase of well-being, development of production, national industry and railways, technical progress, enlightenment, national health care acquired self-sufficient value and became the symbol of the epoch. Moscow municipal authorities took into consideration the current needs of the city inhabitants in their architectural and town-building policy, like any other authority of other towns in Russia during that time.

Never before such representative cultural and educational departments and educational institutions of all ranks were constructed in Moscow in such quantity and so quickly. Never before such quantity of all-Russia, local and branch exhibitions were carried out so widely. Never before so many hospitals and alms houses were constructed, so much attention was turned to the city arrangement, development of all types of transport and communication.

In the second half of the 19th century a complex of constant metallic bridges across the main waterways of the ancient capital – the Moscow-river and the Yauza – was constructed for the first time as an action at the city-wide scale. For some time Vsekhsvjatskiy or the Big Stone bridge, constructed by the time when the cathedral of Christ the Saviour was freed from the scaffoldings, was the only constant bridge across the Moscow river. The others were wooden, which were dismantled during the water flood. In 1860-1890 the construction of bridges, connecting the districts behind the Moscow-river with the centre, was conducted systematically by the forces of the municipal authority. Moskvoretskiy bridge became metallic. In 1864 Dorogomilovskiy bridge was built, in 1865-1866 – Krasnokholmskiy bridge, in 1872-1873 – Krymskiy and Yauzskiy bridges, in 1881-1883 – the Big and Small Ustjinskiy bridges. Construction of bridges was accompanied by the works on creation of passages along the river banks, construction and good arrangement of the quays. In 1876 Krasnokholmskaja quay was faced with stone. In 1877-1880 the gala quay in front of the cathedral of Christ the Saviour was built; in 1887-1888 Derbenevskaja dike was built and Novospasskaja quay was faced with stone.

After establishment of city self-authority Moscow municipal authority began a wide construction of municipal services. The water pipe-line was arranged anew, big works were conducted for creation of sewerage system. City laundry and a huge complex of city slaughter-houses were constructed. Doss-houses were constructed in different districts.

For the purpose of increase, as they said then, "of the exterior comfortable arrangement" the municipal authority conducted big work on straightening the streets and creation of new passages. With this purpose in Moscow, like in Petersburg, at the end of the 19th century a new plan of the city regulation was made. In Moscow it was begun in 1886 and finished in 1898.

The general tendency of that time was well seen in the construction policy of Moscow city authority – making the comfortable arrangement of life contextually important, the embodiment of spiritual values of time.

But the reasonable requirement of comfort rather often became a one-sided practicism and even nihilism in respect of historical memorials. The tradition dating from the 18th century, for the first time acquired the technocratic colouring in the 19th century. In order to make the extremely active movement more convenient, Zavalishin offered as one of radical measures to increase the quantity of bridges (which was successively done by the City Council) and to demolish "the useless wall of Kitay-gorod": "With breaking of the wall much place and material would appear, the city would be freed from extra expenses on its maintenance, movement would open in all directions, and the harm of such dark places like Zarjadie and the place between Nikolskaja street and the wall would be liquidated".[4]

Architecture did not avoid nihilism as a phenomenon of spiritual life of the 19th century. In 1860 in both capitals grandiose projects of recreation of the centre by adding a gala avenue or a system of avenues were created practically simultaneously. In Petersburg it was supposed to arrange them by backfilling Catherine's canal. In Moscow such avenue was planned from Kitay-gorod (from Loubjanskaja square) to Kalanchevskaja square, thus connecting the business centre with the transport junction, create Parisian boulevards of some kind, construct four-storey adjoining buildings on them, which were rare in Moscow at that time. This project, being similar with the "Kremlin reconstruction" of Bazhenov by its attitude towards the historical city as to a place without any buildings, anticipated the projects of the early 20th century, 1920s and 1930s. At the same time it was an architectural illustration of D.Zavalishin's article with the title "London, Paris and Moscow". The author admired London and Paris "which were rebuilt and transformed radically, though for different reasons and by other means, Moscow, though much is constructed in it, does not change with the rational purpose. That is why we would like to make some useful instructions for Moscow based on what was done in London and Paris".

But the problem of traffic relief from the railway stations to the centre and back in the growing city in Moscow became

Old Krymskiy bridge. 1873. Photo. 2nd half of the lath century.

Project of Alexander's avenue. Print. 1871.

extremely acute from the middle of the 19th century. Businessmen, engineers, municipal authority tried to solve it by the use of the new mechanical transport – city railways – first on horse, then on electrical traction.

For the first time the idea to create in Moscow new transportation facilities appeared at the beginning of 1860s. In 1863 Basil Alexandrovich Kokorev, a merchant of the first guild from Kazan (one of the known people of Russian and Moscow merchants, who was characterized as economic Slavophil in the famous book "Merchant Moscow" of P.A.Buryshkin), submitted to the General Manager of Communication Ways and Public Buildings an application for arrangement in Moscow of a network of horse railways with the extent of 57 versts 300 sagenes along the main streets in Moscow and to the railway stations with branches to Petrovskiy park and Sokolniki, which was a grandiose enterprise for that time".

A year later, in 1864, Kokorev offered a new variant of a network of horse railways. It was different from the previous one by less length – 48 versts, and by the absence of the Boulevard line, but better though of and more thoroughly developed network of radial lines, which connected the crowded trade streets with the city centre.

The seriousness and thoroughness of the second variant attracts attention. The second variant had all that would make all future projects different: a complex approach to design of the lines of mechanical traffic as a unified whole system, connected with the historically formed structure of the city plan and with the main tendencies of the city development of that time. The transport problem born by the global social and economic processes and concrete needs of the ancient capital of Russia, became since 1860s one of the most important factors of its town-building development, was defined by it and simultaneously influenced it actively. Already the authors of the first projects understood it. V.A.Kokorev's argumentation testifies to it, proving to Moscow authority the necessity to create a network, exactly a network, and not single lines of a horse railway.

In the explanatory note to the project Kokorev mentioned that "horse railways are most necessary for our vast ancient capital, because there is not a big river and canals near it, like in Petersburg, for easy communication by water, which especially developed after river ships appeared... two ways of transportation are left – on foot or by horses, which was very difficult for poor class because of long distances and high prices..."[6]

In this document the new principle was formulated most evidently, which influenced first gradually, then definitely Moscow town-building development, which after the abrogation of serfdom became determining in the growth of business activity, revealing itself in the growth of the city population, development of the railway transportation (city and interurban), industry, trade and the accompanying social and economic changes the tendency to take into account the needs of not well-off plies of population in development of town-building policy.

The sphere of the social care of the municipal authority became the dwelling problem, location of industrial enterprises, development of transportation, education, health care, city comfortable arrangement. Kokorev's program was mentioned in detail because as though a technical and a concrete question turned out to be connected with all the complex of problems which appeared together with the new phenomenon of a big city which in its turn turned out to be inseparable from the new structure of the city life and the new type of the city itself, conditioned by the growth of private business and the scientific and technical progress which accompanied it.

Kokorev's project was not accepted because of the author's pretensions which seemed exaggerated then, who demanded to give him the network of railways at his full disposal for half a century.

After Kokorev's project there were other ones. By the beginning of 1870s there were two lines of horse rail ways in Moscow. One belonged to the plant of Komissarzhevskaja technical school and was used for cargo transportation. The second, built by the military department by the opening of the Polytechnical exhibition in 1872, began from Iverskie gate, passed along Neglinnaja street, boulevards and then to Smolenskiy (now Belorusskiy) railway station.

The city granted the right to construction of the first Moscow network of horse rail ways to the "First society of horse rail ways in Moscow", established in 1871, because exactly this company announced at the auction in April 1872 the least term of the concession – 40 years. By 1875 the construction activity of the First society was over.

As a result of it, besides the rail ways and the vans in Moscow buildings appeared of new denomination – van barracks, as they called then tram depots, repair workshops (in the outskirts of the city), pavilions at the stops in the city centre. "These pavilions shall be wooden, light and elegant and maintained in good condition during all the period of validity of the concession. The dimensions and the facades of these pavilions shall be approved by Duma."

Moscow city department occupied sun active position from the very beginning in the business of arrangement of the city mechanical communication facilities, preferring such projects that stipulated networks of rail ways, the purpose of which was to solve the city problems as a whole.

The success of the activity of the First society of horse rail ways and its drawback at the same time was the fact that the ring lines were not developed enough, which stimulated creation of new projects. At the end of 1883 engineer A.P.Gorchakov got the concession for 45 years for implementation of the project developed by him of the 2nd network of about 30 versts. His project was based, on the one hand, on Kokorev's ideas about creation of the Boulevard and Garden lines, and on the other hand, on his own idea about creation of the Circuit rail way that was to connect Moscow railway stations and the main production enterprises. The main purpose of the project remained the same: to relieve the horse transport in Moscow and to make easier the connection between the central districts and the suburbs and the suburbs with each other. Two years later Gorchakov managed to organize a Belgian joint-stock company for construction and use of the new network of horse rail ways. By 1887 the network which consisted of Dolgorukovskaja radial branch and two circuit ones, was finished. Later it was added by the line to Petrovskiy park and to the Vorobjovy hills and the steam line to Petrovskoe-Razumovskoe.

During the period from 1860 to 1880 the above-said turn happened: the place of the most intensive growth of population and the focus of active construction activity became the city outskirts. At the same time another turn happened. The municipal authority understood the necessity of construction development and became an important factor, regulating it and ruling the construction policy. One of the most effective instruments of regulation of the city construction and town-building development became the municipal public transport. Its direct influence on the destiny of the city was absolutely inadequate in relation to the influence of the transport buildings themselves on the city look. Thus was the characteristic feature of town-building factors in the second half of the 19th century – direct disproportion between their actual influence on the destiny of the city and architectural expression of what comprised the individuality of the city ensemble.

Already by the end of 1880s in Moscow the first signs of insufficiency of the existing rail ways were found. Proposals about creation of new improved transport facilities were submitted. The First society cartage rail ways intended to make rope traction in Taganskaja line, and in 1895 submitted and offer to Duma about installation of electrical traction, as an experiment, in Dolgorikovskaja line, which connected Strastnaja square with Smolenskiy railway station and further with Petrovskiy park.

The profitability of the line increased twice at once. It induced a whole flow of applications to Duma about transfer of the rail ways to electrical traction.

After long discussions the Municipal Department adopted the decision about redemption before the due time of the lines of the First society for the property of the city and about transfer of the existing network of the cartage rail ways to electrical traction, its modernization and development. The decision was made due to the burning necessity: the prices for flats grew and the dwelling construction in the centre was stopping, the quantity of population in the outskirts increased rapidly. "The situation," according to the formulation of the experts of the City Council, – became close to the critical". As a result, the main task of the municipal policy in the sphere of construction of the city rail ways became the determining of the optimal direction of the lines. The laying was to be conducted in accordance with the process of decentralization of population, provide a convenient, cheap and fast communication between the centre and the outskirts.

The redemption by Moscow municipal department of the lines of cartage rail ways and creation of a new modernized network of electrical rail ways was based on the program, which was strictly followed by the Municipal department since the late 19th century till the revolution.

In the second half of the 19th century in Moscow streets asphalt appeared together with cobble-stone pavement. In 1883 on the Big Stone Bridge and on the highway in front of the cathedral of Christ the Saviour the first electrical lamps were installed. At the beginning electricity was considered as an esthetic factor. Architect I.E.Bondarenko remembered about his studies in the art school: "After school we went to look at two lamps in front of Dusso hotel in Theatre passage, like at a rarity,.. there were Yablochkov's high lamps with soft blue-lilac light near the cathedral of Christ the Saviour". "All Moscow, – tells writer N.D.Teleshov, – gathered to look at these few lamps, like at a miracle".[7]

Moscow municipal department conducted an active construction socially oriented policy. It improved the sanitary situation, the municipal services and comfortable arrangement of the city. It built city hospitals, asylums, educational institutions. It stimulated the charity activity of merchants in creation of asylums, hospitals etc. All this allowed a contemporary to state: 1860-1890 was a golden time in Moscow life, an epoch of constant growth of economy and culture. "The best municipal authority in Russia, an exemplary organization of schools, a big quantity of educational institutions, a beautiful look of the city, which was at the level of European comfortable arrangement – all was created during these years. Moscow was Europeanized but did not become a standard European city. All this made Moscow life colourful and individual till our time".[8]

Renovation of the Centre

In spite of the growth of population, active construction, appearance in 1880-1890 of multi-storey buildings, the authors, who wrote about Moscow after the reforms, still were inclined to emphasize its specialities, which did not change: picturesqueness of the city landscape, beauty and variety of views, unrepeatable old Russian and at the same time Moscow look, plenty of temples, among which now the cathedral of Christ the Saviour is distinguished by its dimensions and the beauty of location.

I.E.Zabelin: "Moscow spread so freely with its settlements and country cottages and in such a beautiful place that it is rightfully considered to be one of the most picturesque cities of Europe... Being in the East, Moscow could not develop according to the Western sample, with which it, besides all, did not agree in belief and some political principles... At attentive close consideration the Eastern look of Moscow turns out to be a creation, in the full meaning of the word, of Russian people".[9]

P.D.Boborykin: "Moscow is so rich in views that it is possible to count up to a hundred points in the city itself and near by, from where the panorama is equally attractive... the cathedral of Christ the Saviour occupies now a special position in Moscow panorama... from the bell-tower of John the Great, all this landscape, which has become now one of the best adornments of Moscow, merges more with the general view of the quay, standing out with all its majesty... There is hardly at least one temple in Western Europe, which stood at a short distance so advantageously and beautifully as the cathedral of Christ the Saviour..."[10]

"Incorrectness", irregularity of Moscow do not irritate now. Besides that, if up to the first third of the 19th century Moscow was striving to be similar to Petersburg in regularity, from the time of the reign of Nicholas I an opposite tendency appeared: to add to Petersburg the look of a Russian town. It resulted in construction of temples in Russian style and in an effort to place them closer to the rivers and canals in order to add "Russian" colouring to Petersburg panoramas. And nevertheless, Petersburg, which seems dull, monotonous, not national, is often opposed to picturesque Moscow which is admired for its unrepeatable individuality. Boborykin, who glorified Moscow, wrote: "A marvelous life in this pot-bellied and juicy Moscow!.. In Petersburg it is physically impossible to feel like that. Eyes deaden. There is a line everywhere – straight, slow, dreary... When you ride, you see the same houses, the same avenue... Nothing characteristic, individual, unimported".[11]

In the second half of the 19th century the renovation of Moscow centre continued in Russian style. Exactly the Russian style as an expression of the idea of the national system and nationality united both periods. In all the rest – geographically, contextually, in the genre, – both periods opposed each other.

The main construction of the second half of the 19th century was connected not with the Kremlin and gala panoramas of the Moscow-river banks, but with the interior territory – Red Square, the squares and streets surrounding Kitay-gorod. Functionally and in genre this period was represented by the types of civil buildings expressing the main ideals of the epoch, – museums, buildings of people's power and theatres. Town-building undertakings expressed the ideas of the national system and the nationality freely, with out an influence of the state power, being the result of the initiative of scientific and public organizations, private people, municipal authority.

The conception of Moscow city centre of the second half of the 19th – beginning of the 20th century was partially similar to the town-building of the epoch of classicism of the second half of the 18th – the first third of the 19th centuries. In both cases the main attention was turned to the reconstruction of the system of the squares, bounding two territories of the historical centre, surrounded by wooden walls. But it was realized in unthinkable forms during the period of classicism and unique in their own way even in Russia – in the forms of ancient Russian architecture. Another approach and contents changed radically the look of the central streets and squares. Classical Moscow contemplated its sense and meaning in the contrast with the historical antiquities and the ancient centre. Moscow of the epoch of eclecticism and modernism, feeling its unsimilarity and up-to-date style, was trying to emphasize at the same time the connection of ages. Interaction and concordance of the new with the ancient acquired a conceptual sense and became a self-sufficient value.

Development of business life and formation of Moscow railway junction changed the hierarchy of the streets and territories in Moscow. The prevailing position, like in the first half of the 18th century, was returned to the territories and streets of the North-Eastern direction. But the reason of revival of the former importance of Nikolskaja, Iljinka, Varvarka, Pokrovka and their continuations in Bely and Zemljanoy towns, was different. Now they connected Moscow trade-business centre with the main quantity of railway stations, situated in North-Eastern outskirts. As a result, together with the Southern, gala facade of the ancient capital, turned to the Moscow-river, the North-Eastern and Eastern facades of Moscow centre were formed. The square system around the Kremlin and Kitay-gorod was the main gala facade personifying Moscow trade-transport functions.

The process of recreation of the historical centre in Russian style, began. Red and Voskresenskaja squares, Theatre passage were reconstructed and practically rebuilt, losing its classical look. The renovation of Loubjanskaja, New and Iljinskaja squares begun in the second half of the 19th century, was over in the early 20th century. During that time Old and Varvarinskaja squares completely changed their look too. A semi-circle of squares was formed around the Kremlin and Kitay-gorod.

Red Square, remaining the main square of Moscow and of its trade centre, with construction of the Historical museum turned into the square of sciences, enlightenment, culture. The Polytechnical exhibition of 1872 initiated creation of the museum, the exhibition was timed to the 200th anniversary of Peter I and the results of the latest development of Russia after the abrogation of serfdom. Its exhibits gave life to the biggest museums of the country – Historical and Polytechnical. The temporary wooden pavilions of the exhibition, implemented in the forms of the national architecture and richly decorated with carving, were situated in the territory of Alexandrovskiy garden, on the quay of the Moscow-river, in the Kremlin and Varvarskaja square, where the section of care of people's morals with a wooden building of a dismantable theatre, constructed according to V.A.Hartman's project, who had taken this principle from booths of people's outdoor fetes. The location of the exhibition pavilions showed how closely the ideas of the scientific and technical progress were interconnected with the idea of the national history, the symbol of which the Kremlin is, with a new understanding of a holiday entertainment. Due to the exhibition Alexandrovskiy garden became, though temporary, a variation of a national park. A national park – a city park, the semantics of which was full of reminiscences of the national history, was a typical result of the historical thinking of the 19th century. Its variations are widely presented in European capitals – Paris, Budapest. In the latter it is, like in Moscow, situated at the foot of the ancient fortress in the historical centre of the Hungarian capital.

Functioning of the Polytechnical exhibition in Moscow turned into one of variants of all-national all-estate holiday. The poetic style of the exhibition's architecture included in itself the experience of design of pavilions of national outdoor fetes and public parks. In this context the symbolics of the choice of exactly Russian style for the exhibition, timed to the 200th anniversary of Peter I, looked especially important. It was also symbolical that for the gala celebration of this event not Petersburg, but Moscow was chosen – the territory of its historical centre. The exhibition was organized on the initiative and by the efforts of the Society of amateurs of the natural science, anthropology and ethnography at Moscow University, i.e. by private people, and meant the appearance of the new historiosophic conception. It coincided with the beginning of the new town-building period in Russia and in Moscow – with the liquidation of the centralized leadership of the city construction and transfer of these functions to the bodies of the municipal authority, i.e. with the city reform of 1870. Both phenomena were of one rank. Expressing the new conception of Russia, they made an impact on the interpretation of its historical past, first of all at such a crucial turn of history as comprehension of the role of Peter I.

According to the new historical conception Peter's deed – the fore-father of new Russia – was an all-national deed. The contents of the exhibition and essence of its architectural and artistic program were to prove it by the style of the pavilion in Russian folk-peasant variant, by the use of wood as the national material, by the arrangement of the exhibition not only in the heart of Russia – Moscow, but in the heart of Moscow. A special pavilion, dedicated to Peter, was built, where he was shown, first of all, as a toiler (as Pushkin wrote: "he was a constant worker on the throne") and a person equal and related in this quality to his people. The world view of the second half of the 19th beginning of the 20th centuries added historical importance to any work, including production of material values, and so their creators – people. The theme Peter – a toiler was the main one in the cycle of lectures timed to the anniversary and the exhibition and read by S.M.Solovjov. Peter's dislike of Moscow was forgotten. People's rumour that Peter was antichrist was forgotten too. The official opening of the exhibition was signified by a gala meeting of Peter's jolly boat – the grandfather of Russian fleet and its installation in a special pavilion at the foot of the Kremlin wall. According to the symbolics of this act in the Kremlin, in Moscow a new Russia was born, its creation was rooted in the national history and is a continuation of the history of Moscow Rusj.

The importance of the Polytechnical exhibition was exclusively big in the architectural history not only of Moscow, but all Russia. From it the new stage of exhibition architecture began. Since then special exhibition pavilions were constructed for the exhibits; most often wooden, in Russian style.

The polytechnical exhibition gave an impulse to another renovation of Moscow historical centre and most important – in the national style. It made legal the opportunity which had not been practiced in the civil construction before.

Simultaneously with the pavilions of the Polytechnical exhibition in Moscow Porokhovtschikov's mansion appeared in Starokonjushenny lane (1872, A.L.Gun), wooden, in Russian style, adorned with rich carving. According to A.L.Gun's project the hall of the known restaurant "Slavjanskiy Bazar" was arranged in Russian style. Cloth with national embroidery was widely used in interiors together with carving, like in the spectators' hall of the National theatre of the Polytechnical exhibition.

The care for the unity of the ensemble, comprehension of the role of the historical holy things – the Kremlin and Kitay-gorod wall, the striving to create the new in direct connection with the past showed most early in the building of the Historical museum (1875-1833, V. Shervud and A. Semenov). Shervud, who was the leader in development of the ideological and symbolical basis of the project, used the same material as for ancient buildings for the facing of the facades of the Historical museum – red brick (it was also presumed to adorn the facade with tiles), decorative details taken from the architecture of the 16th-17th cen-

Putilov's Pavilion made of glass and metal for the Politechnical Exhibition of 1872 in Moscow at the Kremlin Embankment. Engraving portraying arrival of Peter 1st boat.

Upper (1888-1894, architect A.N.Pomerantsev, engineer V.G.Shukhov) and the Middle (1889-1891, architect R.I.Klein) trade rows in Red Square. View ot the cathedral of St.Basil.

turies, and, which was most important, tried to make the composition and the silhouette of the museum corresponding to the surrounding ancient memorials. Recomprehension of the symmetrical-axial composition, characteristic for the after-Petrine architecture, plenty of towers of different height, allowed Shervud to obtain the organic combination with the architecture of the cathedral of St. Basil. The porches and towers of the Historical museum also combine with the Kremlin, which inspired the general compositional design of the museum with the towers situated along the perimetre of the building's volume.

Periphery placement of the towers of the Historical museum, their subordination to the towers of the Kremlin show another aspect of the architectural and town-building role of the museum – a certain centrifugal character. Due to the multi-tower style the museum was included into the system of accents of "the secondary" order – the towers of Iverskie gate of Kitay-gorod, which connected Red Square with Tverskaja street, the towers of the Coin Yard, Kazanskiy cathedral, the towers and temples of Kitay-gorod. With the help of the spatial visual connections the closed ensemble of Red Square acquired some "openness", became a component of the buildings in the adjoining territories.

The construction of the Historical museum initiated the changes of the look of Red Square. The main square of the ancient capital out of a similarity of a Roman forum turned into a symbol of the national system and the nationality, into a direct continuation of the Kremlin and the cathedral of St.-Basil. At the end of the 19th century on the opposite side from the Kremlin two new buildings of the Upper and the Middle trade rows were constructed. Not only the look, but the sense of the square changed radically.

In the composition of the Upper trade rows (GUM, arch. A.N.Pomerantsev) two rows of accents exist – a system of towers, emphasizing the main elements of the symmetrical and axial composition and even the rhythm of the windows with casings, which at the bottom have the archy form of guest yards, traditional for Russia. There is a "round dance" of towers on the first plan of the cathedral of St. Basil. The towers of the Upper trade rows are repeated and supported by the towers of the Historical museum, Iverskie gate. Coin Yard, the bell-tower of the cathedral of the "Kazan" Icon of the Theotokos. The theme of the extended facade of the Upper trade rows with the even rhythm of windows is continued by the Middle trade rows. They fully correspond to the building of the Upper, as they were constructed according to R.I.Klein's project, who got the second award in

Upper and Middle trade rows in Red Sqaure. View of Voskresenskie gate from the cathedral of St. Basil.

Red Square and the Kremlin. View from Vasilievskaja street.
Photo. Late 19th – early 20th centuries.

the competition for the building of the Upper trade rows. If to look at the Upper and Middle rows from the side of the Historical museum, the entire building dominates, the vertical accents of which, corresponding to the extent of the Kremlin wall create a quiet background for contemplation of the cathedral of St.Basil.

Reconstruction of Red Square entailed creation of several more ensembles directly connected with it: entrance to Iljinka, flanked by the Upper and Middle rows and Vetoshny passage made parallely to Red Square. It is bounded by similar facades of two blocks of Upper rows – of the main volume standing out here with its back facade, and the comparatively not big additional, situated on the other side of the new passage. From the side of Bely town the perspective of the passage is closed by the central part of the former Zaikonospasskie trade rows crowned with a high roof (1890s, M.T.Preobrazhenskiy). During creation of Vetoshny passage the mode, characteristic for classicism, of similar arrangement of the street sides, was used, closed by the side of the main building in this ensemble (Theatre square in Moscow and Rossi street in Petersburg). In Moscow of the second half of the 19th century this mode was revived again, but with use of other stylistic forms. Besides Vetoshny passage, it is possible to name Tretjakovskiy passage (1870-1872, A.S.Kaminskiy), Petrovskie lines (1876, B.V.Freidenberg).

Tretjakovskiy passage is a huge trade-official complex, constructed at the expense of brothers Paul and Sergius Tretjakovs, creators of the famous Tretjakovskaja gallery. It connected Kitay-gorod – a business centre and the focus of wholesale trade – with the main trade streets of Moscow – Neglinnaja, Petrovka, Kuznetskiy bridge, Rozhdestvenka, Sofiyka. Actually a new passage was created, closed at both ends by blocks with the arches of the passage in the centre. Three blocks: one going through the wall of Kitay-gorod and two longitudinal, extended along the passage itself had facades in Russian style, corresponding by the look and silhouette to the ancient towers and the wall of Kitay-gorod. The facade of the block looking at Nikolskaja street, in accordance with the character of the architecture of the near by buildings is in the style of Renaissance. A similar mode was used twenty years later, in 1890s by architect A.E.Erikhson during design of Ferein's drug store. Different facades of this building looking at Nikolskaja street and Tretjakovskiy passage, were also finished with the use of different stylistic forms – the facade looking at Nikolskaja street was of Renaissance-baroque style, the facade looking at the wall of Kitay-gorod had a tower and brick facing of the walls reminding of the medieval time.

By the same considerations – closeness to the ancient memorials, the wish to keep the historical colouring of the place, the decision to change the so called Italian style of the initial project of the Polytechnical museum (arch.N.A.Shokhin) into Russian (arch.I.A.Monigetti)was dictated. The Museum building with richly adorned facades and the house of Moscow merchant society, situated behind the wall of Kitay-gorod, created an unrepeatable colouring of the Old square with its ancient and new buildings which existed in concordance.

The ensemble which renovated fully the look of Voskresenskaja square, was based on the same principles. The side of the square turned to the Kremlin, Kitay-gorod, Red Square, was built in Russian style. It was presumed to construct the main building of the square – the City Duma – in the place of today's Historical museum, and the latter was to be along the longitudinal side of Red Square between Nikolskaja and Senate towers of the Kremlin (approximately where the mausoleum is now). However, the plot, more favourable from the town-building point of view, was donated gratis to the Museum by Duma as to the more important building. It was decided to build the City Duma in the place of the old Offices according to D.N.Chichagov's project. There is much in common with the Historical museum in its look and composition – red facing brick of the walls, decoration taken from temple architecture of the 17th century, synthesis of symmetrical and axial and even-metrical composition.

Near the City Duma, behind the wall of Kitay-gorod the building of the Synodal Publishing house was. In the late 19th century architect A.I.Artleben restored the previous and rose a new block in the style of Russian buildings of the middle of the 17th century.

The opposite in relation to the Duma side of Voskresenskaja square, which transferred to Theatre square, was built in the forms of classical architecture, being in harmony with its buildings.

The agricultural museum which was to be constructed in Alexandrovskiy garden near the Kremlin wall and was not realized for the lack of money, was designed in Russian style.

The hotels, which retained their names and the former monastery representations in Kitay-gorod were built in Russian style, thus emphasizing the succession and connection with the old buildings. In difference to them exchanges, offices, banks

Tretiakovskiy passage. Photo. 1880s.

*The Voskresenskaya (of Resurrection) Square.
The Historical Museum and Voskresenskiye Gates with the Chapel
of Iverskaya Mother of God. End of the 19th century.*

*Polytechnical Museum in Old Square (beginning of the construction
of 1847-1877, architect I.A.Monigetti, N.A.Shokhin). Photo. 1880s.*

were designed in European style. However, the wish to keep the look of historical Moscow with the verticles of its "forty of forties" temples was evident in the construction of the second half of the 19th century in the squares and in the streets around Kitay-gorod and in it.

The memorial to grenadiers who died near Plevna during the Russian-Turkish war (1887, O. Shervud), was built in Russian style in the shape of an ancient Russian hip roof chapel. The hip roof of this memorial, the building of the chapel constructed in 1860 in the square of Iljinskie gate, the tower on the side facade of the new block of the Polytechnical museum created a "round dance" of verticles, included into the system of ancient memorials represented by the tower of Iljinskie gate and the cupolas of the church of St.Nicholas "The Big Cross".

The buildings of different denomination, which appeared from 1860 to 1910 near the ancient buildings of Kitay-gorod – the walls, the passage tower and the church of St.Nicholas "The Big Cross", which were different in style, dimensions, silhouette, not losing their individuality, with a rare art, skill and tact added and enriched each other. In the ensemble of the square of Iljinskie gate there are those general features which made Moscow architecture of the middle of the 19th – beginning of the 20th centuries exclusively individual, not like Petersburg. Variety, picturesqueness, irregularity of verticle accents. Besides that exactly these verticles created the basis of the new wholeness of this square. The verticles of 1860-1910 were in interaction with the verticles of the ancient temple and the tower, revived the interconnections characteristic for an ancient Russian town, the upper part of which rose above the space which was wider that the street and the square. The Kitay-gorod wall was not an obstacle to this unity. Due to the visual connections of the vertical volumes the space was also understood as a whole.

The practice of enrichment of the existing system of verticals of towers, temples and bell-towers with new ones in Russian style, which became a characteristic feature of Moscow in 1830-1850, acquired a new life in the second half of the 19th century. Increase of the Russian look of the square of Iljinskie gate was not an exception. On the contrary, it became a rule.

The same process of enrichment and an original concentration of verticals in the main point of a highway connecting the centre – the Kremlin, Red Square with the new transport centre – Kalanchevskaja square, was demonstrated by Loubjanskaja square and Nikolskaja street. The majestic hip roof chapel of Great Martyr Panteleimon (arch. A.S. Kaminskiy) was built on Varvarinskaja square in front of Varvarinskaja tower, near Nikolskaja tower of Kitay-gorod and the church of the "Vladimir Icon of the Theotokos. The chapel of St.Alexander Nevskiy in memory of the soldiers who died during the Russian-Turkish war, was raised in Moiseevskaja square near the church of Great Martyr George on the Krasnaja hill (which was in the place of the building, constructed in 1930 according to I.V.Zholtovskiy's project). In 1830-1890 the Kremlin and Kitay-gorod was surrounded by a ring of verticals of new chapels and bell-towers, supported by the towers of secular buildings – the tower of Tretjakivskiy passage, the tower of Loubjanskiy passage constructed in 1902 (arch.I.I.Kondarenko, now there is the department store "Children's World" in its place).

Preservation of two huge systems of fortifications, with orientation at which new ensembles were created in the centre, allows to refer Moscow to the quantity of unique cities. The after-reform Moscow corresponds to the notion of a big city in all aspects. It is unique because not only the old part, but all system of medieval fortifications became an integral component of new ensembles.

Historism runs through town-building of the middle of the 19th – beginning of the 20th centuries. It was a general feature of the time. Its different forms in their own way, but brightly and expressively showed themselves in the town-building development of European capitals: in Budapest, London, Prague, Vienna, Tallinn, Vilnius and many others. Moscow uniqueness is in another thing. No capital in the world can compete with it in the wholeness of two of four systems of the medieval fortifications, which bounded the town at a certain time and became its main town-forming structures, actively influencing new ensembles.

*Varvarinskaja tower in Kitay-gorod with the chapel of "Bogolyubskaja"
Icon of the Theotokos (1880, architect N.V.Nikitin).*

Square of IUinskie gate with the chapel-memorial to the grenadiers who died near Plevna.

The ensembles of the squares of the North-Eastern part of Kitay-gorod were constructed on the same basis as Red Square: the buildings, which made them finished and closed, were added by verticals along the perimetre, uniting the space of the squares and connecting with the outside space. The facade style and limitness of space, characteristic for the regular town-building, was combined with the interaction of the vertical accents, characteristic for Ancient Russia, uniting the city space.

At the end of the 19th century in the Kremlin the memorial to Alexander II appeared, the only construction of that time which anyway, enriches sufficiently the ensemble and the panorama from the side of the Moscow-river. The bronze statue made by A.M.Opekushin presented the tsar "in full general's form and in emperor's porphirion, i.e. in the vestments in which he was crowned... the left hand holds a sceptre, and the right hand is stretched to people as though meaning the given charities".[12] It stood under a canopy in the centre of a high terrace, the upper edge of which adjoined the edge of the Kremlin hill, and the low one went out to the alley of the Low Kremlin Garden, which led to the church of Sts.Constantine and Helen. The upper square of the terrace was fringed with an archy gallery. "It represented as though a big emperor's forum, like the forums of Ancient Rome and Tsargrad". The terrace looked like a fortress wall with mishukulis, "so that it is in accordance with the walls of Moscow Kremlin... Rising above the merlons of the Southern Kremlin wall, it partially renewed its previous look, for in ancient times it was bounded by double walls from the side of the river".

The architecture, unusual for secular memorials, allowed to settle several architectural and town-building tasks at once. Due to the specialities of the composition and of the silhouette, the memorial of Alexander II complied organically the Kremlin panorama from the side of Zamoskvorechie and Moskvoretskiy bridge. The architectural design of the statue did not let it get lost in the space of the Kremlin squares at the background of the bell-tower of John the Great and Spasskaja tower near by. Besides that, according to the author's opinion, artist P.V.Zhukovskiy, a son of poet V.A.Zhukovskiy, "the canopy (36,2 m high, E.K.) will add to the memorial a sacred character in the eyes of people, our people are used to seeing canopies above especially sacred places (in the church, above the altar tables, above the tsar's and the patriarch's seats, and in palaces – above thrones".[13]

All the above-said allows to read the complicated symbolics of the memorial. The terracr was similar to the Kremlin wall with its fortress look and at the same time symbolized a forum due to the gallery. i.e. the memorial was analogized to the Kremlin-forum, expressing the idea Moscow – the Third Rome. At the same time, the canopy sanctified the tsar's personality, who died from a bomb of a terrorist. Not only the general architectural form, but the finishing of the canopy's interior contained the key to the sense of all the memorial. In accordance with the fact that precise knowledge was so loved in the 19th century, in the canopy's cupola a short chronicle of the emperor's life was placed: the date of birth, the date of coronation. Including the emperor's statue, the canopy became a symbol of the empire: it was adorned with the coat of arms of all its parts. The analogy of the gallery to forums of Rome and Tsargrad was also significant: the gallery's vaults were adorned with the portraits of the Russian tsars, finished by a portrait of Nicholas I – the father of Alexander II.

The memorial of Alexander II testified that the idea of the national system did not disappear out of art, though the theory of its application became much more narrow.

Construction in the City

Moscow ensemble as an architectural and town-building whole remained strikingly variable in the second half of the 19th – beginning of the 20th centuries. Each part of it was relatively autonomous and had its own specifics and individuality. In 1870s an original look of "Moscow City" began to form, as they like to call Kitay-gorod now – the next component of Moscow historical centre after the Kremlin.

In the second half of the 19th – beginning of the 20th centuries Kitay-gorod retained its trade function, but its character changed completely. Before the reforms the main quantity of trade buildings was concentrated in the ancient part of Moscow: in the squares around the Kremlin and in Kitay-gorod. After the reforms dwelling houses disappeared from Kitay-gorod. Its territory became the centre of wholesale, of warehouses, offices, trade houses, banks and hotels, restaurants, at the tables of which transactions for millions were concluded during the exchange hours. The ancient fortress wall, making it a separate

Chapel of Great Martyr Panteleimon, the church of the Vladimir Icon of the Theotokos and Hikolskaja tower of Kitay-gored. View from the inside passage along the wall. Photo. Late 19th century.

town-building territory, contradicted it to some extent to the rest of Moscow.

In accordance with the specific function of Kitay-gorod the specific features of its buildings were formed. It is the only Moscow ensemble, all the space of which is gala, architecturally expressive. The big quantity of internal passages, in spite of the high prices for the land, is striking. It is not often possible to find out where you are: in a lane or an inside yard, because together with the official street passages there are a lot of unofficial ones.

Being created in order to make the cargo transportation convenient, they make up an entire system together with the inside yards. The back facades are not different from the front ones, creating the representative look of "Moscow City". Similar inside yards and passages began to be arranged in other parts of the city too with construction of big dwelling houses-complexes or houses-hotels. However, in the second half of the 19th century they were a rare phenomenon outside Kitay-gorod, being used in single cases (Petrovskie lines were an internal yard which became a city street), while in Kitay-gorod they became a rule.

There was another speciality – different buildings were constructed immediately adjacent to each other, while blocks of one building were often separated and had long yards open at the street. The reason is in the specialization of the district, in the necessity to provide uninterrupted delivery and unloading of cargo, to make the access to the office or a warehouse beautiful and easily approached. The look and structure of many buildings is similarly unusual: narrow, long blocks of shops and offices, separated by big passages. The type of buildings was formed which is known in Moscow only in Kitay-gorod – certain passages under the open sky with galleries. Each shop or an office has their own entrance on the ground floor, and on the second floor there is a gallery on iron columns, to which an external pig iron staircase leads.

Numerous representations of rich monasteries (of St.Joseph, abbot of Volokolamsk, of Novgorod, of the Lavra of the Holy Trinity-St.Sergius – one of the biggest and most beautiful buildings in lljinka street with a corner tower, the first 5-storey building in Moscow), situated in Kitay-gorod, were constructed like temples, in Russian style. Barns, shops, cafes, notary offices were situated in them.

The re-assessment of values of the second half of the 19th century changed the look of the habitual stores and barns. They turned into respectable offices and banks. In 1870-1880 in the finishing of the facades "of the manufacturing and trade firms, mostly of the textile and spinning business", according to P.F.Boborykin's words, the novelties appeared – windows and doors "with expensive glass in oak and walnut doors with figures and pig iron boards", "with sagene mirror windows".[14] They added richness, respectability, solidness to the look of buildings. New buildings of offices and banks turned into the symbol and token of time.

Wholesale, ousted out of Kitay-gorod, management boards of firms and banks, which were not quick enough to capture a place there, concentrated near it in Bely town in the streets Mjasnitskaja, Pokrovka, Soljanka, as well as in the streets, which had been known since ancient time by their active trade – Kuznetskiy bridge, Petrovka, Sofiyka, Neglinka, Sretenka, Stoleshnikov lane, Tverskaja and Big Dmitrovka. In this part of Bely town fashionable shops, passages, state and other banks, hotels were built. During the second half of the 19th century the Northern, North-Eastern and Eastern parts of Bely town lost their nobility look completely and became the focus of trade and business life.

In the North, North-East and East of Moscow there was the main quantity of railway stations. The streets, connecting Moscow business centre – Kitay-gorod, with railway stations, were the first which radically changed the look and specialization, earlier than others got trade and business buildings. The same was going on in the neighbouring parts of Bely town, and their trade-business character showed in the adjoining territories of Zemljanoy town and behind it.

Vast spreading of the trade and business buildings appeared due to new, absolutely unknown factors in town-building. Traditional town-making formations, whether in Ancient Russia or till the middle of the 19th century, were located in the centre during the New time and represented the biggest, socially and artistically important complexes.

Anyway in the town-building of the second half of the 19th – beginning of the 20th centuries new extremely strong objects appeared in the outskirts.

There were several such town-building factors. All of them referred to the sphere of productional and technical or productional and economic activity.

Corner of Kuznetskiy bridge and Neglinnaja street. House of Moscow Merchants Society (1888-1892, architect A.S.Kaminskiy) and Dzhamagarov's passage (1877, architect A. Nezanov). Photo. Late 19th century.

Dzhamagarov's passage in Kuznetskiy bridge.

The first most important town-building factor of productional and economic character was the railway construction for Moscow. After Moscow-Petersburg rail way in 1860s other were constructed. During the first ten years after the reforms the main points of the majority of Moscow rail ways were constructed. An absolutely new phenomenon – Moscow railway junction – appeared in Russia.

Absence or presence of a railway in the middle of the 19th – beginning of the 20th centuries was the factor which decided the destiny of settlements, a quick growth of some, stagnation of others. In Moscow, due to its central situation in European Russia the roads from all the four parts of the world joined. Dependence between the factors of intensive railway construction and the growth of Moscow was not so evident, as for the relatively small towns like Novorossiysk or Novosibirsk, Eniseysk or Krasnojarsk, but it was not less active due to this. Exactly the railway construction, making the ancient capital all-Russian railway junction, railway capital, conditioned its turning into the centre of all-Russian trade, Russian-wide trade base and warehouse, the biggest business and industrial centre. The importance of this factor in Moscow history is a little obscure due to its position of one of the two capitals. Nevertheless, the first wave of the intensive growth of all quantitative indices, characterizing the quantity of population, increase of the speed and volume of construction, of buildings dimensions coincided with the time of the first railway boom in 1860 – beginning of 1870s and was the result of the impulse given at that time.

The principle of location of the railway stations in Moscow demonstrated evidently the attitude to this type of constructions, characteristic in Russia. All of them were situated in the outskirts of that time, outside the Garden Ring and the Camer-Collezhskiy bank. It distinguished Russia from Western Europe acutely, where the buildings of railway stations were constructed among dense city buildings, often becoming, like in Paris or Budapest, a part of a gala ensemble of the most important capital highways.

Before that Moscow history had been developing centrifugally: from the centre to the outskirts. The railway construction and appearance of the railway junction changed the situation sharply.

Simultaneously with the turn of rail ways into the most important town-building factor, and of the districts near the railway stations – into the real new hearths of construction activity, it began to move in the direction opposite the traditional one: from the outskirts to the centre. As though two flows of construction activity appeared, which moved in the direction of each other. At the same time, while the centre of Moscow was becoming a business one, the move of the inhabitants from the centre to the outskirts became more evident.

The change of the look of the centre and the outskirts was going on in conformity with their functional specialization. In the centre the quantity of floors and the density of buildings increased first of all. The former nobility streets of Bely town, adjoining Kitay-gorod, most earlier turned into trade and banking, and if there were still dwelling buildings, now they were not the houses and estates of rich nobility, but multi-apartment multi-storey leased houses with shops and offices on the ground floors. In the outskirts near the railway stations buildings with not many floors dominated.

In the second half of the 19th century another process extremely characteristic for Moscow, became notable and spread in the territory of Bely and Zemljanoy towns: construction on the waste land, flower gardens and vegetable gardens, habitual for Moscow, superstructure of yard blocks, i.e. making the district more dense. All these processes were described by the contemporaries.

L.V.Dalj, more famous by his works about the history of ancient Russian architecture, noted that Moscow would have kept its patriarchal look for a long time, "if it did not become the centre of all Russian rail ways... Speculation was devoted to the construction business and Moscow got an absolutely another character. All the near by territory of the railway stations were built in and are built in with endless rows of two-storey buildings... These houses gradually occupy the waste land along the Garden Ring, bounding Moscow.

The second rank was made by the superstructures of the third floors constructed on stone two-storey houses of the old school, within the borders between the Garden Ring and Kitay-gorod. Here a lot of rooms on the ground floors were arranged for stores, the upper floors were alloted for flats and furnished apartments"[15].

In 1870s the type of industial buildings was formed – multi-storeyed, with an even rhythm of huge windows, a little rounded at the top. The buildings acquired their expressive look due to artistically made utilitarian elements – material (its colour, texture, masonry), as well as dimensions, form, rhythm of the windows. It was a style of practical construction, of industry and transport.

Factories gave life to new city formations – manufacturing settlements. Besides industrial and administrative and economic buildings at the factories dwelling houses appeared. More prescient businessmen already during the time of the industrial overturn began to turn a factory into a small self-sufficient settlement with its own schools and hospitals.

Appearance of large manufacturing districts was another sign of urbanizing Moscow of the second half of the 19th century.

During the pre-reforms period in 1/5 of Moscow territory (inside the Garden Ring) nearly half of Moscow population lived. Behind the Garden Ring the outskirts began. Thirty-forty years later the quiet Moscow outskirts near the railway stations turned into vivid manufacturing districts "of an absolutely original type. Two of them were the biggest: Kozhevnicheskiy and Presnenskiy, but i'n the other outskirts, especially in Sutschovo and at Preobrazhenskaja frontier post there were also many factories. In the narrow lanes of Kozhevniki huge factories closed the sky and turned the passages into dark corridors; instead of the former idyllic silence now the din of machines reigns here". Rapid construction turned the outskirts into vast construction sites. By the end of the century here two thirds of the city population lived – nearly 700 thousand people.

The railway stations and the industrial construction are remarkable also because they represent the second pole or another variation, in comparison with temple and civil architecture, of revival of the national (ancient Russian) and medieval town-building tradition. But there was also an essential difference. The national tradition in architecture was revived consciously and spontaneously. Consciously – in the address to the national inheritance, during design of buildings, which were mentioned above. Spontaneously – in similar principles of formation expressed in direct turning of the useful into the architecturally expressive, as well as in the typologically similar town-forming influence of separate buildings or complexes on the construction in the near by districts and the city as a whole. The latter, as it was already mentioned, included first of all railway stations and industrial enterprises. Their structural and town-building influence exceeded very much the architectural and artistic one. In a big city, especially in a capital like Moscow, the visual connection between the town-forming elements is lost. More than that, generally the industrial architecture was not considered an art then, but absolutely utilitarian construction. The specific expressiveness of factory buildings was not regarded as artistic yet. The situation began to change in the early 20th century.

In Moscow outskirts (like in any other big city) behind the Garden Ring and the Camer-Collezhskiy bank an entire suburban zone – a focus of industrial enterprises, country cottage settlements and districts of cheap dwelling construction – began to form, closely connected with the economics, culture and life of Moscow.

City entertainment gardens acquired a new life. In the middle of the 19th century the most famous city public parks were located in Sokolniki and in Petersburg highway, in far away outskirts and near the city. In the second half of the 19th century they appeared in the city itself. The most famous were the gardens in Petrovskiy park with exotic names like "Algambra", "Eldorado", "Mauritania", and within the city border "Hermitage" (the old one in the district of Bozhedomka) and "Chicago" (then "Aquarium").

The city entertainment park of the second half of the 19th-beginning of the 20th centuries was a child of folk town culture, combining features of outdoor fete with enlightenment and historism of the 19th century. It grew out of private Moscow gardens, beautifully described by M.P.Zagoskin. It was an original ideal world to spend a holiday.

The garden "Chicago" (later "Aquarium") was one of the late creations of magician and wizard" of Russian theatre M.V.Leontovskiy. Leontovskiy established fairy-play on the Russian stage; the same fairy-play he created in entertainment parks. The entrance into "Aquarium" was, like now, from the side of the Garden Ring (not far from the Concert Hall after P.I.Chaykovskiy). Descriptions of journalists allow to some extent to recreate the world of an old Russian city holiday. Coming into the garden a visitor got on a ground decorated with figures of famous people and legendary heroes. Not far from the ground there was a splendid German castle – a pub with a statue of Bismark, pavilions in Russian, French, Mexican style. On the roof of the latter an alarm system was, with the help of which "the magician and wizard" managed the fete. In the depth of the ground there was a theatre for 720 seats and boxes, an open stage with galleries in Pompeian style and a grotto, big sparkling fountains, a Chinese pagoda with a dragon and plenty of other stalls.

In 1897-1898 the garden got another owner and was renamed into "Aquarium". Among the buildings a summer concert hall "Olympia" appeared, artificial grottos, fountains and waterfalls, artificial brooks, cascades falling into big aquariums with fish. After the world exhibition of 1900 in Paris "tin architecture" became modern, and the author of the project for "Aquarium" A.N.Novikov designed three new cabinets under a moresque cupola with decorations of tin-plate in the depth of the garden, following the style of the exhibition pavilions.

At the end of the 19th – beginning of the 20th centuries the crossing of Theatre and Voskresenskaja squares and Theatre passage turned into an original theatre-concert point. Close to the Big and Small theatres in Theatre square and near it the first private theatres were constructed: Shalaputin's theatre in front of the Maly (Small); not far from the square there was Solodovnikov's theatre (now the Theatre of Musical Comedy in Bid Dmitrovka street), Lianozov's theatre, later the Art Theatre in Kamergerskiy lane, Korsh's theatre in Bogoslovskiy lane (now a branch of the Art Theatre in Moskvina street), the theatre Paradiza in Sobinovskiy lane near Big Nikitskaja (now the theatre after Majakovskiy). During design of public buildings together with classical forms the forms of Russian style were widely used, especially in the theatres. The properties of Moscow University were intensively built in (new educational blocks were constructed, the Zoological museum, the library, a house for the teachers (arch.K.M.Bykovskiy). Not far from the University and the theatre Paradiza in Big Nikitskaja street the Moscow conservatoire was built. Together with the special buildings for theatres, theatre halls were arranged in dwelling houses: the theatre of Brenko in Malkielj's house in Tverskaja street, near Strastnaja square (1880s, M.N.Chichagov), theatre-studio of the Art Theatre in Guirsh's house in Povarskaja street (about 1905, I.A.Ivanov-Shits), the concert hall in Small Bronnaja street (1897, I.P.Mashkov) etc.

Thus, different parts of Bely town got different specialization. The Eastern and North-Eastern parts, adjoining Kitay-gorod and being connected with the railway stations and the trade and business parts, were opposed by the Northern and Western parts. Their specialization, mostly educational, was predetermined by Theatre square with the buildings of the emperor's theatres and a complex of buildings of Moscow University. The new theatres, museums, libraries, which appeared in this part of the city at that time, were also close to them. For instance, the Museum of Fine Art after A. S. Pushkin (1898-1912, R.I.Klein) was built very close to Rumjantsev's museum and the building of a picture gallery, specially constructed for it at the beginning of the century.

Differentiation of streets in accordance with their functional denomination was going on in Zamoskvorechie. The streets, leading to Moskvoretskiy bridge and adjoining Paveletskiy railway station – Pjatnitskaja, Novokuznetskaja, were mostly of trade and business character; Ordynka, Big and Small Poljanka and Yakimanka were of dwelling character. In front of the bridge in Balchug and on the "isle" because of construction of a flour market in Bolotnaja square another district of business life was formed – mostly trade and industrial. The Eastern part of the "isle", adjoining Moskvoretskiy bridge and the streets leading to Red Square and Kitay-gorod, represented as though small, a little less fashionable Kitay-gorod with mostly trade-warehouse specialization and hotels; the Western – with the industrial. Here multi-storey red brick blocks of the known confectionery factory Einem were constructed, the central city electrical station of Moscow trams, List's metallic plant. The Eastern end of the "isle" also acquired the industrial character: another electrical station was built on Raushskaja quay.

But the construction of electrical stations was begun by the first of them in the mere heart of Bely town near the Nobility Assembly and the future theatre of Solodovnikov at the corner of Big Dmitrovka and Georgievskiy lane (in the territory of the former monastery of Great Martyr George). The change of the buildings' denomination here reflects symbolically and eloquently the change of priorities.

Korsh's theatre (today it is a branch of Moscow Art Theatre after A.P.Chekhov) in Bogoslovskiy lane (1885, architect M.N.Chichagov). Photo. Late 19th century.

In Moscow outskirts, beginning from the second half of the 19th century, construction of public buildings developed – medical, charity, educational. Turning into a noticeable phenomenon of cultural and social life, equal in its importance with the trade and industrial development of Moscow, they became a certain step in its architectural and town-building development. At the turn of the 19th-20th centuries in the outskirts of the ancient capital several big districts of medical-educational complexes were formed: the former Sokolnichie field in the area of Stromynka street – in the East, Devichie field and the area of Big and Small Tsaritsynskaya streets – in the West, the district of Big and Small Kaluzhskajas, Donskaja street, Shabolovka and Big Serpukhovskaja streets – in the South and South-West. Like the main industrial-transportational districts the place of their location was the territory between the Garden Ring and Camer-Collezhskiy bank. With undoubtful similarity of functions of these districts (cultural, educational, medical, charity) certain characteristic features of their specialization could be seen, partially rooted in the buildings of these suburban territories at the end of the 18th – beginning of the 19th centuries. The districts of the former Sokolnishie field and Stromynka was mostly the district of hospital complexes and alms houses. Similar specialization characterized the districts of Big and Small Kaluzhskajas, Donskaja and Shabolovskaja streets, which was started by the construction of Golitsyn's (arch.M.F.Kazakov) and the first city hospital (arch.O.I.Bove), Miusskaja square and Miusskaja streets, the area of Devichie field (Big and Small Pirogovskaja streets) – that was mostly the district of educational departments. On Devichie field at the end of the 19th century the clinics of Moscow University were constructed (arch.M.D. Bykovskiy), the archive of the Ministry of Foreign Affairs, in the early 20th century – the building of High girls' school (arch.S.U.Solovjov), of the Municipal elementary school (arch. A.A.Ostrogradskiy), the kindergarten after Keljina (arch.S.U.Zelenko) and others. The character of Mius district, built in mainly in the early 20th century, was determined by the buildings of two Shelaputin's schools, Archaeological institute, the national university after Shanjavskiy (1910-1912, I.A.Ivanov-Shits).

During the last 40 years of the 19th century the total quantity of buildings increased five times. Parallely to the growth of the speed and volume of construction the increase of dimensions and height of buildings was going on, constructed mainly in the centre. However, they did not influence the city look as a whole. From 36 thousand dwelling houses at the end of the 19th century in Moscow there were only two thousand 3-storey and about 500 4-5-storey buildings (0,15%). Thus, 93% of all dwelling houses in Moscow were small 1-2 -storey buildings. By the end of the 19th century Moscow remained the city of small buildings.

In the second half of the 19th century the new socially oriented types of cultural educational buildings appeared – national theatres, national houses (libraries, reading-halls). In the early 20th century new types of business and entertainments buildings was added. All the set of buildings was a model of the epoch's consciousness, the business activity of which was inseparable from the care about the well-being of people and their enlightenment, and the historism of thinking made to feel vividly the connection of the past with the present, besides, the past, like the present was comprehended first of all as the history of people and the nation. The theme of historical memory acquired an independent importance then. The Kremlin, though it did not completely lose its administrative and political functions, was comprehended first of all as the national holy thing and a memorial.

The theme of memory was expressed in another thing. For the first time after the beginning of the 19th century, when a monument to Minin and Pozharskiy was installed in Red Square, in the second half of the 19th – beginning of the 20th centuries

Novokuznetskaja street. Buildings of the late 19th century.

a series of sculptural monuments was built. They were installed mainly in Boulevard Ring, the squares on the crossing of the radial and the circuit highways. For instance, for the monument to A.S.Pushkin Strastnaja square was chosen – the end of Tverskoy boulevard, the place on the crossing of Tverskaja street and Boulevard ring. The monument to the heroes of Plevna was situated in the same way – on the crossing of the radial streets and the boulevard near the fortress walls of Kitay-gorod. For the sculptural monuments of the early 19th century the similar places were chosen. The monument to Gogolj was installed on the crossing of Prechistenskiy boulevard and Znamenka street, the monument to the first publisher John Fedorov – in the public garden near the wall of Kitay-gorod. In each of these latter cases the choice was made according to the memoriality of the place, besides the considerations of town-building character: Gogolj died in the house, situated not far from Arbatskie gate in Nikitskiy boulevard, John Fedorov printed his famous Acts of the Apostles in the building which was in the place of the future Synodal printing house, not far from the wall of Kitay-gorod.

In the second half of the 19th century merchants began to leave the habitual areas of their living in Zamoskvorechie and to settle in traditional nobiliary districts: in Povarskaja, Big Nikitskaja, Ostozhenka, Arbat, Prechistenka streets. The place of the biggest construction of mansions of the second half of the 19th – beginning of the 20th centuries: the lanes, adjoining the Boulevard Ring, of the Northern and Western parts of Bely town, but mainly – Zemljanoy town, Zamoskvorechie. In the other territories of Bely town there was nearly no place left for mansions.

In the mansions, constructed most often in Russian style, "terem" (chamber) style prevailed, where each volume had its own finishing different from others, but the frontality of composition was still preserved and orientation of the main facades at contemplation from the street (Igumnov's house in Big Yakimanka, two houses of P.I.Tchukin in Small Gruzinskaja – architects A.E.Erikhson and B.G.Freidenberg).

Simultaneously in 1890s the mansions appeared, the composition of which presumed availability of free space, though it was in accordance with the street space. Their multi-volume style was counted on walking around, picturesqueness, changeability of the look newly opening from each point of view. Each picture seen at a certain moment did not have completeness and changed into another one.

Some of mansions like Z.G.Morozova's house in Spiridonovka (1893, F.O.Shekhelj), were situated in the depth of the yard, though the most extended facade, parallel to the street, corresponded to its direction. But most often the mode was used when the main com-

Monument to A. S. Pushkin in Tverskoy boulvard. Photo. Late 19th century.

plicated, picturesque volume of the building with roofs of different forms, was situated away from the street. At the same time one of its parts, most often a porch (the house of Svjatopolk-Chetvertinskaja in Povarskaja street) or a rizalit stood out to the red line (the mansion of F.O.Shekhtelj in Trekhprudny lane, 1896). It was a combination of two principles – the frontal-facade and centrical. By the fact that one of the volumes was brought out to the red line a building belonged to the street space and the picturesque-rhythmical composition was counted on observance around. Such buildings should be situated inside a free space, in the centre of an estate, like in Ancient Russia chambers and temples were placed. There are not many such mansions in Moscow of the end of the 19th century, they appeared only by its expiration.

The composition of the majority of mansions was subordinated to the street. Contemplation from the street was determining. The side facades as a rule remained secondary, yard facades were interpreted more expressively only if there was a front yard behind the building.

In the mansions, designed with separation from the street and counted on preservation of similar expressiveness of different facades from different points of view, the alignment of the street and front space, traditionally consolidated from the reign of Peter I, changed. Thus the undermining of the norms of regular town-building, enforced two centuries ago, began, gradually and from the bottom, without the government's interference and independently from it.

The picturesqueness and rhythmic structure of the mansions, especially of those designed with separation from the street red line, stipulated interaction of the street and yard space. Thus the frontality was abandoned, the transfer from the street to the yard facades was smooth and unnoticeable, there was no former hierarchy of facades: orientation of one facade at the street was characterized by its location, but not by the significance in the system of the composition.

New signs most early appeared on the mansions built not in classical styles: Gothic (the mansion of Z.G.Morozova in Spiridonovka, arch. F.0.Shekhtelj; the mansion of Bakhrushin in Luzhnetskaja streep, arch. K.K.Guippius), as well as in Russian style. Many mansions, in spite of Gothic forms, had all signs of modernism. Others, with all their innovations, remained within the framework of eclecticism (the mansion of lgumnov in Russian style, in Yakimanka street, arch. N.I.Pozdeev; the house of Svjatopolk-Chetvertinskaja in Povarskaja street, arch. P.S.Boytsov in the style of French Renaissance). Mansions even in such exotic style like Portuguese Renaissance – manuello were built (the mansion of A.A.Morozov in Vozdvizhenka street, arch. V.A.Mazyrin), in Greek style (the mansion of Popov on Smolenskiy boulevard, arch. A.I.Rezanov) etc.

The intensive construction conducted in the second half of the 19th century in all Moscow territory, began to liquidate the difference between the buildings in the streets and in the lanes, the centre and the outskirts. In the lanes of Bely and Zemljanoy towns, especially in the part adjoining the Big Stone bridge, "the isle" and Bolotnaja square, in the territory between Zemljanoy town and Camer-Collezhskiy bank in 1880-1890 big 5-storey apartment houses were built (sometimes with semi-basements), which sometimes were equal or exceeded in dimensions, richness of finishing of the facades in big streets, increasing the traditionally different look and character of buildings, the difference in the quantity of floors of dwelling and public buildings, so typical for Moscow of the 18th century. In the second half of the 19th century this contrast increased with construction of multi-flat leased houses.

For leased houses the dimension, was one of the signs, expressing the hierarchy of values. For the first time the type of an ordinary dwelling building was "extolled" to the level of one of the leading types of buildings. Leased houses were analogized to mansions in significance and orientation at general samples, but exceeded them in dimensions. The majority of such buildings was built in 1890s – during the construction and railway boom after 1870s. In 1890s the streets leading to the railway stations were intensively built in:

Novokuznetskaja, Pjatnitskaja and Poljanka streets lead to Paveletskiy railway station; Novoslobodskaja street – to Savelovskiy railway station; to Rizhskiy railway station – Metschanskaja streets, to Brjanskiy railway station – the district of Dorogomilovo and Smolenskaja square. In difference to the early construction in the districts of the railway stations big leased houses were spread here. Domination of multi-flat dwelling houses at the ends of highways, connecting the railways with the centre, was distinctive, the constructions seemed to be moving in direction of each other.

The ensemble compositions of Moscow streets were reached by the unity of compositional principles, use of little modes. In the historicism more definitely than in romanticism the tendency to the merging of traditions of different character was expressed In architectural practice the tendency included different stylistic directions, the sources at which architects oriented and used, the forms, accents and compositional schemes different in their meaning.

The historic essence of the second half of the 19th century included recomprehension of a number of modes of architecture of baroque and classicism. From classicism the modes of the so called town-building level were taken. Thus was, for instance, the address to effective plastic accents, to the practice of use of corner compositions and emphasizing of corners by rounding them and by cupolas, creation of effective accents on facades. In classicism it was porticos, in historical essence – attics, figured pediments, tower-like tops, cupolas. Their intensiveness and wide spreading contradicted the program neutralization of facades in 1830-1850.

The traditions of baroque were re-comprehended also radically in the historical essence, but mainly at the level-of style. They were similar in the original baroque interpretation of architectural forms: love to the juicy plastics of facades, rhythmic richness of compositions, plenty of decorations. The social status of buildings was absolutely different from both baroque and classicism.

During the second half of the 19th century in the centre of Moscow the turn to entire building in of the street front was over. It was especially evident inside Bely town. The look of the streets was formed by buildings facades merging into an entire street facade.

Another speciality in the look of the after-reform Moscow, like of any Russian town (except its Southern and Middle Asia regions) – was the great role of small buildings. It dominated in the territory between Zemljanoy town and Camer-Collezhskiy bank, merging into one whole with the buildings of the country-side. Its spreading, even domination in the suburbs of the towns was a traditional Russian feature. In the second half of the 19th century wooden architecture as a self-sufficient phenomenon of the national culture and the culture of

N. Igumnov's mansion in Big Yakimanka (1888, architect N. Pozdeev).

certain social ply was reabilitated. It came into town again as a new social and artistic phenomenon, as a fact of return to the national individuality and as an expression of the growth of self-consciousness of the low social plies. Peasants announced about themselves as an independent social power or, more exactly, got the opportunity to make such statement several years before the abrogation of serfdom. And though inside the city the wooden buildings of peasant type kept in the conditions of rapidly urbanizing Moscow only in the suburbs, but the wideness of this suburban region and, mainly, its existence added to Moscow the national colouring characteristic for Russian towns.

In the wooden buildings two directions in architecture became closer: created according to the projects of educated architects and folk masters. National architecture and architecture created on the basis of its traditions, merged in the wooden city dwelling buildings into one whole cultural, historical and artistic phenomenon. The districts built in with such houses were so wide, and their influence on the look and ensemble of the city and its specific Russian colouring was so important that it allows to speak about the wooden buildings in Russian towns of the second half of the 19th – beginning of the 20th centuries as an original social-historical, cultural and architectural-artistic phenomenon within the scale of the world architecture, and to see in the combination of the stone and wooden buildings in the centre the national specific feature of a Russian historical town, which was fully characteristic for its ancient capital.

But there was a sufficient quantity of wooden buildings in Russian style in Moscow centre. They were temporary buildings of different kinds. All bridges got pavilions of the society for saving in water – wooden, adorned with carving. The same pavilions filled in public gardens and parks, wooden summer stages, summer theatres and restaurants were built in Russian style.

Temples of the Second Half of the 19th Century

The second half of the 19th century revealed an absolutely opposite attitude to temple building in comparison with 1830-1850. There were several reasons for it as always. One of them was mentioned already: the transfer of the leadership of construction business from the government to the city authority. The municipal authority were busy first of all with economic affairs stimulated by the general progress in the social and economic life. So the situation allowed to state: from the second half of the 19th century under the attack of the increased dimensions of civil buildings, and mainly by the attitude to them as to the most important ones from the practical point of view, the artistic-contextual role of cult buildings began to decrease in the city ensembles. In the second half of the 19th century this process became irrevocable. "During our time many churches in the capital of Russian orthodox world, the churches of "the third Rome" could cry about how their native city disgraces, represses and stifles them... devouring them cold-heartedly and ruthlessly in the turbid waves of their "modern" trade industrial affairs... The changed way of social life changed the attitude of secular buildings to the holy ones. The city takes care of many "worldly" things , grows not each day, but each hour... it cannot give away the land in order that the temples could remain among the previous spatiousness...".[16]

The author of these words priest N.Skvortsov emphasized the connection between the change of the attitude to temples and one-sided concentration on the worldly success. "City, the centre of secular worldly affairs cannot but oust temples and will oust them more with its one-sided success".[17] And further the author gave examples of the loss by temples of their town-forming importance because of construction around them of big public and trade buildings and turning of the representations into their variation.

Moscow has plenty of monastery representations, "which serve a good source of income which grows in accordance with the development of trade... the owners take good advantage of their good profit, take an active part in construction of buildings", overwhelming churches: "...the temple of St.Prophet Elijah in lljinka street was closed not only by the blocks of trade rows, but by Novgorod representation". The house of the Lavra of the Holy Trinity-St.Sergius adjoined closely Novgorod representation. It "exceeds in beauty and hight all buildings in lljinka street, gives big profit from the rooms leased for the tavern, shops and barns, but, unfortunately, does not give place to any department corresponding to the activity and testaments of the founder of the Lavra and to the doctrine about the Holy Trinity, the icon of which, nevertherless, beautifies the gate of the house between the boards of the textile manufacturers and a notary.

In the same way the building of the museum of such branch of knowledge of which people are mostly proud – Polytechnical – represents a majestic building in comparison with the temple of Great Martyr George in front of it. The temple of Great Martyr George in Mokhovaja street is closed by the building of another temple – the temple of Science – of Moscow University."[18]

In Moscow and Petersburg this process began in Petrine time. N.Skvortsov indicated that in order to free space for the Arsenal the church of the Entry of God Jesus Christ into Jerusalem was demolished. At the same time the practice of demolishing because of town-building reasons remained exceptional. But increase of dimensions and quantity of secular buildings leads to their background temples losing their significance. And this factor is not only of architectural and town-building character, because through it the world view prevailing in the society is expressed. Being in sorrow about the lost leading importance of temples in Moscow panoramas and buildings in the second half of the 19th century, Skvortsov emphasized the exclusive position of the cathedral of Christ the Saviour in Moscow. But here the author really exaggerated. In Moscow from the 18th century two tendencies were in struggle – one secular, governmental or business, the other – the church tendency. Often the same forces expressed and materialized both of them. In Moscow, like in other towns, first in architecture of baroque, later in classicism and romanticism, the striving to increase the dimensions of temples and bell-towers showed. This tendency did not disappear in the second half of the 19th century. On the one hand, in 1871 the offer appeared to demolish the church of the Holy Trinity in Nikitniki in Kitay-gorod for the purpose to construct in its place some business buildings. The church was saved by the interference of Moscow Archaeological Society. On the other hand, the process of super-construction and reconstruction of the existing temples and bell-towers and construction of new ones did not stop both in historical and new Moscow districts. It is difficult, however, to outline some dominating tendency for the second half of the 19th century. Churches were built according to the needs, though their location was always aligned with the existing ensembles, added and enriched them.

In addition to the above-mentioned chapels of St.Alexander Nevskiy in Moiseevskaja square (1883, D.N.Chichagov), Plevnenskaja chapel-memorial in lljinskiy public park (1887, V.O.Shervud), the chapel of "Bogoliubsk" Icon of the Theotokos inside Varvarinskaja tower of Kitay-gorod and an open chapel near this tower (1880, N.V.Nikitin), the chapel of Great Martyr Panteleimon in Nikolskaja street (1881-1883, A.S.Kaminskiy) the newly constructed temples should be mentioned: the church of St.Gregory the Theologian in Bogoslovskiy lane (today Moskvina street, the public park near house 1/30, 1876-1879, A.S.Kaminskiy), the church of "Kazan" Icon of the Theotokos in Big Yakimanka near Kaluzhskie gate, also on the place of a disassembled temple (1886, N.V.Nikitin), the church of Iberon Icon of the Theotokos of the Iberon community of sisters of mercy (Big Poljanka, 20, 1896-1901, S.K.Rodionov), the church of the Intercession in Kudrino in Kudrinskaja square.

A number of temples was built in the outskirts which were intensively constructed at that time: in Marjina Woods (Sheremetjevskaja street, 13, the corner of the 13th passage of Marjina Woods, 1899-1901), the church of St.Tykhon Miracle-worker of Zadons in Sokolniki (Mayskiy lane, 1876). The latter, like many temples of countryside settlements, was built from wood and adorned generously with carving. The policy of intensive temple construction, dating from the late 18th century, continued for spreading of orthodoxy in the districts, inhabited mostly by old believers. In 1895 at the expense of the brothers Bakhrushin the church of St.Basil the Confessor was founded in the New village between the New and Prolomnaja streets (arch.A.P.Popov). The usual superstructures and enlargements of temples continued. A refectory and a bell-tower were added to the church of St.Prophet Elijah in 2nd Obydenny lane (1868, A.S.Kaminskiy), the refectory was reconstructed and the bell-tower got a superstructure of the church of St.Prophet Elijah in Vorontsavo field (1876-1878, P.P.Zykov), a new refectory and bell-tower were constructed for the church of St.Nicholas the Miracle-worker in the New settlement (Dolgorukovskaja street, 23a; 1903, S.F.Voskresenskiy). In 1900-1903 a huge house of the representation of the Balaam monastery (2nd Tverskaja-Yamskaja street, 52) with the church of Sts.Sergius and Herman the Miracle-workers of Balaam, for 1000 people (1900-1903, A.I.Roop). A new block with the church of St-Sergius of Radonezh was constructed at the representation of the Holy Trinity-St.Sergius Lavra in 2nd Troitskiy lane, a chapel of St.Nicholas the Miracle-Worker at the church of St.Basil, archbishop of Caesarea was constructed in 1st Tverskaja-Yamskaja street, in memory of the wedding of their Emperor's Majesty (founded in 1899, arch. F.O.Shekhtelj). Besides that temples were constructed in large hospital-charity complexes.

However, in comparison with 1830-1860 not only the scale of temple construction decreased. It stopped being the subject of constant attention of the authority on the part of the government and the church, becoming in a way a private affair of believers. It was a result of the change of direction of the merchant construction and the system of preferences in the policy of the municipal authority. The authority, among which the leaders were merchants, concentrated on the activity in the sphere of the city comfortable arrangement. It was accompanied by allocation of merchants capitals to charity. In the volume of investments in the second half of the 19th century it increased the investments into construction of temples and was considered a God-serving deed of prior importance. This new worldview phenomenon was described by contemporaries. "In Moscow merchant society there is the ancient Russian idea about a merchant-guest till now, owning big economic power, but being able to serve their native city and the country with his capitals. In Russian idea "money are never the purpose of existence: there is soul, the care of which is more important and more necessary than money. Beginning from bylina's Sadco, Hovgorod guest, Russian merchants were occupied with construction of churches... Donations to churches and monasteries continue in the 19th century too, but in the second half with the cultural growth of Moscow merchants their capitals were widely used in different spheres of science, art and charity... Simple enumeration of what was created by merchants could occupy several pages".[19] "Behind a merchant there sometimes is a whole world of different requirements and burning needs of people and the state, in the name of which he began to speak, without shyness, for he feels his force in this authorization and in this solidarity of his interests with the national interests".[20]

Church of the Kazan Icon of the Theotokos
near Kaluzhskie gate in Big Yakimanka
(1876-1886, architect W.V.Nikitin; did not keep till now).

Withdrawal of capital out of church construction to charity meant significant changes in merchants' worldview. Development of merchants charity and reduction of investment into temple construction were interconnected phenomena.

The temple construction in Moscow of the second half of the 19th century was incomparable in scale, and most important in contents with the temple contsruction of 1830-1860. The government kept from the leadership of temple building in the capitals. Participation of Alexander III in determination of the style of church construction was limited by the wish to see a temple-memorial in Russian style in the place of the deathly injury of his father in Petersburg on the quay of Catherine's canal.

The epoch of great reforms did not spread on temple-building, which in the ancient capital in the second half of the 19th century developed as though by its own momentum. This situation was radically different from the province, where exactly at this time the biggest churches and cathedrals were built, determining the look and panorama of towns. And from Petersburg, where temple construction was conducted equally intensively in the second third, the second half of the 19th and the beginning of the 20th centuries. In Moscow two highest points of temple construction, though induced by different reasons, took place in 1830-1860 and in the early 20th century.

There was a little different situation in the monastery construction. In the second half of the century in Moscow and near by three new monasteries appeared. In 1862 Alexander II certified the application of the Holy Synod about arrangement in Moscow in Vsekhsvjatskoe cemetery (of All Saints) behind the Rogozhskaja frontier post of a convent in the memory of liberation of peasants from serfdom. In 1890 in Novoslobodskaja street a convent of the Icon of the Theotokos "The Joy of All the Afflicted" was open (1893-1894 according to the project of architect Vladimirov the temples of this monastery were constructed). In 1876 outside the borders of Moscow of that time Golutvinkkiy monastery of Kazan Icon of the Theotokos was founded. In the monastery of St.Alexius, moved to Krasnoe village because of the construction of the cathedral of Christ the Saviour, a huge church of All Saints was constructed in 1887-1891 (arch. A.A.Nikiforov).

In the architecture of new temples and monasteries in 1870-1890 the style of the city settlement architecture of the middle of the 17th century of Moscow, partially Yaroslavsko-Kostromskaja schools, was renewed. The turn to this style was symptomatic. The stylistic and esthetic similarity of the architecture of the 17th century and the second half of the 19th century was based on the similarity of social basis. It was born by the mass comprehension of a Russian town. It is a national settlement art. Its customers were the merchants. Exactly because of this Russian style, addressing in temple construction to the inheritance of the 17th century, turned out to be extremely tenacious and not sensitive to the influence of modernism, retaining its viability at the beginning of the 20th century too. Designers of monastery representations turned to the tradition of the 17th century too. The second widely spread direction in the church architecture was based on the tradition of the Byzantine temple architecture, but adapted it to the three-part structure of a Russian parish temple with a bell-tower and a refectory (the church of the Kazan Icon of the Theotokos near Kaluzhskie gate, the church of St.Gregory the Theologian in Bogoslovskiy lane).

However the ousting of temples to the second place in Moscow construction of the second half of the 19th century and in the early 20th century was rather relative then. Only in the centre temples turned out to be enveloped by multi-storey buildings. In the main Moscow territory they still dominated in the city panorama. And in the view at the Kremlin and at Zamoskvorechie. The temple of St.Gregory the Theologian, included into the general row of buildings and the temple of St.Prophet Elijah, which became a part of new trade blocks, were only the prerequisites of the process, which will be continued in the early 20th century.

---

[1] Architect's Guide around Moscow, published by Moscow Architectural Society for the members of 2nd congress of Russian architects in Moscow. ed. I.P.Mashkov. M., 1895, p. 99.
[2] Today's Economy of Moscow. Ed. I.A.Verner, M., 1913, p. 1.
[3] Shtromberg M.A. City Rail Ways in Moscow and Other Big Cities and Their Social Importance. M., 1912, p. 13.
[4] Zavalishin D. London, Paris and Moscow // Russian Records. 1866, August, p. 627-628.
[5] As above, p. 617.
[6] RGIA f. 1639, op. 1, 1863, d. 165, 11. 1-3 ob.
[7] Teleshev N.D. Moscow in Foremer Times. // Moscow Antiquity. M., 1989, p. 426-427.
[8] Vasilich. Moscow. 1850-1910 // Moscow in its Past and Present, iss. XI, M., 1912, p. 19.
[9] Zabelin I.E. Moscow // Moscow and Its Life. Comp.R.Kumov. Spb., 1904, p. 206-208.
[10] Boborykin P.D. Moscow Panorama // Moscow and Its Life..., p. 211, 212, 216.
[11] Boborykin P.D., Kitay-gorod..., p. 33.
[12] Description of the Project, Certified by the Highest Authority, of the Memorial to Emperor Alexander II in Moscow Kremlin, made by artist P.Zhukovskiy and civil engineer N.Sultanov. M., 1890, p. 2.
[13] As above, p. 3.
[14] Sokolovskiy E. Correspondence from Moscow // Architect, 1873, No. 2, p. 28-29.
[15] Dalj L.V. Construction Activity in Moscow //Architect, 1876, No. 4, p. 39-40.
[16] Priest Skvortsov N. The Cry of Moscow Churches // Russian archive. 1893, No. 6, p. 288.
[17] As above, p. 188-289.
[18] As above, p. 293, 297.
[19] Vasilich G. Moscow 1850-1910 // Moscow in Its Past and Present, iss. IX, M., 1912, p. 22.
[20] Quot.: Buryshkin P.A. The above works, 8.

CHAPTER SIX

The Turn of the Century – the Turn of Age

State Emblem of Russian Empire.

Square of Iljinskie gate. There is the North Insurance Society (1910-1916, architects I. Rerberg, M. Peretjatkovich, V. Oltarzhevskiy) behind Iljinskaja tower of Kitay-gored. Photo. Early 20th century.

Varvarinskaja square. On the right – Varvarinskaja tower of Kitay-gorod, on the left – Offices building and the hotel "Business Yard" (1912-1914, architect I.S.Kuznetsov). Post-card. Early 20th century.

Project of Kazanskiy railway station (1917, architect A.V.Tschusev together with A. Snigarev, N. Tamonkin and others). Perspective.

Emperor Nicholas II (1896-1917). Lithography of V. Fers.

Yaroslavskiy railway station (1902-1904, architect F.O.Shekhtel).
Photo. Early 20th century.

Theatre Square and the hotel "Metropol".

The border of the 19th – the 20th centuries was one of the greatest historical turns in the history of Russia, Moscow, Moscow architecture. Anyway, this phenomenon is characteristic not only for this period, a turn of a century was always crucial.

Urbanisation and Moscow Look

In the historical and town-buildings development of Moscow this turn had its own specialities. All the periods considered till the present moment offered their own conception of the centre, in the look and contents of which the concrete historical individuality of that time expressed itself most fully. The border of the 19th – 20th centuries did not offer such conception. The city and its centre developed as though under their own momentum, growing only quantitative indices. Both the city and its centre continued to function and construct on the basis of social, economic and technical factors, which appeared in 1830-1850 and became absolutely definite in the second half of the 19th century. However, the quantitative indices acquired the significance of qualitative factors. The industrial overturn, when the construction of rail ways, development of trade and industry for the first time became town-forming factors, was followed by the industrial and commercial overturn.

Something of the kind happened in the sphere of development of style. At the end of the 19th – beginning of the 20th centuries the second stage of eclecticism – historicism was still valid. At its background at the end of 1890 modernism appeared, and during 1900-1910 – neoclassicism.

The period considered in this chapter was unique, because it was complicated, contradicting, variable and cannot be in general. For the first time since the turn of the 18th century the directions of social and spiritual ideals had the opportunity of free expression in architecture.

Before the middle of the 19th century objective circumstances precluded such opportunity: the state policy in the sphere of architecture with an equally hard system of regulation and control. At the same time the policy of Nicholas I in architecture for the first time gave the opportunity to express one's cultural preferences to low plies of society. In temple architecture there was the opportunity now to turn to ancient orthodox sources, in the civil architecture – to the modes and compositions spread in the first third of the 19th century in the dwelling constructions of merchants, petty bourgeois, artisans. At the same time there was architecture of high culture.

In the second half of the 19th century popular tastes expressed themselves otherwise. Self-consciousness of the third estate declared about itself in the free choice of style. It was a unique period in the history of architecture, when the norms of high architecture were interpreted and subordinated to different tastes. It was an original city people's architecture, created upon the order of many customers by people, who got academic education in conformity with the norms of high style.

Architecture of the early 20th century was a direct antipode to the architecture of the second half of the 19th century in this sense. Mass taste was still reflected in wooden buildings of Moscow, which till 1930 was loyal to the modes and poetic style, born in 1860-1870. At the end of the 19th – beginning of the 20th centuries like in the second half of the 19th century the government did not participate in the leadership of architectural and artistic process in big cities of the European part, especially in the capitals. This stipulation is not random, in the Asian part of Russia, especially in Siberia and in the Far East the situation was different. So during this transfer from the New Time to the Newest a unique situation appeared in Russia for all the historical period from the 18th till the early 20th centuries. As architecture was in the sphere of the interests of high culture again, for the first time in two centuries the opportunity appeared of simultaneous functioning of a number opposite, antagonistic ideas and conceptions and their realization in corresponding styles or directions. These ideas or styles did not have a general character. At the same time they were evident first of all in architecture of the capital cities – Moscow and Petersburg.

The variations of the modernism style are meant here, as well as the avant-garde, neo-classicism. Each of the above phenomena represented a certain conception and its own viewpoint, showing those qualities of inseparability and unmergeability of the ends and beginnings, about which A.A.Blok wrote.

Appearance of the neo-Russian style was connected with Russia, with Abramtsev's circle. This phenomenon, principally different from the Russian style of the second half of the 19th century, was similar to the ideas stated by N.F.Fedorov, V.S.Solovjov, Russian religious philosophers of the early 20th century. Its contents were based on the expression of the Russian idea with its thesis of spiritual renovation on the basis of orthodoxy and with the idea about the historical mission of Russia dating from the formula Moscow – the Third Rome, by means of architecture. A queer fact testified to the viability and prevalence of it. When in 1912 the Balkan war began, one of representatives of the numerous Morozov's family – A.I.Morozov sent to the Holy Synod money stipulated for the return of the church of St.Sophia in Constantinople to its initial function of a Christian temple.

The Russian style did not die in the civil architecture either. This speciality was characteristic mainly for Moscow. There

Alexeevskiy people's house (early 190s; did not keep till now). Access park pavilions. Photo. Early 20th century.

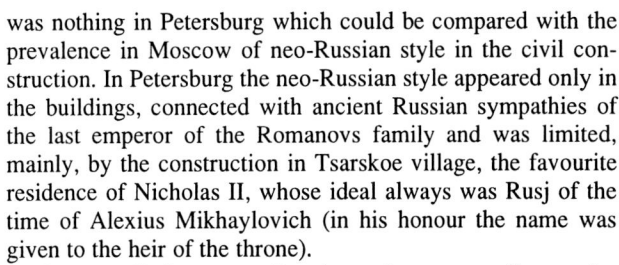

National University after L.A.Shanjavskiy in Miusskaja square (1910-1913, architect I. Ivanov-Shits). Photo. Early of the 20th century.

was nothing in Petersburg which could be compared with the prevalence in Moscow of neo-Russian style in the civil construction. In Petersburg the neo-Russian style appeared only in the buildings, connected with ancient Russian sympathies of the last emperor of the Romanovs family and was limited, mainly, by the construction in Tsarskoe village, the favourite residence of Nicholas II, whose ideal always was Rusj of the time of Alexius Mikhaylovich (in his honour the name was given to the heir of the throne).

In contradiction to neo-Russian style corresponding, mainly, to the Russian idea and orthodoxy, modernism ("pure" modernism, international variant of modernism) can be considered an expression of esthetic utopia. It was based on the idea of spiritual and ennobling influence of beauty and was expressed mostly in mansions and leased houses, i.e. in the types of buildings, where a person spends most of his time, and in the buildings of cultural-educational denomination. It is characteristic that all three theatres constructed in Moscow in the early 20th century: Art Theatre (F.Shekhtelj), Guirsh (I.A.Ivanov-Shits, the corner of Merzljakovskiy lane and Povarskaja street, did not keep till now), Omon (M.A.Durnov) were in the style of modernism.

Strict or rational modernism prevailed in the buildings of banks, offices and trade companies, in industrial buildings, situated within the city boundary limited by the Camer-Collezhskiy bank. It was not adequate to what was connected with the appearing of openly technocratic ideas. In the first projects of Moscow metro (1898-1902 and 1912-1913) for the first time the attitude to the engineering was shown, for instance, to the new means of mechanical transport, as to a self-sufficient, not only practically useful, but also of spiritual value. In this

sense it is possible to see some architectural analogue of futurism and avant-garde in these projects.

Finally, in 1910s neo-classicism claimed to be a self-sufficient style. In neo-classicism the admiration of the beauty of Russian architecture of the New Time, of the "discovery" of Peter's period in Russian history as a phenomenon of the national culture and art was inseparable from the admiration of the strong state power which made possible the realization of the beautiful and grandiose architectural creations of the 18th – beginning of the 19th centuries.

Different styles and directions aligned differently with the main direction of town-building development of Moscow – with its rapid growth and turning into a big city.

Moscow of the late 19th – early 20th centuries lived through another process of intensive urbanization following after the second half of the 19th century. The ancient capital began to lose the features of patriarchality irrevocably. There was active construction on waste land, gardens, outskirts. Moscow was still the second big city after Petersburg in Russia and one of the most dynamically developing cities of the world. In a quarter of a century – from 1895 to 1917 Moscow population, including the outskirts, grew more than twice. At the beginning of 1917 there were more than two million people (2017,1) in it. The growth was due to the newcomers: they comprised 4/5 of the total quantity of inhabitants of the ancient capital. The tendency to increase of the peed of the population growth was continuous. In 1897-1902 population grew at the average in 2,9% annually, in the next five years – in 2.9%, in 1907-1912 – in 4,4%, reaching the apogee during the years of World War I – 4,94%. In 1907-1913 Moscow population was growing as quickly as the population of New-York, twice more

Tverskaja street. View from Kamergerskiy lane. Second building on the right is Savvinskoe representation (1907, architect I. Kuznetsov). Photo. Early 20th century.

City people's house in Vvedenskaja square (1903, architect I. Ivanov-Shits).

quickly than the population of Vienna and 4 times quicker than that of Paris.[1]

In the short period from the late 19th – beginning of the 20th centuries two high points in the construction activity took place: it was the end of the 1890s – beginning of the 1900s – the eve of the first Russian revolution – and 1908 – 1914. The last five-seven pre-war years were the years of unknown construction boom. Its volume and speed left behind all the other periods of rapid construction. Only the dwelling square annually put into operation comprised more than 200,000 m^2. Describing the results of the construction season in 1911 the journal "Zodchiy" ("Architect") wrote: "The last year fully justified the hopes for intensive construction activity: almost in all districts old buildings were rapidly extended and new ones were constructed... There was a rather vivid construction activity in Petersburg, where the per cent of 5-6-storey buildings turned out to be unusually high both in the centre and in the suburbs. The construction season in Moscow was even more active, where only 5-7-storey buildings were constructed in the quantity of 3 thousand last summer..."[2]

Construction in Moscow, not limited by the emperor's decree, like in Petersburg, about the biggest hight of 21 m, was unrestrained in its growth. On the eve of World War I the construction of 7-storey buildings became a norm. More often the buildings were constructed of 8, sometimes 9, 10 even 11 floors. For description of this fact the word "skyscraper", loaned from the USA, is used. But 11 floors did not become the limit for Moscow either. In 1913 architect V.A.Tschuko designed a 12-storey leased house of Moscow School of Painting, Sculpture and Architecture at the corner of Volkhonka street and Small Znamenskiy lane (near the Museum of Fine Art), architect I.P. Mashkov designed a 13-storey leased house at the corner of Skobelevskaja square, Tverskaja street and Glinitschevskiy lane. In difference to the American, all Moscow skyscrapers were dwelling. They were more modest in their sizes than the American ones and traditional in the construction (brick walls, ferro-concrete ceilings, carcase structure was used only for the ground or the first floors, allotted for offices or shops).

In the same way the history of New-York skyscrapers began. The new structures and new aesthetics came when the houses rose much higher than 10 floors. Then the article of L.Salliven "High office buildings from artistic point of view" appeared.[3]

At the beginning of 1880s Boborykin compared Moscow with the biggest industrial-trade cities of the world, certain symbols of the rapid development of capitalism of the second half of the century – Manchester, London and New-York. Moscow of the early 20th century, retaining the similarity to London, showed even more features which made it similar to New-York. Situated on the periphery of European civilization cities, which were not capitals, turned into the main economic centres of two huge continental powers. "The city space of Moscow and New-York was transformed by two forces: capitalism and modern transport".

In Moscow "the motive force" first was the intertown transport – rail ways. The advantageous geographical situation of Moscow in the centre of the Russian land made it the focus of the national railway system. The rail ways connected Moscow not only with the main regions of Russia, but the centre of Europe, thus finishing with supremacy of Petersburg as the window to Europe and to the world space. After the creation of Moscow railway junction development of the city network of railway transport followed, first horse trams, then electrical trams, and finally the metro.

The ensemble of the new urbanizing Moscow of the early 20th century was formed by the combination of multi-storey

The house of the city elementary college in Big Tsaritsinskaja street
(1909, architect A. Ostrogradskiy).

multi-flat dwelling houses with trade-office, bank and industrial buildings, situated inside the city borders, as well as with public buildings of mass denomination like hospitals, alms houses and educational departments of different level and profile. The quantity of theatres increased. New types of cultural buildings appeared intended for mass visitors – cinemas, people's houses, people's theatres, people's universities. First covered stadiums and skating rinks, kindergartens were designed.

The construction boom of the 20th century included all Moscow, spreading to the undeveloped outskirts. In the centre it showed in the increase of the density of the buildings and construction in the place of small buildings of multi-storey giants. As the avalanche construction was equally spread in the centre and the outskirts there is the reason to speak about another tendency which appeared in the early 20th century – the tendency to level the hight and density of buildings in the outskirts and in the centre. Only the tendency is meant here, not the actual situation. In reality there were differences and very big ones.

The construction of multi-storey leased houses began to interfere into the traditional aristocratic, built in mostly with mansions quiet dwelling districts of Moscow. They appeared in Arbat, Ostozhenka, Prechistenka and their lanes, in Povarskaja, Big and Small Nikitskaja, Big and Small Dmitrovka streets. Sometimes they date back to the beginning of 1900, however their main quantity was built on the eve of World War I – in the first half of 1910.

Moscow of the early 20th century represented an impressive picture of intensively urbanized large Russian historical city. Its construction was a striking mixture of ultra modern style and patriarchality, contrasting combinations of multi-storey huge buildings and small houses of 1-2 floors in one street or lane. This picture was most characteristic for the Western areas of Bely, Western and South-Western areas of Zemljanoy towns, Zamoskvorechie.

But Moscow remained the city of contrasts in a wider sense. It was not only the contrast of the densely built in stone houses centre and the small-storey mostly wooden buildings in the outskirts, but also the contrast of the suburban districts with the prevalence of the artisan and small factory production and the districts with developed factory industry. In the early 20th century, though Moscow still remained the city with developed textile industry, in it the engineering industry and metal working were spread too.

I. Sytin's printing house in Tverskaja street (1905, architect A. Erikhson). Photo. Early 20th century.

The city look was changed by the urbanization in the wide meaning of the word, including the technical progress, development of transport, electrical light. The city look was changed acutely by huge window openings of office, bank, trade houses, shop windows of the ground floors of leased houses lit during the dark time with electrical light which seemed blinding then. The advertisements changed the city look too. The tempo of life changed, its rhythm and order.

Architects, engineers and workers built from brick, ferro-concrete and glass new urbanistic Moscow. Poets imprinted in the word its changed look, more exactly the look of the districts which by their unsimilarity to the past arousing admiration and worry:

*"In place of wings skyscrapers rose
And shameless style of modernism is shining"* –
wrote V.Ya.Brjusov

One of the first singers of the appearing urbanized environment V.Shershenevich became:

*Ten-storey fancies were heaping up on each other,
The city poured cries, squeals and rumble spray...
Motors reared and brought out the drunk soul,
Drunk from the noise like from a glass of whisky.*

Or:

*I love only the rumble of avenues,
Only the roar of motors, I despise silence...
And the lamps, skyscrapers and billboards
Are whirling in the strophes, forgetting the measures.*

The rapidly changing life aroused admiration, frightened and worried. The coming of disturbing and menacing events was felt, which made the poet expect the events of the new century with fear, which being a finale of a whole epoch in the history of Russia "Predicts, blowing the veins, ruining all borders, unheard of changes, unknown revolts".

People, who were not only the witnesses of the changes, but partially the creators of new Moscow, tried to look into the future of the 20th century. A year before the beginning of World War I a correspondent of the newspaper "Moscow Voice", hiding behind the initials V.M., published an interview with architects, painters, clerks of the municipal department. They stated unanimously the end of old Moscow. They were also unanimous in their prognosis: the old Moscow – a unique Russian historical city was leaving for the past irrevocably. The difference was only in the attitude to this fact. The material had an eloquent title: "Moscow, losing its look".

"Moscow with its patteren churches, colourful cupolas of bell-towers, with its towers and walls, with small quiet houses, has been remarkable among other towns with its exclusive appearance since ancient time.

In recent time this appearance began to change rapidly. Multi-storey, ugly, without any style houses like plane boxes are growing, old buildings are demolished, – and a question arises – is Moscow not in danger of losing its character, its incomparable look and becoming a usual standard city of European-wide style?

Our associate talked about with a number of competent people".

V.M.Vasnetsov. The famous artist was indignant at the spreading of the new style, at that Nouveau Empire of "decadent manner, which is used more and more to the detriment of development of Russian architecture".

He supposed that the main task of Russian architecture was to find out the forms of the national architecture...

V.K.Trutovskiy. A guide of the Arsenal thought that Moscow was losing: its face. – And I think – it is for the worse...

N.V.Tschenkov. The chief of the commission for the city comfortable arrangement:

– Moscow must acquire a European look. Historical memorials and buildings will, certainly remain, but today's Asian character of the city – all these curved streets, incorrect planning of buildings and strange colour of the houses – must be liquidated...

Soon Moscow became a fully European city. In 1914 electricity was everywhere, boulevards were remade in the foreign

The Medvednikov's hospital and alms house in Big Kaluzhskaja street (1904-1905, architect S. Solovjov).

manner, greenery on them was increased, in ugly squares, like Kudrinskaja, splendid fountains were made; streets were repaved.

Architect R.I.Klein. The builder of the museum of Alexander III supposed that "Moscow was not able to preserve its ancient colouring".[4]

The material, published two years later in 1915, summed up these considerations.

"... The first ten years of the new century were full of rapid exterior re-arrangement of Moscow. 4-, 5- and 6-storey houses were growing like mushrooms, changing radically the look of the most patriarchal streets. The smart looking tram, that has ousted the horse tram, gets to the most deaf places and shortens the distance between the centre and the outskirts. Divisions of the best trade companies are built in the outskirts; finally the streets, shining with windows of shops and electrical light, acquired if not fully European, but rich and smart appearance. The original face of the first capital was formed little by little into a modern big city of classical type... Moscow showed such unusual power of its promising development which gave it the right for economic supremacy among other cities of Russia, without exception of Peterburg".[5]

Modernism, Neoclassicism...

The unity of the general direction of the functional originality and the direction of the construction activity did not mean preservation of Kitay-gorod unchanged. Exactly in the early 20th century it was renovated radically, which was especially evident at the background of Red and Voskresenskaja squares, which kept their look till the second half of the 19th century. The importance of the squares around Kitay-gorod grew rapidly, being connected with the railway stations and the main business and trade streets, – with its Northern, North-Eastern and Eastern parts. The wall of Kitay-gorod was bounded anew by the buildings of the 20th century. At the corner of Theatre square and passage the big hotel "Metropol" was constructed. It was one of the first big buildings in Moscow in the style of modernism. Here an opera theatre, exhibition halls, cinema, a skating rink, restaurants were to be placed. The program was inspired by S.I.Mamontov's dream – the soul and organizer of Moscow Mamontov's circle – about an exit of high art into the midst of people's life, into the streets and squares, about spiritualizing and adornment of life with really beautiful creations.

Such building, bringing beauty into the midst of ordinary life, was to become Yaroslavsky railway station according to F.O.Shekhtelj's project – the first big building in Moscow in the style of national-romantic variant of modernism (neo-Russian style). By Yaroslavsky railway station the road from Moscow to the Russian North was opened, the architecture of which became a synonym of the real national art not spoiled by the foreign and city influence. In the look of the building the architect tried to express a certain formula of the Russian in architecture. But it was only the exterior side of the building. The essence of its contents was in the concealed dream and supertask of modernism about beauty, reforming and spiritualizing life.

Further, in the direction from the North to the East, behind the wall of Kitaygorod one after another at the beginning of the 20th century Kaljazinskoe monastery representation (arch. G.A.Makaev), the building of Moscow merchants society, the block situated at the corner of Small Cherkasskiy lane and New square (arch.F.O.Shekhtelj), the building of the Northern Insurance Society at the corner of the square of Iljinskie gate and Iljinka street (I.I.Rerberg, V.K.Oltarzhevskiy, M.M.Peretjatkovich) were constructed; on the other side of Iljinka street along the wall of Kitay-gorod and Old Square – two big trade-banking buildings of Titov and Armand (V.V.Shervud), the trade house and hotel of Boyar Yard (F.O.Shekhtelj) and, finally, bounding Varvarskaja square and flanking the passage at both sides, the office-banking building of 1900s and a huge complex of "Business Yard" (arch.I.S.Kuznetsov) were constructed. A row of new trade-banking buildings appeared inside Kitay-gorod: the trade block of the Monastery of the Annunciation, the trade house of Arshinov, the Rjabushinskiys' bank, etc.

The row of the new business multi-storey buildings along the wall of Kitay-gorod, certainly, looked especially impressive. It can be considered an image of some kind, a presentation card of new Moscow. It was a personification of its industrial and economic power and simultaneously an enormous historical path. It was the most evident expression of the mentality of the early 20th century, represented by the masterpieces of old Moscow modernism. The gala facade of Kitay-gorod was a certain materialization of the new idea about an ideal city, of its aspect connected with creation of technical and economic power of its time.

At the border of the 19th-20th centuries the notions of the contemporaneity and creation acquired a self-sufficient value. At that time a special philosophy of creation was developed (the books of P.Engelmeier and N.A.Berdjaev about this problem in Russia). At the same time, in the early 20th century the ideas about comfort and technical achievements also acquired a self-sufficient value, creating the ground for absolutization of

City kindergarten after Keljina in Big Tsaritsynskaja (Pirogovskaja) street (early laics, architects A. Zelenko, I. Kondakov). Photo. Early 20th century.

View from Varvarinskie gate of Kitay-gored at the square of Iljinskie gate. On the right – the hotel and the office building "Boyards Yard" (1899-1901, architect F. Shekhtel). Photo. Early 20th century.

The house of Moscow Merchants Society in Small Cherkasskiy lane (1909-1911, architect F.Shekhtel).

engineering and speed. Finally, the beginning of the 20th century – the beginning of a new century felt acutely the unrepeatable individuality of its time its unsimilarity to anything which was before. The requirement of contemporaneity acquired program character, became a sign of the new artistic style in Russia, besides that turned into a term, giving the name to the new architectural style – modernism.

The trade and business buildings in Kitay-gorod were the apotheosis of utilitarism in modernism, which, however, never resulted in absolutizing of engineering, material, construction, function. It was architecture in the best meaning of the word – it was high art. Its creators never limited themselves by purely pragmatical tasks. But in this art there was the danger of reducing .architecture to the level of simple satisfaction of practical needs, as there were no contents in it. This special care of modernism about beauty, spiritualizing the constructive scheme, was the result of the effort to avoid pragmatism in architecture.

The composition of the trade, office, banking and industrial buildings was simple. In the basis of it there was a system of vertical columns, which went through all floors and expressed on the facades by vertical tractions – this was the main theme of a facade. Horizontal divisions corresponding to the division into floors, window openings, which occupied due to an inside carcase the distance between two rows of vertical columns – the second theme subordinated to the first one and interacting with it. The compositional scheme of Moscow trade-office buildings was similar to that of Chicago school. It was one of the most interesting creations of Moscow architecture. Up-to-date materials corresponded to the ultramodern compositions – glazed or mat facing brick, concrete stucco, large mirror glasses. The prevalence of opening from transparent glass looked like an effort to overcome the natural heaviness, making contemporaries to admire "the sun in the shining shop windows".

Technical novelties were comprehended like an aesthetic category. The arouse admiration of the power of human intellect, becoming a symbol of victory over space and heaviness A.I.Tsvetaeva remembered about the constructions which made all Moscow worried by their unprecedentedness: "The second novelty (the first was the start of the first electrical tram – E.K.), which lit Moscow and made it shining, was the multi-storey shop Mure and Meriliz... during a long time before it was opened, Muscovites had walked around the site, which rose higher to the sky... sparkled with glass... walked and looked before the windows became aquariums of light full of magic of objects flowing in this water of light".[6] This shining light, associated with beautiful, was one of the symbols of modernism.

In the early 20th century the process of turning of radial streets of Bely town leading to Kitay-gorod, into trade-business ones, continued. The streets Tverskaja, Mjasnitskaja, Marosseyka, Pokrovka, Big and Small Louhjanka, Big Cmitrovka became such streets, as well as Loubjanskaja square, Kuznetskiy bridge, Petrovka and Vozdvizhenka streets, Stoleshnikov lane. They continued to be renovated but in an absolutely different style.

The corners of the trade-business buildings of Kitay-gorod were accentuated, which was partially their specific feature. The towers of the northern Insurance Company in Iljinka strert, of the houses of Titov and Armand, the rizalit-tower of the Boyars Yard, the portico and cupola on the corner of the Business Yard were the result of town-building considerations, the effort to create a visual connection between the newly constructed buildings and towers of Kitay-gorod, and referring to the Northern Insurance Company, its architectural style corresponded to the near by church of St.Nicholas "The Big Cross".

The creators of the projects of the early 20th century did not use the mode characteristic for the second half of the 19th century, of similarity of stylistic forms, confining themselves to the rhythmic correspondence of volumes. The facade of the Boyars Yard repeated the outline of the wall of Kitay-gorod extending at its foot. The small tower of the Boyars Yard, situated on the axis of the tower of the Kitay-gorod wall, connected two constructions different in time and character into one whole, creating the unrepeatable look of "new Moscow", combining the antiquity and ultramodernism contrastingly and organically.

In the same way the placement of the cupola and portico on the rounded corner of the Business Yard can be explained. The pediment and portico created a vertical especially noticeable at the background of even windows of the huge buildings. Its silhouette, dimensions, proportions were in concordance with the silhouette and proportions of Varvarinskaja tower and the chapel near it. The ensemble of the square was constructed on the basis of the harmony between vertical accents and relatively neutral planes of the new offices blocks and the ancient capital.

The creators of the new trade-banking buildings had to take into consideration the near by temples: Shekhtelj – the church of the Georgian Icon of the Theotokos in Nikitniki, Kuznetsov – the church of All Saints in Kulishki, Rerberg, Peretjatkovich and 0ltarzhevskiy – the church of St.Nicholas "The Big Cross". In all cases one typical mode was used. A new building was located in the depth of a quarter, leaving an op en ground in front of a temple. The zone of a temple's influence became smaller because of the huge dimensions of new buildings.

The same principle of arrangement of special open small yards for churches which were near new buildings, was used during construction in the early 20th century of huge dwelling multi-flat houses-complexes. For instance, the blocks of the huge leased house of the First Russian Insurance Company at the corner of Kuznetskiy bridge and Big Loubjanka (1905-1907, L.N.Benua and A.I.Gunst), flanking a big front yard, stood aside to give place for the church of the Entry of the Theotokos into the Temple. The church turned out to be on the main axis of all the complex, becoming its integral and at the same time organizing part.

The character of combination of the old and the new in the construction of the early 20th century was more complicated than in the second half of the 19th century. The similarity of forms, the unity of style were not considered necessary now. The unity was based on more complicated conformities – in the silhouettes and volumes – the principles typologically similar to those used in Ancient Russia. What developed spontaneously in the second half of the 19th century, became a comprehended mode in the early 20th century.

The example with the building of the Russian Insurance Company allows to remember "the second type of buildings, which especially influenced and changed the Moscow look and turned it into the city of "skyscrapers". The leased houses were Moscow skyscrapers. The increase of the quantity of floors and dimensions of buildings was an uneven and delayed process in Moscow in comparison with Petersburg. But this tendency became irrevocable. Buildings of 5-7 floors became a norm. There were confirmations to it everywhere – in the centre and the outskirts. There was a huge 8-storey house of 1910s in Kudrinskaja square, which remained there till 1950s. The same houses were constructed in Sadovaja-Spasskaja, 19 (L.Shishkovskaja), in Arbat, 35 and 51. At the corner of Sadovo-Triumfalnaja and Oruzheyny lane an 11-storey house appeared (1900s, K.K.Nirenzee). At the corner of Volkhonka street and Small Znamenskiy lane in the plot of the Moscow School of Painting, Sculpture and Architecture V.A.Tschuko was entrusted to design a 12-storey house, instead of an 8-storey one first ordered in 1912.

There was another situation in designing of the leased house of the Mekk at the corner of Tverskaja street, Skobelevskaja square and Glinitschevskiy lane. Archive materials kept the projects of a gradually decreasing building from 13, 11 and, finally, 9 floors. The last variant was certified by the City Council in June of 1915, however it was mentioned that "not seeing any legal reasons for refusal", construction of this building was considered "rather undesirable", because "due to its disproportion the 9-storey building can harm the look of the square and the buildings situated in it".

Besides the continuous growth of dimensions and the quantity of floors of multi-flat leased houses there was another speciality which became a tendency in 1900s and was used much in the construction practice in 1910s. The essence of these searches was connected with the mastering of the internal space, turning it from an absolutely utilitarian into an artistically expressive one, corresponding to the norms of hygiene and suitable for a wide use – for relaxation of the dwellers, for children's games. This led to increase of internal yards up to the dimensions of small squares, to appearance of space between street buildings, to arrangement of the system of internal open front yards and inter-yards passages. Huge complexes of complicated configuration were united into architecturally organized compositions, breaking the habitual front of street buildings, beginning the transfer from the construction along the perimeter with closed internal yards to a free construction by separately placed buildings, characteristic for the 20th century, with a rather relative separation of street and yard space.

The best known example of such constructions is the huge complex at the corner of the streets Soljanka and Zabelina, built in the plot of the Moscow Merchant Society in 1912-1915. Construction of the same huge complexes was planned in Big Nikitskaja, in Tverskaja in the place of the post office, in Arbatskaja square, in Big Sukharevskaja, in the large plot which led to Mjasnitskaja and Sadovo-Spasskaja streets and Ulanskiy lane etc.

The use of the novelties of the architectural style, increase of dimensions of the most spread type of buildings meant the turning of a leased house into one of the leading types of buildings of city construction. This, in its turn testified to the deepest reassessment of values, to the turning of the need to satisfy the most urgent requirements of a maximum quantity of people into a social and moral category. Design of an individual dwelling (now it was a mansion) and mass dwelling of all kinds (leased houses of much comfort; workers' settlements and towns-gardens) became an architectural and social task of first priority. More exactly, social orientation became a synonym of a highest pithiness.

Merchants club in Small Dmitrovka (today Chekhov street). 1907-1908, architect I. Ivanov-Shits. Photo. Early 20th century.

Together with multi-flat leased houses, which were a whole world, where opposite tendencies of a big city combined, like depersonalization and respect to the personality of a separate man, – the mansions of the early 20th century embodied all variations of spiritual searches, connected with the world of a separate man.

Mansions of modernism, especially created by such a great architect of the 20th century like F.O.Shekhtelj, were subordinated to creation of all-penetrating world of beauty and spiritualness, transformation of the utilitarian and comfortable into the lofty and fine. They were the mansions of Rjabushinskiy and Derozhinskaja and the mansions created according to the projects of another well known master of modernism – L.N. Kekushev, the mansions designed by S.U.Solovjov, U.Valkot etc.

The mansions of neo-classicism were similar to modernism by their care about beauty and the belief in its transforming power, and different by the program retrospectivism, construction of an ideal environment for a separate person with the help of the norms of art which seemed immortal. In the quiet corners of Prechistenka, Ostozhenka, Povarskaja, Big Nikitskaja streets the mansions of modernism, situated near each other, created a special world of silence and comfort. The unsimilarity of the program "up-to-date" forms of the first and accentuated classical order forms of the second was softened by the general impression of the internal contradiction of the artistic image and the forced interpretation of the artistic expressiveness of the whole and the parts. The composition of the mansions of modernism inherited the principles of the mansions of historicism of 1890s, which were constructed with a space between them and the street. Multivolumeness and asymmetry of their composition presumed a round walk and turned into a focus, attracting and organizing the street and yard space, showing an evident striving to integration of both with an absolutely clear their separation.

The mansions of neo-classicism represented an opposite pole to the modernism of Moscow architecture. Many of them revived not only the forms, but the spatial schemes of regular construction. But not less quantity of them demonstrated an original merging of artistic-rhythmical compositions of modernism with order forms of classical architecture. In a number of mansions of neo-classicism the mode of stylization, characteristic for modernism, was reborn – accentuated, hypertrophic recreation of the past architectural forms taken for the basis. In Moscow neo-classicism it showed in a deliberate tension, plasticity of forms, especially of columns, which came from the

Kiev railway station (1912-1917, architects I. Rerberg, V. Oltarzhevskiy, engineer V. Shukhov).

order archaic temples of Ancient Greece in Pestum, accepted by Moscow architects of the early 19th century and reborn a century later.

In the mansions of modernism and neo-classicism unsimilarity of artistic images is striking, as well as the world views which they symbolize. The same unsimilarity was in the projects of other buildings, but, probably in the mansions, which expressed most brightly the basic principles of the world view of the early 20th century with its cult of individuality, it was most evident. Architecture is the most abstract symbolic art. Only instrumental music can compete with this speciality. This comparison suits best of all the Moscow architecture of the early 20th century.

Moscow in difference to Petersburg and big West European cities did not know the division of the city territory, which formed in the late 19th – early 20th century, into the multistorey densely constructed centre and the outskirts with small houses.

Zemljanoy town remained in the early 20th century a mainly dwelling district. The streets crossing it were built in with big dwelling and public buildings. In Small Dmitrovka not far from the monastery of the Passions, a merchants club was constructed, at the corner of Sadovaja and Tverskaja streets – the theatre Omona. In Karetny row a theatre for 5000 seats (1915, I.P.Mashkov) was designed. However the lanes, and a number of the streets, for instance, Povarskaja, Small and even Big Nikitskaja remained the places where the mansions of high aristocracy were concentrated, as well as of merchants and intellectuals. The Eastern district of Zemljanoy town was mainly merchant. The Northern part from Small Nikitskaja to Tverskaja were in a way the Latin quarter of Moscow. The district of Tsve..oy boulevard and Sretenka in the North-East were built in with not rich houses of small sellers and clerks. The vivid trade radial streets Arbat, Tverskaja, Sretenka, Mjasnitskaja, Pokrovka, which were a direct continuation of the trade-business streets of Bely town, contrasted with the quiet mainly dwelling character of the main territory of Zemljanoy town. Through them the communication between the centre and the railway stations was implemented.

Mainly the dwelling character was retained by the merchant Zamoskvorechie, built in by small houses, adjoining the only relatively active trade street – Pjatnitskaja. The exception were the Northern territories of Zamoskvorechie – Balchug and Boloto, adjoining Kitay-gorod and continuing directly its trade-warehouse function.

Moscow suburban region was the territory bordered by Camer-Collezhskiy bank, – the most spatious and of different character. Here, in the place of waste land and gardens the economy of Moscow railway junction with passengers and cargo stations was formed, with workshops and depot.

Together with the tendency to the merging of industrial and railway junctions, near town industrial regions (mainly to the North and East from Moscow) with the city ones, another one appeared. Construction of country houses began near the rail ways and stations (mainly in the South, West and North-West), which before the revolution was located in the nearest zone of 10 kilometres from Moscow (within the limits of today's city boundary). At the border of the 19th – 20th centuries a new town-building notion appeared – Big Moscow, the social economic and cultural wholeness of the city territory and the nearest regions, in 1917 officially enlisted in the city structure.

In the early 20th century in Moscow town-building factors were revived on a new spire, which in the second half of the 19th century turned it into a new type of a big city. Three new railway stations appeared in Moscow – Paveletskiy, Savelovskiy and Rizhskiy, Brestskiy (Belorusskiy) was renovated and extended significantly. An overbridge was constructed, which transformed the traditional gala entrance into Moscow – Tverskaj frontier post. The symbols of two epochs were together: not far from the railway station there was the Triumphal arch with the cordeguardias, to them from Petersburg avenue the most up-to-date overbridge led with lamps and grilles in the style of modernism. In 1902—1904 Yaroslavskiy railway station was rebuilt, acquiring a modern look due to the extension of the Northern roads to Archangelsk and Murmansk. Before the revolution and World War I such railway stations in the ancient capital were rebuilt turning into the biggest with platforms as Kazanskiy and Brjanskiy (Kievskiy). The first like Yaroslavskiy in front of it, was in neo-Russian style. The second, in honour of the 100th anniversary of the Patriotic war in 1812, celebrated widely and in gala style, as well as due to the specialities of its location near the road to Borodino and village Phimi, was in the style of neo-classicism.

The district of the Kievskiy railway station was turned into a colossal ensemble – a memorial to a great event in the life of Russia. Dorogomilovskiy bridge got the name of Borodinskiy. At one side of it there was an orthodox church; for the anniversary a church for old believers was constructed on the opposite side of Dorogomilovskaja street. The access to the bridge turned out to be flanked at both sides (an ancient Russian tradition). The perspective of Dorogomilovskaya street was completed with the tower of the railway station.

Extension of the old railway stations and construction of new ones became an architectural expression of another turning of the railway transport into a forceful town-building factor. It gave an impulse to a new construction in Moscow and promised to give a more forceful impulse to its development in future. However its natural development was interrupted sharply at the moment of its increasing ascent.

The beginning of World War I did not interrupt a very intensive private construction. In 1915 the government had to adopt the law about its termination in order not to attract the working force and means from the construction works of strategic importance. The construction of the state and military-strategic importance stopped only after October 1917, which put an end to the grandiose plans of Moscow municipal department. But the works, conducted at the beginning of the 20th century in Moscow, were immense and are an eloquent expression of the economic upsurge at the border of the 19th-20th centuries and especially of its real rise on the eve of the first word war.

Railway Transport in the Town-building Conception

The policy of the municipal authority from the moment of the enforcement of the city self-authority was closely connected with the vital social-economic needs of the city. At the sane time during comparison of the policy conducted in the second half of the 19th and in the late 19th – early 20th centuries there were its own specialities. In the first case, the general city problems were of first priority – the water pipe-line, sewage, slaughter houses, electrical light, health care. In the early 20th century these problems were still important, but the main attention was turned to another thing and acquired an evident social character. The municipal department began to work more on settlement of the problems which were not connected at first sight. It was the dwelling need (the need in cheap, but comfortable and up-to-date houses), assistance in development of the outskirts, development of the city mechanical railway transport, provision of a quick and comfortable connection between the centre and the rapidly developing outskirts. Moscow grew due to the inflow of people. "Economically unprovided people, searching for work, poured into the capital and was thrown outside the borders of the city... this new "move" of population was as big historical event as, on the contrary, its concentration in the cities was".[7]

In the early 20th century the enthusiasm of conquering space and time, which appeared due to the new transportation means – rail ways, trams, automobiles, planes, -showed itself widely and variably in architecture.

The vans of the horse and electrical rail ways and electrical columns changed sufficiently the look of Moscow streets. As for the city rail ways, they turned into one of the most important factors of town-building development of separate districts, especially the outskirts. With developments of the new communication means, new types of buildings appeared, new complexes began to form themselves – pavilions for passengers at the tramway stops and stations, electrical stations and sub-stations, tramway depots and repair workshops. Most important, all the communications and buildings, connected with the municipal transport, were designed according to a system, as one whole, taking into consideration the specialities of the city plan and trying to make the process of the mass dwelling construction orderly and organized.

The planned creation of the network of the tram ways 200 versts Iong, began at once after the project, approved by the Duma in 1902, was certified at the Ministry of Communication Ways. The project was designed according to two principles. "The tramway network helps more correct and even distribution of the population in the city, inducing the ebb of the population from the city centre to the periphery, making the crowd in the centre less, stimulating the construction in the suburbs, thus improving the dwelling and sanitary conditions of the capital's life...".[8]

During the design of the network of the tramway lines it became clear that the transportation problem could not be solved by itself, separately from the dwelling problem. "It is time to stop regarding the house construction as a private affair".[9] "The municipal rail ways are one of the links in the chain of the measures which comprise the city dwelling policy".[10]

The network of the city tram ways designed in 1901, reached 230 versts in 1911. Ten years later the planned work for creation of the network of the municipal tram ways was over. Moscow got "a system of quick, cheap and convenient communication ways, which was not inferior to the network of other European capitals in its wideness and the quantity of branches".

In 1912, together with the rail ways, Moscow also got a ramified system of the complexes and buildings serving the tram ways, which influenced noticeably the look of the central streets and the suburban districts. It included the Central electrical station, situated on the Isle, created by the mouths of the Moscow-river and the Overflow canal.

Temple of the Kazan Icon of the Theotokos in Kaluzhskaja square.

The energy worked out by the Central station, was transferred to the sub-stations, where the constant current of high voltage was inverted to alternating current. By 1912 in Moscow different districts 9 sub-stations were constructed: Miusskaja, Novinskaja, Central, Zamoskvoretskaja, Rogozhskaja, Krasnopridnaja, Loubjanskaja, Sokolnicheskaja and Metschanskaja. In difference to the substations the tram depots and the Central repair workshops were situated only in the suburbs. By 1912 7 tram depots, which had similar planning and composition of the premises, were constructed: Presnenskiy, Miusskiy, Rjazanskiy, Sokolnicheskiy, Zolotorozhskiy, Zamoskvoretskiy and Uvarovskiy.

The stops also got their architectural design. In Strastnaja square, near the Tverskaja frontier post, in Petrovskiy park and near the Sokolnicheskaja frontier post special pavilions appeared with waiting rooms for the public and rest rooms for the personnel working at the tramway lines. Modest wooden pavilions fit with glass were more numerous, they were installed by 1913 in Theatre, Sukharevskaja, Kudrinskaja, Loubjanskaja, Ekaterininskaja, Kalanchevskaja squares, in the square of the Red gate and in Smolenskiy market.

In 1913, taking into consideration the necessity of development of the tramway network, the decision about construction of a second Central electrical station was adopted. For it the land near the monastery of St.Simon was chosen, on the high unflooded bank of the Moscow-river. There was a number of reasons for the choice of the place: the closeness of a branch of the Kazanskaja rail way; the decision about the laying of the Simonovskaja tramway line, for which the district dwellers asked; the planned arrangement of a coil warehouse here. Besides the construction of the second electrical station the project for creation of a new tramway line stipulated also construction of a permanent bridge across the Moscow-river instead of the scow one and arrangement of Simonovskaja quay, which was a continuation of Krutitskaja one. The need in construction of a new bridge increased rapidly after the Paveletskiy railway station was opened, because of the growth of the intensive movement along the Kazanskaja rail way, for the account of which the first bridge was built, because a lot of factories on Derbenevskaja quay appeared.

The construction of Moscow circuit rail way, 55 km long with 14 stations, 2 stopping points, 10 viaducts, 72 bridges, 4 of which were across the Moscow-river, and two – Sergievskiy and Nikolaevskiy (called so in the memory of the grand prince, killed by Kaljaev and in honour of the emperor) were situated near the Entertainment garden and the Vorobjovy hills, was a unique construction affair in its type and grandiosity.

The route of the Circuit railway during its design and construction already, and certainly after its completion, turned into a place of attraction of construction of factories and plants, especially in relatively empty places. It began the formation of the second industrial area or its second semi-circle, situated to the North, North-East, East, South-East and the South from Moscow. It is enough to give the example of creation of the plant AMO (an automobile one, where the brothers Rjabushinskies bought the control of the company). For its construction the place near the station Kozhukhovo was chosen, connected with the branches of Paveletskaja and Moscow-Kazan railways.

By the moment when the construction of the road was finished it was connected with 22 branches: it was planned to connect it with 11 more branches in future for transportation of local cargo and development of the passenger transport.

The appearance of an original internal Northern railway semi-circle was simultaneous and connected with the idea of arrangement of the Circuit railway: Brestskiy (Belorusskiy), Savelovskiy, Peterburgskiy, Kazanskiy railway stations were connected by railways. One of the points of these works became arrangement of the viaducts across Petersburg highway and leading to Kalanchevskaja square in the area of Domnikovskaja street near Kazanskiy railway station.

During five years of 1898-1902 – the time of an especially active growth of Moscow and the second after-reforms period of construction boom – the projects were created which connected the town-building development of Moscow with creation of different systems of mechanical transport, including the first projects of the metro for Moscow and Petersburg.

The project of Moscow metro, developed by engineers P.I.Balinskiy and E.K.Knorre, stipulated arrangement of land lines as trestle bridges, underground lines as trenches and a usual railway road. Together with transportation lines the project stipulated creation of two gala avenues, cardinally changing the look of the main Moscow streets, leading to the Kremlin from the railway stations. The first one, which was supposed to be called the avenue of Nicholas II, began from Petrovsky palace. Its route coincided with the route of Petersburg highway, and then from the square of the Tverskaja frontier post (today of the Belorusskiy railway station) it extended, repeating the direction of the First Tverskaja-Yamskaja and Tverskaja streets and finished in Voskresenskaja square (of the Revolution) between the buildings of the Arsenal and the Historical museum. A part of the metro line, designed by Knorre and Balinskiy, (from Petrovskiy palace to Red Square) stretched under the ground, under Nikolaevskiy avenue.

Arrangement of the second avenue – Sergievskiy – revived the idea of 1860s. It was supposed to extend it from Loubjanskaja square through Mjasnitskaja street along the straight line to Kalanchevskaja square with its three railway stations. The avenue was to become a component of the second metre diameter, which stretched from the centre to Sokolniki and further till the crossing with the Circular road, and on the opposite side from the centre to Zamoskvorechie to the crossing with the line of Paveletskaja railway road.

The project of arrangement of the avenues was especially detailed. The Joint-Stock Company, built by Knorre and Balinskiy, searched for the right to buy a huge territory of 100 sagenes (213 m) wide along all the length of the designed avenues. The central part of the future avenues, 30 sagenes wide, the company was obliged to allot to the city authority: here creation of the traffic part, boulevards, pavements, sewers was planned. In the rest of the avenue, 35 sagenes wide in each part, construction of new gala buildings was planned. "Arrangement of city highways, – the authors emphasized, – is only a function of all the project offered for Moscow, i.e. without roads of high speed the arrangement of the avenues itself cannot be implemented from the financial point of view".[11]

Here, perhaps for the first time in Russia, we see such frank and evident technocratic-nihilistic approach to the plan and historically formed city buildings. For the designers creation of new avenues was only a function of the metro line laid by them, its representative arrangement in the shape of a gala avenue, connecting in the shortest way the railway stations and the city centre. It seems that the grandiose projects of 1920-1930 came from the project of Knorre and Balinskiy. Their creators easily designed very wide straight highways and gigantic squares in connection with the planned construction of the Palace of Labour, Narkomtjazhprom or the Palace of Soviets, like their spiritual fathers like Knorre and Balinskiy, their attitude to Moscow was like to a territory, not as to a city with its real historical buildings. There is another significant fact. The routes of Nikolaevskiy and Sergievskiy avenues anticipated also partially realized the stipulations of the general plan of Moscow reconstruction of 1935 with its widened and rebuilt Gorkiy street and the projects of creation of Novokirovskiy avenue.

The project was declined after acute criticism on the part of the Municipal Department, Moscow Archaeological Society and the Government Commission.

It is necessary to pay attention to the reasons why it was done so. Trestle bridges and trenches made the crossing of many streets impossible. Two city gardens – Alexandrovskiy and Loubjanskiy – and the boulevards, where the trestle bridges would be constructed, would be actually liquidated as the places of rest, because in them trestle bridges would be constructed as well. And there was another argument. The project ignored the historically formed buildings. A whole built in quarter was allocated for the Central railway station and for this it was planned to demolish the church of St.Nicholas (in the former Moskvoretskaja street which does not exist now) behind the cathedral of St.Basil. Besides that in different parts of the city 8 more churches were to be demolished. Realization of the project could decrease the level of the city comfortable arrangement, deteriorate the sanitary conditions, damage the spiritual and material interests of the citizens. "It seems, – the conclusion said, – that the designers of the project forgot that they deal with an ancient city, which has been formed for centuries, and is of immense historical and economic, importance, and supposed that they were working in the place which was to be inhabited".[12]

On 23rd of November of the same 1902 a conclusion of Moscow Archaeological Society was sent to the Ministry of Internal Affairs to V.K.Pleve. Its main idea was that one which was only partially touched upon in the testimonial of Moscow Department. The document is extremely burning.

"The project of Mr.Knorre and Mr.Balinskiy is astonishing with its impudent encroachment on what is dear in the city of Moscow to all Russian people, for whom Moscow is a holy

"Future Moscow". Postcard. 1913.

Mansions of K. Rutkhel and M. Yakunchikova (architect V. Valkot) in Mertvy lane (today N. Ostrovskiy street). Early 20th century.

thing according to historical memory and ancient buildings and a deeply venerated memorial.

The inexplicable attitude to the holy things is shown, if the project is realized, in the infringement of the wholeness of the cathedral of the Kazan Icon of the Theotokos for an arrangement of a tunnel under it and in the fact that it did not spare the orthodox churches: of St. Nicholas "Mjasnitskiy", of Martyrs Florus and Laurus, of St.Prophet John the Predecessor, of the Entry of the Theotokos into the Temple in Loubjanka, of Great Martyr George on the Krasnaya hill, of St.Nicholas in Gnezdniki, of the Resurrection in Brjusov lane, of St.Nicholas "Moskvoretskiy". All these temples, dating from the 17th and even 16th centuries, were to be, according to the project of Knorre and Balinskiy, alienated and demolished. The other temples, for example, the church of the Three Hierarchs near Krasnye gate, the church of St.Nicholas the Miracle-worker in Ordynka, the church of the Holy Spirit near Prechistenskie gate and others were to be belittled in their splendour because of the closeness of the trestle bridge which in some places was at the distance of three arshins from the temples...

Regarding the civil memorials of Moscow we see that Krasnye gate is covered by the trestle bridge; Sukharevskaja tower is not only covered by the trestle bridge, but the bridge's station is adjoined to it. A railway station is planned in the place allocated for the memorial to Gogolj. The trestle bridge makes the view at the monument to "Pushkin absolutely ugly. Near the cathedral of Christ the Saviour the way from the temple down to the river is cut by the trestle bridge, which goes near the memorial to Alexander III, covering the view at the memorial from the Kremlin.

The view at the Kremlin itself, the pride of Moscow, was disfigured by the road from the side of the Kremlin gardens. Here in the first garden the road stretched as an open trench, then on the land and under Troitskiy bridge, renovated nowadays in its ancient view. This bridge is to be remade for the road to pass. Then the road goes by the trestle bridge, across Borovitskiy bridge in front of the tower itself, so that they would go to Borovitskie gate under the trestle bridge".[13]

The Municipal Department had to return to the question about the metro construction in 1911, when the insufficiency of the tramway network became evident, and the metro projects were sent to Moscow City Duma from private bodies.

It is necessary to outline the general features of all the metro projects, which could influence Moscow look especially, reflecting the idea about the city centre of that time, as of a derivative from the transportation and warehouse junction. For the first time the construction idea was identified with absolutely utilitarian needs, which were a motif for large construction works: the metro would serve the passenger and cargo movement; the railway stations were to be connected with the centre by an underground road, where the Central railway station, the Central cold-storage warehouse and a cargo railway station were to be constructed.

In Knorre's project of 1912 an absolutely technical undertaking acquired the importance of a town-forming factor of first priority. The project stipulated recreation of Moscow central ensemble by construction not far from the Kremlin and Kitay-gorod of gigantic Central stations – for passengers and for perishable goods. They were to become the "geometrical centre of Moscow and simultaneously – the centre of all the capital life".[14]

The "American project" of Ya.I.Utin, A.I.Vyshegradskiy, A.I.Guchkov, A.I.Gennert and a citizen of the USA D.Hof was in the manner of Knorre's project.

A tunnel connecting the railway stations, which took 80% of all the passengers movement, led to the Central passengers railway station. Like in Knorre's project, it was offered to construct it in the place, which had become the main point of the crossing of the land routes of the municipal transport – near Loubjanskaja square, in the territory of two quarters, bounded by Neglinny and Theatre passages, Loubjanskaja square and Sofiyka street. It was planned to locate the station itself under this plot. In the land part, which would have consisted of multi-storey buildings (in one of the projects they had 22 floors which was a real skyscraper), arrangement of business and service premises for shops, offices, banks, hotels was planned.

The authors of the project from the City Department tried to use rational ideas of the projects of private businessmen: division of the passengers and cargo lines (K.K.Ruin), creation of three main underground highways, crossing Moscow with their diameters and connecting all the railway stations with the centre (the Tverskaja frontier post – Loubjanskaja square – Pokrovskaja frontier post; Kalanchevskaja square – Loubjanskaja square – Smolenskiy market – Kiev-Voronezh road; the Krestovskaja frontier post – Loubjanskaja sguare – Serpukhovskaja sauare).

The creators of the city project rejected the joint in one place of the Central passengers railway station and the Central market or a food-storage warehouse. Like all the stations within the borders of Camer-Collezhskiy bank the main station in Loubjanskaja sguare was designed under the ground, two exits were stipulated – from Vladimirskie gate of Kitay-gorod wall and to the building of the insurance company "Rossija". Based on the ten-year experience of creation of the network of the tramway lines, the authors of the city project stipulated in it the creation of a system of buildings for production and distribution of electrical energy at once. For production of electrical energy it was presumed to construct the Central electrical station, for its convertion – 13 substations (3 city and 10 suburban ones for the parts of the railway road situated out side the official city border).

The projects of transformation of Moscow centre, connected with the metro laying, were not found. But absolutely amazing postcards kept till our time, published (and the coincidence of the dates does not seem to be random) in 1913 by the consociation Einem under the name "Moscow in future", where the centre of Moscow was shown as the designers of the metro projects saw it. The squares bearing the well-known names are unrecognizable. They are full of skyscrapers. There is a station of the "Air and Earth Communication" here too. As it was presumed to complete the construction of the metro lines by 1921 the possibility of Moscow transformation as it is shown in the postcards, did not seem so far away. The belief in the coming and fast changes reflected the real situation. Another great change in the look of the ancient capital, the most cardinal in its history, war coming. The tempo of life, which changed considerably with appearance of the mechanical transportation facilities, first of the rail ways, then the tramways increased rapidly with the appearance of the transport of the 20th century – automobiles, planes, metro. Not only the ancient traditions changed, hut the ideas about space and time changed, which had existed since the time of the wheel invention and domestication of a horse.

During development of the preliminary, and then the technical project of the metro in the first half of the 1910s there was no doubt in its realization. Though World War I, which began in 1914, postponed the beginning of the construction which had been planned for that year, first for 1915, then 1916, and, finally, for 1917, their completion was invariably planned for 1921.

The beginning of the metro construction was postponed till 1917 because of the offer of the City Duma to conduct the next All Russia Exhibition in Moscow not later than in the spring of 1916, locating it in Khodynskoe field, where in 1882 such an exhibition took place already.

Because of the political events of 1917, beyond the power of the City Duma, and the Civil war which followed them, the metro construction and putting into operation of the first metro lines was postponed for nearly twenty years.

Temple-building

In the early 20th century only three temples were constructed, which were artistically and contextually significant. It was the church of the Intercession in the convent of Sts. Martha and Mary of sisters of mercy, the cathedral of St.Prince Alexander Nevskiy in Miusskaja sguare and the church of the Resurrection near the Sokolnicheskaja frontier post.

St.Martha-St.Mary convent of the sisters of mercy belonged to the new type of communities which appeared in the 19th century and being close to monasteries in its rule and conditions of life, was not a monastery in the full meaning of the word: the majority of sisters did not give monastic vows, the main goal of the community was to help laymen. Besides St.Martha-St.Mary convent there were other communities of sisters of mercy, which had been established earlier and were similar to it: of the Iberon Icon of the Theotokos in Poljanka street, of the Intercession in Pokrovskaja street and of St.Alexander in Hospital square.

The name given to St.Martha-St.Mary convent by its founder grand princess Elizabeth Fedorovna, reflected in general the contents of the monastery construction in the 19th-20th centuries. There was the similarity of the phylosophic understanding of the Russian idea of life reformation with the help of orthodoxy and the Christian doctrine. According to the idea of the founder the convent "was destined to be as though the house of St.Lazarus where Christ the Saviour was so often. The convent's sisters were called to combine St.Mary's high fate, listening to the eternal words of life, and St.Martha's service, because they took care of the suffering brothers who represented Christ".[15]

The church of the Intercession, being a part of the community's ensemble, was situated in the depth of the plot behind the fence and did not influence the street look. However, it is of very high architectural and artistic importance. It was one of the masterpieces of the Neo-Russian style, remarkable by the open use of stylization – a new, in relation to the second half of the 19th century, mode of a creative interpretation of an architectural sample by enlargement of forms, accentuated smoothness of the lines, smoothing out of the corners and unnoticeable transfer from one form to another. All this was to make the temples of the beginning of the century different from the overdecorated style of the second half of the 19th century.

Among the architects of the early 20th century there were the masters who devoted themselves mainly to design of temples, which was a new phenomenon of the New Time for Russia. Neither the 18th, nor the 19th centuries – had known anything of the kind. A.V.Tschusev was one of such architects. His creative work was remarkable with its inventiveness. He preferred the Novgorod and Pskov sample of the 12th and 14th-15th centuries, accentuating with the help of stylization the lapidary style, from the beginning characteristic for the temples of that time, sculptural style of volumes and thus making the look of the designed temples archaic.

The church of the Resurrection near the Sokolnichja frontier post (1909-1913, P.A.Tolstykh) was cross-like in the plan with a hip roof and with its nine cupolas (one – on the hip roof, four – adjoining the hip roof, and four – on the side volumes) created a wonderful image of a town-temple, extremely spread in the wooden carving of the Russian North, and in, so called, Calvary crosses. Adopted by architects from masters of folk art, the expressive symbolics, the beauty of the rhythm and laconism of a composition were introduced in the religious art in the early 20th century and were the source of inspiration during design of temples, iconostases, church clothes etc. The point is that in the early 20th century a "discovery" of some epochs of history of the fatherland art, which had been out of the sphere of high art till then, took place. It was mentioned already that the first impulse for development of neo-classicism was the discovery of the art of the 18th – beginning of the 19th century as a phenomenon of the national culture. The "discovery" of the national art of the Russian North was not of less importance for development of the fatherland art: it was acknowledged a pure expression of the Russian in the Russian art, not muddied by foreign and heterodox influences. Ancient Russian icon-painting was "discovered" as a phenomenon of high art of the world level. These facts were accompanied by reconsideration of the ancient Russian architecture, "discovered" in the reign of Nicholas Pavlovich, good examples of which are the churches of the Intercession in Ordynka and of the Resurrection in Socolniki.

The cathedral of St.Prince Alexander Nevskiy promised to be the greatest after the cathedral of Christ the Saviour in its dimensions and in town-building importance, it was built in the memory of the 50th anniversary of the liberation of the peasants from

Church of the Intercession in St.Martha-St.Mary convent in Big Ordynka (1908-1912, architect A. V. Tschusev).

the serfdom. The idea about immortalization of this event by the way traditional for orthodox nations – by construction of a temple – appeared at once after the issue of the manifesto. Though during 43 years which passed since the event the sum required for the construction, was not collected, in 1904 the territory for the future construction was sanctified in Miusskaja square. The place for the temple was chosen according to the recommendation of Moscow clergymen in the actively built in Moscow suburb. The construction began in the year of the anniversary, 1911, according to the project of architect A.N.Pomerantsev.

Miusskaja sqare was chosen for construction of the biggest temple of the early 20th century not accidentally. In the area of Petersburg highway there was a very active construction close to Belorusskiy and Savelovskiy railway stations in the late 19th-early 20th centuries. Along the highway another district began to be formed which was characterized by charity-cultural orientation. In 1900-1912 in Miusskaja square the university of Shinjavskiy, an industrial school, Abrikosov's maternity home and a building of Moscow Archaeological Institute were built. Further along Petersburg highway in Khodynskoe field Soldatenkovskaja (today Botkinskaja) hospital was open in 1910 (the author of the project of the hospital and the university was I.A.Ivanov-Shits).

The main intensive charity-memorial construction was developed in the area of the highway during World War I. In 1915 at the expense of A.l.Konshina in Petrovskiy park an infirmary for crippled soldiers was created as a small settlement. This specialization of the district began to get formed at the end of 1870s. Then in 1878 in Petersburg highway, a verst before Vsekhsvjatskiy, an Alexandrovskoe refuge appeared for crippled and old soldiers, in 1893 a refuge-hospital for crippled officers appeared. A big stone hip roof temple with a hip roof bell-tower was constructed in memory of the martyr decease of Alexander II according to the project of A.P.Popov and A.N.Kozlov in 1881-1883. Soon after the murder of grand prince Sergius Alexandrovich his widow grand princess Elizabeth Fedorovna arranged in Vsekhsvjatskaja bosk St.Sergius-St.Elizabeth labour refuge for crippled soldiers of the Russian-Japanese war. Near the refuge there was a school with an artisan department for the soldiers' children. The church, situated on the third floor of the main building, was emphasized by a cupola with a cross.

A Brethren cemetery was to become a natural finish of the grandiose district of the memorial-charity buildings, immortalizing the memory of Muscovites who died in World War I and about the warriors who died from wounds in Moscow hospitals. For this in the district of Peschanye streets of our time the city bought an estate with a park in 1915. Here in 1915-1918 according to the project of A.V.Tschusev the church of the Transfiguration was built at the expense of A.M. and M.V.Katkovs in the memory of their sons who died in the war. At the same time the city entrusted architector R.l.Klein, the author of the projects of the Museum of Fine Art, the department store of Mure and Meriliz and Borodinskiy bridge, to create a project of cemetery with a church-memorial and two galleries adjoining it. The galleries were allotted for museums. In one of them it was planned to exhibit materials about the war, in the other – war trophies. In February of 1915 the cemetery with a temporary channel was opened and the first burials were done.

The church of the Transfiguration, built according to Tschusev's project, recreated his favourite temples of Novgorod and Pskov. The belfry on a high basement with a slope staircase leading to it, played a great role in the composition and was equal to the temple in its height. The monumental belfry, repeating the belfry at the temple of the former estate of Boris Godunov in Vjazemy, acquired a special significance in this composition. The chime of its bell was to remind about those who had died in the war.

In general the amount of temple-building, which was reduced sufficiently in the second half of the 19th century in comparison with 1830-1860, continued to decrease. However the situation would look different if to take into consideration the scale of construction of the hospital and charity buildings and complexes, there was always a church in each of them. There were domestic churches also in the majority of the newly constructed educational buildings. To this rather significant quantity of temples a big quantity of old believers' and heterodox temples can be added.

The scale of construction of temples for old believers was especially surprising, the impulse to which was given by the law of the 17th of October, 1905, about the liberty of belief. Less than in ten years 15 new temples were constructed in Moscow. Their main quantity was concentrated in the restrict of the Pokrovskaja and Rogozhskaja frontier posts, where traditionally old believers lived. The big buildings changed the look of the suburbs, built in by small, often wooden houses. The most grandiose buildings were constructed in the previous nestles of old believers. In the Rogozhskoe cemetery a temple-bell-tower of the Resurrection in the memory of the Unsealing of the altars (1906-1912, F.F.Gornostaev) and the cathedral of the Assumption in Apukhtinka (1907 N.D.Polikarpov; Novoselenskiy lane, 6). The dimensions of temples corresponded to their importance and the contents of their consecrations and forms. Orientation at Moscow architecture of the 15th-16th centuries prevailed in the temples constructed upon the order of old believers. In this way the old believers seemed to declare that it was they who were the real guides of the orthodox testimonies and it was they who kept the traditions of the anscestors and the majesty of the Christian ideas and the idea about Moscow as the Third Rome and the striving to make it similar to Jerusalem. It is even more important because,

Old believers' church of the Intercession of Ostozhenskaja community in Ushakovskiy (today Turchaninovskiy lane) in Ostozhenka (1908-1910, architects V. Adamovich, V. Majat). Photo. Early 20th century.

Loubjanskaja square. View at Theatre passage.
Photo. Early 20th century.

if to exclude Moscow and Petersburg, the latest artistic search in the sphere of the temple architecture connected with the neo-Russian style, would turn out to be represented mainly by the old believers' temples.

The temples in the neo-Russian style – a national romantic variant of modernism – were constructed, except the temples of old believers, at the expense of enlightened customers in the estates, for instance, in Talashkino of princess Tenisheva near Smolensk, in Natalievka of Kharitonenko in the former Kharkovskaja domain or in Ostashevo of Constantine Romanov not far from Mozhaysk.

The second speciality of the temples of old believers, which was equally characteristic for buildings in Moscow and Russia, was the individuality of consecrations, closely connected with orientation at Moscow architecture of the 15th-16th centuries. It is common knowledge that Moscow in religious symbolics is the House of the Theotokos: the main city cathedral was consecrated to the Assumption. But Moscow is the capital of Russia. The idea about the special protection of the Theotokos of Russian land was supported also by the holiday of the Intercession, which became a purely Russian feast. Declaring themselves direct successors of traditions of orthodox Russia of that time, when they comprehended their historical mission of the keepers of real belief, the old believers consecrated their temples mainly to the holidays of the Theotokos, most often to the Intercession and the Assumption. The list of consecrations of the temples of old believers in Moscow proves it: the church of the Assumption in Apukhtinka, the churches of the Intercession: of the Ostozhenskaja community in Ushakovskiy lane in Ostozhenka street (1908-1910, V.A.Adamovich and V.M.Majat); of the 2nd community of Pomorskoe marriage concession in Tokmakov lane (1907-1908, I.E.Bondarenko); of the Zamoskvoretskaja community in Novokuznetskaja street (1910, V.Desjatov); of the Karinkinskaja community in Big Vokzalny lane, today Fakeljny lane (after 1905): the church of the Nativity of Christ, the Assumption and St.Nicholas the Miracle-worker of the lst community of the Pomorskoe marriage concession in Big Perevedenovskiy lane (founded in 1908). Two churches of old believers in Moscow were constructed in the name of the Entry of the Theotokos into the Temple – of Nikolsko-Rogozhskaja community at the corner of Small Andronievskaja and 3rd Rogozhskaja streets (1912, I.K.Bondarenko), of the Vvedenskaja community in Generalnaja, today Elektrozavodskaja street (1912). The church of the Tikhvin Icon of the Theotokos was constructed by the Tikhvinskaja community of old believers in Khavskaja (the corner of Serpukhovskoy bank) street in 1912-1914.

The second quantitative group of churches of old believers was consecrated to the beloved Saint – St.Nicholas the Miracle-worker: the church of the Svjato-Nikolaevskaja community (1912, Martjanov; Lefortovskiy lane, 8), on the Vargunskaja hill at the corner of Smolenskaja street and the quay of Borodinskiy bridge (1915, V.D.Adamovich), at the corner of the street Butyrskiy bank, 8 and the former Tsarskiy, today Zastavny lane (1910-1912, A.M.Gurzhienko). The only exception was the church of Great Martyr Catherine in Devkin lane (now Baumanskaja street). For this domestic church, situated in the depth of the yard, in 1915 a multi-tier bell-tower, brought out to the street red line, was constructed according to the project of architect N.N.Blagovetschenskiy.

The same rule is seen in the consecrations of the domestic churches. From 11 temples 7 were consecrated to the Theotokos: three – to the Assumption, two – to the Intercession and the Entry of the Theotokos into the Temple, to the Kazan Icon of the Theotokos; 4 temples were consecrated to St.Nicholas the Miracle-worker. The same situation was in Borovsk – a large centre of old believers, where protopope Habakkuk was kept in prison and where boyarynia Morozova was buried. In the small town one of three temples of old believers was consecrated to All Saints and two to the Intercession; the temple of the lst community was consecrated in 1908, and of the 2nd community – in 1912.[17]

Contextual principles of architecture were directly connected with the consecrations of the temples. In Moscow this correspondence is less evident. The rule characteristic for the province, is hardly seen in the consecrations of Moscow temples. It is seen best of all in the new settlements in Siberia and the Far East, especially in the area of the Great Siberian road. In the late 19th-early 20th centuries temples were the only sphere of architecture, where the policy of the official national system was expressed. And it was most evident in the consecrations of the temples. An absolute majority of temples was consecrated to the divine protectors of the emperors and empresses – alive and deceased, of Alexander II and Alexander III (to St.Prince Alexander Nevskiy), of Nicholas II, to the Saint protectors of the members of the emperor's family. Plenty of temples, like the chapel of the church of St.Basil the Great, archbishop of Caesaria in Tverskaja street, were constructed in the memory of state events, connected with the life of emperors – weddings, coronations, the miraculous saving of Alexander III during the railway accident at the station Borki. There were even the temples consecrated to the voyage of the future empress Alexander Fedorovna to the province. In this sense the consecrations of temples of old believers were directly opposite to consecrations of orthodox temples. In the temples of old believers it was not of monarchist character.

The architecture of temples of old believers was a program one. The church-bell-tower of the Resurrection and the memory of the Unsealing of the altars of their temples, which became a symbol of the acquired freedom of belief, were not consecrated to the Resurrection by accident. For old believers this event was really associated with the resurrection for the new life. The project of F.F.Gornostaev, presented to the competition, was accepted for implementation, because its composition and even location in the ensemble of the cemetery were full of symbolics. There was no neutral detail. The temple-bell-tower combined the typologic features of a cathedral and an on-gate monastery bell-tower. Three cupolas of the longitudinal facade symbolized the Holy Trinity. The arcature belt was contemplated like the belt of the cathedral of the Assumption in the Kremlin. The central part of the temple-bell-tower, standing forward and rising above the side parts, represented a very high pillar-like volume with open arches of the bells at the top, crowned by a cupola. The height of the bell-tower could be compared with the height of John the Great and its finish could be referred to the project of rebuilding of the Kremlin by Boris

Godunov with his idea – the Holy of the Holiest – of creation there of an analogue of the Jerusalem ensemble.

A similar content and similar mode of expression could be seen in the cathedral of the Assumption in Apukhtinka. Its consecration and the look came from the Kremlin prototype, but reproduced it in an enlarged and especially monumental variant.

As it was said above, in the early 20th century some architects began to specialize mainly in design of temples, for instance, V.A.Pokrovskiy, A.V.Tschusev, S.S.Krichinskiy. I.E.Bondarenko most often designed temples for old believers. According to his projects three temples in Moscow and a number of temples near the city, in Povolzhie and even in Riga, were built. For Bondarenko creation of new and unprecedented, address to the early Moscow samples and their brave individualized interpretation in modernism were characteristic. Being closely connected with the Mamontov's circle with its adherence to the revival of the Russian national traditions, for instance of Moscow colourfulness, and the idea of revival of majolica as a new material, the architect used majolica images and colourful tiles in his work. In his compositions the ultramodern – a wide use of iron concrete large beams – was combined with the archaic. Bondarenko widely used the multi-volume style, so loved by Moscow architecture.

Architects V.D.Adamovich and V.M.Majat, who worked in 1910s mainly upon the orders of the Rjabushinskiys, combined in their projects Novgorod and Pskov samples with Moscow traditions, for instance with hip roof bell-towers.

The orthodox temples and those of old believers complimented the colourful look of Moscow of the early 20th century – a city of skyscrapers, big factories and one- or two-storey mansions, big department stores and banks, a city of futuristic projects and intensive temple-construction, which transformed together with such buildings like water towers of the Krestovskaja frontier post, – the look of the outskirts.

* * *

By a strange or perhaps a significant coincidence the year of 1917 was to be really a border in the life of Russia and Moscow. The first half of this year determined the sharp change in the destiny of Russia – the Fevralskaja revolution took place. Emperor Nicholas II abdicated.

The first half of 1917 was to be a new turn in the capital's history of town-building. The regulating and controlling functions of the municipal department began to increase, the social orientation and transfer from private construction to municipal augmented.

In the early 1917 Moscow municipal department developed the report "About the general plan of improvement of Moscow buildings". In order ''to liquidate the spontaneous growth of Moscow and absolutely orderless construction in its territory'' the report stipulated:

"1. To reconsider the plan of Moscow regulation, which has been certified by the Highest authority, from the point of view of the trade and industrial life and dwelling conditions.

2. In the offer of adjoinment of the outskirts to develop a detailed plan of Moscow construction.

3. To establish a special earth fund with allocation to it (for the purchase of land plots) of about three million roubles from the supposed city loan of 37 million roubles.

4. To appeal about an issue of obligatory decrees stipulating the norms of height of buildings, passages, the quantity of buildings, the space between the buildings etc. for the district.

5. To introduce an actual technical control of the constructions during all the period of their implementation, with the right to suspend incorrect constructions...

6. To assist cooperative commercial construction as the one having no profiteering character.

7. To establish sanitary supervision and card registration of all property.

Project of Moscow metro (1902, engineer P. Balinskiy, E. Knorre). Water-colour N. Karazin.

8. To assist the general price decrease of construction materials with their delivery by the municipal ways in Moscow''.

Thus, the regular town-building, which was summed up in the determination of the street network and the general sanitary norms, was to be substituted by the system of strict supervision, leadership of the construction according to the concrete certified plan, and the policy of satisfaction of the need of not well-off people was to be conducted.

On 23rd of May, 1917, Moscow outskirts, which had merged with it long ago into one economic, cultural, architectural, town-building whole, were included into Moscow borders officially. The circu railway became its border.

In 1917 Moscow lived with the feeling of big changes. They were to be favourable, if to take into account the energetic actions undertaken by the Municipal Department. October of 1917 put an end to it. The anxious feeling expressed in the work of symbolists and the architecture of modernism, justified itself. "I think that there is a feeling of a catastrophe in the hearts of the people of the recent generations, caused by the extreme accumulation of facts, some of which have happened already, the others are bound to happen" – A.A.Blok wrote in 1908, comprehending the results of the first Russian revolution of 1905-1907 and being afraid of the coming of new one.

---

1 Moscow History. V. 5, M., 1955, p. 15.
2 Architect, 1912, No. 4, p. 32.
3 Bler A.R. Moscow – New-York, architectural tendencies in the cities' development at the border of the centuries // Moscow journal, 1922, No. 2, p. 14.
4 V.M. Moscow losing its face // Moscow Voice. 1913, 8th of January.
5 Sinegub E. Moscow in 19th and in the early 20th centuries // Moscow. Guide-book, edited by E.A.Zvjagintsev, M.N.Kovalevskiy, M.S.Sergeev, K.V.Sivkov. V., 1915, p. 117, 212.
6 Tsvetaeva A.I. Memoirs. M., 1974, p. 21.
7 Shtromberg M.A. City railway roads in Moscow and other big cities and their social importance. M., 1912, p. 36-37.
8 News of Moscow City Duma, 1907, No. 11, p. 18.
9 Shtromberg M.A. The above works. P. 283.
10 As above, p. 296.
11 RGIA f. 273, op. 6, 1912, d. 1868, 11. 36 ob., 38, 52-52 ob. As above f. 1287, op. 4, 1902-1903, d. 329, 1. 303 ob.
12 RGIA f. 1287, op. 44, 1901-1902, d. 290, 11. 231 ob. 234, 235-235 ob.
13 RGIA f. 1287, op. 44, 1901-1902, d. 290, 11. 230-231.
14 RGIA f. 1288, op. 23, 1912, d. 5, 11. 75-75 ob.
15 New Martyrs of Russia // Composed by priest M.Polskiy. Jordanville, 1949, V.I, p. 270-285. Quot.: Palamarchuk P.P. The above works, p. 538.
16 The analysis was made on the basis of the data published in v. 4 of P.P.Palamarchuk's ''Forty of Forties'', in Parisien issue, where the author wrote under the pen-name of Stephan Zvonarev, because the book was published in the time of the USSR.
17 Osipov V.I., Osipov A.I. On the question about the time when the temples of old believers were built in the town of Borovsk // Bulletin of the Russian Historical Association Verkhnee Poochie. Kaluga, 1994, p. 23-25.
18 Architect, 1917, No. 4, p. 27.

СОБОРЪ СВЯТЫХЪ НОВОМУЧЕНИКОВЪ РОССІЙСКИХЪ Ѿ БЕЗБОЖНИКОВЪ ИЗБІЕННЫХЪ

Afterword

850th anniversary of Moscow is a jubilee date of the city foundation, evolution of its image during one thousand years and a moment on the way of transformations. This complicated century-old, multi-ply image embodies the history of the state and the national culture, many demilishings and revivals of the city, it expresses the purposes of the social structure of all the previous generations of Russia. Moscow image embodies the main symbol of the mission of the nation and the state.

As it is known, memorials of history and culture express most fully and visually the image of the world which is clear and close to us. Exactly in the memorials people see the images of the Fatherland, whether it is a modest country side landscape with a temple or a majestic city – the guards of people's memory and consciousness. In all times memorials contained the main spiritual values of peoples, which was presented by them to the world.

Historical Moscow is not only a collective image of Russian society. People's memory about numerous sufferings and disasters in the fight for independence and freedom of the Motherland, about military valour, glory and Russian State System, about national holy things is concentrated in it. Moscow is a fundamental depository of the national memory, which became the basis of our historical, social and moral consciousness.

Everyone knows Pushkin's words: "Moscow, there is so much merged in this sound for a Russian heart, this sound echoes so much in it!" We often hear them and often pronounce. But, unfortunately, we much more seldom think about their deep innermost meaning. The words: "Moscow is the heart of our Motherland" seem habitual to us. Certainly it is the capital of a huge state. Vast lands of the Eurasian continent gathered together under its "banners". The events, which happened and happen in it, gave and give rise to new social reforms, influencing the destiny of all the mankind.

However, what was the source of this notion "the heart of the Motherland?" What does it mean to each of us? What did exactly "merge" in this sound? What attracting power is there in this image?

Does not it conceal the mystery of Russian life? What contains the legendary enveloping power of Russia and the discouraging helplessness in arrangement of its own every day well-being? Why was it able to stand up against so many invasions of the great people of the East and the West and was her destiny to fall so swiftly because of the bolsheviks' plot?

In certain time it was possible not only to stand up against the enemies, but to create a powerful state, which gathered together the nations and lands that had been hostile before, turning them into allies, retaining their national culture and giving them the opportunity to develop using their own resources with attraction of the richness of all the state, which had been gained by sacrificial service to the Fatherland. And as a result the whole world was stricken by the unprecedented genocide of the Russians and many other native nations of the country, by total and rapid destruction of the national history and culture, of those holy things, for which Russian people fought to death with enemies.

Some religious men, assessing the history, think that Holy Russia have chosen such way to the Truth, undertaking the mission of cross burden of keeping the holiness of the New Testament in love for people, the mission to repeat in the scale of a country the sacrificial feat for atonement of the world's sins and to be crucified together with Christ to mocking, outrage and detraction of an insane crowd. But to resurrect with hope like Him!

Pre-Petrine Moscow Russia was formed in fight with Moslem and catholic-Protestant people. It became possible to stand up against constant invasions and destructions, not to become slaves, only gathering all forces of Russian orthodox lands. But how was it possible to gather forces, if each prince was striving for grand princehood in union with the powerful neighbour-enemy, repressing and robbing his brother? Only the national self-consciousness, turning up at the border between life and death, could become the basis for the union.

In creation of an integral state John I Kalita relied on the national self-consciousness, in which the moral commandment of social and private life – to guard piously orthodox holy things at the price of one's own life, rooted. It was necessary to understand and realise this moral principle in policy in order to defend the country by the united forces of the neighbours, who defended the centre, where the spiritual treasures of these lands were kept.

Byzantine orthodox tradition of the symphony between the church and the kingdom, a pontiff and a prince, a patriarch and a tsar was based on the double entity of the image of Christ – a priest for ever after the order of Melchizedek and the King of kings. In this symphony the role of a pontiff was in sanctifying of God's Home-building on the earth in the image of the Church as the Ark of salvation through the likening to the Archetype, and a prince and a tsar of the state were the defenders and collectors of orthodox holy things.

The image of collecting of holy things was embodied in Moscow after metropolitanoPeter had brought the hierarchs' department here from Vladimir and later the main Russian holy thing – the Vladimir icon of the Most Holy Theotokos, the Protector of orthodoxy had been brought. His statement about the destiny of the new capital is well known: "... there will be an immeasurable quantity of monasteries and this town will be called the Second Jerusalem and it will be very powerful not only in Russia, but it will be glorious in all the parts of the world and possess many hordes from the Southern sea to the cold ocean".

They began to bring to Moscow national holy things that had been in the capitals of grand princely domains before, and then local holy things that were to become of national importance were brought. There were venerated icons of the main Russian cities, icon-banners of military troops, icon-protectors of towns in the lower tier of the iconostasis in the cathedral of the Assumption in the Kremlin, a pantheon of Russian Saints appeared on the arcature belt of the cathedral's facades, a majestic chorus of bells was collected on the belfry, which had been brought from different lands and spread around the blissful news of the New Testament.

Temple's construction symbolically reflected the moral world of the Christian space in the image of the universal synaxis, constantly serving the divine liturgy of the New Testament of the union between God and man through Jesus Christ. These main holy things were concentrated not only in the images of icons, paintings, bells, temples. From the time of christening of Russia the embodiment of the similarity of each town to the Archetype of the Divine City became the key basis of the tradition.

Historians of town-building and architecture note that all the life circle of man from birth to death and Resurrection among Saints got spiritual meaning and sanctified embodiment. Likening of man to the Archetype of God's Son acquired the basis of creation of a new life. When a person was born, he or she was measured and according to these dimensions an icon of the Saint or the holiday, connected with this event was painted. Temple's Adytum was measured by an icon, a monastery or a kremlin were measured by temples module, a town was measured by a module of a monastery or a kremlin, and a town, in its turn, was a measure of a space of a sacral kingdom. All the circle of man's life activity was realised by praying service to the Divine Fatherland. All the developed natural environment was blissfully sanctified and organised according to the Christian doctrine. "We made all subjects around us live and pray", Sergius Esenin wrote in "Mary's Keys".

Christian world view, realized in icon similarity, temple similarity, town similarity to the Archetype, was developed everywhere in European civilization. The Archetype of the Divine Town was at the basis of forming of many capitals, being an icongraphical reflection of Palestinian Jerusalem and the Divine City from the Apocalypse of St.John the Theologian.

The Archetype of the Divine City was specifically embodied in the towns of Roman and Byzantine Empires, of Kiev and Vladimir Rusj, the successor of which Moscow Rusj became. This Christian world view through the principle of likening to the Archetypes of Christ and the Divine City became the source for collection of archetypal holy things, then the lands which were to be defended by the state and people in unity, so that first to survive and defend the national culture, then to turn the neighbours-enemies into allies and brothers by their participation in the defence of common holy things, in order to implement people's moral mission of universal life by the sanctified central power.

The image of collecting of holy things in Moscow was the basic principle, the main testament of the authority till the epoch of Peter I. Holy Russia revealed itself to the peoples of all the world in the image of Moscow likened to the moral collective Archetype of the Divine City. Comprehending itself as the "Third Rome", it tried to embody the ideals of the kingdoms of the ancient peoples – the first Rome and Constantinople, which became the "Second Rome", the kingdoms which expressed the ideas of the Western and Eastern world civilizations.

The best masters of Europe, Asia, from the centres of which Russia inherited its traditions, were attracted to this work. Like the symbolical meaning of temple's four walls, signifying the peoples going to God from the four parts of the world, capitals in the image of the Divine City were also built by the peoples, attracted by the authorities from the four parts of the world.

Thus, in the image of Sacred Moscow Russia collected world spiritual holy things, assimilating the experience of the West and the East. It accumulated the striving of these peoples for spiritual life, to develop it more fully, implanting each discovery of the general human experience in the souls of Russian people.

The culture of pre-Petrine Moscow Rusj testifies in its icons, temples and towns to the exalted comprehension of the spiritual world of the Word and the Image. Moscow became the top of the culture of pre-Petrine Russia, an apocalyptical image of the Divine City, the spiritual highest point of the world, after which "there will not be any fourth Rome".

Man's spiritual-moral consciousness, on which the foundation of Moscow pre-Petrine Russia was built, led to the highest images of a personality and a social arrangement, provided people with national way of life and formed an individual look in the world. Thus, the collection of spiritual holy things created the kingdoms's power, gave rise to the irrepressible swift development of Moscow Rusj, which rose from ashes in front of dumbfounded Europe as a Eurasian state, full of dignity and power, of fabulous beauty likened to the Divine City.

Peter I, continueing the tradition of collecting holy things, was able to understand that Rusj could not be the orthodox world power anymore, which gathered together the world peoples, without learning West-European values.

After his travel to Europe Peter I understood, perhaps, that Russia, in spite of its huge resources, turned out to be more poor that European nations in the standard of life because of its historical development, and Peter connected the richness of Europeans with the intensive social activity and expansion of sea trade. So Peter brought forward before Russia the following task: to use the undeveloped and hidden richness of the country for the service to the Fatherland by beneficial trade with Europe in exchange to its experience. As for the strategic purpose, it was the mastering of its spiritual values.

By that time Russia, at the will of Peter I, lost the order of Pontificate in the spiritual organisation of people's life, and the Ark of salvation of Holy Russia took the one-sided course of self-establishment, not of the divine rise.

In the new man of Italian Renaissance and in European democracy, which gave rise to social activity of European nations, Russia saw by Peter's eyes other spiritual values, that developed on the soil of Catholicism and Protestantism. Peter changed radically the basis of social development through new forms of state arrangement using the experience of European powers, with material accumulation of richness. Foreign influences made a strong impact on Russia in all spheres of social life, from authority to upbringing. Class differences became more active than before, with sharp separation of the nobility and raznochinny (intellectuals not belonging to the gentry) estates, who got European education.

If pre-Petrine Rusj treasured the Archetypal holy things, implanting images of the Divine City everywhere, after-Petrine Russia in each epoch turned into the modern images of a new European style of life: baroque, rococo, classicism, Empire, pseudo-Gothic... "Peter I purified our eyes by the purgatory of European enlightenment", as Gogol formulated precisely and to the point the essence of this process. The former personality depreciated under the pressure of the new enlightenment based on the outward social reformation of public relations.

Today's literary critics note, that great predictor Gogol touched the kernel of the matter. The image of "dead souls", deprived of the gift of the Holy Spirit, – the Evangelical image of Adam's expulsion from the Paradise – symbolized the stray souls of all orthodox Russia in Peter's time. Simultaneously with the change of the way of life the look of all the society, that had the European education, changed, when progressive people became sometimes German, Dutch, English, French... Until, finally, our "chatskiys", "onegins" and "pecherins" turned into Russia's dead souls in the next generation.

The liberal-democratic movement of occidentophils and Slavophils made the society turn its attention to its own national roots. The ways of Russia's development were the main reason of the struggle between them because of different assessment of the role of Peter's reforms and influences of European culture. Occidentophils spoke for further democratic reforms according to the experience of the advanced West. Slavophils, relying on the wholesome world view of old Russia, which was still retained by people, saw Russia's development not only in state and social reforms, but, first of all, in the interior reforming of the world of today's educated man.

The new type of Europeanised thinking justified the existing reality as the highest form of development, rising up a spiral, and the New Testament became only the beginning of the new history, but not the Alfa and Omega of eschatologic life, not the point, to which Christian development is striving inevitably. However, the corrupted man could be reformed by the moral Archetype, which was at the basis of the spiritual "genesis" of private and social culture of ancient Russia, not by the logic of social development.

The epoch of Peter I extended the borders of spiritual influence of Russian culture through the implanting in the state of European values, first hostile to people, which in a hundred and a half years, being remelted in the creative purgatory of Russia, gave to the world the Russian Renaissance represented by Pushkin and Gogol, Belinskiy and Herzen, Chaykovskiy and Glinka, Ivanov and Brjulov, Dostoevskiy and Tolstoy... Due to Peter's reforms, which shook "dead souls" of ancient Russia, Russia of the 19th century became part of European culture, but not civilization yet, because Russian Empire of that time have not mastered the European experience of democratic government.

The 19th century merged organically European education with the culture of ancient Russia, besides European education, implanted in the spiritual world of Russian man, expressed most fully the national character with the moral basis of the general human mission. "In Russia it is possible now to become a Hercules everywhere, – Gogol wrote, any position and place requires this quality. Each of us so disgraced the worthiness of our position and place (all places are worthy) that Herculean power is needed to rise them to their appropriate height. I heard that great walk of life which is not possible for any other nation now, because only here there is such space and only this soul is capable of Herculean power".

Europe watched Russia in Suvorov's marches and in France thrown down, but accepted it in new Russian personalities, which won the heart of a European man, disclosing such abyss of fall and ascension, that since then the matter concerning the mystery of Russian life has remained unsolved.

Russia of the 19th century got a new type of creative personality of Renaissance, however the epoch of Petrine social reforms did not expire. (comprehending the experience of European development and culture, Russia could not stop halfway, discovering the results of the new type of personality of Renaissance in itself, which conformed to the epoch, it was necessary to realize the progressive European social ideas, in order to become a rightful participant of European civilization.

Many Russian philosophers, thinking about the qualities of Russian spirit, made a paradoxical resolution, unacceptable for a normal European consciousness. The nature of Russian spirit is of such quality that resisting new and alien to it, it unwillingly, with love and sympathy comprehended the essence and inevitability of its corruption, being carried away by the outward world. The effort to push away this outward world was always in vain. Winning battles in the field, we opened our houses to foreigners carelessly, cordially and with hospitality. In this way it was with the Tatars, Poles, Germans, French... We learned the inclinations, character, fashion, habits of our invaders, we admired and venerated their abilities and talents. All of them were our teachers.

Gogol noted in the most subtle way the world sensitiveness and responsiveness of Russian man, with the loss of which his "dead soul" acquires opposite features – selfishness and mercilessness. This speciality also leads to all-world consequences, probably, fatal ones.

Each collision with a new power of the outside world, penetrating into the depth of people's soul, loosened, but extended the borders of Russian spirit, and it only became stronger due to these temporary falls, overcoming it by the force of internal freedom and morals, learning strange elements like its own, thus reforming its being.

Revolutionary transformations of the 20th century shook the basis of social life. After the murder of tsar Nicholas II with his family and relatives, Russia lost its rank of a Kingdom, but acquired the rank of Pontificate represented by a new Patriarch. The Ark of salvation of Holy Russia was enveloped by the sacrificial fire of purification from the foul of Petrine epoch. Qualitatively new, "unique" in their importance for the world's destiny social values of a new social structure of life, different from the West, but having accumulated its achievements and experience, appeared. It seemed that orthodox holy things could become now common for all nations, independent from their origin and religion, besides reflecting the deepest hopes and strivings of the world nations.

The experience, knowledge, richness, accumulated and collected by generations of the mankind, which embodied the moral attitude to the world, were to belong to each personality. From the educated estate this main richness was to be transferred to the working estate, so that each one could possess the moral values, which could enrich his or her personality up to the height of understanding of the mission, when the labour of each personality would become a moral-creative service to the Divine Fatherland. The collected spiritual and moral richness was to be disclosed and returned to all nations, to each person. This was to be the high essence of the revolution. The best representatives of Russian democracy dreamed about it.

In reality all was otherwise, and only the results of the Second World War showed the real importance of these holy things, for the sake of saving of what was left from them Russian people showed unprecedented resistance to the national socialism. By the greatest, boundless tension of all the kept moral powers of Russian people, who united in this resistance world nations, by an enormous priceless sacrifice it became possible to defeat the invasion of the evolution's "dead souls" from the West. Half of the East and West took the path of new reforms. The image of nations-brothers who participated in the process of gathering of an integral social Fatherland, was introduced among the nations of the Eastern Europe and Asia. These new "values", remelted in the crucible of social transformations, are the bitter experience and a lesson for the mankind.

If in the gathering of Russian lands Moscow – an image of the Divine City – was in the centre, and in the establishment of Russian Empire Petersburg – Paradise – an image of earthly Eden – was in the centre, at the stage of the gathering of "social Fatherland" the superstate union with a new master of "dead souls" became the basis of the gathering which was an apocalyptical image of new great Babylon of the Party-Fornicatress – an antichurch.

Today the way and quality of life of all our society is assessed according to Historical Moscow, it is a criteria and measure of the attitude of people and the government to what way and by what means it implements its vocation in the world. How we understand today the place of Historical Sacred Moscow in Moscow of today and future, how we show this understanding to the people of the planet, what we create – hell or paradise. That is the key matter of our concrete moral position in the world. In the conditions of responsibility for the world's destiny the image of Historical Moscow acquires exclusive importance in cultural and spiritual goals of the mankind.

The social consciousness, having lost the moral categories of good and evil, the historical memory, lost the immunity in the programming of consciousness of an ordinary person and became ecologically dangerous for life, leading it to the edge of the apocalyptic catastrophe in its relations with the world.

A monstrous outrage upon the memory of those who died for the Fatherland would be considered only an attempt to foul the symbolical grave of an unknown soldier near the Kremlin wall. But for some reason during more than half a century all our soviet society, our fathers and grandfathers watched indifferently the scoffing of "dead souls" at the real pillars of culture and at the national holy things: temple-memorials of military valour, built in honour of the most important events in the history of the Russian State: Kulikovskaja battle, liberation of Moscow in 1612 and the defeat of Napoleon's horde in 1812. The Pantheon of glory and sacrificial service to the Fatherland around the Kremlin sacred walls was annihilated systematically and in a vandal way. In 1936 the cathedral of the Kazan Icon of the Most Holy Theotokos, built by Demetrius Pozharskiy in Red Square near the graves of heroic Russian warriors, was destroyed. Is not it a blasphemy that in their place an entertainment pavilion was installed, and a public toilet was arranged in the place of the sacred cemetery. The cathedral of Christ the Saviour – a donation of grateful successors to the heroes of 1812, raised at the money collected by all Russia, was exploded mercilessly. In its place a construction of a new Babylonian tower – the Palace of Congresses – was started.

These tragic historical facts, carefully kept in secret in the time of totalitarism, appeal to our consciousness like an alarm bell... Each cell in human body has a genetic code of all the organism. Like this quality, a man, having a "genetic" code of world culture and understanding its sacral character, acquires the understanding of all the spiritual body of the mankind. It is possible to say that in the image of Historical Moscow, as in the social and moral top of development, the national and world holy things were gathered and concentrated.

Understanding of Historical Moscow as an icon of the Divine City allows each of us to comprehend the main wealth of the mankind – the spiritual world of the Word and the Archetype, where the spiritual holy things of the mankind were gathered due to Russia's life experience.

Russia have stopped long ago to be only a nation, having accumulated sacrificially the spiritual world of the Word and the Image, each discovery, each living cell of human experience.

The image of Historical Moscow contains the holiness of the Fatherland, signifying the revival and salvation of Russia. All of us are to understand and appreciate the responsibility of each of us for our deeds in this great mission of collective creation on the testimonies of the New Testament.

During the last three-five years – a minor period according to historical measures Moscow revived thousands of memorials of history and culture. First of all these are temples, nearly all of which were transferred to its legal owner – Russian Orthodox Church They are numerous houses, mansions and estates, restored and well arranged as a result of the policy of privatization and market economy, when the owners of memorials became the bodies interested in restoration, in difference to the previous years. Finally, they are dozens of newly recreated Moscow holy things, fully annihilated during the years of theomachism.

By the 850th anniversary of Moscow the inhabitants and guests of the capital will see many revived masterpieces, new town-building ensembles, organically included into historical quarters and providing today's needs of the city. Moscow Government understands clearly the role and importance of the capital's historical image. Including new pages into this great town-building chronicle of Russia, the inhabitants comprehend their responsibility before history, so the Government's decisions concerning the reconstruction are carefully examined by specialists, scientific and creative people. The recreated cathedral of the Kazan Icon of the Most Holy Theotokos, Voskresenskie gate with the chapel of the Iveron Icon in Red Square, the cathedral of Christ the Saviour, reconstruction of Manege Square, creation of the monumental complex on the Poklonnaja hill are the evident proofs of revival of the historical took of the capital and Russia. And all this is not a rapid preparation for a sequential jubilee, but a long-term strategic policy of Moscow Government, dev eloped with consideration of the bitter experience of thoughtless decisions. At the same time it is not a return to the past, but a new comprehension of historical and sacral images in the state's life as of the carriers of moral basis of all today's civilization. Without which it is not possible to imagine Russia with its great Christian mission of service to the mankind.

Editor-in-chief V.A.Vinogradov

ЗАЧАТЕЙСКОИ Д МОНАСТЫРЬ	АЛЕКСЕЕВСКОИ Д МНТРЬ	ЖИВОНАЧАЛНОИ ТРЦЫ СЕРГИЕ МНТРЬ	ДАНИЛОВСКОИ МНТРЬ
НИКИЦКОИ Д МОНАСТЫРЬ	СТРАСНОИ Д МОНАСТЫРЬ	НИКОЛАЕВСКО УГРЕСКОИ Д МНТРЬ	ЦРЬ ВХОДЯЩИ
ГЕОРГИЕВСКОИ Д МОНАСТЫРЬ	МОИСЕЕВСКОИ Д МНТРЬ	СПАСКОИ МОНАСТЫРЬ	
ВАРСОНОФЬЕВСКОИ Д МНТРЬ	РОЖЕСТВЕНСКОИ Д МНТРЬ	ВОЗДВИЖЕНСКОИ МОНАСТЫРЬ	СПАСЪ СИМОНОВЪ МОНАСТЫРЬ

Edited and printed by Publishing House AO "Moscow Textbooks"

Publishing House AO "Moscow Textbooks". **General director S.M.LINOVICH**
© Conception of the edition of V.A.VINOGRADOV
© Design and the model: G.A.KOMAROV, V.A.VINOGRADOV
Authors: V.A.VINOGRADOV (the leader),
E.I.KIRICHENKO, G.A.KOMAROV, T.A.KORYUKINA, G.Ya.MOKEEV
Literature edition: N.N.VIZZHILIN, T.A.KORYUKINA
Translate by I.M. KOUDRIAVTSEVA
Editor of the English text: O.E. KOUDRIAVTSEVA
Photo of the jacket: V.A.SVERDLOV from the original of G.A.KOMAROV
in the text: N.N.ALEXEEV, V.M.RUDCHENKO, E.V.SHVED
Computer imposing: K.S.DONCHUK, S.B.MILOVIDOV
Art editor: Ya.B.MALOGOLOVKINA
Colour separation: N.V.BALASHOV, V.N.KOZLJAEV, S.N.KAVERIN
Montage: M.A.PAVLOVA
Printing: V.A.MAKHOV

The first end sheet: view of the Kremlin from Zamoskvorechie. Pikar,s print. 18th century
The second end sheet: the reigning city of Moscow with the monasteries. Splint of 18th century

MOSCOW, 850TH ANNIVERSARY
Edit.No.071230 of 27.10.95
Signed for printing on 17.08.96
Format 60 X 90 1/8. Bleached paper.
Offset printing. Phis. print. sh. 46
Run of 10 000 copies. Order No. 4266

Printed by AO "Moscow Textbooks"
125252, Moscow, Zorgue str., 15

Post-printing works:
Order of the Work Red Banner
GUPP "Children's Book" of Roskompechatj
127018, Moscow, Sutschevskiy bank, 49

Department of Printing and Information of Moscow Government

Contents

BOOK TWO IMAGES OF MOSCOW of the 18th – beginning 20th century 199

INTRODUCTION. Two centuries in the architectural history of Moscow *(Kirichenko E. I.)* 203
Peter's reign – the beginning of epochal change in national history and culture 204
Character of Legal Relations of the Government and the Church of 18th – Beginning 20th Century *(Glagolev A.N.)* 206
Town Actions and Orthodox Traditions *(Romanov G. A.)* 208

Chapter 1. THE SECOND CAPITAL OF RUSSIAN EMPIRE *(Kirichenko E.I.)* 215
Russia Before Peter's Time 219
Town-building policy of Peter's reign 220
"Moscow – the Third Rome". Reconsideration of the Traditional Formula in the Light of the Imperial Idea ...222
Antique motif in the triumphal constructions of Peter the Great in Moscow *(Natschokina M. V.)* 224
State-Imperial Idea in Development of Moscow 227
Temples of Peter's Reign 229
1730s-1750s. Town-Building Ideas during the Reign of Anna Ioannovna and Elizabeth Petrovna ..232
Temples of 1730-1750 234
Two Tendencies in the Civil Architecture of Moscow ..238

Chapter 2. NOBILIARY CAPITAL OF RUSSIA *(Kirichenko E.I.)* 241
Moscow and Petersburg – Two Capitals of Russia 246
Projects and practice of Recreation of the Historical Centre 248
Reconstruction of the Historical Towns on the Principles of Regularity and the Architectural and Town-building Destiny of Moscow. The Plan of 1775 252
Correct Architecture and Style "Gothically" Incorrect 256
Nobility Estate in Moscow 258
Ideas of Enlightenment and Construction of Public and Administrative Buildings in Moscow. 262
Christian Universalism of State Policy and Temple Architecture 264

Chapter 3. BURNT AND REVIVED MOSCOW *(Pokrovskaja Z. K.)* 269
New Ensemble of the Centre 277
Public Buildings 282
Construction of Temples 284
Triumphal Arch 288
Moscow Mansion and City Estate 289

Chapter 4. TWO SYMBOLS OF MOSCOW *(Kirichenko E.I.)* 293
Tsargrad and Manchester 299
Cathedral of Christ the Saviour 302
Conception of the Capital City Centre in 1830-1850 306
Renovation of the Verticals System................307
New Regular Ensembles 310
Industrial Construction 313

Chapter 5. MERCHANT MOSCOW *(Kirichenko E.I.)* 317
Moscow – Merchant Capital of Russia 325
City Reform of 1870s 327
Renovation of the Centre 331
Construction in the City 336
Temples of the Second Half of the 19th Century 342

Chapter 6. THE TURN OF THE CENTURY – THE TURN OF AGE *(Kirichenko E.I.)* 345
Urbanization and Moscow Look 347
Modernism, Neoclassicism... 351
Railway Transport in the Town-building Conception 354
Temple-building 358

AFTERWORD *(Vinogradov V.A.)* 363

Contents

A WORD ABOUT MOSCOW OF THE CITY MAYOR Yuriy LUZHKOV 2
**ADDRESS TO THE READERS
OF THE HOLIEST PATRIARCH OF MOSCOW AND ALL RUSSIA ALEXIUS II** 6
PREFACE 12

BOOK ONE — ANCIENT MOSCOW 13

INTRODUCTION 19
Theology of Image (Uspenskiy L.A.) 19
About the Prototype (Uspenskiy L. A.) 20
Figuratively-Symbolical Language
of Sacred Town (Vinogradov V.A.) 22
About the Anniversary Date (G. Mokeev) 23

Chapter 1. FORGOTTEN MOSCOVJ (G. Mokeev) 26
Historical news 30
Moscovj-Land 31
The Town of Power 33
Nestle of the centre's settlements 36
Cherished holy places 37
Yuri "Long Hands" 38
Christening, the first churches 39
About Church (priest Troitskiy N) 42

Chapter 2. DOMAIN CAPITAL TOWN
(G. Mokeev) 47
Moscow was not built at once 51
The First Prince – Vladimir Vsevolodovich 52
Moscow Domain 54
First Stone Church 55
About Town 57
Church's Object Symbolics (priest Lebedev L.) 58

Chapter 3. THE TABLE RUSSIAN LAND
(G. Mokeev). 63
The First Grand Prince 68
First builder of Table Moscow 70
The Preceptor and Warrior 71
Stone Wooden Kremlin 74
About The Holy Russia 76
Theology of Russian Land (priest Lebedev L.) 79

Chapter 4. THE CAPITAL OF GREAT RUSSIA
(G. Mokeev) 89
Liberation From The Yoke 94
The Kremlin 95
Hierarch and the First Tsar 100
Kitay-Gorod 101

The Tsar and the First Patriarch 104
Bely – Tsar' Town 105
Skorodom 106
System of Planning 108
Monuments of Syntaxis Russia 112

Chapter 5. REGAL MOSCOW
(Koudriavtsev M.P.) 113
Riverine Ensembles and the Natural "Bowl" 120
Moscow Temples (G. Mokeev) 124
The Centre of the Capital. Zamoskvorechie 131
Monastery Complexes 137
Town-building Composition 139
The Memorial of Military Glory 141

Chapter 6. THE SYMBOL OF HOLY RUSSIA
(Koudriavtsev M.P., Mokeev G.Ya.) 145
"The House of the Most Holy Theotokos" 149
"The Second Jerusalem" 151
"The Third Rome" 155
"The Heavenly Town" 160

Chapter 7. THE PHENOMENON OF HOLY
RUSSIA in divine revelation of Moscow 165
Red Square – the Temple Under the Open Sky
(Koudriavtsev M.P., Koudriavtseva T.N.) 170
**Religious processions as an image
of oecumenical divine service** (Romanov G.A.) 174
Influence of Byzantium on Russian Capitals 175
Synodal Procession of Russian Church 175
The Image of the Procession of Saints 177
The New Town of New Constantine 178
Ecumenical Annual Divine Service 179
The Rite at the Frontal Place 182
Forty of Forties – the Image of the Concluding Procession. 184
Processions of the Troubled Time 184
Spasskie Gate and the Image
of the Entry of the Lord Jesus Christ into Jerusalem 186
"The Town of Moscow" in Ecumenical Processions ... 189
**"It is Common Knowlege, that the Earth
begins From the Kremlin"** (Romanov G.A.) 190